Enterprise JavaBeans™

Other Java™ resources from O'Reilly

Related titles

Java™ in a Nutshell
Head First Java™
Head First EJB™
Programming Jakarta Struts
Tomcat: The Definitive Guide
Learning Java™
Java™ Extreme Programming Cookbook
Java™ Servlet and JSP™ Cookbook™
Hardcore Java™
JavaServer™ Pages

Java Books Resource Center

java.oreilly.com is a complete catalog of O'Reilly's books on Java and related technologies, including sample chapters and code examples.

OnJava.com is a one-stop resource for enterprise Java developers, featuring news, code recipes, interviews, weblogs, and more.

Conferences

O'Reilly Media, Inc. brings diverse innovators together to nurture the ideas that spark revolutionary industries. We specialize in documenting the latest tools and systems, translating the innovator's knowledge into useful skills for those in the trenches. Visit *conferences.oreilly.com* for our upcoming events.

Safari Bookshelf (*safari.oreilly.com*) is the premier online reference library for programmers and IT professionals. Conduct searches across more than 1,000 books. Subscribers can zero in on answers to time-critical questions in a matter of seconds. Read the books on your Bookshelf from cover to cover or simply flip to the page you need. Try it today with a free trial.

FOURTH EDITION

Enterprise JavaBeans™

Richard Monson-Haefel

JBoss Workbook by Bill Burke and Sacha Labourey

O'REILLY®

Beijing · Cambridge · Farnham · Köln · Paris · Sebastopol · Taipei · Tokyo

Enterprise JavaBeans™, Fourth Edition
by Richard Monson-Haefel
JBoss Workbook by Bill Burke and Sacha Labourey

Printed in the United States of America.

The JBoss Workbook section of the book was previously published as *JBoss 3.2 Workbook for Enterprise JavaBeans, Third Edition*.

Published by O'Reilly Media, Inc., 1005 Gravenstein Highway North, Sebastopol, CA 95472.

O'Reilly books may be purchased for educational, business, or sales promotional use. Online editions are also available for most titles (*safari.oreilly.com*). For more information, contact our corporate/institutional sales department: (800) 998-9938 or *corporate@oreilly.com*.

Editor: Mike Loukides

Production Editor: Colleen Gorman

Cover Designer: Hanna Dyer

Interior Designer: David Futato

Printing History:

June 1999:	First Edition.
March 2000:	Second Edition.
September 2001:	Third Edition.
June 2004:	Fourth Edition.

This book uses RepKover™, a durable and flexible lay-flat binding.

ISBN: 0-596-00530-X
[M]

For my wife and best friend,
Hollie

Table of Contents

Part II. JBoss Workbook

Preface

Author's Note

In the winter of 1997, I was consulting on an e-commerce project that was using Java RMI. Not surprisingly, the project failed because Java RMI didn't address performance, scalability, failover, security, or transactions, all of which are vital in a production environment. Although the outcome of that project is not unique to Java RMI—I have seen the same thing happen with CORBA—the timing of the project was especially interesting. Enterprise JavaBeans™ was first introduced by Sun Microsystems at around that time, and had Enterprise JavaBeans (EJB) been available earlier, that same project probably would have succeeded.

At the time I was working on that ill-fated Java RMI project, I was also writing a column for *JavaReport Online* called "The Cutting Edge." The column covered what were then new Java technologies such as the Java Naming and Directory Interface™ (JNDI) and the JavaMail™ API. I was actually looking for a new topic for the third installment of "The Cutting Edge" when I discovered the first public draft of Enterprise JavaBeans, Version 0.8. I had originally heard about this technology in 1996, but this was the first time that public documentation had been made available. Having worked on CORBA, Java RMI, and other distributed object technologies, I knew a good thing when I saw it and immediately began writing an article about this new technology.

That seems like eons ago. Since I published that article in March 1998, literally thousands of articles on EJB have been written, and several books on the subject have come and gone. This book, now in its fourth edition, has kept pace with four versions of the EJB specification in last five years. As the newest version of the specification takes flight, and a slew of new books on the subject debut, I can't help but remember the days when the words "Enterprise JavaBeans" drew blank looks from just about everyone. I'm glad those days are over.

What Is Enterprise JavaBeans?

When Java™ was first introduced in the summer of 1995, most of the IT industry focused on its graphical user interface characteristics and the competitive advantage it offered in terms of distribution and platform independence. Those were interesting times. The applet was king, and only a few of us were attempting to use Java on the server side. In reality, we spent about half of our time coding and the other half trying to convince management that Java was not a fad.

Today, the focus has broadened considerably: Java has been recognized as an excellent platform for creating enterprise solutions, specifically for developing distributed server-side applications. This shift has much to do with Java's emerging role as a universal language for producing implementation-independent abstractions for common enterprise technologies. The JDBC™ API is the first and most familiar example. JDBC (Java Database Connectivity) provides a vendor-independent Java interface for accessing SQL relational databases. This abstraction has been so successful that it's difficult to find a relational database vendor that doesn't support JDBC. Java abstractions for enterprise technologies have expanded considerably to include JNDI for abstracting directory services, JTA (Java Transaction API) for abstracting access to transaction managers, JMS (Java Message Service) for abstracting access to different message-oriented middleware products, and more.

Enterprise JavaBeans, first introduced as a draft specification in late 1997, has since established itself as one of the most important Java enterprise technologies provided by Sun Microsystems. EJB provides an abstraction for component transaction monitors (CTMs), which represent the convergence of two technologies: traditional transaction-processing (TP) monitors (such as CICS, TUXEDO, and Encina), and distributed object services (such as CORBA, DCOM, and native Java RMI). Combining the best of both technologies, component transaction monitors provide a robust, component-based environment that simplifies distributed development while automatically managing the most complex aspects of enterprise computing, such as object brokering, transaction management, security, persistence, and concurrency.

Enterprise JavaBeans defines a server-side component model that allows business objects to be developed and moved from one brand of EJB container to another. A component (i.e., an enterprise bean) presents a programming model that allows the developer to focus on its business purpose. An EJB server is responsible for making the component a distributed object and for managing services such as transactions, persistence, concurrency, and security. In addition to defining the bean's business logic, the developer defines the bean's runtime attributes in a way that is similar to choosing the display properties of visual widgets. The transactional, persistence, and security behaviors of a component can be defined by choosing from a list of properties. The end result is that EJB makes developing distributed-component systems that are managed in a robust transactional environment much easier. For developers and corporate IT shops that have struggled with the complexities of delivering mission-critical, high-performance distributed systems using CORBA, DCOM, or Java RMI, EJB provides a far simpler and more productive platform on which to base development efforts.

When Enterprise JavaBeans 1.0 was finalized in 1998, it quickly became a de facto industry standard. Many vendors announced their support even before the specification was finalized. Since that time, EJB has been enhanced three times. The specification was updated in 1999, to Version 1.1, and again in 2001, to Version 2.0, which was covered in the second and third editions of this book. The most recent revision to the specification, Version 2.1, is covered by this, the fourth edition of *Enterprise JavaBeans*. This edition also covers EJB 2.0, which is for the most part a subset of the functionality offered by EJB 2.1.

Products that conform to the EJB standard have come from every sector of the IT industry, including the TP monitor, CORBA ORB, application server, relational database, object database, and web server industries. Some of these products are based on proprietary models that have been adapted to EJB; many more wouldn't even exist without EJB.

In short, Enterprise JavaBeans 2.1 and 2.0 provide a standard distributed-component model that greatly simplifies the development process and allows beans developed and deployed on one vendor's EJB server to be easily deployed on a different vendor's EJB server. This book will provide you with the foundation you need to develop vendor-independent EJB solutions.

Who Should Read This Book?

This book explains and demonstrates the fundamentals of the Enterprise JavaBeans 2.1 and 2.0 programming models. Although EJB makes distributed computing much simpler, it is still a complex technology that requires a great deal of time and study to master. This book provides a straightforward, no-nonsense explanation of the underlying technology, Java classes and interfaces, component model, and runtime behavior of Enterprise JavaBeans. It includes material that is backward-compatible with EJB 2.0 and provides special notes and chapters when there are significant differences between 2.1 and 2.0.

Although this book focuses on the fundamentals, it's not a "dummies" book. Enterprise JavaBeans is an extremely complex and ambitious enterprise technology. While using EJB may be fairly simple, the amount of work required to understand and master EJB is significant. Before reading this book, you should be fluent in the Java language and have some practical experience developing business solutions. Experience with distributed object systems is not a must, but you will need some experience with JDBC (or at least an understanding of the basics) to follow the examples in this book.

If you are unfamiliar with the Java language, I recommend *Learning Java* by Patrick Niemeyer and Jonathan Knudsen; this book was formerly *Exploring Java* (O'Reilly). If you are unfamiliar with JDBC, I recommend *Database Programming with JDBC and Java* by George Reese (O'Reilly). If you need a stronger background in distributed computing, I recommend *Java Distributed Computing* by Jim Farley (O'Reilly).

Organization

This book is organized into two parts: the technical manuscript followed by the JBoss workbook. The technical manuscript explains what EJB is, how it works, and when to use it. The JBoss workbook provides step-by-step instructions for installing, configuring, and running the examples from the manuscript on the JBoss 3.0 Application Server.

Part I: The Technical Manuscript

The technical manuscript is covered in Chapters 1–19 and is about 90% of the content for this book. Chapters 1–18 were written by yours truly, Richard Monson-Haefel, while Chapter 19 was written by Keyton Weissenger and Shy Aberman. Here is a summary of these chapters and their content.

Chapter 1, *Introduction*
: This chapter defines component transaction monitors and explains how they form the underlying technology of the Enterprise JavaBeans component model.

Chapter 2, *Architectural Overview*
: This chapter defines the architecture of the Enterprise JavaBeans component model and examines the difference between the three basic types of enterprise beans: entity beans, session beans, and message-driven beans.

Chapter 3, *Resource Management and the Primary Services*
: This chapter explains how the EJB-compliant server manages an enterprise bean at runtime.

Chapter 4, *Developing Your First Enterprise Beans*
: This chapter walks the reader through the development of some simple enterprise beans.

Chapter 5, *The Remote and Local Client View*
: This chapter explains in detail how enterprise beans are accessed and used by remote, local, and web service client applications.

Chapter 6, *CMP: Basic Persistence*
: This chapter provides an explanation of how to develop basic container-managed entity beans.

Chapter 7, *CMP: Entity Relationships*
: This chapter picks up where Chapter 6 left off, expanding your understanding of container-managed persistence to complex bean-to-bean relationships.

Chapter 8, *CMP: EJB QL*
: This chapter addresses the Enterprise JavaBeans Query Language (EJB QL), which is used to query EJBs and to locate specific entity beans in EJB 2.1 and 2.0 container-managed persistence.

Chapter 9, *Bean-Managed Persistence*
: This chapter covers the development of bean-managed persistence beans including when to store, load, and remove data from the database.

Chapter 10, *The Entity-Container Contract*
: This chapter covers the general protocol between an entity bean and its container at runtime and applies to both container-managed persistence and bean-managed persistence.

Chapter 11, *Session Beans*
: This chapter shows how to develop stateless and stateful session beans.

Chapter 12, *Message-Driven Beans*
: This chapter shows how to develop message-driven beans in EJB 2.1 and 2.0.

Chapter 13, *Timer Service*
: This chapter shows how to use the Timer service in EJB 2.1

Chapter 14, *EJB 2.1: Web Service Standards*
: This chapter explains Web services standards, XML, SOAP, WSLD, and UDDI.

Chapter 15, *EJB 2.1 and Web Services*
: This chapter discusses how Web services are supported in EJB using the JAX-RPC API.

Chapter 16, *Transactions*
: This chapter provides an in-depth explanation of transactions and describes the transactional model defined by Enterprise JavaBeans.

Chapter 17, *J2EE*
: This chapter provides an overview of J2EE v1.4 and explains how EJB 2.1 fits into this new platform.

Chapter 18, *XML Deployment Descriptors*
: This chapter provides an in-depth explanation of the XML deployment descriptors used in EJB 2.0 and 2.1.

Chapter 19, *EJB Design in the Real World*
: This chapter provides some basic design strategies that can simplify your EJB development efforts and make your EJB system more efficient.

Part II: The JBoss Workbook

The JBoss workbook is an update of the JBoss workbook that was published as a supplement to the third edition of this book. The JBoss workbook shows how to execute the examples from this book on the JBoss 4.0 Application Server. It's indispensible to readers who want to code while learning and see the examples from the book run on a real application server.

The previous edition of this book published the JBoss Workbook as a separate title along with three other workbooks for J2EE 1.3 SDK, IBM WebSphere and BEA WebLogic. All of the workbooks were critical successes and popular with readers, but they were not a very big commercial success—you could download them for free—and were difficult to manage. For this edition, we decided to develop one workbook to reduce expenses. We also decided to bind it with the rest of the book to make your life easier—you don't have to buy it separately or download it off the Web.

The JBoss workbook is really excellent and I'm proud to include it in this book. It was written by Bill Burke and Sacha Labourey, two of the people behind JBoss and acknowledged experts in their fields. That said, I want to make it clear to readers that I'm not endorsing JBoss over other J2EE application servers. The JBoss workbook is included in this edition for pragmatic reasons:

- JBoss supported most, if not all, EJB 2.1 features when this book was in the final weeks of development—most of the other vendors did not.
- Bill Burke and Sacha Labourey were willing to commit the time and effort to update their workbook and have it ready for in time for printing. They are also willing to keep it updated as new JBoss versions come out.
- JBoss is free, and in a time when application servers cost tens, if not hundreds of thousands of dollars to deploy, it's a better choice for developers who are learning how to develop EJB for the first time.

The JBoss workbook shows how to execute examples from most of the chapters in this book—basically any chapter with at least one significant example is covered by the workbook. You'll want to read the introduction to the workbook to set up JBoss and configure it for the examples. After that, just go to the workbook chapter that matches the chapter you're reading. For example, if you are reading Chapter 6 on basic container-managed persistence, use the "Chapter 6 Exercises" section of the workbook to develop and run the examples on JBoss.

Software and Versions

This book covers Enterprise JavaBeans Versions 2.1 and 2.0. It uses Java language features from the Java 1.2 platform including JDBC. Because the focus of this book is on developing vendor-independent Enterprise JavaBeans components and solutions,

I have stayed away from proprietary extensions and vendor-dependent idioms. Any EJB-compliant server can be used with this book, but you should be familiar with your server's specific installation, deployment, and runtime-management procedures to work with the examples. A workbook for the JBoss Application Server is included at the end of this book to help you get started.

EJB 2.1 and 2.0 have a lot in common, but when they differ, chapters or sections within a chapter that are specific to each version are clearly marked. Feel free to skip version-specific sections that do not concern you. Unless indicated, the source code in this book has been written for both EJB 2.1 and 2.0.

Conventions

The following typographical conventions are used in this book:

Italic
: Used for filenames and pathnames, hostnames, domain names, URLs, and email addresses. *Italic* is also used for new terms where they are defined.

`Constant width`
: Used for code examples and fragments, XML elements and tags, and SQL commands, table names, and column names. `Constant width` is also used for class, variable, and method names and for Java keywords used within the text.

`Constant width bold`
: Used for emphasis in some code examples.

`Constant width italic`
: Used to indicate text that is replaceable. For example, in *`BeanName`*`PK`, you would replace *`BeanName`* with a specific bean name.

Indicates a tip, suggestion, or general note.

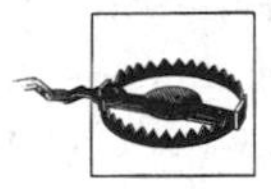

Indicates a warning or caution.

An Enterprise JavaBean consists of many parts; it's not a single object, but a collection of objects and interfaces. To refer to an enterprise bean as a whole, we use its business name in Roman type, followed by the acronym EJB. For example, we will refer to the Customer EJB when we want to talk about the enterprise bean in general. If we put the name in a constant-width font, we are referring explicitly to the bean's remote interface; thus, `CustomerRemote` is the remote interface that defines the business methods of the Customer EJB.

Comments and Questions

Please address comments and questions concerning this book to the publisher:

O'Reilly Media, Inc.
1005 Gravenstein Highway North
Sebastopol, CA 95472
(800) 998-9938 (in the United States or Canada)
(707) 829-0515 (international or local)
(707) 829-0104 (fax)

There is a web page for this book, which lists errata, examples, and any additional information. You can access this page at:

http://www.oreilly.com/catalog/entjbeans4/

To comment on or ask technical questions about this book, send email to:

bookquestions@oreilly.com

For more information about books, conferences, software, Resource Centers, and the O'Reilly Network, see the O'Reilly web site at:

http://www.oreilly.com

The author maintains a web site for the discussion of EJB and related distributed computing technologies at *http://www.jmiddleware.com*. jMiddleware.com provides news about this book as well as code tips, articles, and an extensive list of links to EJB resources.

Acknowledgments

The credit for this book's development and delivery is shared by many individuals. Michael Loukides, my editor, was pivotal to the success of every edition of this book. Without his experience, craft, and guidance, this book would not have been possible. I'm also greatful to the co-authors who contributed greatly to the success of this fourth edition. The JBoss workbook was written by Bill Burke and Sacha Labourey. It's a significant contribution and I'm proud to have their names on the cover of this book. Keyton Weissenger and Shy Aberman collaborated to produce Chapter 19, which is an excellent overview of real-world EJB design and performance issues—that chapter is based on hard-earned experience deploying several EJB production systems.

Many expert technical reviewers helped ensure that the material was technically accurate and true to the spirit of Enterprise JavaBeans. Of special note are Lance Anderson, Bill Burke, Dave Cronin, James Pinpin, Tom Mars, and Ricky Yim. They contributed greatly to the technical accuracy of this book and brought a combination of industry and real-world experience to bear, helping to make this one of the best books on Enterprise JavaBeans published today.

I would also like to thank the folks at TheServerSide.com and everyone in the community who provided valuable feedback, including (in alphabetical order) Michael Boyd, Ravi Brewster, Patrick De Clercq, Peter Durcansky, Sudheer Fernades, Vick Fisher, Thomas Foersch, John Guthrie, George Jiang, Markus Knauss, Madhusudhan Konda, Ravi Kyamala, Lee Yeow Leong, David McCann, Olav Nybo, Sunil Patil, Zheng Ping, Manfred Rosenboom, Viviane Costa Silva, Simon Spruzen, Bob Stine, Dave Tuke, Ray Yan, Chunshui Yu, and Ping Zheng.

Special thanks also go to Greg Nyberg, Hemant Khandelwal, Kyle Brown, Robert Castaneda, Joe Fialli, Anil Sharma, Seth White, Evan Ireland, David Chappell (the .NET guy), Jim Farley, Prasad Muppirala, Sriram Srinivasan, Anne Thomas, Ian McCallion, Tim Rohaly, James D. Frentress, Andrzej Jan Taramina, Marc Loy, Don Weiss, Mike Slinn, and Kevin Dick. The contributions of these technical experts were critical to the technical and conceptual accuracy of earlier editions of this book. Others I would like to thank include Maggie Mezquita, Greg Hartzel, John Klug, and Jon Jamsa of BORN Information, all of whom suffered though the first draft of the first edition so long ago to provide valuable feedback.

Thanks also to Vlad Matena and Mark Hapner of Sun Microsystems, the primary architects of Enterprise JavaBeans; Linda DeMichiel, EJB 2.1/2.0 specification lead; and all the other EJB 2.1 expert group members.

Finally, I extend the most sincere gratitude to my wife, Hollie, for supporting and assisting me through the five years of painstaking research and writing that were required to produce four editions of this book. Without her unfailing support and love, this book would not have been completed.

PART I
The Technical Manuscript

CHAPTER 1

Introduction

This book is about Enterprise JavaBeans 2.1, the latest version of the Enterprise JavaBeans specification. It also covers Enterprise JavaBeans 2.0, which is still in widespread use. Just as the Java platform has revolutionized the way we think about software development, the Enterprise JavaBeans (EJB) specification has revolutionized the way we think about developing mission-critical enterprise software. It combines server-side components with distributed object technologies, asynchronous messaging, and web services to greatly simplify the task of application development. It automatically takes into account many of the requirements of business systems, including security, resource pooling, persistence, concurrency, and transactional integrity.

This book shows you how to use Enterprise JavaBeans to develop scalable, portable business systems. But before we can start talking about EJB itself, we'll need a brief introduction to the technologies addressed by EJB, such as component models, distributed objects, asynchronous messaging, and web services. It's particularly important to have a basic understanding of component transaction monitors, the technology that lies beneath EJB. In Chapter 2 and Chapter 3, we'll look at EJB itself and see how enterprise beans are put together. The rest of the book is devoted to developing enterprise beans for an imaginary business and discussing advanced issues.

It is assumed that you're already familiar with Java; if you're not, *Learning Java*, by Patrick Niemeyer and Josh Peck (O'Reilly), is an excellent introduction. This book also assumes that you're conversant in the JDBC API, or at least in SQL. If you're not familiar with JDBC, see *Database Programming with JDBC and Java* by George Reese (O'Reilly).

One of Java's most important features is platform independence. Since it was first released, Java has been marketed as "write once, run anywhere." While the hype has gotten a little heavy-handed at times, code written with Sun's Java programming language is remarkably platform-independent. Enterprise JavaBeans isn't just platform-independent—it's also implementation-independent. If you've worked with JDBC, you know a little about what this means. Not only can the JDBC API run on a Windows machine or on a Unix machine, it can also access relational databases of many different vendors (DB2, Oracle, MySQL, SQLServer, etc.) by using different JDBC drivers. You don't have to code to a particular database implementation—just change JDBC drivers, and you change databases.* It's the same with EJB. Ideally, an EJB component—an enterprise bean—can run in any application server that implements the EJB specification.† This means that you can develop and deploy your EJB business system in one server, such as BEA's WebLogic, and later move it to a different EJB server, such as Pramati, Sybase EAServer, IBM's WebSphere, or an open source project such as Apache Geronimo, OpenEJB, JOnAS, or JBoss. Implementation independence means that your business components are not dependent on the brand of server, which gives you many more options before, during, and after development and deployment.

Server-Side Components

Object-oriented languages such as Java, C++, and C# are used to write software that is flexible, extensible, and reusable—the three axioms of object-oriented development. In business systems, object-oriented languages are used to improve development of GUIs, to simplify access to data, and to encapsulate the business logic. The encapsulation of business logic into business objects is a fairly recent focus in the information-technology industry. Business is fluid, which means that a business's products, processes, and objectives evolve over time. If the software that models the business can be encapsulated into business objects, it becomes flexible, extensible, and reusable, and therefore evolves as the business evolves.

A server-side component model may define an architecture for developing *distributed business objects* that combines the accessibility of distributed object systems with the fluidity of objectified business logic. Server-side component models are used on the middle-tier application servers, which manage the components at runtime and make them available to remote clients. They provide a baseline of functionality that makes it easy to develop distributed business objects and assemble them into business solutions.

Server-side components can also be used to model other aspects of a business system, such as presentation and routing. The Java servlet, for example, is a server-side component that is used to generate HTML and XML data for the presentation layer of a three-tier architecture. EJB 2.1 message-driven beans, which are discussed later in this book, are server-side components that can be used to consume and process asynchronous messages.

* In some cases, differences in database vendor's support for SQL may require customization of SQL statements used in development.

† Provided that the bean components and EJB servers comply with the specification, and no proprietary functionality is used in development.

Server-side components, like other components, can be bought and sold as independent pieces of executable software. They conform to a standard component model and can be executed without direct modification in a server that supports that component model. Server-side component models often support attribute-based programming, which allows the runtime behavior of the component to be modified when it is deployed, without having to change the programming code in the component. Depending on the component model, the server administrator can declare a server-side component's transactional, security, and even persistence behavior by setting these attributes to specific values.

As an organization's services, products, and operating procedures evolve, server-side components can be reassembled, modified, and extended so that the business system reflects those changes. Imagine a business system as a collection of server-side components that model concepts such as customers, products, reservations, and warehouses. Each component is like a Lego(™) block that can be combined with other components to build a business solution. Products can be stored in the warehouse or delivered to a customer; a customer can make a reservation or purchase a product. You can assemble components, take them apart, use them in different combinations, and change their definitions. A business system based on server-side components is fluid because it is objectified, and it is accessible because the components can be distributed.

Enterprise JavaBeans Defined

Sun Microsystems' definition of the Enterprise JavaBeans architecture is:

> The Enterprise JavaBeans architecture is a component architecture for the development and deployment of component-based distributed business applications. Applications written using the Enterprise JavaBeans architecture are scalable, transactional, and multi-user secure. These applications may be written once, and then deployed on any server platform that supports the Enterprise JavaBeans specification.*

That's a mouthful, but it's not atypical of how Sun defines many of its Java technologies—have you ever read the definition of the Java language itself? It's about twice as long. This book offers a shorter definition of EJB:

> Enterprise JavaBeans is a standard server-side component model for distributed business applications.

This means the EJB offers a standard model for building server-side components that represent both business objects (customers, items in inventory, and the like) and business processes (purchasing, stocking, and so on). Once you have built a set of components that fit the requirements of your business, you can combine them to create business applications. On top of that, as "distributed" components, they don't all

* Sun Microsystems' *Enterprise JavaBeans Specification, v2.1*, Copyright 2002 by Sun Microsystems, Inc.

have to reside on the same server. Components can reside wherever it's most convenient: a Customer component can "live" near the Customer database, a Part component can live near the inventory database, and a Purchase business-process component can live near the user interface. You can do whatever's necessary for minimizing latency, sharing the processing load, or maximizing reliability.

Distributed Object Architectures

To understand EJB, you need to understand how distributed objects work. Distributed object systems are the foundation for modern three-tier architectures. In a three-tier architecture, as shown in Figure 1-1, the presentation logic resides on the client (first tier), the business logic resides on the middle tier (second tier), and other resources, such as the database, reside on the backend (third tier).

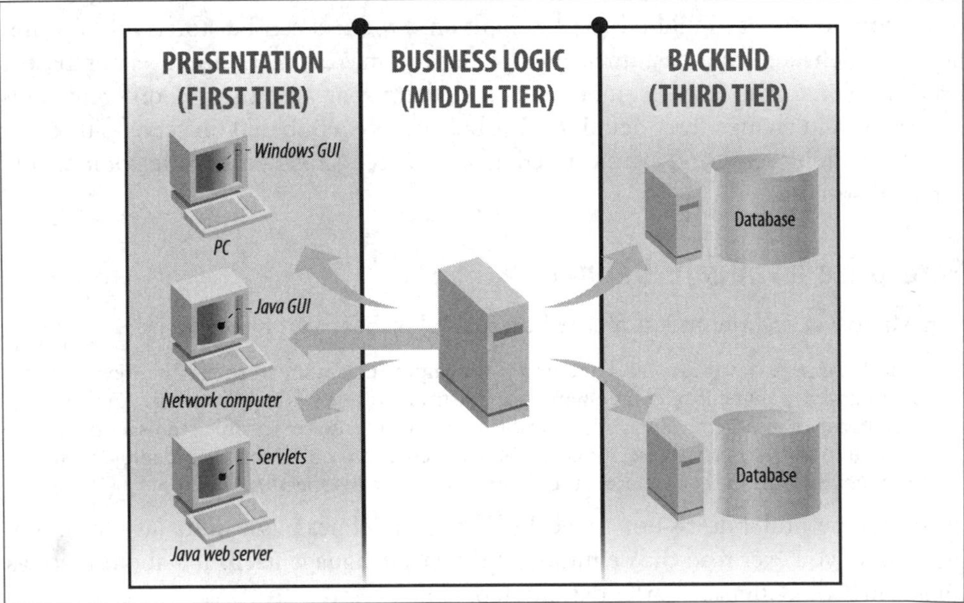

Figure 1-1. Three-tier architecture

All distributed object protocols are built on the same basic architecture, which is designed to make an object on one computer look like it's residing on a different computer. Distributed object architectures are based on a network communication layer that is really very simple. Essentially, there are three parts to this architecture: the business object, the skeleton, and the stub.

The *business object* resides on the middle tier. It's an instance of an object that models the state and business logic of some real-world concept, such as a person, order, or account. Every business object class has matching stub and skeleton classes built specifically for that type of business object. For example, a distributed business object called `Person` would have matching `Person_Stub` and `Person_Skeleton` classes. As shown in Figure 1-2, the business object and skeleton reside on the middle tier, and the stub resides on the client.

The *stub* and the *skeleton* are responsible for making the business object on the middle tier look as if it is running locally on the client machine. This is accomplished through some kind of *remote method invocation* (RMI) protocol. An RMI protocol is used to communicate method invocations over a network. CORBA, Java RMI, and Microsoft .NET all use their own RMI protocols.* Every instance of the business object on the middle tier is wrapped by an instance of its matching skeleton class. The skeleton is set up on a port and IP address and listens for requests from the stub, which resides on the client machine and is connected via the network to the skeleton. The stub acts as the business object's surrogate on the client and is responsible for communicating requests from the client to the business object through the skeleton. Figure 1-2 illustrates the process of communicating a method invocation from the client to the server object and back. The stub and the skeleton hide the communication specifics of the RMI protocol from the client and the implementation class, respectively.

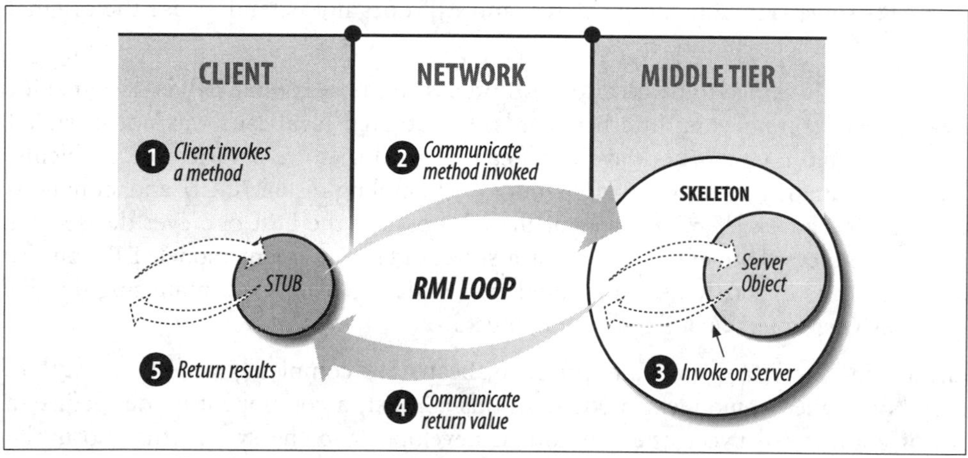

Figure 1-2. RMI loop

The business object implements a public interface that declares its business methods. The stub implements the same interface as the business object, but the stub's methods do not contain business logic. Instead, the business methods on the stub implement whatever networking operations are required to forward the request to the business object and receive the results. When a client invokes a business method

* The acronym "RMI" isn't specific to Java RMI. This section uses the term RMI to describe distributed object protocols in general. Java RMI is the Java language version of a distributed object protocol.

on the stub, the request is communicated over the network by streaming the name of the method invoked, and the values passed in as parameters, to the skeleton. When the skeleton receives the incoming stream, it parses the stream to discover which method is requested, then invokes the corresponding business method on the business object. Any value that is returned from the method invoked on the business object is streamed back to the stub by the skeleton. The stub then returns the value to the client application as if it had processed the business logic locally.

Component Models

The term "component model" has many different interpretations. Enterprise JavaBeans specifies a *server-side* component model. Using a set of classes and interfaces from the `javax.ejb` package, developers can create, assemble, and deploy components that conform to the EJB specification.

The original JavaBeans is also a component model, but it's not a server-side component model like EJB. Other than sharing the name "JavaBeans," these two component models are completely unrelated. In the past, a lot of the literature referred to EJB as an extension of the original JavaBeans, but this is a misrepresentation. The two APIs serve very different purposes, and EJB does not extend or use the original JavaBeans component model.

JavaBeans is intended to be used for *intra*process purposes, while EJB is designed for *inter*process components. In other words, the original JavaBeans was not intended for distributed components. JavaBeans can be used to solve a variety of problems, but it is primarily used to build clients by assembling visual (GUI) and nonvisual widgets. It's an excellent component model, possibly the best one ever devised for intraprocess development, but it's not a server-side component model. EJB, on the other hand, is explicitly designed to address issues involved with managing distributed business objects in a three-tier architecture.

Given that JavaBeans and Enterprise JavaBeans are completely different, why are they both called component models? In this context, a component model defines a set of contracts between the component developer and the system that hosts the component. The contracts express how a component should be developed and packaged. Once a component is defined, it becomes an independent piece of software that can be distributed and used in other applications. A component is developed for a specific purpose but not a specific application. In the original JavaBeans, a component might be a push button or a spreadsheet that can be used in any GUI application according to the rules specified in the original JavaBeans component model. In EJB, there are several different types of components: components that represent entities in a database (*entity beans*) have a slightly different contract with their container than components that represent business processes (*session beans*). For example, a component might be a Customer business object, represented by an entity bean, that can be deployed in any EJB server and used to develop any business application that needs a customer business object. Another type of component might be a MakePurchase object, represented by a session bean, that models what happens when a customer buys a particular product. (Although the act of making a purchase isn't itself represented in a database, a purchase involves a complex interaction between a customer, a sales person, inventory, accounts receivable, and possibly other entities.) The MakePurchase object has a different contract with its container than the Customer object, but it too can still be deployed in any EJB server and used in any business application that needs to support purchases. A third type of EJB, the MessageDrivenBean, has a slightly different contract with its container—but it, too, can be deployed in any EJB server.

Competing Component Models: Microsoft's .NET Framework

Enterprise JavaBeans did not appear out of nowhere; it is one of a number of component transaction monitors (CTMs), which in turn have their origin in older transaction processing monitors (like Tuxedo) and Object Request Brokers. However, the most important competition for EJB is Microsoft's .NET framework. .NET has its origins in the Microsoft Transaction Server (MTS), which was arguably the first commercially available CTM. MTS was later renamed COM+. Microsoft's COM+ is based on the Component Object Model (COM), originally designed for use on the desktop but eventually pressed into service as a server-side component model. For distributed access, COM+ clients use the Distributed Component Object Model (DCOM).

When MTS was introduced in 1996, it was an exciting development because it provided a comprehensive environment for business objects. With MTS, application developers could write COM components without worrying about system-level concerns. Once a business object was designed to conform to the COM model, MTS (and now COM+) took care of everything else, including transaction management, concurrency, and resource management.

Since then, COM+ has become part of Microsoft's .NET Framework. The core functionality provided by COM+ services remains essentially the same in .NET, but the way it appears to a developer has changed significantly. Rather than writing components as COM objects, .NET Framework developers build applications as *managed objects*. All managed objects, and in fact all code written for the .NET Framework, depends on a Common Language Runtime (CLR). For Java-oriented developers, the CLR is much like a Java virtual machine (VM), and a managed object is analogous to an instance of a Java class; i.e., to a Java object.

The .NET Framework provides first-class support for web services via the SOAP (Simple Object Access Protocol) protocol, which enables business components in the .NET world to communicate with applications on any other platform written in any language. This can potentially make business components in .NET universally accessible, a feature that is not easily dismissed. In fact, .NET was the impetus that motivated Sun Microsystems to extend EJB and the rest of the J2EE platform to support web services. Microsoft's .NET platform represents the greatest threat to the dominance of the Java platform since the Java programming language was introduced in 1995.

Although the .NET Framework provides many interesting features, it falls short as an open standard. The COM+ services in the .NET Framework are Microsoft's proprietary CTM, which means that using this technology binds you to the Microsoft platform. If your company plans to deploy server-side components on a non-Microsoft platform, .NET is not a viable solution. In addition, the COM+ services in the .NET Framework are focused on stateless components; there's no built-in support for persistent transactional objects. Although stateless components can offer higher performance, business systems need the kind of flexibility offered by CTMs, which include stateful and persistent components.

Benefits of a Standard Server-Side Component Model

What does it mean to be a standard server-side component model? Quite simply, it means that you can develop business objects using the Enterprise JavaBeans component model and expect them to work in any application server that supports the complete EJB specification. This is a pretty powerful statement, because it largely eliminates the biggest problem faced by potential customers of Microsoft .NET products: fear of vendor "lock-in." With a standard server-side component model, customers can commit to using an EJB-compliant application server with the knowledge that they can migrate to a better server if one becomes available. Obviously, care must be taken when using proprietary extensions developed by vendors, but this is nothing new. Even in the relational database industry—which has been using the SQL standard for a couple of decades—optional proprietary extensions abound.

Having a standard server-side component model has benefits beyond implementation independence. A standard component model provides a vehicle for growth in the third-party products. If numerous vendors support EJB, creating add-on products and component libraries is more attractive to software vendors. The IT industry has seen this type of cottage industry grow up around other standards, such as SQL; hundreds of add-on products can now be purchased to enhance business systems with data that is stored in SQL-compliant relational databases. Report-generating tools and data-warehouse products are typical examples. The GUI component industry has also seen the growth of its own third-party products. A healthy market for component libraries already exists for GUI component models such as Sun's original JavaBeans component model.

Many third-party products for Enterprise JavaBeans exist today. Add-on products for credit-card processing, legacy database access, and other business services have been introduced for various EJB-compliant systems. These types of products make development of EJB systems simpler and faster than the alternatives, making the EJB component model attractive to corporate IT and server vendors alike. The market for prepackaged EJB components is growing in several domains, including sales, finance, education, web-content management, collaboration, and other areas.

Asynchronous Messaging

In addition to supporting RMI-based distributed business objects, Enterprise JavaBeans supports asynchronous messaging. An asynchronous messaging system allows two or more applications to exchange information in the form of messages. A message, in this case, is a self-contained package of business data and network routing headers. The business data contained in a message can be anything—depending on the business scenario—and usually contains information about some business transaction. In enterprise systems, messages inform an application of some event or occurrence in another system.

Asynchronous messages may be transmitted from one application to another on a network using message-oriented middleware (MOM). MOM products ensure that messages are properly distributed among applications. In addition, MOM usually provides fault-tolerance, load-balancing, scalability, and transactional support for enterprises that need to reliably exchange large quantities of messages. MOM vendors use different message formats and network protocols for exchanging messages, but the basic semantics are the same. An API is used to create a message, give it a payload (application data), assign it routing information, and then send the message. The same API is used to receive messages produced by other applications.

In modern enterprise-messaging systems, applications exchange messages through virtual channels called *destinations*. When you send a message, it's addressed to a destination, not to a specific application. Any application that subscribes or registers an interest in that destination may receive that message. In this way, the applications that receive messages and those that send messages are decoupled. Senders and receivers are not bound to each other in any way and may send and receive messages as they see fit.

Enterprise JavaBeans integrates the functionality of MOM into its component model. This integration extends the EJB platform so that it supports both RMI and asynchronous messaging. EJB 2.0 and 2.1 support asynchronous messaging through the Java Message Service (JMS) and a new component called the message-driven bean. In addition to JMS, message-driven beans in EJB 2.1 can support other synchronous and asynchronous messaging systems.

Java Message Service

Each MOM vendor implements its own networking protocols, routing, and administration facilities, but the basic semantics of the developer API provided by different MOMs are the same. It's this similarity in APIs that makes the Java Message Service (JMS) possible.

JMS is a vendor-agnostic Java API that can be used with many different MOM vendors. JMS is very similar to JDBC in that an application developer can reuse the same API to access many different systems. If a vendor provides a compliant service provider for JMS, the JMS API can be used to send messages to and receive messages from that vendor. For example, you can use the same JMS API to send messages with Progress's SonicMQ as with IBM's MQSeries.

Message-Driven Beans and J2eeCA 1.5

Enterprise JavaBeans 2.0 introduced a new kind of component, called a *message-driven bean*, which is a kind of standard JMS bean. It can receive and send asynchronous JMS messages, and can easily interact with other EJBs.

EJB 2.1 extends the programming model of the message-driven bean beyond JMS to any messaging system. While vendors must continue to support JMS-based message-driven beans (JMS-MDBs), other types of messaging systems are also allowed. It's likely that vendors will develop new message-driven bean types to support all kinds of protocols, including SMTP for email, SNMP for device control, peer-to-peer protocols (e.g., BEEP and Jabber) and many other open and proprietary messaging systems. In addition, the message-driven bean has become an elegant option for serving connections to legacy transaction processing systems like CICS, IMS, openUTM, and others.

The expansion of message-driven beans in EJB 2.1 to other protocols is made possible by the new J2EE Connector Architecture (J2eeCA 1.5), which defines a portable programming model for interfacing with enterprise information systems. The use of J2eeCA in J2EE is analogous to the use of USB in computer hardware. A computer that supports USB can interface with just about any USB-compliant device. Similarly, an EJB 2.1 container that supports J2eeCA 1.5 can interface with any J2eeCA 1.5–compliant resource. For example, if XYZ Vendor creates a new message-driven bean component for their proprietary messaging system based on J2eeCA 1.5, that component will be portable across all EJB 2.1–compliant servers. Figure 1-3 illustrates how a J2eeCA for a messaging system integrates with EJB 2.1.

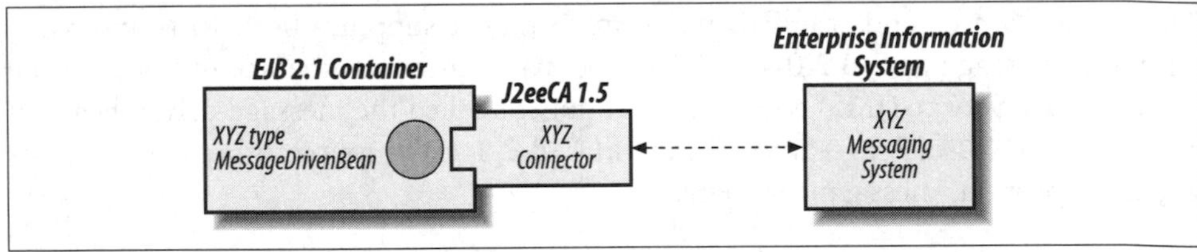

Figure 1-3. EJB 2.1 message-driven beans and J2eeCA 1.5

Message-driven beans in EJB 2.1 and 2.0 allow other applications to send messages that can be captured and processed by the EJB application. This feature allows EJB applications to better integrate with legacy and other proprietary systems.

Web Services

Web services represent the latest wave in distributed computing, and perhaps the most important innovation since the introduction of Java in 1995 and XML in 1998. Although the term "web services" is bandied about quite a bit, arriving at a concrete definition is difficult because web services is, at the highest level, not specific to any particular technology or platform. It's often defined in fairly abstract terms like "a substrate for building distributed applications using software running on different operating systems and devices"* or "self-contained, self-describing, modular applications that can be published, located, and invoked across the Web."† Of course, these quotes are taken out of context, but that's the essential point: you need some kind of context to define web services. Here's my definition of web services that has meaning in the context of J2EE, EJB, .NET, and most other web services platforms:

> Web services are network applications that use SOAP and WSDL to exchange information in the form of XML documents.

To understand this definition, you need to understand SOAP and WSDL. Here are brief definitions of these terms.

SOAP 1.1
: SOAP (Simple Object Access Protocol) is an XML grammar developed by Microsoft, IBM, and others, that is currently under the auspices of the W3C. It's an application protocol used in both RPC and asynchronous messaging. SOAP is very flexible and extensible and, unlike its predecessors (DCE RPC, CORBA IIOP, Java RMI-JRMP, and DCOM), it's been endorsed and adopted by just about every major vendor. (If you're not familiar with XML, see *Java and XML* by Brett McLaughlin (O'Reilly) or *XML in a Nutshell* by Elliotte Rusty Harold (O'Reilly).

WSDL 1.1
: The Web Service Description Language (WSDL) is another XML grammar, developed by Microsoft and IBM under the auspices of the W3C. It is an XML-based IDL (Interface Definition Language) that can be used to describe web services, including the kind of message format expected, the Internet protocol used, and the Internet address of the web service.

Web services are truly platform-independent. Although Java RMI and CORBA IIOP also claim to be platform-independent, in fact these older technologies require their own platforms. To use Java RMI, you need a Java virtual machine and the Java programming language; a program written in Visual Basic or C++ can't interact with a Java program using RMI. CORBA IIOP is also restrictive, because the IIOP protocol usually requires an elaborate infrastructure like a CORBA ORB, which limits devel-

* Tim Ewald, "The Web Services Idea," July 12, 2002, Microsoft.com (*http://msdn.microsoft.com/webservices/understanding/readme/default.asp*).

† Doug Tidwell, "Web services—the Web's next revolution," November 29, 2000, IBM.com (*http://www-105.ibm.com/developerworks/education.nsf/webservices-onlinecourse-bytitle/BA84142372686CFB862569A400601C18?OpenDocument*).

opers to those few vendors that support CORBA, or to the Java environment (which includes built-in support for CORBA IIOP).

Web services, on the other hand, are not tied to a specific platform like the JVM or to a technology infrastructure like CORBA because they focus on the protocols used to exchange messages—SOAP and WSDL—not the implementation that supports those protocols. In other words, you can build web services on any platform, using any programming language any way you please.

EJB 2.1 allows enterprise beans to be exposed as web services, so that their methods can be invoked by other J2EE applications as well as applications written in other programming languages on a variety of platforms. Web services in EJB 2.1 supports both RPC-style and document-style messaging. Support for web services is based on a new web service API: JAX-RPC. Web services and the use of JAX-RPC is covered in detail in Chapter 14.

Titan Cruises: An Imaginary Business

To make things a easier and more fun, we discuss all the concepts in this book in the context of an imaginary business, a cruise line called Titan. A cruise line makes a particularly interesting example because it incorporates several different businesses: it has ship cabins that are similar to hotel rooms; it serves meals like a restaurant; it offers various recreational opportunities; and it needs to interact with other travel businesses.

This type of business is a good candidate for a distributed object system because many of the system's users are geographically dispersed. Commercial travel agents, for example, who need to book passage on Titan ships need to access the reservation system. Supporting many—possibly hundreds—of travel agents requires a robust transactional system to ensure agents have access and reservations are completed properly.

Throughout this book, we will build a fairly simple slice of Titan's EJB system that focuses on the process of making a reservation for a cruise. This exercise will give us an opportunity to develop Ship, Cabin, TravelAgent, ProcessPayment, and other enterprise beans. In the process, you will need to create relational database tables for persisting data used in the example. It is assumed that you are familiar with relational database management systems and that you can create tables according to the SQL statements provided. EJB can be used with any kind of database or legacy application, but the relational database is most commonly understood database technology, so I have chosen this as the persistence layer.

What's Next?

To develop business objects using EJB, you have to understand the life cycles and architecture of EJB components. This means understanding the concepts of how EJB's components are managed and made available as distributed objects. Developing an understanding of the EJB architecture is the focus of the next two chapters.

CHAPTER 2

Architectural Overview

In order to use Enterprise JavaBeans effectively, you need to understand the EJB architecture. This chapter explores the core of the EJB architecture: how enterprise beans are distributed as business objects. Chapter 3 explores the services and resource-management techniques supported by EJB.

In order to be truly versatile, the EJB component design had to be smart. For application developers, assembling enterprise beans requires little or no expertise in the complex system-level issues that often plague three-tier development efforts. While EJB makes the process easier for application developers, it also provides EJB server developers with a great deal of flexibility in how they support the EJB specification.

The Enterprise Bean Component

Enterprise JavaBeans server-side components come in three fundamentally different types: *entity, session,* and *message-driven beans*. Both session and entity beans are RMI-based server-side components that are accessed using distributed object protocols. Message-driven beans process messages from non-RMI systems like Java Message Service, legacy systems, and web services. All EJB servers must at least support a JMS-based message driven bean, but they may also support other types of message-driven bean.

A good rule of thumb is that entity beans model business concepts that can be expressed as nouns. For example, an entity bean might represent a customer, a piece of equipment, an item in inventory, or even a place. In other words, entity beans model real-world objects; these objects are usually persistent records in some kind of database. Our hypothetical cruise line will need entity beans that represent cabins, customers, ships, etc.

Session beans are extensions of the client application that manage processes or tasks. A Ship bean provides methods for doing things directly to a ship, but doesn't say anything about the context under which those actions are taken. Booking passengers on the ship requires that we use a Ship bean, but it also requires a lot of things that have nothing to do with the ship itself: we'll need to know about passengers, ticket rates, schedules, and so on. A session bean is responsible for this kind of coordination. Session beans tend to manage particular kinds of activities, such as the act of making a reservation. They have a lot to do with the relationships between different entity beans. A TravelAgent session bean, for example, might make use of a Cruise, a Cabin, and a Customer—all entity beans—to make a reservation.

Similarly, message-driven beans coordinate tasks involving other session and entity beans. Message-driven beans and session beans differ primarily in how they are accessed. While a session bean provides a remote interface that defines which methods can be invoked, a message-driven bean subscribes to or listens for messages. It responds by processing the message and managing the actions that other beans take. For example, a ReservationProcessor message-driven bean would receive asynchronous messages—perhaps from a legacy reservation system—from which it would coordinate the interactions of the Cruise, Cabin, and Customer beans to make a reservation.

The activity that a session or message-driven bean represents is fundamentally transient: you start making a reservation, you do a bunch of work, and then it's finished. The session and message-driven beans do not represent things in the database. Obviously, session and message-driven beans have lots of side effects on the database; in the process of making a reservation, you might create a new Reservation by assigning a Customer to a particular Cabin on a particular Ship. All of these changes would be reflected in the database by actions on the respective entity beans. Session and message-driven beans like TravelAgent and ReservationProcessor, which are responsible for making a reservation on a cruise, can even access a database directly and perform reads, updates, and deletes to data. But there's no TravelAgent or ReservationProcessor record in the database—once the bean has made the reservation, it waits to process another.

What makes the distinction between the different types of beans difficult to understand is that it's extremely flexible. The relevant distinction for Enterprise JavaBeans is that an entity bean has persistent state; session and message-driven beans model interactions but do not have persistent state.

Classes and Interfaces

A good way to understand the design of enterprise beans is to look at how you'd go about implementing one. To implement entity and session enterprise beans, you need to define the component interfaces,* a bean class, and a primary key:

* There are basically three kinds of component interfaces: remote, local, and endpoint. The remote and local interfaces are supported by both EJB 2.1 and 2.0, while the endpoint component interface is new in EJB 2.1 and is not supported by EJB 2.0.

Remote interface

The remote interface defines the bean's business methods which can be accessed from applications outside the EJB container: the business methods a bean presents to the outside world to do its work. The remote interface extends `javax.ejb.EJBObject`, which in turn extends `java.rmi.Remote`. It is used by session and entity beans in conjunction with the remote home interface.

Remote home interface

The home interface defines the bean's life-cycle methods which can be accessed from applications outside the EJB container: the life-cycle methods for creating new beans, removing beans, and finding beans. The home interface extends `javax.ejb.EJBHome`, which in turn extends `java.rmi.Remote`. It is used by session and entity beans in conjunction with the remote interface.

Local interface

The local interface for an enterprise bean defines business methods that can be used by other beans in the same EJB container: the business methods a bean presents to other beans running in the same JVM. It allows beans to interact without the overhead of a distributed object protocol, which improves their performance. The local interface extends `javax.ejb.EJBLocalObject`. It is used by session and entity beans in conjunction with the local home interface.

Local home interface

The local home interface defines life-cycle methods that can be used by other beans in the same EJB container; that is, the life-cycle methods a bean presents to other beans running in the same JVM. It allows beans to interact without the overhead of a distributed object protocol, which improves their performance. The local home interface extends `javax.ejb.EJBLocalHome`. It is used by session and entity beans in conjunction with the local interface.

Endpoint interface

The endpoint interface defines business methods that can be accessed from applications outside the EJB container via SOAP. The endpoint interface is based on JAX-RPC (Java API for XML-RPC) and is designed to adhere to the SOAP and WSDL standards. The endpoint interface extends `java.rmi.Remote`. It can be used only by stateless session beans. There is no home interface associated with the endpoint interface.

Message interface

Message-driven beans implement the message interface, which defines the methods by which messaging systems, such as Java Message Service, can deliver messages to the bean.

Bean class

The session and entity bean classes implement the bean's business and life-cycle methods. Note that the bean class usually does not implement the remote or local component interfaces, but it may implement the endpoint interface.

However, the bean class must have methods matching the signatures of the methods defined in the remote, local, and endpoint interfaces, and must have methods corresponding to some of the methods in both the remote and local home interfaces. If this sounds perfectly confusing, it is. In addition, an entity bean must implement `javax.ejb.EntityBean`; a session bean must implement `javax.ejb.SessionBean`. The `EntityBean` and `SessionBean` extend `javax.ejb.EnterpriseBean`.

A message-driven bean implements one or more message delivery methods (e.g., `onMessage( )`) defined in a message interface. The container calls these methods when a new messages arrives. The message-driven bean class must also implement `javax.ejb.MessageDrivenBean`. EJB 2.1 and 2.0 containers must support JMS-based message-driven beans, which implement the `javax.jms.MessageListener` interface. EJB 2.1 also supports message-driven beans that process messages from other types of messaging systems with their own message interfaces. The `MessageDrivenBean`, like the `EntityBean` and the `SessionBean`, extends the `javax.ejb.EnterpriseBean` interface.

Primary key

The primary key is a class that provides a pointer into the database. Only entity beans need a primary key. The principal requirement for this class is that it implements `java.io.Serializable`.

Local interfaces provide a way for beans in the same container to interact efficiently. Calls to methods in the local interface don't involve RMI; the methods in the local interfaces don't need to declare that they throw `RemoteException`, and so on. An enterprise bean isn't required to provide a local interface if you know when you're developing the bean that it will interact only with remote or Web service clients. Likewise, an enterprise bean doesn't need to provide a remote or an endpoint interface if you know it will be called only by enterprise beans in the same container. You can provide any combination of local, remote, and endpoint interfaces.

The complexity comes about because enterprise beans exist in the middle—between some kind of client software and some kind of database. The client never interacts with a bean class directly; it always uses the methods of the entity or session bean's component interfaces to do its work, interacting with stubs that are generated automatically. (For that matter, a bean that needs the services of another bean is just another client: it uses the same stubs, rather than interacting with the bean class directly.) Although the local and local home interfaces do not involve RMI, they still represent a stub or a proxy to the bean class. While there is no network, the stubs allow the container to monitor the interactions between beans and to apply security and transactions as appropriate.

It's important to note that message-driven beans don't support remote, local, or endpoint component interfaces, but they may become the client of other session or entity beans and interact with those beans through their component interfaces. The entity and session beans with which the message-driven bean interact may be located in the same container, in which case the message-driven bean uses their local component interfaces, or they may be located in a different address space and EJB container, in which case the remote or endpoint component interfaces are used.

There are also many interactions between an enterprise bean and its *container* (Many people use the terms "container" and "server" interchangeably, which is understandable because the difference between the terms isn't clearly defined.) The container is responsible for creating new instances of beans, making sure they are stored properly by the server, and so on. Tools provided by the container's vendor do a tremendous amount of work behind the scenes. At least one tool takes care of creating the mapping between entity beans and records in the database. Other tools generate code based on the component interfaces and the bean class itself. The code generated does things like create the bean, store it in the database, and so on.

Naming conventions

Before going on, let's establish some conventions. When we speak about an enterprise bean as a whole—its component interfaces, bean class, and so forth—we will call it by its common business name, followed by EJB. For example, an enterprise bean that is developed to model a cabin on a ship will be called the Cabin EJB. Notice that we don't use a constant-width font for "Cabin," because we are referring to all the parts of the bean (the component interfaces, bean class, etc.) as a whole, not just to one particular part, such as the remote interface or bean class. The term *enterprise bean* or *bean* denotes any kind of bean, including entity, session, and message-driven beans. *Entity bean* denotes an entity-type enterprise bean; *session bean* denotes a session-type enterprise bean; and *message-driven bean* denotes a message driven-type enterprise bean. The acronym MDB is frequently used in place of the term "message-driven bean."

We also use suffixes to distinguish between local, remote, and endpoint component interfaces. When we are talking about the remote interface of the Cabin EJB, we will combine the common business name with the word *Remote*. For example, the remote interface for the Cabin EJB is called the `CabinRemote` interface. The local interface of the Cabin EJB would be the `CabinLocal` interface. The endpoint interface for the Cabin EJB-based web service would be `CabinWS` (WS stands for Web Service). The home interfaces add the word *Home* to the mix. The remote and local home interfaces for the Cabin EJB would be `CabinHomeRemote` and `CabinHomeLocal`, respectively.* The bean class is always the common business name, followed by the word *Bean*. For example, the Cabin EJB's bean class would be named `CabinBean`.

* The endpoint interface does not have a corresponding home interface.

These naming conventions are used for clarity; they are not prescriptive or even recommended for use in production. Once you understand the differences between the component interfaces and the different types of beans, you can use any naming strategy you wish.

The remote interface

Having introduced the machinery, let's look at how to build an entity bean with remote component interfaces. In this section, we examine the Cabin EJB, an entity bean that models a cabin on a cruise ship. Let's start with its remote interface.

We'll define the remote interface for a Cabin bean using the `CabinRemote` interface, which defines business methods for working with cabins. All remote interface types extend the `javax.ejb.EJBObject` interface:

```
import java.rmi.RemoteException;

public interface CabinRemote extends javax.ejb.EJBObject {
    public String getName( ) throws RemoteException;
    public void setName(String str) throws RemoteException;
    public int getDeckLevel( ) throws RemoteException;
    public void setDeckLevel(int level) throws RemoteException;
}
```

These are methods for naming the cabin and setting the cabin's deck level; you can probably imagine lots of other methods that you'd need, but this is enough to get started. All of these methods declare that they throw `RemoteException`, which is required of all methods on remote component interfaces. EJB requires the use of Java RMI-IIOP conventions with remote component interfaces, although the underlying protocol can be CORBA IIOP, Java Remote Method Protocol (JRMP), or some other protocol. Java RMI-IIOP will be discussed in more detail in the next chapter.

The remote home interface

The remote home interface defines life-cycle methods used by clients of entity and session beans for locating enterprise beans. The remote home interface extends `javax.ejb.EJBHome`. We'll call the home interface for the Cabin bean `CabinHomeRemote`, and define it like this:

```
import java.rmi.RemoteException;
import javax.ejb.CreateException;
import javax.ejb.FinderException;

public interface CabinHomeRemote extends javax.ejb.EJBHome {
    public CabinRemote create(Integer pk)
        throws CreateException, RemoteException;
    public CabinRemote findByPrimaryKey(Integer id)
        throws FinderException, RemoteException;
}
```

The `create( )` method is responsible for initializing an instance of our bean. If your application needs them, you can provide other `create( )` methods with different arguments. For example, you could provide a `create( )` method that initializes the cabin's deck and name.

The `findByPrimaryKey( )` method, with a single argument, is required, and allows you to look up a particular Cabin given its primary key. You are free to define other methods that provide convenient ways to look up Cabin beans—for example, you might want to define a method called `findByShip( )` that returns all the cabins on a particular ship. Find methods like these are used in *entity beans* but not in *session* or message-driven beans.

The bean class

Now let's look at an actual entity bean. Here's the code for the `CabinBean`; it's a sparse implementation, but it shows how the pieces fit together:

```
import javax.ejb.EntityContext;

public abstract class CabinBean implements javax.ejb.EntityBean {

    public Integer ejbCreate(Integer pk){
        setId(id);
        return null;
    }
    public void ejbPostCreate(Integer pk){
        // do nothing
    }

    public abstract String getName( );
    public abstract void setName(String str);

    public abstract int getDeckLevel( );
    public abstract void setDeckLevel(int level);

    public abstract Integer getId( );
    public abstract void setId(Integer pk);

    public void setEntityContext(EntityContext ctx){
        // empty implementation
    }
    public void unsetEntityContext( ){
        // empty implementation
    }
    public void ejbActivate( ){
        // empty implementation
    }
    public void ejbPassivate( ){
        // empty implementation
    }
    public void ejbLoad( ){
```

```
            // empty implementation
        }
        public void ejbStore(){
            // empty implementation
        }
        public void ejbRemove(){
            // empty implementation
        }
    }
```

Notice that the CabinBean class is abstract, as are several of the methods that access or update the bean's persistent state. Also notice that there are no instance fields to hold the state information these methods access. The abstract methods (and the missing fields) are implemented by the container system automatically. Container-managed entity beans are the only beans that are declared as abstract with abstract accessor methods. You won't see abstract classes and methods in session or message-driven beans.

The set and get methods for the cabin's name and deck level are the CabinBean's business methods; they match the business methods defined by the EJB's remote interface, CabinRemote. The business methods are the only methods visible to the client application; the other methods are visible only to the EJB container or the bean class itself. For example, the setId( )and getId( ) methods are defined in the bean class but not in the remote interface, which means they cannot be called by the entity bean's client. The other methods are required by the EJB component model and are not part of the bean class's public business definition.

The ejbCreate( ) and ejbPostCreate( ) methods initialize the instance of the bean class when a new cabin record is ready to be added to the database. The last seven methods in the CabinBean are defined in the javax.ejb.EntityBean interface. These methods are life-cycle callback methods. The EJB container invokes these callback methods on the bean class when important life-cycle events occur. The ejbRemove( ) method, for example, notifies an entity bean that its data is about to be deleted from the database. The ejbLoad( ) and ejbStore( ) methods notify the bean instance that its state is being read or written to the database. The ejbActivate( ) and ejbPassivate( ) methods notify the bean instance that it is about to be activated or deactivated, a process that conserves memory and other resources. setEntityContext( ) enables the EJB container to give the bean information about itself and its surroundings. unsetEntityContext( ) is called by the EJB container to notify the bean instance that it is about to be dereferenced for garbage collection.

All these callback methods provide the bean class with *notifications* when an action is about to be taken, or was just taken, on the bean's behalf by the EJB server. These notifications simply inform the bean of an event; the bean doesn't have to do anything about it. The callback notifications tell the bean where it is during its lifecycle, when it is about to be loaded, removed, deactivated, and so on. Because the callback methods are defined in the javax.ejb.EntityBean interface, the entity bean class must implement them, but it isn't required to do anything meaningful with the methods if it doesn't need to. Our bean, the `CabinBean`, won't need to do anything when these callback methods are invoked, so these methods are empty implementations. Details about these callback methods, when they are called, and how a bean should react to them are covered in Chapter 10.

The primary key

The primary key is a pointer that helps locate data that describes a unique record or entity in the database; it is used in the `findByPrimaryKey()` method of the home interface to locate a specific entity. Primary keys are defined by the bean developer and must be some type of serializable object. The Cabin EJB uses a simple `java.lang.Integer` type as its primary key. It's also possible to define custom primary keys, called *compound primary keys*, which represent complex primary keys consisting of several different fields. Primary keys are covered in detail in Chapter 10.

What about session beans?

`CabinBean` is an entity bean, but a session bean wouldn't be all that different. It would extend `SessionBean` instead of `EntityBean` and would have an `ejbCreate()` method that would initialize the bean's state, but no `ejbPostCreate()`. Session beans do not have `ejbLoad()` or `ejbStore()` methods, because session beans are not persistent. While session beans have a `setSessionContext()` method, they do not have an `unsetSessionContext()` method. Session beans have `ejbActivate()` and `ejbPassivate()` methods, which are used by stateful session beans to manage conversational state. Finally, session beans provide an `ejbRemove()` method, which notifies the bean that the client no longer needs it. However, this method doesn't tell the bean that its data is about to be removed from the database, because a session bean doesn't represent data.

Session beans don't have a primary key. That's because session beans are not persistent themselves, so there is no need for a key that maps to the database. Session beans are covered in detail in Chapter 11.

What about message-driven beans?

Message-driven beans (MDBs) implement a message interface; they don't implement remote, local, endpoint, or home interfaces. The message-driven bean defines a few callback methods and one or more message delivery methods. The callback methods include the `ejbCreate()` method, which is called when the bean class is first created; the `ejbRemove()` method, called when the bean instance is about to be discarded from the system (usually when the container doesn't need it any longer); and the `setMessageDrivenContext()` method. The kind of message delivery methods implemented by the MDB depend on the type of messaging service it supports. For example, a JMS-based MDB, which all EJB containers must support, must implement the `onMessage( )` method, which is called every time a new asynchronous JMS message is delivered. The message-driven bean doesn't define the `ejbPassivate( )`, `ejbActivate( )`, `ejbLoad( )`, or `ejbStore( )` methods because it doesn't need them.

Message-driven beans don't have a primary key, for the same reason that session beans don't. They are not persistent, so there is no need for a key to the database. Message-driven beans are covered in detail in Chapter 12.

Deployment Descriptors and JAR Files

The interfaces and classes we have discussed don't address how beans are managed at runtime. We didn't talk about how beans interact with security, transactions, naming, and other services common to distributed object systems. These types of primary services are handled automatically by the EJB container, but that prompts the question, "How does the EJB container know how to handle security, transactions, and so on?" The EJB container gets this kind of runtime information from *deployment descriptors*.

Deployment descriptors allow us to customize an EJB's runtime behavior without having to change the software itself. Deployment descriptors are also similar to the property sheets used in Visual Basic and PowerBuilder. Where property sheets allow us to describe the runtime attributes of visual widgets (background color, font size, etc.), deployment descriptors allow us to describe runtime attributes of server-side components (security, transactional context, etc.).

When a bean class and its interfaces have been defined, a deployment descriptor for the bean is created and populated with data about the bean. Integrated development environments (IDEs) that support development of Enterprise JavaBeans often allow developers to set up the deployment descriptors they need using visual utilities like property sheets. After the developer has set all of the bean's properties, the deployment descriptor is saved to a file. Once the deployment descriptor is completed and saved to a file, the bean can be packaged in a JAR file for deployment.

JAR (Java Archive) files are ZIP files that package Java classes and other resources that are ready to be used in some type of application. JARs are used for packaging applets, Java applications, JavaBeans, web applications (servlets and JSPs), and Enterprise JavaBeans. A JAR file containing one or more enterprise beans includes the bean classes, component interfaces, and supporting classes for each bean. It also contains one deployment descriptor, which is used for all the beans in the JAR file. When a bean is deployed, the JAR file's location is given to the container's deployment tools.

When the container opens the JAR file, it reads the deployment descriptor to learn about the bean and how it should be managed at runtime. The deployment descriptor tells the deployment tools what kind of beans are in the JAR file (*session*, *entity*, or *message-driven*), how they should be managed in transactions, who has access to the beans at runtime, and other information. The person deploying the bean can alter some of these settings, such as transactional and security access attributes, to customize the bean for a particular application. Most container tools provide user-friendly property sheets for reading and altering the deployment descriptor when the bean is deployed.

When Enterprise JavaBeans 1.0 was released, serializable classes were used for the deployment descriptor. Starting with Enterprise JavaBeans 1.1, the serializable deployment descriptor classes used in EJB 1.0 were dropped in favor of a more flexible file format based on the Extensible Markup Language (XML). The XML deployment descriptors are text files structured according to a standard schema (XML Schema in EJB 2.1 and Document Type Definition (DTD) in EJB 2.0) that can be extended so the type of deployment information stored evolves as the specification evolves. Chapter 17 provides a detailed description of XML deployment descriptors. The following sections provide a brief overview of XML deployment descriptors.

EJB 2.1: Deployment descriptor

The following descriptor might be used to describe the Cabin bean in EJB 2.1:

```
<?xml version="1.0" encoding="UTF-8"?>
<ejb-jar xmlns="http://java.sun.com/xml/ns/j2ee"
         xmlns:xsi="http://www.w3.org/2001/XMLSchema-instance"
         xsi:schemaLocation="http://java.sun.com/xml/ns/j2ee
                             http://java.sun.com/xml/ns/j2ee/ejb-jar_2_1.xsd"
         version="2.1">

    <enterprise-beans>
        <entity>
            <ejb-name>CabinEJB</ejb-name>
            <home>com.titan.CabinHomeRemote</home>
            <remote>com.titan.CabinRemote</remote>
            <ejb-class>com.titan.CabinBean </ejb-class>
            <persistence-type>Container</persistence-type>
            <prim-key-class>java.lang.Integer</prim-key-class>
            <reentrant>False</reentrant>
        </entity>
    </enterprise-beans>
</ejb-jar>
```

The first element in an EJB 2.1 deployment descriptor declares the document to be an XML document conformant with XML Version 1.0, and the character encoding, normally UTF-8.

The root element is the `ejb-jar` element. It declares the namespace of the EJB 2.1 XML Schema as well as the schema's location. In addition, the `ejb-jar` element declares the version of EJB supported, which in the case of EJB 2.1 is version "2.1".

EJB 2.0: Deployment descriptor

The following descriptor might be used to describe the Cabin bean in EJB 2.0:

```
<!DOCTYPE ejb-jar PUBLIC "-//Sun Microsystems, Inc.//DTD EnterpriseJavaBeans 2.0//EN"
"http://java.sun.com/dtd/ejb-jar_2_0.dtd">

<ejb-jar>
    <enterprise-beans>
        <entity>
            <ejb-name>CabinEJB</ejb-name>
            <home>com.titan.CabinHomeRemote</home>
            <remote>com.titan.CabinRemote</remote>
            <ejb-class>com.titan.CabinBean </ejb-class>
            <persistence-type>Container</persistence-type>
            <prim-key-class>java.lang.Integer</prim-key-class>
            <reentrant>False</reentrant>
        </entity>
    </enterprise-beans>
</ejb-jar>
```

The first element in an EJB 2.0 deployment descriptor is <!DOCTYPE>. This element describes the organization that defined the DTD for the XML document, supplies the DTD's version, and provides a URL for the DTD. The DTD describes how a particular XML document is structured.

EJB 2.1 and 2.0: Elements of the XML deployment descriptor

Now, let's look more closely at the information in the deployment descriptor. Note that the deployment descriptor for a real bean would have a lot more information; this example simply illustrates the type of information you'll find in a deployment descriptor. Here's what the individual elements mean:

<ejb-jar>
: The root of the XML deployment descriptor. All other elements must be nested below this one. It must contain one <enterprise-beans> element and may contain other optional elements.

<enterprise-beans>
: Contains declarations for all the enterprise beans described by this XML document. It may contain <entity>, <session>, or <message-driven> (EJB 2.0) elements, which describe entity, session, and message-driven enterprise beans, respectively.

<entity>
: Describes an entity bean and its deployment information. There must be one of these elements for every entity bean described by the XML deployment descriptor. While this deployment descriptor describes a single entity bean, the <session> element is used in the same way to describe a session bean. The <message-driven> element is different, as it does not define any component interfaces.

`<ejb-name>`
: The descriptive name of the enterprise bean. It is the name used for the enterprise bean in conversation, when talking about the bean component as a whole.

`<home>`
: The fully qualified class name of the remote home interface. This interface defines the life-cycle behaviors (create, find, remove) of the enterprise bean to its clients outside the container system.

`<remote>`
: The fully qualified class name of the remote interface. This interface defines the enterprise bean's business methods to its clients outside the container system.

`<ejb-class>`
: The fully qualified class name of the bean class. This class implements the business methods of the bean.

`<prim-key-class>`
: The fully qualified class name of the enterprise bean's primary key. The primary key is used to find the bean data in the database.

The `<persistence-type>` and `<reentrant>` elements express the persistence strategy and concurrency policies of the entity bean. These elements are explained in more detail later in the book.

As you progress through this book, you will be introduced to the elements that describe concepts that have not been covered yet, so don't worry about knowing all of the elements you might find in a deployment descriptor.

EJB Objects and EJB Home

The entity and session beans both declare the component interfaces that their clients use to access them. (Message-driven beans are a very different kind of animal). In EJB 2.0, clients outside the container system always use the enterprise bean's remote component interfaces. In EJB 2.1, clients outside the container system have the option of accessing stateless session beans as Web services. For both EJB 2.1 and 2.0, clients within the same J2EE system (i.e., enterprise beans, Servlets, and JSPs) can use local component interfaces to interact. This section explains how the component interfaces are connected to instances of the bean class at runtime.

Now that you have a basic understanding of some of an enterprise bean's parts (component interfaces, bean class, and deployment descriptor), it's time to talk more precisely about how these parts come together inside an EJB container system. Unfortunately, we can't talk as precisely as we'd like. There are a number of ways for an EJB container to implement these relationships; we'll show some of the possibilities. Specifically, we'll talk about how the container implements the component interface of entity and session beans, so that clients—either applications outside the container or other co-located enterprise beans—can interact with and invoke methods on the bean class.

The two missing pieces are the EJB object itself and the EJB home. You will probably never see the EJB home and EJB object classes because their class definitions are proprietary to the vendor's EJB implementation and are generally not made public. This practice is useful because it represents a separation of responsibilities along areas of expertise. As an application developer, you are intimately familiar with how your business environment works and needs to be modeled, so you will focus on creating the applications and beans that describe your business. System-level developers, the people who write EJB servers, don't understand your business, but they do understand how to develop CTMs and support distributed objects. It makes sense for system-level developers to apply their skills to the mechanics of managing distributed objects, but leave the business logic to you, the application developer. Let's talk briefly about the EJB object and the EJB home so the missing pieces in the big picture are understandable.

The EJB object

This chapter has said a lot about a bean's remote and local interfaces, which extend the `EJBObject` and the `EJBLocalObject` interfaces, respectively. Who implements these interfaces? Clearly, the stub does: we understand that much. But what about the server side?

On the server side, an EJB object is an object that implements the remote and/or local interfaces of the enterprise bean. The EJB object is generated by your EJB container and wraps the enterprise bean instance—that is, an instance of the enterprise bean class you've created (in our example, the `CabinBean`) on the server—and expands its functionality to include `javax.ejb.EJBObject` and/or `javax.ejb.EJBLocalObject` behavior. This object works with the container to apply transactions, security, and other system-level operations to the bean at runtime.

We're forced to use "and/or" a lot when talking about which interface the EJB object implements. That's because enterprise beans in EJB can declare the local interface, the remote interface, or both! In EJB 2.1, stateless session beans can also implement an *endpoint* interface, which turns it into a Web service. (The endpoint interface and Web services are addressed separately in Chapter 14.) Regardless of which interfaces the bean implements, we can think of the EJB object as implementing both. In reality, there may be a special EJB object for the remote interface and another special EJB object for the local interface of each enterprise bean; that depends on how the vendor chooses to implement it. But that distinction, while it matters to EJB vendors, isn't visible to EJB developers.

A vendor can use a number of strategies to implement the EJB object. Figure 2-1 illustrates two possibilities using the `CabinRemote` interface. The same implementation strategies apply to the `CabinLocal` and `javax.ejb.EJBLocalObject` interfaces.

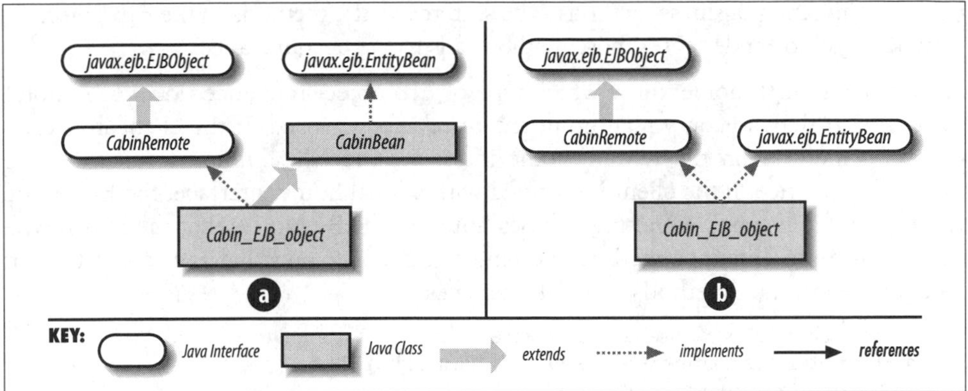

Figure 2-1. Two ways to implement the EJB object

In Figure 2-1(a), the EJB object class actually extends the bean class, adding functionality specific to the EJB container. In Figure 2-1(b), the bean class is no longer included in the model. In this case, the EJB object has both the proprietary implementation required by the EJB container and bean class method implementations that were copied from the bean class's definition.

The EJB object design shown in Figure 2-1(a) is perhaps the most common. But other implementations are used; it shouldn't make a difference which one your vendor has chosen. The bottom line is that you never really know much about the EJB object: its implementation is up to the vendor. Knowing that the EJB object exists answers a lot of questions about how enterprise beans are structured. But everything a client (including other enterprise beans) needs to know about an enterprise bean is described by the remote and home interfaces.

The EJB home

The EJB home is a lot like the EJB object. It's another class that's generated automatically when you install an enterprise bean in a container. It implements all the methods defined by the home interfaces (local and/or remote) and is responsible for helping the container manage the bean's life cycle. The EJB home is responsible for locating, creating, and removing enterprise beans. These tasks may involve working with the EJB server's resource managers, instance pooling, and persistence mechanisms, the details of which are hidden from the developer.

For example, when a create method is invoked on a home interface, the EJB home creates an instance of the EJB object that references a bean instance of the appropriate type. Once the bean instance is associated with the EJB object, the instance's matching `ejbCreate()` method is called. In the case of an entity bean, a new record is inserted into the database. With session beans, the instance is simply initialized. Once the `ejbCreate()` method has completed, the EJB home returns a remote or local reference (i.e., a stub) for the EJB object to the client. The client can then work with the EJB object by invoking business methods. The stub relays the methods to the EJB object; in turn, the EJB object delegates those method calls to the bean instance.

How does the EJB home know which type of EJB object reference (local or remote) to return? It depends on which home interface is being used. If the client invokes a `create( )` method on the remote home interface, the EJB home returns a remote interface reference. If the client is working with a local home interface, the EJB home returns a reference implementing the local interface. EJB requires that the return type of remote home interface methods be remote interfaces and that the return type of local home interface methods be local interfaces:

```
// The Cabin EJB's remote home interface
public interface CabinHomeRemote extends javax.ejb.EJBHome {
    public CabinRemote create(Integer pk)
        throws CreateException, RemoteException;
    public CabinRemote findByPrimaryKey(Integer id)
        throws FinderException, RemoteException;
}

// The Cabin EJB's local home interface
public interface CabinHomeLocal extends javax.ejb.EJBLocalHome {
    public CabinLocal create(Integer pk)
        throws CreateException;
    public CabinLocal findByPrimaryKey(Integer id)
        throws FinderException;
}
```

Figure 2-2 illustrates the architecture of EJB with the EJB home and EJB object implementing the home interface and remote or local interface. The bean class is wrapped by the EJB object. Remember, though, that this is only an illustration. "EJB object" and "EJB home" are simply terms to describe the EJB container's responsibilities for supporting the component interfaces. In reality, we have no idea how the vendor chose to implement the EJB object and EJB home, since they are only logical constructs and may not have equivalent software counterparts.

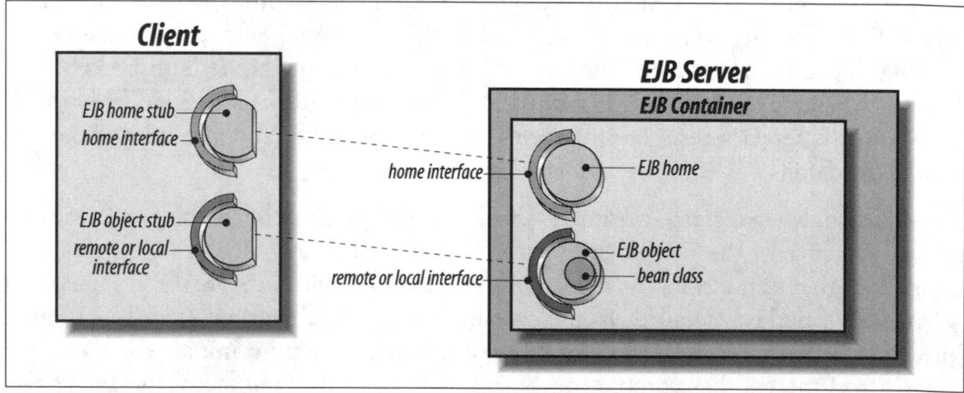

Figure 2-2. EJB architecture

Deploying a bean

After the files that define the bean (the component interfaces and the bean classes) have been packaged into a JAR file, the bean is ready to be deployed; that is, it can be added to an EJB container so it can be accessed as a distributed component. During the deployment process, tools provided by the EJB container vendor generate the EJB object and EJB home classes by examining the deployment descriptor and the other interfaces and classes in the JAR file.

Using Enterprise Beans

Let's look at how a client would use an enterprise bean to do something useful. We'll start with the Cabin EJB defined earlier. A cabin is a thing or place with a description that is stored in a database. To make the example a little more real, assume that there are other entity beans: Ship, Cruise, Ticket, Customer, Employee, and so on.

Getting Information from an Entity Bean

Imagine that a GUI client needs to display information about a particular cruise: the cruise name, the ship name, and a list of cabins. Using the cruise ID obtained from a text field, we can use our beans to look up data about the cruise. Here's the code:

```
CruiseHomeRemote cruiseHome = ... ; // use JNDI to get the home
// Get the cruise ID text field 1.
String cruiseID = textField1.getText( );
// Create an EJB primary key from the cruise ID.
Integer pk = new Integer(cruiseID);
// Use the primary key to find the cruise.
CruiseRemote cruise = cruiseHome.findByPrimaryKey(pk);
// Set text field 2 to show the cruise name.
textField2.setText(cruise.getName( ));
// Get a remote reference to the ship that will be used
// for the cruise from the cruise bean.
ShipRemote ship = cruise.getShip( );
// Set text field 3 to show the ship's name.
textField3.setText(ship.getName( ));

// Get all the cabins on the ship.
Collection cabins = ship.getCabins( );
Iterator cabinItr = cabins.iterator( );

// Iterate through the enumeration, adding the name of each cabin
// to a list box.
while(cabinItr.hasNext( ))
    CabinRemote cabin = (CabinRemote)cabinItr.next( );
    listBox1.addItem(cabin.getName( ));
}
```

We start by getting a remote reference to the EJB home for an entity bean that represents a cruise. We need a remote reference rather than a local one because the client is an application located outside the EJB container. It's not shown in the example, but references to the EJB home are obtained using JNDI. JNDI is a powerful API for locating resources, such as remote objects, on networks. JNDI lookups are covered in subsequent chapters.

We read a cruise ID from a text field, use it to create a primary key, and use that primary key together with the EJB home to get a `CruiseRemote` reference. This reference implements the bean's business methods. Once we have the appropriate Cruise EJB, we can ask the bean to give us a remote reference to a Ship EJB that represents the ship used for the cruise. We can then call the `ship.getCabins()` method to get a `Collection` of remote Cabin EJB references from the Ship EJB, and, with the Cabin EJBs in hand, we can retrieve and display the names of the Cabin EJBs.

Modeling Taskflow with Session Beans

Entity beans are useful for representing data and describing business concepts that can be expressed as nouns, but they're not very good at representing a process or a task. A Ship bean provides methods and behavior for doing things directly to a ship, but it does not define the context under which these actions are taken. The previous example retrieved data about cruises and ships; we could also have modified this data. With enough effort, we could have figured out how to book a passenger—perhaps by adding a Customer EJB to a Cruise EJB, or adding a customer to a list of passengers maintained by the ship. We could try to shove methods for accepting payment and other tasks related to booking into our GUI client application, or even into the Ship or Cabin EJBs, but that's a contrived and inappropriate solution. We don't want business logic in the client application—that's why we went to a multitier architecture in the first place. Similarly, we don't want this kind of logic in our entity beans that represent ships and cabins. Booking passengers on a ship or scheduling a ship for a cruise are the types of activities or functions of the business, not the Ship or the Cabin bean, and are therefore expressed in terms of a process or task.

Session beans act as agents that manage business processes or tasks for the client; they're the appropriate place for business logic. A session bean is not persistent; nothing in a session bean maps directly into a database or is stored between sessions. Session beans work with entity beans, data, and other resources to control *taskflow*. Taskflow is the essence of any business system, because it expresses how entities interact to model the actual business. Session beans control tasks and resources but do not themselves represent data.

The term "taskflow" was coined specifically for this book. It's derived from the term "workflow," which is frequently used to describe the management of business processes that may span several days with lots of human intervention. In contrast to workflow, the term taskflow is used in this book to describe the interactions of beans within a single transaction that takes only a few seconds to execute.

The following code demonstrates how a session bean designed to make cruise-line reservations might control the taskflow of other entity and session beans. Imagine that a piece of client software, in this case a user interface, obtains a remote reference to a TravelAgent session bean. Using the information entered into text fields by the user, the client application books a passenger on a cruise:

```
// Get the credit card number from the text field.
String creditCard = textField1.getText( );
int cabinID = Integer.parseInt(textField2.getText( ));
int cruiseID = Integer.parseInt(textField3.getText( ));

// Create a new Reservation session passing in a reference to a
// customer entity bean.
TravelAgent travelAgent = travelAgentHome.create(customer);

// Set cabin and cruise IDs.
travelAgent.setCabinID(cabinID);
travelAgent.setCruiseID(cruiseID);

// Using the card number and price, book passage.
// This method returns a Ticket object.
TicketDO ticket = travelAgent.bookPassage(creditCard, price);
```

This is a fairly *coarse-grained* abstraction of the process of booking a passenger: most of the details are hidden from the client. Hiding the *fine-grained* details of taskflow is important because it provides the system with flexibility as it evolves: we know that we will always want to book passengers, but the process for booking a passenger may change.

Course-grained and fine-grained are terms that are sometimes used to describe the level of detail exposed by the public interface of a component. A component whose public interfaces exposes a lot of detail about how the component funtions is called fine-grained. Components that provide a public interface but do not expose the details of its operation are called coarse-grained. When dealing with remote clients, coarse-grained interfaces are usally prefered because they are more flexible—the client doesn't have to be aware of all the nitty-gritty details of how the component works.

The following listing shows some of the code for the `TravelAgentBean`. The `bookPassage( )` method works with three entity beans, the Customer, Cabin, and Cruise EJBs, and another session bean, the ProcessPayment EJB. The ProcessPayment EJB provides several methods for making a payment, including check, cash, and credit card. In this case, we use the ProcessPayment bean to make a credit card payment. Once payment has been made, a serializable `TicketDO` object is returned to the client.

```
public class TravelAgentBean implements javax.ejb.SessionBean {
    public CustomerRemote customer;
```

```
    public CruiseRemote cruise;
    public CabinRemote cabin;

    public void ejbCreate(CustomerRemote cust){
        customer =cust;
    }
    public TicketDO bookPassage(CreditCardDO card,double price)
        throws IncompleteConversationalState {
        if (customer == null ||cruise == null ||cabin == null){
            throw new IncompleteConversationalState( );
        }
        try {
            ReservationHomeRemote resHome = (ReservationHomeRemote)
                getHome("ReservationHome",ReservationHomeRemote.class);
            ReservationRemote reservation =
                resHome.create(customer,cruise,cabin,price,new Date( ));
            ProcessPaymentHomeRemote ppHome = (ProcessPaymentHomeRemote)
                getHome("ProcessPaymentHome",ProcessPaymentHomeRemote.class);

            ProcessPaymentRemote process = ppHome.create( );
            process.byCredit(customer,card,price);

            TicketDO ticket = new TicketDO(customer,cruise,cabin,price);
            return ticket;
        }catch(Exception e){
            throw new EJBException(e);
        }
    }

// More business methods and callback methods follow
}
```

This example leaves out some details, but it demonstrates the difference in purpose between a session bean and an entity bean. Entity beans represent the behavior and data of a business object, while session beans model the taskflow. The client application uses the TravelAgent EJB to perform a task using other beans. For example, the TravelAgent EJB uses a ProcessPayment EJB and a Reservation EJB in the process of booking passage. The ProcessPayment EJB processes the credit card, and the Reservation EJB records the actual reservation in the system. Session beans can also be used to read, update, and delete data that can't be adequately captured in an entity bean. Session beans don't represent records or data in the database, but they can access data.

All of the work performed by the TravelAgent session bean could have been coded in the client application. Having the client interact directly with entity beans is a common but troublesome design approach because it ties the client directly to the details of the business tasks. As a result, any changes in the way entity beans interact requires changes to the client, and it's very difficult to reuse the code that models the taskflow.

Session beans allow clients to perform tasks without being concerned with the details that make up the task. A developer can update the session bean, possibly changing the taskflow, without affecting the client code. In addition, if the session bean is properly defined, other clients that perform the same tasks can reuse it. The Process-Payment session bean, for example, can be used in many areas besides reservations, including retail and wholesale sales. For example, the ship's gift shop could use the ProcessPayment EJB to process purchases. As a client of the ProcessPayment EJB, the TravelAgent EJB doesn't care how ProcessPayment works; it's only interested in the ProcessPayment EJB's coarse-grained interface, which validates and records charges.

Moving taskflow logic into a session bean also simplifies the client application and reduces network traffic. Excessive network traffic is a common problem for distributed object systems: it can overwhelm the server and clog the network, hurting response time and performance. Session beans, if used properly, can reduce network traffic by limiting the number of requests needed to perform a task. The user of session beans keeps the interaction between the beans involved in a taskflow on the server. One method invocation on the client application results in many method invocations on the server, but the network sees only the traffic produced by the client's call to the session bean. In the TravelAgent EJB, the client invokes `bookPassage()`; in turn, `bookPassage()` makes several method invocations on other enterprise beans. Furthermore, the TravelAgent bean may be in the same container as the other beans, and therefore can use the local interfaces, further reducing network traffic. For the network cost of one method invocation, the client gets several method invocations.

In addition, session beans reduce the number of network connections that the client needs. The cost of maintaining many network connections can be high, so reducing the number of connections each client needs improves the performance of the system as a whole. Figure 2-3 compares the network traffic and connections generated by a client that uses only entity beans to those generated by a client that uses session beans.

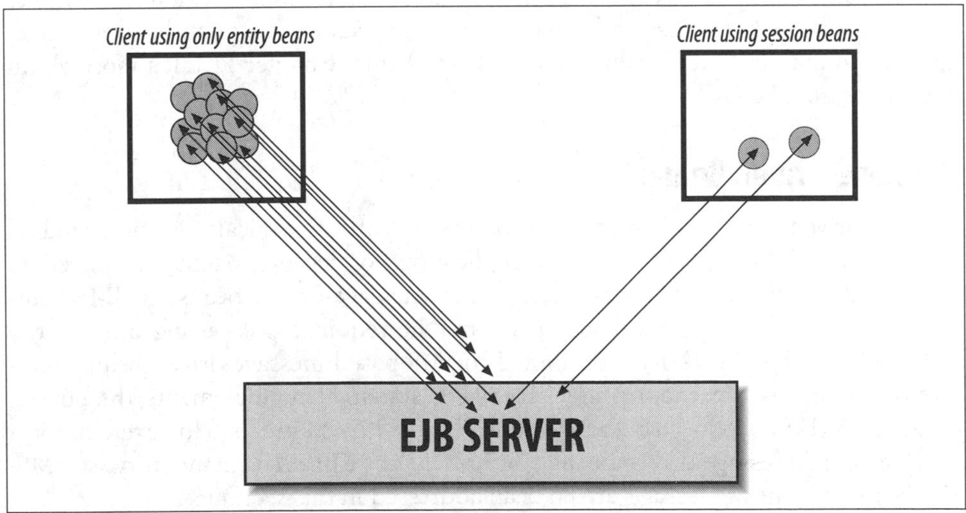

Figure 2-3. Session beans reduce network traffic and thin down clients

Session beans also limit the number of stubs used on the client, which saves the client memory and processing cycles. This may not seem like a big deal, but without the use of session beans, a client might be expected to manage hundreds or even thousands of remote references at one time. In the TravelAgent EJB, for example, the `bookPassage()` method works with several remote references, but the client is exposed only to the TravelAgent's remote reference.

Stateless and stateful session beans

Session beans can be either *stateful* or *stateless*. Stateful session beans maintain *conversational state* when used by a client. Conversational state is not written to a database; it's information that is kept in memory while a client carries on a conversation with an enterprise bean, and is lost when the conversation ends or if the EJB container crashes. For example, a client making a reservation through the TravelAgent bean may call the methods that set cabin and cruise IDs. These IDs are part of the session's conversational state, and affect the behavior of subsequent method calls, such as the call to `bookPassage()` that makes the actual reservation. Conversational state is kept for only as long as the client application is actively using the bean. Once the client shuts down or releases the TravelAgent EJB, the conversational state is lost forever. Stateful session beans are not shared among clients; they are dedicated to the same client for the life of the enterprise bean.

Stateless session beans do not maintain any conversational state. Each method is completely independent and uses only data passed in its parameters. The ProcessPayment EJB is a perfect example of a stateless session bean: it doesn't need to maintain any conversational state from one method invocation to the next. All the information needed to make a payment is passed into the `byCreditCard()` method. Stateless session beans provide better performance and consume fewer resources than entity and stateful session beans because a few stateless session bean instances can serve hundreds and possibly thousands of clients. Chapter 11 talks more about stateless session beans.

Message-Driven Beans

Message-driven beans are integration points for other applications interested in working with EJB applications. Java applications or legacy systems that need to access EJB applications can send messages to message-driven beans via JMS. This bean processes those messages and performs the required tasks using other entity and session beans. EJB 2.1 is not limited to JMS-based message-driven beans: message-driven beans can support any messaging system that implements the correct J2eeCA 1.5 (J2EE Connector Architecture Version 1.5) contracts. However, support for JMS-based message-driven beans (JMS-MDBs) in EJB 2.1 is mandatory, so JMS-MDBs are the type of message-driven bean addressed in this section.

In many ways, JMS-MDBs fulfill the same role as stateless session beans: they manage the taskflow of entity and session beans. The task is initiated by an asynchronous message sent by an application using JMS. Unlike session beans, which respond to business methods invoked on their component interfaces, a JMS-MDB responds to messages delivered through its `onMessage( )` method. Since the messages are asynchronous, the client that sends them doesn't expect a reply. The messaging client simply sends the message and forgets about it.

As an example, we can recast the TravelAgent EJB developed earlier as the ReservationProcessor JMS message-driven bean:

```
public class ReservationProcessorBean implements javax.ejb.MessageDrivenBean,
    javax.jms.MessageListener {

    public void onMessage(Message message) {
        try {
            MapMessage reservationMsg = (MapMessage)message;

            Integer customerPk = (Integer)reservationMsg.getObject("CustomerID");
            Integer cruisePk = (Integer)reservationMsg.getObject("CruiseID");
            Integer cabinPk = (Integer)reservationMsg.getObject("CabinID");
            double price = reservationMsg.getDouble("Price");

            CreditCardDO card = getCreditCard(reservationMsg);
            CustomerRemote customer = getCustomer(customerPk);
            CruiseLocal cruise = getCruise(cruisePk);
            CabinLocal cabin = getCabin(cabinPk);

            ReservationHomeLocal resHome = (ReservationHomeLocal)
                jndiContext.lookup("java:comp/env/ejb/ReservationHome");
            ReservationLocal reservation =
                resHome.create(customer,cruise,cabin,price,new Date( ));

            Object ref = jndiContext.lookup("java:comp/env/ejb/ProcessPaymentHome");
            ProcessPaymentHomeRemote ppHome = (ProcessPaymentHomeRemote)
                PortableRemoteObject.narrow(ref,ProcessPaymentHomeRemote.class);

            ProcessPaymentRemote process = ppHome.create( );
            process.byCredit(customer,card,price);

        } catch(Exception e) {
            throw new EJBException(e);
        }
    }
   // More helper methods and callback methods follow
}
```

All the information about the reservation is obtained from the message delivered to the MDB. JMS messages can take many forms; the `javax.jms.MapMessage` used in this example carries name-value pairs. Once the information is gathered from the message and the enterprise bean references are obtained, the reservation is processed in the same way as it was in the session bean. The only difference is that a `TicketDO` object isn't created and returned to the caller; message-driven beans don't have to respond to the caller.

Regardless of the messaging system, message-driven beans do not maintain any conversational state. Each new message is independent of the previous messages. The message-driven bean is explained in detail in Chapter 12.

The Bean-Container Contract

The environment that surrounds the beans on the EJB server is often called the *container*. The container is more a concept than a physical construct. It acts as an intermediary between the bean and the EJB server. It manages the EJB objects and EJB homes and helps these constructs to manage bean resources and provide services such as transactions, security, concurrency, and naming at runtime. The distinction between the container and the server is not clearly defined, but the EJB specification defines the component model in terms of the container's responsibilities, so we will follow that convention here.

Enterprise bean components interact with the EJB container through a well-defined component model. The `EntityBean`, `SessionBean`, and `MessageDrivenBean` interfaces provide callback methods that notify the bean class of life-cycle events. At runtime, the container invokes these methods on the bean instance when relevant events occur. For example, when the container is about to write an entity bean instance's state to the database, it first calls the bean instance's `ejbStore( )` method. This call gives the bean instance an opportunity to do cleanup on its state before it's written to the database. The `ejbLoad( )` method is called just after the bean's fields are populated from the database, providing the bean developer with an opportunity to manage the bean's state before the first business method is called.* Other callback methods can be used by the bean class in a similar fashion. EJB defines when these various callback methods are invoked and what can be done within their contexts.

While the bean interfaces require implementations of all the callback methods, those implementations don't have to be meaningful. The method body of any or all of the callback methods can be left empty, and often is. Beans that implement callback methods usually access resources that aren't managed by the EJB system. Enterprise beans that wrap legacy systems often fall into this category.

`javax.ejb.EJBContext` is an interface implemented by the container and is also part of the bean-container contract. Entity beans use a subclass of `javax.ejb.EJBContext` called `javax.ejb.EntityContext`. Session beans use a subclass called `javax.ejb.SessionContext`. Message-driven beans use the subclass `javax.ejb.MessageDrivenContext`. These

* The `ejbLoad( )` and `ejbStore( )` behavior illustrated here is for container-managed persistence. With bean-managed persistence, the behavior is slightly different. This distinction is examined in detail in Chapter 10.

`EJBContext` types provide the bean with information about its environment: its container, the client using the enterprise bean, and the bean itself. The bean can use this information while processing requests from clients and callback methods from the container.

An enterprise bean's interface with the container also includes a JNDI namespace, called the *environment naming context*, which the bean can use to look up the resources it needs (including other beans). The JNDI environment naming context and the `EJBContext` (and its subclasses) are described in more detail in Chapters 10, 11, and 12.

Summary

This chapter covered a lot of ground describing the basic architecture of an EJB system. At this point, you should understand that beans are business object components. The home interfaces define life-cycle methods for creating, finding, and destroying beans, and the remote and local interfaces define the public business methods of the bean. Message-driven beans do not have component interfaces. The bean class is where the state and behavior of the bean are implemented.

There are three basic kinds of beans: entity, session, and message-driven. Entity beans are persistent and represent a person, place, or thing. Session beans are extensions of the client and embody a process or a taskflow that defines how other beans interact. Session beans are not persistent: they receive their state from the client, and they live only as long as the client needs them. Message-driven beans are integration points that allow other applications to interact with EJB applications using JMS or, in EJB 2.1, some other J2eeCA 1.5–compliant resource. Message-driven beans, like stateless session beans, are not persistent and do not maintain conversational state.

The EJB object and EJB home are conceptual constructs that delegate method invocations to session and entity beans from the client and help the container to manage the enterprise bean at runtime. The clients of entity and session beans do not interact with the instances of the bean class directly. Instead, the client software interacts with stubs, which are connected to the EJB object and EJB home. The EJB object implements the remote and/or local interface and expands the bean class's functionality. The EJB home implements the home interface and works closely with the container to create, locate, and remove beans.

Beans interact with their containers through the well-defined bean-container contract. This contract provides callback methods, the `EJBContext`, and the JNDI environment-naming context. The callback methods notify the bean class that it is involved in a life-cycle event. The `EJBContext` and JNDI environment-naming context provide the bean instance with information about its environment.

CHAPTER 3

Resource Management and the Primary Services

Chapter 2 discussed the basic architecture of Enterprise JavaBeans, including the relationship between the bean class, the component interfaces, the EJB object and EJB home, and the EJB container. These artifacts define a common model for distributed server-side components. But the common model for distributed objects isn't enough to make EJB interesting or even particularly useful. EJB servers also manage the resources used by beans, and can manage thousands, even millions of distributed objects simultaneously. They must manage how distributed objects use memory, threads, database connections, processing power, and more. Furthermore, the EJB specification defines interfaces that help developers take advantage of these common practices.

In particular, EJB servers support six primary services: concurrency, transaction management, persistence, object distribution, naming, and security. These services provide the kind of infrastructure that is necessary for a successful three-tier system. Enterprise JavaBeans also supports two additional services: asynchronous messaging and a timer service.

This chapter discusses the resource-management facilities and the primary services that are available to Enterprise JavaBeans.

Resource Management

A large business system with many users can easily require thousands of objects—even millions of objects—to be in use simultaneously. As the number of interactions among these objects increases, concurrency and transactional concerns can degrade the system's response time and frustrate users. EJB servers increase performance by synchronizing object interactions and sharing resources.

There is a relationship between the number of clients and the number of distributed objects that are required to service them. Not surprisingly, the larger the client population, the more distributed objects are needed. At some point, the increase in clients affects performance and diminishes throughput. EJB explicitly supports two mechanisms that make it easier to manage large numbers of beans at runtime: instance pooling and activation. In addition, EJB supports the use of the J2EE Connector Architecture (J2EE Connectors) for managing resource connections. As the number of distributed objects and clients increase, the number of resource connections also increases. J2EE Connectors work with the EJB container to manage connections to databases, enterprise messaging, ERP, legacy systems, and other types of resources.

Instance Pooling

The concept of pooling resources is nothing new. It's common to pool database connections so that the business objects in the system can share database access. This trick reduces the number of database connections needed, which reduces resource consumption and increases throughput. The J2EE Connector Architecture (J2eeCA) is frequently the mechanism employed by EJB containers when pooling connections to databases and other resources, and is covered a little later. Most EJB containers also apply resource pooling to server-side components; this technique is called *instance pooling*. Instance pooling reduces the number of component instances—and therefore resources—needed to service client requests. In general, it is also less expensive to reuse pooled instances than to create and destroy instances.

As you already know, clients of session and entity beans interact with the beans through the remote and local interfaces implemented by EJB objects. Client applications never have direct access to the actual bean. Similarly, JMS clients never interact with JMS-based message-driven beans (JMS-MDBs) directly. They send messages that are routed to the EJB container system. The EJB container then delivers these messages to the proper message-driven instance.

Instance pooling is possible because clients never access beans directly. Therefore, there's no fundamental reason to keep a separate copy of each enterprise bean for each client. The server can keep a much smaller number of enterprise beans around to do the work, reusing each enterprise bean instance to service different requests. Although this sounds like a resource drain, when done correctly, it greatly reduces the resources required to service all the client requests.

The entity bean life cycle

To understand how instance pooling works, let's examine the life cycle of an entity bean. Entity beans exist in one of three states:

No state
: When a bean instance is in this state, it has not yet been instantiated. We identify this state to provide a beginning and an end for the life cycle of a bean instance.

Pooled state
: When an instance is in this state, it has been instantiated by the container but has not yet been associated with an EJB object.

Ready state
: When a bean instance is in this state, it has been associated with an EJB object and is ready to respond to business method invocations.

Each EJB vendor implements instance pooling differently, but all instance-pooling strategies attempt to manage collections of bean instances so that they are quickly accessible at runtime. To set up an instance pool, the EJB container creates several instances of a bean class and holds them until needed. As clients make business-method requests, bean instances from the pool are assigned to the EJB objects associated with the clients. When the EJB object doesn't need the instance, it's returned to the instance pool. An EJB server maintains instance pools for every type of bean deployed. Every instance in an instance pool is *equivalent*—they are treated equally. Instances are selected arbitrarily from the instance pool and assigned to EJB objects as needed.

After the bean instance is placed in the pool, it gets a reference to a `javax.ejb.EJBContext`. The `EJBContext` provides an interface that the bean can use to communicate with the EJB environment. This `EJBContext` becomes more useful when the bean instance moves to the Ready state. When a client uses an EJB home to obtain a remote or local reference to a bean, the container responds by creating an EJB object. Once created, the EJB object is assigned a bean instance from the instance pool. When a bean instance is assigned to an EJB object, it officially enters the Ready state. From the Ready state, a bean instance can receive requests from the client and callbacks from the container. Figure 3-1 shows the sequence of events that results in an EJB object wrapping a bean instance and servicing a client.

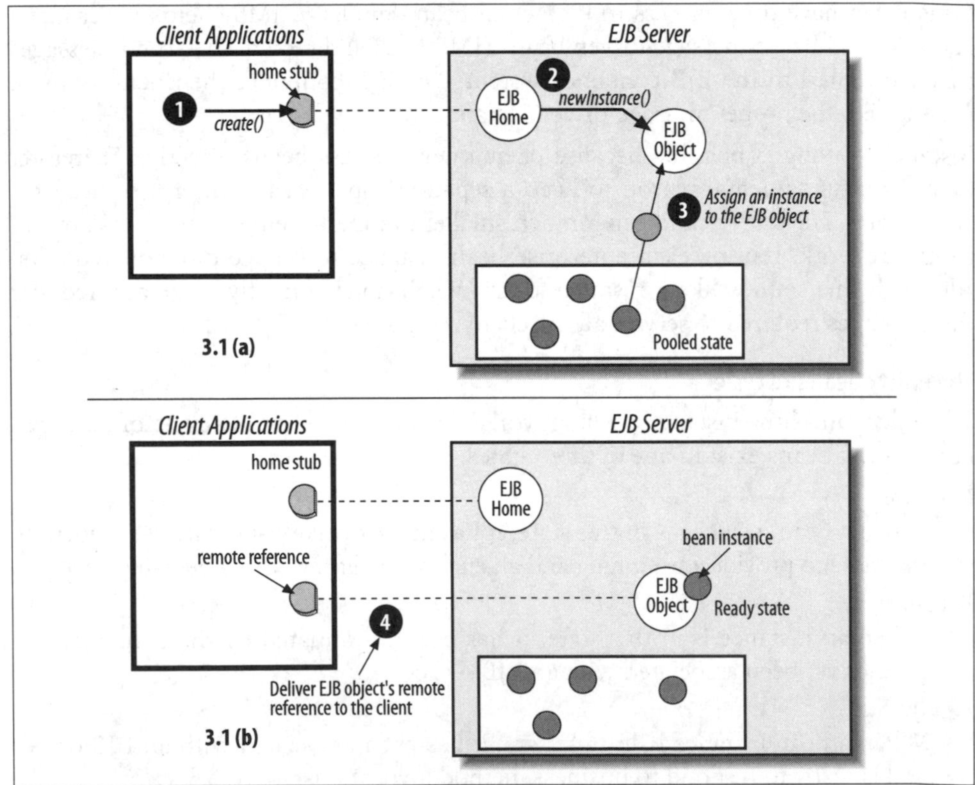

Figure 3-1. A bean moves from the instance pool to the Ready state

When a bean instance moves into the Ready state, the `EJBContext` takes on new meaning. The `EJBContext` provides information about the client that is using the bean. It also provides the instance with access to its own EJB home and EJB object, which is useful when the bean needs to pass references to itself or to other enterprise beans, or when it needs to create, locate, or remove beans of its own class. So the `EJBContext` is not a static class; it is an interface to the container, and its state changes as the instance is assigned to different EJB objects.

When the client is finished with a bean's remote reference, either the remote reference passes out of scope or one of the bean's remove methods is called.* At this point, the bean instance is disassociated from the EJB object and returned to the instance pool. Bean instances can also be returned to the pool during lulls between client requests. If a client request is received and no bean instance is associated with the EJB object, an instance is retrieved from the pool and assigned to the EJB object. This is called *instance swapping*. After the bean instance returns to the instance pool, it is again available to service a new client request. Figure 3-2 illustrates the life cycle of a bean instance.

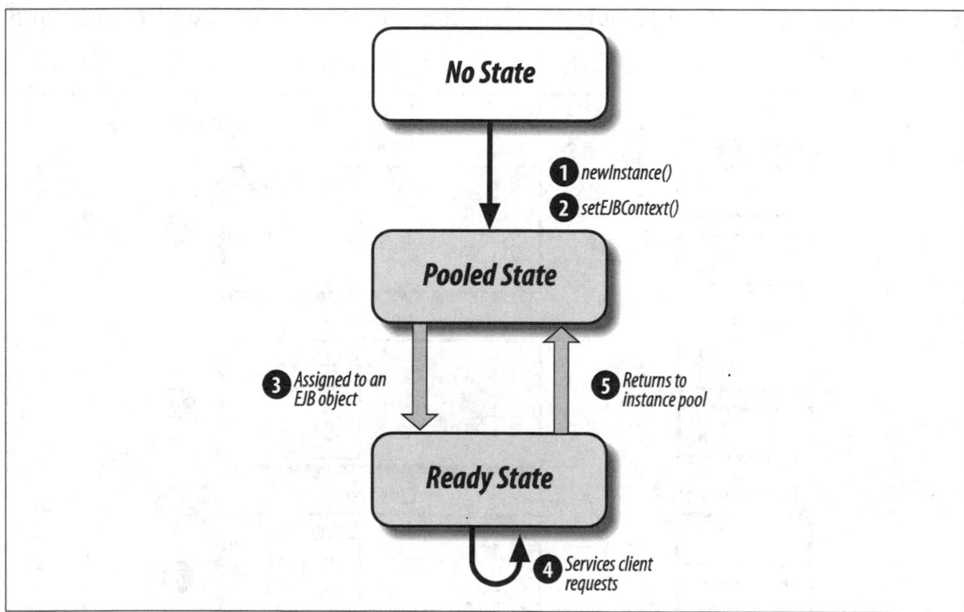

Figure 3-2. Life cycle of a bean instance

The number of instances in the pool fluctuates as instances are assigned to EJB objects and returned to the pool. The container can also manage the number of

* The `EJBHome`, `EJBLocalHome`, `EJBObject`, and `EJBLocalObject` interfaces all define methods that can be used to remove a bean.

instances in the pool, increasing the count when client activity increases and lowering the count during less active periods.

Instance swapping

Stateless session beans offer a particularly powerful opportunity to leverage instance pooling. Because a stateless session bean does not maintain any state between method invocations, every method invocation operates independently, performing its task without relying on instance variables. This means that any stateless session instance can service requests for any EJB object of the proper type. The container can therefore swap bean instances in and out between method invocations.

Figure 3-3 illustrates instance swapping between stateless session bean method invocations. In Figure 3-3 (a), instance A is servicing a business method invocation delegated by EJB object 1. Once instance A has serviced the request, it moves back to the instance pool (Figure 3-3 (b)). When a business method invocation on EJB object 2 is received, instance A is associated with that EJB object for the duration of the operation (Figure 3-3 (c)). While instance A is servicing EJB object 2, another method invocation is received by EJB object 1 from the client and is serviced by instance B (Figure 3-3 (d)).

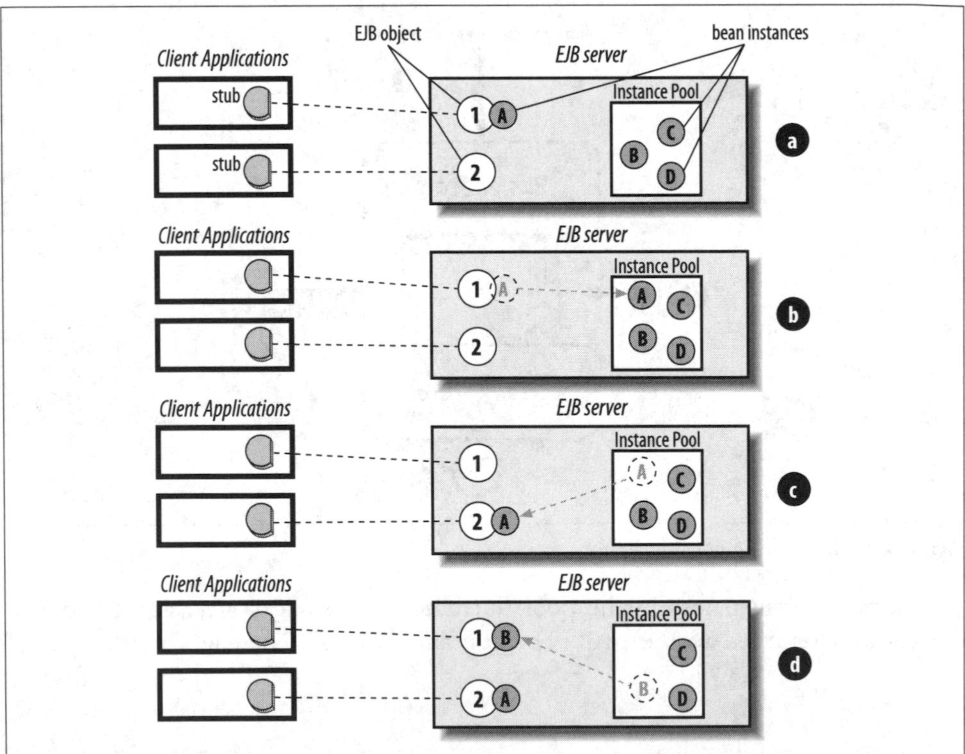

Figure 3-3. Stateless session beans in a swapping strategy

Using this swapping strategy allows a few stateless session bean instances to serve hundreds of clients, because the amount of time it takes to perform most method invocations is typically much shorter than the pauses between method invocations. When a bean instance is finished servicing a request for an EJB object, it is immediately made available to any other EJB object that needs it. This allows fewer stateless session instances to service more requests, which decreases resource consumption and improves performance.

Stateless session beans are declared "stateless" in the deployment descriptor. Nothing in the class definition marks a session bean as being stateless or stateful. Once a bean class is deployed as stateless, the container assumes that no conversational state is maintained between method invocations. So a stateless bean can have instance variables, but because bean instances can be servicing several different EJB objects, they should not be used to maintain conversational state.

Message-driven beans and instance pooling

Message-driven beans, like stateless session beans, do not maintain state specific to a client request, which makes them excellent candidates for instance pooling.

In most EJB containers, each type of message-driven bean has its own instance pool that services incoming messages. JMS-MDBs subscribe to a specific message destination, which is a kind of address used when sending and receiving messages. When a JMS client sends an asynchronous message to a destination, the message is delivered to the EJB containers of the beans that subscribe to the destination. The EJB container determines which JMS-MDB subscribes to that destination, then chooses an instance of that type from the instance pool to process the message. Once the JMS-MDB instance has finished processing the message (when the `onMessage( )` method returns), the EJB container returns the instance to its instance pool. Figure 3-4 illustrates how client requests are processed by an EJB container.

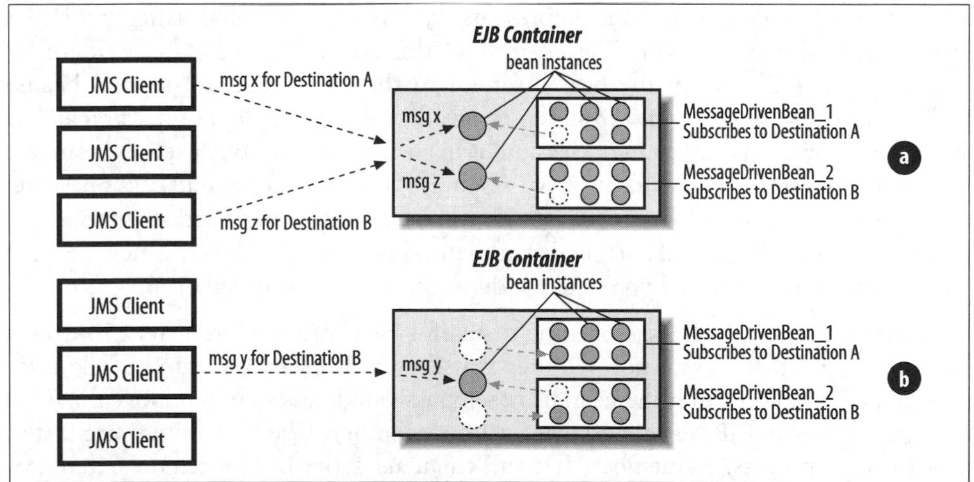

Figure 3-4. JMS-MDB instance pooling

In Figure 3-4 (a), the top JMS client delivers a message to Destination A and the bottom JMS client delivers a message to Destination B. The EJB container chooses an instance of MessageDrivenBean_1 to process the message intended for Destination A and an instance of MessageDrivenBean_2 to process the message intended for Destination B. The bean instances are removed from the pool and used to process the messages.

A moment later in Figure 3-4 (b), the middle JMS client sends a message to Destination B. At this point, the first two messages have already been processed and the container is returning the instances to their respective pools. As the new message comes in, the container chooses a new instance of MessageDrivenBean_2 to process the message.

JMS-MDBs are always deployed to process messages from a specific destination. In the above example, instances of MessageDrivenBean_1 process messages only for Destination A, while instances of MessageDrivenBean_2 process messages only for Destination B. Several messages for the same destination can be processed at the same time. If, for example, a hundred messages for Destination A arrive at the same time, the EJB container simply chooses a hundred instances of MessageDrivenBean_1 to process the incoming messages; each instance is assigned a message.

EJB 2.1 has expanded the role of message-driven beans beyond JMS so that they can support other messaging services and APIs. This opens the message-driven bean up to just about any kind of resource, including messaging systems other than JMS, ERP systems like SAP, and legacy systems like IMS. Regardless of the type of resource represented by the message-driven bean, the instances of the bean type will be pooled in the same way as the JMS-MDBs.

The Activation Mechanism

Unlike other enterprise beans, stateful session beans maintain state between method invocations. *Conversational state* represents the continuing conversation with the stateful session bean's client. The integrity of this conversational state needs to be maintained for the life of the bean's service to the client. Stateful session beans, unlike stateless session, entity, and message-driven beans, do not participate in instance pooling. Instead, stateful session beans use activation to conserve resources. When an EJB server needs to conserve resources, it can evict stateful session beans from memory. When a bean is evicted, its conversational state is serialized to a secondary storage. When a client invokes a method on the EJB object, a new stateful instance is instantiated and populated with the state from the initial bean.

Passivation is the act of disassociating a stateful bean instance from its EJB object and saving its state. Passivation requires that the bean instance's state be held relative to its EJB object. After the bean has been passivated, it is safe to remove the bean instance from the EJB object and evict it from memory. Clients are unaware of the deactivation process. Remember that the client uses the bean's remote reference, which is implemented by an EJB object, and therefore does not directly communicate with the bean instance. As a result, the client's connection to the EJB object can be maintained while the bean is passivated.

Activating a bean is the act of restoring a stateful bean instance's state relative to its EJB object. When a method on the passivated EJB object is invoked, the container automatically creates a new instance and sets its fields equal to the data stored during passivation. The EJB object can then delegate the method invocation to the bean as normal. Figure 3-5 shows activation and passivation of a stateful bean. In Figure 3-5 (a), the bean is being passivated. The state of instance B is read and held relative to the EJB object it was serving. In Figure 3-5 (b), the bean has been passivated and its state preserved. Here, the EJB object is not associated with a bean instance. In Figure 3-5 (c), the bean is being activated. A new instance, instance C, has been instantiated and associated with the EJB object and is in the process of having its state populated with the state held relative to the EJB object.

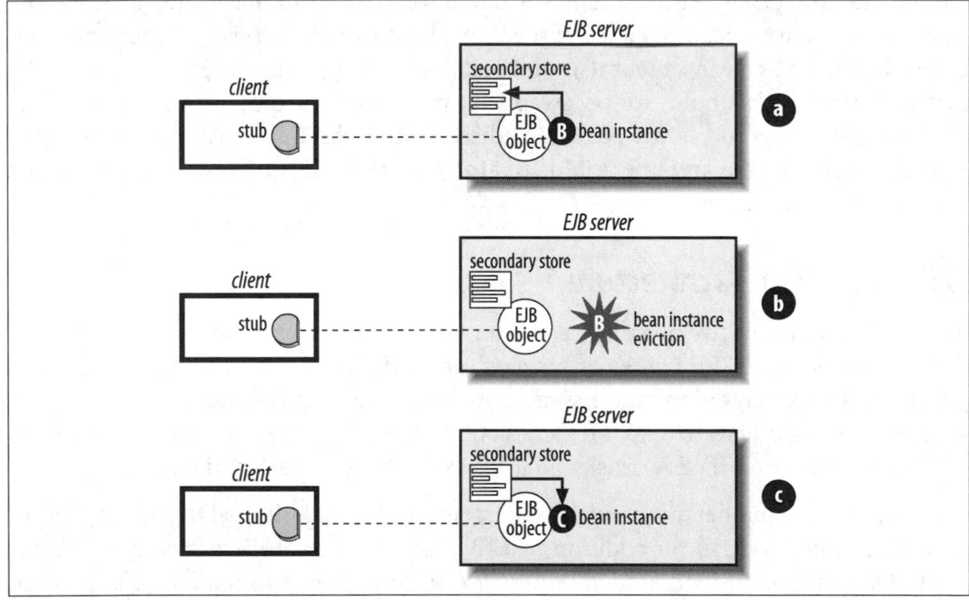

Figure 3-5. The passivation and activation processes

The exact mechanism for activating and passivating stateful beans is up to the vendor. Each stateful bean is serializable and thus provides at least one way of preserving its state, but vendors are free to choose other serialization techniques. Note that the transient property is not treated as you might expect when activating a passivated bean. In Java serialization, transient fields are always set to the initial value for that field type when the object is deserialized. `Integers` are set to `0`, `Booleans` to `false`, object references to `null`, and so on. In EJB, transient fields are not necessarily set back to their initial values but can maintain their original values, or any arbitrary value, after being activated. Take care when using transient fields, since their state following activation is implementation-specific.

The activation process is supported by the life-cycle callback methods discussed in Chapter 2. The `ejbActivate()` method i activation callback methodss called immediately following the successful activation of a bean instance, and can be used to reset transient fields to an initial value. `ejbPassivate()` is called immediately prior to passivation of the bean instance. These two methods are especially helpful if the bean instance maintains connections to resources that need to be closed or freed prior to passivation and reobtained following activation. Because the stateful bean instance is evicted from memory, open connections to resources are not maintained. The exceptions are remote references to other beans and the `SessionContext`, which must be maintained with the serialized state of the bean and reconstructed when the bean is activated. EJB also requires that the references to the JNDI environment context, component interfaces, and the `UserTransaction` object be maintained through passivation.

Unlike stateful beans, entity beans do not have conversational state; instead, the state of each entity bean instance is saved in the database. However, the activation callback methods (`ejbActivate()` and `ejbPassivate()`) are used to notify the instance when it's about to be swapped in or out of the instance pool. The `ejbActivate()` method is invoked immediately after the bean instance is swapped into the EJB object, and the `ejbPassivate()` method is invoked just before the instance is swapped out.

J2EE Connector Architecture

The J2EE Connector Architecture defines an interface between Enterprise Information Systems (EISs) and J2EE container systems (i.e., EJB and Servlet containers). EIS is a generic term for any information system, including relational database servers, message-oriented middleware (e.g., MQSeries and SonicMQ), CORBA, ERP systems (e.g., SAP, PeopleSoft, and JD Edwards), and legacy systems (e.g., IMS and CICS).

J2EE defines a number of standard enterprise APIs, including JDBC, JMS, JNDI, Java IDL, and JavaMail, in addition to EJB. Each of these APIs provides a vendor-neutral API for a specific kind of enterprise information system. JDBC is used to exchange information with relational databases; JMS is for message-oriented middleware; JNDI is for naming and directory services; JavaMail is for electronic mail systems; and Java IDL is for CORBA. Requiring support for these APIs ensures that the enterprise beans that use them are portable across EJB vendors.

Although the enterprise APIs are vendor-agnostic, the products behind the APIs are always proprietary. When an enterprise bean uses the enterprise APIs, it's the responsibility of the EJB container to pool and maintain the EIS connections, enroll the EIS in transactions, propagate security credentials, etc. These tasks often require the EJB container to interact with the underlying EIS in ways not addressed by the generic APIs. In effect, each J2EE vendor had to write proprietary code to manage each brand of EIS. Faced with this situation, J2EE vendors chose which EISs they would support for each standard API. This situation had a significant impact on the brands of EIS an EJB vendor could be expected to support: for example, vendor A might support JDBC connectivity to Oracle, while vendor B supports only DB2.

J2EE Connectors 1.0 for EJB 2.0 and 2.1

EJB 2.0 required support for the new J2EE Connector Architecture, which went a long way to solving this problem. The J2eeCA defines an interface between enterprise information systems and EJB containers. It establishes a set of Java interfaces that the EIS must implement in order to be J2EE Connector–compliant. These interfaces define a very general and portable Service Provider Interface (SPI) for creating EIS connections, managing connections in a pool, enrolling connections into transactions, and exchanging security information. The J2eeCA essentially hides the differences between proprietary infrastructures so that EJB container vendors can develop one set of code to manage all J2eeCA-compliant EISs.

While the J2eeCA standardizes the SPI, it has little or no impact on the APIs that you, the developer, use. A JDBC provider (a.k.a. driver) that is J2eeCA-compliant has the same API as one that's not. From the perspective of the application developer, nothing's changed, but under the hood of the EJB container, a single set of code can be used to manage all EISs. The benefit is that you can plug any J2eeCA-compliant EIS into your EJB container system. You don't have to worry about the EIS vendor you choose: as long as its API is J2EE Connector–compliant, it will work with any EJB 2.0 or 2.1 vendor.

While Version 1.0 of the J2EE Connector Architecture solved some important problems, it didn't support the *push* model for messaging. Several EISs push data to clients, without the clients explicitly making a request—for example, JMS. JMS allows clients to receive messages by subscribing to a destination. In this case, the EIS, the message-oriented middleware, is pushing messages to the clients.

J2EE Connectors 1.5 for EJB 2.1

EJB 2.1 requires support for J2EE Connector Architecture 1.5, which also supports the push model. To support the push model, J2eeCA 1.5 uses the message-driven bean programming model. Specifically, it defines a container-connector interface that allows incoming messages, sent asynchronously from the EIS, to be processed by message-driven beans. For example, vendor X could develop a J2EE Connector for a Mail Delivery Agent (MDA), which is software that delivers Internet email. Vendor X defines a message-listening interface, the `EmailListener`, that can be implemented to create an Email Message-Driven Bean (Email-MDB) for processing email. As the MDA receives email from the Internet, it pushes them to the EJB container, which delegates each message to an instance of the Email-MDB. The application developer then writes an Email-MDB that implements the `javax.ejb.MessageDrivenBean` interface as well as the `com.xvendor.EmailListener` interface. Once the Email-MDB is created and deployed, it can process incoming messages.

Primary Services

Many value-added services are available for distributed applications. This book looks at eight value-added services called the *primary services* because they are required to complete the Enterprise JavaBeans platform. The primary services include concurrency, transactions, persistence, distributed objects, asynchronous messaging, timer, naming, and security. EJB servers automatically manage all the primary services. This capability relieves the application developers from the task of mastering these complicated services. Instead, developers can focus on defining the business logic that describes the system and leave the system-level concerns to the EJB server. The following sections describe each of the primary services and explain how they are supported by EJB.

Concurrency

Concurrency is important to all the bean types, but it has different meanings for each type.

Concurrency with session and entity beans

Session beans do not support concurrent access. This limitation makes sense if you consider the nature of stateful and stateless session beans. A stateful bean is an extension of one client and serves only that client. It doesn't make sense to make stateful beans concurrent if they are used only by the clients that created them. Stateless session beans don't need to be concurrent because they don't maintain state that needs to be shared. The scope of the operations performed by a stateless bean is limited to the scope of each method invocation. Because neither stateful nor stateless session beans represent shared data, there is no need for concurrency.

Entity beans represent data that is shared and may be accessed concurrently. Entity beans are shared components. In Titan's EJB system, for example, there are three ships: *Paradise*, *Utopia*, and *Valhalla*. At any given moment the Ship entity bean that represents the *Utopia* might be accessed by hundreds of clients. To make concurrent access to entity beans possible, the EJB container needs to protect the data represented by the shared bean, while allowing many clients to access the bean simultaneously.

In a distributed object system, problems arise when you attempt to share distributed objects among clients. If two clients are both using the same EJB object, how do you keep one client from writing over the changes of the other? If, for example, one client reads the state of an instance just before a different client makes a change to the same instance, the data the first client read becomes invalid. Figure 3-6 shows two clients sharing the same EJB object.

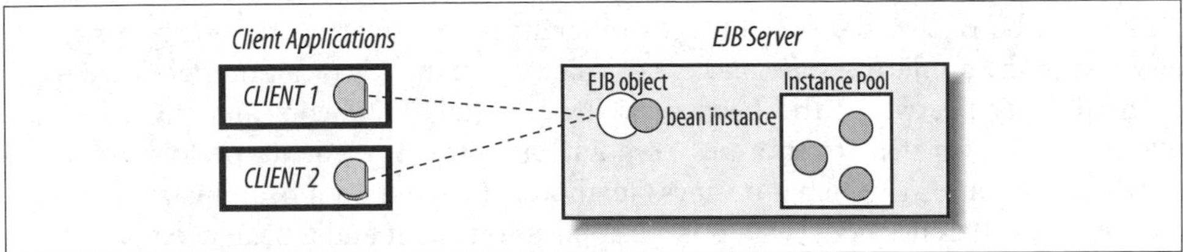

Figure 3-6. Clients sharing access to an EJB object

EJB addresses the dangers associated with concurrency in entity beans by prohibiting concurrent access to bean instances. In other words, several clients can be connected to one EJB object, but only one client thread can access the bean instance at a time. If, for example, one of the clients invokes a method on the EJB object, no other client can access that bean instance until the method invocation is complete. In fact, if the method is part of a larger transaction, the bean instance cannot be accessed at all, except within the same transactional context, until the entire transaction is complete.

Since EJB servers handle concurrency, a bean's methods do not have to be made thread-safe. In fact, the EJB specification prohibits use of the `synchronized` keyword. Prohibiting the use of the thread synchronization primitives prevents developers from thinking that they control synchronization and enhances the performance of bean instances at runtime. In addition, the EJB specification explicitly prohibits beans from creating their own threads. In other words, as a bean developer, you cannot create a thread within a bean. The EJB container has to maintain complete control over the bean in order to properly manage concurrency, transactions, and persistence. Allowing the bean developer to create arbitrary threads would compromise the container's ability to track what the bean is doing and make it impossible for the container to manage the primary services.

Reentrance

When talking about concurrency in entity beans, we need to discuss the related concept of *reentrance*. Reentrance is when a thread of control attempts to reenter a bean instance; for example, bean A calls bean B, which in turn calls bean A. In EJB, entity-bean instances are nonreentrant by default, which means that loopbacks like the one just described are not allowed.

Remember that entity and session beans interact using objects that implement each other's remote and local interfaces, and do not interact directly. In other words, when bean A operates on bean B, it does so the same way an application client would: by using B's remote or local interface as implemented by an EJB object. This allows the EJB container to interpose between method invocations from one bean to the next in order to apply security and transaction services.

While most bean-to-bean interactions take place using local reference of enterprise beans that are in the same container, occasionally beans interact using remote references. When interactions between beans take place using remote references, the beans can be relocated—possibly to a different server—with little or no impact on the rest of the application. Regardless of whether remote or local interfaces are used, from the perspective of the bean servicing the call, all clients are created equal. Figure 3-7 shows that, from a bean's point of view, only clients perform business method invocations. When a business method is invoked on a bean instance, it cannot tell the difference between a remote application client and a bean client.

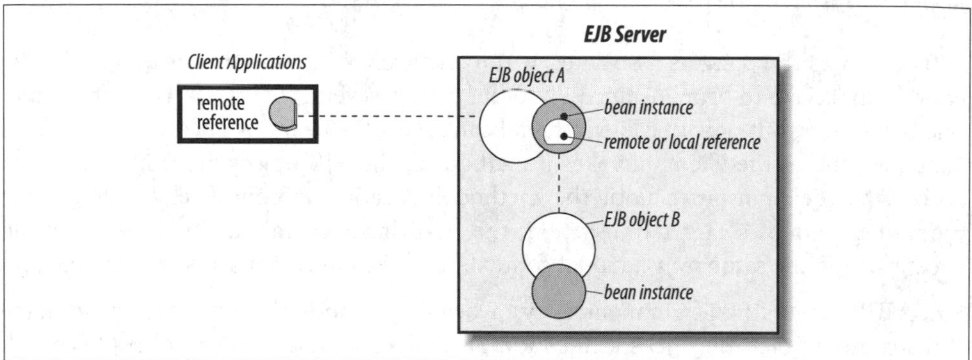

Figure 3-7. Beans access each other through EJB objects

A *loopback* occurs when bean A invokes a method on bean B that then attempts to make a call back to bean A. In Figure 3-8, client 1 invokes a method on bean A. In response to the method invocation, bean A invokes a method on bean B. At this point, there is no problem because client 1 controls access to bean A, and bean A is the client of bean B. If, however, bean B attempts to call a method on bean A, it is blocked because the thread has already entered bean A. By calling its caller, bean B is performing a loopback. This is illegal by default, because EJB doesn't allow a thread of control to reenter a bean instance.

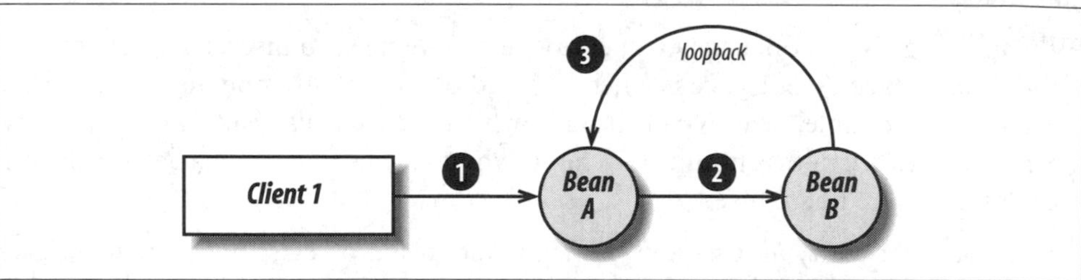

Figure 3-8. A loopback scenario

Session beans can never be reentrant, and throw an exception if a loopback is attempted. Entity beans can be configured to allow reentrance, although it is discouraged by the specification.

Reentrance is not relevant to message-driven beans because they do not respond to RMI calls, as session and entity beans do. Furthermore, EJB 2.1 endpoint interfaces may only be implemented by stateless session beans, which may not be reentrant.

The problem with reentrance is that client access to a bean is synchronized so that only one client can access any given bean at a time. Reentrance addresses a thread of control—initiated by a client request—that attempts to reaccess a bean instance. The problem with reentrant code is that the EJB object, which intercepts and delegates method invocations, cannot differentiate between reentrant code and multithreaded access within the same transactional context. (You'll read more about transactional context in Chapter 14.) If you permit reentrance, you also permit multithreaded access to the bean instance. Multithreaded access to a bean instance can result in corrupted data because threads affect each other's work when they try to accomplish their separate tasks.

It's important to remember that reentrant code is different from a bean instance that simply invokes its own methods at an instance level. In other words, method `foo( )` on a bean instance can invoke its own public, protected, default, or private methods directly as much as it wants. Here is an example of intra-instance method invocation that is perfectly legal:

```
public HypotheticalBean extends EntityBean {
    public int x;

    public double foo( ) {
        int i = this.getX( );
        return this.boo(i);
    }
    public int getX( ) {
        return x;
    }
    private double boo(int i) {
        double value = i * Math.PI;
        return value;
    }
}
```

The business method `foo( )` invokes `getX( )` and then a private method, `boo( )`. The method invocations within the body of `foo( )` are intra-instance invocations and are not considered reentrant.

Concurrency with message-driven beans

In message-driven beans, concurrency refers to the processing of more than one message at a time. If message-driven beans could process only a single message at time, they would be practically useless in a real-world application because they couldn't handle heavy message loads. As Figure 3-9 illustrates, if three messages are delivered to a specific destination from three different clients at the same time, three instances of a single JMS-MDB that subscribes or listens to that destination can be used to process the messages simultaneously.

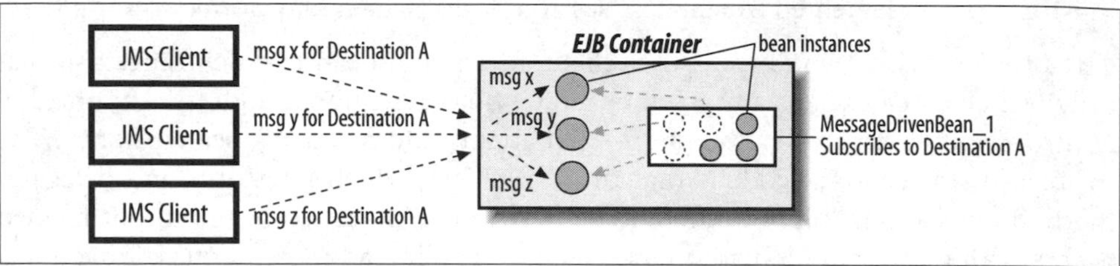

Figure 3-9. Concurrent processing with message-driven beans

Message-driven beans that implement APIs other than JMS benefit from the same concurrency controls as JMS-MDBs. Message-driven beans of all kinds are pooled and used to process incoming messages concurrently so that hundreds, possibly thousands, of messages can be handled simultaneously.*

Transactions

A *transaction* is a unit-of-work or a set of tasks executed together. Transactions are atomic; in other words, all the tasks in a transaction must be completed together for the transaction to be considered a success. In the previous chapter, we used the TravelAgent bean to describe how a session bean controls the interactions of other beans. Here is a code snippet showing the bookPassage( ) method described in Chapter 2:

```
public TicketDO bookPassage(CreditCardDO card,double price)
    throws IncompleteConversationalState {
    if (customer == null ||cruise == null ||cabin == null) {
        throw new IncompleteConversationalState( );
    }
    try {
        ReservationHomeRemote resHome = (ReservationHomeRemote)
            getHome("ReservationHome",ReservationHomeRemote.class);
        ReservationRemote reservation =
            resHome.create(customer,cruise,cabin,price,new Date( ));
        ProcessPaymentHomeRemote ppHome = (ProcessPaymentHomeRemote)
            getHome("ProcessPaymentHome",ProcessPaymentHomeRemote.class);

        ProcessPaymentRemote process = ppHome.create( );
        process.byCredit(customer,card,price);
```

* In reality, it's very difficult to process anything simultaneously without multiple processors, but conceptually this statement is true. Multiple threads in the same VM or multiple VMs on the same processor (computer chip) imitate simultaneous processing.

```
            TicketDO ticket = new TicketDO(customer,cruise,cabin,price);
            return ticket;
        } catch(Exception e) {
            throw new EJBException(e);
        }
    }
```

The `bookPassage( )` method consists of two tasks that must be completed together: the creation of a new Reservation EJB and the processing of the payment. When the TravelAgent EJB is used to book a passenger, the charges to the passenger's credit card and the creation of the reservation must both be successful. It would be inappropriate for the ProcessPayment EJB to charge the customer's credit card if the creation of a new Reservation EJB fails. Likewise, you can't make a reservation if the customer credit card is not charged. An EJB server monitors the transaction to ensure that all the tasks are completed successfully.

Transactions are managed automatically; as a bean developer, you don't need to use any APIs to manage a bean's involvement in a transaction. Simply declaring the transactional attribute at deployment time tells the EJB server how to manage the bean at runtime. EJB does provide a mechanism that allows beans to manage transactions explicitly, if necessary. Setting the transactional attributes during deployment is discussed in Chapter 14, as is explicit management of transactions and other transactional topics.

Persistence

Entity beans represent the behavior and data associated with real-world people, places, or things. Unlike session and message-driven beans, entity beans are persistent, which means that the state of an entity is saved in a database. Persistence allows entities to be durable, so that both their behavior and their data can be accessed at any time without concern that the information will be lost because of a system failure.

When a bean's state is automatically managed by a persistence service, the container is responsible for synchronizing the entity bean's instance fields with the data in the database. This automatic persistence is called *container-managed* persistence. When a bean is designed to manage its own state, as is often the case when dealing with legacy systems, it is called *bean-managed* persistence.

Each vendor gets to choose its own mechanism for implementing container-managed persistence, but the vendor's implementation must support the EJB callback methods and transactions. The most common mechanisms used in persistence by EJB vendors are *object-to-relational* persistence and *object database* persistence.

Object-to-relational persistence

Object-to-relational persistence is the most common persistence mechanism used in EJB servers today. Object-to-relational persistence involves mapping an entity bean's state to relational database tables and columns.

In Titan's system, the CabinBean models the concept of a ship's cabin. The CabinBean defines three fields: name, deckLevel, and id. The abbreviated definition of the CabinBean looks like this:

```
public abstract class CabinBean implements javax.ejb.EntityBean {

    public abstract String getName( );
    public abstract void setName(String str);

    public abstract int getDeckLevel( );
    public abstract void setDeckLevel(int level);

    public abstract Integer getId( );
    public abstract void setId(Integer id);

}
```

The abstract accessor methods represent the entity bean's container-managed fields. When an entity bean is deployed, the container implements these "virtual" fields for the bean, so it is convenient to think of the abstract accessor methods as describing persistent fields. For example, when talking about the state represented by the setName( )/getName( ) abstract accessor method, we refer to it as the name field. Similarly, getId( )/setId( ) represents the id field, and getDeckLevel( )/setDeckLevel( ) represents the deckLevel field.

With object-to-relational database mapping, the fields of an entity bean correspond to columns in a relational database. The Cabin's name field, for example, maps to the column labeled NAME in a table called CABIN in Titan's relational database. Figure 3-10 shows a graphical depiction of this type of mapping.

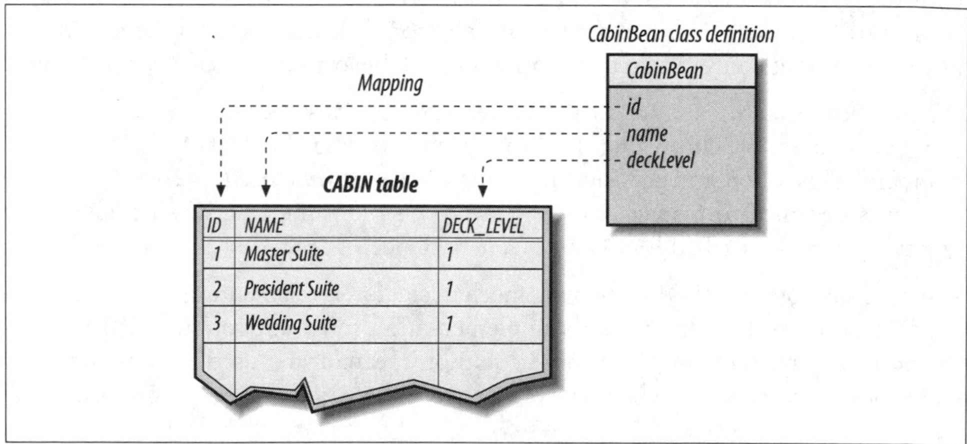

Figure 3-10. Object-to-relational mapping of entity beans

Many EJB systems provide wizards or administrative interfaces for mapping relational database tables to the fields of entity-bean classes. Using these wizards, mapping entities to tables is fairly straightforward and usually takes place at deployment time. Figure 3-11 shows Pramati Application Server's object-to-relational mapping wizard.

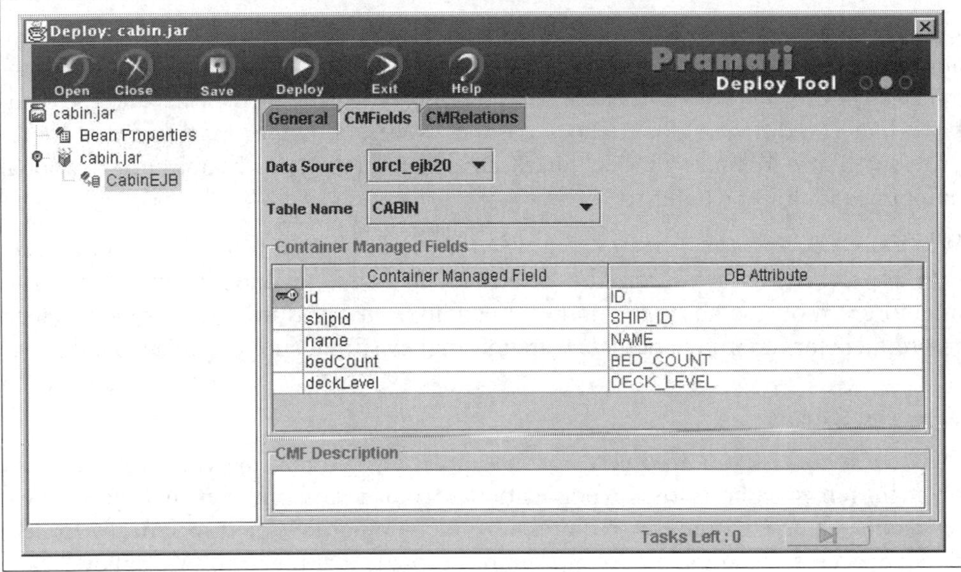

Figure 3-11. Pramati object-to-relational mapping wizard

Once a bean's fields are mapped to the relational database, the container takes over the responsibility of keeping the state of an entity-bean instance consistent with the corresponding tables in the database. This process is called *synchronizing* the state of the bean instance. In the case of `CabinBean`, bean instances map one-to-one to rows in the `CABIN` table of the relational database. When a change is made to a Cabin EJB, it is written to the appropriate row in the database. Sometimes, bean types map to more than one table. These are more complicated mappings, often requiring a SQL join and multiple updates.

In addition, container-managed persistence defines entity-bean relationship fields, which allow entity beans to have one-to-one, one-to-many, and many-to-many relationships with other beans. Entity beans can maintain collections of other entity beans or single references. The container-managed persistence model is covered in Chapters 6, 7, and 8.

In addition to synchronizing the state of an entity, EJB provides mechanisms for creating and removing entities. Calls to the EJB home to create and remove entities result in the insertion or deletion of records in the database. Because each entity stores its state in a database table, new records (and therefore bean identities) can be added to tables from outside the EJB system. In other words, inserting a record into the `CABIN` table—whether done by EJB or by direct access to the database—creates a new Cabin entity.

It's not created in the sense of instantiating a Java object, but rather in the sense that the data that describes a Cabin entity has been added to the system.

Object database persistence

Object-oriented databases are designed to preserve object types and object graphs, and therefore are a good match for components written in an object-oriented language such as Java. They offer a cleaner mapping between entity beans and the database than a traditional relational database. However, container-managed persistence provides a programming model that can accommodate both object-to-relational mapping and object databases.

While object databases perform well when it comes to very complex object graphs, they are still not as standardized as relational databases, making it more difficult to migrate from one database to another. In addition, fewer third-party products (such as products for reporting and data warehousing) exist that support object databases.

Legacy persistence

EJB can be used to put an object wrapper on legacy systems, systems that are based on mainframe applications, or nonrelational databases. Container-managed persistence in such an environment requires an EJB container designed specifically for legacy data access. Vendors might, for example, provide mapping tools that allow beans to be mapped to IMS, CICS, b-trieve, or some other legacy application.

Container-managed versus bean-managed persistence

Regardless of the type of legacy system, container-managed persistence is preferable to bean-managed persistence. With container-managed persistence, the bean's state is managed automatically, a process that is more efficient at runtime and more productive during bean development. Many projects, however, require that beans obtain their states from legacy systems that are not supported by the EJB vendor. In these cases, developers must use bean-managed persistence, which means the developer doesn't use the automatic persistence service of the EJB server. BMP is also used by third-party persistence providers that support nontraditional database systems. These third-party products will generate BMPs automatically and use J2eeCA to obtain transactionally safe access to a database not normally supported by the EJB vendor. Chapters 6 through 9 describe container-managed and bean-managed persistence in detail.

Distributed Objects

When we discuss the component interfaces and other EJB interfaces and classes used on the client, we are talking about the client's view of the EJB system. The *EJB client view* doesn't include the EJB objects, the EJB container, instance swapping, or any of the other implementation specifics. As far as a remote client is concerned, a bean is defined by its remote interface and home interface or endpoint interface. Everything else is invisible, including the mechanism used to support distributed objects. As long as the EJB server supports the EJB client view, any distributed object protocol can be used. EJB 2.0 requires that every EJB server support Java RMI-IIOP, but it doesn't limit the protocols an EJB server can support to just Java RMI-IIOP (the Java RMI API using the CORBA IIOP protocol). EJB 2.1 also requires support for SOAP 1.1 via the JAX-RPC API.

Regardless of the protocol, the server must support Java clients using the Java EJB client API, which means that the protocol must map to the Java RMI-IIOP or the JAX-RPC programming model. Figure 3-12 illustrates the Java language EJB API supported by different distributed object protocols.

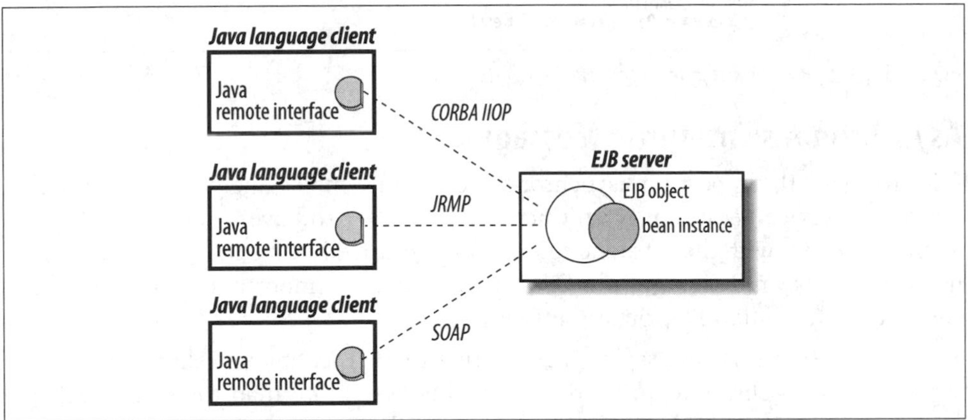

Figure 3-12. Java EJB client view supported by various protocols

EJB also allows servers to support access to beans by clients written in languages other than Java. An example of this capability is the EJB-to-CORBA mapping defined by Sun.* This document describes the CORBA Interface Definition Language (IDL) that can be used to access enterprise beans from CORBA clients. A CORBA client can be written in any language, including C++, Smalltalk, Ada, and even COBOL. The mapping also includes details about supporting the Java EJB client view, as well as details on mapping the CORBA naming system to EJB servers and distributed transactions across CORBA objects and beans. Another example is the EJB-to-SOAP mapping based on JAX-RPC. It allows SOAP client applications written in languages such as VisualBasic.NET, C#, and Perl to access stateless session beans. Figure 3-13 illustrates the possibilities for accessing an EJB server from different distributed object clients.

* Sun Microsystems' *Enterprise JavaBeans to CORBA Mapping, Version 1.1*, by Sanjeev Krishnan..

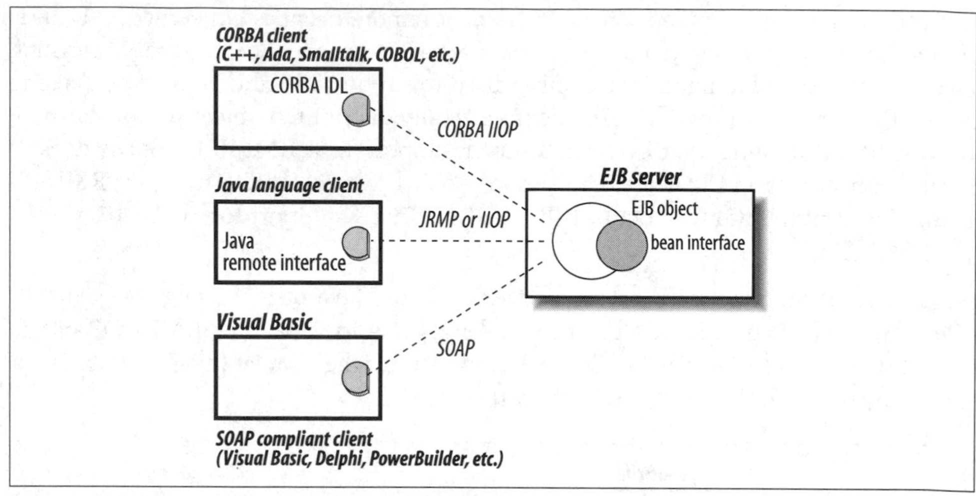

Figure 3-13. EJB accessed from different distributed clients

Asynchronous Enterprise Messaging

Prior to EJB 2.0, support for asynchronous enterprise messaging was not considered a primary service because it wasn't necessary in order to have a complete EJB platform. However, with the introduction of message-driven beans in EJB 2.0, asynchronous enterprise messaging with JMS has become so important that it has been elevated to the status of a primary service.

Support for enterprise messaging requires that the EJB container reliably route messages from JMS clients to JMS-MDBs. This involves more than the simple delivery semantics associated with email or even the JMS API. With enterprise messaging, messages must be reliably delivered, which means that a failure while delivering the message may require the JMS provider to attempt redelivery.* What's more, enterprise messages may be persistent, which means they are stored to disk or to a database until they can be properly delivered to their intended clients. Persistent messages also must survive system failures; if the EJB server crashes, these messages must still be available for delivery when the server comes back up. Most importantly, enterprise messaging is transactional. That means if a JMS-MDB fails while processing a message, that failure will abort the transaction and force the EJB container to redeliver the message to another message-driven bean instance.

In addition message-driven beans, stateless session beans and entity beans can also send JMS messages. Sending messages can be as important to Enterprise JavaBeans as delivery of messages to JMS-MDB—support for both facilities tends to go hand in hand.

* Most EJB vendors will place a limit on the number of times a message can be redelivered. If redelivery is attemped too many times, the message might be placed in a "dead message" repository, where it can be reviewed by an administrator.

In EJB 2.0, supporting JMS-MDBs required tight coupling between the EJB container and the JMS message router; as a result, many EJB container systems could only support a limited number of JMS providers. This changed in EJB 2.1, which requires support for Java Connector API Version 1.5. J2EE Connectors provides better support for asynchronous communication systems such as JMS, which means that JMS-MDBs have become more of a pluggable service in the EJB platform. Any JMS provider that supports the J2eeCA can send messages to a JMS message-driven bean.

EJB 2.1 : Timer Service

Enterprise JavaBeans 2.1 introduced a new primary service, the Timer Service. The Timer Service can be used to schedule notifications that are sent to enterprise beans at specific times. Timers are useful in many different applications. For example, a banking system may set timers on mortgage accounts to check for past-due payments. A stock-trading system might allow timers to be set on "buy limit orders." A medical claims system may set timers for automatic fraud audits of individual medical records. Timers can also be used in applications like self-auditing systems and batch processing.

Timers can be set on entity, stateless session, and message-driven beans. With session and entity beans, the bean sets the timers itself. For example, when a mortgage loan is created, the entity bean that represents the loan might set a past-due timer when the loan is created, and reset the timer whenever a payment is made. Some EJB container systems may support message-driven bean timers, which are configured at deployment time and perform batch processing at regular intervals. The Timer Service is covered in detail in Chapter 13.

Naming

All naming services do essentially the same thing: they provide clients with a mechanism for locating distributed objects or resources. To accomplish this, a naming service must provide two things: object binding and a lookup API. *Object binding* is the association of a distributed object with a natural language name or identifier. The `CabinHomeRemote` object, for example, might be bound to the name "CabinHomeRemote" or "room." A binding is really a pointer or an index to a specific distributed object. A *lookup API* provides the client with an interface to the naming system. Simply put, lookup APIs allow clients to connect to a distributed service and request a remote reference to a specific object.

Enterprise JavaBeans mandates the use of JNDI as a lookup API on Java clients. JNDI (Java Naming and Directory Interface) supports just about any kind of naming and directory service. Although JNDI can become extraordinarily complex, the way it's used in J2EE applications is usually fairly simple. Java client applications can use JNDI to initiate a connection to an EJB server and to locate a specific EJB home. The following code shows how the JNDI API might be used to locate and obtain a reference to the EJB home CabinHomeRemote:

```
javax.naming.Context jndiContext = new javax.naming.InitialContext( );
Object ref = jndiContext.lookup("java:comp/env/ejb/CabinHomeRemote");
CabinHomeRemote cabinHome = (CabinHomeRemote)
    PortableRemoteObject.narrow(ref, CabinHomeRemote.class);

Cabin cabin = cabinHome.create(382, "Cabin 333",3);
cabin.setName("Cabin 444");
cabin.setDeckLevel(4);
```

The properties passed into the constructor of InitialContext tell the JNDI API where to find the EJB server and what JNDI service provider (driver) to load. The Context.lookup( ) method tells the JNDI service provider the name of the object to return from the EJB server. In this case, we are looking for the home interface to the Cabin EJB. Once we have the Cabin EJB's home interface, we can use it to create new cabins and access existing cabins.

There are many different kinds of directory and naming services; EJB vendors can choose the one that best meets their needs, but all vendors must support the CORBA naming service in addition to any other directory services they choose to support.

Security

Enterprise JavaBeans servers can support as many as three kinds of security:

Authentication
: Simply put, authentication validates the identity of the user. The most common kind of authentication is a simple login screen that requires a username and a password. Once users have successfully passed through the authentication system, they are free to use the system. Authentication can also be based on secure ID cards, swipe cards, security certificates, and other forms of identification. While authentication is the primary safeguard against unauthorized access to a system, it is fairly crude because it doesn't police an authorized user's access to resources within the system.

Access control
: Access control (a.k.a. authorization) applies security policies that regulate what a specific user can and cannot do. Access control ensures that users access only those resources for which they have been given permission. Access control can police a user's access to subsystems, data, and business objects, or it can monitor more general behavior. Certain users, for example, may be allowed to update information while others are allowed only to view the data.

Secure communication
: Communication channels between a client and a server are frequently the focus of security concerns. A channel of communication can be secured by encrypting the communication between the client and the server. When communication is

secured by encryption, the messages passed are encoded so that they cannot be read or manipulated by unauthorized individuals. This normally involves the exchange of cryptographic keys between the client and the server. The keys allow the receiver of the message to decode the message and read it.

Most EJB servers support secure communication—usually through the Secure Sockets Layer (SSL) protocol—and some mechanism for authentication, but Enterprise JavaBeans specifies only access control in its server-side component models. Authentication may be specified in subsequent versions, but secure communication will probably never be specified because it is independent of the EJB specification and the distributed object protocol.

Although authentication is not specified in EJB, it is often accomplished using the JNDI API. For example, a client using JNDI can provide authenticating information using the JNDI API to access a server or resources in the server. This information is frequently passed when the client attempts to initiate a JNDI connection to the EJB server. The following code shows how the client's password and username are added to the connection properties used to obtain a JNDI connection to the EJB server:

```
properties.put(Context.SECURITY_PRINCIPAL, userName );
properties.put(Context.SECURITY_CREDENTIALS, userPassword);

javax.naming.Context jndiContext = new javax.naming.InitialContext(properties);
Object ref= jndiContext.lookup("CabinHomeRemote");
CabinHomeRemote cabinHome = (CabinHome)
    PortableRemoteObject.narrow(ref, CabinHomeRemote.class);
```

EJB specifies that every client application accessing an EJB system must be associated with a security identity. The security identity represents the client as either a user or a role. A user might be a person, security credential, computer, or even a smart card. Normally, the user is a person whose identity is assigned when she logs in. A role represents a grouping of identities and might be something like "manager," which is a group of user identities that are considered managers at a company.

When a remote client logs on to the EJB system, it is associated with a security identity for the duration of that session. The identity is found in a database or directory specific to the platform or EJB server. This database or directory is responsible for storing individual security identities and their memberships to groups. Once a remote client application has been associated with a security identity, it is ready to use beans to accomplish some task. When a client invokes a method on a bean, the EJB server implicitly passes the client's identity with the method invocation. When the EJB object or EJB home receives the method invocation, it checks the identity to ensure that the client is allowed to invoke that method.

Role-driven access control

In Enterprise JavaBeans, the security identity is represented by a `java.security.Principal` object. The `Principal` acts as a representative for users, groups, organizations, smart cards, and so on to the EJB access-control architecture. Deployment descriptors include tags that declare which logical roles are allowed to access which bean methods at runtime. The security roles are considered logical roles because they do not directly reflect users, groups, or any other security identities in a specific operational environment. Instead, security roles are mapped to real-world user groups and users when the bean is deployed. This mapping allows a bean to be portable; every time the bean is deployed in a new system, the roles can be mapped to the users and groups specific to that operational environment.

Here is a portion of the Cabin EJB's deployment descriptor that defines two security roles, `ReadOnly` and `Administrator`:

```
<security-role>
    <description>
        This role is allowed to execute any method on the bean
        and to read and change any cabin bean data.
    </description>
    <role-name>
        Administrator
    </role-name>
</security-role>

<security-role>
    <description>
        This role is allowed to locate and read cabin info.
        This role is not allowed to change cabin bean data.
    </description>
    <role-name>
        ReadOnly
    </role-name>
</security-role>
```

The role names in this descriptor are not reserved or special names with predefined meanings; they are simply logical names chosen by the bean assembler. In other words, the role names can be anything you want.* Once the `<security-role>` tags are declared, they can be associated with methods in the bean using `<method-permission>` tags. Each `<method-permission>` tag contains one or more `<method>` tags, which identify the bean methods associated with one or more logical roles identified by the `<role-name>` tags. The `<role-name>` tags must match the names defined by the `<security-role>` tags:

```
<method-permission>
    <role-name>Administrator</role-name>
    <method>
        <ejb-name>CabinEJB</ejb-name>
        <method-name>*</method-name>
    </method>
</method-permission>
```

* For a complete understanding of XML, including specific rules for tag names and data, see *Learning XML* by Erik Ray (O'Reilly).

```
<method-permission>
    <role-name>ReadOnly</role-name>
    <method>
        <ejb-name>CabinEJB</ejb-name>
        <method-name>getName</method-name>
    </method>
    <method>
        <ejb-name>CabinEJB</ejb-name>
        <method-name>getDeckLevel</method-name>
    </method>
    <method>
        <ejb-name>CabinEJB</ejb-name>
        <method-name>findByPrimaryKey</method-name>
    </method>
</method-permission>
```

In the first `<method-permission>`, the `Administrator` role is associated with all methods on the Cabin EJB, which is denoted by specifying the wildcard character (*) in the `<method-name>` of the `<method>` tag. In the second `<method-permission>`, the `ReadOnly` role is limited to accessing only three methods: `getName( )`, `getDeckLevel( )`, and `findByPrimaryKey( )`. Any attempt by a `ReadOnly` role to access a method that is not listed in the `<method-permission>` results in an exception. This kind of access control makes for a fairly fine-grained authorization system.

Since a single deployment descriptor can describe more than one enterprise bean, the tags used to declare method permissions and security roles are defined in a special section of the deployment descriptor. This allows several beans to share the same security roles. The location of these tags and their relationship to other sections of the deployment descriptor is covered in more detail in Chapter 17.

The person who deploys the bean must examine the `<security-role>` information and map each logical role to a user group. The deployer need not be concerned with what roles go to which methods; rely on the descriptions given in the `<security-role>` tags to determine matches based on the description of the logical role. This relieves the deployer, who may not be a developer, from having to understand how the bean works in order to deploy it. Figure 3-14 shows the same enterprise bean deployed in two different environments (labeled X and Z). In each environment, the user groups are mapped to their logical roles in the XML deployment descriptor so that specific user groups have access privileges to specific methods on specific enterprise beans. The `ReadOnly` role is mapped to those groups that should be limited to the get accessor methods and the find method. The `Administrator` role is mapped to those user groups that should have privileges to invoke any method on the Cabin EJB.

The access control described here is implicit; once the bean is deployed, the container takes care of checking that users access only those methods for which they have permission. When a client invokes a method on a bean, the client's `Principal` is checked to see if it is a member of a role mapped to that method. If it's not, an exception is thrown and the client is denied permission to invoke the method. If the client is a member of a privileged role, the method is invoked.

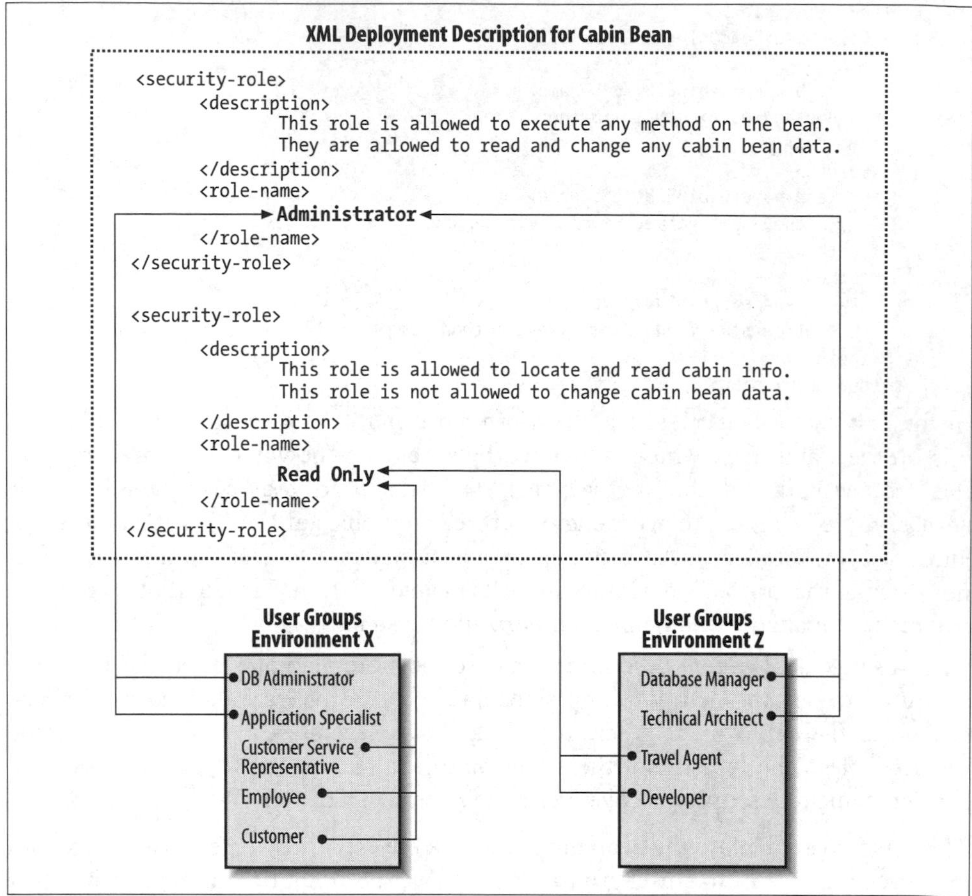

Figure 3-14. Mapping roles in the operational environment to logical roles in the deployment descriptor

A client's `Principal` is propagated from one bean invocation to the next, ensuring that its access is controlled whether or not it invokes a bean method directly. For example, propagation prevents a user in a ReadOnly role from legitimately invoking a method on some bean, which in turn invokes a method that is prohibited to a ReadOnly user. This propagation can be overridden by specifying that the enterprise bean executes under a different security identity, called the *runAs* security identity (discussed later in this chapter).

Unchecked methods

In EJB, a set of methods can be designated as *unchecked*, which means that the security permissions are not checked before the method is invoked. An unchecked method can be invoked by any client, no matter what role it is using. To designate a method or methods as unchecked, use the <method-permission> element and replace the <role-name> element with an empty <unchecked> element:

```
<method-permission>
    <unchecked/>
    <method>
        <ejb-name>CabinEJB</ejb-name>
        <method-name>*</method-name>
    </method>
    <method>
        <ejb-name>CustomerEJB</ejb-name>
        <method-name>findByPrimaryKey</method-name>
    </method>
</method-permission>
<method-permission>
    <role-name>administrator</role-name>
    <method>
        <ejb-name>CabinEJB</ejb-name>
        <method-name>*</method-name>
    </method>
</method-permission>
```

This declaration tells us that all the methods of the Cabin EJB, as well as the Customer EJB's `findByPrimaryKey()` method, are unchecked. Although the second <method-permission> element gives the administrator permission to access all the Cabin EJB's methods, this declaration is overridden by the unchecked method permission. Unchecked method permissions always override all other method permissions.

The runAs security identity

In addition to specifying the `Principal`s that have access to an enterprise bean's methods, the deployer can also specify the runAs `Principal` for the entire enterprise bean. The runAs security identity was originally specified in EJB 1.0, abandoned in EJB 1.1, and then reintroduced in EJB 2.0 and modified so that it is easier for vendors to implement.

While the <method-permission> elements specify which `Principal`s have access to the bean's methods, the <security-identity> element specifies under which `Principal` the method will run. In other words, the runAs `Principal` is used as the enterprise bean's identity when it tries to invoke methods on other beans—however, this identity isn't necessarily the same as the identity that's currently accessing the bean. For example, the following deployment descriptor elements declare that the `create()` method can be accessed only by `JimSmith` but that the Cabin EJB always runs under the `Administrator` security identity:

```
<enterprise-beans>
...
    <entity>
        <ejb-name>CabinEJB</ejb-name>
        ...
        <security-identity>
            <run-as>
```

```
                <role-name>Administrator</role-name>
            </run-as>
        </security-identity>
        ...
    </entity>
...
</enterprise-beans>
<assembly-descriptor>
<security-role>
    <role-name>Administrator</role-name>
</security-role>
<security-role>
    <role-name>JimSmith</role-name>
</security-role>
...
<method-permission>
    <role-name>JimSmith</role-name>
    <method>
        <ejb-name>CabinEJB</ejb-name>
        <method-name>create</method-name>
    </method>
</method-permission>
...
</assembly-descriptor>
```

This kind of configuration is useful when the enterprise beans or resources accessed in the body of the method require a Principal that is different from the one used to gain access to the method. For example, the create( ) method might call a method in enterprise bean X that requires the Administrator security identity. If we want to use enterprise bean X in the create( ) method, but we want only Jim Smith to create new cabins, we would use the <security-identity> and <method-permission> elements together to give us this kind of flexibility: the <method-permission> for create( ) would specify that only Jim Smith can invoke the method, and the <security-identity> element would specify that the enterprise bean always runs under the Administrator security identity. To specify that an enterprise bean will execute under the caller's identity, the <security-identity> role contains a single empty element, the <use-caller-identity> element. For example, the following declarations specify that the Cabin EJB always executes under the caller's identity, so if Jim Smith invokes the create( ) method, the bean will run under the JimSmith security identity:

```
<enterprise-beans>
...
    <entity>
        <ejb-name>CabinEJB</ejb-name>
        ...
        <security-identity>
            <use-caller-identity/>
        </security-identity>
        ...
    </entity>
...
</enterprise-beans>
```

Figure 3-15 illustrates how the runAs `Principal` can change in a chain of method invocations. Notice that the runAs `Principal` is the `Principal` used to test for access in subsequent method invocations.

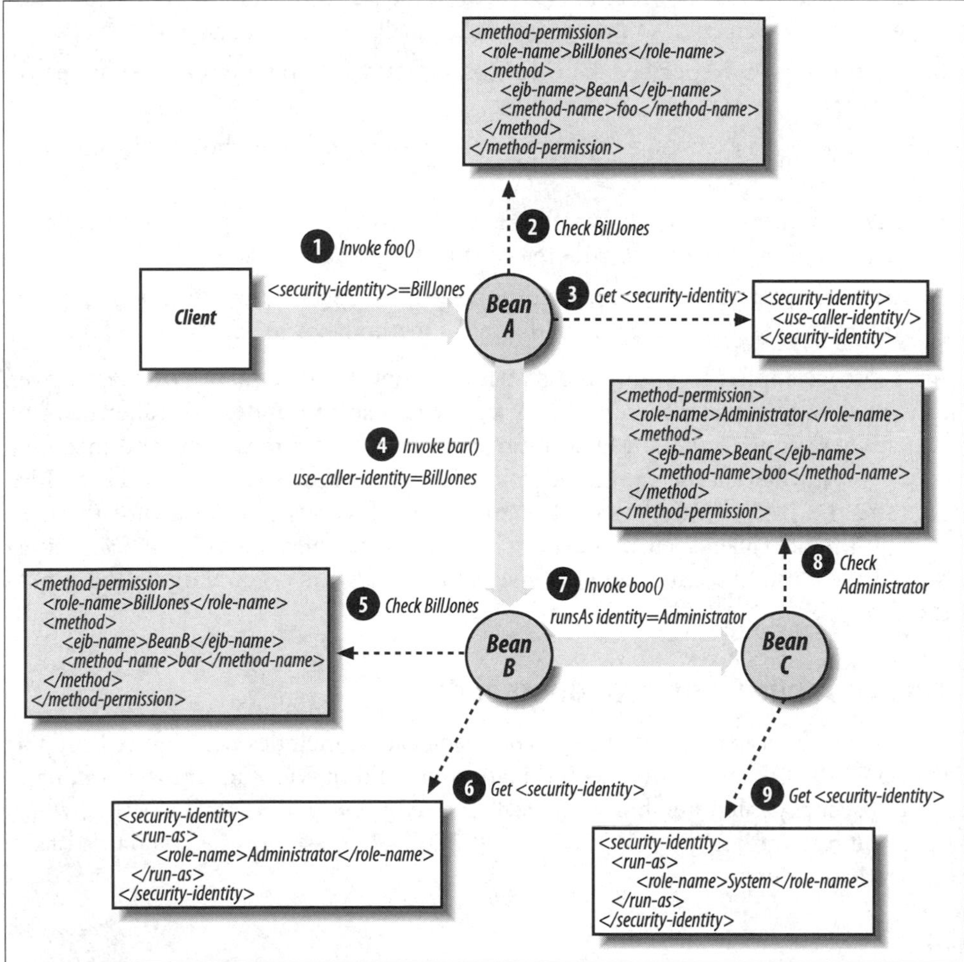

Figure 3-15. runAs identity

Here's what's going on in Figure 3-15:

1. The client, who is identified as `BillJones`, invokes the method `foo()` on enterprise bean A.
2. Before servicing the method, enterprise bean A checks to see if `BillJones` is included in the `<method-permission>` elements for `foo()`. It is.
3. The `<security-identity>` of enterprise bean A is declared as `<use-caller-identity>`, so the `foo()` method executes under the caller's `Principal`; in this case, it's `BillJones`.

4. While `foo( )` is executing, it invokes method `bar( )` on enterprise bean B using the `BillJones` security identity.
5. Enterprise bean B checks the `foo( )` method's `Principal` (`BillJones`) against the allowed identities for method `bar( )`. `BillJones` is included in the `<method-permission>` elements, so the method `bar( )`is allowed to execute.
6. Enterprise bean B specifies the `<security-identity>` to be the runAs `Principal` of `Administrator`.
7. While `bar( )` is executing, enterprise bean B invokes the method `boo( )` on enterprise bean C.
8. Enterprise bean C checks whether `bar( )`'s runAs `Principal` (`Administrator`) is included in the `<method-permission>` elements for method `boo( )`. It is.
9. The `<security-identity>` for enterprise bean C specifies a runAs `Principal` of `System`, the identity under which the `boo( )` method executes.

This protocol applies to entity and stateless session beans equally. Message-driven beans have only a runAs identity; they will never execute under the caller identity, because there is no "caller." Message-driven beans process messages, and incoming messages don't have a meaningful identity. These messages are not considered RMI calls, and the JMS clients that send them are not directly associated with the messages. With no caller security identity to propagate, message-driven beans must always have a runAs security identity specified, and always execute under that runAs `Principal`.

Primary Services and Interoperability

Interoperability is a vital part of EJB. The specification includes the required support for Java RMI-IIOP for remote method invocation, and provides for transaction, naming, and security interoperability. EJB 2.1 also requires support for JAX-RPC, which itself requires support for SOAP 1.1 and WSDL 1.1; these are the standards of the web services industry.

IIOP

EJB requires vendors to provide an implementation of Java RMI that uses the CORBA 2.3.1 IIOP protocol. The goal of this requirement is that J2EE servers will be able to interoperate, so that J2EE components (enterprise beans, applications, servlets, and JSPs) in one J2EE server can access enterprise beans in a different J2EE server. The Java RMI-IIOP specification standardizes the transfer of parameters, return values, and exceptions, as well as the mapping of interfaces and value objects to the CORBA IDL.

Vendors may support protocols other than Java RMI-IIOP, as long as the semantics of the RMI interfaces adhere to the types allowed in RMI-IIOP. This constraint ensures that a client's view of EJB is consistent, regardless of the protocol used in remote invocations.

Transaction interoperability between containers for two-phase commits is an optional but important feature of EJB. It ensures that transactions started by a J2EE web component propagate to enterprise beans in other containers. The EJB specifications detail how two-phase commits are handed across EJB containers as well as how transactional containers interact with nontransactional containers.

EJB also addresses the need for an interoperable naming service for looking up enterprise beans. It specifies CORBA CosNaming as the interoperable naming service, defining how the service must implement the IDL interfaces of beans in the CosNaming module and how EJB clients use the service over IIOP.

EJB provides security interoperability by specifying how EJB containers establish trust relationships and how containers exchange security credentials when J2EE components access enterprise beans across containers. EJB containers are required to support the Secure Sockets Layer (SSL 3.0) protocol and the related IETF-standard Transport Layer Security (TLS 1.0) protocol for secure connections between clients and enterprise beans.

While IIOP has been around for a long time and offers interoperability in a number of areas, the truth is it hasn't been very successful. There are a variety of reasons why IIOP has not been the silver bullet it was intended to be, but perhaps the biggest reason is complexity. Although IIOP is platform-independent, it's not trivial for vendors to implement. In addition, there appear to be numerous gaps in the IIOP and other CORBA protocols, which cause interoperability problems when actually deployed in a production environment. It's rare to hear of real-world systems that have successfully deployed interoperating EJB systems based on IIOP. The solution the industry seems to have latched onto is web services, which depend on SOAP and WSDL as the bases for interoperability.

SOAP and WSDL

SOAP (Simple Object Access Protocol) is the primary protocol used by web services today. It's based on XML and can be used for both RPC and document (asynchronous) style messaging. The fact that SOAP is based on XML means that it's fairly easy to support. Any platform (operating system, programming language, software application, etc.) that can create HTTP network connections and parse XML can handle the SOAP protocol. This is why SOAP has gained widespread acceptance in a short period of time. There are over 70 SOAP toolkits (code libraries) available today for just about every modern programming environment, including Java, .NET, JavaScript, C, C++, VisualBasic, Delphi, Perl, Python, Ruby, SmallTalk, and others.

WSDL (Web Service Description Language) is the IDL of the web services. A WSDL document is an XML file that describes what web services a company supports, as well as the protocols, message formats, and network addresses of those web services. WSDL documents are highly structured, so that they can be used to autogenerate RPC stubs and other software interfaces for communicating with web services. Although WSDL documents are open enough to describe any type of service, they are typically used to describe web services that use the SOAP protocol.

WSDL and SOAP are normally used in combination. They form the building blocks for other interoperability standards covering security, transaction, orchestration, enterprise messaging, and a cornucopia of other topics. There is a lot of overlap among different groups that are developing infrastructure protocols based on SOAP and WSDL, and as a result, there are a lot of conflicting and immature standards. SOAP and WSDL have a lot of promise, but it's still too soon to say whether web services will solve the interoperability problems that have plagued enterprise computing since the beginning. It's likely that SOAP, WSDL, and the infrastructure protocols based on these standards will go further than IIOP, DCOM, and other predecessors, but they won't be a silver bullet. Web services are covered in more detail in Chapter 14.

What's Next?

The first three chapters of this book gave you a foundation on which to develop Enterprise JavaBeans components and applications. While we haven't gone into detail, we've shown you most of the topics that you'll be dealing with. Beginning with Chapter 4, you will develop your own beans and learn how to apply them in EJB applications.

CHAPTER 4

Developing Your First Enterprise Beans

One of the most important features of EJB is that enterprise beans have the ability to work with containers from different vendors. However, that doesn't mean that selecting a server and installing your enterprise beans on that server are trivial processes.

Choosing and Setting Up an EJB Server

The EJB server you choose should provide a utility for deploying enterprise beans. It doesn't matter whether the utility is command-line oriented or graphical, as long as it does the job. The deployment utility should allow you to work with prepackaged enterprise beans, i.e., enterprise beans that have already been developed and archived in a JAR file. Finally, the EJB server must support an SQL-standard relational database that is accessible using JDBC. For the database, you should have privileges sufficient for creating and modifying a few simple tables in addition to normal read, update, and delete capabilities. If you have chosen an EJB server that does not support a SQL-standard relational database, you may need to modify the examples to work with the product you are using.

This book does not say very much about how to install and deploy enterprise beans. That task is largely server-dependent. We'll provide some general ideas about how to organize JAR files and create deployment descriptors, but for a complete description of the deployment process, you'll have to refer to your vendor's documentation.

Setting Up Your Java IDE

To get the most from this chapter, it helps to have an IDE that has a debugger and allows you to add Java files to its environment. Several Java IDEs—such as BEA's Weblogic Workshop, IBM's Eclipse, Borland's JBuilder, and Sun's Forte—fulfill this requirement. Some EJB products, such as IBM's WebSphere and BEA's Weblogic, are tightly coupled with an IDE that makes life a lot easier when it comes to writing, deploying, and debugging your applications.

Once you have an IDE set up, you need to include the Enterprise JavaBeans and other J2EE packages which will be provided by your application server vendor—usually in a single JAR file (e.g., *j2ee.jar*).

Developing an Entity Bean

There's no better place to start than the Cabin EJB, which we have been examining throughout the previous chapters. The Cabin EJB is an entity bean that encapsulates the data and behavior associated with a cruise ship cabin in Titan's business domain.

Cabin: The Remote Interface

When developing an entity bean, we first want to define its remote interface. The remote interface defines the bean's business purpose; the methods of this interface must capture the concept of the entity. We defined the remote interface for the Cabin EJB in Chapter 2; here, we add two new methods for setting and getting the ship ID and the bed count. The ship ID identifies the ship to which the cabin belongs, and the bed count tells how many people the cabin can accommodate:

```
package com.titan.cabin;

import java.rmi.RemoteException;

public interface CabinRemote extends javax.ejb.EJBObject {
    public String getName( ) throws RemoteException;
    public void setName(String str) throws RemoteException;
    public int getDeckLevel( ) throws RemoteException;
    public void setDeckLevel(int level) throws RemoteException;
    public int getShipId( ) throws RemoteException;
    public void setShipId(int sp) throws RemoteException;
    public int getBedCount( ) throws RemoteException;
    public void setBedCount(int bc) throws RemoteException;
}
```

The `CabinRemote` interface defines four properties: `name`, `deckLevel`, `shipId`, and `bedCount`. *Properties* are attributes of an enterprise bean that can be accessed by public set and get methods.

Notice that we have made the `CabinRemote` interface a part of a new package named `com.titan.cabin`. Place all the classes and interfaces associated with each type of bean in a package specific to the bean. Because our beans are for the use of the Titan cruise line, we placed these packages in the `com.titan` package hierarchy. We also created directory structures that match package structures. If you are using an IDE that works directly with Java files, create a new directory called *dev* (for development) and create the directory structure shown in Figure 4-1. Copy the `CabinRemote` interface into your IDE and save its definition to the *cabin* directory. Compile the `CabinRemote` interface to ensure that its definition is correct. The *CabinRemote.class* file, generated by the IDE's compiler, should be written to the *cabin* directory, the same directory as the *CabinRemote.java* file. The rest of the Cabin bean's classes will be placed in this same directory.

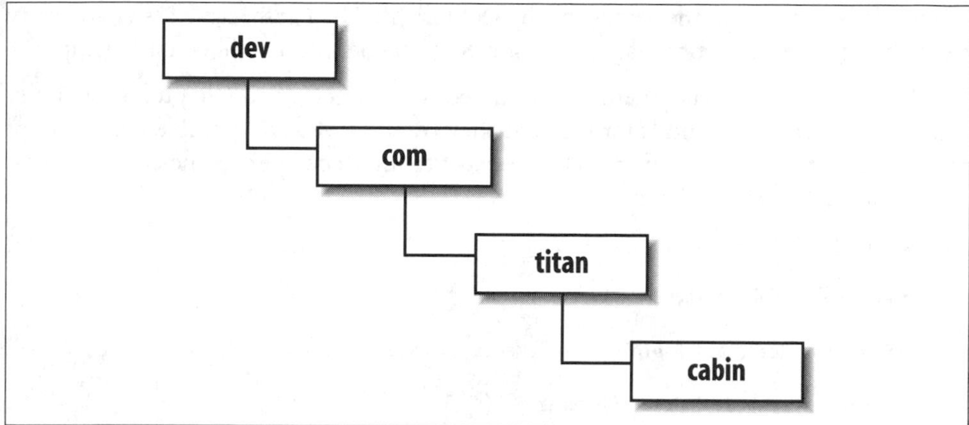

Figure 4-1. Directory structure for the Cabin bean

CabinHome: The Remote Home Interface

Once we have defined the remote interface of the Cabin EJB, we have defined the remote view of this simple entity bean. Next, we need to define the Cabin EJB's remote home interface, which specifies how the enterprise bean can be created, located, and destroyed by remote clients; in other words, the Cabin EJB's life-cycle behavior. Here is a complete definition of the `CabinHomeRemote` home interface:

```
package com.titan.cabin;

import java.rmi.RemoteException;
import javax.ejb.CreateException;
import javax.ejb.FinderException;

public interface CabinHomeRemote extends javax.ejb.EJBHome {

    public CabinRemote create(Integer id)
        throws CreateException, RemoteException;

    public CabinRemote findByPrimaryKey(Integer pk)
        throws FinderException, RemoteException;
}
```

The `CabinHomeRemote` interface extends `javax.ejb.EJBHome` and defines two life-cycle methods: `create()` and `findByPrimaryKey()`. These methods create and locate remote references to Cabin EJBs. Remove methods (for deleting enterprise beans) are defined in the `javax.ejb.EJBHome` interface, so the `CabinHomeRemote` interface inherits them.

CabinBean: The Bean Class

We have now defined the remote client-side API for creating, locating, using, and removing the Cabin EJB. Now we need to define `CabinBean`, the class that provides the implementation on the server for the Cabin EJB. The `CabinBean` class is an entity bean that uses container-managed persistence, so its definition will be fairly simple.

In addition to the callback methods discussed in Chapter 2 and Chapter 3, we must also define accessor methods for the `CabinRemote` interface and an implementation of the create method defined in the `CabinHomeRemote` interface. Here is the complete definition of the `CabinBean` class:

```
package com.titan.cabin;

import javax.ejb.EntityContext;

public abstract class CabinBean implements javax.ejb.EntityBean {

    public Integer ejbCreate(Integer id){
        this.setId(id);
        return null;
    }
    public void ejbPostCreate(Integer id){

    }
    public abstract void setId(Integer id);
    public abstract Integer getId( );

    public abstract void setShipId(int ship);
    public abstract int getShipId( );

    public abstract void setName(String name);
    public abstract String getName( );

    public abstract void setBedCount(int count);
    public abstract int getBedCount( );

    public abstract void setDeckLevel(int level);
    public abstract int getDeckLevel( );

    public void setEntityContext(EntityContext ctx) {
        // Empty implementation.
    }
    public void unsetEntityContext( ) {
        // Empty implementation.
    }
    public void ejbActivate( ) {
        // Empty implementation.
    }
    public void ejbPassivate( ) {
        // Empty implementation.
    }
    public void ejbLoad( ) {
```

```
        // Empty implementation.
    }
    public void ejbStore() {
        // Empty implementation.
    }
    public void ejbRemove() {
        // Empty implementation.
    }
}
```

The CabinBean class can be divided into two sections for discussion: declarations for the container-managed fields and the callback methods.

Container-managed fields

The CabinBean defines several pairs of abstract accessor methods. For example, setName( ) and getName( ) are a pair of abstract accessor methods. These methods are responsible for setting and getting the entity bean's name field. When the bean is deployed, the EJB container automatically implements all the abstract accessor methods so that the bean state can be synchronized with the database. These implementations map the abstract accessor methods to fields in the database. Although all the abstract accessor methods have corresponding methods in the remote interface, CabinRemote, it's not necessary that they do so. Some accessor methods are for the entity bean's use only and are never exposed to the client through the remote or local interfaces. Note that, unlike the matching methods in the remote interface, the abstract accessor methods do not throw RemoteExceptions.

It's customary to consider the abstract accessor methods as providing access to virtual fields and to refer to those fields by their method names, less the get or set prefix. For example, the getName( )/setName( ) abstract accessor methods define a virtual *container-managed persistence* (CMP) field called name (the first letter is always changed to lowercase). The getDeckLevel( )/setDeckLevel( ) abstract accessor methods define a virtual CMP field called deckLevel, and so on.

The name, deckLevel, shipId, and bedCount fields represent the Cabin EJB's persistent state. They will be mapped to the database at deployment time. These fields are also publicly available through the entity bean's remote interface. Invoking the getBedCount( ) method on a CabinRemote EJB object causes the container to delegate that call to the corresponding getBedCount( ) method on the CabinBean instance.

There is no requirement that CMP fields must be exposed. The id field is another container-managed field, but its abstract accessor methods are not exposed to the client through the CabinRemote interface. This field is the primary key of the Cabin EJB; it's the entity bean's index to its data in the database. It's bad practice to expose the primary key of an entity bean—you don't want client applications to be able to change that key.

The callback methods

The CabinHomeRemote interface defines one create( ) method, so there is only one corresponding ejbCreate( ) method and one ejbPostCreate( ) method defined by the CabinBean class. When a client invokes the create( ) method on the remote home interface, it is delegated to a matching ejbCreate( ) method on the entity bean instance. The ejbCreate( ) method initializes the fields; in the case of the CabinBean, it sets the id field.

Although it's not required by the EJB specification, *some* J2EE application vendors insist that ejbCreate() throw a javax.ejb.CreateException—this is true of the J2EE 1.4 SDK. This has never been a requirement, but it's an issue that continues to crop up every time there is a new edition of this book.

The ejbCreate( ) method always returns the primary key type; with container-managed persistence, this method returns the null value. It's the container's responsibility to create the primary key. Why does it return null? This convention makes it easier for EJB vendors that support container-managed persistence using bean-managed persistence—it's a technique that is more common in EJB 1.1. Bean-managed persistence beans, which are covered in Chapter 10, always return the primary key type.

Once the ejbCreate( ) method has executed, the ejbPostCreate( ) method is called to perform any follow-up operations. The ejbCreate( ) and ejbPostCreate( ) methods must have signatures that match the parameters and (optionally) the exceptions of the home interface's create( ) method. The ejbPostCreate( ) method is used to perform any postprocessing on the bean after it is created, but before it can be used by the client. Both methods will execute, one right after the other, when the client invokes the create( ) method on the remote home interface.

The findByPrimaryKey( ) method is not defined in container-managed bean classes. Instead, find methods are generated at deployment and implemented by the container. With bean-managed entity beans, find methods must be defined in the bean class. In Chapter 10, when you develop bean-managed entity beans, you will define the find methods in the bean classes you develop.

The CabinBean class implements javax.ejb.EntityBean, which defines seven callback methods: setEntityContext( ), unsetEntityContext( ), ejbActivate( ), ejbPassivate( ), ejbLoad( ), ejbStore( ), and ejbRemove( ). The container uses these callback methods to notify the CabinBean of certain events in its life cycle. Although the callback methods are implemented, the implementations are empty. The CabinBean is simple enough that it doesn't need to do any special processing during its life cycle. When we study entity beans in more detail in Chapter 6 through Chapter 11, we will take advantage of these callback methods.

The Deployment Descriptor

You are now ready to create a deployment descriptor for the Cabin EJB. The deployment descriptor performs a function similar to a properties file. It describes which classes make up an enterprise bean and how the enterprise bean should be managed at runtime. During deployment, the deployment descriptor is read and its properties are displayed for editing. The deployer can then modify and add settings as appropriate for the application's operational environment. Once the deployer is satisfied with the deployment information, she uses it to generate the entire supporting infrastructure needed to deploy the enterprise bean in the EJB server. This may include resolving enterprise bean references, adding the enterprise bean to the naming system, and generating the enterprise bean's EJB object and EJB home, persistence infrastructure, transactional support, and so forth.

Although most EJB server products provide a wizard for creating and editing deployment descriptors, we will create ours directly so that the enterprise bean is defined in a vendor-independent manner. This requires some manual labor, but it gives you a much better understanding of how deployment descriptors are created. Once the deployment descriptor is finished, the enterprise bean can be placed in a JAR file and deployed on any EJB-compliant server of the appropriate version. An XML deployment descriptor has been created for every example in this book; they are available from the download site.

Vendors often require that you include vendor-specific deployment files along with the standard ones. This is an unfortunate situation that impacts portability, but something you need to be aware of. Consult your vendor's documentation to discover what additional configuration files they require.

Throughout this book, we show both the EJB 2.1 and EJB 2.0 code when they are different. In many cases, the component interfaces are the same; however, XML deployment descriptors will be different because EJB 2.1 uses XML Schema, while EJB 2.0 uses an XML DTD. This is the case with the Cabin EJB.

EJB 2.1: The Cabin EJB's deployment descriptor

Here's the deployment descriptor for the Cabin bean in EJB 2.1:

```
<?xml version="1.0" encoding="UTF-8" ?>
<ejb-jar
     xmlns="http://java.sun.com/xml/ns/j2ee"
     xmlns:xsi="http://www.w3.org/2001/XMLSchema-instance"
     xsi:schemaLocation="http://java.sun.com/xml/ns/j2ee
                         http://java.sun.com/xml/ns/j2ee/ejb-jar_2_1.xsd"
     version="2.1">
    <enterprise-beans>
        <entity>
```

```
            <ejb-name>CabinEJB</ejb-name>
            <home>com.titan.cabin.CabinHomeRemote</home>
            <remote>com.titan.cabin.CabinRemote</remote>
            <ejb-class>com.titan.cabin.CabinBean</ejb-class>
            <persistence-type>Container</persistence-type>
            <prim-key-class>java.lang.Integer</prim-key-class>
            <reentrant>False</reentrant>
            <abstract-schema-name>Cabin</abstract-schema-name>
            <cmp-field><field-name>id</field-name></cmp-field>
            <cmp-field><field-name>name</field-name></cmp-field>
            <cmp-field><field-name>deckLevel</field-name></cmp-field>
            <cmp-field><field-name>shipId</field-name></cmp-field>
            <cmp-field><field-name>bedCount</field-name></cmp-field>
            <primkey-field>id</primkey-field>
            <security-identity><use-caller-identity/></security-identity>
        </entity>
    </enterprise-beans>
    <assembly-descriptor>
    ...
    </assembly-descriptor>
</ejb-jar>
```

The ejb-jar element declares its namespace, the XSI namespace, and the location of the XML Schema that is used to validate it. The meaning of namespaces and XML schemas are described in more detail in Chapter 16.

EJB 2.0: The Cabin EJB's deployment descriptor

In EJB 2.0, the deployment descriptor is based on an XML DTD and looks like this:

```
<?xml version="1.0" encoding="UTF-8" ?>
<!DOCTYPE ejb-jar PUBLIC "-//Sun Microsystems, Inc.//DTD Enterprise
JavaBeans 2.0//EN" "http://java.sun.com/dtd/ejb-jar_2_0.dtd">

<ejb-jar>
    <enterprise-beans>
        <entity>
            <ejb-name>CabinEJB</ejb-name>
            <home>com.titan.cabin.CabinHomeRemote</home>
            <remote>com.titan.cabin.CabinRemote</remote>
            <ejb-class>com.titan.cabin.CabinBean</ejb-class>
            <persistence-type>Container</persistence-type>
            <prim-key-class>java.lang.Integer</prim-key-class>
            <reentrant>False</reentrant>
            <abstract-schema-name>Cabin</abstract-schema-name>
            <cmp-field><field-name>id</field-name></cmp-field>
            <cmp-field><field-name>name</field-name></cmp-field>
            <cmp-field><field-name>deckLevel</field-name></cmp-field>
            <cmp-field><field-name>shipId</field-name></cmp-field>
            <cmp-field><field-name>bedCount</field-name></cmp-field>
            <primkey-field>id</primkey-field>
            <security-identity><use-caller-identity/></security-identity>
        </entity>
```

```
    </enterprise-beans>
    <assembly-descriptor>
    ...
    </assembly-descriptor>
</ejb-jar>
```

The <!DOCTYPE> element describes the purpose of the XML file, its root element, and the location of its DTD. The DTD is used to verify that the document is structured correctly. This element is discussed in detail in Chapter 16. EJB 2.0 specifies the ejb-jar_2_0.dtd as its DTD.

EJB 2.1 and 2.0: Defining the XML elements

One important difference between EJB 2.1 and EJB 2.0 is that they use different types of validation for deployment descriptors. EJB 2.0 uses XML DTDs, which have been employed for the past few years to validate the structure of the XML deployment descriptor. XML Schema is a new mechanism for validating deployment descriptors. XML Schema can validate not only the structure but also the values used in the deployment descriptor—something DTDs couldn't do well. On the other hand, XML Schema is complex and takes time to master, so there is a price to be paid for the added precision it offers.

The rest of the XML elements are nested one within another and delimited by beginning and ending tags. The structure is not complicated. If you have done any HTML coding, you already understand the format. An element always starts with a *<name_of_tag>* tag and ends with a *</name_of_tag>* tag. Everything in between—even other elements—is part of the enclosing element.

The first major element is the <ejb-jar> element, which is the root of the document. All the other elements must lie within this element. Next is the <enterprise-beans> element. Every bean declared in an XML file must be included in this section. This file describes only the Cabin EJB, but we could define several beans in one deployment descriptor.

The <entity> element shows that the beans defined within this tag are entity beans. Similarly, a <session> element describes session beans; since the Cabin EJB is an entity bean, we don't need a <session> element. In addition to a description, the <entity> element provides the fully qualified class names of the remote interface, home interface, bean class, and primary key. The <cmp-field> elements list all the container-managed fields in the entity bean class. These are the fields that will persist in the database and be managed by the container at runtime. The <entity> element also includes a <reentrant> element that can be set as True or False depending on whether the bean allows reentrant loopbacks or not.

The deployment descriptor also specifies the <security-identity> as <use-caller-identity/>, which simply means the bean propagates the calling client's security identity when it accesses resources or other beans. Security identities are covered in Chapter 3.

The section of the XML file after the <enterprise-beans> element is enclosed by the <assembly-descriptor> element, which describes the security roles and transaction attributes of the bean. In this example, this section of the XML file is the same for both EJB 2.1 and EJB 2.0:

```
<ejb-jar ...>
    <enterprise-beans>
    ...
    </enterprise-beans>

<assembly-descriptor>
        <security-role>
            <description>
                This role represents everyone who is allowed full access
                to the Cabin EJB.
            </description>
            <role-name>everyone</role-name>
        </security-role>

        <method-permission>
            <role-name>everyone</role-name>
            <method>
                <ejb-name>CabinEJB</ejb-name>
                <method-name>*</method-name>
            </method>
        </method-permission>

        <container-transaction>
            <method>
                <ejb-name>CabinEJB</ejb-name>
                <method-name>*</method-name>
            </method>
            <trans-attribute>Required</trans-attribute>
        </container-transaction>

</assembly-descriptor>
</ejb-jar>
```

It may seem odd to separate the <assembly-descriptor> information from the <enterprise-beans> information, since it clearly applies to the Cabin EJB, but in the scheme of things, it's perfectly natural. A single XML deployment descriptor can describe several beans, which might all rely on the same security roles and transaction attributes. To make it easier to deploy several beans together, this common information is grouped in the <assembly-descriptor> element.

There is another (perhaps more important) reason for separating information about the bean itself from the security roles and transaction attributes. Enterprise JavaBeans defines the responsibilities of different participants in the development and deployment of beans. We don't address these development roles in this book because they are not critical to learning the fundamentals of EJB. For now, it's enough to know that the person who develops the beans and the person who assembles the beans into an application have separate responsibilities and therefore deal with separate parts of the XML deployment descriptor. The bean developer is responsible for everything within the `<enterprise-beans>` element; the bean assembler is responsible for everything within the `<assembly-descriptor>`. Throughout this book you will play both roles, developing the beans and assembling them. Other roles you will fill are that of the deployer, who actually loads the enterprise beans into the EJB container, and the administrator, who is responsible for tuning the EJB server and managing it at runtime. In real projects, these roles may be filled by an individual, several different individuals, or even teams.

The `<assembly-descriptor>` contains the `<security-role>` elements and their corresponding `<method-permission>` elements. In this example, there is one security role, `everyone`, which is mapped to all the methods in the Cabin EJB using the `<method-permission>` element. (The * in the `<method-name>` element means "all methods.")

The `<container-transaction>` element declares that all the methods of the Cabin EJB have a `Required` transaction attribute, which means that all the methods must be executed within a transaction. Transaction attributes are explained in more detail in Chapter 14. The deployment descriptor ends with the closing tag of the `<ejb-jar>` element.

Copy the Cabin EJB's deployment descriptor into the *META-INF* directory and save it as *ejb-jar.xml*. You have now created all the files you need to package your Cabin EJB. Figure 4-2 shows all the files that should be in the *dev* directory.

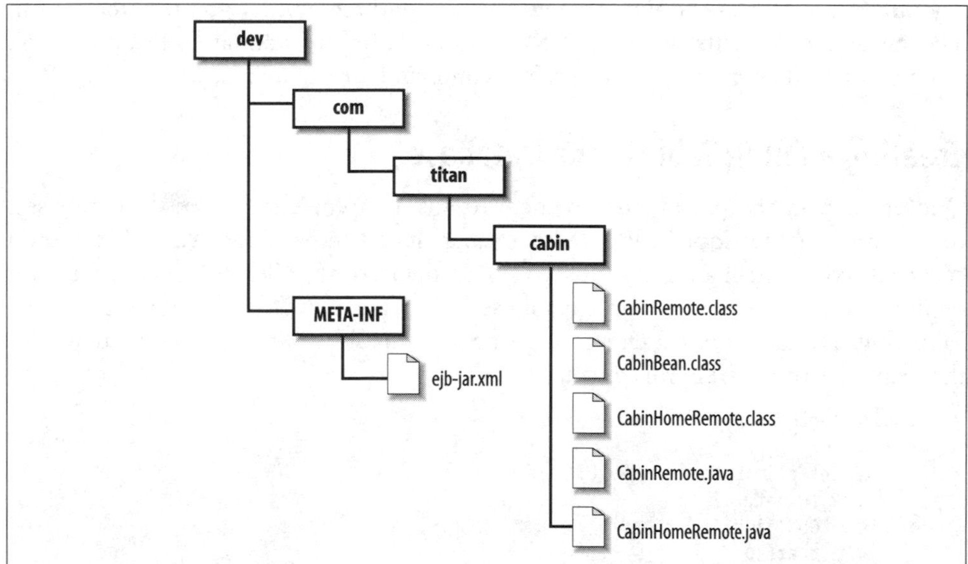

Figure 4-2. The Cabin EJB files

cabin.jar: The JAR File

The JAR file is a platform-independent file format for compressing, packaging, and delivering several files together. Based on the ZIP file format and the ZLIB compression standards, the JAR (Java archive) tool and packages were originally developed to make downloads of Java applets more efficient. As a packaging mechanism, however, the JAR file format is a very convenient way to "shrink-wrap" components and other software for delivery to third parties. In EJB development, a JAR file packages all the classes and interfaces associated with a bean, including the deployment descriptor, into one file.

Creating the JAR file for deployment is easy. Position yourself in the *dev* directory that is just above the *com/titan/cabin* directory tree, and execute the following command:

```
\dev % jar cf cabin.jar com/titan/cabin/*.class META-INF/ejb-jar.xml

F:\..\dev>jar cf cabin.jar com\titan\cabin\*.class META-INF\ejb-jar.xml
```

You might have to create the *META-INF* directory first and copy *ejb-jar.xml* into that directory. The *c* option tells the *jar* utility to create a new JAR file that contains the files indicated in subsequent parameters. It also tells the *jar* utility to stream the resulting JAR file to standard output. The *f* option tells *jar* to redirect the standard output to a new file named in the second parameter (*cabin.jar*). It's important to get the order of the option letters and the command-line parameters to match. You can learn more about the *jar* utility and the `java.util.zip` package in *Java in a Nutshell* by David Flanagan, or *Learning Java* by Pat Niemeyer and Jonathan Knudsen (both published by O'Reilly).

The *jar* utility creates the file *cabin.jar* in the *dev* directory. If you're interested in looking at the contents of the JAR file, you can use any standard ZIP application (WinZip, PKZIP, etc.), or you can use the command *jar tvf cabin.jar*.

Creating a CABIN Table in the Database

One of the primary jobs of a deployment tool is mapping entity beans to databases. In the case of the Cabin EJB, we must map its `id`, `name`, `deckLevel`, `shipId`, and `bedCount` container-managed fields to some data source. Before proceeding with deployment, you need to set up a database and create a `CABIN` table. You can use the following standard SQL statement to create a `CABIN` table that will be consistent with the examples provided in this chapter:

```
create table CABIN
(
    ID int primary key NOT NULL,
    SHIP_ID int,
    BED_COUNT int,
    NAME char(30),
    DECK_LEVEL int
)
```

This statement creates a CABIN table that has five columns corresponding to the container-managed fields in the CabinBean class. Once the table is created and connectivity to the database is confirmed, you can proceed with the deployment process.

Deploying the Cabin EJB

Deployment is the process of reading the bean's JAR file, changing or adding properties to the deployment descriptor, mapping the bean to the database, defining access control in the security domain, and generating any vendor-specific classes needed to support the bean in the EJB environment. Every EJB server product has its own deployment tools, which may provide a graphical user interface, a set of command-line programs, or both. Graphical deployment wizards are the easiest deployment tools to use.

A deployment tool reads the JAR file and looks for *ejb-jar.xml*. In a graphical deployment wizard, the deployment descriptor elements are presented using a set of property sheets similar to those used in environments such as VisualBasic.NET, PowerBuilder, and JBuilder. Figure 4-3 shows the deployment wizard for the J2EE 1.3 SDK (Reference Implementation) server.

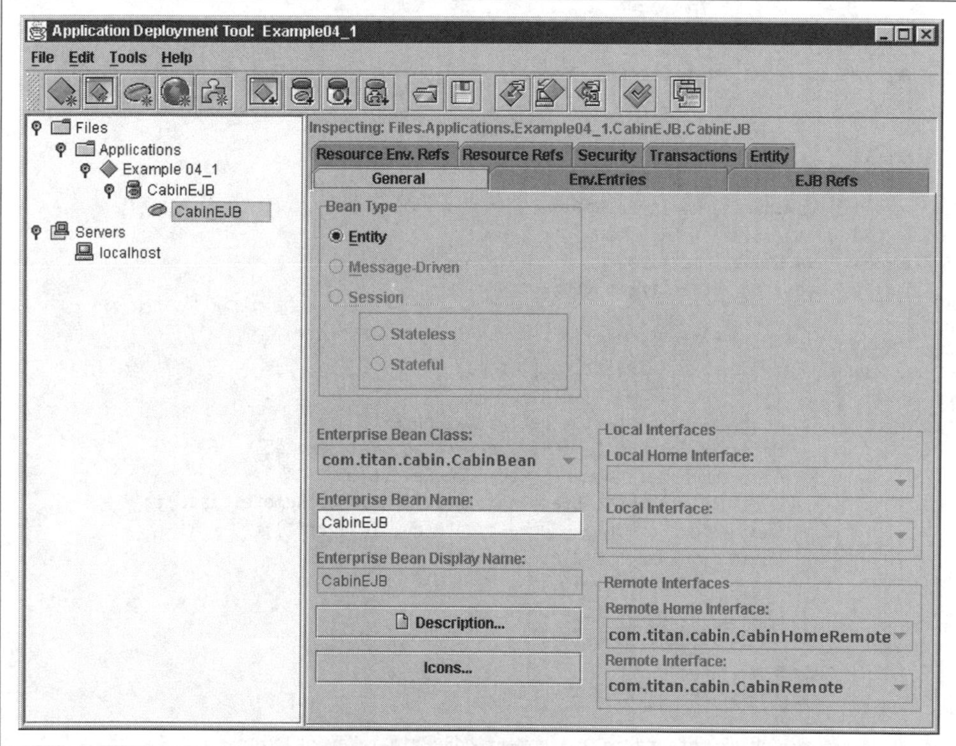

Figure 4-3. J2EE 1.3 SDK Reference Implementation's deployment wizard

The J2EE Reference Implementation's deployment wizard has fields and panels that match the XML deployment descriptor. You can map security roles to user groups, set the JNDI lookup name, map the container-managed fields to the database, etc. EJB deployment tools provide varying degrees of support for mapping container-managed fields to a data source. Some provide sophisticated graphical user interfaces, while others are simpler and less flexible. Fortunately, mapping the `CabinBean`'s container-managed fields to the `CABIN` table is a fairly straightforward process. The documentation for your vendor's deployment tool will show you how to create this mapping. Once you have finished the mapping, you can complete the deployment of the Cabin EJB and prepare to access it from the EJB server.

Creating a Client Application

Now that the Cabin EJB has been deployed, we want to access it from a remote client. In this section, we create a remote client that connects to the EJB server, locates the EJB remote home for the Cabin EJB, and creates and interacts with several Cabin EJBs. The following code shows a Java application that creates a new Cabin EJB, sets its `name`, `deckLevel`, `shipId`, and `bedCount` properties, and then locates it again using its primary key:

```
package com.titan.cabin;

import com.titan.cabin.CabinHomeRemote;
import com.titan.cabin.CabinRemote;

import javax.naming.InitialContext;
import javax.naming.Context;
import javax.naming.NamingException;
import java.rmi.RemoteException;
import java.util.Properties;
import javax.rmi.PortableRemoteObject;

public class Client_1 {
    public static void main(String [] args) {
        try {
            Context jndiContext = getInitialContext( );
            Object ref = jndiContext.lookup("CabinHomeRemote");
            CabinHomeRemote home = (CabinHomeRemote)
                PortableRemoteObject.narrow(ref,CabinHomeRemote.class);
            CabinRemote cabin_1 = home.create(new Integer(1));
            cabin_1.setName("Master Suite");
            cabin_1.setDeckLevel(1);
            cabin_1.setShipId(1);
            cabin_1.setBedCount(3);

            Integer pk = new Integer(1);

            CabinRemote cabin_2 = home.findByPrimaryKey(pk);
            System.out.println(cabin_2.getName( ));
            System.out.println(cabin_2.getDeckLevel( ));
```

```
            System.out.println(cabin_2.getShipId( ));
            System.out.println(cabin_2.getBedCount( ));

        } catch (java.rmi.RemoteException re){re.printStackTrace( );}
          catch (javax.naming.NamingException ne){ne.printStackTrace( );}
          catch (javax.ejb.CreateException ce){ce.printStackTrace( );}
          catch (javax.ejb.FinderException fe){fe.printStackTrace( );}
    }

    public static Context getInitialContext( )
        throws javax.naming.NamingException {

        Properties p = new Properties( );
        // ... Specify the JNDI properties specific to the vendor.
        return new javax.naming.InitialContext(p);
    }
}
```

To access an enterprise bean, a client starts by using JNDI to obtain a directory connection to a bean's container. JNDI is an implementation-independent API for directory and naming systems. Every EJB vendor must provide a directory service that is JNDI-compliant. This means that they must provide a JNDI service provider, which is a piece of software analogous to a driver in JDBC. Different service providers connect to different directory services—not unlike JDBC, where different drivers connect to different relational databases. The `getInitialContext( )` method uses JNDI to obtain a network connection to the EJB server.

The code used to obtain the JNDI `Context` depends on which EJB vendor you use. Consult your vendor's documentation to find out how to obtain a JNDI `Context` appropriate to your product. For example, the code used to obtain a JNDI `Context` in WebSphere might look something like the following:

```
public static Context getInitialContext( )
    throws javax.naming.NamingException {

    java.util.Properties properties = new java.util.Properties( );
    properties.put(javax.naming.Context.PROVIDER_URL, "iiop:///");
    properties.put(javax.naming.Context.INITIAL_CONTEXT_FACTORY,
        "com.ibm.ejs.ns.jndi.CNInitialContextFactory");
    return new InitialContext(properties);
}
```

The same method developed for BEA's WebLogic Server would be different:

```
public static Context getInitialContext( )
    throws javax.naming.NamingException {

    Properties p = new Properties( );
    p.put(Context.INITIAL_CONTEXT_FACTORY,
        "weblogic.jndi.WLInitialContextFactory");
    p.put(Context.PROVIDER_URL, "t3://localhost:7001");
    return new javax.naming.InitialContext(p);
}
```

Once a JNDI connection is established and a context is obtained from the `getInitialContext( )` method, the context can be used to look up the EJB home of the Cabin EJB.

```
Object ref = jndiContext.lookup("CabinHomeRemote");
```

Throughout this book, we'll use lookup names like "CabinHomeRemote" for remote client applications. The actual name you use to do a lookup may be different, depending on the requirements of your vendor. You will need to bind a lookup name to the EJB server's naming service, and some vendors may require a special directory path.

If you are using a standard J2EE component (Servlet, JSP, EJB, or J2EE Application Client), you will not need to set the properties explicitly when creating a JNDI `InitialContext`, no matter which EJB vendor you are using. That's because the JNDI properties can be configured at deployment time and are applied automatically. A J2EE component would obtain its `InitialContext` as follows:

```
public static Context getInitialContext( )
    throws javax.naming.NamingException {

    return new javax.naming.InitialContext( );
}
```

This is simpler and more portable than configuring JNDI properties for simple Java clients. All J2EE components use the same JNDI naming system that enterprise beans use to lookup any service. Specifically, they require that EJB references be bound to the `java:comp/env/ejb/` namespace. For example, for a J2EE component, here's all we need to look up the Cabin EJB:

```
Object ref = jndiContext.lookup("java:comp/env/ejb/CabinHomeRemote");
```

At deployment time you would use the vendor's deployment tools to map that JNDI name to the Cabin EJB's home. In this book, Java client applictions will need to use explicit parameters for JNDI lookups. As an alternative you could use a special J2EE component called a J2EE Application Client, but this type of component is outside the scope of this book. For more information about J2EE Application Client components consult the J2EE 1.3 (for EJB 2.0) or the J2EE 1.4 specifications.

The `Client_1` application uses the `PortableRemoteObject.narrow( )` method to narrow the `Object ref` to a `CabinHomeRemote` reference:

```
Object ref = jndiContext.lookup("CabinHomeRemote");
CabinHomeRemote home = (CabinHomeRemote)
    PortableRemoteObject.narrow(ref,CabinHomeRemote.class);
```

The `PortableRemoteObject.narrow( )` method was first introduced in EJB 1.1 and continues to be used on remote clients in EJB 2.1 and 2.0. It is needed to support the requirements of RMI over IIOP. Because CORBA supports many different languages, casting is not native to CORBA (some languages don't have casting). Therefore, to get a remote reference to `CabinHomeRemote`, we must explicitly narrow the object returned from `lookup( )`. This has the same effect as casting and is explained in more detail in Chapter 5.

The name used to find the Cabin EJB's EJB home is set by the deployer using a deployment wizard like the one pictured earlier. The JNDI name is entirely up to the person deploying the bean; it can be the same as the bean name set in the XML deployment descriptor, or something completely different.

Creating a new Cabin EJB

Once we have a remote reference to the EJB home, we can use it to create a new Cabin entity:

```
CabinRemote cabin_1 = home.create(new Integer(1));
```

We create a new `Cabin` entity using the `create(Integer id)` method defined in the remote home interface of the Cabin EJB. When this method is invoked, the EJB home works with the EJB server to create a Cabin EJB, adding its data to the database. The EJB server creates an EJB object to wrap the Cabin EJB instance and returns a remote reference to the EJB object. The `cabin_1` variable then contains a remote reference to the Cabin EJB we just created. We don't need to use the `PortableRemoteObject.narrow( )` method to get the EJB object from the home reference, because it was declared as returning the `CabinRemote` type; no casting was required. We don't need to explicitly narrow remote references returned by `findByPrimaryKey( )` for the same reason.

With the remote reference to the EJB object, we can update the `name`, `deckLevel`, `shipId`, and `bedCount` of the Cabin EJB:

```
CabinRemote cabin_1 = home.create(new Integer(1));
cabin_1.setName("Master Suite");
cabin_1.setDeckLevel(1);
cabin_1.setShipId(1);
cabin_1.setBedCount(3);
```

Figure 4-4 shows how the relational database table we created should look after this code has been executed. It should contain one record.

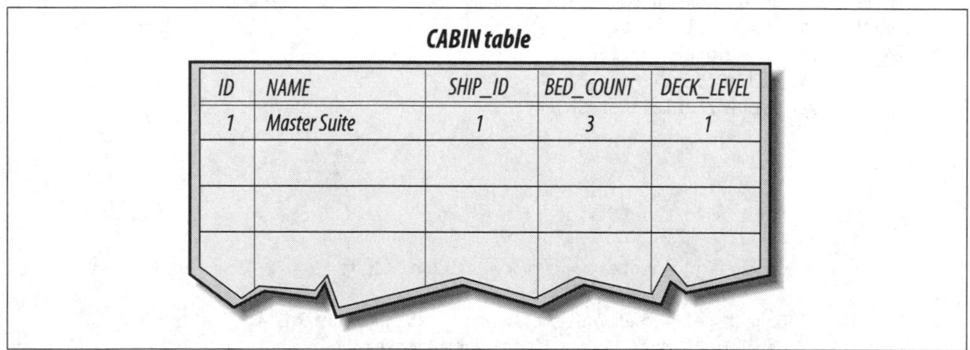

CABIN table

ID	NAME	SHIP_ID	BED_COUNT	DECK_LEVEL
1	Master Suite	1	3	1

Figure 4-4. CABIN table with one cabin record

A client locates entity beans using the findByPrimaryKey( ) method in the home interface. To look up the Cabin bean we just created, we create a primary key of the correct type—in this case, Integer. When we invoke the finder method on the home interface using the primary key, we get back a remote reference to the EJB object. We can now interrogate the remote reference returned by findByPrimaryKey( ) to get the Cabin EJB's name, deckLevel, shipId, and bedCount:

```
Integer pk = new Integer(1);

CabinRemote cabin_2 = home.findByPrimaryKey(pk);
System.out.println(cabin_2.getName( ));
System.out.println(cabin_2.getDeckLevel( ));
System.out.println(cabin_2.getShipId( ));
System.out.println(cabin_2.getBedCount( ));
```

We are ready to create and run the Client_1 application. Compile the client application and deploy the Cabin EJB into the container system (see the JBoss Workbook section of this book, Exercise 4.1). Then run the Client_1 application. The output should look something like this:

```
Master Suite
1
1
3
```

Congratulations! You just created and used your first entity bean. Of course, the client application doesn't do much. Before going on to create session beans, create another client that adds some test data to the database. Here we'll create Client_2, which is a modification of Client_1 that populates the database with a large number of cabins for three different ships:

```
package com.titan.cabin;

import com.titan.cabin.CabinHomeRemote;
import com.titan.cabin.CabinRemote;

import javax.naming.InitialContext;
import javax.naming.Context;
import javax.naming.NamingException;
import javax.ejb.CreateException;
import java.rmi.RemoteException;
import java.util.Properties;
import javax.rmi.PortableRemoteObject;

public class Client_2 {

    public static void main(String [] args) {
        try {
            Context jndiContext = getInitialContext( );

            Object ref = jndiContext.lookup("CabinHomeRemote");
            CabinHomeRemote home = (CabinHomeRemote)
                PortableRemoteObject.narrow(ref,CabinHomeRemote.class);
```

```
            // Add 9 cabins to deck 1 of ship 1.
            makeCabins(home, 2, 10, 1, 1);
            // Add 10 cabins to deck 2 of ship 1.
            makeCabins(home, 11, 20, 2, 1);
            // Add 10 cabins to deck 3 of ship 1.
            makeCabins(home, 21, 30, 3, 1);

            // Add 10 cabins to deck 1 of ship 2.
            makeCabins(home, 31, 40, 1, 2);
            // Add 10 cabins to deck 2 of ship 2.
            makeCabins(home, 41, 50, 2, 2);
            // Add 10 cabins to deck 3 of ship 2.
            makeCabins(home, 51, 60, 3, 2);

            // Add 10 cabins to deck 1 of ship 3.
            makeCabins(home, 61, 70, 1, 3);
            // Add 10 cabins to deck 2 of ship 3.
            makeCabins(home, 71, 80, 2, 3);
            // Add 10 cabins to deck 3 of ship 3.
            makeCabins(home, 81, 90, 3, 3);
            // Add 10 cabins to deck 4 of ship 3.
            makeCabins(home, 91, 100, 4, 3);

            for (int i = 1; i <= 100; i++){
                Integer pk = new Integer(i);
                CabinRemote cabin = home.findByPrimaryKey(pk);
                System.out.println("PK = "+i+", Ship = "+cabin.getShipId( )
                    + ", Deck = "+cabin.getDeckLevel( )
                    + ", BedCount = "+cabin.getBedCount( )
                    + ", Name = "+cabin.getName( ));
            }

        } catch (java.rmi.RemoteException re) {re.printStackTrace( );}
          catch (javax.naming.NamingException ne) {ne.printStackTrace( );}
          catch (javax.ejb.CreateException ce) {ce.printStackTrace( );}
          catch (javax.ejb.FinderException fe) {fe.printStackTrace( );}
    }

    public static javax.naming.Context getInitialContext( )
        throws javax.naming.NamingException{
    Properties p = new Properties( );
    // ... Specify the JNDI properties specific to the vendor.
    return new javax.naming.InitialContext(p);
    }

    public static void makeCabins(CabinHomeRemote home, int fromId,
                                  int toId, int deckLevel, int shipNumber)
        throws RemoteException, CreateException {

    int bc = 3;
    for (int i = fromId; i <= toId; i++) {
        CabinRemote cabin = home.create(new Integer(i));
        int suiteNumber = deckLevel*100+(i-fromId);
        cabin.setName("Suite "+suiteNumber);
```

```
            cabin.setDeckLevel(deckLevel);
            bc = (bc==3)?2:3;
            cabin.setBedCount(bc);
            cabin.setShipId(shipNumber);
            }
        }
    }
```

Create and run the `Client_2` application against the Cabin EJB we deployed earlier. `Client_2` lists all the Cabin EJBs it added to the database:

```
PK = 1, Ship = 1, Deck = 1, BedCount = 3, Name = Master Suite
PK = 2, Ship = 1, Deck = 1, BedCount = 2, Name = Suite 100
PK = 3, Ship = 1, Deck = 1, BedCount = 3, Name = Suite 101
PK = 4, Ship = 1, Deck = 1, BedCount = 2, Name = Suite 102
PK = 5, Ship = 1, Deck = 1, BedCount = 3, Name = Suite 103
PK = 6, Ship = 1, Deck = 1, BedCount = 2, Name = Suite 104
PK = 7, Ship = 1, Deck = 1, BedCount = 3, Name = Suite 105
...
```

We now have 100 cabin records in our `CABIN` table, representing 100 cabin entities in our EJB system. This amount provides a good set of test data for the session bean we will create in the next section, and for subsequent examples throughout the book.

Developing a Session Bean

Session beans act as agents to the client, controlling taskflow (the business process) and filling the gaps between the representation of data by entity beans and the business logic. Session beans are often used to manage interactions between entity beans and can perform complex manipulations of beans. Since we have defined only one entity bean so far, we will start by manipulating this bean. The interactions of entity beans within session beans is explored in greater detail in Chapter 11.

Client applications and other beans use the Cabin EJB in a variety of ways. Some of these uses were predictable when the Cabin EJB was defined, but many were not. After all, an entity bean represents data—in this case, data describing a cabin. The uses to which we put that data change over time—hence the importance of separating the data itself from the taskflow. In Titan's business system, for example, we may need to list and report on cabins in ways that were not predictable when the Cabin EJB was defined. Rather than change the Cabin EJB every time we need to look at it differently, we will obtain the information we need using a session bean. The definition of an entity bean should only be changed within the context of a larger process—for example, a major redesign of the business system.

We'll start developing a TravelAgent EJB that is responsible for the taskflow of booking a passage on a cruise. This session bean will be used in client applications accessed by travel agents throughout the world. In addition to booking tickets, the TravelAgent EJB provides information about which cabins are available on the cruise. In this chapter, we develop the first implementation of this listing behavior.

The "list cabins" behavior will be used to provide customers with a list of cabins that can accommodate their needs. The Cabin EJB does not directly support this kind of list, nor should it. The list we need is specific to the TravelAgent EJB, so it's the TravelAgent EJB's responsibility to query the Cabin EJB and produce the list.

Start by creating a development directory for the TravelAgent EJB, as we did for the Cabin EJB. Name this directory *travelagent* and nest it below the */dev/com/titan* directory, which also contains the *cabin* directory (see Figure 4-5). Place all the Java files and the XML deployment descriptor for the TravelAgent EJB into the *travelagent* directory.

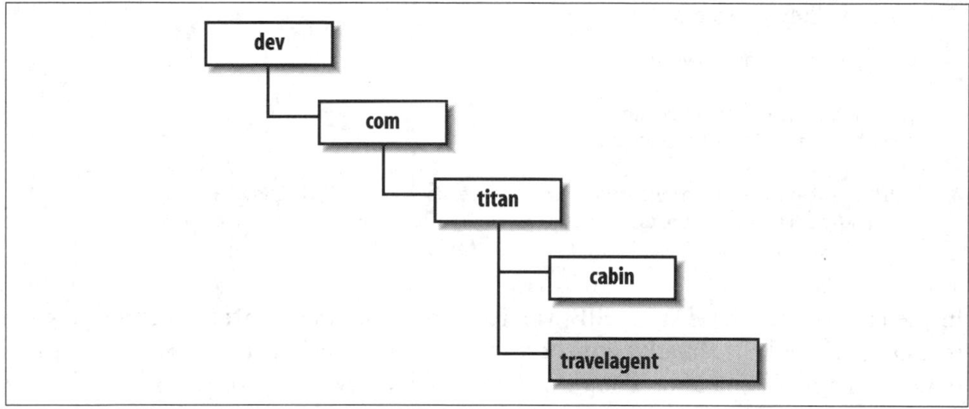

Figure 4-5. Directory structure for the TravelAgent EJB

TravelAgentRemote: The Remote Interface

As before, we start by defining the remote interface so that our focus is on the business purpose of the bean, rather than its implementation. Starting small, we know that the TravelAgent EJB will need to provide a method for listing all the cabins available with a specified bed count for a specific ship. We'll call that method `listCabins( )`. Since we need only a list of cabin names and deck levels, we'll define `listCabins( )` to return an array of `Strings`. Here's the remote interface for `TravelAgentRemote`:

```
package com.titan.travelagent;

import java.rmi.RemoteException;
import javax.ejb.FinderException;

public interface TravelAgentRemote extends javax.ejb.EJBObject {

    // String elements follow the format "id, name, deck level"
    public String [] listCabins(int shipID, int bedCount)
        throws RemoteException;
}
```

TravelAgentHomeRemote: The Remote Home Interface

The second step in the development of the TravelAgent EJB bean is to create the remote home interface. The remote home interface for a session bean defines the create methods that initialize a new session bean for use by a client.

Find methods are not used in session beans; session beans do not represent data in the database, so a find method would not be meaningful. A session bean is dedicated to a client for the life of that client (or less). For the same reason, we don't need to worry about primary keys—since session beans don't represent persistent data, we don't need a key to access that data.

```
package com.titan.travelagent;

import java.rmi.RemoteException;
import javax.ejb.CreateException;

public interface TravelAgentHomeRemote extends javax.ejb.EJBHome {
    public TravelAgentRemote create( )
        throws RemoteException, CreateException;
}
```

In the case of the TravelAgent EJB, we need only a simple `create( )` method to get a reference to the bean. Invoking this `create( )` method returns the TravelAgent EJB's remote reference, which the client can use for the reservation process.

TravelAgentBean: The Bean Class

Using the remote interface as a guide, we can define the `TravelAgentBean` class that implements the `listCabins( )` method. Here's the definition of `TravelAgentBean` for this example:

```
package com.titan.travelagent;

import com.titan.cabin.CabinRemote;
import com.titan.cabin.CabinHomeRemote;
import java.rmi.RemoteException;
import javax.naming.InitialContext;
import javax.naming.Context;
import java.util.Properties;
import java.util.Vector;
import javax.rmi.PortableRemoteObject;
import javax.ejb.EJBException;


public class TravelAgentBean implements javax.ejb.SessionBean {

    public void ejbCreate( ) {
    // Do nothing.
    }
    public String [] listCabins(int shipID, int bedCount) {
```

```
        try {
            javax.naming.Context jndiContext = new InitialContext( );
            Object obj = jndiContext.lookup("java:comp/env/ejb/CabinHomeRemote");

            CabinHomeRemote home = (CabinHomeRemote)
                PortableRemoteObject.narrow(obj,CabinHomeRemote.class);

            Vector vect = new Vector( );
            for (int i = 1; ; i++) {
                Integer pk = new Integer(i);
                CabinRemote cabin;
                try {
                    cabin = home.findByPrimaryKey(pk);
                } catch(javax.ejb.FinderException fe) {
                    break;
                }
                // Check to see if the bed count and ship ID match.
                if (cabin.getShipId( ) == shipID &&
                    cabin.getBedCount( ) == bedCount) {
                    String details = i+","+cabin.getName( )+
                                    ","+cabin.getDeckLevel( );
                    vect.addElement(details);
                }
            }

            String [] list = new String[vect.size( )];
            vect.copyInto(list);
            return list;

        } catch(Exception e) {throw new EJBException(e);}
    }

    public void ejbRemove( ){}
    public void ejbActivate( ){}
    public void ejbPassivate( ){}
    public void setSessionContext(javax.ejb.SessionContext cntx){}
}
```

In order to examine the listCabins( ) method in detail, let's address the implementation in pieces, starting with the use of JNDI to locate the CabinHomeRemote:

```
javax.naming.Context jndiContext = new InitialContext( );

Object obj = jndiContext.lookup("java:comp/env/ejb/CabinHomeRemote");

CabinHomeRemote home = (CabinHomeRemote)
    javax.rmi.PortableRemoteObject.narrow(obj, CabinHomeRemote.class);
```

Beans are clients to other beans, just like client applications. This means that they must interact with other beans in the same way that J2EE application clients interact with beans. For one bean to locate and use another bean, it must first locate and obtain a reference to the bean's EJB home. This is accomplished using the JNDI default context, which is the JNDI context that the container provides automatically when you create a new instance of the InitialContext. You don't need to set any properties on the InitialContext when using a standard J2EE component (EJB, Servlet/JSP, or J2EE Application Client).

All beans have their own default JNDI context called the environment naming context, which was discussed briefly in Chapter 3. The default context exists in the name space (directory) called "java:comp/env" and its subdirectories. When the bean is deployed, any beans it uses are mapped into the subdirectory "java:comp/env/ejb", so that bean references can be obtained at runtime through a simple and consistent use of the JNDI default context. We'll come back to this when we look at the deployment descriptor for the TravelAgent EJB.

Once the remote EJB home of the Cabin EJB has been obtained, we can use it to produce a list of cabins that match the parameters passed into the method. The following code loops through all the Cabin EJBs and produces a list that includes only those cabins in which the ship and bed count are specified:

```
Vector vect = new Vector( );
for (int i = 1; ; i++) {
    Integer pk = new Integer(i);
    CabinRemote cabin;
    try {
        cabin = home.findByPrimaryKey(pk);
    } catch(javax.ejb.FinderException fe){
        break;
    }
    // Check to see if the bed count and ship ID match.
    if (cabin.getShipId() == shipID && cabin.getBedCount( ) == bedCount) {
        String details = i+","+cabin.getName()+","+cabin.getDeckLevel( );
        vect.addElement(details);
    }
}
```

This method iterates through all the primary keys, obtaining a remote reference to each Cabin EJB in the system and checking whether its shipId and bedCount match the parameters passed. The for loop continues until a FinderException is thrown, which will probably occur when a primary key that isn't associated with a bean is used. (This isn't the most robust code possible, but it will do for now.) Following this block of code, we simply copy the Vector's contents into an array and return it to the client.

While this is a very crude approach to locating the right Cabin EJBs—we will define a better method in Chapter 11—it is adequate for our current purposes. The purpose of this example is to illustrate that the taskflow associated with this listing behavior is not included in the Cabin EJB, nor is it embedded in a client application. Taskflow logic, whether it's a process like booking a reservation or like obtaining a list, is placed in a session bean.

The TravelAgent EJB's Deployment Descriptor

The TravelAgent EJB uses an XML deployment descriptor similar to the one used for the Cabin entity bean. The following sections contain the *ejb-jar.xml* file used to deploy the TravelAgent bean in EJB. Chapter 11 describes how to deploy several beans in one deployment descriptor, but for now the TravelAgent and Cabin EJBs are deployed separately.

EJB 2.1: Deployment descriptor

In EJB 2.1, the deployment descriptor for the TravelAgent EJB looks like this:

```
<?xml version="1.0" encoding="UTF-8" ?>
<ejb-jar
     xmlns="http://java.sun.com/xml/ns/j2ee"
     xmlns:xsi="http://www.w3.org/2001/XMLSchema-instance"
     xsi:schemaLocation="http://java.sun.com/xml/ns/j2ee
                         http://java.sun.com/xml/ns/j2ee/ejb-jar_2_1.xsd"
     version="2.1">
    <enterprise-beans>
        <session>
            <ejb-name>TravelAgentEJB</ejb-name>
            <home>com.titan.travelagent.TravelAgentHomeRemote</home>
            <remote>com.titan.travelagent.TravelAgentRemote</remote>
            <ejb-class>com.titan.travelagent.TravelAgentBean</ejb-class>
            <session-type>Stateless</session-type>
            <transaction-type>Container</transaction-type>
            <ejb-ref>
                <ejb-ref-name>ejb/CabinHomeRemote</ejb-ref-name>
                <ejb-ref-type>Entity</ejb-ref-type>
                <home>com.titan.cabin.CabinHomeRemote</home>
                <remote>com.titan.cabin.CabinRemote</remote>
            </ejb-ref>
            <security-identity><use-caller-identity/></security-identity>
        </session>
    </enterprise-beans>
    <assembly-descriptor>
    ...
    </assembly-descriptor>
</ejb-jar>
```

EJB 2.0: Deployment descriptor

In EJB 2.0, the deployment descriptor for the TravelAgent EJB looks like this:

```
<?xml version="1.0" encoding="UTF-8" ?>
<!DOCTYPE ejb-jar PUBLIC "-//Sun Microsystems, Inc.//DTD Enterprise
JavaBeans 2.0//EN" "http://java.sun.com/dtd/ejb-jar_2_0.dtd">
<ejb-jar>
    <enterprise-beans>
        <session>
            <ejb-name>TravelAgentEJB</ejb-name>
            <home>com.titan.travelagent.TravelAgentHomeRemote</home>
```

```
            <remote>com.titan.travelagent.TravelAgentRemote</remote>
            <ejb-class>com.titan.travelagent.TravelAgentBean</ejb-class>
            <session-type>Stateless</session-type>
            <transaction-type>Container</transaction-type>
            <ejb-ref>
                <ejb-ref-name>ejb/CabinHomeRemote</ejb-ref-name>
                <ejb-ref-type>Entity</ejb-ref-type>
                <home>com.titan.cabin.CabinHomeRemote</home>
                <remote>com.titan.cabin.CabinRemote</remote>
            </ejb-ref>
            <security-identity><use-caller-identity/></security-identity>
        </session>
    </enterprise-beans>
    <assembly-descriptor>
    ...
    </assembly-descriptor>
</ejb-jar>
```

EJB 2.0 and 1.1: Defining the XML elements

The only significant difference between the 2.1 and 2.0 deployment descriptors is that EJB 2.1 declares the use of an XML Schema for validation while EJB 2.0 uses a DTD.

Other than the `<session-type>` and `<ejb-ref>` elements, the TravelAgent EJB's XML deployment descriptor should be familiar: it uses many of the same elements as the Cabin EJB's. The `<session-type>` element can be `Stateful` or `Stateless`, to indicate which type of session bean is used. In this case, we are defining a stateless session bean.

The `<ejb-ref>` element is used at deployment time to map the bean references used within the TravelAgent EJB. In this case, the `<ejb-ref>` element describes the Cabin EJB, which we already deployed. The `<ejb-ref-name>` element specifies the name that must be used by the TravelAgent EJB to obtain a reference to the Cabin EJB's home. The `<ejb-ref-type>` tells the container what kind of bean it is, `Entity` or `Session`. The `<home>` and `<remote>` elements specify the fully qualified interface names of the Cabin's home and remote bean interfaces.

When the bean is deployed, the `<ejb-ref>` will be mapped to the Cabin EJB in the EJB server. This is a vendor-specific process, but the outcome should always be the same. When the TravelAgent EJB does a JNDI lookup using the context name "`java:comp/env/ejb/CabinHomeRemote`", it obtains a remote reference to the Cabin EJB's home. The purpose of the `<ejb-ref>` element is to eliminate network-specific and implementation-specific use of JNDI to obtain remote bean references. This makes a bean more portable, because the network location and JNDI service provider can change without affecting the bean code or even the XML deployment descriptor.

While we haven't yet created a local interface for our beans, it's always preferable to use local references instead of remote references when beans access each other within the same server. Local references are specified using the `<ejb-local-ref>` element, which looks just like the `<ejb-ref>` element.

The <assembly-descriptor> section of the deployment descriptor is the same for EJB 2.1 and EJB 2.0:

```
<assembly-descriptor>
    <security-role>
        <description>
            This role represents everyone who is allowed full access
            to the TravelAgent EJB.
        </description>
        <role-name>everyone</role-name>
    </security-role>

    <method-permission>
        <role-name>everyone</role-name>
        <method>
            <ejb-name>TravelAgentEJB</ejb-name>
            <method-name>*</method-name>
        </method>
    </method-permission>

    <container-transaction>
        <method>
            <ejb-name>TravelAgentEJB</ejb-name>
            <method-name>*</method-name>
        </method>
        <trans-attribute>Required</trans-attribute>
    </container-transaction>
</assembly-descriptor>
```

Deploying the TravelAgent EJB

Once you've defined the XML deployment descriptor, you are ready to place the TravelAgent EJB in its own JAR file and deploy it into the EJB server. Use the same process to JAR the TravelAgent EJB as you used for the Cabin EJB. Shrink-wrap the TravelAgent EJB class and its deployment descriptor into a JAR file and save the file to the *com/titan/travelagent* directory:

```
\dev % jar cf travelagent.jar com/titan/travelagent/*.class META-INF/ejb-jar.xml

F:\..\dev>jar cf travelagent.jar com\titan\travelagent\*.class META-INF\ejb-jar.xml
```

You might have to create the *META-INF* directory first, and copy *ejb-jar.xml* into that directory. The TravelAgent EJB is now complete and ready to be deployed.

To make your TravelAgent EJB available to a client application, you need to use the deployment utility or wizard of your EJB server. The deployment utility reads the JAR file to add the TravelAgent EJB to the EJB server environment. Unless your EJB server has special requirements, it is unlikely that you will need to change or add any new attributes to the bean. You will not need to create a database table, since the TravelAgent EJB is using the Cabin EJB and is not itself persistent. However, you will need to map the <ejb-ref> element in the TravelAgent EJB's deployment descriptor to the Cabin EJB. Your EJB server's deployment facilities provides a mechanism for accomplishing this task (see Exercise 4.2 in the Workbook).

Creating a Client Application

To show that our session bean works, we'll create a simple client application that uses it. This client produces a list of cabins assigned to ship 1 with a bed count of 3. Its logic is similar to the client we created earlier to test the Cabin EJB: it creates a context for looking up `TravelAgentHomeRemote`, creates a TravelAgent EJB, and invokes `listCabins( )` to generate a list of the cabins available. Here's the code:

```
import com.titan.travelagent.TravelAgentRemote;
import com.titan.travelagent.TravelAgentHomeRemote;

import javax.naming.InitialContext;
import javax.naming.Context;
import javax.naming.NamingException;
import javax.ejb.CreateException;
import java.rmi.RemoteException;
import java.util.Properties;
import javax.rmi.PortableRemoteObject;

public class Client_3 {
    public static int SHIP_ID = 1;
    public static int BED_COUNT = 3;

    public static void main(String [] args) {
        try {
            Context jndiContext = getInitialContext( );

            Object ref = jndiContext.lookup("TravelAgentHomeRemote");
            TravelAgentHomeRemote home = (TravelAgentHomeRemote)
                PortableRemoteObject.narrow(ref,TravelAgentHomeRemote.class);

            TravelAgentRemote travelAgent = home.create( );

            // Get a list of all cabins on ship 1 with a bed count of 3.
            String list [] = travelAgent.listCabins(SHIP_ID,BED_COUNT);

            for(int i = 0; i < list.length; i++){
                System.out.println(list[i]);
            }

        } catch(java.rmi.RemoteException re){re.printStackTrace( );}
            catch(Throwable t){t.printStackTrace( );}
    }
    static public Context getInitialContext( ) throws Exception {
        Properties p = new Properties( );
        // ... Specify the JNDI properties specific to the vendor.
        return new InitialContext(p);
    }
}
```

When you have successfully run `Client_3`, the output should look like this:

```
1,Master Suite                ,1
3,Suite 101                   ,1
5,Suite 103                   ,1
7,Suite 105                   ,1
9,Suite 107                   ,1
12,Suite 201                   ,2
14,Suite 203                   ,2
16,Suite 205                   ,2
18,Suite 207                   ,2
20,Suite 209                   ,2
22,Suite 301                   ,3
24,Suite 303                   ,3
26,Suite 305                   ,3
28,Suite 307                   ,3
30,Suite 309                   ,3
```

You have now successfully created the first piece of the TravelAgent session bean—a method that obtains a list of cabins by manipulating the Cabin EJB entity.

CHAPTER 5

The Remote and Local Client View

Developing the Cabin EJB and the TravelAgent EJB may have raised your confidence, but it also may have raised a lot of questions. We have glossed over most of the details involved in developing, deploying, and accessing the enterprise beans. In this chapter and the ones that follow, we will peel away the layers of the Enterprise JavaBeans onion to expose the details of EJB application development.

This chapter focuses specifically on the client's remote and local view of entity and session beans. The endpoint view, which is used by Web service clients to access stateless session beans, is significantly different and is addressed separately in the Web services chapter, Chapter 14. Message-driven beans are not covered in this chapter either—they are covered in detail in Chapter 12.

Locating Beans with JNDI

In Chapter 4, the client application started by creating an `InitialContext`, which it then used to get a remote reference to the homes of the Cabin and TravelAgent EJBs. The `InitialContext` is part of a larger API called the Java Naming and Directory Interface (JNDI). We use JNDI to look up an EJB home in an EJB server just like we might use a phone book to find the home number of a friend or business associate.

JNDI is a standard Java package that provides a uniform API for accessing a wide range of services. It is somewhat similar to JDBC, which provides uniform access to different relational databases. Just as JDBC lets us write code that doesn't care whether it's talking to an Oracle database or a DB2 database, JNDI lets us write code that can access different directory and naming services, including the naming services provided by EJB servers. EJB servers are required to support JNDI by organizing beans into a directory structure and providing a JNDI driver, called a *service provider*, for accessing that directory structure. Using JNDI, an enterprise can organize its beans, services, data, and other resources in a unified directory.

Two of JNDI's greatest features are that it is virtual and dynamic. JNDI is virtual because it allows one directory service to be linked to another through simple URLs. The URLs in JNDI are analogous to HTML links. Just as an HTML link allows you to download a new page without worrying about the server on which that page is located, JNDI lets us drill down through directories to files, printers, and EJB home objects without knowing where the resources—or even the directory servers holding information about the resources—are located. The directories and subdirectories can be located in the same host or physically hosted at different locations. As developers or administrators, we can create virtual directories that span a variety of services over many different physical locations.

JNDI is dynamic because it allows the JNDI drivers (a.k.a. service providers) for specific types of directory services to be loaded at runtime. A driver maps a specific kind of directory service into the standard JNDI class interfaces. When a link to a different directory service is chosen, the driver for that type of directory service is automatically loaded from the directory's host, if it is not already resident on the user's machine. Automatically downloading JNDI drivers makes it possible for a client to navigate across arbitrary directory services without knowing in advance what kinds of services it is likely to find.

After the client application locates and obtains a remote reference to the EJB home using JNDI, the client can use the EJB home to obtain an EJB object reference to an enterprise bean. In Chapter 4 the client applications used the method `getInitialContext( )` to get a JNDI `InitialContext` object, which looked like this:

```
public static Context getInitialContext()
    throws javax.naming.NamingException {

    Properties p = new Properties();
    // ... Specify the JNDI properties specific to the vendor.
    return new javax.naming.InitialContext(p);
}
```

An *initial context* is the starting point for any JNDI lookup—it's similar in concept to the root of a filesystem. The way an initial context is created is peculiar, but not fundamentally difficult. We start with a properties table of type `Properties`. This is essentially a hash table to which we add various values that determine the kind of initial context you get. Of course, as mentioned in Chapter 4, this code depends on how our EJB vendor has implemented JNDI. For example, with the Pramati Application Server, `getInitialContext( )` might look something like this:

```
public static Context getInitialContext() throws Exception {
    Hashtable p = new Hashtable();
    p.put(Context.INITIAL_CONTEXT_FACTORY,
         "com.pramati.naming.client.PramatiClientContextFactory");
    p.put(Context.PROVIDER_URL, "rmi://127.0.0.1:9191");
    return new InitialContext(p);
}
```

For a more detailed explanation of JNDI, see O'Reilly's *Java Enterprise in a Nutshell* by David Flanagan, Jim Farley, William Crawford, and Kris Magnusson.

The Remote Client API

Enterprise bean developers are required to provide a bean class, component interfaces, and, for entity beans, a primary key. The component interfaces and primary key class are visible to the client; the bean class itself is not. The component interfaces and primary key contribute to the client-side API in EJB.

Any client, whether it is in the same container system or not, may use the *Remote Client API*, which means that it may use the remote interface, the remote home interface, and Java RMI to access entity and session beans. Enterprise beans that are located in the same EJB container have the option of using the *Local Client API*. The Local Client API provides local component interfaces and avoids the restrictions and overhead of the Remote Client API. This section examines the remote component interfaces and the primary key, as well as other Java types that make up EJB's remote client-side API.

Java RMI-IIOP

Enterprise JavaBeans defines an enterprise bean's remote client API in terms of Java RMI-IIOP, which enforces compliance with CORBA. This means that the underlying protocol used by remote clients to access enterprise beans can be anything the vendor wants as long as it supports the types of interfaces and arguments that are compatible with Java RMI-IIOP. However, in addition to any proprietary protocols, vendors must also support the CORBA IIOP 1.2 protocol as defined in the CORBA 2.3.1 specification.

To use the Remote Client API, define your component interfaces and argument types so that they comply with Java RMI-IIOP types. It's not all that difficult to comply with this restriction. The next few sections discuss the Java RMI-IIOP programming model for EJB.

Java RMI return types, parameters, and exceptions

As an implementation of Java RMI, Java RMI-IIOP must first comply with the basic restrictions of Java RMI. We'll first take a look at Java RMI restrictions and then proceed to examine addition restrictions imposed by Java RMI-IIOP.

The supertypes of the remote home interface and remote interface, `javax.ejb.EJBHome` and `javax.ejb.EJBObject`, both extend `java.rmi.Remote`. As `Remote` interface subtypes, they are expected to adhere to the Java RMI specification for `Remote` interfaces.

Return types and parameters

The remote component interfaces must follow several guidelines, some of which apply to the return types and parameters that are allowed. There are two kinds of return and parameter types: *declared* types, which are checked by the compiler, and *actual* types, which are checked by the runtime. Java RMI requires the use of actual types. The actual types used in the java.rmi.Remote interfaces must be primitives, java.rmi.Remote types, or serializable types (including the String type). java.rmi.Remote types and serializable types do not have to implement java.rmi.Remote and java.io.Serializable explicitly. For example, the java.util.Collection type, which does not explicitly extend java.io.Serializable, is a perfectly valid return type for a remote finder method, provided that the concrete class implementing Collection, the actual type, does implement java.io.Serializable.

Java RMI has no special rules regarding declared return types or parameter types. At runtime, a type that is not a java.rmi.Remote type is assumed to be serializable; if it is not, an exception is thrown. The actual type that is passed cannot be checked by the compiler; it must be checked at runtime.

Here is a list of the types that can be passed as parameters or returned in Java RMI:

Primitives
: These include byte, boolean, char, short, int, long, double, and float.

Java serializable types
: Any class that implements or any interface that extends java.io.Serializable.

Java RMI remote types
: Any class that implements or any interface that extends java.rmi.Remote.

Serializable objects are passed by copy (a.k.a. passed by value), not by reference, which means that changes in a serialized object on one tier are not automatically reflected on the others. Objects that implement Remote, like TravelAgentRemote or CabinRemote, are passed as *remote references*, which are a little different. A remote reference is a Remote interface implemented by a distributed object stub. When a remote reference is passed as a parameter or returned from a method, the stub is serialized and passed by value, not the object referenced by the stub. In Chapter 11, the home interface for the TravelAgent EJB is modified so that the create( ) method takes a reference to a Customer EJB as its only argument:

```
public interface TravelAgentHomeRemote extends javax.ejb.EJBHome {
    public TravelAgentRemote create(CustomerRemote customer)
        throws RemoteException, CreateException;
}
```

The customer argument is a remote reference to a Customer EJB that is passed into the create( ) method. When a remote reference is passed or returned in Enterprise JavaBeans, the EJB object stub is passed by copy. The copy of the EJB object stub points to the same EJB object as the original stub. Therefore, both the enterprise bean instance and the client have remote references to the same EJB object. Changes made on the client using the remote reference will be reflected when the enterprise bean instance uses the same remote reference. Figures 5-1 and 5-2 show the difference between a serializable object and a remote reference argument.

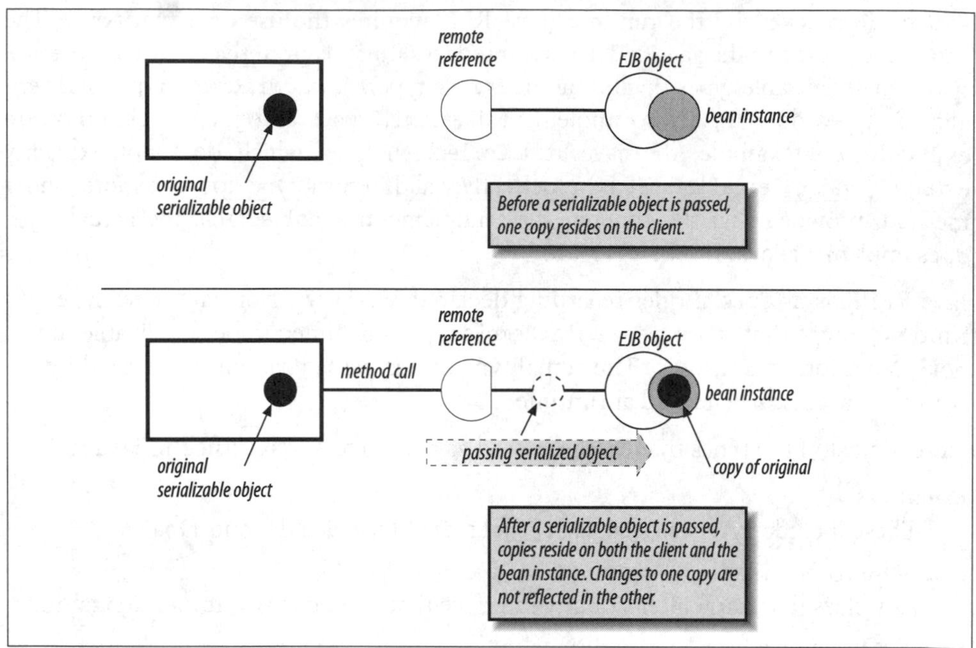

Figure 5-1. Serializable arguments

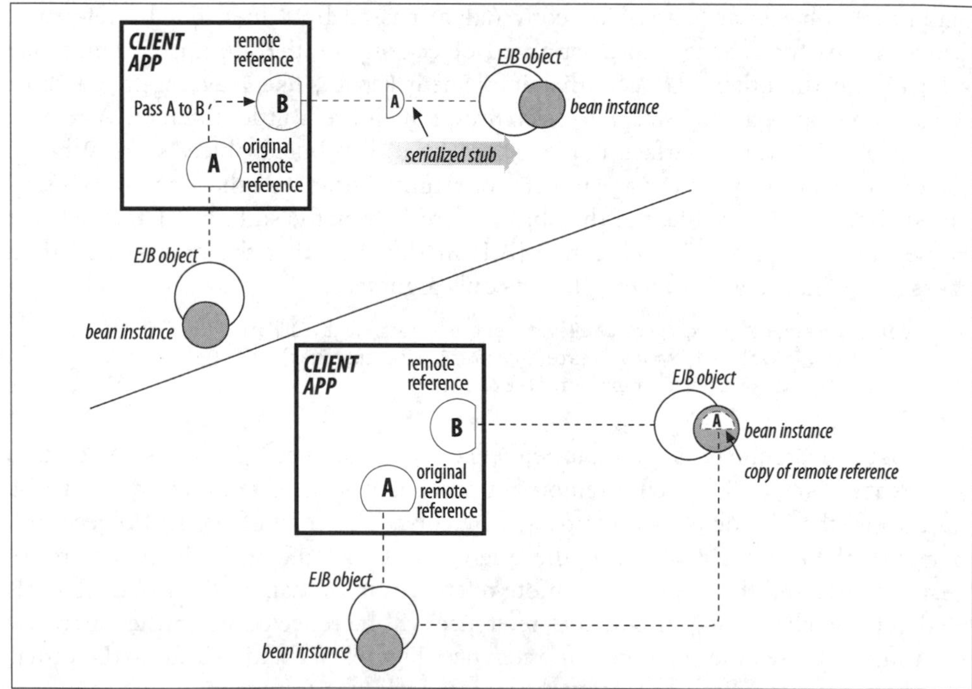

Figure 5-2. Remote reference arguments in RMIExceptions

The RMI specification states that every method defined in a `Remote` interface must throw the `java.rmi.RemoteException`. The `RemoteException` is used when problems occur with distributed object communications, such as a network failure or inability to locate the object server. `Remote` interfaces can also throw application-specific exceptions (exceptions defined by the application developer). The following code shows the remote interface to the TravelAgent EJB discussed in Chapter 2. The `bookPassage( )` method in the `TravelAgentRemote` interface throws the `RemoteException` (as required) in addition to an application exception, `IncompleteConversationalState`:

```
public interface TravelAgentRemote extends javax.ejb.EJBObject {

    public void setCruiseID(int cruise)
        throws RemoteException, FinderException;
    public int getCruiseID( ) throws RemoteException;

    public void setCabinID(int cabin)
        throws RemoteException, FinderException;
    public int getCabinID( ) throws RemoteException;

    public int getCustomerID( ) throws RemoteException;

    public Ticket bookPassage(CreditCardRemote card, double price)
        throws RemoteException,IncompleteConversationalState;

    public String [] listAvailableCabins(int bedCount)
        throws RemoteException;

}
```

Java RMI-IIOP type restrictions

Along with the Java RMI programming model, Java RMI-IIOP imposes restrictions on the remote interfaces and value types used in the Remote Client API. The restrictions are born of limitations in the Interface Definition Language (IDL) upon which CORBA IIOP 1.2 is based. The exact nature of these limitations is outside the scope of this book. Here are two; the others, like IDL name collisions, are rarely encountered:*

- Method overloading is restricted; a remote interface may not directly extend two or more interfaces that have methods with the same name (even if their arguments are different). A remote interface may, however, overload its own methods and extend a remote interface with overloaded method names. Overloading is viewed, here, as including overriding. Figure 5-3 illustrates both of these situations.
- Serializable types must not directly or indirectly implement the `java.rmi.Remote` interface.

* To learn more about CORBA IDL and its mapping to the Java language, consult "The Common Object Request Broker: Architecture and Specification" and "The Java Language to IDL Mapping," both available at the OMG web site (*http://www.omg.org*).

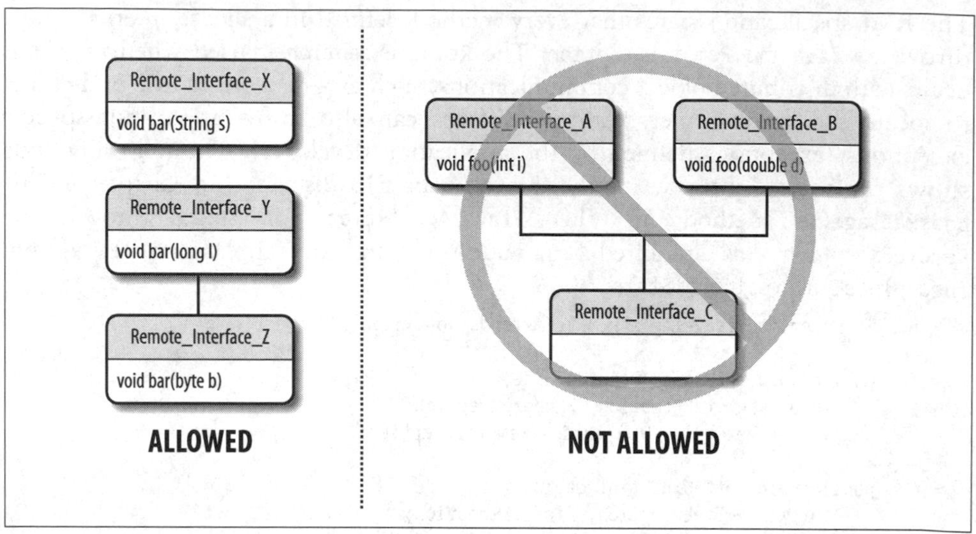

Figure 5-3. Overloading rules for remote interface inheritance

Explicit narrowing using PortableRemoteObject

In Java RMI-IIOP, remote references must be explicitly narrowed using the `javax.rmi.PortableRemoteObject.narrow( )` method. The typical practice in Java is to cast the reference to the more specific type:

```
javax.naming.Context jndiContext;
...
CabinHomeRemote home =
    (CabinHomeRemote)jndiContext.lookup("CabinHomeRemote");
```

The `javax.naming.Context.lookup( )` method returns an `Object`. In EJB's Local Client API, we can assume that it is legal to cast the return argument. However, the Remote Client API must be compatible with Java RMI-IIOP, which means that clients must adhere to limitations imposed by the IIOP 1.2 protocol. To accommodate all languages, many of which have no concept of casting, IIOP 1.2 does not support stubs that implement multiple interfaces. The stub returned in IIOP implements only the interface specified by the return type of the remote method that was invoked. If the return type is `Object`, as is the remote reference returned by the `lookup( )` method, the stub will implement only methods specific to the `Object` type.

Of course, some means for converting a remote reference from a more general type to a more specific type is essential in an object-oriented environment. In Java RMI-IIOP, the mechanism is `javax.rmi.PortableRemoteObject.narrow( )`. Remember that while the Remote Client API requires that we use Java RMI-IIOP reference and argument types, the wire protocol need not be IIOP 1.2. Other protocols besides IIOP may also require explicit narrowing.

To narrow the return value of the Context.lookup( ) method to the appropriate type, we must explicitly ask for a remote reference that implements the interface we want:

```
import javax.rmi.PortableRemoteObject;
...
javax.naming.Context jndiContext;
...
Object ref = jndiContext.lookup("CabinHomeRemote");
CabinHomeRemote home = (CabinHomeRemote)
    PortableRemoteObject.narrow(ref, CabinHomeRemote.class);
```

The narrow( ) method takes two arguments: the remote reference that is to be narrowed and the type to which it should be narrowed. When it has executed, it returns a stub that implements the specified Remote interface. Because the stub is known to implement the correct type, we can then use Java's native casting to narrow the stub to the correct Remote interface.

The narrow( ) method is used only when a remote reference to an EJB home or EJB object is returned without a specific Remote interface type. This occurs in six circumstances:

1. When a remote EJB home reference is obtained using the javax.naming.Context.lookup( ) method:

    ```
    Object ref = jndiContext.lookup("CabinHomeRemote");
    CabinHomeRemote home = (CabinHomeRemote)
        PortableRemoteObject.narrow(ref, CabinHomeRemote.class);
    ```

2. When a remote EJB object reference is obtained from a Collection or Enumeration returned by a remote home interface finder method:

    ```
    ShipHomeRemote shipHome = ... // get ship home
    Enumeration enum = shipHome.findByCapacity(2000);
    while(enum.hasMoreElements( )){
        Object ref = enum.nextElement( );
        ShipRemote ship = (ShipRemote)
            PortableRemoteObject.narrow(ref, ShipRemote.class);
        // do something with Ship reference
    }
    ```

3. When a remote EJB object reference is obtained using the javax.ejb.Handle.getEJBObject( ) method:

    ```
    Handle handle = .... // get Handle
    Object ref = handle.getEJBObject( );
    CabinRemote cabin = (CabinRemote)
    PortableRemoteObject.narrow(ref,CabinRemote.class);
    ```

4. When a remote EJB home reference is obtained using the javax.ejb.HomeHandle.getEJBHome( ) method:

    ```
    HomeHandle homeHdle = ... // get home Handle
    EJBHome ref = homeHdle.getEJBHome( );
    CabinHomeRemote home = (CabinHomeRemote)
        PortableRemoteObject.narrow(ref, CabinHomeRemote.class);
    ```

5. When a remote EJB home reference is obtained using the `javax.ejb.EJBMetaData.getEJBHome( )` method:

   ```
   EJBMetaData metaData = homeHdle.getEJBMetaData( );
   EJBHome ref = metaData.getEJBHome( );
   CabinHomeRemote home = (CabinHomeRemote)
       PortableRemoteObject.narrow(ref, CabinHomeRemote.class);
   ```

6. When a wide remote EJB object type is returned from any business method; here is a hypothetical example:

   ```
   // Officer extends Crewman
   ShipRemote ship = // get Ship remote reference
   CrewmanRemote crew = ship.getCrewman("Burns", "John", "1st Lieutenant");
   OfficerRemote burns = (OfficerRemote)
       PortableRemoteObject.narrow(crew, OfficerRemote.class);
   ```

`PortableRemoteObject.narrow( )` is not required when the remote type is specified in the method signature. This is true of the *create* and *find* methods (see the section "Creating and finding beans" later in this chapter) in remote home interfaces that return a single bean. For example, the `create( )` and `findByPrimaryKey( )` methods defined in the `CabinHomeRemote` interface (Chapter 4) do not require the use of the `narrow( )` method because these methods already return the correct EJB object type. Business methods that return the correct type do not need to use the `narrow( )` method either, as the following code illustrates:

```
/* The CabinHomeRemote.create( ) method specifies
 * the CabinRemote interface as the return type,
 * so explicit narrowing is not needed.*/
CabinRemote cabin = cabinHome.create(new Integer(12345));

/* The CabinHomeRemote.findByPrimaryKey( ) method specifies
 * the CabinRemote interface as the return type,
 * so explicit narrowing is not needed.*/
CabinRemote cabin = cabinHome.findByPrimaryKey(new Integer(12345));

/* The ShipRemote.getCrewman( ) business method specifies
 * the CrewmanRemote interface as the return type,
 * so explicit narrowing is not needed.*/
CrewmanRemote crew = ship.getCrewman("Burns", "John",
    "1st Lieutenant");
```

The Remote Home Interface

The remote home interface provides life-cycle operations and metadata. When we use JNDI to access a bean, we obtain a remote reference, or stub, to the bean's EJB home, which implements the remote home interface. Every bean type may have one home interface, which extends the `javax.ejb.EJBHome` interface:

```
public interface javax.ejb.EJBHome extends java.rmi.Remote {
    public abstract EJBMetaData getEJBMetaData( )
        throws RemoteException;
    public HomeHandle getHomeHandle( )
```

```
        throws RemoteException;
    public abstract void remove(Handle handle)
        throws RemoteException, RemoveException;
    public abstract void remove(Object primaryKey)
        throws RemoteException, RemoveException;
}
```

Removing beans

The `EJBHome.remove( )` methods are responsible for deleting an enterprise bean. The argument is either the `javax.ejb.Handle` of the enterprise bean or, if it's an entity bean, its primary key. The `Handle` is discussed in more detail later, but it is essentially a serializable pointer to a specific enterprise bean. When either of the `EJBHome.remove( )` methods is invoked, the remote reference to the enterprise bean on the client becomes invalid: the stub to the enterprise bean that was removed no longer works. If for some reason the enterprise bean can't be removed, a `RemoveException` is thrown.

The impact of the `EJBHome.remove( )` on the enterprise bean itself depends on the type of bean. For session beans, the `EJBHome.remove( )` methods end the session's service to the client. When `EJBHome.remove( )` is invoked, the remote reference to the session bean becomes invalid, and any conversational state maintained by the session bean is lost. The TravelAgent EJB you created in Chapter 4 is stateless, so no conversational state exists.

When a `remove()` method is invoked on an entity bean, the remote reference becomes invalid, and any data it represents is deleted from the database. This operation is destructive because once an entity bean has been removed, the data it represents no longer exists. The difference between using a `remove( )` method on a session bean and using `remove( )` on an entity bean is similar to the difference between hanging up on a telephone conversation and actually killing the caller on the other end.

The following code fragment is taken from the `main( )` method of a client application similar to the clients we created to exercise the Cabin and TravelAgent EJBs. It shows that we can remove enterprise beans using a primary key (for entity beans only) or a `Handle`. Removing an entity bean deletes the entity from the database; removing a session bean results in the remote reference becoming invalid. Here's the code:

```
Context jndiContext = getInitialContext( );

// Obtain a list of all the cabins for ship 1 with bed count of 3.

Object ref = jndiContext.lookup("TravelAgentHomeRemote");
TravelAgentHomeRemote agentHome = (TravelAgentHomeRemote)
    PortableRemoteObject.narrow(ref,TravelAgentHomeRemote.class);

TravelAgentRemote agent = agentHome.create( );
String list [] = agent.listCabins(1,3);
System.out.println("1st List: Before deleting cabin number 30");
```

```
for(int i = 0; i < list.length; i++){
    System.out.println(list[i]);
}

// Obtain the home and remove cabin 30. Rerun the same cabin list.

ref = jndiContext.lookup("CabinHomeRemote");
CabinHomeRemote c_home = (CabinHomeRemote)
    PortableRemoteObject.narrow(ref, CabinHomeRemote.class);

Integer pk = new Integer(30);
c_home.remove(pk);
list = agent.listCabins(1,3);
System.out.println("2nd List: After deleting cabin number 30");
for (int i = 0; i < list.length; i++) {
    System.out.println(list[i]);
}
```

First, the application creates a list of cabins, including the cabin with the primary key 30. Then it removes the Cabin EJB with this primary key and creates the list again. The second time the iteration is performed, cabin 30 is not listed; the `listCabin()` method will be unable to find a cabin with a primary key equal to 30 because the bean and its data are no longer in the database. The output should look something like this:

```
1st List: Before deleting cabin number 30
1,Master Suite                  ,1
3,Suite 101                     ,1
5,Suite 103                     ,1
7,Suite 105                     ,1
9,Suite 107                     ,1
12,Suite 201                    ,2
14,Suite 203                    ,2
16,Suite 205                    ,2
18,Suite 207                    ,2
20,Suite 209                    ,2
22,Suite 301                    ,3
24,Suite 303                    ,3
26,Suite 305                    ,3
28,Suite 307                    ,3
29,Suite 309                    ,3
30,Suite 309                    ,3
2nd List: After deleting cabin number 30
1,Master Suite                  ,1
3,Suite 101                     ,1
5,Suite 103                     ,1
7,Suite 105                     ,1
9,Suite 107                     ,1
12,Suite 201                    ,2
14,Suite 203                    ,2
16,Suite 205                    ,2
18,Suite 207                    ,2
20,Suite 209                    ,2
```

```
22,Suite 301                    ,3
24,Suite 303                    ,3
26,Suite 305                    ,3
28,Suite 307                    ,3
29,Suite 308                    ,3
```

Bean metadata

`EJBHome.getEJBMetaData()` returns an instance of `javax.ejb.EJBMetaData` that describes the remote home interface, remote interface, and primary key classes and indicates whether the enterprise bean is a session or entity bean.* This type of metadata is valuable to Java tools such as IDEs that have wizards or other mechanisms for interacting with an enterprise bean from a client's perspective. A tool could, for example, use the class definitions provided by the `EJBMetaData` with Java reflection to create an environment in which deployed enterprise beans can be "wired" together by developers. Of course, information such as the JNDI names and URLs of the enterprise beans is also needed.

Most application developers rarely use the `EJBMetaData`. Knowing that it's there, however, is valuable when we need to create code generators or some other automatic facility. In those cases, familiarity with the Reflection API is necessary.† The following code shows the interface definition for `EJBMetaData`. Any class that implements the `EJBMetaData` interface must be serializable; it cannot be a stub to a distributed object. This allows IDEs and other tools to save the `EJBMetaData` for later use:

```
public interface javax.ejb.EJBMetaData {
    public abstract EJBHome getEJBHome( );
    public abstract Class getHomeInterfaceClass( );
    public abstract Class getPrimaryKeyClass( );
    public abstract Class getRemoteInterfaceClass( );
    public abstract boolean isSession( );
    public abstract boolean isStatelessSession( )
}
```

The following code shows how the `EJBMetaData` for the Cabin EJB could be used to get more information about the enterprise bean. Notice that there is no way to get the bean class using the `EJBMetaData`; the bean class is not part of the client API and therefore doesn't belong to the metadata. Here's the code:

```
Context jndiContext = getInitialContext( );

Object ref = jndiContext.lookup("CabinHomeRemote");
CabinHomeRemote c_home = (CabinHomeRemote)
    PortableRemoteObject.narrow(ref, CabinHomeRemote.class);
```

* Message-driven beans don't have component interfaces and can't be accessed by Java RMI-IIOP.

† The Reflection API is outside the scope of this book, but it is covered in *Java in a Nutshell*, by David Flanagan (O'Reilly).

```
EJBMetaData meta = c_home.getEJBMetaData( );

System.out.println(meta.getHomeInterfaceClass().getName( ));
System.out.println(meta.getRemoteInterfaceClass().getName( ));
System.out.println(meta.getPrimaryKeyClass().getName( ));
System.out.println(meta.isSession( ));
```

This application creates output like the following:

```
com.titan.cabin.CabinHomeRemote
com.titan.cabin.CabinRemote
java.lang.Integer
false
```

In addition to providing the class types of the enterprise bean, the `EJBMetaData` makes the remote EJB home available for the bean. Once we get the remote EJB home from the `EJBMetaData`, we can obtain references to the remote EJB object and perform other functions. In the following code, we use the `EJBMetaData` to get the primary key class, create a key instance, obtain the remote EJB home, and get a remote reference to the EJB object for a specific cabin entity from the EJB home:

```
Object primKeyType = meta.getPrimaryKeyClass( );
if(primKeyType instanceof java.lang.Integer){
    Integer pk = new Integer(1);

    Object ref = meta.getEJBHome( );
    CabinHomeRemote c_home2 = (CabinHomeRemote)
        PortableRemoteObject.narrow(ref,CabinHomeRemote.class);

    CabinRemote cabin = c_home2.findByPrimaryKey(pk);
    System.out.println(cabin.getName( ));
}
```

The HomeHandle

The `HomeHandle` is accessed by calling `EJBHome.getHomeHandle( )`. This method returns a `javax.ejb.HomeHandle` object that provides a serializable reference to an enterprise bean's remote home. The `HomeHandle` allows a remote home reference to be stored and used in the future. It is similar to the `javax.ejb.Handle` and is discussed in more detail a little later.

Creating and finding beans

In addition to the standard `javax.ejb.EJBHome` methods that all remote home interfaces inherit, the remote home interfaces also include special create and find methods—find methods are used with entity beans only. The following code shows the remote home interface defined for the Cabin EJB:

```
public interface CabinHomeRemote extends javax.ejb.EJBHome {
    public CabinRemote create(Integer id)
        throws CreateException, RemoteException;
```

```
    public CabinRemote findByPrimaryKey(Integer pk)
        throws FinderException, RemoteException;
}
```

Create methods throw a CreateException if something goes wrong during the creation process; find methods throw a FinderException if there is an error. Since these methods are defined in an interface that subclasses Remote, they must also declare that they throw the RemoteException.

It is up to the bean developer to define the appropriate create and find methods in the remote home interface. CabinHomeRemote currently has only one create method, which creates a cabin with a specified ID, and one find method, which looks up an enterprise bean, given its primary key. However, it is easy to imagine methods that would create and find a cabin with particular properties—for example, a cabin with three beds, or a deluxe cabin with blue wallpaper.

Beginning with EJB 2.0, the create method names can have suffixes. In other words, all create methods can take the form create<*SUFFIX*>( ). For example, the Customer EJB might define a remote home interface with several create methods, each of which takes a different Integer type parameter and has a different method name:

```
public interface CustomerHome extends javax.ejb.EJBHome {

    public CustomerRemote createWithSSN(Integer id, String socialSecurityNumber)
        throws CreateException, RemoteException;

    public CustomerRemote createWithPIN(Integer personalIdNumber)
        throws CreateException, RemoteException;

    public CustomerRemote createWithBLN(Integer id, String businessLicenseNumber)
        throws CreateException, RemoteException;

    public Customer findByPrimaryKey(Integer id)
        throws FinderException, RemoteException;
}
```

While the use of a suffix in the create method names is allowed, it is not required. You can name all your create methods create(...) and differentiate them by their parameters (method overloading).

The create and find methods defined in the remote home interfaces are straightforward and easy for the client to use. The create methods must match the ejbCreate( ) and ejbPostCreate( ) methods of the bean class. The create( ), ejbCreate( ), and ejbPostCreate( ) methods match when they have the same parameters, when the arguments are of the same type and in the same order, and when their method names are the same. This way, when a client calls the create method on the home interface, the call can be delegated to the corresponding ejbCreate( ) and ejbPostCreate( ) methods on the bean instance.

For bean-managed entities, every find<*SUFFIX*>( ) method in the home interface must correspond to an ejbFind<*SUFFIX*>( ) method in the bean itself. Container-managed entities do not implement ejbFind( ) methods in the bean class; the EJB container supports find methods automatically. You will discover more about how to implement the ejbCreate( ), ejbPostCreate( ), and ejbFind( ) methods in the bean in Chapters 6 through 10.

Home methods

In addition to find and create methods, the home interface of entity beans may also define *home methods*. A home method is a business method that can be invoked on the home interface (local or remote) and is not specific to one bean instance. For example, the Cabin EJB could define a home method, getDeckCount( ), which returns the number of cabins on a specific deck level:

```
public interface CabinHomeRemote extends javax.ejb.EJBHome {
    public CabinRemote create(Integer id)
        throws CreateException, RemoteException;

    public CabinRemote findByPrimaryKey(Integer pk)
        throws FinderException, RemoteException;

    public int getDeckCount(int level) throws RemoteException;
}
```

Any method in the home interface that is not a create or find method is assumed to be a home method and should have a corresponding ejbHome( ) method in the bean class, as shown here:

```
public class CabinBean implements javax.ejb.EntityBean{
    public int ejbHomeGetDeckCount(int level){
        // implement logic to determine deck count
    }
    ...
}
```

Clients can use home methods from the enterprise bean's home interface. The client does not need a reference to a specific EJB object:

```
Object ref = jndiContext.lookup("CabinHome");
CabinHomeRemote home = (CabinHomeRemote)
    PortableRemoteObject.narrow(ref, CabinHomeRemote.class);

int count = home.getDeckCount(2);
```

Home methods are only available to entity beans. They can be used for generic business logic that applies changes across a group of entity beans or obtains information that is not specific to any single entity bean. Home methods are discussed in more detail in Chapter 10.

The Remote Interface

The business methods of an enterprise bean can be defined by the bean's remote interface. The `javax.ejb.EJBObject` interface, which extends the `java.rmi.Remote` interface, is the base class for all remote interfaces. Here is the remote interface for the TravelAgent bean we developed in Chapter 4:

```
public interface TravelAgentRemote extends javax.ejb.EJBObject {

    public String [] listCabins(int shipID, int bedCount)
        throws RemoteException;
}
```

Figure 5-4 shows the `TravelAgentRemote` interface's inheritance hierarchy.

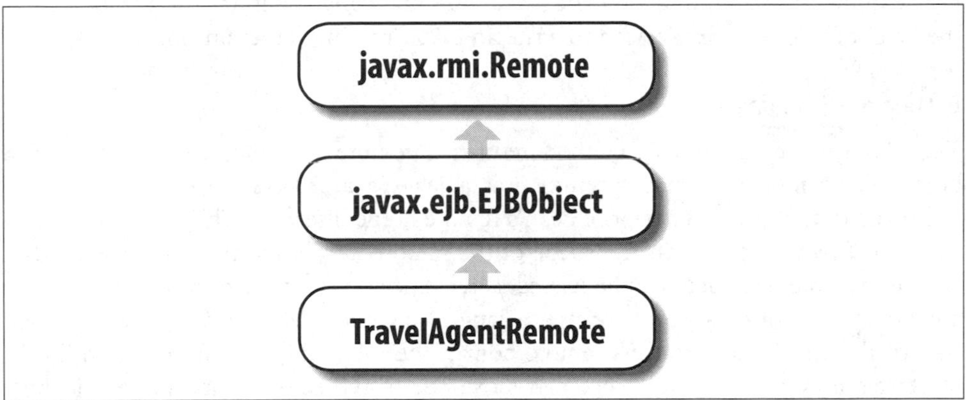

Figure 5-4. Enterprise bean interface inheritance hierarchy

Remote interfaces are focused on the business problem and do not include methods for system-level operations such as persistence, security, concurrency, or transactions. System-level operations are handled by the EJB server, which relieves the client developer of many responsibilities. All remote interface methods for beans must throw a `java.rmi.RemoteException`, which identifies problems with distributed communications. In addition, methods in the remote interface can throw custom exceptions to indicate abnormal business-related conditions or errors in executing the business method. You will learn more about defining custom exceptions in Chapters 11 and 15. To deploy the example discussed in this section, see Exercise 5.1 in the Workbook.

EJBObject, Handle, and Primary Key

All remote interfaces extend the `javax.ejb.EJBObject` interface, which provides a set of utility methods and return types. These methods and return types are valuable in managing the client's interactions with beans. Here is the definition of `EJBObject`:

```
public interface javax.ejb.EJBObject extends java.rmi.Remote {
    public abstract EJBHome getEJBHome( )
        throws RemoteException;
```

```
    public abstract Handle getHandle( )
        throws RemoteException;
    public abstract Object getPrimaryKey( )
        throws RemoteException;
    public abstract boolean isIdentical(EJBObject obj)
        throws RemoteException;
    public abstract void remove( )
        throws RemoteException, RemoveException;
}
```

When the client obtains a reference to the remote interface, it is actually obtaining a remote reference to an EJB object. The EJB object implements the remote interface by delegating business method calls to the bean class; it provides its own implementations for the `EJBObject` methods, which return information about the corresponding bean instance on the server. The server automatically generates the EJB object, so the bean developer doesn't need to write an `EJBObject` implementation.

Getting the EJBHome

The `EJBObject.getEJBHome( )` method returns a remote reference to the bean's EJB home. The remote reference is returned as a `javax.ejb.EJBHome` object, which can be narrowed to the specific enterprise bean's remote home interface. This method is useful when an EJB object has left the scope of the remote EJB home that manufactured it. Because remote references can be passed as references and returned from methods, like any other Java object, a remote reference can quickly find itself in a completely different part of the application from its remote home. The following code is contrived, but it illustrates how a remote reference can move out of the scope of its home, and how `getEJBHome( )` can be used to get a new reference to the EJB home at any time:

```
public static void main(String [] args) {
    try {
        Context jndiContext = getInitialContext( );
        Object ref = jndiContext.lookup("TravelAgentHomeRemote");
        TravelAgentHomeRemote home = (TravelAgentHomeRemote)
            PortableRemoteObject.narrow(ref,TravelAgentHomeRemote.class);

        // Get a remote reference to the bean (EJB object).
        TravelAgentRemote agent = home.create( );
        // Pass the remote reference to some method.
        getTheEJBHome(agent);

    } catch (java.rmi.RemoteException re){re.printStackTrace( );}
      catch (Throwable t){t.printStackTrace( );}
}

public static void getTheEJBHome(TravelAgentRemote agent)
    throws RemoteException {

    // The home interface is out of scope in this method,
    // so it must be obtained from the EJB object.
    Object ref = agent.getEJBHome( );
```

```
        TravelAgentHomeRemote home = (TravelAgentHomeRemote)
            PortableRemoteObject.narrow(ref,TravelAgentHomeRemote.class);
        // Do something useful with the home interface.
    }
```

Primary key

`EJBObject.getPrimaryKey()` returns the primary key for an entity bean, and isn't supported by EJB objects that represent other types of beans. To better understand the nature of a primary key, we need to look beyond the boundaries of the client's view into the EJB container's layer.

The EJB container is responsible for the persistence of entity beans, but the exact mechanism for persistence is up to the vendor. To locate an instance of a bean in a persistent store, the data that makes up the entity must be mapped to some kind of unique key. In relational databases, data is uniquely identified by one or more column values that can be combined to form a primary key. In an object-oriented database, the key wraps an object ID (OID) or some kind of database pointer. Regardless of the mechanism—which isn't really relevant from the client's perspective—the unique key for an entity bean's data is represented by the primary key, which is returned by the `EJBObject.getPrimaryKey()` method.

The primary key can be used to obtain remote references to entity beans using the `findByPrimaryKey()` method:

```
Context jndiContext = getInitialContext();

Object ref = jndiContext.lookup("CabinHomeRemote");
CabinHomeRemote home = (CabinHomeRemote)
    PortableRemoteObject.narrow(ref,CabinHomeRemote.class);

CabinRemote cabin_1 = home.create(new Integer(101));
Integer pk = (Integer)cabin_1.getPrimaryKey();
CabinRemote cabin_2 = home.findByPrimaryKey(pk);
```

In this code, the client creates a Cabin EJB, retrieves its primary key, and then uses the key to get a new reference to the same Cabin EJB. Thus, we have two variables, `cabin_1` and `cabin_2`, that are remote references to EJB objects. The variables both reference the same Cabin bean, with the same underlying data, because they have the same primary key.

A primary key is only valid for the correct bean in the correct container. For example, imagine that a third-party vendor sells the Cabin EJB as a product. The vendor sells the Cabin EJB to both Titan and a competitor. Both companies deploy the entity bean using their own relational databases with their own data. As you would expect, both cruise companies have a Cabin bean with a primary key equal to 20, but they represent different cabins for different ships. The Cabin EJBs come from different EJB containers, so their primary keys are not equivalent.* Every entity EJB object

* This is, of course, not true if both Cabin EJBs use the same database, which is common in a clustered scenario.

has a unique identity within its EJB home. If two EJB objects have the same home and same primary key, they are considered identical.

A primary key must implement the `java.io.Serializable` interface. This means that a primary key can always be obtained from an EJB object, stored on the client using the Java serialization mechanism, and deserialized when needed. When a primary key is deserialized, it can be used to obtain a remote reference to the same entity bean using `findByPrimaryKey( )`, provided that the key is used on the correct remote home interface and container. Preserving the primary key using serialization might be useful if the client application needs to access specific entity beans at a later date.

The following code shows a primary key that is serialized and then deserialized:

```
// Obtain cabin 101 and set its name.
Context jndiContext = getInitialContext( );

Object ref = jndiContext.lookup("CabinHomeRemote");
CabinHomeRemote home = (CabinHomeRemote)
    PortableRemoteObject.narrow(ref, CabinHomeRemote.class);

Integer pk_1 = new Integer(101);
CabinRemote cabin_1 = home.findByPrimaryKey(pk_1);
cabin_1.setName("Presidential Suite");

// Serialize the primary key for cabin 101 to a file.
FileOutputStream fos = new FileOutputStream("pk101.ser");
ObjectOutputStream outStream = new ObjectOutputStream(fos);
outStream.writeObject(pk_1);
outStream.flush( );
outStream.close( );
pk_1 = null;

// Deserialize the primary key for cabin 101.
FileInputStream fis = new FileInputStream("pk101.ser");
ObjectInputStream inStream = new ObjectInputStream(fis);
Integer pk_2 = (Integer)inStream.readObject( );
inStream.close( );

// Reobtain a remote reference to cabin 101 and read its name.
CabinRemote cabin_2 = home.findByPrimaryKey(pk_2);
System.out.println(cabin_2.getName( ));
```

Comparing beans for identity

The `EJBObject.isIdentical( )` method compares two EJB object remote references. It's worth considering why `Object.equals( )` isn't sufficient for comparing EJB objects. An EJB object is a distributed object stub and therefore contains a lot of networking and other state. As a result, references to two EJB objects may be unequal, even if they both represent the same unique bean. The `EJBObject.isIdentical( )` method returns true if two EJB object references represent the same bean, even if the EJB object stubs are different object instances.

The following code starts by creating two remote references to the TravelAgent EJB. These remote EJB objects both refer to the same type of enterprise bean; comparing them with `isIdentical()` returns `true`. The two TravelAgent EJBs were created separately, but because they are stateless, they are equivalent. If TravelAgent EJB had been a stateful bean, the outcome would have been different. Comparing two stateful beans results in `false` because stateful beans have conversational state, which makes them unique. When we use `CabinHomeRemote.findByPrimaryKey()` to locate two EJB objects that refer to the same Cabin entity bean, we know the entity beans are identical, because we used the same primary key. In this case, `isIdentical()` also returns `true`:

```
Context ctx  = getInitialContext();

Object ref = ctx.lookup("TravelAgentHomeRemote");
TravelAgentHomeRemote agentHome =(TravelAgentHomeRemote)
    PortableRemoteObject.narrow(ref, TravelAgentHomeRemote.class);

TravelAgentRemote agent_1 = agentHome.create();
TravelAgentRemote agent_2 = agentHome.create();
boolean x = agent_1.isIdentical(agent_2);
// x will equal true; the two EJB objects are equal.

ref = ctx.lookup("CabinHomeRemote");
CabinHomeRemote c_home = (CabinHomeRemote)
    PortableRemoteObject.narrow(ref, CabinHomeRemote.class);

Integer pk_1 = new Integer(101);
Integer pk_2 = new Integer(101);
CabinRemote cabin_1 = c_home.findByPrimaryKey(pk_1);
CabinRemote cabin_2 = c_home.findByPrimaryKey(pk_2);
x = cabin_1.isIdentical(cabin_2);
// x will equal true; the two EJB objects are equal.
```

The `Integer` primary key used in the Cabin bean is simple. More complex, custom-defined primary keys require us to override `Object.equals()` and `Object.hashCode()` for the `EJBObject.isIdentical()` method to work. Chapter 10 discusses the development of more complex custom primary keys, which are called *compound primary keys*.

Removing beans

The `EJBObject.remove()` method removes session and entity beans. The impact of this method is the same as the `EJBHome.remove()` method. For session beans, `remove()` releases the session and invalidates the remote EJB object reference. For entity beans, the data that the bean represents is deleted from the database and the remote reference becomes invalid. The following code shows the `EJBObject.remove()` method in use:

```
Context jndiContext = getInitialContext();

Object ref = jndiContext.lookup("CabinHomeRemote");
CabinHomeRemote c_home = (CabinHomeRemote)
    PortableRemoteObject.narrow(ref,CabinHomeRemote.class);
```

```
Integer pk = new Integer(101);
CabinRemote cabin = c_home.findByPrimaryKey(pk);
cabin.remove( );
```

The `remove( )` method throws a `RemoveException` if for some reason the reference can't be deleted.

The enterprise bean Handle

The `EJBObject.getHandle( )` method returns a `javax.ejb.Handle` object. The `Handle` is a serializable reference to the remote EJB object. A `Handle` allows us to recreate a remote EJB object reference that points to the same type of session bean or the same unique entity bean from which the `Handle` originated. The client can save the `Handle` using Java serialization and then deserialize it to obtain a reference to the original EJB object.

Here is the interface definition of the `Handle`:

```
public interface javax.ejb.Handle {
    public abstract EJBObject getEJBObject( )
      throws RemoteException;
}
```

The `Handle` interface specifies only one method, `getEJBObject( )`. Calling this method returns the remote EJB object from which the `Handle` was created. Once we've gotten the object back, we can narrow it to the appropriate remote interface type. The following code shows how to serialize and deserialize an EJB `Handle` on a client:

```
// Obtain cabin 100.
Context jndiContext = getInitialContext( );

Object ref = jndiContext.lookup("CabinHomeRemote");
CabinHomeRemote home = (CabinHomeRemote)
    PortableRemoteObject.narrow(ref,CabinHomeRemote.class);

Integer pk_1 = new Integer(100);
CabinRemote cabin_1 = home.findByPrimaryKey(pk_1);

// Serialize the Handle for cabin 100 to a file.
Handle handle = cabin_1.getHandle( );
FileOutputStream fos = new FileOutputStream("handle100.ser");
ObjectOutputStream outStream = new ObjectOutputStream(fos);
outStream.writeObject(handle);
outStream.flush( );
fos.close( );
handle = null;

// Deserialize the Handle for cabin 100.
FileInputStream fis = new FileInputStream("handle100.ser");
ObjectInputStream inStream = new ObjectInputStream(fis);
handle = (Handle)inStream.readObject( );
fis.close( );
```

```
// Reobtain a remote reference to cabin 100 and read its name.

ref = handle.getEJBObject( );
CabinRemote cabin_2 = (CabinRemote)
    PortableRemoteObject.narrow(ref, CabinRemote.class);

if(cabin_1.isIdentical(cabin_2))
    // This will always be true.
```

At first glance, the Handle and the primary key appear to do the same thing, but in truth they are very different. Using the primary key requires us to have the correct remote EJB home—if we no longer have a reference to the EJB remote home, we must look up the container using JNDI and get a new home. Only then can we call findByPrimaryKey( ) to locate the actual enterprise bean. Here's how this might work:

```
// Obtain the primary key from an input stream.
Integer primaryKey = (Integer)inStream.readObject( );

// The JNDI API is used to get a root directory or initial context.
javax.naming.Context ctx = new getInitialContext( );

// Using the initial context, obtain the EJBHome for the Cabin bean.

Object ref = ctx.lookup("CabinHomeRemote");
CabinHomeRemote home = (CabinHomeRemote)
    PortableRemoteObject.narrow(ref,CabinHomeRemote.class);

// Obtain a reference to an EJB object that represents the entity instance.
CabinRemote cabin_2 = home.findByPrimaryKey(primaryKey);
```

The Handle object is easier to use because it encapsulates the details of doing a JNDI lookup on the container. With a Handle, the correct EJB object can be obtained in one method call, Handle.getEJBObject( ), rather than the three method calls needed to look up the context, get the home, and find the actual bean. Furthermore, while the primary key can obtain remote references to unique entity beans, it is not available for session beans; Handle, on the other hand, can be used with either type of enterprise bean. This makes using a Handle more consistent across bean types.

Consistency is good in its own right, but it isn't the whole story. Normally, we think of session beans as not having identifiable instances because they exist for only the life of the client session, but this is not exactly true. We have mentioned (but not yet shown) stateful session beans, which retain state information between method invocations. Two instances of a stateful session beans are not equivalent. A Handle allows us to work with a stateful session bean, deactivate the bean, and then reactivate it at a later time. A client could, for example, be using a stateful session bean to process an order when the process is interrupted for some reason. Instead of losing all the work performed in the session, a Handle can be obtained from the EJB object and the client application can be closed down. When the user is ready to continue the order, the Handle can be used to obtain a reference to the stateful session EJB object. Note that this process is not necessarily fault-tolerant. If the EJB server goes down or crashes, the stateful session bean is lost and the Handle is useless. It's also possible for the session bean to time out, which would cause the container to remove it from service. If this happens, the session bean is no longer available to the client.

HomeHandle

The javax.ejb.HomeHandle is similar to javax.ejb.Handle. Just as the Handle is used to store and retrieve references to remote EJB objects, the HomeHandle is used to store and retrieve references to remote EJB homes. In other words, the HomeHandle can be stored and later used to access an EJB home's remote reference the same way that a Handle can be serialized and later used to access an EJB object's remote reference. Here's how the HomeHandle can be obtained, serialized, and used:

```
// Obtain cabin 100.
Context jndiContext = getInitialContext( );

Object ref = jndiContext.lookup("CabinHomeRemote");
CabinHomeRemote home = (CabinHomeRemote)
    PortableRemoteObject.narrow(ref,CabinHomeRemote.class);

// Serialize the HomeHandle for the Cabin bean.
HomeHandle homeHandle = home.getHomeHandle( );
FileOutputStream fos = new FileOutputStream("handle.ser");
ObjectOutputStream outStream = new ObjectOutputStream(fos);
outStream.writeObject(homeHandle);
outStream.flush( );
fos.close( );
homeHandle = null;

// Deserialize the HomeHandle for the Cabin bean.
FileInputStream fis = new FileInputStream("handle.ser");
ObjectInputStream inStream = new ObjectInputStream(fis);
homeHandle = (HomeHandle)inStream.readObject( );
fis.close( );

EJBHome homeRef = homeHandle.getEJBHome( );
CabinHomeRemote home2 = (CabinHomeRemote)
    PortableRemoteObject.narrow(homeRef,CabinHomeRemote.class);
```

Inside the Handle

Thinking about how Handles might be implemented gives us a better understanding of how they work. (Just remember that each vendor has its own implementation, which may be completely different from the implemenation we'll discuss.) Here's an implementation of a Handle for an entity bean:

```
package com.titan.cabin;

import javax.naming.InitialContext;
import javax.naming.Context;
```

```
import javax.naming.NamingException;
import javax.ejb.EJBObject;
import javax.ejb.Handle;
import java.rmi.RemoteException;
import java.util.Properties;
import javax.rmi.PortableRemoteObject;

public class VendorX_CabinHandle
    implements javax.ejb.Handle, java.io.Serializable {

    private Integer primary_key;
    private String home_name;
    private Properties jndi_properties;

    public VendorX_CabinHandle(Integer pk, String hn, Properties p) {
        primary_key = pk;
        home_name = hn;
        jndi_properties = p;
    }

    public EJBObject getEJBObject( ) throws RemoteException {
        try {
            Context ctx = new InitialContext(jndi_properties);

            Object ref = ctx.lookup(home_name);
            CabinHomeRemote home =(CabinHomeRemote)
                PortableRemoteObject.narrow(ref,CabinHomeRemote.class);

            return home.findByPrimaryKey(primary_key);
        } catch (javax.ejb.FinderException fe) {
            throw new RemoteException("Cannot locate EJB object",fe);
        } catch (javax.naming.NamingException ne) {
            throw new RemoteException("Cannot locate EJB object",ne);
        }
    }
}
```

Our implementation encapsulates the JNDI lookup and the use of the home's `findByPrimaryKey( )` method, so any change that invalidates the key also invalidates preserved `Handle` objects that depend on that key. Additionally, the `Handle` assumes that the networking configuration and naming—the IP address of the EJB server and the JNDI name of the bean's home—remain stable. If the EJB server's network address changes or the name used to identify the home changes, the `Handle` becomes useless.

In addition, some vendors choose to implement a security mechanism in the `Handle` that prevents its use outside the scope of the client application that originally requested it. How this mechanism would work is unclear, but the security limitation it implies should be considered before attempting to use a `Handle` outside the client's scope. To deploy the example in this section, see Exercise 5.2 in the Workbook.

The Local Client API

Enterprise JavaBeans were originally defined in terms of remote interfaces, such as the ones we've been discussing. The use of remote interfaces gave a nice, clean design: beans and bean clients did not need to worry about where other beans were located, because all bean references were treated as remote references. Beans always communicated with each other using Java RMI.

But in the real world, when two or more enterprise beans interact, they are usually *co-located*; that is, they are deployed in the same EJB container system and execute within the same Java Virtual Machine. In this case, RMI really isn't necessary, and imposes overhead that we'd rather do without. Why treat all beans as remote objects if, in fact, they are often local? EJB 2.0 introduced the Local Client API to give developers control over whether beans should be accessed as remote objects, using RMI, or as local objects.

In EJB 2.0 and 2.1, session and entity beans can implement either remote or local component interfaces, or both. Any type of enterprise bean (entity, session, or message-driven) can become a co-located client of a session or entity bean; for example, a message-driven bean can call methods on co-located entity beans using its local component interfaces. The Local Client API is similar to the Remote Client API, but it is less complicated. The Local Client API is composed of two interfaces, the local and local home interfaces, which are similar to the remote and remote home interfaces.

The Local Interface

The local interface, like the remote interface, defines business methods that can be invoked by other co-located beans (co-located clients). These business methods must match the signatures of business methods defined in the bean class. For example, the `CabinLocal` interface is the local interface defined for the Cabin EJB:

```
package com.titan.cabin;

import javax.ejb.EJBException;

public interface CabinLocal extends javax.ejb.EJBLocalObject {
    public String getName( ) throws EJBException;
    public void setName(String str) throws EJBException;
    public int getDeckLevel( ) throws EJBException;
    public void setDeckLevel(int level) throws EJBException;
    public int getShipId( ) throws EJBException;
    public void setShipId(int sp) throws EJBException;
    public int getBedCount( ) throws EJBException;
    public void setBedCount(int bc) throws EJBException;
}
```

The `CabinLocal` interface is basically the same as the `CabinRemote` interface we developed in Chapter 4, with a couple of key differences. Most importantly, the `CabinLocal` interface extends the `javax.ejb.EJBLocalObject` interface, rather than

EJBObject, and its methods do not throw the java.rmi.RemoteException. Here's the definition of the EJBLocalObject interface:

```
package javax.ejb;

import javax.ejb.EJBException;
import javax.ejb.RemoteException;

public interface EJBLocalObject {
    public EJBLocalHome getEJBLocalHome( ) throws EJBException;
    public Object getPrimaryKey( ) throws EJBException;
    public boolean isIdentical(EJBLocalObject obj) throws EJBException;
    public void remove( ) throws RemoveException, throws EJBException;
}
```

The methods in the EJBLocalObject interface should be familiar to you already. The getEJBLocalHome( ) method returns a local home object; getPrimaryKey( ) returns the primary key (entity beans only); isIdentical( ) compares two local EJB objects; and remove( ) removes the enterprise bean. These methods work just like their corresponding methods in the javax.ejb.EJBObject interface.

It's also important to notice the differences between EJBLocalObject and EJBObject. EJBLocalObject does not extend the java.rmi.Remote interface, because it is not a remote object. Nor does EJBLocalObject define a getHandle( ) method; handles are not relevant when the client and the enterprise bean are located in the same EJB container system. The Handle is a serializable reference that makes it easier for a remote client to obtain a reference to an enterprise bean from a remote node. Since co-located beans are located in the same container system, not across a network, the Handle object is not necessary.

The EJBLocalObject and the local interfaces that extend it do not throw a java.rmi.RemoteException, which is no longer needed. Instead, the local interfaces and EJBLocalObject throw EJBException. This exception is thrown by the container when some kind of system error occurs or when transaction errors cause the bean instance to be discarded. EJBException is a subtype of the java.lang.RuntimeException and is therefore an unchecked exception. Unchecked exceptions do not have to be declared in the throws clause of the local component interfaces and do not require the client to explicitly handle them using try/catch blocks. However, we choose to declare the EJBException in the method signatures of the CabinLocal interface in order to communicate to the client application that this type of exception is possible.

The Local Home Interface

The local home interface, like the remote home interface, defines life-cycle methods that can be invoked by other beans located in the same container. The life-cycle methods of the local home interface include find, create, and remove methods similar to those of the remote home interface. Here's the definition of CabinHomeLocal, the local home interface of the Cabin EJB:

```
package com.titan.cabin;

import javax.ejb.EJBException;
import javax.ejb.CreateException;
import javax.ejb.FinderException;

public interface CabinHomeLocal extends javax.ejb.EJBLocalHome {

    public CabinLocal create(Integer id)
        throws CreateException, EJBException;

    public CabinLocal findByPrimaryKey(Integer pk)
        throws FinderException, EJBException;
}
```

The `CabinHomeLocal` interface is similar to its counterpart, `CabinHomeRemote`, which we developed in Chapter 4. However, `CabinHomeLocal` extends `javax.ejb.EJBLocalHome` and does not throw the `RemoteException` from its create and find methods. You may also have noticed that the `create( )` and `findByPrimaryKey( )` methods return an instance of the `CabinLocal` interface, not the remote interface of the Cabin EJB. The create and find methods of local home interfaces always return EJB objects that implement the enterprise bean's local interface.

Local interfaces must always extend the `EJBLocalHome` interface, which is much simpler than its remote counterpart, `EJBHome`:

```
package javax.ejb;

import javax.ejb.RemoveException;
import javax.ejb.EJBException;

public interface EJBLocalHome {
    public void remove(Object primaryKey)
        throws RemoveException, EJBException;
}
```

Unlike the `EJBHome`, the `EJBLocalHome` does not provide `EJBMetaData` and `HomeHandle` accessors. The `EJBMetaData` object, which is primarily used by visual development tools, is not needed for co-located beans. In addition, the `HomeHandle` is not relevant to co-located client beans any more than the `Handle` was, because co-located beans do not need special network references. The `EJBLocalHome` does define a `remove( )` method that takes the primary key as its argument; this method works the same as its corresponding method in the remote `EJBObject` interface.

Deployment Descriptor

When an enterprise bean uses local component interfaces, the interfaces must be declared in the XML deployment descriptor. Here are the changes we need to make to the deployment descriptor for the Cabin bean:

```
<!DOCTYPE ejb-jar PUBLIC "-//Sun Microsystems, Inc.//DTD Enterprise
JavaBeans 2.0//EN" "http://java.sun.com/dtd/ejb-jar_2_0.dtd">
```

```
<ejb-jar>
    <enterprise-beans>
        <entity>
            <ejb-name>CabinEJB</ejb-name>
            <home>com.titan.cabin.CabinHomeRemote</home>
            <remote>com.titan.cabin.CabinRemote</remote>
            <local-home>com.titan.cabin.CabinHomeLocal</local-home>
            <local>com.titan.cabin.CabinLocal</local>
            <ejb-class>com.titan.cabin.CabinBean</ejb-class>
```

In addition to adding the `<local-home>` and `<local>` elements, the `<ejb-ref>` element is changed to an `<ejb-local-ref>` element, indicating that a local EJB object is being used instead of a remote one:

```
<ejb-local-ref>
    <ejb-ref-name>ejb/CabinHomeLocal</ejb-ref-name>
    <ejb-ref-type>Entity</ejb-ref-type>
    <local-home>com.titan.cabin.CabinHomeLocal</local-home>
    <local>com.titan.cabin.CabinLocal</local>
</ejb-local-ref>
```

Using the Local Client API

We can easily redesign the TravelAgent EJB developed in Chapter 4 so that it uses the Cabin EJB's local component interfaces instead of the remote component interfaces:

```
public String [] listCabins(int shipID, int bedCount) {

    try {
        javax.naming.Context jndiContext = new InitialContext( );
        CabinHomeLocal home = (CabinHomeLocal)
            jndiContext.lookup("java:comp/env/ejb/CabinHomeLocal");

        Vector vect = new Vector( );
        for (int i = 1; ; i++) {
            Integer pk = new Integer(i);
            CabinLocal cabin;
            try {
                cabin = home.findByPrimaryKey(pk);
            } catch(javax.ejb.FinderException fe) {
                break;
            }
            // Check to see if the bed count and ship ID match.
            if (cabin.getShipId( ) == shipID &&
                cabin.getBedCount( ) == bedCount) {
                String details =
                i+","+cabin.getName()+","+cabin.getDeckLevel( );
                vect.addElement(details);
            }
        }

        String [] list = new String[vect.size( )];
        vect.copyInto(list);
```

```
            return list;

        } catch(NamingException ne) {
            throw new EJBException(ne);
        }
    }
```

Three small changes are needed. The most important change is using local component interfaces for the Cabin EJB instead of remote interfaces. We do not need to use the `PortableRemoteObject.narrow( )` method when obtaining the Cabin EJB's home object because we are not accessing the home across the network; we are accessing the home object from the same JVM, so there's no problem with a regular Java cast. Eliminating this method call makes the code much easier to read. We also changed the `try/catch` block to catch the `javax.naming.NamingException` rather than the `EJBException` thrown by the local component interface methods. It is easier to allow those exceptions to propagate directly to the container, where they can be handled better. Chapter 15 covers exception handling in detail. To deploy the examples in this section, see Exercise 5.3 in the Workbook.

When to Use Local Component Interfaces

Entity and session beans can provide either local or remote component interfaces, or they may use both so that the bean is accessible from remote and local clients. Whenever we have enterprise beans accessing each other from within the same container system, we must seriously consider using local component interfaces, as their performance is likely to be better than that of remote component interfaces.

However, relying on the Local Client API eliminates the location transparency of enterprise bean references. In other words, if we provide only a local client API, we cannot move the bean to a different server. The Remote Client API allows us to move enterprise beans from one server to another without impacting the bean code.

The Local Client API also passes object arguments by reference from one bean to another, as illustrated in Figure 5-5. This means that an object passed from enterprise bean A to enterprise bean B is referenced by both beans, so if B changes its values, A will see those changes.

With the Remote Client API, objects' arguments (parameters or return values) are always copied, so changes made to one copy are not reflected in the other (see Figure 5-1).

Passing by reference can create some pretty dangerous situations if the enterprise beans that share the object reference are not coded carefully. In most cases, it is best to pass immutable objects without copying them first.

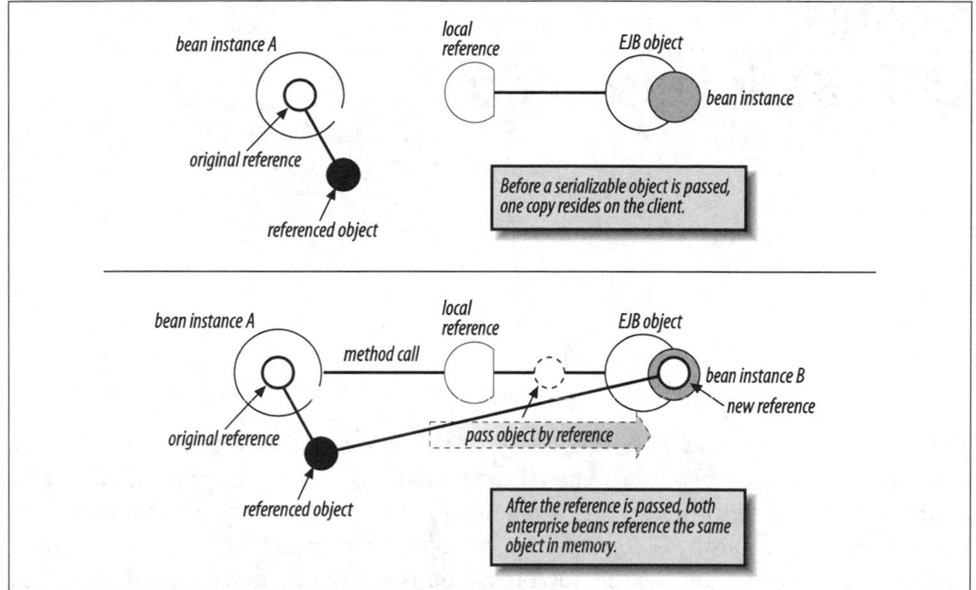

Figure 5-5. Passing by reference with the Local Client API

Are Local Component Interfaces Necessary?

Why is the Local Client API needed at all? Wouldn't it have been possible to amend the specification of the Remote Client API to account for co-located container optimizations, making those optimizations standard, configurable attributes in the deployment descriptor? The only problem with that solution is semantics. The remote interfaces extend `java.rmi.Remote`, and all subtypes of the `java.rmi.Remote` interface are required to throw `java.rmi.RemoteException` types from methods. It may have been difficult for developers to distinguish between a co-located EJB object and a remote EJB object, which is an important distinction if one is passing objects by reference while the other passes them by copy.

However, it can also be difficult for some EJB developers to use both the Remote and Local Client APIs correctly and effectively. With local component interfaces, we are locked into a single JVM, and we cannot move beans from one container to the next at will. The arguments for and against the local component interfaces both have their merits. Whether we agree with the need for the Local Client API or not, local interfaces are here to stay, and we must learn to use them appropriately.

CHAPTER 6

CMP: Basic Persistence

In this chapter, we'll take a thorough look at the process of developing entity beans. A good rule of thumb is that entity beans model business concepts that can be expressed as nouns. Although this is a guideline rather than a requirement, it helps determine when a business concept is a candidate for implementation as an entity bean. In grammar school, you learned that nouns are words that describe a person, place, or thing. The concepts of "person" and "place" are fairly obvious: a person EJB might represent a customer or passenger, and a place EJB might represent a city or port-of-call. Similarly, entity beans often represent "things": real-world objects like ships, credit cards, and abstractions such as reservations. Entity beans describe both the state and behavior of real-world objects and allow developers to encapsulate the data and business rules associated with specific concepts; a Customer EJB encapsulates the data and business rules associated with a customer, for example. This makes it possible for data associated with a concept to be manipulated consistently and safely.

In Titan's cruise ship business, we can identify hundreds of business concepts that are nouns and, therefore, could conceivably be modeled by entity beans. We've already seen a simple Cabin EJB in Chapter 4, and we'll develop Customer and Address EJBs in this chapter. Titan could clearly make use of a Cruise EJB, a Reservation EJB, and many others. Each of these business concepts represents data that needs to be tracked and possibly manipulated.

Entities represent data in the database, so changes to an entity bean result in changes to the database. That's ultimately the purpose of an entity bean: to provide programmers with a simpler mechanism for accessing and changing data. It is much easier to change a customer's name by calling `Customer.setName()` than by executing an SQL command against the database. In addition, using entity beans provides opportunities for software reuse. Once an entity bean has been defined, its definition can be used throughout Titan's system in a consistent manner. The concept of a customer, for example, is used in many areas of Titan's business, including booking, accounts receivable, and marketing. A Customer EJB provides Titan with one complete way of accessing customer information, and thus it ensures that access to the information is consistent and simple. Representing data as entity beans can make development easier and more cost-effective.

When a new entity EJB is created, a new record must be inserted into the database and a bean instance must be associated with that data. As the EJB is used and its state changes, these changes must be synchronized with the data in the database: entries must be inserted, updated, and removed. The process of coordinating the data represented by a bean instance with the database is called *persistence*.

There are two basic types of entity beans, distinguished by how they manage persistence: container-managed persistence beans and bean-managed persistence beans. For *container-managed persistence* beans (frequently called CMP beans), the container knows how a bean instance's persistence and relationship fields map to the database and automatically takes care of inserting, updating, and deleting the data associated with entities in the database. Entity beans using *bean-managed persistence* do all this work manually: the bean developer must write the code to manipulate the database. The EJB container tells the bean instance when it is safe to insert, update, and delete its data from the database, but it provides no other help.

This chapter and the two that follow focus on entity beans that use container-managed persistence. In EJB 2.1 and EJB 2.0, the data associated with an entity bean can be much more complex than in earlier versions. Container-managed beans can have relationships with other entity beans, a function that was not well supported in the older version—as a result, vendors sometimes offered proprietary solutions that were not portable. In addition, container-managed beans can be finer in granularity so that they can easily model things such as the address, line item, or cabin. The Customer EJB that we'll define in this chapter has relationships with several other entities, including the Address, Phone, CreditCard, Cruise, Ship, Cabin, and Reservation EJBs. In the next few chapters, you'll learn how to use EJB's support for bean-to-bean relationships, and will also come to understand their limitations. In addition, in Chapter 8, you will learn about the Enterprise JavaBeans Query Language (EJB QL), which is used to define how the find methods and select methods should behave at runtime.

The Abstract Programming Model

In CMP, the container automatically manages the entity beans' state. The container takes care of enrolling the entity bean in transactions and persisting its state to the database. The developer describes the attributes and relationships of an entity bean using *virtual* persistence fields and relationship fields. They are called virtual fields because the bean developer does not declare these fields explicitly; instead, abstract accessor (get and set) methods are declared in the entity bean class. The implementations of these methods are generated at deployment time by the EJB vendor's container tools. It's important to remember that the terms *relationship field* and *persistence field* refer to the abstract accessor methods and not to actual fields declared in the classes.

In Figure 6-1, the Customer EJB has six accessor methods. The first four read and update the last and first names of the customer. These are examples of *persistence* fields: simple direct attributes of the entity bean. The last two accessor methods obtain and set references to the Address EJB through its local interface, `AddressLocal`. This is an example of a *relationship* field called the `homeAddress` field.

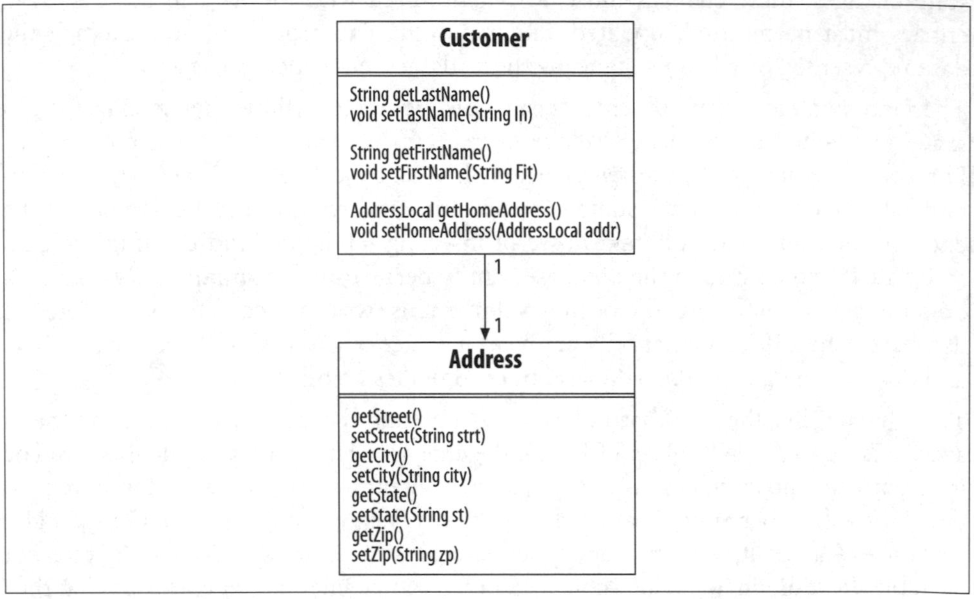

Figure 6-1. Class diagram of Customer and Address EJBs

Abstract Persistence Schema

The CMP entity bean classes are defined using abstract accessor methods that represent virtual persistence and relationship fields. As already mentioned, the actual fields themselves are not declared in the entity classes. Instead, the characteristics of these fields are described in the XML deployment descriptor used by the entity bean. The abstract persistence schema is the set of XML elements in the deployment descriptor that describe the relationship fields and the persistence fields. Together with the abstract accessor methods and some help from the deployer, the container tool will have enough information to map the entity and its relationships to other entity beans to the database.

Container Tools and Persistence

One of the responsibilities of the vendor's container-deployment tool is generating concrete implementations of the abstract entity beans. The concrete classes generated by the container tool are called *persistence classes*. Instances of the persistence classes are responsible for working with the container to read and write data between the entity bean and the database at runtime. Once the persistence classes are generated, they can be deployed into the EJB container. The container informs the *persistence instances* (instances of persistence classes) when it's a good time to read and write data to the database.

The persistence classes may include database access logic optimized for a particular database, database schema, or database configuration. Persistence classes may employ optimizations such as lazy loading and optimistic locking to further improve performance. Because the EJB container generates the persistence classes at deployment time, including the database access logic, bean developers do not have to write the database access code themselves. As an EJB developer, you will never have to deal with database access code when working with CMP entities. In fact, you probably won't have access to the persistence classes that contain that logic, because they are generated by the container tool automatically and aren't available to the bean developer.

Figures 6-2 and 6-3 show different container tools, both of which are being used to map the Customer entity bean to a relational database.

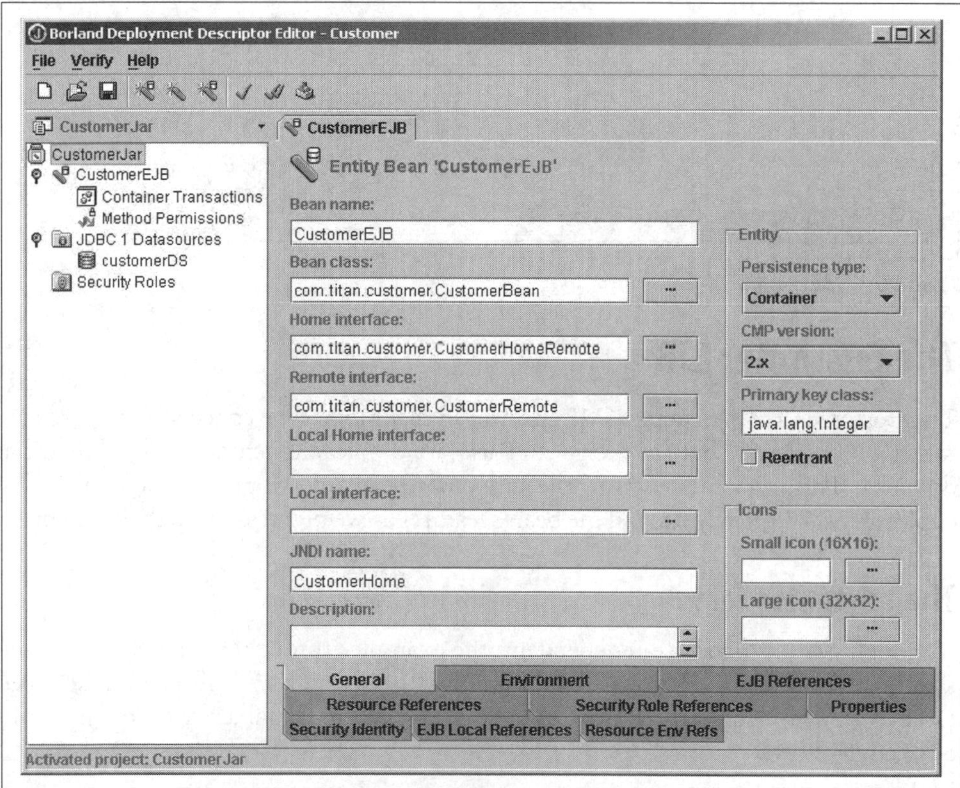

Figure 6-2. Borland AppServer deployment tool

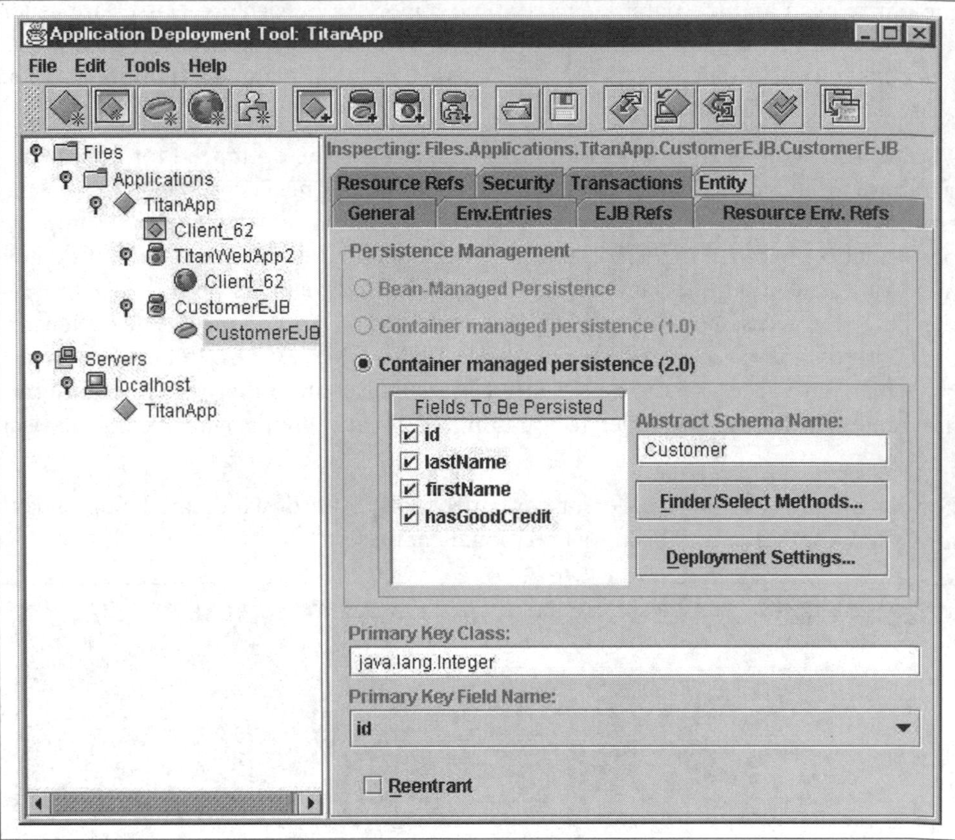

Figure 6-3. J2EE 1.3 SDK deployment tool

The Customer EJB

The Customer EJB is a simple CMP entity bean that models the concept of a cruise customer or passenger, but its design and use are applicable across many commercial domains. This section introduces the Customer bean's development, packaging, and deployment. We greatly expand the bean's features as we progress through the chapter.

The Customer Table

Although CMP is database-independent, the examples throughout this book assume that you are using a relational database. This means that we will need a `CUSTOMER` table from which to get our customer data. The relational database table definition in SQL is as follows:

```
CREATE TABLE CUSTOMER
(
    ID INT PRIMARY KEY NOT NULL,
```

```
        LAST_NAME CHAR(20),
        FIRST_NAME CHAR(20)
    )
```

The CustomerBean

The CustomerBean class is an abstract class that the container uses for generating a concrete implementation, the persistence entity class. The mechanism used by the container for generating a persistence entity class varies, but most vendors generate a subclass of the abstract class provided by the bean developer (see Figure 6-4).

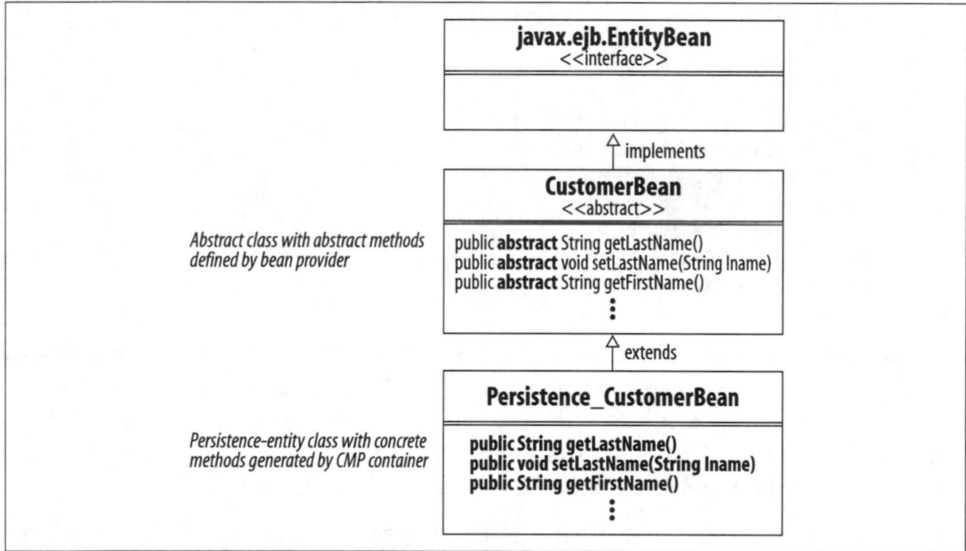

Figure 6-4. The container tool typically extends the bean class

The bean class must declare accessor (set and get) methods for each persistence field and relationship field defined in the deployment descriptor. The container needs both the abstract accessor methods (defined in the entity bean class) and the XML elements of the deployment descriptor to fully describe the bean's persistence schema. In this book, the entity bean class is always defined before the XML elements, because it's a more natural approach for most Java developers. Here is a very simple definition of the CustomerBean class:

```
package com.titan.customer;

import javax.ejb.EntityContext;

public abstract class CustomerBean implements javax.ejb.EntityBean {

    public Integer ejbCreate(Integer id){
        setId(id);
        return null;
    }
```

```
    public void ejbPostCreate(Integer id){
    }

    // abstract accessor methods

    public abstract Integer getId( );
    public abstract void setId(Integer id);

    public abstract String getLastName( );
    public abstract void setLastName(String lname);

    public abstract String getFirstName( );
    public abstract void setFirstName(String fname);

    // standard callback methods

    public void setEntityContext(EntityContext ec){}
    public void unsetEntityContext( ){}
    public void ejbLoad( ){}
    public void ejbStore( ){}
    public void ejbActivate( ){}
    public void ejbPassivate( ){}
    public void ejbRemove( ){}
}
```

The CustomerBean class is required to be abstract in order to reinforce the idea that the CustomerBean is not deployed directly. Since abstract classes cannot be instantiated, this class must be subclassed by a persistence class generated by the deployment tool. When generating the persistence class, the deployment tool must generate the accessor methods, which are themselves declared as abstract.

The CustomerBean extends the javax.ejb.EntityBean interface, which defines several callback methods, including setEntityContext( ), unsetEntityContext( ), ejbLoad( ), ejbStore( ), ejbActivate( ), ejbPassivate( ), and ejbRemove( ). These methods are important for notifying the bean instance about events in its life cycle, but we do not need to worry about them yet. We will discuss these methods in detail in Chapter 10.

The first method in the entity bean class is ejbCreate( ), which takes a reference to an Integer object as its only argument. The ejbCreate( ) method is called when the remote client invokes the create( ) method on the entity bean's home interface. This concept should be familiar, since it's the same way ejbCreate( ) worked in the Cabin bean developed in Chapter 4. The ejbCreate( ) method is responsible for initializing any persistence fields before the entity bean is created. In this first example, the ejbCreate( ) method is used to initialize the id persistence field, which is represented by the setId( )/getId( ) accessor methods.

The return type of ejbCreate( ) is an Integer, which is the *primary key* of the entity bean. The primary key is a unique identifier that can take a variety of forms. In this case, the primary key (the Integer) is mapped to the ID field in the CUSTOMER table. This will become evident when we define the XML deployment descriptor. However, although the return type of the `ejbCreate()` method is the primary key, the value actually returned by the `ejbCreate()` method is `null`. The EJB container and persistence class will extract the primary key from the bean when it is needed. See the sidebar "Why ejbCreate() Returns Null" for an explanation of `ejbCreate()`'s return type.

Why ejbCreate() Returns Null

In EJB 1.0, the first release of EJB, the `ejbCreate()` method in container-managed persistence was declared as returning void, while the `ejbCreate()` method in bean-managed persistence returns the primary key type. However, in EJB 1.1 it was changed to the primary key type, with an actual return value of null.

EJB 1.1 changed the return value of `ejbCreate()` from void to the primary key type to facilitate subclassing; i.e., to make it easier for a bean-managed entity bean to extend a container-managed entity bean. In EJB 1.0, this was not possible because Java doesn't allow you to overload methods with different return values. Changing this definition allowed a bean-managed entity bean to extend a container-managed bean, which in turn allowed vendors to support CMP by extending a container-managed bean with an automatically generated bean-managed bean—a fairly simple solution to a difficult problem.

With the changes made to CMP starting in EJB 2.0, this little trick has become less useful. The abstract persistence schema of EJB CMP beans is, in many cases, too complex for a simple BMP container. However, it remains in the specification for backward compatibility and to facilitate bean-managed persistence subclassing, if needed.

The `ejbPostCreate()` method performs initialization after the entity bean is created but before it services any requests from the client. Usually, this method is used to perform work on the entity bean's relationship fields, which can occur only after the bean's `ejbCreate()` method has been invoked and added to the database. For each `ejbCreate()` method, there must be a matching `ejbPostCreate()` method that has the same method name and arguments but returns void. This pairing of `ejbCreate()` and `ejbPostCreate()` ensures that the container calls the correct methods together. We'll explore the use of the `ejbPostCreate()` later; for now, it's not needed, so its implementation is left empty.

The abstract accessor methods (`setLastName()`, `getLastName()`, `setFirstName()`, `getFirstName()`) represent the persistence fields in the `CustomerBean` class. When the bean is processed by a container, these methods will be implemented by a persistence class based on the abstract persistence schema (XML deployment descriptor elements), the particular EJB container, and the database used. Basically, these methods fetch and update values in the database and are not implemented by the bean developer.

The Remote Interface

We need a CustomerRemote interface for the Customer EJB, because the bean will be accessed by clients outside the container system. The remote interface defines the business methods that clients use to interact with the entity bean. The remote interface should define methods that model the public aspects of the business concept being modeled; that is, those behaviors and data that should be exposed to client applications. Here is the remote interface for CustomerRemote:

```
package com.titan.customer;
import java.rmi.RemoteException;

public interface CustomerRemote extends javax.ejb.EJBObject {

    public String getLastName( ) throws RemoteException;
    public void setLastName(String lname) throws RemoteException;

    public String getFirstName( ) throws RemoteException;
    public void setFirstName(String fname) throws RemoteException;
}
```

Any methods defined in the remote interface must match methods defined in the bean class. In this case, the accessor methods in the CustomerRemote interface match persistence field accessor methods in the CustomerBean class—with a few exceptions, methods in the remote interface can match any business method in the bean class

While remote methods can match persistence fields and other business methods in the bean class, the specification prohibits the remote methods from matching callback methods (ejbRemove( ), ejbActivate( ), ejbLoad( ), etc.) or relationship fields—relationship fields are used to access other entity beans. In addition, remote methods may not modify any container-managed persistence fields that are part of the primary key of an entity bean. Notice that the remote interface does not define a setId( ) method, which would allow it to modify the primary key.

The Remote Home Interface

The remote home interface of any entity bean is used to create, locate, and remove entities from the EJB container. Each entity bean type may have its own remote home interface, local home interface, or both. As explained in Chapter 5, the remote and local home interfaces perform essentially the same function. The home interfaces define three basic kinds of methods: home business methods, zero or more create methods, and one or more find methods. The create( ) methods act like remote constructors and define how new entity beans are created. In our remote home interface, we provide only a single create( ) method, which matches the corresponding ejbCreate( ) method in the bean class. The find method is used to locate a specific Customer EJB using the primary key as a unique identifier.

Here is the complete definition of the CustomerHomeRemote interface:

```
package com.titan.customer;

import java.rmi.RemoteException;
import javax.ejb.CreateException;
import javax.ejb.FinderException;

public interface CustomerHomeRemote extends javax.ejb.EJBHome {

    public CustomerRemote create(Integer id)
        throws CreateException, RemoteException;

    public CustomerRemote findByPrimaryKey(Integer id)
        throws FinderException, RemoteException;

}
```

A create( ) method may be suffixed with a name in order to further qualify it when overloading method arguments. This is useful if we have two different create( ) methods that take arguments of the same type. For example, we could declare two create( ) methods for Customer that both declare an Integer and a String argument. The String argument might be a Social Security number (SSN) in one case and a tax identification number (TIN) in another—individuals have Social Security numbers while corporations have tax identification numbers. Here's how these methods might look:

```
public interface CustomerHomeRemote extends javax.ejb.EJBHome {

    public CustomerRemote createWithSSN(Integer id, String socialSecurityNumber)
        throws CreateException, RemoteException;

    public CustomerRemote createWithTIN(Integer id, String taxIdentificationNumber)
        throws CreateException, RemoteException;

    public CustomerRemote findByPrimaryKey(Integer id)
        throws FinderException, RemoteException;
 }
```

Each create<SUFFIX>( ) method must have a corresponding ejbCreate<SUFFIX>( ) in the bean class. For example, the CustomerBean class needs to define ejbCreateWithSSN( ) and ejbCreateWithTIN( ) methods as well as matching ejbPostCreateWithSSN( ) and ejbPostCreateWithTIN( ) methods. We are keeping this example simple, so we need only one create( ) method and, therefore, no suffix.

Enterprise JavaBeans specifies that create( ) methods in the remote home interface must throw the javax.ejb.CreateException. In the case of container-managed persistence, the container needs a common exception for communicating problems that may occur during the create process.

Entity remote home interfaces must define a findByPrimaryKey( ) method that takes the entity bean's primary key type as its only argument. No matching method needs to be defined in the entity bean class. The implementation of `findByPrimaryKey()` is generated automatically. At runtime, the `findByPrimaryKey()` method automatically locates and returns a remote reference to the entity bean with the matching primary key.

The bean developer can also declare other find methods. For example, the `CustomerHomeRemote` interface could define a `findByLastName(String lname)` method that locates all the Customer entities with the specified last name. These types of find methods are automatically implemented by the deployment tool based on the method signature and an EJB QL statement. EJB QL is similar to SQL but is specific to EJB. Custom finder methods and EJB QL are discussed in detail in Chapter 8.

The XML Deployment Descriptor

CMP entity beans must be packaged with an XML deployment descriptor that describes the bean and its abstract persistence schema. With many commercial containers, the bean developer is not directly exposed to the deployment descriptor, but instead uses the container's deployment tools to package beans. In this book, however, I describe the deployment descriptor in detail so you have a full understanding of its content and organization.

Here is the complete XML deployment descriptor for the Customer EJB in EJB 2.1. Many of the elements in this descriptor should be familiar from Chapter 4; we will focus on the new elements:

```
<?xml version="1.0" encoding="UTF-8" ?>
<ejb-jar
     xmlns="http://java.sun.com/xml/ns/j2ee"
     xmlns:xsi="http://www.w3.org/2001/XMLSchema-instance"
     xsi:schemaLocation="http://java.sun.com/xml/ns/j2ee
                         http://java.sun.com/xml/ns/j2ee/ejb-jar_2_1.xsd"
     version="2.1">

    <enterprise-beans>
        <entity>
            <ejb-name>CustomerEJB</ejb-name>
            <home>com.titan.customer.CustomerHomeRemote</home>
            <remote>com.titan.customer.CustomerRemote</remote>
            <ejb-class>com.titan.customer.CustomerBean</ejb-class>
            <persistence-type>Container</persistence-type>
            <prim-key-class>java.lang.Integer</prim-key-class>
            <reentrant>False</reentrant>
            <cmp-version>2.x</cmp-version>
            <abstract-schema-name>Customer</abstract-schema-name>
            <cmp-field><field-name>id</field-name></cmp-field>
            <cmp-field><field-name>lastName</field-name></cmp-field>
            <cmp-field><field-name>firstName</field-name></cmp-field>
            <primkey-field>id</primkey-field>
            <security-identity><use-caller-identity/></security-identity>
        </entity>
    </enterprise-beans>
```

```
    <assembly-descriptor>
        <security-role>
            <role-name>Employees</role-name>
        </security-role>
        <method-permission>
            <role-name>Employees</role-name>
            <method>
                <ejb-name>CustomerEJB</ejb-name>
                <method-name>*</method-name>
            </method>
        </method-permission>
        <container-transaction>
            <method>
                <ejb-name>CustomerEJB</ejb-name>
                <method-name>*</method-name>
            </method>
            <trans-attribute>Required</trans-attribute>
        <container-transaction>
    </assembly-descriptor>
</ejb-jar>
```

The deployment descriptor for EJB 2.0 is exactly the same, except that it uses XML DTD instead of XML Schema, so the first tag in the EJB 2.0 deployment descriptor is the document declaration followed by the <ejb-jar> element.

```
<?xml version="1.0" encoding="UTF-8" ?>
<!DOCTYPE ejb-jar PUBLIC "-//Sun Microsystems, Inc.//DTD Enterprise
JavaBeans 2.0//EN" "http://java.sun.com/dtd/ejb-jar_2_0.dtd">

<ejb-jar>
    ...
</ejb-jar>
```

The first few elements in the Customer EJB's deployment descriptor should be familiar; they declare the Customer EJB name, (CustomerEJB) as well as its home, remote, and bean class. The <security-identity> element should also be familiar, as well as the <assembly-descriptor> elements, which declare the security and transaction attributes of the bean. In this case, they state that all employees can access any CustomerEJB method and that all methods use the Required transaction attribute.

Container-managed persistence entities also need to declare a persistence type, version, and whether they are reentrant. These elements are declared under the <entity> element.

The <persistence-type> element tells the container system whether the bean will be a container-managed persistence entity or a bean-managed persistence entity. In this case it's container-managed, so we use Container. Had it been bean-managed, the value would have been Bean.

The <cmp-version> element is optional; it tells the container system which version of container-managed persistence is being used. The value of the <cmp-version> element can be either 2.x or 1.x. The 2.x designator is used for EJB 2.1 and 2.0, while

1.x is used for EJB 1.1. EJB 2.1 and 2.0 containers are required to support EJB 1.1 CMP for backward compatibility. If it is not declared, the default value is 2.x. It's not really needed here, but it's specified as an aid to other developers who might read the deployment descriptor.

The <reentrant> element indicates whether reentrant behavior is allowed. In this case the value is False, which indicates that the CustomerEJB is not reentrant (i.e., loopbacks are not allowed). A value of True would indicate that the CustomerEJB is reentrant and that loopbacks are permitted.

The entity bean must also declare its container-managed persistence fields and its primary key:

```
<entity>
    <ejb-name>CustomerEJB</ejb-name>
    <home>com.titan.customer.CustomerHomeRemote</home>
    <remote>com.titan.customer.CustomerRemote</remote>
    <ejb-class>com.titan.customer.CustomerBean</ejb-class>
    <persistence-type>Container</persistence-type>
    <prim-key-class>java.lang.Integer</prim-key-class>
    <reentrant>False</reentrant>
    <cmp-version>2.x</cmp-version>
    <cmp-field><field-name>id</field-name></cmp-field>
    <cmp-field><field-name>lastName</field-name></cmp-field>
    <cmp-field><field-name>firstName</field-name></cmp-field>
    <primkey-field>id</primkey-field>
</entity>
```

The container-managed persistence fields are the id, lastName, and firstName, as indicated by the <cmp-field> elements. The <cmp-field> elements must have matching accessor methods in the CustomerBean class. As you can see in Table 6-1, the values declared in the <field-name> element match the names of abstract accessor methods we declared in the CustomerBean class.

Table 6-1. Field names for abstract accessor methods

CMP field	Abstract accessor method
id	public abstract Integer getId( ) public abstract void setId(Integer id)
lastName	public abstract String getLastName( ) public abstract void setLastName(String lname)
firstName	public abstract String getFirstName( ) public abstract void setFirstName(String lname)

CMP requires that the <field-name> values start with a lowercase letter. The names of the matching accessor methods take the form get<field-name>( ), set<field-name >( ) (the first letter of the field name is capitalized). The return type of the get method and the parameter of the set method determine the type of the <cmp-field>. It's the convention of this book, but not a requirement of CMP, that field names with multiple words are declared using "camel case," in which each new word starts with a capital letter (e.g., lastName).

Finally, we declare the primary key using two fields, <prim-key-class> and <primkey-field>. <prim-key-class> indicates the type of the primary key, and <primkey-field> indicates which of the <cmp-field> elements designates the primary key. The Customer EJB uses a *single-field* primary key, in which the bean's identifier is composed of a single container-managed field. The <primkey-field> must be declared if the entity bean uses a single-field primary key. *Compound* primary keys, which use more than one of the persistence fields as a key, are often used instead. In this case, the bean developer creates a custom primary key. The <prim-key-class> element is always required, whether it's a single-field, compound, or unknown primary key. Unknown keys use a field that may not be declared in the bean at all. The different types of primary keys are covered in more detail in Chapter 10.

The EJB JAR File

Now that you have created the interfaces, bean class, and deployment descriptor, you're ready to package the bean for deployment. As you learned in Chapter 4, the JAR file provides a way to "shrink-wrap" a component so it can be deployed in an EJB container. The command for creating a new EJB JAR file is:

```
\dev % jar cf customer.jar com/titan/customer/*.class
com/titan/customer/META-INF/ejb-jar.xml

F:\..\dev>jar cf cabin.jar com\titan\customer\*.class com\titan\customer
\META-INF\ejb-jar.xml
```

There are a number of tools that create the XML deployment descriptor and package the enterprise bean into a JAR file automatically. Some of these tools even create the home and remote interfaces automatically, based on input from the developer.

Deployment

Once the CustomerEJB is packaged in a JAR file, it's ready to be deployed in an EJB container. The point is to map the container-managed persistence fields of the bean to fields or data objects in the database. (Earlier in this chapter, Figure 6-2 and Figure 6-3 showed two visual tools used to map the Customer EJB's persistence fields.) In addition, the security roles need to be mapped to the subjects in the security realm of the target environment and the bean needs to be added to the naming service and given a JNDI lookup name (name binding).

The Client Application

The Client application is a remote client to the CustomerEJB that creates several customers, finds them, and then removes them. Here is the complete definition of the Client application:

```
import javax.naming.InitialContext;
import javax.naming.Context;
import javax.naming.NamingException;
import java.util.Properties;
```

```
public class Client {
    public static void main(String [] args)) throws Exception {
        //obtain CustomerHome
        Context jndiContext = getInitialContext( );
        Object obj=jndiContext.lookup("CustomerHomeRemote");
        CustomerHomeRemote home = (CustomerHomeRemote)
            javax.rmi.PortableRemoteObject.narrow(obj,CustomerHomeRemote.class);
        //create Customers
        for(int i =0;i <args.length;i++){
            Integer primaryKey =new Integer(i);
            String firstName = args [i ];
            String lastName = args [i ];
            CustomerRemote customer = home.create(primaryKey);
            customer.setFirstName(firstName);
            customer.setLastName(lastName);
        }
        //find and remove Customers
        for(int i = 0;i < args.length;i++){
            Integer primaryKey = new Integer(i);
            CustomerRemote customer = home.findByPrimaryKey(primaryKey);
            String lastName = customer.getLastName( );
            String firstName = customer.getFirstName( );
            System.out.print(primaryKey+"=");
            System.out.println(firstName+""+lastName);
            //remove Customer
            customer.remove( );
        }
    }
    public static Context getInitialContext(
        throws javax.naming.NamingException {
        Properties p =new Properties( );
        //...Specify the JNDI properties specific to the vendor.
        return new javax.naming.InitialContext(p);
    }
}
```

The `Client` application creates several Customer EJBs, sets their first and last names, prints out the persistence field values, and then removes the entities from the container system and, effectively, the database. To deploy the examples in this section, see Exercise 6.1 in the Workbook.

Persistence Fields

Container-managed persistence (CMP) fields are virtual fields whose values map directly to the database. Persistence fields can be Java serializable types and Java primitive types. Java serializable types implement the `java.io.Serializable` interface. Most deployment tools easily handle `java.lang.String`, `java.util.Date`, and the primitive wrappers (`Byte`, `Boolean`, `Short`, `Integer`, `Long`, `Double`, and `Float`), because these types of objects are part of the Java core and map naturally to database fields.

The CustomerEJB declares three serializable fields, id, lastName, and firstName, which map naturally to the INT and CHAR fields of the CUSTOMER table in the database.

You can also define your own serializable types, called *dependent value classes*, and declare them as CMP fields. However, I recommend that you do not use custom serializable objects as persistence field types unless it is absolutely necessary—they are usually recommended for unstructured types, such as multimedia data (images, blobs, etc.). Arbitrary dependent value classes usually will not map naturally to database types, so they must be stored in their serializable forms in some type of binary database field.

Serializable objects are always returned as copies and not references, so modifying a serializable object will not impact its database value. The value of a serializable object must be updated using the set<field-name> method.

The primitive types (byte, short, int, long, double, float, and boolean) are also allowed to be CMP fields. These types are easily mapped to the database and are supported by all deployment tools. As an example, the CustomerEJB might declare a boolean that represents a customer's credit worthiness:

```
public abstract class CustomerBean implements javax.ejb.EntityBean {

    public Integer ejbCreate(Integer id){
        setId(id);
        return null;
    }

    // abstract accessor methods

    public abstract boolean getHasGoodCredit( );
    public abstract void setHasGoodCredit(boolean creditRating);
    ...
}
```

You must add a database field, HAS_GOOD_CREDIT, to the CUSTOMER table for the hasGoodCredit persistent field. Depending on the kind of database you are using, this field may be a BIT, INT, BOOLEAN, or something else. For example, Oracle and DB2 use an INT field:

```
CREATE TABLE CUSTOMER
{
    ID INT PRIMARY KEY,
    LAST_NAME CHAR(20),
    FIRST_NAME CHAR(20),
    HAS_GOOD_CREDIT INT
}
```

Other databases use different data types for the HAS_GOOD_CREDIT field:

- In Oracle, it should be INT.
- In DB2 UDB, it should be INT.

- In SQL*Server, it should be BIT.
- In Sybase ASE, it should be BIT.
- In Cloudscape, it should be BOOLEAN.
- In PointBase, it should be BOOLEAN.

This is an unfortunate SQL portability problem that occurs when you're using different database technologies, but it's the only inconsistency I discovered while testing the code for this book. Before adding the HAS_GOOD_CREDIT field to the CUSTOMER table, check your vendor's documentation to determine the field type.

Dependent Value Classes

Dependent value classes are custom serializable objects that can be used as persistence fields (although this use is not recommended). They are useful for packaging data and moving it between an entity bean and its remote clients. They separate the client's view of the entity bean from its abstract persistence model, which makes it easier for the entity bean class to change without affecting existing clients.

The remote interface methods of an entity bean should be defined independently of the abstract persistence schema. In other words, you should design the remote interfaces to model the business concepts, not the underlying persistence programming model. Dependent value classes can help separate a remote client's view from the persistence model by providing objects that fill the gaps in these perspectives.

For example, the CustomerEJB could be modified so that its lastName and firstName fields are not exposed to remote clients through their accessor methods. This is a reasonable design approach, since most clients access the entire name of the customer at once. The remote interface might be modified to look like:

```
import java.rmi.RemoteException;

public interface CustomerRemote extends javax.ejb.EJBObject {

    public Name getName( ) throws RemoteException;
    public void setName(Name name) throws RemoteException;

}
```

This remote interface is simpler than the one we saw earlier. It allows the remote client to get all the name information in one method call instead of two, reducing network traffic and improving performance for remote clients. The use of the Name object is also more consistent with how the client interacts with the Customer EJB.

To implement this interface, the CustomerBean class adds a business method that matches the remote interface methods. The setName( ) method updates the lastName and firstName fields, while the getName( ) method constructs a Name object from these fields:

```
import javax.ejb.EntityContext;

public abstract class CustomerBean implements javax.ejb.EntityBean {

    public Integer ejbCreate(Integer id){
        setId(id);
        return null;
    }
    public void ejbPostCreate(Integer id) {
    }

    // business methods
    public Name getName( ) {
        Name name = new Name(getLastName(),getFirstName( ));
        return name;
    }
    public void setName(Name name) {
        setLastName(name.getLastName( ));
        setFirstName(name.getFirstName( ));
    }

    // abstract accessor methods
    public abstract String getLastName( );
    public abstract void setLastName(String lname);

    public abstract String getFirstName( );
    public abstract void setFirstName(String fname);
```

The getName( ) and setName( ) methods are business methods, not abstract persistence methods. Entity beans can have as many business methods as needed. Business methods introduce business logic to the Customer EJB; otherwise, the bean would be only a data wrapper. For example, validation logic could be added to the setName( ) method to ensure that the data is correct before applying the update. In addition, the entity bean class can use other methods that help with processing data—these are just instance methods and may not be exposed as business methods in the remote interface.

How dependent value classes are defined is important to understanding how they should be used. The Name dependent value class is defined as:

```
public class Name implements java.io.Serializable {
    private String lastName;
    private String firstName;

    public Name(String lname, String fname){
        lastName = lname;
        firstName = fname;
    }
    public String getLastName( ) {
        return lastName;
```

```
        }
        public String getFirstName( ) {
            return firstName;
        }
    }
```

You'll notice that the Name dependent value class has get accessor methods but not set methods. It's immutable. This is a design strategy used in this book, not a requirement of the EJB specification. By making dependent values immutable, we ensure that remote clients cannot change the Name object's fields. The reason for this design is simple: the Name object is a copy, not a remote reference. Changes to Name objects are not reflected in the database. Making the Name immutable helps to ensure that clients do not mistake this dependent value for a remote object reference, thinking that a change to the Name object is automatically reflected in the database. To change the customer's name, the client is required to create a new Name object and use the setName( ) method to update the Customer EJB.

The following listing illustrates how a client would modify the name of a customer using the Name dependent value class:

```
// find Customer
customer = home.findByPrimaryKey(primaryKey);
name = customer.getName( );
System.out.print(primaryKey+" = ");
System.out.println(name.getFirstName()+" "+name.getLastName( ));

// change Customer's name
name = new Name("Monson-Haefel", "Richard");
customer.setName(name);
name = customer.getName( );
System.out.print(primaryKey+" = ");
System.out.println(name.getFirstName()+" "+name.getLastName( ));
```

The output will look like this:

```
1 = Richard Monson
1 = Richard Monson-Haefel
```

Defining the bean's interfaces according to business concepts and not the underlying data is not always reasonable, but you should try to employ this strategy when the underlying data model doesn't clearly map to the business purpose or concept being modeled by the entity bean. The bean's interfaces may be used by developers who know the business but not the abstract programming model. It is important to them that the entity beans reflect the business concept. In addition, defining the interfaces independently of the persistence model enables the component interfaces and persistence model to evolve separately. This allows the abstract persistence programming model to change over time, and allows for new behavior to be added to the entity bean as needed.

Dependent value classes should not be used indiscriminately. Generally speaking, it is foolish to use dependent value classes when a CMP field will do just fine. For example, checking a client's creditworthiness before processing an order can be accomplished easily using the getHasGoodCredit( ) method directly. In this case, a dependent value class would serve no purpose. Exercise 6.2 in the Workbook shows how to deploy these examples on the JBoss server.

Relationship Fields

Entity beans can form relationships with other entity beans. In Figure 6-1, at the beginning of this chapter, the Customer EJB has a one-to-one relationship with the Address EJB. The Address EJB is a fine-grained business object that should always be accessed in the context of another entity bean, which means it should have only local interfaces and not remote interfaces. An entity bean can have relationships with many different entity beans at the same time. For example, we could easily add relationship fields for Phone, CreditCard, and other entity beans to the Customer EJB. At this point, we're choosing to keep the Customer EJB simple.

Using Figure 6-1 as a guide, we define the Address EJB as follows:

```
package com.titan.address;

import javax.ejb.EntityContext;

public abstract class AddressBean implements javax.ejb.EntityBean {

    public Integer ejbCreateAddress(String street, String city,
        String state, String zip)
    {
         setStreet(street);
         setCity(city);
         setState(state);
         setZip(zip);
         return null;
    }
    public void ejbPostCreateAddress(String street, String city,
        String state, String zip) {
    }

    // persistence fields

    public abstract Integer getId( );
    public abstract void setId(Integer id);
    public abstract String getStreet( );
    public abstract void setStreet(String street);
    public abstract String getCity( );
    public abstract void setCity(String city);
    public abstract String getState( );
    public abstract void setState(String state);
    public abstract String getZip( );
    public abstract void setZip(String zip);
```

```
    // standard callback methods

    public void setEntityContext(EntityContext ec){}
    public void unsetEntityContext( ){}
    public void ejbLoad( ){}
    public void ejbStore( ){}
    public void ejbActivate( ){}
    public void ejbPassivate( ){}
    public void ejbRemove( ){}
}
```

The AddressBean class defines several persistence fields (street, city, state, and zip) and an ejbCreateAddress( ) method, which is called when a new Address EJB is created. The persistence fields are represented by abstract accessor methods. These abstract methods are matched with XML deployment descriptor elements. At deployment time, the container maps the Customer and Address EJB's persistence fields to the database. This means there must be a table in our relational database that contains columns matching the persistence fields in the Address EJB. In this example, we will use a separate ADDRESS table for storing address information:

```
CREATE TABLE ADDRESS
(
    ID INT PRIMARY KEY NOT NULL,
    STREET CHAR(40),
    CITY CHAR(20),
    STATE CHAR(2),
    ZIP CHAR(10)
)
```

The ID column in this table is an auto-increment field, created automatically by the database or container system. It is the primary key of the Address EJB. Once the bean is created, its primary key must never again be modified. When primary keys are autogenerated values, such as the ID column in the ADDRESS table, the EJB container obtains the primary key value from the database.

The other columns in this table correspond to the Address bean's persistence fields. Entity beans do not have to define all the columns in the corresponding table as persistence fields. In fact, there's no requirement that an entity bean correspond to a single table; it may be persisted to columns in several different tables. The bottom line is that the container allows the abstract persistence schema of an entity bean to be mapped to a database in a variety of ways, allowing a clean separation between the persistence classes and the database.

In addition to the bean class, we must define the local interface for the Address EJB. This interface allows the EJB to be accessed by other entity beans (namely, the Customer EJB) within the same address space or process:

```
// Address EJB's local interface
public interface AddressLocal extends javax.ejb.EJBLocalObject {
    public String getStreet( );
    public void setStreet(String street);
```

```
        public String getCity( );
        public void setCity(String city);
        public String getState( );
        public void setState(String state);
        public String getZip( );
        public void setZip(String zip);
    }

    // Address EJB's local home interface
    public interface AddressHomeLocal extends javax.ejb.EJBLocalHome {
        public AddressLocal createAddress(String street,String city,
            String state,String zip) throws javax.ejb.CreateException;
        public AddressLocal findByPrimaryKey(Integer primaryKey)
            throws javax.ejb.FinderException;
    }
```

You may have noticed that the `ejbCreate( )` method of the `AddressBean` class and the `findByPrimaryKey( )` method of the home interface both define the primary key type as `java.lang.Integer`. The primary key is generated automatically. Most EJB vendors allow entity beans' primary keys to be mapped to autogenerated fields. If your vendor does not support autogenerated primary keys, you must set the primary key's value in the `ejbCreate( )` method.

The relationship field for the Address EJB is defined in the `CustomerBean` class using an abstract accessor method, the same way that persistence fields are declared. In the following code, the `CustomerBean` has been modified to include the Address EJB as a relationship field:

```
import javax.ejb.EntityContext;
import javax.ejb.CreateException;

public abstract class CustomerBean implements javax.ejb.EntityBean {
    ...

    // persistence relationship
    public abstract AddressLocal getHomeAddress( );
    public abstract void setHomeAddress(AddressLocal address);

    // persistence fields
    public abstract boolean getHasGoodCredit( );
    public abstract void setHasGoodCredit(boolean creditRating);
    ...
```

The `getHomeAddress( )` and `setHomeAddress( )` accessor methods are self-explanatory; they allow the bean to access and modify its `homeAddress` relationship. The name of the accessor method is determined by the name of the relationship field, as declared in the deployment descriptor. In this case, we have named the customer's address `homeAddress`, so the corresponding accessor method names will be `getHomeAddress( )` and `setHomeAddress( )`.

To accommodate the relationship between the Customer EJB and the home address, a foreign key, `ADDRESS_ID`, is needed in the `CUSTOMER` table. The foreign key points to the ADDRESS record. In practice, it would be more common to give the ADDRESS table a foreign key to the CUSTOMER table. However, the schema used here demonstrates alternative database mappings:

```
CREATE TABLE CUSTOMER
(
    ID INT PRIMARY KEY NOT NULL,
    LAST_NAME CHAR(20),
    FIRST_NAME CHAR(20),
    ADDRESS_ID INT
)
```

When a new Address EJB is created and set as the Customer EJB's homeAddress relationship, the Address EJB's primary key is placed in the ADDRESS_ID column of the CUSTOMER table:

```
// get local reference
AddressLocal address = ...

// establish the relationship
customer.setHomeAddress(address);
```

To give the Customer a home address, we need to deliver the address information to the Customer. This appears to be a simple matter of declaring matching setHomeAddress( )/getHomeAddress( ) accessors in the remote interface, but it's not! While it's valid to make persistence fields available to remote clients, persistence relationships are more complicated. The remote interface of a bean is not allowed to expose its relationship fields. In the case of the homeAddress field, we have declared the type to be AddressLocal, which is a local interface, so the setHomeAddress( )/getHomeAddress( ) accessors cannot be declared in the remote interface of the Customer EJB. The reason for this restriction on remote interfaces is fairly simple: the EJBLocalObject, which implements the local interface, is optimized for use within the same address space or process as the bean instance and is not capable of being used across the network. In other words, references that implement the local interface of a bean cannot be passed across the network, so a local interface cannot be declared as a return type of a parameter of a remote interface.

Local interfaces (interfaces that extend javax.ejb.EJBLocalObject), on the other hand, can expose any kind of relationship field. With local interfaces, the caller and the enterprise bean being called are located in the same address space, so they can pass around local references without a problem. For example, if we had defined a local interface for the Customer EJB, it could include a method that allows local clients to access its Address relationship directly:

```
public interface CustomerLocal extends javax.ejb.EJBLocalObject {
    public AddressLocal getHomeAddress( );
    public void setHomeAddress(AddressLocal address);
}
```

When it comes to the Address EJB, it's better to define a local interface only because it's such a fine-grained bean. To get around remote-interface restrictions, the business methods in the bean class exchange address data instead of Address references. For example, we can declare a method in the Customer bean that allows the client to send address information:

```
public abstract class CustomerBean implements javax.ejb.EntityBean {

    public Integer ejbCreate(Integer id) {
        setId(id);
        return null;
    }
    public void ejbPostCreate(Integer id) {
    }
    // business method
    public void setAddress(String street,String city,String state,String zip) {
        try {

            AddressLocal addr = this.getHomeAddress( );
            if(addr == null) {
                // Customer doesn't have an address yet. Create a new one.
                InitialContext cntx = new InitialContext( );
                AddressHomeLocal addrHome = (AddressHomeLocal)
                     cntx.lookup("java:comp/env/ejb/AddressHomeLocal");
                addr = addrHome.createAddress(street,city,state,zip);
                this.setHomeAddress(addr);
            } else {
                // Customer already has an address. Change its fields.
                addr.setStreet(street);
                addr.setCity(city);
                addr.setState(state);
                addr.setZip(zip);
            }

        } catch(Exception e) {
            throw new EJBException(e);
        }
    }

    ...
```

The setAddress( ) business method in the CustomerBean class is also declared in the remote interface of the Customer EJB, so it can be called by remote clients:

```
public interface CustomerRemote extends javax.ejb.EJBObject {

    public void setAddress(String street,String city,String state,String zip)
    throws RemoteException;

    public Name getName( ) throws RemoteException;
    public void setName(Name name) throws RemoteException;

    public boolean getHasGoodCredit( ) throws RemoteException;
    public void setHasGoodCredit(boolean creditRating) throws RemoteException;

}
```

When the CustomerRemote.setAddress( ) method is invoked on the CustomerBean, the method's arguments are used to create a new Address EJB and set it as the homeAddress relationship field, if one doesn't already exist. If the Customer EJB already has a homeAddress relationship, that Address EJB is modified to reflect the new address information.

When creating a new Address EJB, the home object is obtained from the JNDI ENC (environment naming context) and its createAddress( ) method is called. This results in the creation of a new Address EJB and the insertion of a corresponding ADDRESS record into the database. After the Address EJB is created, it's used in the setHomeAddress( ) method. The CustomerBean class must explicitly call the setHomeAddress( ) method, or the new address will not be assigned to the customer. Creating an Address EJB without assigning it to the customer results in a *disconnected* Address EJB. More precisely, it results in an ADDRESS record in the database that is not referenced by any CUSTOMER records. Disconnected entity beans are fairly normal and even desirable in many cases. In this case, however, we want the new Address EJB to be assigned to the homeAddress relationship field of the Customer EJB.

The viability of disconnected entities depends, in part, on the referential integrity of the database. For example, if the referential integrity allows only non-null values for the foreign key column, creating a disconnected entity may result in a database error.

When the setHomeAddress( ) method is invoked, the container links the ADDRESS record to the CUSTOMER record automatically. In this case, it places the ADDRESS primary key in the CUSTOMER record's ADDRESS_ID field and creates a reference from the CUSTOMER record to the ADDRESS record.

If the Customer EJB already has a homeAddress, we want to change its values instead of creating a new Address EJB. We don't need to use setHomeAddress( ) if we are simply updating the values of an existing Address EJB, because the Address EJB we modified already has a relationship with the entity bean.

We also want to provide clients with a business method for obtaining a Customer EJB's home address information. Since we are prohibited from sending an instance of the Address EJB directly to the client (because it's a local interface), we must package the address data in some other form and send that to the client. There are two solutions to this problem: acquire the remote interface of the Address EJB and return that; or return the data as a dependent value object.

We can obtain the remote interface for the Address EJB only if one is defined. The Address EJB is too fine-grained to justify creating a remote interface, but in many other circumstances, a bean may indeed want to have a remote interface. If, for example, the Customer EJB referenced a SalesPerson EJB, the CustomerBean could convert the local reference into a remote reference. This would be done by accessing the local EJB object, getting its primary key (EJBLocalObject.getPrimaryKey( )), obtaining the SalesPerson EJB's remote home from the JNDI ENC, and then using the primary key and remote home reference to find a remote interface reference:

```
public SalesRemote getSalesRep(){
    SalesLocal local = getSalesPerson();
    Integer primKey = local.getPrimaryKey();
    InitialContext cntx = new InitialContext();
    Object ref = cntx.lookup("java:comp/env/ejb/SalesHomeRemote");
    SalesHomeRemote home = (SalesHomeRemote)
        PortableRemoteObject.narrow(ref, SalesHomeRemote.class);

    SalesRemote remote = home.findByPrimaryKey( primKey );
    return remote;
}
```

The other option is to use a dependent value to pass the Address EJB's data between remote clients and the Customer EJB. This is the approach recommended for fine-grained beans like the Address EJB—we don't want to expose these beans directly to remote clients. The following code shows how the `AddressDO` dependent value class is used in conjunction with the local component interfaces of the Address EJB (the `DO` in `AddressDO` is a convention used in this book—it's a qualifier that stands for "dependent object"):

```
public abstract class CustomerBean implements javax.ejb.EntityBean {

    public Integer ejbCreate(Integer id) {
        setId(id);
        return null;
    }
    public void ejbPostCreate(Integer id) {
    }
    // business method
    public AddressDO getAddress() {
        AddressLocal addrLocal = getHomeAddress();
        if(addrLocal == null) return null;
        String street = addrLocal.getStreet();
        String city = addrLocal.getCity();
        String state = addrLocal.getState();
        String zip = addrLocal.getZip();
        AddressDO addrValue = new AddressDO(street,city,state,zip);
        return addrValue;
    }
    public void setAddress(AddressDO addrValue)
        throws EJBException {

        String street = addrValue.getStreet();
        String city = addrValue.getCity();
        String state = addrValue.getState();
        String zip = addrValue.getZip();

        AddressLocal addr = getHomeAddress();

        try {
```

```
        if(addr == null) {
            // Customer doesn't have an address yet. Create a new one.
            InitialContext cntx = new InitialContext( );
            AddressHomeLocal addrHome = (AddressHomeLocal)
                  cntx.lookup("java:comp/env/ejb/AddressHomeLocal");
            addr = addrHome.createAddress(street, city, state, zip);
            this.setHomeAddress(addr);
        } else {
            // Customer already has an address. Change its fields.
            addr.setStreet(street);
            addr.setCity(city);
            addr.setState(state);
            addr.setZip(zip);
        }

        } catch(NamingException ne) {
            throw new EJBException(ne);
        } catch(CreateException ce) {
            throw new EJBException(ce);
        }
    }
    ...
```

Here is the definition for an AddressDO dependent value class, which is used by the enterprise bean to send address information to the client:

```
public class AddressDO implements java.io.Serializable {
    private String street;
    private String city;
    private String state;
    private String zip;

    public AddressDO(String street, String city, String state, String zip ) {
        this.street = street;
        this.city = city;
        this.state = state;
        this.zip = zip;
    }
    public String getStreet( ) {
        return street;
    }
    public String getCity( ) {
        return city;
    }
    public String getState( ) {
        return state;
    }
    public String getZip( ) {
        return zip;
    }
}
```

The AddressDO dependent value is immutable: it cannot be altered once it is created. As stated earlier, immutability helps to reinforce the fact that the dependent value class is a copy, not a remote reference. To use the AddressDO, we add accessor methods to the CustomerRemote interface:

```
public interface CustomerRemote extends javax.ejb.EJBObject {

    public void setAddress(AddressDO address) throws RemoteException;
    public AddressDO getAddress( ) throws RemoteException;

    public void setAddress(String street,String city,String state,String zip)
    throws RemoteException;

    public Name getName( ) throws RemoteException;
    public void setName(Name name) throws RemoteException;

    public boolean getHasGoodCredit( ) throws RemoteException;
    public void setHasGoodCredit(boolean creditRating) throws RemoteException;

}
```

You can now use a client application to test the Customer EJB's relationship with the Address EJB. Here is the client code that creates a new Customer, gives it an address, and then changes the address:

```
import javax.naming.InitialContext;
import javax.rmi.PortableRemoteObject;
import javax.naming.Context;
import javax.naming.NamingException;
import java.util.Properties;

public class Client {
    public static void main(String [] args) throws Exception {
        // obtain CustomerHomeRemote
        Context jndiContext = getInitialContext( );
        Object obj=jndiContext.lookup("CustomerHomeRemote");
        CustomerHomeRemote home = (CustomerHomeRemote)
            javax.rmi.PortableRemoteObject.narrow(obj,
            CustomerHomeRemote.class);

        // create a Customer
        Integer primaryKey = new Integer(1);
        CustomerRemote customer = home.create(primaryKey);

        // create an address
        AddressDO address = new AddressDO("1010 Colorado",
            "Austin", "TX", "78701");
        // set address
        customer.setAddress(address);

        address = customer.getAddress( );

        System.out.print(primaryKey+" = ");
        System.out.println(address.getStreet( ));
        System.out.println(address.getCity( )+","+
                           address.getState( )+" "+
                           address.getZip( ));
```

```
        // create a new address
        address = new AddressDO("1600 Pennsylvania Avenue NW",
            "DC", "WA", "20500");

        // change Customer's address
        customer.setAddress(address);

        address = customer.getAddress( );

        System.out.print(primaryKey+" = ");
        System.out.println(address.getStreet( ));
        System.out.println(address.getCity( )+","+
                           address.getState( )+" "+
                           address.getZip( ));

        // remove Customer
        customer.remove( );
    }

    public static Context getInitialContext( )
        throws javax.naming.NamingException {
        Properties p = new Properties( );
        // ... Specify the JNDI properties specific to the vendor.
        //return new javax.naming.InitialContext(p);
        return null;
    }
}
```

The following listing shows the EJB 2.1 deployment descriptor for the Customer and Address EJBs. You don't need to worry about the details of the deployment descriptor yet; it will be covered in depth in Chapter 7.

```
<?xml version="1.0" encoding="UTF-8" ?>
<ejb-jar
     xmlns="http://java.sun.com/xml/ns/j2ee"
     xmlns:xsi="http://www.w3.org/2001/XMLSchema-instance"
     xsi:schemaLocation="http://java.sun.com/xml/ns/j2ee
                         http://java.sun.com/xml/ns/j2ee/ejb-jar_2_1.xsd"
     version="2.1">

    <enterprise-beans>
        <entity>
            <ejb-name>CustomerEJB</ejb-name>
            <home>com.titan.customer.CustomerHomeRemote</home>
            <remote>com.titan.customer.CustomerRemote</remote>
            <ejb-class>com.titan.customer.CustomerBean</ejb-class>
            <persistence-type>Container</persistence-type>
            <prim-key-class>java.lang.Integer</prim-key-class>
            <reentrant>False</reentrant>
            <cmp-version>2.x</cmp-version>
            <abstract-schema-name>Customer</abstract-schema-name>
            <cmp-field><field-name>id</field-name></cmp-field>
            <cmp-field><field-name>lastName</field-name></cmp-field>
            <cmp-field><field-name>firstName</field-name></cmp-field>
```

```
            <primkey-field>id</primkey-field>
            <security-identity><use-caller-identity/></security-identity>
        </entity>
        <entity>
            <ejb-name>AddressEJB</ejb-name>
            <local-home>com.titan.address.AddressHomeLocal</local-home>
            <local>com.titan.address.AddressLocal</local>
            <ejb-class>com.titan.address.AddressBean</ejb-class>
            <persistence-type>Container</persistence-type>
            <prim-key-class>java.lang.Integer</prim-key-class>
            <reentrant>False</reentrant>
            <cmp-version>2.x</cmp-version>
            <abstract-schema-name>Address</abstract-schema-name>
            <cmp-field><field-name>id</field-name></cmp-field>
            <cmp-field><field-name>street</field-name></cmp-field>
            <cmp-field><field-name>city</field-name></cmp-field>
            <cmp-field><field-name>state</field-name></cmp-field>
            <cmp-field><field-name>zip</field-name></cmp-field>
            <primkey-field>id</primkey-field>
            <security-identity><use-caller-identity/></security-identity>
        </entity>
    </enterprise-beans>
    <relationships>
        <ejb-relation>
            <ejb-relation-name>Customer-Address</ejb-relation-name>
            <ejb-relationship-role>
                <ejb-relationship-role-name>
                    Customer-has-an-Address
                </ejb-relationship-role-name>
                <multiplicity>One</multiplicity>
                <relationship-role-source>
                    <ejb-name>CustomerEJB</ejb-name>
                </relationship-role-source>
                <cmr-field>
                    <cmr-field-name>homeAddress</cmr-field-name>
                </cmr-field>
            </ejb-relationship-role>
            <ejb-relationship-role>
                <ejb-relationship-role-name>
                    Address-belongs-to-Customer
                </ejb-relationship-role-name>
                <multiplicity>One</multiplicity>
                <relationship-role-source>
                    <ejb-name>AddressEJB</ejb-name>
                </relationship-role-source>
            </ejb-relationship-role>
        </ejb-relation>
    </relationships>
    <assembly-descriptor>
        <security-role>
            <role-name>Employees</role-name>
        </security-role>
        <method-permission>
            <role-name>Employees</role-name>
```

```
            <method>
                <ejb-name>CustomerEJB</ejb-name>
                <method-name>*</method-name>
            </method>
            <method>
                <ejb-name>AddressEJB</ejb-name>
                <method-name>*</method-name>
            </method>
        </method-permission>
        <container-transaction>
            <method>
                <ejb-name>AddressEJB</ejb-name>
                <method-name>*</method-name>
            </method>
            <method>
                <ejb-name>CustomerEJB</ejb-name>
                <method-name>*</method-name>
            </method>
            <trans-attribute>Required</trans-attribute>
        </container-transaction>
    </assembly-descriptor>
</ejb-jar>
```

The EJB 2.0 deployment descriptor looks the same, except it uses a document declaration that points to a DTD instead referencing an XML Schema. Here's the difference:

```
<?xml version="1.0" encoding="UTF-8" ?>
<!DOCTYPE ejb-jar PUBLIC "-//Sun Microsystems, Inc.//DTD Enterprise
JavaBeans 2.0//EN" "http://java.sun.com/dtd/ejb-jar_2_0.dtd">

<ejb-jar>
   ...
</ejb-jar>
```

Exercise 6.3 in the Workbook shows how to deploy this example on the JBoss server.

CHAPTER 7

CMP: Entity Relationships

Chapter 6 covered basic container-managed persistence (CMP), including container-managed persistence fields and an introduction to a basic container-managed relationship field. This chapter develops the Customer EJB and discusses the seven relationships that entity beans can have with each other.

In order to model real-world business concepts, entity beans must be capable of forming complex relationships. Chapter 6 demonstrated a one-to-one relationship between the Customer and Address EJBs. This relationship was unidirectional: the Customer had a reference to the Address, but the Address did not have a reference back to the Customer. This is a perfectly legitimate relationship, but other relationships are possible. For example, each Address could also reference its Customer, a bidirectional, one-to-one relationship in which both participants maintain references to each other. Entity beans can also have one-to-many, many-to-one, and many-to-many relationships. For example, the Customer EJB may have many phone numbers, but each phone number belongs to only one Customer (a one-to-many relationship). A Customer may have been on many Cruises, and each Cruise has many Customers (a many-to-many relationship).

The Seven Relationship Types

Seven types of relationships can exist between EJBs. There are four types of cardinality: *one-to-one*, *one-to-many*, *many-to-one*, and *many-to-many*. In addition, each relationship can be either *unidirectional* or *bidirectional*. These options seem to yield eight possibilities, but if you think about it, you'll realize that one-to-many and many-to-one bidirectional relationships are actually the same thing. Thus, there are only seven distinct relationship types. To understand relationships, it helps to think about some simple examples:

One-to-one, unidirectional

The relationship between a customer and an address. You clearly want to be able to look up a customer's address, but you probably don't care about looking up an address's customer.

One-to-one, bidirectional
The relationship between a customer and a credit card number. Given a customer, you obviously want to be able to look up his credit card number. Given a credit card number, it is also conceivable that you would want to look up the customer who owns the credit card.

One-to-many, unidirectional
The relationship between a customer and a phone number. A customer can have many phone numbers (business, home, cell, etc.). You might need to look up a customer's phone number, but you probably wouldn't use one of those numbers to look up the customer.

One-to-many, bidirectional
The relationship between a cruise and a reservation. Given a reservation, you want to be able to look up the cruise for which the reservation was made. And given a particular cruise, you want to be able to look up all reservations. (Note that a many-to-one bidirectional relationship is just another perspective on the same concept.)

Many-to-one, unidirectional
The relationship between a cruise and a ship. You want to be able to look up the ship that will be used for a particular cruise, and many cruises share the same ship, though at different times. It's less useful to look up the ship to see which cruises are associated with it, although if you want this capability, you can implement a many-to-one bidirectional relationship.

Many-to-many, unidirectional
The relationship between a reservation and a cabin. It's possible to make a reservation for multiple cabins, and you clearly want to be able to look up the cabin assigned to a reservation. However, you're not likely to want to look up the reservation associated with a particular cabin. (If you think you need to do so, implement it as a bidirectional relationship.)

Many-to-many, bidirectional
The relationship between a cruise and a customer. A customer can make reservations on many cruises, and each cruise has many customers. You want to be able to look up both the cruises on which a customer has a booking, and the customers that will be going on any given cruise.

Abstract Persistence Schema

In Chapter 6, you learned how to form a basic relationship between the Customer and Address entity beans using the abstract programming model. In reality, the abstract programming model is only half of the equation. In addition to declaring abstract accessor methods, a bean developer must describe the cardinality and direction of the entity-to-entity relationships in the bean's deployment descriptor. This step is handled in the `<relationships>` section of the XML deployment descriptor. As we discuss each type of relationship, we will examine both the abstract programming model and the XML elements. The purpose of this section is to introduce you to the basic elements used in the XML deployment descriptor, to better prepare you for subsequent sections on specific relationship types.

In this book we always refer to the Java programming idioms used to describe relationships—specifically, the abstract accessor methods—as the *abstract programming model*. When referring to the XML deployment descriptor elements, we use the term *abstract persistence schema*. In the EJB specification, the term "abstract persistence schema" actually refers to both the Java idioms and the XML elements, but this book separates these concepts so we can discuss them more easily.

An entity bean's abstract persistence schema is defined in the `<relationships>` section of the XML deployment descriptor for that bean. The `<relationships>` section falls between the `<enterprise-beans>` section and the `<assembly-descriptor>` section.

```
<ejb-jar>
    <enterprise-beans>
    ...
    </enterprise-beans>
    <relationships>
        <ejb-relation>
        ...
        </ejb-relation>
        <ejb-relation>
        ...
        </ejb-relation>
    </relationships>
    <assembly-descriptor>
    ...
    </assembly-descriptor>
</ejb-jar>
```

Defining relationship fields requires an `<ejb-relation>` element for each entity-to-entity relationship. For each set of abstract accessor methods that define a relationship field, there must be an `<ejb-relation>` element in the deployment descriptor. EJB requires the entity beans that participate in a relationship to be defined in the same XML deployment descriptor.

Here is a partial listing of the deployment descriptor for the Customer and Address EJBs, with emphasis on the elements that define the relationship:

```
<ejb-jar ...>
    ...
    <enterprise-beans>
        <entity>
            <ejb-name>CustomerEJB</ejb-name>
            <local-home>com.titan.customer.CusomterHomeLocal</local-home>
            <local>com.titan.customer.CustomerLocal</local>
            ...
        </entity>
        <entity>
```

```
            <ejb-name>AddressEJB</ejb-name>
            <local-home>com.titan.address.AddressHomeLocal</local-home>
            <local>com.titan.address.AddressLocal</local>
            ...
        </entity>
        ...
    </enterprise-beans>

    <relationships>
        <ejb-relation>
            <ejb-relation-name>Customer-Address</ejb-relation-name>
            <ejb-relationship-role>
                <ejb-relationship-role-name>
                    Customer-has-an-Address
                </ejb-relationship-role-name>
                <multiplicity>One</multiplicity>
                <relationship-role-source>
                    <ejb-name>CustomerEJB</ejb-name>
                </relationship-role-source>
                <cmr-field>
                    <cmr-field-name>homeAddress</cmr-field-name>
                </cmr-field>
            </ejb-relationship-role>
            <ejb-relationship-role>
                <ejb-relationship-role-name>
                    Address-belongs-to-Customer
                </ejb-relationship-role-name>
                <multiplicity>One</multiplicity>
                <relationship-role-source>
                    <ejb-name>AddressEJB</ejb-name>
                </relationship-role-source>
            </ejb-relationship-role>
        </ejb-relation>
    </relationships>
</ejb-jar>
```

Every relationship may have a relationship name, which is declared in the `<ejb-relation-name>` element. This serves to identify the relationship for individuals reading the deployment descriptor or for deployment tools, but it's not required.

Every `<ejb-relation>` element has exactly two `<ejb-relationship-role>` elements, one for each participant in the relationship. In the previous example, the first `<ejb-relationship-role>` declares the Customer EJB's role in the relationship. We know this because the `<relationship-role-source>` element specifies the `<ejb-name>` as `CustomerEJB`. `CustomerEJB` is the `<ejb-name>` used in the Customer EJB's original declaration in the `<enterprise-beans>` section. The `<relationship-role-source>` element's `<ejb-name>` must always match an `<ejb-name>` element in the `<enterprise-beans>` section.

The `<ejb-relationship-role>` element also declares the cardinality, or *multiplicity*, of the role. The `<multiplicity>` element can either be `One` or `Many`. In this case, the Customer EJB's `<multiplicity>` element has a value of `One`, which means that every

Address EJB has a relationship with exactly *one* Customer EJB. The Address EJB's `<multiplicity>` element also specifies `One`, which means that every Customer EJB has a relationship with exactly one Address EJB. If the Customer EJB had a relationship with many Address EJBs, the Address EJB's `<multiplicity>` element would be set to `Many`.

In Chapter 6, the Customer EJB had abstract accessor methods for getting and setting the Address EJB in the `homeAddress` field, but the Address EJB did not have abstract accessor methods for the Customer EJB. In this case, the Customer EJB maintains a reference to the Address EJB, but the Address EJB doesn't maintain a reference back to the Customer EJB. This is a unidirectional relationship, which means that only one of the entity beans in the relationship maintains a container-managed relationship field.

If the bean described by the `<ejb-relationship-role>` element maintains a reference to the other bean in the relationship, that reference must be declared as a *container-managed relationship field* in the `<cmr-field>` element. The `<cmr-field>` element is declared under the `<ejb-relationship-role>` element:

```
<ejb-relationship-role>
    <ejb-relationship-role-name>
        Customer-has-an-Address
    </ejb-relationship-role-name>
    <multiplicity>One</multiplicity>
    <relationship-role-source>
        <ejb-name>CustomerEJB</ejb-name>
    </relationship-role-source>
    <cmr-field>
        <cmr-field-name>homeAddress</cmr-field-name>
    </cmr-field>
</ejb-relationship-role>
```

EJB requires that the `<cmr-field-name>` begin with a lowercase letter. For every relationship field defined by a `<cmr-field>` element, there must be a pair of matching abstract accessor methods in the bean class. One method in this pair must be defined with the method name `set<cmr-field-name>( )`, with the first letter of the `<cmr-field-name>` value changed to uppercase. The other method is defined as `get<cmr-field-name>( )`, also with the first letter of the `<cmr-field-name>` value in uppercase. In the previous example, the `<cmr-field-name>` is `homeAddress`, which corresponds to the `getHomeAddress( )` and `setHomeAddress( )` abstract accessor methods defined in the `CustomerBean` class:

```
// bean class code
public abstract void setHomeAddress(AddressLocal address);
public abstract AddressLocal getHomeAddress( );

// XML deployment descriptor declaration
<cmr-field>
    <cmr-field-name>homeAddress</cmr-field-name>
</cmr-field>
```

The return type of the `get<cmr-field-name>()` method and the parameter type of the `set<cmr-field-name>()` must be the same. The type must be the local interface of the entity bean that is referenced or one of two `java.util.Collection` types. In the case of the `homeAddress` relationship field, we are using the Address EJB's local interface, `AddressLocal`. Returning a collection is discussed later in this chapter.

Now that we have established a basic understanding of how elements are declared, we are ready to discuss each of the seven types of relationships. In the process, we will introduce additional entity beans that have relationships with the Customer EJB, including the CreditCard, Phone, Ship, and Reservation EJBs.

It's important to understand that although entity beans may have both local and remote interfaces, a container-managed relationship field can use only the entity bean's local interface when persisting a relationship. So, for example, it is illegal to define an abstract accessor method that has an argument type of `javax.ejb.EJBObject` (a remote interface type). All container-managed relationships are based on `javax.ejb.EJBLocalObject` (local interface) types.

Database Modeling

This chapter discusses several different database table schemas. These schemas demonstrate possible relationships between entities in the database; they don't represent the only way to implement these relationships, or even the best way. For example, the Address-Customer relationship is implemented by having the `CUSTOMER` table maintain a foreign key to the `ADDRESS` table. This is not how most databases will be organized—instead, they will probably use a link table or have the `ADDRESS` table maintain a foreign key to the `CUSTOMER`. The difference really isn't important for the purposes of this book, as EJB's container-managed persistence can support different database organizations. If you have the luxury of defining your own database schema, organize your database in whatever way makes the most sense for your application. If you've inherited a database schema, container-managed persistence should be flexible enough to support the database organization you already have.

Throughout this chapter, we assume that the database tables are created before the EJB application—in other words, that the EJB application is mapped to a legacy database. Some vendors offer tools that generate tables automatically according to the relationships defined between the entity beans. These tools may create schemas that are very different from the ones explored here. In other cases, vendors that support established database schemas may not have the flexibility to support the schemas illustrated in this chapter. As an EJB developer, you must be flexible enough to adapt to the facilities provided by your EJB vendor.

One-to-One, Unidirectional Relationship

An example of a one-to-one, unidirectional relationship is the one between the Customer EJB and the Address EJB defined in Chapter 6. In this example, each Customer has exactly one Address, and each Address has exactly one Customer. Which bean references which determines the direction of navigation. While the Customer has a reference to the Address, the Address doesn't reference the Customer. The relationship is therefore unidirectional—you can only go from the Customer to the Address, not the other way around. In other words, an Address EJB has no idea who owns it. Figure 7-1 shows this relationship.

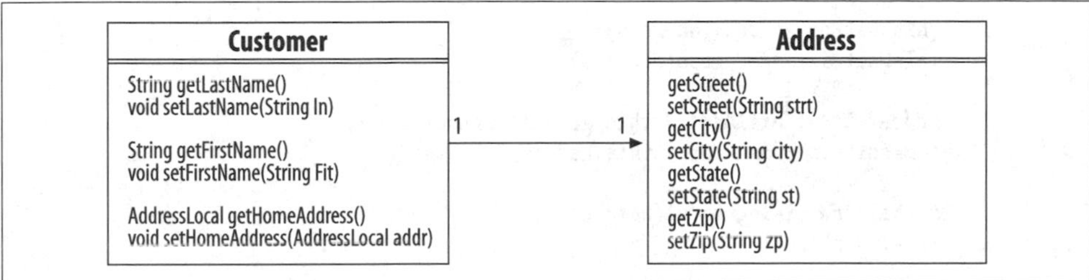

Figure 7-1. One-to-one, unidirectional relationship

Relational database schema

As shown in Figure 7-2, one-to-one, unidirectional relationships normally use a fairly typical relational database schema in which one table contains a foreign key (pointer) to another table. In this case, the `CUSTOMER` table contains a foreign key to the `ADDRESS` table, but the `ADDRESS` table doesn't contain a foreign key to the `CUSTOMER` table. This allows records in the `ADDRESS` table to be shared by other tables, a scenario explored in the "Many-to-Many, Unidirectional Relationship" section.

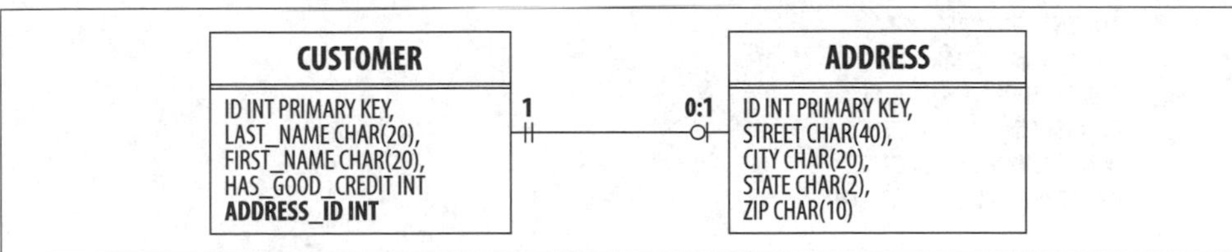

Figure 7-2. One-to-one, unidirectional relationship in RDBMS

Abstract programming model

In unidirectional relationships (navigated only one way), only one of the enterprise beans defines abstract accessor methods that let it get or set the other bean in the relationship. Thus, inside the `CustomerBean` class, you can call the `getHomeAddress()`/`setHomeAddress()` methods to access the Address EJBs, but there are no methods inside the `AddressBean` class to access the Customer EJB.

The Address EJB can be shared between relationship fields of the same enterprise bean, but it cannot be shared between Customer EJBs. If, for example, the Customer EJB defines two relationship fields, billingAddress and homeAddress, as one-to-one, unidirectional relationships with the Address EJB, these two fields can reference the same Address EJB:

```
public abstract class CustomerBean implements javax.ejb.EntityBean {
    ...
    public void setAddress(String street,String city,String state,String zip) {
        ...

        address = addressHome.createAddress(street, city, state, zip);

        this.setHomeAddress(address);
        this.setBillingAddress(address);

        AddressLocal billAddr = this.getBillingAddress( );
        AddressLocal homeAddr = this.getHomeAddress( );

        if(billAddr.isIdentical(homeAddr))
        // always true

        ...
    }
    ...
}
```

If at any time you want to make the billingAddress different from the homeAddress, you can simply set it equal to a different Address EJB. Sharing a reference to another bean between two relationship fields in the same entity is sometimes very convenient, though. In order to support this type of relationship, a new billing address field might be added to the CUSTOMER table:

```
CREATE TABLE CUSTOMER
(
    ID INT PRIMARY KEY,
    LAST_NAME CHAR(20),
    FIRST_NAME CHAR(20),
    HAS_GOOD_CREDIT INT,
    HOME_ADDRESS_ID INT,
    BILLING_ADDRESS_ID INT
)
```

As the earlier example shows, it is possible for two fields in a bean (in this case, the homeAddress and billingAddress fields in the Customer EJB) to reference the same relationship (i.e., a single Address EJB) if the relationship type is the same. However, it is not possible to share a single Address EJB between two different Customer EJBs. If, for example, the home Address of Customer A were assigned as the home Address of Customer B, the Address would be moved, not shared, so that Customer A wouldn't have a home Address any longer. As you can see in Figure 7-3, Address 2 is initially assigned to Customer B, but becomes disconnected when Address 1 is reassigned to Customer B.

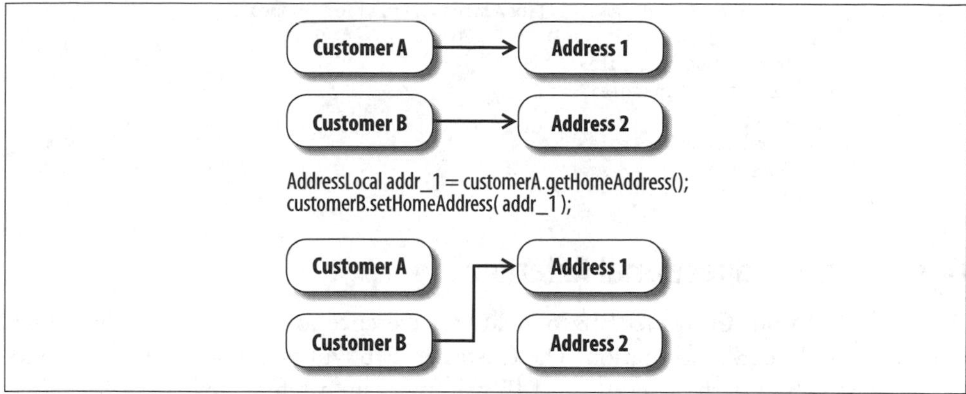

Figure 7-3. Exchanging references in a one-to-one, unidirectional relationship

This seemingly strange side effect is a result of how the relationship is defined. The Customer-to-Address EJB relationship was defined as one-to-one, so the Address EJB can be referenced by only one Customer EJB.

If the Customer EJB does not have an Address EJB associated with its `homeAddress` field, the `getHomeAddress( )` method will return `null`. This is true of all container-managed relationship fields that reference a single entity bean.

Abstract persistence schema

We defined the XML elements for the Customer-Address relationship earlier in this chapter, so we won't go over them again. The `<ejb-relation>` element used in that section declared a one-to-one, unidirectional relationship. If, however, the Customer EJB maintained two relationship fields with the Address EJB—`homeAddress` and `billingAddress`—each of these relationships would have to be described in its own `<ejb-relation>` element:

```
<relationships>
    <ejb-relation>
        <ejb-relation-name>Customer-HomeAddress</ejb-relation-name>
        <ejb-relationship-role>
            ...
            <cmr-field>
                <cmr-field-name>homeAddress</cmr-field-name>
            </cmr-field>
        </ejb-relationship-role>
        <ejb-relationship-role>
            ...
        </ejb-relationship-role>
    </ejb-relation>
    <ejb-relation>
        <ejb-relation-name>Customer-BillingAddress</ejb-relation-name>
        <ejb-relationship-role>
            ...
            <cmr-field>
```

```
                <cmr-field-name>billingAddress</cmr-field-name>
            </cmr-field>
        </ejb-relationship-role>
        <ejb-relationship-role>
            ...
        </ejb-relationship-role>
    </ejb-relation>
</relationships>
```

One-to-One, Bidirectional Relationship

We can expand our Customer EJB to include a reference to a CreditCard EJB, which maintains credit card information. The Customer EJB will maintain a reference to its CreditCard EJB, and the CreditCard EJB will maintain a reference back to the Customer—this makes good sense, since a CreditCard should be aware of who owns it. Since each CreditCard has a reference back to one Customer and each Customer references one CreditCard, we have a one-to-one bidirectional relationship.

Relational database schema

The CreditCard EJB has a corresponding `CREDIT_CARD` table, so we need to add a `CREDIT_CARD` foreign key to the `CUSTOMER` table:

```
CREATE TABLE CREDIT_CARD
(
    ID INT PRIMARY KEY NOT NULL,
    EXP_DATE DATE,
    NUMBER CHAR(20),
    NAME CHAR(40),
    ORGANIZATION CHAR(20),
    CUSTOMER_ID INT
)

CREATE TABLE CUSTOMER
(
    ID INT PRIMARY KEY,
    LAST_NAME CHAR(20),
    FIRST_NAME CHAR(20),
    HAS_GOOD_CREDIT INT,
    HOME_ADDRESS_ID INT,
    BILLING_ADDRESS_ID INT,
    CREDIT_CARD_ID INT
)
```

One-to-one, bidirectional relationships may model relational database schemas in which the two tables hold foreign keys for one another (specifically, two rows in different tables point to each other). Figure 7-4 illustrates how this schema would be implemented for rows in the `CUSTOMER` and `CREDIT_CARD` tables.

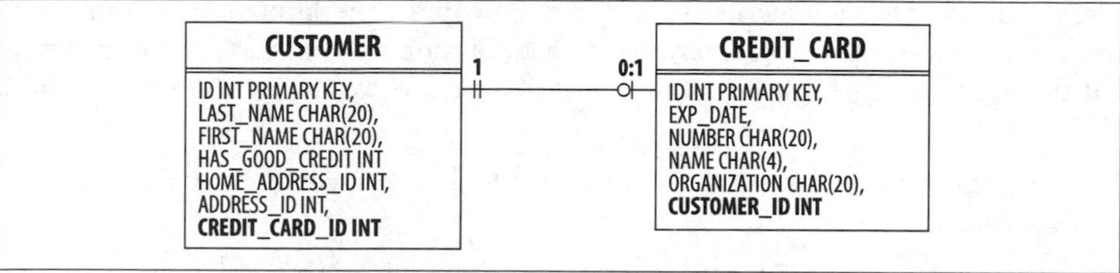

Figure 7-4. One-to-one, bidirectional relationship in RDBMS

It is also possible for a one-to-one, bidirectional relationship to be established through a linking table, in which each foreign key column must be unique. Using a linking table is convenient when you do not want to impose relationships on the original tables. We will use linking tables in one-to-many and many-to-many relationships later in this chapter. The abstract persistence schema of an entity bean may map to a variety of database schemas; the database schemas used in these examples are only a few possiblities.

Abstract programming model

To model the relationship between the Customer and CreditCard EJBs, we need to declare a relationship field named `customer` in the `CreditCardBean` class:

```
public abstract class CreditCardBean extends javax.ejb.EntityBean {

    ...

    // relationship fields
    public abstract CustomerLocal getCustomer( );
    public abstract void setCustomer(CustomerLocal local);

    // persistence fields
    public abstract Integer getId( );
    public abstract void setId(Integer id);
    public abstract Date getExpirationDate( );
    public abstract void setExpirationDate(Date date);
    public abstract String getNumber( );
    public abstract void setNumber(String number);
    public abstract String getNameOnCard( );
    public abstract void setNameOnCard(String name);
    public abstract String getCreditOrganization( );
    public abstract void setCreditOrganization(String org);

    // standard callback methods
    ...

}
```

We use the Customer EJB's local interface (assume one has been created), because relationship fields require local interface types. All the relationships explored in the rest of this chapter assume local interfaces. Of course, the limitation of using local interfaces instead of remote interfaces is that you don't have location transparency. All the entity beans must be located in the same process or Java Virtual Machine (JVM).

We can also add a set of abstract accessor methods in the `CustomerBean` class for the `creditCard` relationship field:

```
public abstract class CustomerBean implements javax.ejb.EntityBean {
    ...
    public abstract void setCreditCard(CreditCardLocal card);
    public abstract CreditCardLocal getCreditCard( );
    ...
}
```

Although a `setCustomer( )` method is available in the `CreditCardBean`, we do not have to set the Customer reference on the CreditCard EJB explicitly. When a CreditCard EJB reference is passed into the `setCreditCard( )` method on the `CustomerBean` class, the EJB container automatically establishes the customer relationship on the Credit-Card EJB to point back to the Customer EJB:

```
public abstract class CustomerBean implements javax.ejb.EntityBean {
    ...
    // The setCreditCard() business method uses the setCreditCard( ) abstract accessor
    public void setCreditCard(Date exp, String numb, String name, String org)
        throws CreateException {
        ...

        card = creditCardHome.create(exp,numb,name,org);

        // the CreditCard EJB's customer field will be set automatically
        this.setCreditCard(card);
        CustomerLocal customer = card.getCustomer( );

        if(customer.isIdentical(ejbContext.getEJBLocalObject( ))
        // always true

        ...
    }
    ...
}
```

The rules for sharing a single bean in a one-to-one, bidirectional relationship are the same as those for one-to-one, unidirectional relationships. While the CreditCard EJB may be shared between relationship fields of the same Customer EJB, it can't be shared between different Customer EJBs. As Figure 7-5 shows, assigning Customer A's `CreditCard` to Customer B disassociates that `CreditCard` from Customer A and moves it to Customer B.

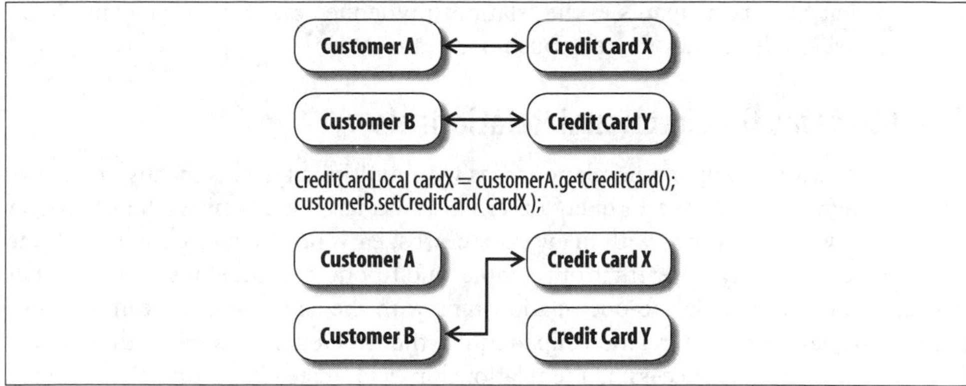

Figure 7-5. Exchanging references in a one-to-one, bidirectional relationship

Abstract persistence schema

The `<ejb-relation>` element that defines the Customer-to-CreditCard relationship is similar to the one used for the Customer-to-Address relationship, with one important difference—both `<ejb-relationship-role>` elements have a `<cmr-field>`:

```
<relationships>
    <ejb-relation>
        <ejb-relation-name>Customer-CreditCard</ejb-relation-name>
        <ejb-relationship-role>
            <ejb-relationship-role-name>
                Customer-has-a-CreditCard
            </ejb-relationship-role-name>
            <multiplicity>One</multiplicity>
            <relationship-role-source>
                <ejb-name>CustomerEJB</ejb-name>
            </relationship-role-source>
            <cmr-field>
                <cmr-field-name>creditCard</cmr-field-name>
            </cmr-field>
        </ejb-relationship-role>
        <ejb-relationship-role>
            <ejb-relationship-role-name>
                CreditCard-belongs-to-Customer
            </ejb-relationship-role-name>
            <multiplicity>One</multiplicity>
            <relationship-role-source>
                <ejb-name>CreditCardEJB</ejb-name>
            </relationship-role-source>
            <cmr-field>
                <cmr-field-name>customer</cmr-field-name>
            </cmr-field>
        </ejb-relationship-role>
    </ejb-relation>
</relationships>
```

The fact that both participants in the relationship define `<cmr-field>` elements (relationship fields) tells us that the relationship is bidirectional.

One-to-Many, Unidirectional Relationship

Entity beans can also maintain relationships with multiplicity. This means one entity bean can aggregate or contain many other entity beans. For example, the Customer EJB may have relationships with many Phone EJBs, each of which represents a phone number. This is very different from simple one-to-one relationships—or, for that matter, from multiple one-to-one relationships with the same type of bean. One-to-many and many-to-many relationships require the developer to work with a collection of references when accessing the relationship field, instead of a single reference.

Relational database schema

To illustrate a one-to-many, unidirectional relationship, we will use a new entity bean, the Phone EJB, for which we must define a table, the `PHONE` table:

```
CREATE TABLE PHONE
(
    ID INT PRIMARY KEY NOT NULL,
    NUMBER CHAR(20),
    TYPE INT,
    CUSTOMER_ID INT
)
```

One-to-many, unidirectional relationships between the `CUSTOMER` and `PHONE` tables could be implemented in a variety of ways. For this example, we chose to have the `PHONE` table include a foreign key to the `CUSTOMER` table.

The table of aggregated data can maintain a column of nonunique foreign keys to the aggregating table. In the case of the Customer and Phone EJBs, the `PHONE` table maintains a foreign key to the `CUSTOMER` table, and one or more `PHONE` records may contain foreign keys to the same `CUSTOMER` record. In other words, in the database, the `PHONE` records point to the `CUSTOMER` records. In the abstract programming model, however, it is the Customer EJB that points to the Phone EJBs—two schemas are reversed. How does this work? The container system hides the reverse pointer so that it appears as if the Customer is aware of the Phone EJB, and not the other way around. When you ask the container to return a `Collection` of Phone EJBs (invoking the `getPhoneNumbers()` method), it queries the `PHONE` table for all the records with a foreign key matching the Customer EJB's primary key. The use of reverse pointers in this type of relationship is illustrated in Figure 7-6.

This database schema illustrates that the structure and relationships of the actual database can differ from the relationships as defined in the abstract programming model. In this case, the tables are set up in reverse, but the EJB container system will manage the beans to meet the specification of the bean developer. When you are

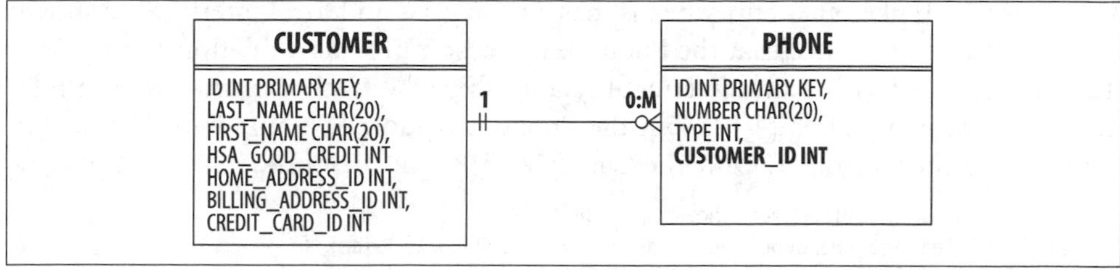

Figure 7-6. One-to-many, unidirectional relationship in RDBMS using reverse pointers

dealing with legacy databases (i.e., databases that were established before the EJB application), reverse-pointer scenarios like the one illustrated here are common, so supporting this kind of relationship mapping is important.

A simpler implementation of the Customer-Phone relationship could use a link table that maintains two columns with foreign keys pointing to both the `CUSTOMER` and `PHONE` records. We could then place a constraint on the `PHONE` foreign key column in the link table to ensure that it contains only unique entries (i.e., that every phone has only one customer), while allowing the `CUSTOMER` foreign key column to contain duplicates. The advantage of the link table is that it doesn't impose the relationship between the `CUSTOMER` and `PHONE` records onto either of the tables.

Abstract programming model

In the abstract programming model, we represent multiplicity by defining a relationship field that can point to many entity beans. To do this, we employ the same abstract accessor methods we used for one-to-one relationships, but this time we set the field type to either `java.util.Collection` or `java.util.Set`. The `Collection` maintains a homogeneous group of local EJB object references, which means it contains many references to one kind of entity bean. The `Collection` type may contain duplicate references to the same entity bean, while the `Set` type may not.

For example, a Customer EJB may have relationships with several phone numbers (e.g., a home phone, work phone, cell phone, fax, etc.), each represented by a Phone EJB. Instead of having a different relationship field for each of these Phone EJBs, the Customer EJB keeps all the Phone EJBs in a collection-based relationship field, which can be accessed through abstract accessor methods:

```
public abstract class CustomerBean implements javax.ejb.EntityBean {
    ...
    // relationship fields
    public abstract Collection getPhoneNumbers( );
    public abstract void setPhoneNumbers(Collection phones);

    public abstract AddressLocal getHomeAddress();( )
    public abstract void setHomeAddress(AddressLocal local);
    ...
```

The Phone EJB, like other entity beans, has a bean class and local interface, as shown in the next listing. Notice that the PhoneBean doesn't provide a relationship field for the Customer EJB. It's a unidirectional relationship; the Customer maintains a relationship with many Phone EJBs, but the Phone EJBs do not maintain a relationship field back to the Customer. Only the Customer EJB is aware of the relationship:

```
// the local interface for the Phone EJB
public interface PhoneLocal extends javax.ejb.EJBLocalObject {
    final public static byte HOME_PHONE = (byte)1;
    final public static byte WORK_PHONE = (byte)2;
    final public static byte CELL_PHONE = (byte)3;

    public String getNumber( );
    public void setNumber(String number);
    public byte getType( );
    public void setType(byte type);
}

// the bean class for the Phone EJB
public abstract class PhoneBean implements javax.ejb.EntityBean {

    public Integer ejbCreate(String number, byte type) {
        setNumber(number);
        setType(type);
        return null;
    }
    public void ejbPostCreate(String number,byte type) {
    }

    // persistence fields
    public abstract Integer getId( );
    public abstract void setId(Integer id);
    public abstract String getNumber( );
    public abstract void setNumber(String number);
    public abstract byte getType( );
    public abstract void setType(byte type);

    // standard callback methods
    ...
}
```

To illustrate how an entity bean uses a collection-based relationship field, we define a method in the `CustomerBean` class that allows remote clients to add new phone numbers. The method, `addPhoneNumber( )`, uses the phone number arguments to create a new Phone EJB and then add that Phone EJB to a collection-based relationship field named `phoneNumbers`:

```
public abstract class CustomerBean implements javax.ejb.EntityBean {

    // business methods
    public void addPhoneNumber(String number, byte type) {
```

```
        InitialContext jndiEnc = new InitialContext( );
        PhoneHomeLocal phoneHome =  (PhoneHomeLocal)
           jndiEnc.lookup("java:comp/env/ejb/PhoneHomeLocal");
        PhoneLocal phone = phoneHome.create(number,type);

        Collection phoneNumbers = this.getPhoneNumbers( );
        phoneNumbers.add(phone);

    }
    ...
    // relationship fields
    public abstract java.util.Collection getPhoneNumbers( );
    public abstract void setPhoneNumbers(java.util.Collection phones);

    ...
```

Note that we created the Phone EJB first, then added it to the phoneNumbers collection-based relationship. We obtained the phoneNumbers Collection object from the getPhoneNumbers( ) accessor method, then added the new Phone EJB to the Collection just as we would add any object to a Collection. Adding the Phone EJB to the Collection causes the EJB container to set the foreign key on the new PHONE record so that it points back to the Customer EJB's CUSTOMER record. If we had used a link table, a new link record would have been created. From this point forward, the new Phone EJB will be available from the phoneNumbers collection-based relationship.

You can also update or remove references using the accessor methods. The following code defines two methods in the CustomerBean class that allow clients to remove or update phone numbers in the bean's phoneNumbers relationship field:

```
public abstract class CustomerBean implements javax.ejb.EntityBean {

    // business methods
    public void removePhoneNumber(byte typeToRemove) {

        Collection phoneNumbers = this.getPhoneNumbers( );
        Iterator iterator = phoneNumbers.iterator( );
        while(iterator.hasNext( )) {
            PhoneLocal phone = (PhoneLocal)iterator.next( );
            if(phone.getType( ) == typeToRemove) {
                iterator.remove(phone);
                break;
            }
        }
    }
    public void updatePhoneNumber(String number,byte typeToUpdate) {
        Collection phoneNumbers = this.getPhoneNumbers( );
        Iterator iterator = phoneNumbers.iterator( );
        while(iterator.hasNext( )) {
            PhoneLocal phone = (PhoneLocal)iterator.next( );
            if(phone.getType( ) == typeToUpdate) {
                phone.setNumber(number);
                break;
```

```
            }
        }
    }
    ...
    // relationship fields
    public abstract Collection getPhoneNumbers( );
    public abstract void setPhoneNumbers(Collection phones);
```

In the removePhoneNumber( ) business method, a Phone EJB with the matching type was found and then removed from the collection-based relationship. The phone number is not deleted from the database; it's just disassociated from the Customer EJB (i.e., it is no longer referenced by a Customer). Figure 7-7 shows what happens when a Phone EJB reference is removed from the collection-based relationship.

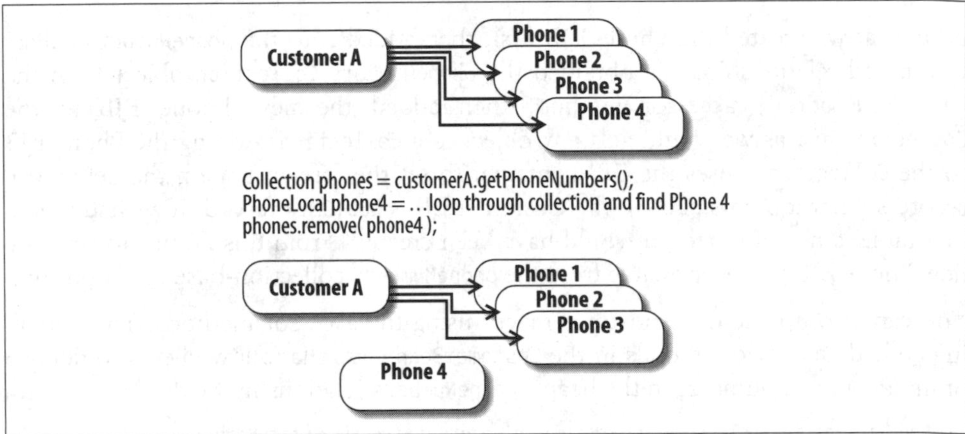

Figure 7-7. Removing a bean reference from a relationship-field collection

The updatePhoneNumber( ) method actually modifies an existing Phone EJB, changing its state in the database. The Phone EJB is still referenced by the collection-based relationship, but its data has changed.

The removePhoneNumber( ) and updatePhoneNumber( ) methods illustrate that a collection-based relationship can be accessed and updated just like any other Collection object. In addition, a java.util.Iterator can be obtained from the Collection object for looping operations. However, you should exercise caution when using an Iterator over a collection-based relationship. You must not add elements to or remove elements from the Collection object while you are using its Iterator. The only exception to this rule is that the Iterator.remove( ) method may be called to remove an entry. Although the Collection.add( ) and Collection.remove( ) methods can be used in other circumstances, calling these methods while an Iterator is in use results in a java.util.IllegalStateException exception.

If no beans have been added to the phoneNumbers relationship field, the getPhoneNumbers( ) method returns an empty Collection object. The Collection object used with the relationship field is implemented by the container system, proprietary to the vendor, and tightly coupled with the inner workings of the container. This allows the EJB container to implement performance enhancements such as lazy loading or optimistic concurrency without exposing those mechanisms to the bean developer.* Application-defined Collection objects may be used with container-manager relationship fields only if the elements are of the proper type. For example, it is legal to create a new Collection object and then add that Collection object to the Customer EJB using the setPhoneNumbers( ) method:

```
public void addPhoneNumber(String number, String type) {

    ...
    PhoneLocal phone = phoneHome.create(number,type);

    Collection phoneNumbers = java.util.Vector( );
    phoneNumbers.add(phone);

    // This is allowed
    this.setPhoneNumbers(phoneNumbers);

}

// relationship fields
public abstract Collection getPhoneNumbers( );

public abstract void setPhoneNumbers(Collection phones);
```

We have used the getPhoneNumbers( ) method extensively, but have not yet used the setPhoneNumbers( ) method. In most cases, this method will not be used, because it updates an entire collection of phone numbers. However, it can be useful for exchanging like relationships between entity beans.

If two Customer EJBs want to exchange phone numbers, they can do so in a variety of ways. The most important thing to keep in mind is that a Phone EJB, as the subject of a one-to-many, unidirectional relationship, may reference only one Customer EJB. It can be copied, so that both Customers have Phone EJBs with similar data, but the Phone EJB itself cannot be shared.

Imagine that Customer A wants to transfer all of its phone numbers to Customer B. It can accomplish this using Customer B's setPhoneNumbers( ) method, as shown in the following listing (we assume the Customer EJBs are interacting through their local interfaces):

```
CustomerLocal customerA = ... get Customer A
CustomerLocal customerB = ... get Customer B
```

* A Collection from a collection-based relationship that is materialized in a transaction cannot be modified outside the scope of that transaction. See Chapter 14 for more details.

```
Collection phonesA = customerA.getPhoneNumbers( );
customerB.setPhoneNumbers( phonesA );

if( customerA.getPhoneNumbers().isEmpty( ))
    // this will be true
if( phonesA.isEmpty( )) )
    // this will be true
```

As Figure 7-8 illustrates, passing one collection-based relationship to another disassociates those relationships from the first bean and associates them with the second. In addition, if the second bean already has a `Collection` of Phone EJBs in its `phoneNumbers` relationship field, those beans are bumped out of the relationship and disassociated from the bean.

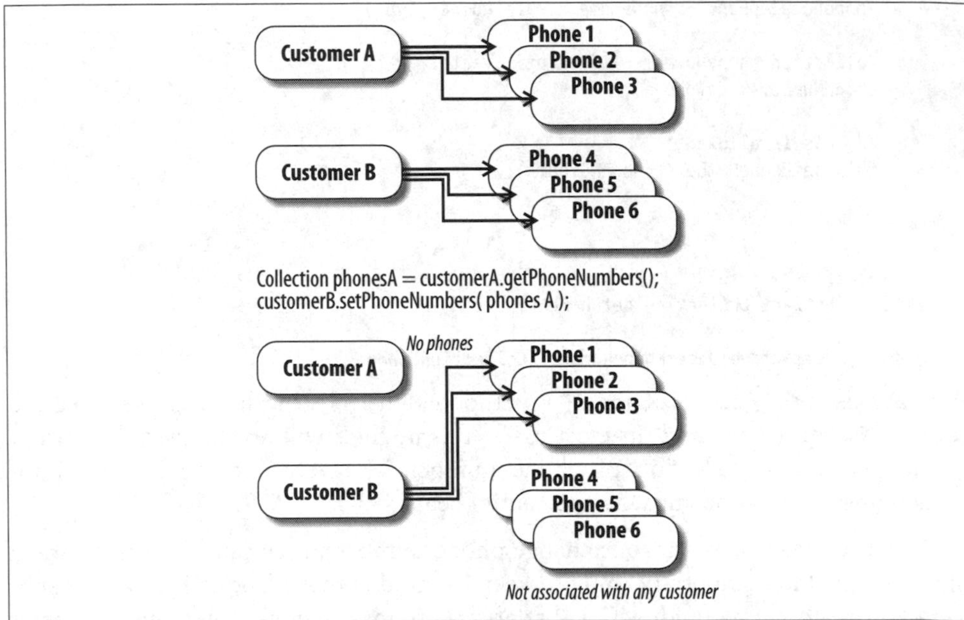

Figure 7-8. Exchanging a relationship collection in a one-to-many, unidirectional relationship

The result of this exchange may be counterintuitive, but it is necessary to uphold the multiplicity of the relationship, which says that the Phone EJB may have only one Customer EJB. This explains why Phone EJBs 1, 2, and 3 don't reference both Customers A and B, but it doesn't explain why Phone EJBs 4, 5, and 6 are disassociated from Customer B. Why isn't Customer B associated with all the Phone EJBs? The reason is purely a matter of semantics, since the relational database schema wouldn't technically prevent this from occurring. The act of replacing one `Collection` with another by calling `setPhoneNumbers(Collection collection)` implies that Customer B's initial `Collection` object is no longer referenced.

In addition to moving whole collection-based relationships between beans, it is possible to move individual Phone EJBs between Customers. These cannot be shared either. For example, if a Phone EJB aggregated by Customer A is added to the relationship collection of Customer B, that Phone EJB changes so that it's now referenced by Customer B instead of Customer A, as Figure 7-9 illustrates.

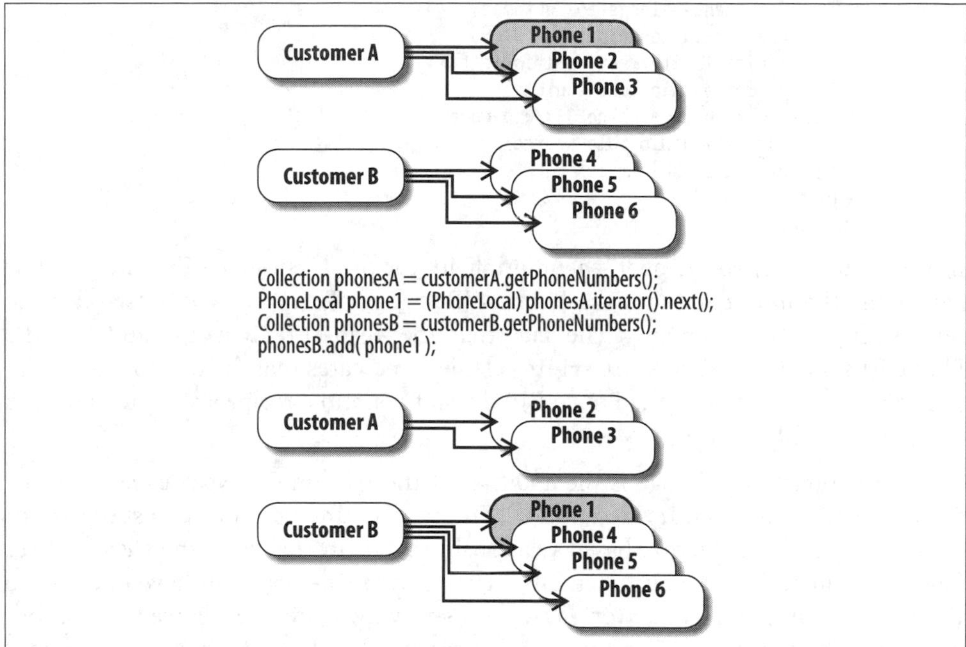

Figure 7-9. Exchanging a bean in a one-to-many, unidirectional relationship

Once again, it's the multiplicity of the relationship that prevents Phone 1 from referencing both Customer A and Customer B.

Abstract persistence schema

The abstract persistence schema for one-to-many, unidirectional relationships has a few significant differences from the `<ejb-relation>` elements seen so far:

```
<relationships>
    <ejb-relation>
        <ejb-relation-name>Customer-Phones</ejb-relation-name>
        <ejb-relationship-role>
            <ejb-relationship-role-name>
                Customer-has-many-Phone-numbers
            </ejb-relationship-role-name>
            <multiplicity>One</multiplicity>
            <relationship-role-source>
                <ejb-name>CustomerEJB</ejb-name>
            </relationship-role-source>
```

```
            <cmr-field>
                <cmr-field-name>phoneNumbers</cmr-field-name>
                <cmr-field-type>java.util.Collection</cmr-field-type>
            </cmr-field>
        </ejb-relationship-role>
        <ejb-relationship-role>
            <ejb-relationship-role-name>
                Phone-belongs-to-Customer
            </ejb-relationship-role-name>
            <multiplicity>Many</multiplicity>
            <relationship-role-source>
                <ejb-name>PhoneEJB</ejb-name>
            </relationship-role-source>
        </ejb-relationship-role>
    </ejb-relation>
</relationships>
```

In the `<ejb-relation>` element, the multiplicity for the Customer EJB is declared as `One`, while the multiplicity for the Phone EJB is `Many`. These keywords establish the relationship as one-to-many. The fact that the `<ejb-relationship-role>` for the Phone EJB doesn't specify a `<cmr-field>` element indicates that the one-to-many relationship is unidirectional; the Phone EJB doesn't contain a reciprocating reference to the Customer EJB.

The most interesting change is the addition of the `<cmr-field-type>` element in the Customer EJB's `<cmr-field>` declaration. The `<cmr-field-type>` must be specified for a bean that has a collection-based relationship field (in this case, the `phoneNumbers` field maintained by the Customer EJB). The `<cmr-field-type>` can have one of two values, `java.util.Collection` or `java.util.Set`, which are the allowed collection-based relationship types. In a future specification, the allowed types for collection-based relationships may be expanded to include `java.util.List` and `java.util.Map`, but these are not yet supported. Exercise 7.1 in the Workbook shows how to deploy this example on the JBoss server.

The Cruise, Ship, and Reservation EJBs

By now, I imagine that you're bored by all these phone numbers, credit cards, and addresses. To make things more interesting, we are going to introduce some more entity beans so that we can model the remaining four relationships: many-to-one unidirectional, one-to-many bidirectional, many-to-many bidirectional, and many-to-many unidirectional.

In Titan's reservation system, every customer (a.k.a. passenger) can be booked on one or more cruises. Each booking requires a reservation. A reservation may be for one or more (usually two) passengers. Each cruise requires exactly one ship, but each ship may be used for many cruises throughout the year. Figure 7-10 illustrates these relationships.

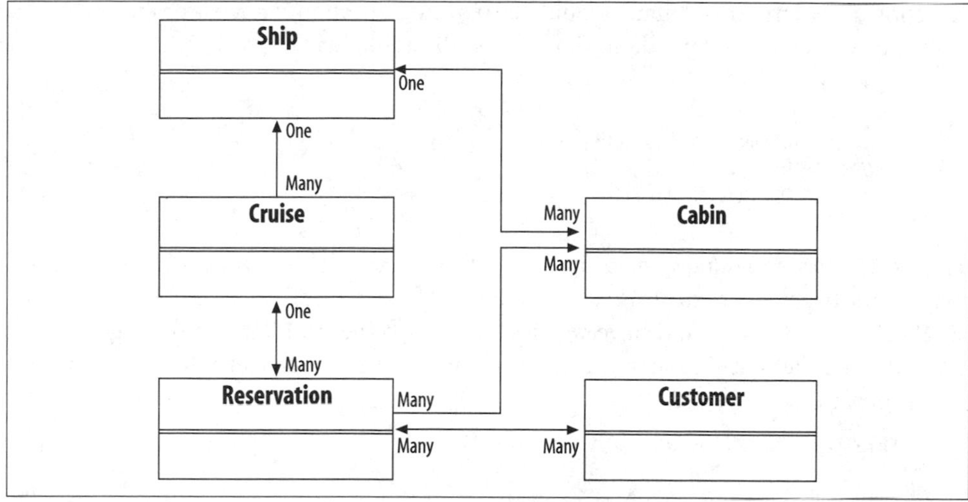

Figure 7-10. Cruise, Ship, Reservation, Cabin, and Customer class diagram

Many-to-One, Unidirectional Relationship

Many-to-one unidirectional relationships result when many entity beans reference a single entity bean, but the referenced entity bean is unaware of the relationship. In the Titan Cruise business, for example, the concept of a cruise can be captured by a Cruise EJB. As shown in Figure 7-10, each Cruise has a many-to-one relationship with a Ship. This relationship is unidirectional; the Cruise EJB maintains a relationship with the Ship EJB, but the Ship EJB does not keep track of the Cruises for which it is used.

Relational database schema

The relational database schema for the Cruise-to-Ship relationship is fairly simple; it requires that the `CRUISE` table maintain a foreign key column for the `SHIP` table, with each row in the `CRUISE` table pointing to a row in the `SHIP` table. The `CRUISE` and `SHIP` tables are defined below; Figure 7-11 shows the relationship between these tables in the database.

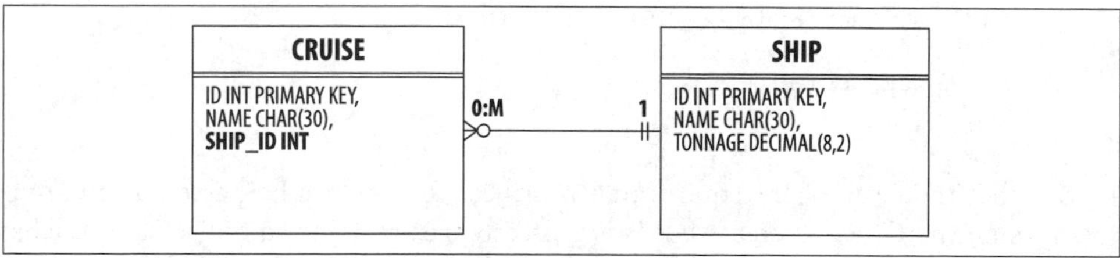

Figure 7-11. Many-to-one, unidirectional relationship in RDBMS

An enormous amount of data would be required to adequately describe an ocean liner, but we'll use a simple definition of the SHIP table here:

```
CREATE TABLE SHIP
(
    ID INT PRIMARY KEY NOT NULL,
    NAME CHAR(30),
    TONNAGE DECIMAL (8,2)
)
```

The CRUISE table maintains data on each cruise's name, ship, and other information that is not germane to this discussion. (Other tables, such as RESERVATIONS, SCHEDULES, and CREW, would have relationships with the CRUISE table through linking tables.) We'll keep it simple and focus on a definition that is useful for the examples in this book:

```
CREATE TABLE CRUISE
(
    ID INT PRIMARY KEY NOT NULL,
    NAME CHAR(30),
    SHIP_ID INT
)
```

Abstract programming model

In the abstract programming model, the relationship field is of type ShipLocal and is maintained by the Cruise EJB. The abstract accessor methods are similar to those defined in the previous examples:

```
public abstract class CruiseBean implements javax.ejb.EntityBean {
    public Integer ejbCreate(String name, ShipLocal ship) {
        setName(name);
        return null;
    }
    public void ejbPostCreate(String name, ShipLocal ship) {
        setShip(ship);
    }
    public abstract Integer getId( );
    public abstract void setId(Integer id);
    public abstract void setName(String name);
    public abstract String getName( );
    public abstract void setShip(ShipLocal ship);
    public abstract ShipLocal getShip( );

    // EJB callback methods
    ...
}
```

Notice that the Cruise EJB requires that a ShipLocal reference be passed as an argument when the Cruise is created; this is perfectly natural, since a cruise cannot exist without a ship. According to the EJB specification, relationship fields cannot be modified or set in the ejbCreate() method. They must be modified in the ejbPostCreate(), a constraint that is followed in the CruiseBean class.

The reason relationships are set in ejbPostCreate() and not ejbCreate() is simple: the primary key for the entity bean may not be available until after ejbCreate() executes. The primary key is needed if the mapping for the relationship uses the key as a foreign key, so assignment of relationships is postponed until the ejbCreate() method completes and the primary key becomes available. This is also true with autogenerated primary keys, which usually require that the insert be done before a primary key can be generated. In addition, referential integrity may specify non-null foreign keys in referencing tables, so the insert must take place first. In reality, the transaction does not complete until both the ejbCreate() and ejbPostCreate() methods have executed, so the vendors are free to choose the best time for database inserts and linking of relationships.

The relationship between the Cruise and Ship EJBs is unidirectional, so the Ship EJB doesn't define any relationship fields, just persistence fields:

```
public abstract class ShipBean implements javax.ejb.EntityBean {

    public Integer ejbCreate(Integer primaryKey,String name,double tonnage) {
        setId(primaryKey);
        setName(name);
        setTonnage(tonnage);
        return null;
    }
    public void ejbPostCreate(Integer primaryKey,String name,double tonnage) {
    }
    public abstract void setId(Integer id);
    public abstract Integer getId();
    public abstract void setName(String name);
    public abstract String getName();
    public abstract void setTonnage(double tonnage);
    public abstract double getTonnage();

    // EJB callback methods
    ...
}
```

This should all be fairly mundane for you now. The impact of exchanging Ship references between Cruise EJBs should be equally obvious. As shown previously in Figure 7-10, each Cruise may reference only a single Ship, but each Ship may reference many Cruise EJBs. If you take Ship A, which is referenced by Cruises 1, 2, and 3, and pass it to Cruise 4, Cruises 1 through 4 will all reference Ship A, as shown in Figure 7-12.

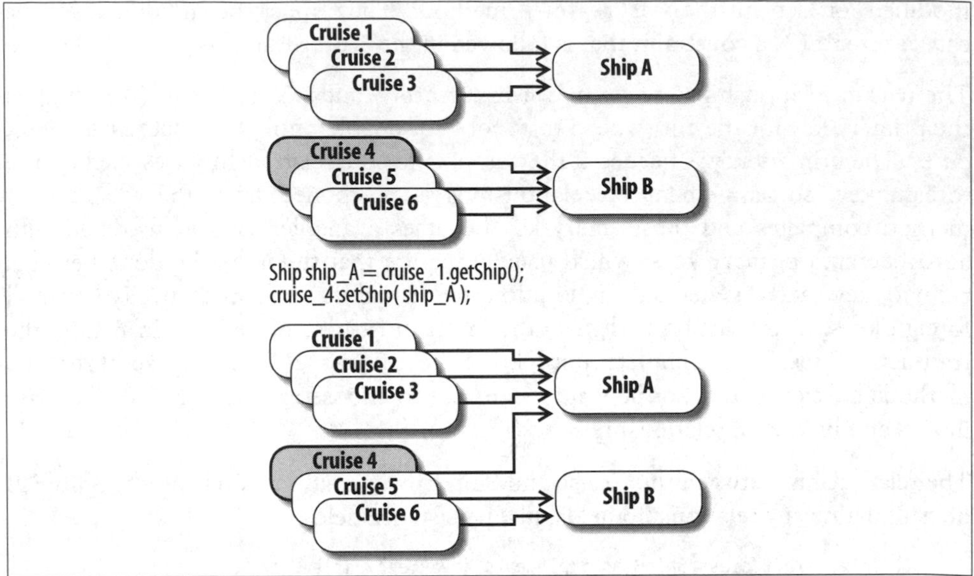

Figure 7-12. Sharing a bean reference in a many-to-one, unidirectional relationship

Abstract persistence schema

The abstract persistence schema is simple in a many-to-one, unidirectional relationship. It uses everything you have already learned, and shouldn't contain any surprises:

```
<ejb-jar>
...
<enterprise-beans>
    <entity>
        <ejb-name>CruiseEJB</ejb-name>
        <local-home>com.titan.cruise.CruiseHomeLocal</local-home>
        <local>com.titan.cruise.CruiseLocal</local>
        ...
    </entity>
    <entity>
        <ejb-name>ShipEJB</ejb-name>
        <local-home>com.titan.ship.ShipHomeLocal</local-home>
        <local>com.titan.ship.ShipLocal</local>
        ...
    </entity>
    ...
</enterprise-beans>

<relationships>
    <ejb-relation>
        <ejb-relation-name>Cruise-Ship</ejb-relation-name>
        <ejb-relationship-role>
            <ejb-relationship-role-name>
                Cruise-has-a-Ship
            </ejb-relationship-role-name>
```

```
            <multiplicity>Many</multiplicity>
            <relationship-role-source>
                <ejb-name>CruiseEJB</ejb-name>
            </relationship-role-source>
            <cmr-field>
                <cmr-field-name>ship</cmr-field-name>
            </cmr-field>
        </ejb-relationship-role>
        <ejb-relationship-role>
            <ejb-relationship-role-name>
                Ship-has-many-Cruises
            </ejb-relationship-role-name>
            <multiplicity>One</multiplicity>
            <relationship-role-source>
                <ejb-name>ShipEJB</ejb-name>
            </relationship-role-source>
        </ejb-relationship-role>
    </ejb-relation>
</relationships>
```

The `<ejb-relationship-role>` of the Cruise EJB defines its multiplicity as `Many` and declares `ship` as its relationship field. The `<ejb-relationship-role>` of the Ship EJB defines its multiplicity as `One` and contains no `<cmr-field>` declaration, because it's a unidirectional relationship.

One-to-Many, Bidirectional Relationship

One-to-many and many-to-one bidirectional relationships sound like they're different, but they're not. A one-to-many, bidirectional relationship occurs when one entity bean maintains a collection-based relationship field with another entity bean, and each entity bean referenced in the collection maintains a single reference back to its aggregating bean. For example, in the Titan Cruise system, each Cruise EJB maintains a collection of references to all the passenger reservations made for that Cruise, and each Reservation EJB maintains a single reference to its Cruise. The relationship is a one-to-many, bidirectional relationship from the perspective of the Cruise EJB, and a many-to-one, bidirectional relationship from the perspective of the Reservation EJB.

Relational database schema

The first table we need is the `RESERVATION` table, which is defined in the following listing. Notice that the `RESERVATION` table contains, among other things, a column that serves as a foreign key to the `CRUISE` table:

```
CREATE TABLE RESERVATION
(
    ID INT PRIMARY KEY NOT NULL,
    AMOUNT_PAID DECIMAL (8,2),
    DATE_RESERVED DATE,
   CRUISE_ID INT
)
```

While the RESERVATION table contains a foreign key to the CRUISE table, the CRUISE table doesn't maintain a foreign key back to the RESERVATION table. The EJB container system can determine the relationship between the Cruise and Reservations EJBs by querying the RESERVATION table, so explicit pointers from the CRUISE table to the RESERVATION table are not required. This illustrates the separation between the entity bean's view of its persistence relationships and the database's actual implementation of those relationships.

The relationship between the RESERVATION and CRUISE tables is shown in Figure 7-13.

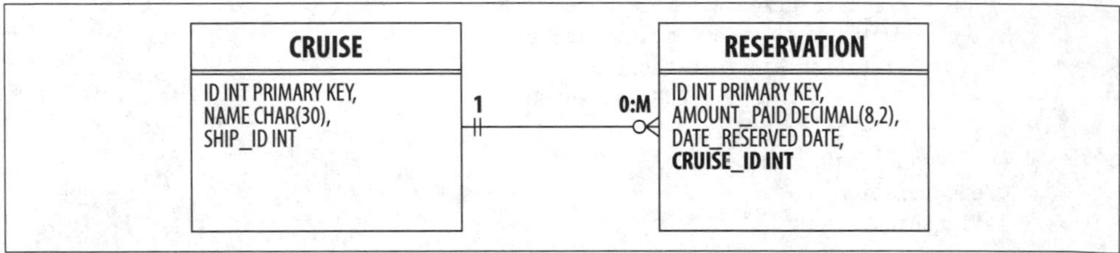

Figure 7-13. One-to-many/many-to-one, bidirectional relationship in RDBMS

As an alternative, we could have used a link table that would declare foreign keys to both the CRUISE and RESERVATION tables. This link table would probably impose a uniqueness constraint on the RESERVATION foreign key to ensure that each RESERVATION record had only one corresponding CRUISE record.

Abstract programming model

To model the relationship between Cruises and Reservations, we first define the Reservation EJB, which maintains a relationship field to the Cruise EJB:

```
public abstract class ReservationBean implements javax.ejb.EntityBean {

    public Integer ejbCreate(CruiseLocal cruise) {
        return null;
    }
    public void ejbPostCreate(CruiseLocal cruise) {
        setCruise(cruise);
    }
    public abstract void setCruise(CruiseLocal cruise);
    public abstract CruiseLocal getCruise( );
    public abstract Integer getId( );
    public abstract void setId(Integer id);
    public abstract void setAmountPaid(float amount);
    public abstract float getAmountPaid( );
    public abstract void setDate(Date date);
    public abstract Date getDate( );

    // EJB callback methods
    ...
}
```

When a Reservation EJB is created, a reference to the Cruise for which it is created must be passed to the create( ) method. Notice that the CruiseLocal reference is set in the ejbPostCreate( ) method, not the ejbCreate( ) method. As stated previously, the ejbCreate( ) method is not allowed to update relationship fields; that is the job of ejbPostCreate( ).

We need to add a collection-based relationship field to the Cruise EJB so that it can reference all the Reservation EJBs that were created for it:

```
public abstract class CruiseBean implements javax.ejb.EntityBean {
    ...
    public abstract void setReservations(Collection res);
    public abstract Collection getReservations( );
    public abstract Integer getId( );
    public abstract void setId(Integer id);
    public abstract void setName(String name);
    public abstract String getName( );
    public abstract void setShip(ShipLocal ship);
    public abstract ShipLocal getShip( );

   // EJB callback methods
    ...
}
```

The interdependency between the Cruise and Reservation EJBs produces some interesting results. For example, the act of creating a Reservation EJB automatically adds that entity bean to the collection-based relationship of the Cruise EJB:

```
CruiseLocal cruise = ... get CruiseLocal reference

ReservationLocal reservation = reservationHomeLocal.create( cruise );

Collection collection = cruise.getReservations( );

if(collection.contains(reservation))
    // always returns true
```

This is a side effect of the bidirectional relationship. Any Cruise referenced by a specific Reservation has a reciprocal reference back to that Reservation. If Reservation X references Cruise A, Cruise A must have a reference to Reservation X. When you create a new Reservation EJB and set the Cruise reference on that bean, the Reservation is automatically added to the Cruise EJB's reservation field.*

Sharing references between beans has some of the ugly consequences we learned about earlier. For example, passing a collection of Reservations referenced by Cruise A to Cruise B actually moves those relationships to Cruise B, so Cruise A has no more Reservations (see Figure 7-14).

* This actually depends in large part on the sequence of operations, the transaction context, and even the isolation levels used in the database. Chapter 14 provides more information on these topics.

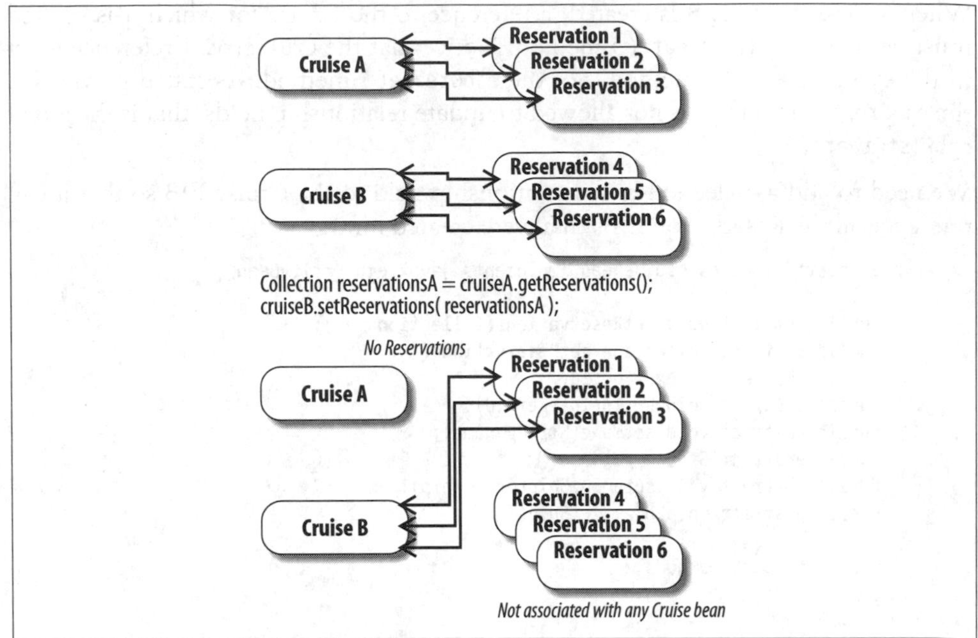

Figure 7-14. Sharing an entire collection in a one-to-many, bidirectional relationship

As with the Customer and Phone EJBs, this effect is usually undesirable and should be avoided; it displaces the set of Reservation EJBs formerly associated with Cruise B.

You can move an entire collection from one bean to another and combine it with the second bean's collection by using the `Collection.addAll( )` method, as shown in Figure 7-15.* If you move Cruise A's collection of references to Cruise B, Cruise A will no longer reference any Reservation EJBs, while Cruise B will reference those it referenced before the exchange as well as those it acquired from Cruise A.

Moving an individual Reservation EJB from one Cruise to another is similar to moving an individual bean in a one-to-many relationship: the result is shown in Figure 7-9, when a Phone was moved from one Customer to another. The net effect of using `Collection.addAll( )` in this situation is the same as using `Collection.add( )` on the target collection for every element in the source collection. In both cases, you move every element from the source collection to the target collection.

Once again, container-managed relationship fields, collection-based or otherwise, must always use the `javax.ejb.EJBLocalObject` (local) interface of a bean and never the `javax.ejb.EJBObject` (remote) interface. It would be illegal to try to add the remote interface of the Reservation EJB (if it has one) to the Cruise EJB's Reservation `Collection`. Any attempt to add a remote interface type to a collection-based relationship field results in a `java.lang.IllegalArgumentException`.

* The `addAll( )` method must be supported by collection-based relationship fields.

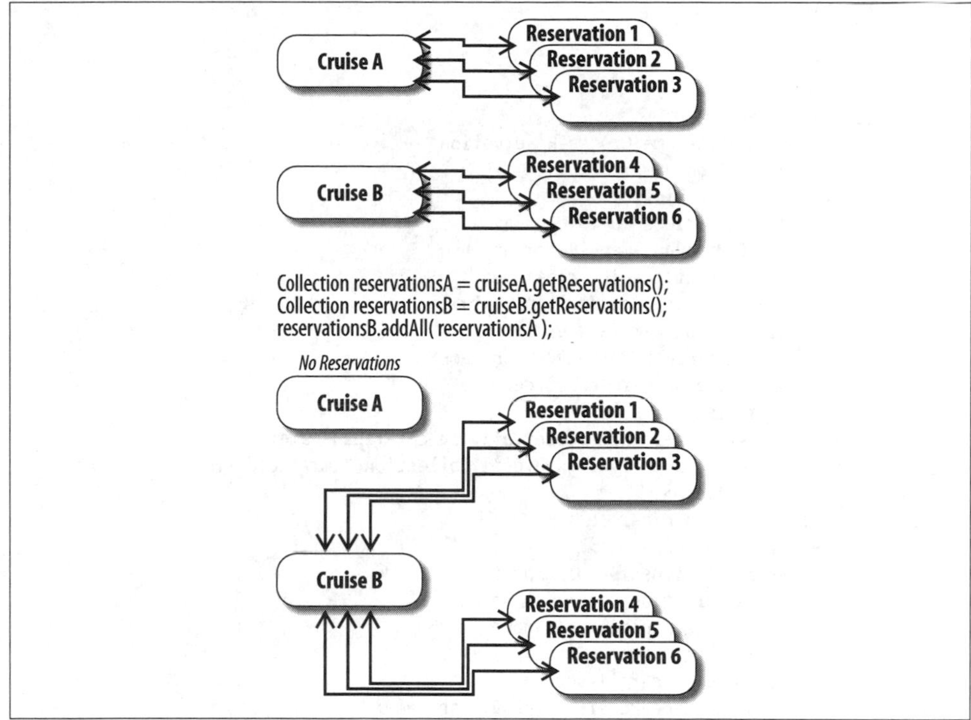

Figure 7-15. Using Collection.addAll() in a one-to-many, bidirectional relationship

Abstract persistence schema

The abstract persistence schema for the Cruise-Reservation relationship doesn't introduce any new concepts. The Cruise and Reservation `<ejb-relationship-role>` elements both have `<cmr-field>` elements. The Cruise specifies `One` as its multiplicity, while Reservation specifies `Many`. Here's the code:

```
<ejb-jar>
...
<enterprise-beans>
    <entity>
        <ejb-name>CruiseEJB</ejb-name>
        <local-home>com.titan.cruise.CruiseHomeLocal</local-home>
        <local>com.titan.cruise.CruiseLocal</local>
        ...
    </entity>
    <entity>
        <ejb-name>ReservationEJB</ejb-name>
        <local-home>
            com.titan.reservations.ReservationHomeLocal
        </local-home>
        <local>com.titan.reservation.ReservationLocal</local>
        ...
```

```
    </entity>
    ...
</enterprise-beans>
<relationships>
    <ejb-relation>
        <ejb-relation-name>Cruise-Reservation
        </ejb-relation-name>
        <ejb-relationship-role>
            <ejb-relationship-role-name>
                Cruise-has-many-Reservations
            </ejb-relationship-role-name>
            <multiplicity>One</multiplicity>
            <relationship-role-source>
                <ejb-name>CruiseEJB</ejb-name>
            </relationship-role-source>
            <cmr-field>
                <cmr-field-name>reservations</cmr-field-name>
                <cmr-field-type>java.util.Collection</cmr-field-type>
            </cmr-field>
        </ejb-relationship-role>
        <ejb-relationship-role>
            <ejb-relationship-role-name>
                Reservation-has-a-Cruise
            </ejb-relationship-role-name>
            <multiplicity>Many</multiplicity>
            <relationship-role-source>
                <ejb-name>ReservationEJB</ejb-name>
            </relationship-role-source>
            <cmr-field>
                <cmr-field-name>cruise</cmr-field-name>
            </cmr-field>
        </ejb-relationship-role>
    </ejb-relation>
</relationships>
```

Many-to-Many, Bidirectional Relationship

Many-to-many, bidirectional relationships occur when many beans maintain a collection-based relationship field with another bean, and each bean referenced in the Collection maintains a collection-based relationship field back to the aggregating beans. For example, in Titan Cruises, every Reservation EJB may reference many Customers (a family can make a single reservation) and each Customer can have many reservations (a person may make more than one reservation). In this many-to-many, bidirectional relationship, the customer keeps track of all of its reservations, and each reservation may be for many customers.

Relational database schema

The RESERVATION and CUSTOMER tables have already been established. To establish a many-to-many, bidirectional relationship, we create the RESERVATION_CUSTOMER_LINK table. This table maintains two foreign key columns: one for the RESERVATION table and another for the CUSTOMER table:

```
CREATE TABLE RESERVATION_CUSTOMER_LINK
(
    RESERVATION_ID INT,
    CUSTOMER_ID INT
)
```

The relationship between the CUSTOMER, RESERVATION, and CUSTOMER_RESERVATION_LINK tables is illustrated in Figure 7-16.

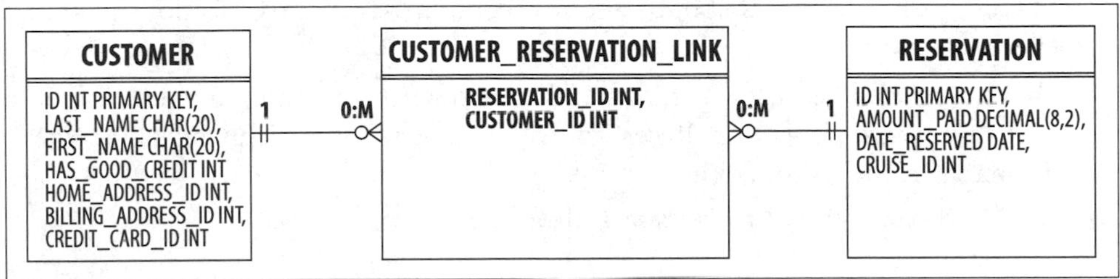

Figure 7-16. Many-to-many, bidirectional relationship in RDBMS

Many-to-many, bidirectional relationships always require a link table in a normalized relational database.

Abstract programming model

To model the many-to-many, bidirectional relationship between the Customer and Reservation EJBs, we need to include collection-based relationship fields in both bean classes:

```
public abstract class ReservationBean implements javax.ejb.EntityBean {

    public Integer ejbCreate(CruiseLocal cruise,Collection customers) {
        return null;
    }
    public void ejbPostCreate(CruiseLocal cruise,Collection customers) {
        setCruise(cruise);
        Collection myCustomers = this.getCustomers();
        myCustomers.addAll(customers);
    }

    public abstract void setCustomers(Set customers);
    public abstract Set getCustomers();
    ...
}
```

The abstract accessor methods defined for the customers relationship field declare the Collection type as java.util.Set. The Set type should contain only unique Customer EJBs and no duplicates. Duplicate Customers would introduce some interesting but undesirable side effects in Titan's reservation system. To maintain a valid passenger count, and to avoid overcharging customers, Titan requires that a Customer be booked only once in the same Reservation. The Set collection type expresses this restriction. The effectiveness of the Set collection type depends largely on referential-integrity constraints established in the underlying database.

In addition to adding the getCustomers()/setCustomers() abstract accessors, we have modified the ejbCreate()/ejbPostCreate() methods to take a Collection of Customer EJBs. When a Reservation EJB is created, it must be provided with a list of Customer EJBs that it will add to its own Customer EJB collection. Container-managed relationship fields cannot be modified in the ejbCreate() method. It's the ejbPostCreate() method's job to modify container-managed relationships fields when a bean is created.

We have also modified the Customer EJB to allow it to maintain a collection-based relationship with all of its Reservations. The Customer EJB now includes a reservations relationship field:

```
public abstract class CustomerBean implements javax.ejb.EntityBean {
    ...
    // relationship fields
    public abstract void setReservations(Collection reservations);

    public abstract Collection getReservations();
    ...
```

When a Reservation EJB is created, it is passed references to its Cruise and to a collection of Customers. Because the relationship is bidirectional, the EJB container automatically adds the Reservation EJB to the reservations relationship field of the Customer EJB. The following code illustrates this:

```
Collection customers = ... get local Customer EJBs
CruiseLocal cruise = ... get a local Cruise EJB
ReservationHomeLocal resHome = ... get local Reservation home

ReservationLocal myReservation = resHome.create(cruise,  customers);

Iterator iterator = customers.iterator();
while(iterator.hasNext()) {
    CustomerLocal customer = (CustomerLocal)iterator.next();
    Collection reservations = customer.getReservations();
    if( reservations.contains( myReservation ))
        // this will always be true
}
```

Exchanging bean references in many-to-many, bidirectional relationships results in true sharing, where each relationship maintains a reference to the transferred collection. This type of relationship is illustrated in Figure 7-17.

Of course, using the setCustomers() or setReservations() method changes the references between the entity bean and the elements in the original collection, but the other relationships held by those elements are unaffected. Figure 7-18 illustrates what happens when an entire collection is shared in a many-to-many bidirectional relationship.

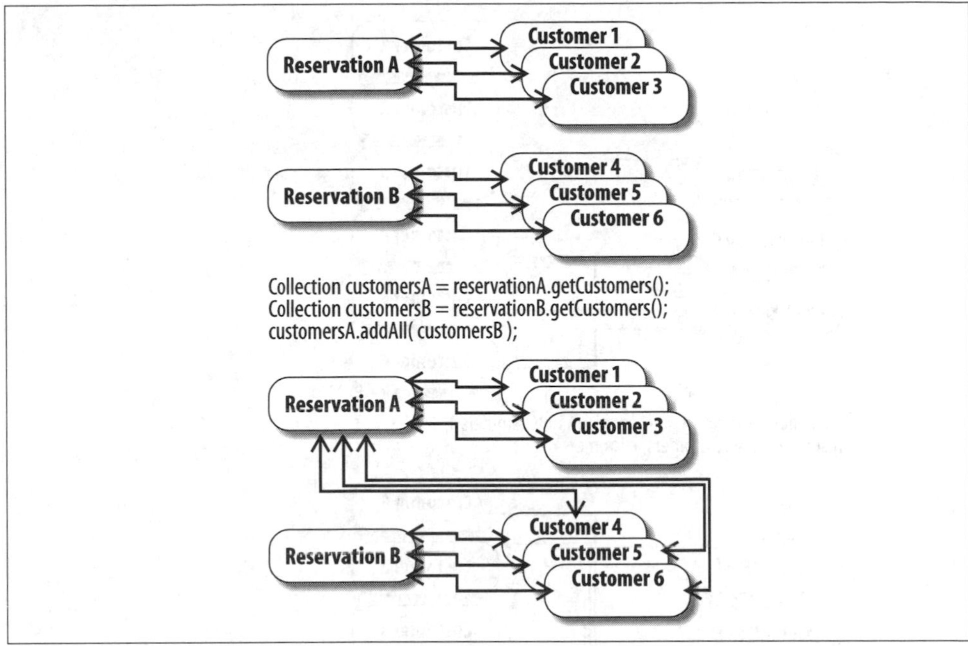

Figure 7-17. Using Collection.addAll( ) in a many-to-many, bidirectional relationship

After the `setCustomers( )` method is invoked on Reservation D, Reservation D's Customers change to Customers 1, 2, and 3. Customers 1, 2, and 3 were also referenced by Reservation A before the sharing operation and remain referenced by Reservation A after it's complete. In fact, only the relationships between Reservation D and Customers 4, 5, and 6 are impacted. The relationship between Customers 4, 5, and 6 and other Reservation EJBs are not affected by the sharing operation. This is a unique property of many-to-many relationships (both bidirectional and unidirectional): operations on the relationship fields affect only those specific relationships; they do not impact either party's relationships with other beans of the same relationship type.

Abstract persistence schema

The abstract persistence schema of a many-to-many, bidirectional relationship introduces nothing new and should contain no surprises. Each `<ejb-relationship-role>` specifies `Many` as its multiplicity and declares a `<cmr-field>` of a specific `Collection` type:

```
<ejb-jar>
...
<enterprise-beans>
    <entity>
        <ejb-name>CustomerEJB</ejb-name>
        <local-home>com.titan.customer.CustomerHomeLocal</local-home>
        <local>com.titan.customer.CustomerLocal</local>
        ...
    </entity>
```

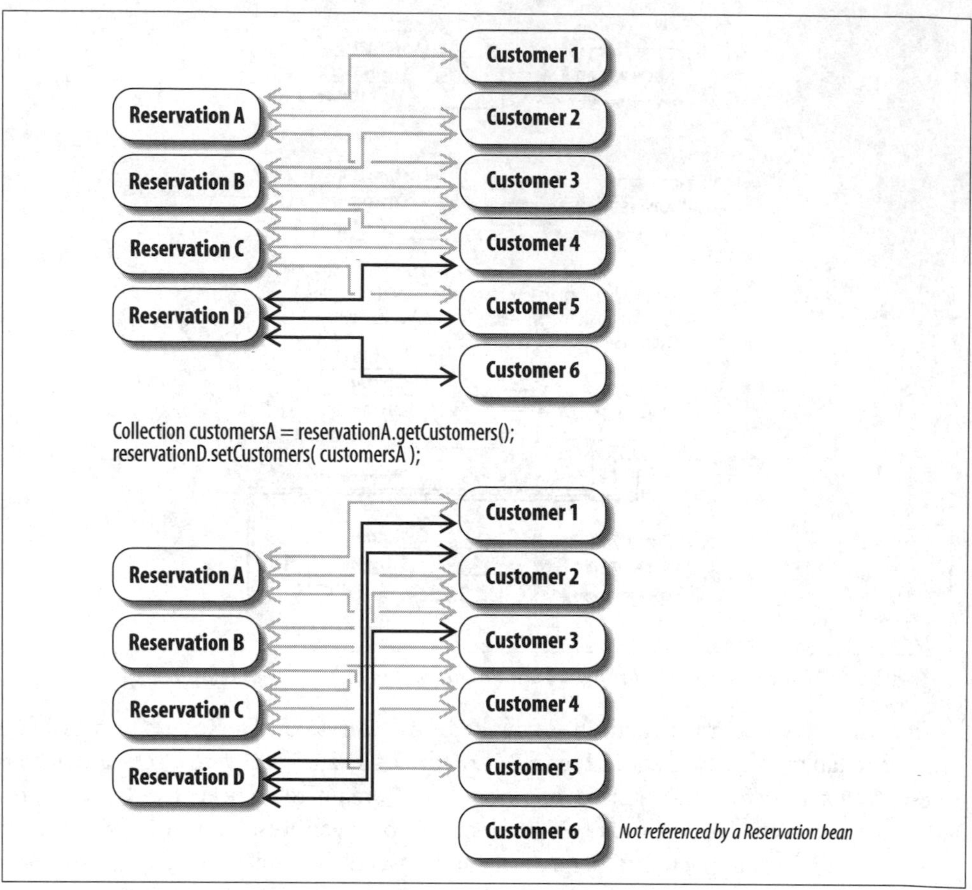

Figure 7-18. Sharing an entire collection in a many-to-many, bidirectional relationship

```
        <entity>
            <ejb-name>ReservationEJB</ejb-name>
            <local-home> com.titan.reservation.ReservationHomeLocal</local-home>
            <local>com.titan.reservation.ReservationLocal</local>
            ...
        </entity>
        ...
    </enterprise-beans>

    <relationships>
        <ejb-relation>
            <ejb-relation-name>Customer-Reservation</ejb-relation-name>
            <ejb-relationship-role>
                <ejb-relationship-role-name>
                    Customer-has-many-Reservations
                </ejb-relationship-role-name>
                <multiplicity>Many</multiplicity>
                <relationship-role-source>
                    <ejb-name>CustomerEJB</ejb-name>
```

```
            </relationship-role-source>
            <cmr-field>
                <cmr-field-name>reservations</cmr-field-name>
                <cmr-field-type>java.util.Collection</cmr-field-type>
            </cmr-field>
        </ejb-relationship-role>
        <ejb-relationship-role>
            <ejb-relationship-role-name>
                Reservation-has-many-Customers
            </ejb-relationship-role-name>
            <multiplicity>Many</multiplicity>
            <relationship-role-source>
                <ejb-name>ReservationEJB</ejb-name>
            </relationship-role-source>
            <cmr-field>
                <cmr-field-name>customers</cmr-field-name>
                <cmr-field-type>java.util.Set</cmr-field-type>
            </cmr-field>
        </ejb-relationship-role>
    </ejb-relation>
</relationships>
```

Many-to-Many, Unidirectional Relationship

Many-to-many, unidirectional relationships occur when many beans maintain a collection-based relationship with another bean, but the bean referenced in the `Collection` does not maintain a collection-based relationship back to the aggregating beans. In Titan's reservation system, every Reservation is assigned a Cabin on the Ship. This allows a Customer to reserve a specific Cabin (e.g., a deluxe suite or a cabin with sentimental significance) on the Ship. In this case, each Reservation may be for more than one Cabin, since each Reservation can be for more than one Customer. For example, a family might make a Reservation for five people for two adjacent Cabins (one for the kids and the other for the parents).

While the Reservation must keep track of the Cabins it reserves, it's not necessary for the Cabins to track all the Reservations made by all the Cruises. The Reservation EJBs reference a collection of Cabin beans, but the Cabin beans do not maintain references back to the Reservations.

Relational database schema

Our first order of business is to declare a `CABIN` table:

```
CREATE TABLE CABIN
(
    ID INT PRIMARY KEY NOT NULL,
    SHIP_ID INT,
    NAME CHAR(10),
    DECK_LEVEL INT,
    BED_COUNT INT
)
```

Notice the CABIN table maintains a foreign key to the SHIP table. While this relationship is important, we don't discuss it because we covered the one-to-many, bidirectional relationship in this chapter. To accommodate the many-to-many, unidirectional relationship between the RESERVATION and CABIN table, we need a RESERVATION_CABIN_LINK table:

```
CREATE TABLE RESERVATION_CABIN_LINK
(
    RESERVATION_ID INT,
    CABIN_ID INT
)
```

The relationship between the CABIN records and the RESERVATION records through the RESERVATION_CABIN_LINK table is illustrated in Figure 7-19.

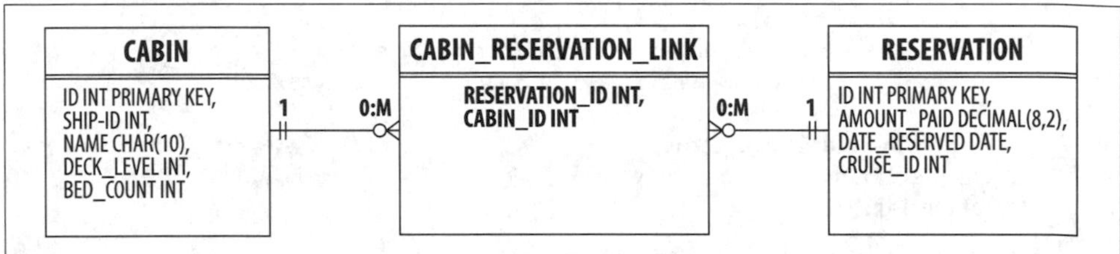

Figure 7-19. Many-to-many, unidirectional relationship in RDBMS

Abstract programming model

To model this relationship, we need to add a collection-based relationship field for Cabin beans to the Reservation EJB:

```
public abstract class ReservationBean implements javax.ejb.EntityBean {
    ...
    public abstract void setCabins(Set cabins);
    public abstract Set getCabins( );
    ...
}
```

In addition, we need to define a Cabin bean. Notice that the Cabin bean doesn't maintain a relationship back to the Reservation EJB. The lack of a container-managed relationship field for the Reservation EJB tells us the relationship is unidirectional:

```
public abstract class CabinBean implements javax.ejb.EntityBean {

    public Integer ejbCreate(ShipLocal ship, String name) {
        this.setName(name);
        return null;
    }
    public void ejbPostCreate(ShipLocal ship, String name) {
        this.setShip(ship);
    }
    public abstract void setShip(ShipLocal ship);
    public abstract ShipLocal getShip( );
    public abstract Integer getId( );
    public abstract void setId(Integer id);
    public abstract void setName(String name);
    public abstract String getName( );
    public abstract void setBedCount(int count);
```

```
        public abstract int getBedCount( );
        public abstract void setDeckLevel(int level);
        public abstract int getDeckLevel( );

        // EJB callback methods
    }
```

Although the Cabin bean doesn't define a relationship field for the Reservation EJB, it does define a one-to-many, bidirectional relationship for the Ship EJB. The effect of exchanging relationship fields in a many-to-many, unidirectional relationship is basically the same as in a many-to-many, bidirectional relationship. Use of the `Collection.addAll( )` operation to share entire collections has the same net effect; the only difference is that the arrows point only one way, instead of both ways.

If a Reservation removes a Cabin bean from its collection-based relationship field, it doesn't affect other Reservation EJBs that reference the Cabin bean (Figure 7-20).

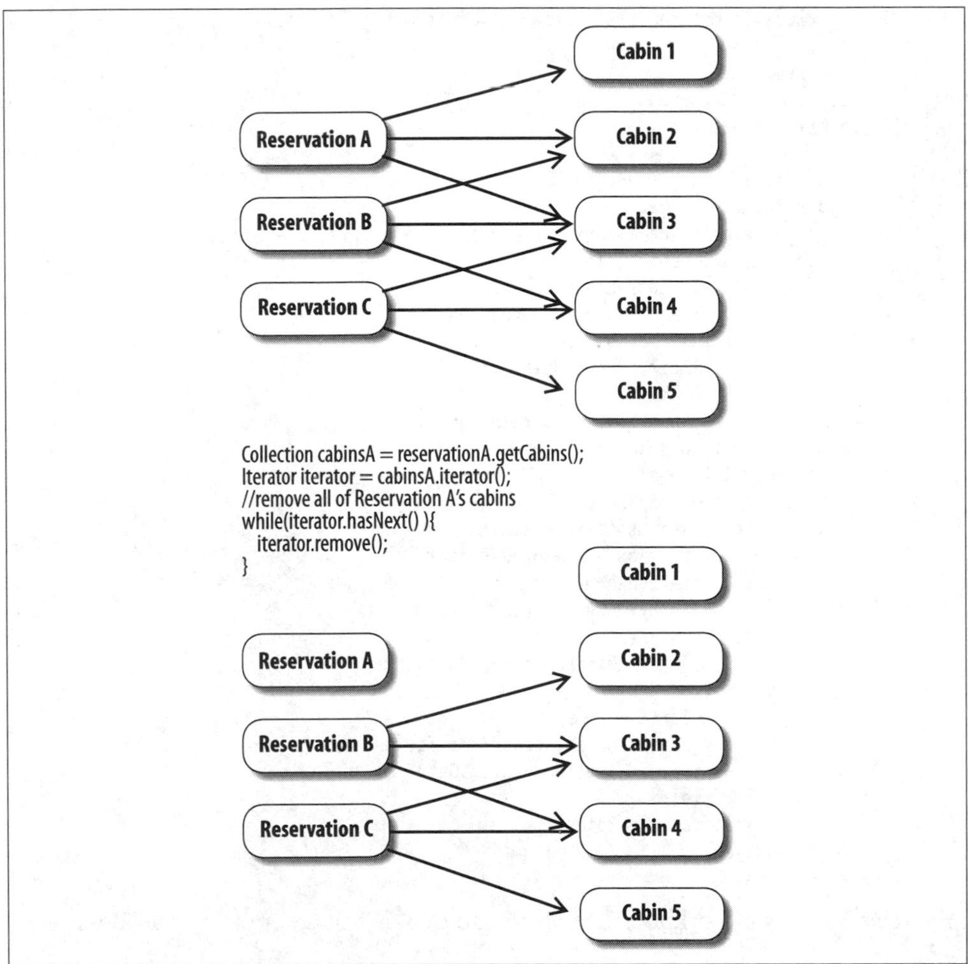

Figure 7-20. Removing beans in a many-to-many, unidirectional relationship

Abstract persistence schema

The abstract persistence schema for the Reservation-Cabin relationship holds no surprises. The multiplicity of both `<ejb-relationship-role>` elements is `Many`, but only the Reservation EJB's `<ejb-relationship-role>` defines a `<cmr-field>`:

```
<ejb-jar>
...
<enterprise-beans>
    <entity>
        <ejb-name>CabinEJB</ejb-name>
        <local-home>com.titan.cabin.CabinHomeLocal</local-home>
        <local>com.titan.cabin.CabinLocal</local>
        ...
    </entity>
    <entity>
        <ejb-name>ReservationEJB</ejb-name>
        <local-home> com.titan.reservation.ReservationHomeLocal</local-home>
        <local>com.titan.reservation.ReservationLocal</local>
        ...
    </entity>
    ...
</enterprise-beans>

<relationships>
    <ejb-relation>
        <ejb-relation-name>Cabin-Reservation</ejb-relation-name>
        <ejb-relationship-role>
            <ejb-relationship-role-name>
                Cabin-has-many-Reservations
            </ejb-relationship-role-name>
            <multiplicity>Many</multiplicity>
            <relationship-role-source>
                <ejb-name>CabinEJB</ejb-name>
            </relationship-role-source>
        </ejb-relationship-role>
        <ejb-relationship-role>
            <ejb-relationship-role-name>
                Reservation-has-many-Customers
            </ejb-relationship-role-name>
            <multiplicity>Many</multiplicity>
            <relationship-role-source>
                <ejb-name>ReservationEJB</ejb-name>
            </relationship-role-source>
            <cmr-field>
                <cmr-field-name>cabins</cmr-field-name>
                <cmr-field-type>java.util.Set</cmr-field-type>
            </cmr-field>
        </ejb-relationship-role>
    </ejb-relation>
</relationships>
```

Exercise 7.2 in the Workbook shows how to deploy this example on the JBoss server.

Co-Location and the Deployment Descriptor

If two entity beans are to have a relationship, they must be deployed by the same deployment descriptor. When deployed together, the entity beans are seen as a single deployment unit or application, in which all the entities are using the same database and are co-located in the same JVM. This restriction makes it possible for the EJB container system to use lazy loading, optimistic concurrency, and other performance optimizations. While it would technically be possible to support relationships across deployments or even across container systems, the difficulty of doing so, combined with the expected degradation in performance, was reason enough to limit relationship fields to entity beans that are deployed together. In the future, entity relationships may be expanded to include remote references to entities deployed in other containers or other JAR files in the same container.

Cascade Delete and Remove

As you learned in Chapter 5, invoking the `remove( )` operation on the EJB home or EJB object of an entity bean deletes that entity bean's data from the database. Deleting the bean's data, of course, has an impact on the relationships that entity bean has with other entity beans.

When an entity bean is deleted, the EJB container first removes it from any relationships it maintains with other entity beans. Consider, for example, the relationship between the entity beans we have created in this chapter (shown in Figure 7-21).

If an EJB application invokes `remove( )` on a CreditCard EJB, the Customer EJB that referenced that bean would have a value of `null` for its `creditCard` relationship field, as the following code fragment illustrates:

```
CustomerLocal customer = ... get Customer EJB
CreditCardLocal creditCard = customer.getCreditCard( );
creditCard.remove( );
if(customer.getCreditCard( ) == null)
    // this will always be true
```

The moment the `remove( )` operation is invoked on the CreditCard EJB's local reference, the bean is disassociated from the Customer bean and deleted. The impact of removing a bean is even more interesting when that bean participates in several relationships. For example, invoking `remove( )` on a Customer EJB will affect the relationship fields of the Reservation, Address, Phone, and CreditCard EJBs. With single EJB object relationship fields, such as the CreditCard EJB's reference to the Customer EJB, the field for the bean that is removed is set to `null`. With collection-based relationship fields, the entity that is deleted is removed from the collection. In some cases, you want the removal of an entity bean to cause a cascade of deletions. For example, if a Customer EJB is removed, we also want the Address EJBs referenced in its `billingAddress` and `homeAddress` relationship field to be deleted, in order to avoid leaving disconnected Address EJBs in the database. The `<cascade-delete>` element

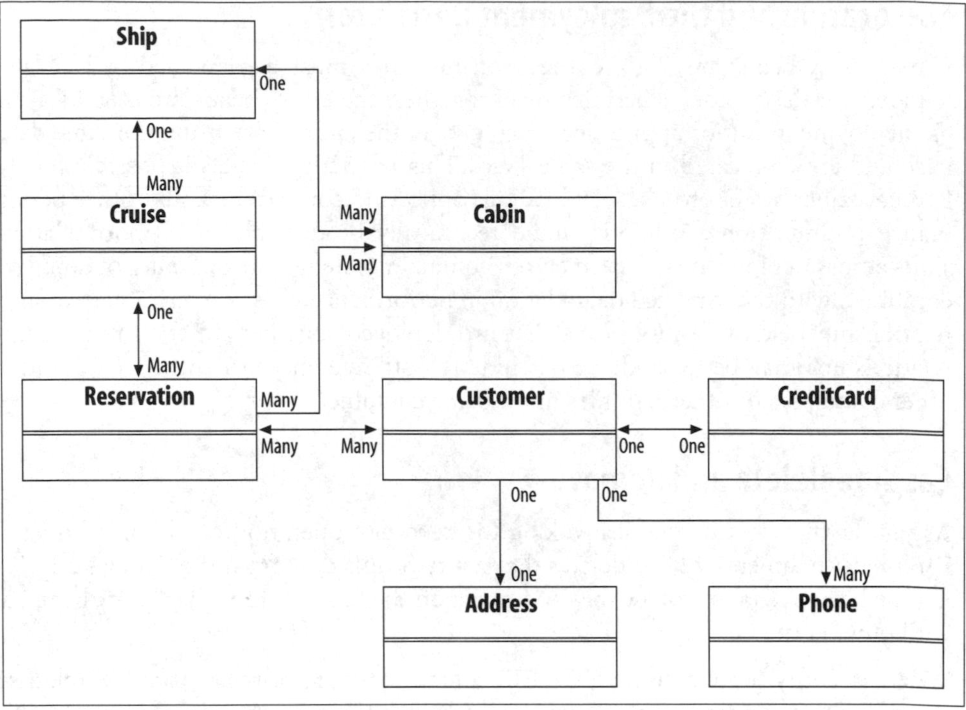

Figure 7-21. Titan Cruises class diagram

requests cascade delete; it can be used with one-to-one or one-to-many relationships. It does not make sense in many-to-many and many-to-one relationships. For example, in the many-to-one relationship between the Reservation and Cruise EJBs, cancellation of a reservation by one passenger should not cancel the cruise itself! In other words, we would not want the deletion of a Reservation EJB to cause the deletion of its Cruise EJB.

Here's how to modify the relationship declaration for the Customer and Address EJBs in order to obtain a cascade delete:

```
<relationships>
    <ejb-relation>
        <ejb-relationship-role>
            <multiplicity>One</multiplicity>
            <relationship-role-source>
                <ejb-name>CustomerEJB</ejb-name>
            </relationship-role-source>
            <cmr-field>
                <cmr-field-name>homeAddress</cmr-field-name>
            </cmr-field>
        </ejb-relationship-role>
        <ejb-relationship-role>
            <multiplicity>One</multiplicity>
            <cascade-delete/>
```

```
            <relationship-role-source>
                <ejb-name>AddressEJB</ejb-name>
            </relationship-role-source>
        </ejb-relationship-role>
    </ejb-relation>
</relationships>
```

If you do not specify a cascade delete, the ADDRESS record associated with the Address EJB is not be removed when the CUSTOMER record is deleted. This can result in a disconnected entity: rows in the database that are not linked to anything. In some cases, we want to specify a cascading delete to ensure that no detached entities remain after a bean is removed. However, it's important to use a cascading delete with care. If, for example, the ADDRESS record associated with an entity bean is shared by other CUSTOMER records (i.e., if two different customers reside at the same residence), we probably do not want it to be deleted when the CUSTOMER record is deleted. A cascade delete can be specified only on an entity bean that has a single reference to the entity being deleted. For example, you can specify a cascade delete in the <ejb-relationship-role> for the Phone EJB in the Customer-Phone relationship if the Customer is deleted, because each Phone EJB is referenced by only one Customer. However, you cannot specify a cascade delete for the Customer EJB in this relationship, because a Customer may be referenced by many Phone EJBs. The entity bean that causes the cascade delete must have a multiplicity of One in the relationship.

A cascade delete affects only the relationship for which it is specified. So, for example, if you specify a cascade delete for the Customer-Phone relationship but not the Customer-HomeAddress relationship, deleting a Customer causes all the Phone EJBs to be deleted, but not the Address EJBs. You must also specify a cascade delete for the Address EJBs if you want them to be deleted.

Cascade delete can propagate through relationships in a chain reaction. For example, if the Ship-Cruise relationship specifies a cascade delete on the Cruise relationship field and the Cruise-Reservation relationship specifies a cascade delete on the Reservation relationship field, when a Ship is removed all of its Cruises and the Reservations for those Cruises will be removed.

Cascade delete is a powerful tool, but it's also dangerous and should be handled with care. The effectiveness of a cascade delete depends in large part on the referential integrity of the database. For example, if the database is set up so that a foreign key must point to an existing record, deleting an entity's data could violate that restriction and cause a transaction rollback.

Exercise 7.3 in the Workbook show how to deploy the examples in this section.

CHAPTER 8

CMP: EJB QL

Find methods have been a part of the Enterprise JavaBeans specification since EJB 1.0. These methods are defined on the entity bean's home interfaces and are used for locating entity beans. All home interfaces must have a findByPrimaryKey( ) method, which takes the primary key of the entity bean as an argument and returns a remote or local reference to that entity bean. For example, the Cruise EJB defines this find method in its home interface as:

```
public CruiseHomeLocal  extends  javax.ejb.EJBLocalHome {
  public Integer create(String name,ShipLocal ship)
    throws CreateException;

  public CruiseLocal findByPrimaryKey(Integer key)
    throws FinderException;
}
```

In addition to the mandatory findByPrimaryKey( ) method, home interfaces can define as many custom find methods as needed. For example, the Cruise EJB might define a method called findByName( ) for locating a Cruise with a specific name:

```
public CruiseHomeLocal extends javax.ejb.EJBLocalHome {
  public Integer create(String name,ShipLocal ship)
    throws CreateException;

  public CruiseLocal findByPrimaryKey(Integer key)
    throws FinderException;

  public CruiseLocal findByName(String cruiseName)
   throws FinderException;
}
```

It's not obvious to the container how a custom find method should behave. In EJB 1.0 and 1.1, vendors came up with their own query languages and methods to specify the behavior of these other solutions. Consequently, the custom methods generally were not portable, and guesswork was required on the part of the deployer to determine how to properly execute queries against them. EJB 2.0 introduced the Enterprise JavaBeans Query Language (EJB QL)—a standard query language for declaring the behavior of custom find methods—and the new select methods. Select methods are similar to find methods, but they are more flexible and are visible to the bean class only. Find and select methods are collectively referred to as *query* methods. EJB 2.1 enhances EJB QL by adding aggregate functions, the ORDER BY clause, and other new features. The differences in EJB QL between EJB 2.1 and EJB 2.0 are clearly stated throughout this chapter.

EJB QL is a declarative query language similar to the Structured Query Language (SQL) used in relational databases, but it is tailored to work with the abstract persistence schema of entity beans. EJB QL queries are defined in terms of the abstract persistence schema of entity beans and not the underlying data store, so they are portable across databases and data schemas. When an entity bean's abstract bean class is deployed, the EJB QL statements are translated into data access code optimized for a specific data store. At runtime, query methods defined in EJB QL usually execute in the native language of the underlying data store. For example, a container that uses a relational database for persistence might translate EJB QL statements into standard SQL 92, while an object-database container might translate the same EJB QL statements into an object query language.

EJB QL makes it possible to define queries that are portable across databases and EJB vendors. The EJB QL language is easy for developers to learn, yet precise enough to be interpreted into native database code. It is a rich and flexible query language that empowers developers, while executing in fast native code at runtime. However, EJB QL is not a silver bullet and is not without its problems, as we'll see later in this chapter.

Declaring EJB QL

EJB QL statements are declared in `<query>` elements in an entity bean's deployment descriptor. In the following listing, the `findByName()` method defined in the Cruise bean's local home interface has its own query element and EJB QL statement:

```
<ejb-jar ...>
    <enterprise-beans>
        <entity>
            <ejb-name>CruiseEJB</ejb-name>
            ...
            <reentrant>False</reentrant>
            <abstract-schema-name>Cruise</abstract-schema-name>
            <cmp-version>2.x</cmp-version>
            <cmp-field>
                    <field-name>name</field-name>
            </cmp-field>
            <primkey-field>id</primkey-field>
            <query>
             <query-method>
               <method-name>findByName</method-name>
               <method-params>
```

```
                <method-param>java.lang.String</method-param>
              </method-params>
            </query-method>
            <ejb-ql>
              SELECT OBJECT(c) FROM Cruise AS c
              WHERE c.name = ?1
            </ejb-ql>
          </query>
      </entity>
    </enterprise-beans>
</ejb-jar>
```

The <query> element contains two primary elements. The <query-method> element identifies a particular find method, and the <ejb-ql> element declares the EJB QL statement. The <query> element binds the EJB QL statement to the proper find method. Don't worry too much about the EJB QL statement just yet; we'll cover that in detail starting in the next section.

Every entity bean that is referenced in an EJB QL statement must have a special designator called an *abstract schema name*, which is declared by the <abstract-schema-name> element. Each element must declare a unique name. These names must be unique: no two entity beans may have the same abstract schema name. In the entity element that describes the Cruise EJB, the abstract schema name is declared as `Cruise`. The <ejb-ql> element contains an EJB QL statement that uses this identifier in its `FROM` clause.

The Query Methods

There are two main types of query methods: find methods and select methods. These are discussed in the following sections.

Find Methods

Find methods are invoked by EJB clients (applications or beans) to obtain EJB object references to specific entity beans. For example, you might call the `findByPrimaryKey( )` method on the Customer EJB's home interface to obtain a reference to a specific Customer bean.

Find methods are always declared in the local and remote home interfaces of an entity bean. Specifying a single remote or local return type for a find method indicates that the method locates only one bean. `findByPrimaryKey( )` obviously returns a single remote reference, because there is a one-to-one correspondence between a primary key's value and an entity. Other single-entity find methods can also be declared. For example, in the following code segment the Customer EJB declares several single-entity find methods, each of which supports a different query:

```
public interface CustomerHomeRemote extends javax.ejb.EJBHome {
    public CustomerRemote findByPrimaryKey(Integer primaryKey)
        throws javax.ejb.FinderException, java.rmi.RemoteException;
```

```
    public CustomerRemote findByName(String lastName, String firstName)
        throws javax.ejb.FinderException, java.rmi.RemoteException;

    public CustomerRemote findBySSN(String socialSecurityNumber)
        throws javax.ejb.FinderException, java.rmi.RemoteException;
}
```

Bean developers can also define multi-entity find methods, which return a collection of EJB objects. The following listing shows a couple of multi-entity find methods:

```
public interface CustomerHomeLocal extends javax.ejb.EJBLocalHome {
    public CustomerLocal findByPrimaryKey(Integer primaryKey)
        throws javax.ejb.FinderException;

    public Collection findByCity(String city,String state)
        throws javax.ejb.FinderException;

    public Collection findByGoodCredit( )
        throws javax.ejb.FinderException;
}
```

To return several references from a find method, you must use a `java.util.Collection` type.* A find method that uses this return type may have duplicates. To avoid duplicates, use the keyword `DISTINCT` in the EJB QL statement associated with the find method. Multi-entity finds return an empty `Collection` if no matching beans are found.

All query methods (find or select) must be declared as throwing the `javax.ejb.FinderException`. Find methods that return a single remote reference throw a `FinderException` if an application error occurs and a `javax.ejb.ObjectNotFoundException` if a matching bean cannot be found. The `ObjectNotFoundException` is a subtype of `FinderException` that is thrown only by single-entity find methods.

With the exception of `findByPrimaryKey( )` methods, all find methods must be declared in `<query>` elements in the bean's deployment descriptor. Query declarations for `findByPrimaryKey( )` methods are not necessary and, in fact, are forbidden. It's obvious what this method should do, and you may not try to change its behavior. The following snippet from the Customer EJB's deployment descriptor shows declarations of two find methods, `findByName( )` and `findByGoodCredit( )`:

```
<query>
    <query-method>
        <method-name>findByName</method-name>
        <method-params>
            <method-param>java.lang.String</method-param>
            <method-param>java.lang.String</method-param>
        </method-params>
    </query-method>
    <ejb-ql>
```

* In The `java.util.Collection` is the only collection type supported for multi-entity find methods in CMP.

```
        SELECT OBJECT(c) FROM Customer AS c
        WHERE c.lastName = ?1 AND c.firstName = ?2
    </ejb-ql>
</query>
<query>
    <query-method>
        <method-name>findByGoodCredit</method-name>
        <method-params/>
    </query-method>
    <ejb-ql>
        SELECT OBJECT(c) FROM Customer AS c
        WHERE c.hasGoodCredit = TRUE
    </ejb-ql>
</query>
```

The `<query>` elements allow the bean developer to associate EJB QL statements with specific find methods. When the bean is deployed, the container attempts to match the find method declared in each of the query elements with find methods in the entity bean's home interfaces. To do so, it matches the values of the `<method-name>` and `<method-params>` elements with method names and parameter types (ordering is important) in the home interfaces.

When two find methods have the same method name and parameters, the query declaration applies to both methods. (This situation occurs when similar find methods are in the local home and remote home interfaces.) The container returns the proper type for each query method: the remote home returns remote EJB objects, and the local home returns local EJB objects. You can therefore define the behavior of both the local and remote home find methods using a single `<query>` element, which is convenient if you want local clients to have access to the same find methods as remote clients.

The `<ejb-ql>` element specifies the EJB QL statement for a specific find method. EJB QL statements can use input parameters (e.g., `?1`, `?2`, ... `?n`), which are mapped to the `<method-param>` elements of the find method, as well as literals (e.g., `TRUE`).

Select Methods

Select methods are similar to find methods, but they are more versatile and can be used only internally, by the bean class. In other words, select methods are private query methods; they are not exposed to an entity bean's interfaces.

Select and find methods also execute in different transaction contexts. The select method executes in the transaction context of the business or callback method that is using it, while the find methods execute according to their own transaction attributes, as specified by the bean provider.

Select methods are declared as abstract methods using the naming convention `ejbSelect<`*`METHOD-NAME`*`>`. Here are four select methods declared in the `AddressBean` class:

```
public class AddressBean implements javax.ejb.EntityBean {
    ...
    public abstract String ejbSelectMostPopularCity( )
        throws FinderException;

    public abstract Set ejbSelectZipCodes(String state)
        throws FinderException;

    public abstract Collection ejbSelectAll( )
        throws FinderException;

    public abstract CustomerLocal ejbSelectCustomer(AddressLocal addr)
        throws FinderException;
    ...
}
```

Select methods can return the values of CMP fields. The `ejbSelectMostPopularCity( )` method, for example, returns a single `String` value, the name of the city referenced by the most Address EJBs.

To return several references from a select method, you must declare the return type to be either a `Collection` or a `Set`.* Which type to return depends on whether you want to allow duplicate values. By definition, a `Set` never contains duplicates, while a `Collection` may have duplicates. Multi-entity selects return an empty `Collection` or `Set` if no matching beans are found. For example, the `ejbSelectZipCodes( )` method returns a `java.util.Set` of `String` values: a unique collection of all the Zip codes declared for the Address EJBs for a specific state.

Like find methods, select methods can declare arguments that limit the scope of the query. For example, the `ejbSelectZipCodes( )` and `ejbSelectCustomer( )` methods declare arguments that limit the scope of the results. These arguments are used as input parameters in the EJB QL statements assigned to the select methods.

Select methods can return local or remote EJB objects. Whether a single-entity select method returns a local or a remote object is determined by the return type of the `ejbSelect( )` method. The `ejbSelectCustomer( )` method, for example, returns a local EJB object, the `CustomerLocal`. This method could easily have been defined to return a remote object by changing the return type to the Customer bean's remote interface (`CustomerRemote`). Multi-entity select methods, which return a collection of EJB objects, return local EJB objects by default. However, you can override this behavior by using the `<result-type-mapping>` element in the select method's `<query>` element.

The following snippet from an XML deployment descriptor declares two select methods. Notice that they are exactly the same as the find method declarations:

```
<query>
    <query-method>
```

* Other collection types, such as `java.util.List` and `java.util.Map`, may be added in future versions.

```
        <method-name>ejbSelectZipCodes</method-name>
        <method-params>
        <method-param>java.lang.String</method-param>
        </method-params>
      </query-method>
      <ejb-ql>
          SELECT a.homeAddress.zip FROM Address AS a
          WHERE a.homeAddress.state = ?1
      </ejb-ql>
  </query>
  <query>
      <query-method>
          <method-name>ejbSelectAll</method-name>
          <method-params/>
      </query-method>
      <result-type-mapping>Remote</result-type-mapping>
      <ejb-ql>
          SELECT OBJECT(a) FROM Address AS a
      </ejb-ql>
  </query>
```

The name given in each `<method-name>` element must match one of the `ejbSelect<METHOD-NAME>()` methods defined in the bean class. This is different from find methods in CMP, which use the names of select methods defined by the bean class.

By default, the `<result-type-mapping>` element in the value of `<result-type-mapping>` can be either `Remote` or `Local`. `Local` indicates that the select method should return local EJB objects; `Remote` indicates remote EJB objects. For a single-entity select, the actual return type of the `ejbSelect()` method must match the `<result-type-mapping>`. In the previous example, the `<result-type-mapping>` element for the `ejbSelectAll()` method is declared as `Remote`, which means the query should return remote EJB object types (i.e., remote references to the Address EJB).*

Select methods can be used to query all the entity beans declared in the same deployment descriptor. Select methods may be called by a bean's `ejbHome()` methods, by any business methods, or by the `ejbLoad()` and `ejbStore()` methods. In most cases, select methods will be called by `ejbHome()` or by business methods in the bean class.

The most important thing to remember about select methods is that while they can do anything find methods can and more, they can be used only by the entity bean class that declares them, not by the entity bean's clients.

* This is illustrative. As a developer, it is unlikely (although possible) that you would define a remote interface for the Address EJB, because it is too fine-grained for use by remote clients.

EJB QL Examples

EJB QL is expressed in terms of the abstract persistence schema of an entity bean: its abstract schema name, CMP fields, and CMR fields. EJB QL uses the abstract schema names to identify beans, the CMP fields to specify values, and the CMR fields to navigate across relationships.

To discuss EJB QL, we will make use of the relationships among the Customer, Address, CreditCard, Cruise, Ship, Reservation, and Cabin EJBs defined in Chapter 7. Figure 8-1 is a class diagram that shows the direction and cardinality (multiplicity) of the relationships among these beans.

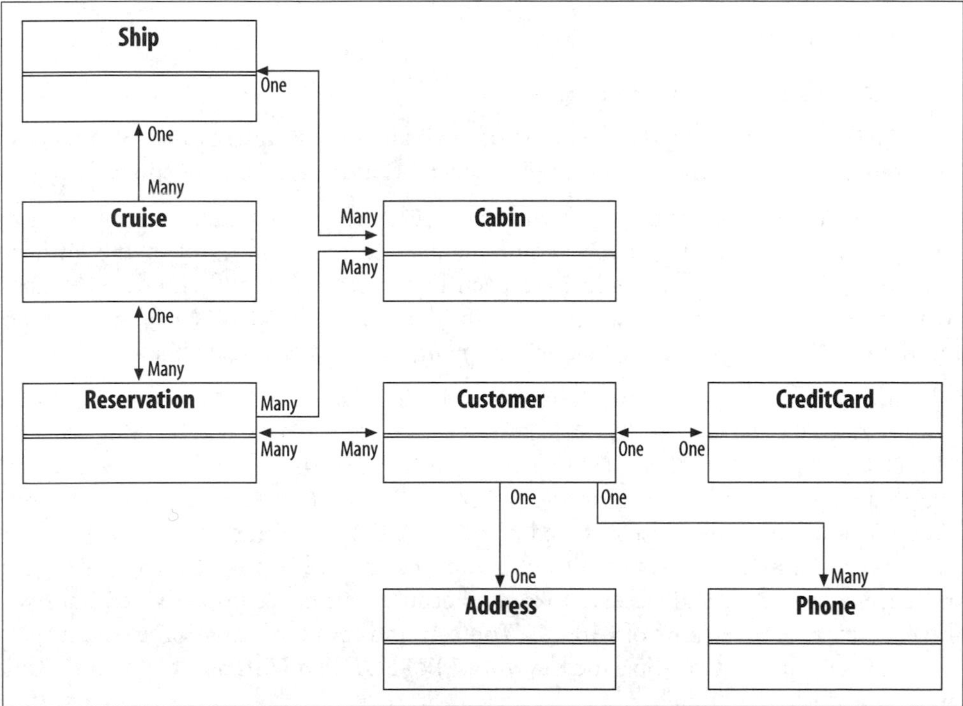

Figure 8-1. Titan Cruises class diagram

Simple Queries

The simplest EJB QL statement has no `WHERE` clause and only one abstract schema type. For example, you could define a query method to select all Customer beans:

```
SELECT OBJECT( c ) FROM Customer AS c
```

The `FROM` clause determines which entity bean types will be included in the select statement (i.e., provides the *scope* of the select). In this case, the `FROM` clause declares the type to be `Customer`, which is the abstract schema name of the Customer EJB.

The AS c part of the clause assigns c as the identifier of the Customer EJB. This is similar to SQL, which allows an identifier to be associated with a table. Identifiers can be any length and follow the same rules that are applied to field names in the Java programming language. However, identifiers cannot be the same as existing <ejb-name> or <abstract-schema-name> values. In addition, identification variable names are *not* case-sensitive, so an identifier of customer would be in conflict with an abstract schema name of Customer. For example, the following statement is illegal because Customer is the abstract schema name of the Customer EJB:

```
SELECT OBJECT( customer ) FROM Customer AS customer
```

The AS operator is optional, but it is used in this book to help make the EJB QL statements more clear. The following two statements are equivalent:

```
SELECT OBJECT(c) FROM Customer AS c

SELECT OBJECT(c) FROM Customer c
```

The SELECT clause determines the type of any values that are returned. In this case, the statement returns the Customer entity bean, as indicated by the c identifier.

The OBJECT( ) operator is required when the SELECT type is a solitary identifier for an entity bean. The reason for this requirement is pretty vague (and in the author's opinion, the specification would have been better off without it), but it is required whenever the SELECT type is an entity bean identifier. The OBJECT( ) operator is not used if the SELECT type is expressed using a *path*, which is discussed below.

Identifiers cannot be EJB QL reserved words. In EJB 2.0, the following words are reserved: SELECT, FROM, WHERE, DISTINCT, OBJECT, NULL, TRUE, FALSE, NOT, AND, OR, BETWEEN, LIKE, IN, AS, UNKNOWN, EMPTY, MEMBER, OF and IS. EJB 2.1 adds 10 new reserved words to this list, which include AVG, MAX, MIN, SUM, COUNT, ORDER, BY, ASC, DESC, and MOD. You shouldn't use these reserved words with EJB 2.0 either, because the queries that use them as identifiers won't be forward compatible with EJB 2.1. It's a good practice to avoid all SQL reserved words, because you never know which ones will be used by future versions of EJB QL. You can find more information in the Appendix ("SQL99 and Vendor-Specific Keywords") of *SQL in a Nutshell* by Kevin E. Kline with David Kline (O'Reilly).

Simple Queries with Paths

EJB QL allows SELECT clauses to return any CMP or single CMR field. For example, we can define a simple select statement to return the last names of all of Titan's customers:

```
SELECT c.lastName FROM Customer AS c
```

The SELECT clause uses a simple path to select the Customer EJB's lastName field as the return type. EJB QL uses the CMP and CMR field names declared in <cmp-field> and <cmr-field> elements of the deployment descriptor. To navigate between fields, use the familiar Java dot (.) operator. The previous EJB QL statement is based on the Customer EJB's deployment descriptor:

```
<enterprise-beans>
    <entity>
        <ejb-name>CustomerEJB</ejb-name>
        <home>com.titan.customer.CustomerHomeRemote</home>
        <remote>com.titan.customer.CustomerRemote</remote>
        <ejb-class>com.titan.customer.CustomerBean</ejb-class>
        <persistence-type>Container</persistence-type>
        <prim-key-class>java.lang.Integer</prim-key-class>
        <reentrant>False</reentrant>
        <abstract-schema-name>Customer</abstract-schema-name>
        <cmp-version>2.x</cmp-version>
        <cmp-field><field-name>id</field-name></cmp-field>
        <cmp-field><field-name>lastName</field-name></cmp-field>
        <cmp-field><field-name>firstName</field-name></cmp-field>
```

You can also use CMR field types in simple select statements. The following EJB QL statement selects all the CreditCard EJBs from all the Customer EJBs:

```
SELECT c.creditCard FROM Customer AS c
```

In this case, the EJB QL statement uses a path to navigate from the Customer EJBs to their `creditCard` relationship fields. The `creditCard` identifier is obtained from the `<cmr-field>` name used in the relationship element that describes the Customer-CreditCard relationship:

```
<enterprise-beans>
    <entity>
        <ejb-name>CustomerEJB</ejb-name>
        ...
        <abstract-schema-name>Customer</abstract-schema-name>
    </entity>
</enterprise-beans>
...
<relationships>
    <ejb-relation>
        <ejb-relation-name>Customer-CreditCard</ejb-relation-name>

        <ejb-relationship-role>
            <ejb-relationship-role-name>
                Customer-has-a-CreditCard
            </ejb-relationship-role-name>
            <multiplicity>One</multiplicity>
            <relationship-role-source>
                <ejb-name>CustomerEJB</ejb-name>
            </relationship-role-source>
         <cmr-field>
             <cmr-field-name>creditCard</cmr-field-name>
         </cmr-field>
        </ejb-relationship-role>
        <ejb-relationship-role>
        ...
```

Paths can be as long as required. It's common to use paths that navigate over one or more CMR fields to end at either a CMR or CMP field. For example, the following EJB QL statement selects all the `city` CMP fields of all the Address EJBs in each Customer EJB:

```
SELECT c.homeAddress.city  FROM Customer AS c
```

In this case, the path uses the abstract schema name of the Customer EJB, the Customer EJB's `homeAddress` CMR field, and the Address EJB's `city` CMP field.

To illustrate more complex paths, we'll need to expand the class diagram. Figure 8-2 shows that the CreditCard EJB is related to a CreditCompany EJB that has its own Address EJB.

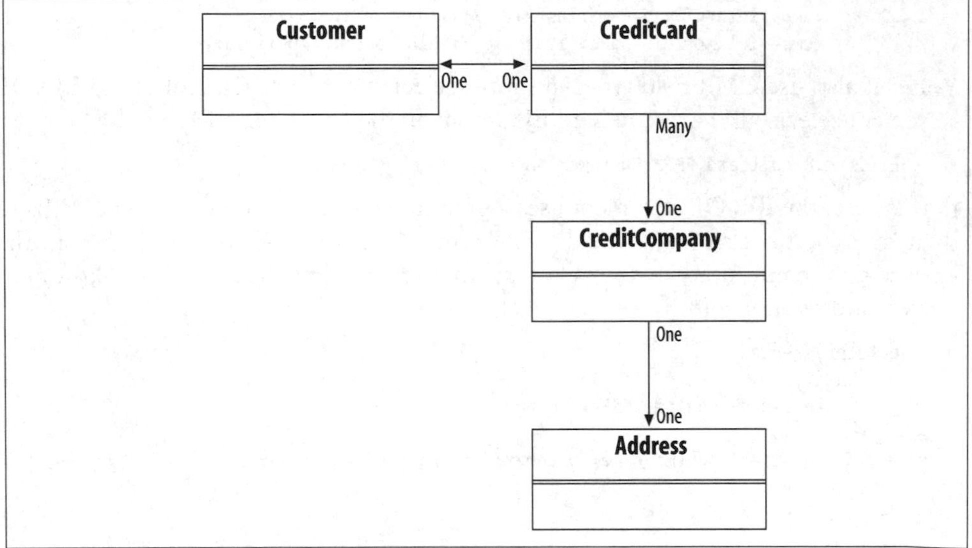

Figure 8-2. Expanded class diagram for CreditCard EJB

Using these relationships, we can specify a more complex path that navigates from the Customer EJB to the CreditCompany EJB to the Address EJB. Here's an EJB QL statement that selects the addresses of all the credit card companies used by Titan's customers:

```
SELECT c.creditCard.creditCompany.address FROM Customer AS c
```

The EJB QL statement could also navigate all the way to the Address bean's CMP fields. The following statement selects all the cities in which the credit card companies that distribute credit cards used by Titan's customers are based:

```
SELECT c.creditCard.creditCompany.address.city FROM Customer AS c
```

Note that these EJB QL statements return `address` CMR fields or `city` CMP fields only for those credit card companies responsible for cards owned by Titan's customers.

The address information of any credit card companies whose cards are not currently used by Titan's customers won't be included in the results.

Paths cannot navigate beyond CMP fields. For example, imagine that the Address EJB uses a `ZipCode` class as its `zip` CMP field:

```
public class ZipCode implements java.io.Serializable {
    public int mainCode;
    public int codeSuffix;
    ...
}
```

You can't navigate to one of the `ZipCode` class's instance fields:

```
// this is illegal
SELECT c.homeAddress.zip.mainCode FROM Customer AS c
```

The paths used in SELECT clauses of EJB QL statements must always end with a single type. They may not end with a collection-based relationship field. For example, the following is not legal because `reservations` is a collection-based relationship field:

```
// this is illegal
SELECT c.reservations FROM Customer AS c
```

In fact, it's illegal to navigate across a collection-based relationship field. The following EJB QL statement is also illegal, even though the path ends in a single-type relationship field:

```
// this is illegal
SELECT c.reservations.cruise FROM Customer AS c
```

If you think about it, this limitation makes sense. You can't use a navigation operator (.) in Java to access elements of a `java.util.Collection` object. For example, if `getReservations( )` returns a `java.util.Collection` type, this statement is illegal:

```
// this is illegal in the Java programming language
customer.getReservations().getCruise( );
```

Referencing the elements of a collection-based relationship field is possible, but it requires the use of an `IN` operator and an identification assignment in the `FROM` clause.

The IN Operator

Many relationships between entity beans are collection-based, and being able to access and select beans from these relationships is important. We've seen that it is illegal to select elements directly from a collection-based relationship. To overcome this limitation, EJB QL introduces the `IN` operator, which allows an identifier to represent individual elements in a collection-based relationship field.

The following query uses the `IN` operator to select the elements from a collection-based relationship. It returns all the reservations of all the customers:

```
SELECT OBJECT( r )
FROM Customer AS c,  IN( c.reservations ) AS r
```

The IN operator assigns the individual elements in the reservations CMR field to the identifier r. Once we have an identifier to represent the individual elements of the collection, we can reference them directly and even select them in the EJB QL statement. We can also use the element identifier in path expressions. For example, the following statement selects every cruise for which Titan's customers have made reservations:

```
SELECT r.cruise
FROM Customer AS c, IN( c.reservations ) AS r
```

The identifiers assigned in the FROM clause are evaluated from left to right. Once you declare an identifier, you can use it in subsequent declarations in the FROM clause. The identifier c, which was declared first, was subsequently used in the IN operator to define the identifier r.

The OBJECT( ) operator is used for single identifiers in the select statement and not for path expressions. While this convention makes little sense, it is required by the EJB specifications. As a rule of thumb, if the select type is a solitary identifier of an entity bean, it must be wrapped in an OBJECT( ) operator. If the select type is a path expression, OBJECT( ) is not necessary.

Identification chains can become very long. The following statement uses two IN operators to navigate two collection-based relationships and a single CMR relationship. While not necessarily useful, this statement demonstrates how a query can use IN operators across many relationships:

```
SELECT cbn.ship
FROM Customer AS c, IN ( c.reservations ) AS r,
IN( r.cabins ) AS cbn
```

To put the examples in this section into action, see Exercise 8.1 in the Workbook.

Using DISTINCT

The DISTINCT keyword ensures that the query does not return duplicates. It is especially valuable when applied to EJB QL statements used by multivalued find methods. Find methods in CMP have only one return type, java.util.Collection, which may include duplicates. For example, the following find method and its associated query will return duplicates:

```
// the find method declared in the remote or local home interface
public java.util.Collection  findAllCustomersWithReservations()

// the EJB QL statement associated with the find method
SELECT OBJECT( cust ) FROM Reservation AS res, IN (res.customers) AS cust
```

If a customer has more than one reservation, there will be duplicate references to that Customer EJB in the result Collection. Using the DISTINCT keyword ensures that each Customer EJB is represented only once in the result:

```
SELECT DISTINCT OBJECT( cust ) FROM Reservation AS res,
IN (res.customers) cust
```

The DISTINCT keyword can also be used with select methods. It works the same way for select methods that have a return type of Collection. If the select method's return type is java.util.Set, the DISTINCT keyword has no effect; the Set object eliminates duplicates by definition.

The WHERE Clause and Literals

You can use literal values to narrow the scope of the elements selected. This is accomplished through the WHERE clause, which behaves in much the same way as the WHERE clause in SQL.

For example, you can define an EJB QL statement that selects all the Customer EJBs that use a specific brand of credit card. The literal in this case is a String literal. Literal strings are enclosed by single quotes. Literal values that include a single quote, like the restaurant name "Wendy's," use two single quotes to escape the quote: 'Wendy''s'. The following statement returns customers that use American Express:

```
SELECT OBJECT( c ) FROM Customer AS c
WHERE c.creditCard.organization = 'American Express'
```

Path expressions in the WHERE clause are used in the same way as in the SELECT clause. When making comparisons with a literal, the path expression must evaluate to a CMP field; you can't compare a CMR field with a literal.

In addition to literal strings, literals can be exact numeric values (long types) and approximate numeric values (double types). Exact numeric literal values are expressed using the Java integer literal syntax (321, -8932, +22). Approximate numeric literal values are expressed using Java floating point literal syntax in scientific (5E3, -8.932E5) or decimal (5.234, 38282.2) notation. For example, the following EJB QL statement selects all the ships that weigh 100,000.00 metric tons:

```
SELECT OBJECT( s )
FROM Ship AS s
WHERE s.tonnage = 100000.00
```

Boolean literal values use TRUE and FALSE. Here's an EJB QL statement that selects all the customers who have good credit:

```
SELECT OBJECT( c ) FROM Customer AS c
WHERE c.hasGoodCredit = TRUE
```

The WHERE Clause and Input Parameters

Query methods (find and select methods) that use EJB QL statements may specify method arguments. *Input parameters* allow those method arguments to be mapped to EJB QL statements and are used to narrow the scope of the query. For example, the `ejbSelectByCity( )` method selects all the customers who reside in a particular city and state:

```
public abstract class CustomerBean implements javax.ejb.EntityBean {
    ...
    public abstract Collection ejbSelectByCity(String city,String state)
        throws FinderException;
    ...
}
```

The EJB QL statement for this method uses the `city` and `state` arguments as input parameters:

```
SELECT OBJECT( c ) FROM Customer AS c
WHERE c.homeAddress.state = ?2
AND c.homeAddress.city = ?1
```

Input parameters use a ? prefix followed by the argument's position, in order of the query method's parameters. In this case, `city` is the first argument listed in the `ejbSelectByCity( )` method and `state` is the second. When a query method declares one or more arguments, the associated EJB QL statement may use some or all of the arguments as input parameters.

Input parameters are not limited to simple CMP field types; they can also be EJB object references. For example, the following find method, `findByShip( )`, is declared in the Cruise bean's local home interface:

```
public interface CruiseLocalHome extends javax.ejb.EJBLocalHome {
    ...
    public Collection findByShip( ShipLocal ship )
        throws FinderException;
}
```

The EJB QL statement associated with this method would use the `ship` argument to locate all the cruises scheduled for the specified Ship bean:

```
SELECT OBJECT( crs ) FROM Cruise AS crs
WHERE crs.ship = ?1
```

When an EJB object is used as an input parameter, the container bases the comparison on the primary key of the EJB object. In this case, it searches through all the Cruise EJBs looking for references to a Ship EJB with the same primary key value as the one the Ship EJB passed to the query method.

The WHERE Clause and Operator Precedence

The `WHERE` clause is composed of conditional expressions that reduce the scope of the query and limit the number of items selected. Several conditional and logical operators can be used in expressions; they are listed below in order of precedence:

- Navigation operator (.)
- Arithmetic operators: +, - unary; *, / multiplication and division; +, - addition and subtraction
- Comparison operators: =, >, > =, <, <=, <> (not equal), `LIKE`, `BETWEEN`, `IN`, `IS NULL`, `IS EMPTY`, `MEMBER OF`
- Logical operators: `NOT`, `AND`, `OR`

The WHERE Clause and CDATA Sections

EJB QL statements are declared in XML deployment descriptors. XML uses the greater than (>) and less than (<) characters as delimiters for tags; using these symbols in the EJB QL statements causes parsing errors unless CDATA sections are used. For example, the following EJB QL statement causes a parsing error, because the XML parser interprets the > symbol as an incorrectly placed XML tag delimiter:

```
<query>
    <query-method>
        <method-name>findWithPaymentGreaterThan</method-name>
        <method-params>
            <method-param>java.lang.Double</method-param>
        </method-params>
    </query-method>
    <ejb-ql>
        SELECT OBJECT( r ) FROM Reservation AS r
        WHERE r.amountPaid  > ?1
    </ejb-ql>
</query>
```

To avoid this problem, place the EJB QL statement in a CDATA section, which takes the form `<![CDATA[`*`literal-text`*`]]>`:

```
<query>
    <query-method>
        <method-name>findWithPaymentGreaterThan</method-name>
        <method-params>
            <method-param>java.lang.Double</method-param>
        </method-params>
    </query-method>
    <ejb-ql>
        <![CDATA[
        SELECT OBJECT( r ) FROM Reservation AS r
        WHERE r.amountPaid  > 300.00
        ]]>
    </ejb-ql>
</query>
```

When an XML processor encounters a CDATA section, it doesn't attempt to parse the contents enclosed by the CDATA section; instead, the parser treats the contents as literal text.*

The WHERE Clause and Arithmetic Operators

The arithmetic operators allow a query to perform arithmetic in the process of doing a comparison. Arithmetic operators can be used only in the `WHERE` clause, not in the `SELECT` clause.

The following EJB QL statement returns references to all the Reservation EJBs that will be charged a port tax of more than $300.00:

```
SELECT OBJECT( r ) FROM Reservation AS r
WHERE (r.amountPaid * .01) > 300.00
```

The rules applied to arithmetic operations are the same as those used in the Java programming language, where numbers are *widened* or *promoted* in the process of performing a calculation. For example, multiplying a `double` and an `int` value requires that the `int` first be promoted to a `double` value. (The result will always be that of the widest type used in the calculation, so multiplying an `int` and a `double` results in a `double` value.)

`String`, `boolean`, and EJB object types cannot be used in arithmetic operations. For example, using the addition operator with two `String` values is considered an illegal operation. There is a special function for concatenating `String` values, covered later in the section titled "The WHERE Clause and Functional Expressions."

The WHERE Clause and Logical Operators

Logical operators such as `AND`, `OR`, and `NOT` operate the same way in EJB QL as their corresponding logical operators in SQL.

Logical operators evaluate only Boolean expressions, so each operand (i.e., each side of the expression) must evaluate to `true` or `false`. Logical operators have the lowest precedence so that all the expressions can be evaluated before they are applied.

The `AND` and `OR` operators don't behave like their Java language counterparts, `&&` and `||`. EJB QL does not specify whether the right-hand operands are evaluated conditionally. For example, the `&&` operator in Java evaluates its right-hand operand *only* if the left-hand operand is `true`. Similarly, the `||` logical operator evaluates the right-hand operand *only* if the left-hand operand is `false`. We can't make the same assumption for the `AND` and `OR` operators in EJB QL. Whether these operators evaluate right-hand operands depends on the native query language into which the state-

* To learn more about XML and the use of CDATA sections, see *XML in a Nutshell* by Elliotte Rusty Harold and W. Scott Means (O'Reilly).

ments are translated. It's best to assume that both operands are evaluated on all logical operators.

`NOT` simply reverses the Boolean result of its operand; expressions that evaluate to the Boolean value of `true` become `false`, and vice versa.

The WHERE Clause and Comparison Symbols

Comparison operators, which use the symbols =, >, >=, <, <=, and <>, should be familiar to you. The following statement selects all the Ship EJBs whose `tonnage` CMP field is greater than or equal to 80,000 tons but less than or equal to 130,000 tons:

```
SELECT OBJECT( s ) FROM Ship AS s
WHERE s.tonnage >= 80000.00 AND s.tonnage <= 130000.00
```

Only the = and <> (not equal) operators may be used on `boolean` and EJB object identifiers. In EJB 2.0, the greater-than and less-than symbols (>, >=, <, <=) can be used only on numeric values. In EJB 2.0, it's illegal to use the greater-than or less-than symbols to compare two `String`s. In EJB 2.1, the greater-than and less-than symbols can also be used with `String` values. However, the semantics of these operations are not defined by the EJB 2.1 specification. Is character case (upper or lower) important? Does leading and trailing whitespace matter? Issues like these affect the ordering of String values. In order for EJB QL to maintain its status as an abstraction of native query languages (e.g., SQL-92, JDOQL, OQL, etc.) it cannot dictate `String` ordering, because native query languages may have very different ordering rules. In fact, even different relational database vendors vary on the question of `String` ordering, which makes it all but impossible to standardize ordering even for SQL "compliant" databases.

Of course, this is all academic if you plan on using the same database well into the future. In such a case, the best thing to do is to examine the documentation for the database you are using to find out how it orders strings in comparisons. This tells you exactly how your EJB QL comparisons will work.

The WHERE Clause and Equality Semantics

While it is legal to compare an exact numeric value (`short`, `int`, `long`) to an approximate numeric value (`double`, `float`), all other equality comparisons must compare the same types. You cannot, for example, compare a `String` value of `123` to the `Integer` literal `123`. However, you can compare two `String` types for equality.

In EJB 2.1, you can compare numeric values for which the rules of numeric promotion apply. For example, a `short` may be compared to an `int`, an `int` to a `long`, etc. EJB 2.1 also states that primitives may be compared to primitive wrappers primitives—the rules of numeric promotion apply.

Where EJB 2.0 was very specific about String type comparisons, saying that they must match exactly, character-for-character, EJB 2.1 drops this requirement, making the evaluation of equality between String types more ambiguous. Again, this ambiguity arises from the differences between kinds of databases (relational versus object-oriented versus file), as well as differences between vendors of relational databases. Consult your vendor's documentation to determine exactly how String equality comparisons are evaluated.

You can also compare EJB objects for equality, but these too must be of the same type. To be more specific, they must both be EJB object references to beans from the same deployment. As an example, the following method finds all the Reservation EJBs made by a specific Customer EJB:

```
public interface ReservationHomeLocal extends EJBLocalHome {
    public Collection findByCustomer(CustomerLocal customer)
        throws FinderException;
    ...
}
```

The matching EJB QL statement uses the customer argument as a parameter:

```
SELECT OBJECT( r )
FROM Reservation r, IN ( r.customers ) AS cust
WHERE  cust = ?1
```

It's not enough for the EJB object used in the comparison to implement the CustomerLocal interface; it must be of the same bean type as the Customer EJB used in the Reservation's customers CMR field. In other words, they must be from the same deployment. Once it's determined that the bean is the correct type, the actual comparison is performed on the beans' primary keys. If they have the same primary key, they are considered equal.

You cannot use java.util.Date objects in equality comparisons. To compare dates, you must use the long millisecond value of the date, which means that the date must be persisted in a long CMP field, not a DateCMP field. The input value or literal must also be a long value. Use the java.util.Calandar class to obtain the long millisecond value of a Date object.

The WHERE Clause and BETWEEN

The BETWEEN clause is an inclusive operator specifying a range of values. In this example, we use it to select all ships weighing between 80,000 and 130,000 tons:

```
SELECT OBJECT( s ) FROM Ship AS s
WHERE s.tonnage BETWEEN 80000.00 AND 130000.00
```

The BETWEEN clause may be used only on numeric primitives (byte, short, int, long, double, float) and their corresponding java.lang.Number types (Byte, Short, Integer, etc.). It cannot be used on String, boolean, or EJB object references.

Using the NOT logical operator in conjunction with BETWEEN excludes the range specified. For example, the following EJB QL statement selects all the ships that weigh less than 80,000 tons or greater than 130,000 tons but excludes everything in between:

```
SELECT OBJECT( s ) FROM Ship AS s
WHERE s.tonnage NOT BETWEEN 80000.00 AND 130000.00
```

The net effect of this query is the same as if it had been executed with comparison symbols:

```
SELECT OBJECT( s ) FROM Ship AS s
WHERE s.tonnage < 80000.00 OR s.tonnage > 130000.00
```

The WHERE Clause and IN

The IN conditional operator used in the WHERE clause is not the same as the IN operator used in the FROM clause. In the WHERE clause, IN tests for membership in a list of literal values. For example, the following EJB QL statement uses the IN operator to select all the customers who reside in a specific set of states:

```
SELECT OBJECT( c ) FROM Customer AS c
WHERE c.homeAddress.state  IN ('FL', 'TX', 'MI', 'WI', 'MN')
```

Applying the NOT operator to this expression reverses the selection, excluding all customers who reside in the list of states:

```
SELECT OBJECT( c ) FROM Customer AS c
WHERE c.homeAddress.state NOT IN ('FL', 'TX', 'MI', 'WI', 'MN')
```

If the field tested is null, the value of the expression is "unknown", which means it cannot be predicted.

In EJB 2.0, the IN operator is limited to evaluating string values. In EJB 2.1, this operator can be used with operands that evaluate to either string or numeric values. For example, the following EJB QL statement uses the IN operator to select all cabins on deck levels 1, 3, 5, and 7:

```
SELECT OBJECT( cab ) FROM Cabin AS cab
WHERE cab.deckLevel IN (1,3,5,7)
```

EJB 2.1 also allows you to use the IN operator with input parameters; EJB 2.0 does not. For example, the following select method returns all the customers who live is the designated states:

```
public Collection ejbSelectCustomersByStates(String state1, String state2, String state3)
```

The EJB QL assigned to this select method would use the input parameters with the IN operator, as shown in the following listing:

```
SELECT OBJECT( c ) FROM Customer AS c
WHERE c.homeAddress.state IN ( ?1, ?2, ?3, 'WI', 'MN')
```

In this case, the input parameters (?1, ?2, and ?3) are combined with string literals ('WI' and 'MN') to show that mixing literal and input parameters is allowed, providing they are "like" types.

The WHERE Clause and IS NULL

The IS NULL comparison operator allows you to test whether a path expression is null. For example, the following EJB QL statement selects all the customers who do not have home addresses:

```
SELECT OBJECT( c ) FROM Customer AS c
WHERE c.homeAddress IS NULL
```

Using the NOT logical operator, we can reverse the results of this query, selecting all the customers who do have home addresses:

```
SELECT OBJECT( c ) FROM Customer AS c
WHERE c.homeAddress IS NOT NULL
```

In EJB 2.0, null fields in comparison operations (e.g., IN and BETWEEN) can cause bizarre side effects. In most cases, evaluating a null field in a comparison operation (other than IS NULL) produces an UNKNOWN result. Unknown evaluations throw the entire EJB QL result set into question. One way to avoid this situation is to require that fields used in the expressions have values. This requires careful programming. To ensure that an entity bean field is never null, you must initialize the field when the entity is created. For primitive values, this not a problem; they have default values, so they cannot be null. Other fields, such as single CMR fields and object-based CMP fields such as String, must be initialized in the ejbCreate( ) and ejbPostCreate( ) methods.

In EJB 2.1, path expressions are composed using "inner join" semantics. If an entity has a null CMR field, any query that uses that field as part of a path expression eliminates that entity from consideration. For example, if the Customer EJB representing "John Smith" has a null value for its address CMR field, then the "John Smith" Customer EJB won't be included in the result set for the following query:

```
SELECT OBJECT( c ) FROM Customer AS c
WHERE c.homeAddress.state = 'TX'
AND c.lastName = 'Smith' AND c.firstName = 'John'
```

This seems obvious at first, but stating it explicitly helps eliminate much of the ambiguity associated with null CMR fields. In EJB 2.0, it was unclear what would happen, which is why it was recommended that all CMR fields have values. This is not necessary in EJB 2.1.

In EJB 2.1, the NULL comparison operator can also be used to test input parameters. In this case, NULL is usually combined with the NOT operator to ensure that an input parameter is not a null value. For example, the query used in conjunction with the ejbSelectByCity( ) method can be modified to test for null input parameters.

```
public abstract class CustomerBean implements javax.ejb.EntityBean {
    ...
    public abstract Collection ejbSelectByCity(String city, String state)
        throws FinderException;
    ...
}
```

The EJB QL statement for this method first checks that the city and state input parameters are not null, and then uses them in comparison operations.

```
SELECT OBJECT( c ) FROM Customer AS c
WHERE ?1 IS NOT NULL AND ?2 IS NOT NULL
AND c.homeAddress.state = ?2
AND c.homeAddress.city = ?1
```

In this case, if either of the input parameters are null values, the query returns an empty Collection, avoiding the possibility of UNKNOWN results from null input parameters.

In EJB 2.1, if the results of a query include a null CMR or CMP field, the results must include null values. For example, the following query selects the Address EJBs customers with the last name "Smith":

```
SELECT c.address FROM Customer AS c
WHERE c.lastName = 'Smith'
```

If the Customer EJB representing "John Smith" has a null value for its address CMR field, the previous query returns a Collection that includes a null value—the null represents the address CMR field of "John Smith"—in addition to a bunch of Address EJB references. EJB 2.0 was not clear on whether null values were returned or not, but EJB 2.1 says they are. You can eliminate null values by including the NOT NULL operator in the query, as shown here:

```
SELECT c.address.city FROM Customer AS c
WHERE c.address.city NOT NULL AND c.address.state = 'FL'
```

The WHERE Clause and IS EMPTY

The IS EMPTY operator allows the query to test whether a collection-based relationship is empty. Remember from Chapter 7 that a collection-based relationship will never be null. If a collection-based relationship field has no elements, it returns an empty Collection or Set.

Testing whether a collection-based relationship is empty has the same purpose as testing whether a single CMR field or CMP field is null: it can be used to limit the scope of the query and items selected. For example, the following query selects all the cruises that have not booked any reservations:

```
SELECT OBJECT( crs ) FROM Cruise AS crs
WHERE crs.reservations IS EMPTY
```

The NOT operator reverses the result of IS EMPTY. The following query selects all the cruises that have at least one reservation:

```
SELECT OBJECT( crs ) FROM Cruise AS crs
WHERE crs.reservations IS NOT EMPTY
```

It is illegal to use IS EMPTY against collection-based relationships that have been assigned an identifier in the FROM clause:

```
// illegal query
SELECT OBJECT( r )
FROM Reservation AS r, IN( r.customers ) AS c
WHERE
r.customers IS NOT EMPTY AND
c.address.city = 'Boston'
```

While this query appears to be good insurance against UNKNOWN results, it's not. It's illegal because the IS EMPTY operator cannot be used on a collection-based relationship identified in an IN operator in the FROM clause. Because the relationship is specified in the IN clause, only those Reservation EJBs that have a nonempty customers field will be included in the query; any Reservation EJB that has an empty CMR field is already excluded because its customers elements cannot be assigned the c identifier.

The WHERE Clause and MEMBER OF

The MEMBER OF operator is a powerful tool for determining whether an EJB object is a member of a specific collection-based relationship. The following query determines whether a particular Customer (specified by the input parameter) is a member of any of the Reservation-Customer relationships:

```
SELECT OBJECT( crs )
FROM Cruise AS crs, IN (crs.reservations) AS res, Customer AS cust
WHERE
cust = ?1
  AND
cust MEMBER OF res.customers
```

Applying the NOT operator to MEMBER OF has the reverse effect, selecting all the cruises on which the specified customer does not have a reservation:

```
SELECT OBJECT( crs )
FROM Cruise AS crs, IN (crs.reservations) AS res, Customer AS cust
WHERE
cust = ?1
  AND
cust NOT MEMBER OF res.customers
```

Checking whether an EJB object is a member of an empty collection always returns false.

The WHERE Clause and LIKE

The LIKE comparison operator allows the query to select String type CMP fields that match a specified pattern. For example, the following EJB QL statement selects all the customers with hyphenated names, like "Monson-Haefel" and "Berners-Lee":

```
SELECT OBJECT( c ) FROM Customer AS c
WHERE c.lastName LIKE '%-%'
```

You can use two special characters when establishing a comparison pattern: `%` (percent) stands for any sequence of characters, and `_` (underscore) stands for any single character. You can use these characters at any location within a string pattern. If a `%` or `_` actually occurs in the string, you can escape it with the \ character. The `NOT` logical operator reverses the evaluation so that matching patterns are excluded. The following examples show how the LIKE clause evaluates `String` type CMP fields:

`phone.number LIKE '617%'`
: True for "617-322-4151"
  False for "415-222-3523"

`cabin.name LIKE 'Suite _100'`
: True for "Suite A100"
  False for "Suite A233"

`phone.number NOT LIKE '608%'`
: True for "415-222-3523"
  False for "608-233-8484"

`someField.underscored LIKE '\_%'`
: True for "_xyz"
  False for "abc"

`someField.percentage LIKE '\%%'`
: True for "% XYZ"
  False for "ABC"

The `LIKE` operator *cannot* be used with input parameters. This is an important point that is confusing to many new EJB developers. The `LIKE` operator compares a `String` type CMP field to a `String` literal. As it is currently defined, it cannot be used in a comparison with an input parameter, because an input parameter is, by definition, unknown until the method is invoked. The comparison pattern must be known at deployment time in order to generate the native query code.

Functional Expressions

In the previous edition of this book, I complained about the limited support for functions in EJB QL. EJB 2.1 has started to address this problem by adding five new aggregate functions for the SELECT clause as well as the MOD function for the WHERE clause.

Functional expressions in the WHERE clause

EJB QL has four functional expressions that allow for simple `String` manipulation and three functional expressions for basic numeric operations. The `String` functions are:

`CONCAT(String1, String2)`
: Returns the `String` that results from concatenating `String1` and `String2`.

`LENGTH(String)`
: Returns an `int` indicating the length of the string.

`LOCATE(String1, String2 [, start])`
: Returns an `int` indicating the position at which `String1` is found within `String2`. If it's present, `start` indicates the character position in `String2` at which the search should start. Support for the `start` parameter is optional; some containers will support it, it while others will not. Don't use it if you want to ensure the query is portable.

`SUBSTRING(String1, start, length)`
: Returns the `String` consisting of length characters taken from `String1`, starting at the position given by `start`.

The `start` and `length` parameters indicate positions in a `String` as integer values. You can use these expressions in the `WHERE` clause to refine the scope of the items selected. Here's how the `LOCATE` and `LENGTH` functions might be used:

```
SELECT OBJECT( c )
FROM Customer AS c
WHERE
LENGTH(c.lastName) > 6
  AND
LOCATE( c.lastName, 'Monson') > -1
```

This statement selects all the customers with `Monson` somewhere in their last name, but specifies that the name must be longer than six characters. Therefore, "Monson-Haefel" and "Monson-Ares" evaluate to `true`, but "Monson" returns `false` because it has only six characters.

The arithmetic functions in EJB QL may be applied to primitive as well as corresponding primitive wrapper types:

`ABS(number)`
: Returns the absolute value of a number (`int`, `float`, or `double`).

`SQRT(double)`
: Returns the square root of a `double`.

`MOD(int, int)`
: EJB 2.1 only. Returns the remainder for the first parameter divided by the second (i.e., MOD(7, 5) is equal to 2).

EJB 2.1: Aggregate functions in the SELECT clause

Aggregate functions are used with queries that return a collection of values. They are fairly simple to understand and can be handy, especially the `COUNT( )` function. It's important to understand that aggregate functions can only be used with select methods, not find methods. The find methods may only return EJB object references (local or remote).

COUNT (identifier or path expression). This function returns the number of items in the query's final result set. The return type is a `long` or `java.util.Long`, depending on whether it is the return type of the query method. For example, the following query provides a count of all the customers who live in Wisconsin:

```
SELECT  COUNT( c )
FROM Customers AS c
WHERE c.address.state = 'WI'
```

The `COUNT( )` function can be used with an identifier, in which case it always counting entities, or with path expressions, in which case it counts either CMR fields or CMP fields. For example, the following statement provides a count of all the Zip codes that start with the characters "554":

```
SELECT  COUNT(c.address.zip)
FROM Customers AS c
WHERE c.address.zip LIKE '554%'
```

In some cases, queries that count a path expression have a corresponding query that can be used to count an identifier. For example, the result of the following query, which counts Customers instead of the `zip` CMP field, is equivalent to the previous query:

```
SELECT COUNT( c )
FROM Customers AS c
WHERE c.address.zip LIKE '554%'
```

MAX(path expression), MIN(path expression). These functions can be used to find the largest or smallest value from a collection of any type of CMP field. They cannot be used with identifiers or paths that terminate in a CMR field. The result type will be the type of CMP field that is being evaluated. For example, the following query returns the highest price paid for a reservation:

```
SELECT MAX( r.amountPaid )
FROM Reservation AS r
```

The `MAX( )` and `MIN( )` functions can be applied to any valid CMP value, including primitive types, Strings, and even serializable objects. The result of applying the `MAX( )` and `MIN( )` functions to serializable objects is not specified, because there is no standard way to determine which serializable object is greater or lesser than another.

The result of applying the `MAX( )` and `MIN( )` functions to a `String` CMP field depends on the underlying data store. This has to do with the inherent problems associated with `String` type comparisons.

AVG(numeric), SUM(numeric). The `AVG( )` and `SUM( )` functions can only be applied to path expressions that terminate in a numeric primitive field (`byte`, `long`, `float`, etc.) or one their corresponding numeric wrappers (Byte, `Long`, `Float`, etc.). The result of a query that uses the `SUM( )` function has the same type as the numeric type it's evaluating. The result type of the `AVG( )` function is a `double` or `java.util.Double`, depending on whether it is used in the return type of the select method.

For example, the following query uses the SUM( ) function to get the total amount paid by all customers for a specific Cruise (specified by input parameter):

```
SELECT SUM( r.amountPaid)
FROM Cruise c, IN( c.reservations) AS r
WHERE  c = ?1
```

DISTINCT, nulls, and empty arguments. The DISTINCT operator can be used with any of the aggregate functions to eliminate duplicate values. The following query uses the DISTINCT operator to count the number of *different* Zip codes that match the pattern:

```
SELECT DISTINCT COUNT(c.address.zip)
FROM Customers AS c
WHERE c.address.zip LIKE '554%'
```

The DISTINCT operator first eliminates duplicate Zip codes; if 100 customers live in the same area with the same Zip code, their Zip code is only counted once. After the duplicates have been eliminated, the COUNT( ) function counts the number of items left.

Any CMP field with a null value is automatically eliminated from the result set operated on by the aggregate functions. The COUNT( ) function also ignores CMP values with null values. The aggregate functions AVG( ), SUM( ), MAX( ), and MIN( ) return null when evaluating an empty collection. For example, the following query attempts to obtain the average price paid by customers for a specific Cruise:

```
SELECT AVG( r.amountPaid)
FROM Cruise As c, IN( c.reservations ) AS r
WHERE c = ?1
```

If the Cruise specified by the input parameter has no reservations, the collection on which the AVG( ) function operates is empty (there are no reservations and therefore no amounts paid). In this case, the select method returns null if it specified a java.lang.Double or java.lang.Float return type. If, however, it returns the select method specified primitive type return value (e.g., double or float), a javax.ejb.ObjectNotFoundException will be thrown.

The COUNT( ) function returns 0 (zero) when the argument it evaluates is an empty collection. If the following query is evaluated on a Cruise with no reservations, the result is 0 (zero) because the argument is an empty collection:

```
SELECT COUNT( r )
FROM Cruise AS c, IN( c.reservations ) AS r
WHERE c = ?1
```

To deploy these examples in an EJB container, see Exercise 8.2 in the Workbook.

EJB 2.1: The ORDER BY Clause

The ORDER BY clause allows you to specify the order of the entities in the collection returned by a query. EJB 2.0 didn't include an ORDER BY clause, and as a result you never knew what order the results would be in. The semantics of the ORDER BY clause are basically the same as in SQL. For example, we can construct a simple query that uses the ORDER BY clause to return an alphabetical list of all of Titan's Customers:

```
SELECT OBJECT( c )
FROM Customers AS c
ORDER BY c.lastName
```

This might return a Collection of Customer EJBs in the following order (assume their last and first names are printed to output):

```
Aares, John
Astro, Linda
Brooks, Hank
.
.
Xerces, Karen
Zastro, William
```

You can use the ORDER BY clause with or without the WHERE clause. For example, we can refine the previous query by listing only those customers who reside in Boston, MA:

```
SELECT OBJECT( c )
FROM Customers AS c
WHERE c.address.city = 'Boston' AND c.address.state = 'MA'
ORDER BY c.lastName
```

The default order of an item listed in the ORDER BY clause is always ascending, which means that the lesser values are listed first and the greatest values last. You can explicitly specify the order as *ascending* or *descending* by using the key words ASC or DESC. The default is ASC. Here's a statement that lists customers in reverse (descending) order:

```
SELECT OBJECT( c )
FROM Customers AS c
ORDER BY c.lastName DESC
```

The results of this query are:

```
Zastro, William
Xerces, Karen
.
.
Brooks, Hank
Astro, Linda
Aares, John
```

You can specify multiple order-by items. For example, you can sort customers by lastName in ascending order and firstName in descending order:

```
SELECT OBJECT( c )
FROM Customers AS c
ORDER BY c.lastName ASC, c.firstName DESC
```

If you have five Customer EJBs with the lastName equal to "Brooks", this query sorts the results as follows:

```
Brooks, William
Brooks, Henry
```

```
Brooks, Hank
Brooks, Ben
Brooks, Andy
```

Although the fields used in the ORDER BY clause must be CMP fields, the value selected can be an entity identifier, a CMR field, or a CMP field. For example, the following query returns an ordered list of all Zip codes:

```
SELECT addr.zip
FROM Address AS addr
ORDER BY addr.zip
```

The following query returns all the Address EJBs for customers named "Smith", ordered by their Zip code.

```
SELECT c.address
FOR Customer AS c
WHERE c.lastName = 'Smith'
ORDER BY c.address.zip
```

You must be careful which CMP fields you use in the ORDER BY clause. If the query selects a collection of entities, than the ORDER BY clause can only be used with CMP fields of the entity type that is selected. The following query is illegal, because the CMP field used in the ORDER BY clause is not a field of the entity type selected:

```
// Illegal EJB QL
SELECT OBJECT( c )
FROM Customer AS c
ORDER BY c.address.city
```

Because the city CMP field is not a direct CMP field of the Customer EJB, you cannot use it in the ORDER BY clause.

A similar restriction applies to CMP results. The CMP field used in the ORDER BY clause must be the same as the CMP field identified in the SELECT clause. The following query is illegal, because the CMP that identified in the SELECT clause is not the same as the one used in the ORDER BY clause:

```
SELECT c.address.city
FROM Customer AS c
ORDER BY c.address.state
```

In the above query, we wanted a list of all the cities ordered by their state. Unfortunately, this is illegal. You can't order by the state CMP field if you are selecting the city CMP field.

Problems with EJB QL

EJB QL is a powerful new tool that promises to improve performance, flexibility, and portability of entity beans in container-managed persistence, but it has some design flaws and omissions.

The OBJECT( ) Operator

The use of the OBJECT( ) operator is cumbersome and provides little or no value to the bean developer. It's trivial for EJB vendors to determine when an abstract schema type is the return value, so the OBJECT( ) operator provides little real value during query translation. In addition, the OBJECT( ) operator is applied haphazardly. It's required when the return type is an abstract schema identifier, but not when a path expression of the SELECT clause ends in a CMR field. Both return an EJB object reference, so the use of OBJECT( ) in one scenario and not the other is illogical and confusing.

When questioned about this, Sun replied that several vendors had requested the use of the OBJECT( ) operator because it will be included in the next major release of the SQL programming language. EJB QL was designed to be similar to SQL because SQL is the query language that is most familiar to developers, but this doesn't mean it should include functions and operations that have no real meaning in Enterprise JavaBeans.

Lack of Support for Date

EJB QL doesn't provide native support for the java.util.Date class. The java.util.Date class should be supported as a natural type in EJB QL. It should be possible, for example, to do comparisons with Date CMP fields and literal and input parameters using comparison operators (=, >, >=, <, <=, <>). It should also be possible to introduce common date functions so that comparisons can be done at different levels, such as comparing the day of the week (DOW( )) or month (MONTH( )), etc. In addition, date literals should be supported. For example, a literal like "2004-04-02" for April 2nd, 2004 should be acceptable as a literal. Of course, supporting Date types and literals in EJB QL is not trivial and problems with interpretation of dates and locales would need to be considered, but the failure to address Date as a supported type is significant.

Limited Functions

While the aggregate functions and functional expressions provided by EJB QL are valuable to developers, many other functions should also be added. For example, CAST( ) (useful for comparing different types) and date functions, such as DOW( ), MONTH( ), etc., could be added. The UPPER( ) and LOWER( ) functional expressions should also be added—they make it possible to do caseless comparisons in the LIKE clause.

EJB 2.1 adds some functions to the SELECT clause, including COUNT( ), SUM( ), AVG( ), MAX( ), and MIN( ).

Multiple SELECT Expressions

In EJB 2.0 and 2.1, EJB QL statements can only declare a single SELECT expression. In other words, it's not possible to SELECT multiple items. The following query is illegal:

```
SELECT addr.city, addr.state
FROM Address AS addr
```

Today, you can only select either the city or the state, but not both.

GROUP BY and HAVING

In SQL, the GROUP BY and HAVING clauses are commonly used to apply stricter organization to a query and narrowing the results for aggregate functions. The GROUP BY clause is usually used in combination with aggregate functions, because it allows you to cluster data by category. For example, the following query provides a count for all the cities in each state:

```
SELECT addr.state, COUNT(addr.city)
FROM Address AS addr
GROUP BY addr.state
```

The HAVING clause is used with a GROUP BY clause and acts as a filter, restricting the final output. The HAVING clause employs aggregate functional expressions using only the identifiers used in the SELECT clause. For example, the following query uses the GROUP BY and HAVING clauses to select and count only the states with more than 200 cities:

```
SELECT addr.state, COUNT(addr.city)
FROM Address AS addr
GROUP BY addr.state
HAVING COUNT(addr.city) > 200
```

Subqueries

Subqueries can be useful; they are common to SQL and some other query languages. A subquery is a SELECT statement inside of another SELECT statement, usually in the WHERE, SELECT, or HAVING clause. For example, the following subquery finds the average amount paid for a reservation, a value that is subsequently used to find all reservations where the amount paid is greater than the average.

```
SELECT  OBJECT(res)
FROM Reservations AS res
WHERE res.amountPaid >=
     ( SELECT AVG(r.amountPaid) FROM Cruise AS c, IN( c.reservations ) AS r
       WHERE c = ?1   )
```

Dynamic Queries

Dynamic queries are supported by most vendors, but not the specification. In EJB 2.0 and 2.1, all EJB QL statements are statically compiled at deployment time. In other words, you can't make up a query on the fly and submit it to the EJB container system. This restriction makes it difficult to create reports and do analysis because you always have to know the queries before the beans are deployed. Most vendors already support dynamic queries—it's a mystery why EJB QL doesn't.

CHAPTER 9

Bean-Managed Persistence

From the developer's point of view, bean-managed persistence (BMP) requires more effort than container-managed persistence, because you must explicitly write the persistence logic into the bean class. In order to write the persistence-handling code into the bean class, you must know what type of database is being used and the how the bean class's fields map to that database.

Given that container-managed persistence saves a lot of work, why would anyone bother with bean-managed persistence? The main advantage of BMP is that it gives you more flexibility in how state is managed between the bean instance and the database. Entity beans that use data from a combination of different databases or other resources such as Enterprise Resource Planning (ERP) or legacy systems can benefit from BMP. Essentially, bean-managed persistence is the alternative to container-managed persistence when the container tools are inadequate for mapping the bean instance's state to the backend databases or resources. In most cases, you won't need to use BMP because most projects use relational databases which are supported by CMP, but BMP remains an excellent alternative when you need to represent data as entities from unsupported resources. When you do use BMP is likely that you will create entity beans that wrapper a J2EE Connector API that is accessing an ERP (e.g., SAP, PeopleSoft, etc.), legacy system (e.g., CICS, IMS, etc.), or proprietary resource of some type. You may also employ the JDO API (Java Data Object) to access an object-oriented database or some other resource. Its also possible that you will use more than one API to present a single view of data from two or more resources.

The primary disadvantage of BMP is obvious: more work is required to define the bean. You have to understand the structure of the database or resource and the APIs that access them, and you must develop the logic to create, update, and remove data associated with entities. This requires diligence in using the EJB callback methods (e.g., `ejbLoad()` and `ejbStore()`) appropriately. In addition, you must explicitly develop the find methods defined in the bean's home interfaces.

The select methods used in container-managed persistence are not supported in bean-managed persistence.

Another disadvantage of BMP is that it ties the bean to a specific database or resource type and structure. Any changes in the database or in the structure of data require changes to the bean instance's definition, and these changes may not be trivial. A bean-managed entity is not as database independent as a container-managed entity, but it can better accommodate a complex or unusual set of data.

To help you understand how BMP works, we will create a new Ship EJB that is similar to the one used in Chapter 7. For BMP, we need to implement the `ejbCreate( )`, `ejbLoad( )`, `ejbStore( )`, and `ejbRemove( )` methods to handle synchronizing the bean's state with the database.

The Remote Interface

We will need a remote interface for the Ship EJB. This interface is basically the same as any other remote or local interface. It defines the business methods used by clients to interact with the bean:

```
package com.titan.ship;

import javax.ejb.EJBObject;
import java.rmi.RemoteException;

public interface ShipRemote extends javax.ejb.EJBObject {
    public String getName( ) throws RemoteException;
    public void setName(String name) throws RemoteException;
    public void setCapacity(int cap) throws RemoteException;
    public int getCapacity( ) throws RemoteException;
    public double getTonnage( ) throws RemoteException;
    public void setTonnage(double tons) throws RemoteException;
}
```

We will not develop a local interface for the bean-managed Ship bean in this chapter; however, bean-managed entity beans can have either local or remote component interfaces, just like container-managed entity beans.

Set and Get Methods

The `ShipRemote` definition uses a series of accessor methods whose names begin with "set" and "get." This is not a required signature pattern, but it is the naming convention used by most Java developers when obtaining and changing the values of object attributes or fields. These methods are often referred to as *setters* and *getters*. These methods should be defined independently of the anticipated storage structure of the data. In other words, you should design the remote interface to model the business concepts, not the underlying data. Just because there's a `getCapacity( )` method doesn't mean that there has to be a `capacity` field in the bean or the database; the `getCapacity( )` method could conceivably compute the capacity from a list of cabins by looking up the ship's model and configuration, or with some other algorithm.

Defining entity business methods according to the business concept and not the underlying data is not always possible, but you should try to employ this strategy whenever you can. The reason is twofold. First, the underlying data doesn't always clearly define the business purpose or concept being modeled by the entity bean. Remote and local interfaces are often used by developers who know the business but not the database configuration. It is important to them that the entity bean reflect the business concept. Second, defining the properties of the entity bean independently of the data allows the bean and data to evolve separately. This is important because it allows a database implementation to change over time; it also allows for new behavior to be added to the entity bean as needed. If the bean's definition is independent of the data source, the impact change is limited.

The Remote Home Interface

Entity beans' home interfaces (local and remote) are used to create, locate, and remove objects from EJB systems. Each entity bean has its own remote or local home interface. The home interface defines two basic kinds of methods: zero or more create methods, and one or more find methods. In this example, the create methods act like remote constructors and define how new Ship EJBs are created. The find methods are used to locate a specific Ship or Ships. The following code contains the complete definition of the `ShipHomeRemote` interface:

```
package com.titan.ship;

import javax.ejb.EJBHome;
import javax.ejb.CreateException;
import javax.ejb.FinderException;
import java.rmi.RemoteException;
import java.util.Collection;

public interface ShipHomeRemote extends javax.ejb.EJBHome {

    public ShipRemote create(Integer id, String name, int capacity, double tonnage)
        throws RemoteException,CreateException;
    public ShipRemote create(Integer id, String name)
        throws RemoteException,CreateException;
    public ShipRemote findByPrimaryKey(Integer primaryKey)
        throws FinderException, RemoteException;

    public Collection findByCapacity(int capacity)
        throws FinderException, RemoteException;
}
```

Enterprise JavaBeans specifies that create methods in the home interface must throw the `javax.ejb.CreateException`. This provides the EJB container with a common exception for communicating problems experienced during the create process.

The `RemoteException` is thrown by all remote interfaces and is used to report network problems that occurred while processing invocations between a remote client and the EJB container system.

The Primary Key

In bean-managed persistence, a primary key can be a serializable object defined specifically for the bean by the bean developer. The primary key defines attributes we can use to locate a specific bean in the database. For the `ShipBean` we need only one attribute, `id`, but in other cases a primary key may have several attributes, which together uniquely identify a bean's data.

We will examine primary keys in detail in Chapter 10; for now, we specify that the Ship EJB uses a simple single-value primary key of type `java.lang.Integer`. The actual persistence field in the bean class is an `Integer` named `id`.

The ShipBean

The `ShipBean` defined for this chapter uses JDBC to synchronize the bean's state to the database. In reality, an entity bean this simple could easily be deployed as a CMP bean. The purpose of this chapter, however, is to illustrate exactly where the resource-access code goes for BMP and how to implement it. When learning about bean-managed persistence, you should focus on when and where the resource is accessed in order to synchronize the bean with the database. The fact that we are using JDBC and synchronizing the bean state against a relational database is not important. The bean could just as easily be persisted to some legacy system, to an ERP application, or to some other resource that is not supported by your vendor's version of CMP.

Here is the complete definition of the `ShipBean`:

```
package com.titan.ship;

import javax.naming.Context;
import javax.naming.InitialContext;
import javax.naming.NamingException;
import javax.ejb.EntityContext;
import java.rmi.RemoteException;
import java.sql.SQLException;
import java.sql.Connection;
import java.sql.PreparedStatement;
import java.sql.DriverManager;
import java.sql.ResultSet;
```

```
import javax.sql.DataSource;
import javax.ejb.CreateException;
import javax.ejb.EJBException;
import javax.ejb.FinderException;
import javax.ejb.ObjectNotFoundException;
import java.util.Collection;
import java.util.Properties;
import java.util.Vector;
import java.util.Collection;

public class ShipBean implements javax.ejb.EntityBean {
    public Integer id;
    public String name;
    public int capacity;
    public double tonnage;

    public EntityContext context;

    public Integer ejbCreate(Integer id, String name, int capacity, double tonnage)
        throws CreateException {
        if ((id.intValue( ) < 1) || (name == null))
            throw new CreateException("Invalid Parameters");
        this.id = id;
        this.name = name;
        this.capacity = capacity;
        this.tonnage = tonnage;

        Connection con = null;
        PreparedStatement ps = null;
        try {
            con = this.getConnection( );
            ps = con.prepareStatement(
                "insert into Ship (id, name, capacity, tonnage) " +
                "values (?,?,?,?)");
            ps.setInt(1, id.intValue( ));
            ps.setString(2, name);
            ps.setInt(3, capacity);
            ps.setDouble(4, tonnage);
            if (ps.executeUpdate( ) != 1) {
                throw new CreateException ("Failed to add Ship to database");
            }
            return id;
        }
        catch (SQLException se) {
            throw new EJBException (se);
        }
        finally {
            try {
                if (ps != null) ps.close( );
                if (con!= null) con.close( );
            } catch(SQLException se) {
                se.printStackTrace( );
            }
        }
```

```
}
public void ejbPostCreate(Integer id, String name, int capacity,
    double tonnage) {
    // Do something useful with the primary key.
}
public Integer ejbCreate(Integer id, String name) throws CreateException {
    return ejbCreate(id,name,0,0);
}
public void ejbPostCreate(Integer id, String name) {
    // Do something useful with the EJBObject reference.
}
public Integer ejbFindByPrimaryKey(Integer primaryKey) throws FinderException {
    Connection con = null;
    PreparedStatement ps = null;
    ResultSet result = null;
    try {
        con = this.getConnection( );
        ps = con.prepareStatement("select id from Ship where id = ?");
        ps.setInt(1, primaryKey.intValue( ));
        result = ps.executeQuery( );
        // Does the ship ID exist in the database?
        if (!result.next( )) {
            throw new ObjectNotFoundException("Cannot find Ship with id = "+id);
        }
    } catch (SQLException se) {
        throw new EJBException(se);
    }
    finally {
        try {
            if (result != null) result.close( );
            if (ps != null) ps.close( );
            if (con!= null) con.close( );
        } catch(SQLException se){
            se.printStackTrace( );
        }
    }
    return primaryKey;
}
public Collection ejbFindByCapacity(int capacity) throws FinderException {
    Connection con = null;
    PreparedStatement ps = null;
    ResultSet result = null;
    try {
        con = this.getConnection( );
        ps = con.prepareStatement("select id from Ship where capacity = ?");
        ps.setInt(1,capacity);
        result = ps.executeQuery( );
        Vector keys = new Vector( );
        while(result.next( )) {
            keys.addElement(result.getObject("id"));
        }
        return keys;

    }
```

```
    catch (SQLException se) {
        throw new EJBException (se);
    }
    finally {
        try {
            if (result != null) result.close( );
            if (ps != null) ps.close( );
            if (con!= null) con.close( );
        } catch(SQLException se) {
            se.printStackTrace( );
        }
    }
}
public void setEntityContext(EntityContext ctx) {
    context = ctx;
}
public void unsetEntityContext( ) {
    context = null;
}
public void ejbActivate( ) {}
public void ejbPassivate( ) {}
public void ejbLoad( ) {

    Integer primaryKey = (Integer)context.getPrimaryKey( );
    Connection con = null;
    PreparedStatement ps = null;
    ResultSet result = null;
    try {
        con = this.getConnection( );
        ps = con.prepareStatement("select name, capacity,
            tonnage from Ship where id = ?");
        ps.setInt(1, primaryKey.intValue( ));
        result = ps.executeQuery( );
        if (result.next( )){
            id =primaryKey;
            name = result.getString("name");
            capacity = result.getInt("capacity");
            tonnage = result.getDouble("tonnage");
        } else {
            throw new NoSuchEntityException( );
        }
    } catch (SQLException se) {
        throw new EJBException(se);
    }
    finally {
        try {
            if (result != null) result.close( );
            if (ps != null) ps.close( );
            if (con!= null) con.close( );
        } catch(SQLException se) {
            se.printStackTrace( );
        }
    }
}
```

```
public void ejbStore( ) {
    Connection con = null;
    PreparedStatement ps = null;
    try {
        con = this.getConnection( );
        ps = con.prepareStatement(
            "update Ship set name = ?, capacity = ?, " +
            "tonnage = ? where id = ?");
        ps.setString(1,name);
        ps.setInt(2,capacity);
        ps.setDouble(3,tonnage);
        ps.setInt(4,id.intValue( ));
        if (ps.executeUpdate( ) != 1) {
            throw new NoSuchEntityException("ejbStore");
        }
    }
    catch (SQLException se) {
        throw new EJBException (se);
    }
    finally {
        try {
            if (ps != null) ps.close( );
            if (con!= null) con.close( );
        } catch(SQLException se) {
            se.printStackTrace( );
        }
    }
}
public void ejbRemove( ) {
    Connection con = null;
    PreparedStatement ps = null;
    try {
        con = this.getConnection( );
        ps = con.prepareStatement("delete from Ship where id = ?");
        ps.setInt(1, id.intValue( ));
        if (ps.executeUpdate( ) != 1) {
            throw new EJBException("ejbRemove");
        }
    }
    catch (SQLException se) {
        throw new EJBException (se);
    }
    finally {
        try {
            if (ps != null) ps.close( );
            if (con!= null) con.close( );
        } catch(SQLException se) {
            se.printStackTrace( );
        }
    }
}
public String getName( ) {
    return name;
}
```

```
    public void setName(String n) {
        name = n;
    }
    public void setCapacity(int cap) {
        capacity = cap;
    }
    public int getCapacity( ) {
        return capacity;
    }
    public double getTonnage( ) {
        return tonnage;
    }
    public void setTonnage(double tons) {
        tonnage = tons;
    }
    private Connection getConnection( ) throws SQLException {
          // Implementations shown below.
    }
}
```

Obtaining a Resource Connection

In order for a BMP entity bean to work, it must have access to the database or resource to which it will persist itself. To get access to the database, the bean usually obtains a resource factory from the JNDI ENC. The JNDI ENC is covered in detail in Chapter 11, but an overview here will be helpful since this is one of the first times it is actually used in this book. The first step in accessing the database is to request a connection from a `DataSource`, which we obtain from the JNDI environment naming context:

```
private Connection getConnection( ) throws SQLException {
    try {
        Context jndiCntx = new InitialContext( );
        DataSource ds = (DataSource)jndiCntx.lookup("java:comp/env/jdbc/titanDB");
        return ds.getConnection( );
    }
    catch (NamingException ne) {
        throw new EJBException(ne);
    }
}
```

In EJB, every enterprise bean has access to its JNDI environment naming context (ENC), which is part of the bean-container contract. The bean's deployment descriptor maps resources such as the JDBC DataSource, JavaMail, J2EE Connector, and Java Message Service to a context (name) in the ENC. This provides a portable model for accessing these types of resources. Here's the relevant portion of the deployment descriptor that describes the JDBC resource:

```
<enterprise-beans>
    <entity>
        <ejb-name>ShipEJB</ejb-name>
```

```
        ...
        <resource-ref>
            <description>DataSource for the Titan database</description>
            <res-ref-name>jdbc/titanDB</res-ref-name>
            <res-type>javax.sql.DataSource</res-type>
            <res-auth>Container</res-auth>
        </resource-ref>
        ...
    </entity>
    ...
</enterprise-beans>
```

The `<resource-ref>` tag is used for any resource (e.g., JDBC, JMS, Connector, JavaMail) that is accessed from the ENC. It describes the JNDI name of the resource (`<res-ref-name>`), the factory type (`<res-type>`), and whether authentication is performed explicitly by the bean or automatically by the container (`<res-auth>`). In this example, we are declaring that the JNDI name `jdbc/titanDB` refers to a `javax.sql.DataSource` resource manager and that authentication to the database is handled automatically by the container. The JNDI name specified in the `<res-ref-name>` tag is always relative to the standard JNDI ENC context name, `java:comp/env`.

When the bean is deployed, the deployer maps the information in the `<resource-ref>` tag to a live database. This is done in a vendor-specific manner, but the end result is the same. When a database connection is requested using the JNDI name `java:comp/jdbc/titanDB`, a `DataSource` for the Titan database is returned. Consult your vendor's documentation for details on how to map the `DataSource` to the database at deployment time.

The `getConnection( )` method provides us with a simple and consistent mechanism for obtaining a database connection for our `ShipBean` class. Now that we have a mechanism for obtaining a database connection, we can use it to insert, update, delete, and find Ship EJBs in the database.

Exception Handling

Exception handling is particularly relevant to this discussion because, unlike in container-managed persistence, in bean-managed persistence the bean developer is responsible for throwing the correct exceptions at the right moments. For this reason, we'll take a moment to discuss the different types of exceptions in BMP. This discussion will be useful when we get into the details of database access and implementing the callback methods.

Bean-managed beans throw three types of exceptions:

Application exceptions

Application exceptions include standard EJB application exceptions and custom application exceptions. The standard EJB application exceptions are `CreateException`, `FinderException`, `ObjectNotFoundException`, `DuplicateKeyException`, and

RemoveException. These exceptions are thrown from the appropriate methods to indicate that a business logic error has occurred. Custom exceptions are exceptions developed for specific business problems. We cover developing custom exceptions in Chapter 11.

Runtime exceptions
Runtime exceptions are thrown from the virtual machine itself and indicate that a fairly serious programming error has occurred. Examples include the NullPointerException and IndexOutOfBoundsException. These exceptions are handled by the container automatically and should not be handled inside a bean method.

You will notice that all the callback methods (ejbLoad( ), ejbStore( ), ejbActivate( ), ejbPassivate( ), and ejbRemove( )) throw an EJBException when a serious problem occurs. All EJB callback methods declare the EJBException and RemoteException in their throws clauses. Any exception thrown from one of the callback methods must be an EJBException or a subclass. The RemoteException type is included in the method signature to support backward compatibility with EJB 1.0 beans. Its use has been deprecated since EJB 1.1. RemoteExceptions should never be thrown by callback methods of EJB 2.0 or EJB 2.1 beans.

Subsystem exceptions
Checked exceptions thrown by other subsystems should be wrapped in an EJBException or application exception and rethrown from the method. Several examples of this can be found in the previous example, in which a SQLException that was thrown from JDBC was caught and rethrown as an EJBException. Checked exceptions from other subsystems, such as those thrown from JNDI, JavaMail, and JMS, should be handled in the same fashion. The EJBException is a subtype of the RuntimeException, so it doesn't need to be declared in the method's throws clause. If the exception thrown by the subsystem is not serious, you can opt to throw an application exception, but this is not recommended unless you are sure of the cause and the effects of the exception on the subsystem. In most cases, throwing an EJBException is preferred.

Exceptions have an impact on transactions and are fundamental to transaction processing. They are examined in greater detail in Chapter 15.

The ejbCreate( ) Method

ejbCreate( ) methods are called by the container when a client invokes the corresponding create( ) method on the bean's home. With bean-managed persistence, the ejbCreate( ) methods are responsible for adding new entities to the database. This means that the BMP version of ejbCreate( ) will be much more complicated than the equivalent methods in container-managed entities; with container-managed beans, ejbCreate( ) doesn't have to do much more than initialize a few fields.

Another difference between bean-managed and container-managed persistence is that the EJB specification states that `ejbCreate( )` methods in bean-managed persistence must return the primary key of the newly created entity. By contrast, in container-managed beans `ejbCreate( )` is required to return `null`.

The following code contains the `ejbCreate( )` method of the `ShipBean`. Its return type is the Ship EJB's primary key, `Integer`. The method uses the JDBC API to insert a new record into the database based on the information passed as parameters:

```
public Integer ejbCreate(Integer id, String name, int capacity, double tonnage)
    throws CreateException {
    if ((id.intValue( ) < 1) || (name == null))
        throw new CreateException("Invalid Parameters");
    this.id = id;
    this.name = name;
    this.capacity = capacity;
    this.tonnage = tonnage;

    Connection con = null;
    PreparedStatement ps = null;
    try {
        con = this.getConnection( );
        ps = con.prepareStatement(
            "insert into Ship (id, name, capacity, tonnage) " +
            "values (?,?,?,?)");
        ps.setInt(1, id.intValue( ));
        ps.setString(2, name);
        ps.setInt(3, capacity);
        ps.setDouble(4, tonnage);
        if (ps.executeUpdate( ) != 1) {
            throw new CreateException ("Failed to add Ship to database");
        }
        return id;
    }
    catch (SQLException se) {
        throw new EJBException (se);
    }
    finally {
        try {
            if (ps != null) ps.close( );
            if (con!= null) con.close( );
        } catch(SQLException se) {
            se.printStackTrace( );
        }
    }
}
```

At the beginning of the method, we verify that the parameters are correct and throw a `CreateException` if the `id` is less than 1 or the `name` is `null`. This shows how you would typically use a `CreateException` to report an application-logic error.

The ShipBean instance fields are initialized using the parameters passed to ejbCreate( ) by setting the instance fields of the ShipBean. We will use these values to manually insert the data into the SHIP table in our database.

To perform the database insert, we use a JDBC PreparedStatement for SQL requests, which makes it easier to see the parameters being used (we could also have used a stored procedure through a JDBC CallableStatement or a simple JDBC Statement object). We insert the new bean into the database using a SQL INSERT statement and the values passed into ejbCreate( ) parameters. If the insert is successful (i.e., no exceptions are thrown), we create a primary key and return it to the container.

If the insert operation is unsuccessful we throw a new CreateException, which illustrates this exception's use in a more ambiguous situation. Failure to insert the record could be construed as an application error or a system failure. In this situation, the JDBC subsystem hasn't thrown an exception, so we shouldn't interpret the inability to insert a record as a failure of the subsystem. Therefore, we throw a CreateException instead of an EJBException. Throwing a CreateException allows the application to recover from the error, a transactional concept that is covered in more detail in Chapter 15.

When the insert operation is successful, the primary key is returned to the EJB container from the ejbCreate( ) method. In this case we simply return the same Integer object passed into the method, but in many cases a new key might be derived from the method arguments. This is especially true when using compound primary keys, which are discussed in Chapter 10. Behind the scenes, the container uses the primary key and the ShipBean instance that returned it to provide the client with a reference to the new Ship entity. Conceptually, this means that the ShipBean instance and primary key are assigned to a newly constructed EJB object, and the EJB object stub is returned to the client.

Our home interface requires us to provide a second ejbCreate( ) method with different parameters. We can save work and write more bulletproof code by making the second method call the first:

```
public Integer ejbCreate(Integer id, String name) throws CreateException {
    return ejbCreate(id,name,0,0);
}
```

The ejbLoad( ) and ejbStore( ) Methods

Throughout the life of an entity, its data will be changed by client applications. In the ShipBean, we provide accessor methods to change the name, capacity, and tonnage of the Ship EJB after it has been created. Invoking any of these accessor methods changes the state of the ShipBean instance, and these changes must be reflected in the database.

In container-managed persistence, synchronization between the entity bean and the database takes place automatically; the container handles it for you. With bean-managed persistence, you are responsible for synchronization: the entity bean must read from and write to the database directly. The container works closely with the BMP entities by advising them when to synchronize their state through the use of two callback methods: `ejbStore( )` and `ejbLoad( )`.

The `ejbStore( )` method is called when the container decides that it is a good time to write the entity bean's data to the database. The container makes these decisions based on all the activities it is managing, including transactions, concurrency, and resource management. Vendor implementations may differ slightly as to when the `ejbStore( )` method is called, but this is not the bean developer's concern. In most cases, the `ejbStore( )` method will be called after one or more business methods have been invoked or at the end of a transaction.

Here is the `ejbStore( )` method for the `ShipBean`:

```
public void ejbStore( ) {
    Connection con = null;
    PreparedStatement ps = null;
    try {
        con = this.getConnection( );
        ps = con.prepareStatement(
            "update Ship set name = ?, capacity = ?, " +
            "tonnage = ? where id = ?");
        ps.setString(1,name);
        ps.setInt(2,capacity);
        ps.setDouble(3,tonnage);
        ps.setInt(4,id.intValue( ));
        if (ps.executeUpdate( ) != 1) {
            throw new EJBException("ejbStore");
        }
    }
    catch (SQLException se) {
        throw new EJBException (se);
    }
    finally {
        try {
            if (ps != null) ps.close( );
            if (con!= null) con.close( );
        } catch(SQLException se) {
            se.printStackTrace( );
        }
    }
}
```

Except for the fact that we are doing an update instead of an insert, this method is similar to the `ejbCreate( )` method we examined earlier. We use a JDBC `PreparedStatement` to execute the SQL `UPDATE` command, and we use the entity bean's persistence fields as parameters to the request. This method synchronizes the database with the state of the bean.

EJB also provides an ejbLoad( ) method that synchronizes the state of the entity with the database. This method is usually called at the start of a new transaction or business-method invocation. The idea is to make sure that the bean always represents the most current data in the database, which could be changed by other beans or other non-EJB applications.

Here is the ejbLoad( ) method for a bean-managed ShipBean class:

```
public void ejbLoad( ) {

    Integer primaryKey = (Integer)context.getPrimaryKey( );
    Connection con = null;
    PreparedStatement ps = null;
    ResultSet result = null;
    try {
        con = this.getConnection( );
        ps = con.prepareStatement(
            "select name, capacity, tonnage from Ship where id = ?");
        ps.setInt(1, primaryKey.intValue( ));
        result = ps.executeQuery( );
        if (result.next( )){
            id = primaryKey;
            name = result.getString("name");
            capacity = result.getInt("capacity");
            tonnage = result.getDouble("tonnage");
        } else {
            throw new EJBException( );
        }
    } catch (SQLException se) {
        throw new EJBException(se);
    }
    finally {
        try {
            if (result != null) result.close( );
            if (ps != null) ps.close( );
            if (con!= null) con.close( );
        } catch(SQLException se) {
            se.printStackTrace( );
        }
    }
}
```

To execute the ejbLoad( ) method, we need a primary key. To get the primary key, we query the bean's EntityContext. Note that we don't get the primary key directly from the ShipBean's id field, because we cannot guarantee that this field is always valid—the ejbLoad( ) method might be populating the bean instance's state for the first time, in which case the fields would all be set to their default values. This situation would occur following bean activation. We can guarantee that the EntityContext for the ShipBean is valid because the EJB specification requires that the bean instance's EntityContext reference be valid before the ejbLoad( ) method can be invoked.

At this point you may want to jump to Chapter 10 and read the section called "EntityContext" to get a better understanding of the EntityContext's purpose and usefulness in entity beans.

The ejbRemove( ) Method

In addition to handling their own inserts and updates, bean-managed entities must handle their own deletions. When a client application invokes the remove method on the EJB home or EJB object, that method invocation is delegated to the bean-managed entity by calling ejbRemove( ). It is the bean developer's responsibility to implement an ejbRemove( ) method that deletes the entity's data from the database. Here's the ejbRemove( ) method for our bean-managed ShipBean:

```
public void ejbRemove( ) {
    Connection con = null;
    PreparedStatement ps = null;
    try {
        con = this.getConnection( );
        ps = con.prepareStatement("delete from Ship where id = ?");
        ps.setInt(1, id.intValue( ));
        if (ps.executeUpdate( ) != 1) {
            throw new EJBException("ejbRemove");
        }
    }
    catch (SQLException se) {
        throw new EJBException (se);
    }
    finally {
        try {
            if (ps != null) ps.close( );
            if (con!= null) con.close( );
        } catch(SQLException se) {
            se.printStackTrace( );
        }
    }
}
```

The ejbFind( ) Methods

In bean-managed persistence, the find methods in the remote or local home interface must match the ejbFind( ) methods in the actual bean class. In other words, for each method named find<*SUFFIX*>( ) in a home interface, there must be a corresponding ejbFind<*SUFFIX*>( ) method in the entity bean class with the same arguments and application exceptions. When a find method is invoked on an EJB home, the container delegates the find( ) method to a corresponding ejbFind( ) method on the bean instance. The bean-managed entity is responsible for locating records that match the find requests. There are two find methods in ShipHomeRemote:

```
public interface ShipHomeRemote extends javax.ejb.EJBHome {

    public ShipRemote findByPrimaryKey(Integer primaryKey)
        throws FinderException, RemoteException;
    public Collection findByCapacity(int capacity)
        throws FinderException, RemoteException;
}
```

Here are the signatures of the corresponding `ejbFind( )` methods in the `ShipBean`:

```
public class ShipBean implements javax.ejb.EntityBean {

    public Integer ejbFindByPrimaryKey(Integer primaryKey)
        throws FinderException {}
    public Collection ejbFindByCapacity(int capacity)
        throws FinderException {}
}
```

Aside from the names, there's a significant difference between these two groups of methods. The find methods in the home interface return either an EJB object implementing the bean's remote interface—in this case, `ShipRemote`–or a collection of EJB objccts in the form of a `java.util.Enumeration` or `java.util.Collection`. The `ejbFind( )` methods in the bean class, on the other hand, return either a primary key for the appropriate bean—in this case, `Integer`—or a collection of primary keys. The methods that return a single value (whether a remote/local interface or a primary key) are used whenever you need to look up a single reference to a bean. If you are looking up a group of references (for example, all ships with a certain capacity), you have to use the method that returns either the `Collection` or `Enumeration` type. In either case, the container intercepts the primary keys and converts them into remote references for the client.

> The EJB specification recommends that bean-managed persistence beans use the `Collection` type instead of the `Enumeration` type. This recommendation is made so that BMP beans are more consistent with CMP beans, which use only the `Collection` type. The `Enumeration` type is an artifact of EJB 1.0 and 1.1 and is maintained for backwards compatibility.

It shouldn't come as a surprise that the type returned—whether it's a primary key or a remote (or local) interface—must be appropriate for the type of bean you're defining. For example, you shouldn't put find methods in a Ship EJB to look up and return Cabin EJB objects. If you need to return collections of a different bean type, use a business method in the remote interface, not a find method from one of the home interfaces.

The EJB container takes care of returning the proper (local or remote) interface to the client. For example, the Ship EJB may define a local and a remote home interface, both of which have a `findByPrimaryKey( )` method. When `findByPrimary( )` is invoked on the local or remote interface, it will be delegated to the ejbFindByPrimary( ) key method. After the ejbFindByPrimaryKey( ) method executes and returns the primary key, the EJB container takes care of returning a ShipRemote or ShipLocal reference to the client, depending on which home interface (local or remote) was used. The EJB container also handles this for multi-entity find methods, returning a collection of remote references for remote home interfaces or local references for local home interfaces.

Both find methods defined in the ShipBean class throw an EJBException if a failure in the request occurs when an SQL exception condition is encountered. findByPrimaryKey( ) throws an ObjectNotFoundException if no records in the database match the id argument. This is exception should always be thrown by single-entity find methods if no entity is found.

The findByCapacity( ) method returns an empty collection if no SHIP records with a matching capacity are found; multi-entity find methods do *not* throw ObjectNotFoundExceptions if no entities are found.

It is mandatory for all entity remote and local home interfaces to include the findByPrimaryKey( ) method. This method returns the remote or local interface type (ShipRemote or ShipLocal). It declares one parameter, the primary key for that bean type. With local home interfaces, the return type of any single-entity finder method is always the bean's local interface. With remote home interfaces, the return type of any single-entity find method is the remote interface. You cannot deploy an entity bean that doesn't include a findByPrimaryKey( ) method in its home interfaces.

Following the rules outlined earlier, we can define two ejbFind( ) methods in ShipBean that match the two find( ) methods defined in the ShipHomeRemote:

```
public Integer ejbFindByPrimaryKey(Integer primaryKey) throws FinderException {
    Connection con = null;
    PreparedStatement ps = null;
    ResultSet result = null;
    try {
        con = this.getConnection( );
        ps = con.prepareStatement("select id from Ship where id = ?");
        ps.setInt(1, primaryKey.intValue( ));
        result = ps.executeQuery( );
        // Does the ship ID exist in the database?
        if (!result.next( )) {
            throw new ObjectNotFoundException("Cannot find Ship with id = "+id);
        }
    } catch (SQLException se) {
        throw new EJBException(se);
    }
    finally {
        try {
            if (result != null) result.close( );
            if (ps != null) ps.close( );
            if (con!= null) con.close( );
        } catch(SQLException se) {
```

```
            se.printStackTrace( );
        }
    }
    return primaryKey;
}
public Collection ejbFindByCapacity(int capacity) throws FinderException {
    Connection con = null;
    PreparedStatement ps = null;
    ResultSet result = null;
    try {
        con = this.getConnection( );
        ps = con.prepareStatement("select id from Ship where capacity = ?");
        ps.setInt(1,capacity);
        result = ps.executeQuery( );
        Vector keys = new Vector( );
        while(result.next( )) {
            keys.addElement(result.getObject("id"));
        }
        return keys;
    }
    catch (SQLException se) {
        throw new EJBException (se);
    }
    finally {
        try {
            if (result != null) result.close( );
            if (ps != null) ps.close( );
            if (con!= null) con.close( );
        } catch(SQLException se) {
            se.printStackTrace( );
        }
    }
}
```

The mandatory findByPrimaryKey( ) method uses the primary key to locate the corresponding database record. Once it has verified that the record exists, it simply returns the primary key to the container, which then uses the key to activate a new instance and associate it with that primary key at the appropriate time. If no record is associated with the primary key, the method throws an ObjectNotFoundException.

The ejbFindByCapacity( ) method returns a collection of primary keys that match the criteria passed into the method. Again, we construct a prepared statement that we use to execute our SQL query. This time, however, we expect multiple results, so we use the java.sql.ResultSet to iterate through the results, creating a vector of primary keys for each SHIP_ID returned.

Find methods are not executed on bean instances that are currently supporting a client application. Only bean instances that are not currently assigned to an EJB object (i.e., instances in the instance pool) are supposed to service find requests, which means that the ejbFind( ) methods in the bean instance have somewhat limited use of the EntityContext. The EntityContext methods getPrimaryKey( ) and getEJBObject( ) will throw exceptions because the bean instance is in the pool and is not associated with a primary key or EJB object when the ejbFind( ) method is called.

Where do the objects returned by find methods originate? This seems like a simple enough question, but the answer is surprisingly complex. Remember that find methods aren't executed by bean instances that are actually supporting the client; rather, the container selects an idle bean instance from the instance pool to execute the method. The container is responsible for creating the EJB objects and local or remote references for the primary keys returned by the ejbFind( ) method in the bean class. As the client accesses these remote references, bean instances are swapped into the appropriate EJB objects, loaded with data, and made ready to service the client's requests.

The Deployment Descriptor

With a complete definition of the Ship EJB, including the remote interface, remote home interface, and primary key, we are ready to create a deployment descriptor. XML deployment descriptors for bean-managed entity beans are a little different from the descriptors we created for the container-managed entity beans in Chapter 6 and Chapter 7. In this deployment descriptor, the <persistence-type> is Bean and there are no <container-managed> or <relationship-field> declarations. We also must declare the DataSource resource factory that we use to query and update the database.

Here is the deployment descriptor for EJB 2.1:

```
<ejb-jar
    xmlns="http://java.sun.com/xml/ns/j2ee"
    xmlns:xsi="http://www.w3.org/2001/XMLSchema-instance"
    xsi:schemaLocation="http://java.sun.com/xml/ns/j2ee
                        http://java.sun.com/xml/ns/j2ee/ejb-jar_2_1.xsd"
    version="2.1">

    <enterprise-beans>

        <entity>
            <description>
                This bean represents a cruise ship.
            </description>
            <ejb-name>ShipEJB</ejb-name>
            <home>com.titan.ship.ShipHomeRemote</home>
            <remote>com.titan.ship.ShipRemote</remote>
            <ejb-class>com.titan.ship.ShipBean</ejb-class>
            <persistence-type>Bean</persistence-type>
            <prim-key-class>java.lang.Integer</prim-key-class>
            <reentrant>False</reentrant>
            <security-identity><use-caller-identity/></security-identity>
            <resource-ref>
```

```
                <description>DataSource for the Titan database</description>
                <res-ref-name>jdbc/titanDB</res-ref-name>
                <res-type>javax.sql.DataSource</res-type>
                <res-auth>Container</res-auth>
            </resource-ref>
        </entity>
    </enterprise-beans>

    <assembly-descriptor>
        <security-role>
            <description>
                This role represents everyone who is allowed full access
                to the Ship EJB.
            </description>
            <role-name>everyone</role-name>
        </security-role>

        <method-permission>
            <role-name>everyone</role-name>
            <method>
                <ejb-name>ShipEJB</ejb-name>
                <method-name>*</method-name>
            </method>
        </method-permission>

        <container-transaction>
            <method>
                <ejb-name>ShipEJB</ejb-name>
                <method-name>*</method-name>
            </method>
            <trans-attribute>Required</trans-attribute>
        </container-transaction>
    </assembly-descriptor>
</ejb-jar>
```

The EJB 2.0 deployment descriptor is exactly the same except for one thing. It uses a DTD instead of XML schema so there is a `<!DOCTYPE>` element declaration instead of XML Schema attribute declarations.

```
<!DOCTYPE ejb-jar PUBLIC "-//Sun Microsystems, Inc.//DTD Enterprise
JavaBeans 2.0//EN" "http://java.sun.com/dtd/ejb-jar_2_0.dtd">

<ejb-jar>
 <enterprise-beans>
```

Exercise 9.1 in the Workbook show how to deploy the examples in this section.

CHAPTER 10

The Entity-Container Contract

Although CMP and BMP entities are programmed differently, their relationships to the container system at runtime is very similar. This chapter covers the relationship between EJBs and their containers. It includes discussions of primary keys, callback methods, and the entity bean life cycle. When differences between CMP and BMP are important, they will be noted.

The Primary Key

A primary key is an object that uniquely identifies an entity bean. A primary key can be any serializable type, including primitive wrappers (`Integer`, `Double`, `Long`, etc.) or custom classes defined by the bean developer. In the Ship EJB discussed in Chapter 7 and Chapter 9, we used the `Integer` type as a primary key. Primary keys can be declared by the bean developer, or the primary key type can be deferred until deployment. We will talk about deferred primary keys later.

Because the primary key may be used in remote invocations, it must adhere to the restrictions imposed by Java RMI-IIOP; that is, it must be a valid Java RMI-IIOP value type. These restrictions are discussed in Chapter 5, but for most cases, you just need to make the primary key serializable. In addition, the primary key must implement `equals( )` and `hashCode( )` appropriately.

EJB allows two types of primary keys: single-field and compound. *Single-field* primary keys map to a single persistence field defined in the bean class. The Customer and Ship EJBs, for example, use a `java.lang.Integer` primary key that maps to the container-managed persistence field named `id`. A *compound* primary key is a custom-defined class that declares several instance variables that map to more than one persistence field in the bean class.

Single-Field Primary Keys

The `String` class and the standard wrapper classes for the primitive data types (`java.lang.Integer`, `java.lang.Double`, etc.) can be used as primary keys. These are referred to as single-field primary keys because they are atomic; they map to one of the bean's persistence fields. Compound primary keys map to two or more persistence fields.

In the Ship EJB, we specified an `Integer` type as the primary key:

```
public interface ShipHomeRemote extends javax.ejb.EJBHome {

    public Ship findByPrimaryKey(java.lang.Integer primarykey)
        throws FinderException, RemoteException;
    ...
}
```

In this case, there must be a single persistence field in the bean class with the same type as the primary key. For the `ShipBean`, the `id` *persistent field* is of type `java.lang.Integer`, one of the single-field primary key types. The term "persistent field" means a container-managed persistent field in CMP entities or a instance field in an BMP entity that maps to the beans state in the database. In container-managed persistence, the primary key type must map to one of the bean's CMP fields. The abstract accessor methods for the `id` field in the `ShipBean` class fit this description:

```
public class ShipBean implements javax.ejb.EntityBean {
    public abstract Integer getId( );
    public abstract void setId(Integer id);
    ...
}
```

The single-field primary key must also map to a CMP field in bean-managed persistence. For the BMP `ShipBean` class defined in Chapter 9, the `Integer` primary key maps to the `id` instance field:

```
public class ShipBean implements javax.ejb.EntityBean {
    public Integer id;
    public String name;
    ...
}
```

In CMP entities, you identify the CMP field that will serve as the single-field primary key using the `<primkey-field>` element in the deployment descriptor. In addition, the `<prim-key-class>` element specifies the type of object used for the primary key class. The CMP Ship EJB discussed in Chapter 7 uses both of these elements when defining the `id` CMP field as the primary key:

```
<entity>
    <ejb-name>ShipEJB</ejb-name>
    <home>com.titan.ShipHomeRemote</home>
    <remote>com.titan.ShipRemote</remote>
    <ejb-class>com.titan.ShipBean</ejb-class>
    <persistence-type>Container</persistence-type>
    <prim-key-class>java.lang.Integer</prim-key-class>
```

```
        <reentrant>False</reentrant>
        <cmp-field><field-name>id</field-name></cmp-field>
        <cmp-field><field-name>name</field-name></cmp-field>
        <cmp-field><field-name>tonnage</field-name></cmp-field>
        <primkey-field>id</primkey-field>
    </entity>
```

In BMP entities you do not specify a `<primkey-field>`, because primary keys are created by the bean code, not the container. However, you are required to identify the `<prim-key-class>` with BMP entities as shown in the following listing.

```
    <entity>
        <ejb-name>ShipEJB</ejb-name>
        <home>com.titan.ShipHomeRemote</home>
        <remote>com.titan.ShipRemote</remote>
        <ejb-class>com.titan.ShipBean</ejb-class>
        <persistence-type>Bean</persistence-type>
       <prim-key-class>java.lang.Integer</prim-key-class>

    </entity>
```

Although primary keys can be primitive wrappers (`Integer`, `Double`, `Long`, etc.), they cannot be primitive types (`int`, `double`, `long`, etc.) because the semantics of the EJB programming model require the use of `Object` type primary keys. For example, the `EJBObject.getPrimaryKey( )` method returns an `Object` type, thus forcing primary keys to be `Objects`. Primitives also cannot be primary keys because primary keys must be managed by `Collection` objects, which work only with `Object` types. Primitives are not `Object` types and do not have `equals( )` or `hashcode( )` methods.

Compound Primary Keys

A compound primary key is a class that implements `java.io.Serializable` and contains one or more public fields whose names and types match a subset of persistence fields in the bean class. They are defined by bean developers for specific entity beans.

For example, if a Ship EJB didn't have an `id` field, we might uniquely identify ships by their names and registration numbers. (We are adding the `registration` persistent field to the Ship EJB for this example.) In this case, the `name` and `registration` persistent fields would become our primary key fields, which match corresponding fields (`NAME` and `REGISTRATION`) in the `SHIP` database table. To accommodate multiple fields as a primary key, we need to define a primary key class.

The convention in this book is to define all compound primary keys as serializable classes with names that match the pattern `BeanNamePK`. In this case we can construct a new class called `ShipPK`, which serves as the compound primary key for our Ship EJB:

```
    public class ShipPK implements java.io.Serializable {
        public String name;
        public String registration;

        public ShipPK( ){
```

```
    }
    public ShipPK(String name, String registration) {
        this.name = name;
        this.registration = registration;
    }
    public String getName( ) {
        return name;
    }
    public String getRegistration( ) {
        return registration;
    }
    public boolean equals(Object obj) {
        if (obj == null || !(obj instanceof ShipPK))
            return false;

        ShipPK other = (ShipPK)obj;
        if(this.name.equals(other.name) &&
            this.registration.equals(other.registration))
            return true;
        else
            return false;

    }
    public int hashCode( ) {
        return name.hashCode()^registration.hashCode( );
    }

    public String toString( ) {
        return name+" "+registration;
    }

}
```

To make the ShipPK class work as a compound primary key, we must make its fields public. This allows the container system to use reflection when synchronizing the values in the primary key class with the persistence fields in the bean class. We must also define equals( ) and hashCode( ) methods to allow the primary key to be easily manipulated within collections by container systems and application developers. We have also overridden the toString( ) method to return a meaningful value. The default implementation defined in Object returns the class name of the object appended to the object identity for that name space.

With CMP entities, it's important to make sure that the variables declared in the primary key have corresponding CMP fields in the entity bean with matching identifiers (names) and data types. This is required so that the container, using reflection, can match the variables declared in the compound key to the correct CMP fields in the bean class. In this case, the name and registration instance variables declared in the ShipPK class correspond to name and registration CMP fields in the Ship EJB, so it's a good match.

With BMP entities, the instance fields of the primary key class are not required to map exactly to corresponding persistent fields in the bean class. The bean class is directly responsible for creating and managing the instance fields of the primary key, not the container. In most cases, however, the instance fields in the primary key will map to persistent fields in the bean class.

The `ShipPK` class defines two constructors: a *no-argument* constructor and an *overloaded* constructor that sets the `name` and `registration` variables. The overloaded constructor is a convenience method for developers that reduces the number of steps required to create a primary key. The no-argument constructor is *required* for container-managed persistence. When a new EJB is created in CMP, the container automatically instantiates the primary key using the `Class.newInstance( )` method and populates it from the bean's container-managed fields. A no-argument constructor must exist in order for this process to work.

To accommodate the `ShipPK`, we change the `ejbCreate( )`/`ejbPostCreate( )` methods on the bean class of both BMP and CMP entities so that they have `name` and `registration` arguments to set the primary key fields in the bean.

Here is how the `ShipPK` primary key class would be used in the CMP `ShipBean` class we developed for in Chapter 7:

```
import javax.ejb.EntityContext;
import javax.ejb.CreateException;

public abstract class ShipBean implements javax.ejb.EntityBean {

    public ShipPK ejbCreate(String name, String registration) {
        setName(name);
        setRegistration(registration);
        return null;
    }
    public void ejbPostCreate(String name, String registration) {
    }
    ...
```

The deployment descriptor for CMP entities is required to define `<cmp-field>` entries that match the instance fields of the compound primary key, but it must *not* define a `<primkey-field>` element. The `<primkey-field>` element is only used with single-field primary keys. The deployment descriptor for CMP entities *must* define a `<prim-key-class>` for compound primary keys, however.

```
<entity>
    <ejb-name>ShipEJB</ejb-name>
    <home>com.titan.ShipHomeRemote</home>
    <remote>com.titan.ShipRemote</remote>
    <ejb-class>com.titan.ShipBean</ejb-class>
    <persistence-type>Container</persistence-type>
        <prim-key-class>com.titan.ShipPK</prim-key-class>
    <reentrant>False</reentrant>
    <cmp-field><field-name>name</field-name></cmp-field>
```

```
        <cmp-field><filed-name>registration</field-name></cmp-field>
        <cmp-field><field-name>tonnage</field-name></cmp-field>
    </entity>
```

Here is how the ShipPK primary key class might be used in the BMP ShipBean class we developed for in Chapter 9:

```
public class ShipBean implements javax.ejb.EntityBean {
    public String name;
    public String registration;

    public ShipPK ejbCreate(String name, String registration){
        this.name = name;
        this.registration = registration;
        ...
        // database insert logic goes here
        ...
        return new ShipPK(name, registration);
    }
```

The deployment descriptor for BMP entities is always required to define the <prim-key-class> for both single-field and compound primary keys as shown in the following listing:

```
<entity>
    <ejb-name>ShipEJB</ejb-name>
    <home>com.titan.ShipHomeRemote</home>
    <remote>com.titan.ShipRemote</remote>
    <ejb-class>com.titan.ShipBean</ejb-class>
    <persistence-type>Bean</persistence-type>
    <prim-key-class>com.titan.ShipPK</prim-key-class>

</entity>
```

The ejbCreate( ) method of both the BMP and CMP entities now declares the ShipPK as the primary key type. The return type of the ejbCreate( ) method must match the primary key type if the primary key is defined or the java.lang.Object type if it is undefined (CMP only).

In container-managed persistence, if the primary key fields are defined—i.e., if they are accessible through abstract accessor methods—they *must* be set in the ejbCreate( ) method. While the return type of the ejbCreate( ) method is always the primary key type, the value returned in CMP must always be null. The EJB container itself takes care of extracting the proper primary key directly. In bean-managed persistence, the bean class is responsible for constructing the primary key and returning it to the container.

The ShipHomeRemote interface for both CMP and BMP entities is modified so that it uses the name and registration arguments in the create( ) method and the ShipPK in the findByPrimaryKey( ) method (EJB requires that we use the primary key type in that method):

```
import java.rmi.RemoteException;
import javax.ejb.CreateException;
```

```
import javax.ejb.FinderException;

public interface ShipHomeRemote extends javax.ejb.EJBHome {

    public ShipRemote create(String name, String registration)
        throws CreateException, RemoteException;

    public ShipRemote findByPrimaryKey(ShipPK primaryKey)
        throws FinderException, RemoteException;

}
```

`setName()` and `setRegistration()`, which modify the `name` and `registration` fields of the Ship EJB, should not be declared in the bean's remote or local interfaces. As explained in the next paragraph, the primary key of an entity bean must *not* be changed once the bean is created. However, methods that simply read the primary key fields (e.g., `getName()` and `getRegistration()`) may be exposed because they don't change the key's values.

CMP requires that the primary key may be set only once, either in the `ejbCreate()` method or, if it's undefined, automatically by the container when the bean is created. Once the bean is created, the primary key fields *must never* be modified by the bean or any of its clients. This is a reasonable requirement that should also be applied to bean-managed persistence beans, because the primary key is the unique identifier of the bean. Changing it could violate referential integrity in the database, possibly resulting in two beans being mapped to the same identifier or breaking any relationships with other beans that are based on the value of the primary key.

Undefined Primary Keys in CMP

Undefined primary keys for container-managed persistence were introduced in EJB 1.1. Basically, undefined primary keys allow the bean developer to defer declaring the primary key to the deployer, which makes it possible to create more portable entity beans.

One problem with container-managed persistence in EJB 1.0 was that the entity bean developer had to define the primary key before the entity bean was deployed. This requirement forced the developer to make assumptions about the environment in which the entity bean would be used, which limited the entity bean's portability across databases. For example, a relational database uses a set of columns in a table as the primary key, to which an entity bean's fields map nicely. An object database, however, uses a completely different mechanism for indexing objects, to which a primary key may not map well. The same is true for legacy systems and Enterprise Resource Planning (ERP) systems.

An undefined primary key allows the deployer to choose a system-specific key at deployment time. An object database may generate an object ID, while an ERP system may generate some other primary key. These keys may be automatically generated by the database or backend system. The CMP bean may need to be altered or extended by the deployment tool to support the key, but this is immaterial to the bean developer; she concentrates on the business logic of the bean and leaves the indexing to the container.

To facilitate the use of undefined primary keys, the CMP bean class and its interfaces use the Object type to identify the primary key. The Ship EJB developed in Chapter 7 could use an undefined primary key. As the following code shows, the Ship EJB's ejbCreate( ) method returns an Object type:

```
public abstract class ShipBean extends javax.ejb.EntityBean {

    public Object ejbCreate(String name, int capacity, double tonnage) {
        ...
        return null;
}
```

The findByPrimaryKey( ) method defined in the local and remote home interfaces must also use an Object type:

```
public interface ShipHomeRemote extends javax.ejb.EJBHome {

    public ShipRemote findByPrimaryKey(Object primaryKey)
        throws javax.ejb.FinderException;

}
```

The Ship EJB's deployment descriptor defines its primary key type as java.lang.Object and does *not* define any <prim-key-field> elements:

```
<ejb-jar>
    <enterprise-beans>
        <entity>
            <ejb-name>ShipEJB</ejb-name>
            ...
            <ejb-class>com.titan.ship.ShipBean</ejb-class>
            <persistence-type>Container</persistence-type>
            <prim-key-class>java.lang.Object</prim-key-class>
            <reentrant>False</reentrant>
            <cmp-field><field-name>name</field-name></cmp-field>
            <cmp-field><field-name>capacity</field-name></cmp-field>
            <cmp-field><field-name>tonnage</field-name></cmp-field>
        </entity>
```

One drawback of using an undefined primary key is that it requires the bean developer and application developer (client code) to work with a java.lang.Object type and not a specific primary key type, which can be limiting. For example, it's not possible to construct an undefined primary key to use in a find method if you don't know its type. This limitation can be quite daunting if you need to locate an entity bean by its primary key. However, entity beans with undefined primary keys can be located easily using other query methods that do not depend on the primary key value, so this limitation is not a serious handicap.

In bean-managed persistence, you can declare an undefined primary key simply by making the primary key type java.lang.Object. However, this is pure semantics; the primary key value will not be auto-generated by the container because the bean developer has total control over persistence. In this case the bean developer would still need to use a valid primary key, but its type would be hidden from the bean clients. This method can be useful if the primary key type is expected to change over time.

The Callback Methods

All entity beans (container- and bean-managed) must implement the javax.ejb.EntityBean interface. The EntityBean interface contains a number of callback methods that the container uses to alert the bean instance of various runtime events:

```
public interface javax.ejb.EntityBean extends javax.ejb.EnterpriseBean {
    public abstract void ejbActivate( ) throws EJBException, RemoteException;
    public abstract void ejbPassivate( ) throws EJBException, RemoteException;
    public abstract void ejbLoad( ) throws EJBException, RemoteException;
    public abstract void ejbStore( ) throws EJBException, RemoteException;
    public abstract void ejbRemove( ) throws EJBException, RemoteException,
        RemoveException;
    public abstract void setEntityContext(EntityContext ctx) throws EJBException,
        RemoteException;
    public abstract void unsetEntityContext( ) throws EJBException,
        RemoteException;
}
```

Each callback method is invoked on an entity bean instance at a specific time during its life cycle.

As described in Chapter 9, BMP beans must implement most of these callback methods to synchronize the bean's state with the database. The ejbLoad( ) method tells the BMP bean when to read its state from the database; ejbStore( ) tells it when to write to the database; and ejbRemove( ) tells the bean when to delete itself from the database.

While BMP beans take full advantage of callback methods, CMP entity beans may not need to use all of them. The persistence of CMP entity beans is managed automatically, so in most cases the resources and logic that might be managed by these methods is already handled by the container. However, a CMP entity bean can take advantage of these callback methods if it needs to perform actions that are not automatically supported by the container.

You may have noticed that each method in the EntityBean interface throws both a javax.ejb.EJBException and a java.rmi.RemoteException. EJB 1.0 required that a RemoteException be thrown if a system exception occurred while a bean was executing a callback method. However, since EJB 1.1 the use of RemoteException in these methods has been deprecated in favor of the javax.ejb.EJBException. EJB 2.0 and EJB 2.1 suggest that the EJBException be thrown if the bean encounters a system error, such as a SQLException, while executing a method. The EJBException is a subclass of RuntimeException, so you don't have to declare it in the method signature. Since the use of the RemoteException is deprecated, you also don't have to declare it when implementing the callback methods either; in fact, it's recommended that you don't.

setEntityContext( ) and unsetEntityContext( )

The first method called after a bean instance is instantiated is setEntityContext( ). As the method signature indicates, this method passes the bean instance a reference to a javax.ejb.EntityContext, which is the bean instance's interface to the container. The purpose and functionality of the EntityContext is covered later in this chapter.

The setEntityContext( ) method is called prior to the bean instance's entry into the instance pool. In Chapter 3, we discussed the instance pool that EJB containers maintain, where instances of entity and stateless session beans are kept ready to use. EntityBean instances in the instance pool are not associated with any data in the database; their state is not unique. When a client requests a specific entity, an instance from the pool is chosen, populated with data from the database, and assigned to service the client. Any nonmanaged resources needed for the life of the instance should be obtained when this method is called. This ensures that such resources are obtained only once in the life of a bean instance. A nonmanaged resource is one that is not automatically managed by the container (e.g., references to CORBA objects). Only resources that are not specific to the entity bean's identity should be obtained in the setEntityContext( ) method. Other managed resources (e.g., Java Message Service factories) and entity bean references are obtained as needed from the JNDI ENC. Bean references and managed resources obtained through the JNDI ENC are not available from setEntityContext( ). The JNDI ENC is discussed later in this chapter.

At the end of the entity bean instance's life, after it is removed permanently from the instance pool and before it is garbage collected, the unsetEntityContext( ) method is called, indicating that the bean instance is about to be evicted from memory by the container. This is a good time to free up any resources obtained in the setEntityContext( ) method.

ejbCreate( )

In a CMP bean, the ejbCreate( ) method is called before the bean's state is written to the database. Values passed in to the ejbCreate( ) method should be used to initialize the CMP fields of the bean instance. Once the ejbCreate( ) method completes, a new record, based on the CMP fields, is written to the database.

In bean-managed persistence, the ejbCreate( ) method is called when it's time for the bean to add itself to the database. Inside the ejbCreate( ) method, a BMP bean must use some kind of API to insert its data into the database.

Each ejbCreate( ) method must have parameters that match a create( ) method in the home interface. If you look at the ShipBean class definition and compare it to the Ship EJB's home interfaces (see Chapter 7 and Chapter 9), you can see how the parameters for the create methods match exactly in type and sequence. This enables the container to delegate each create( ) method invoked on an EJB home to the proper ejbCreate( ) method in the bean instance.

In addition, the ejbCreate( ) method can take the form ejbCreate<*SUFFIX*>( ), which allows for easier method overloading when parameters are the same but the methods act differently. For example, ejbCreateByName(String name) and ejbCreateByRegistration(String registration) would have corresponding create( ) methods defined in the local or home interface, in the form createByName(String name) and createByRegistration(String registration).

The EntityContext maintained by the bean instance does not provide an entity bean with the proper identity until ejbCreate( ) has completed. This means that while the ejbCreate( ) method is executing, the bean instance doesn't have access to its primary key or EJB object. The EntityContext does, however, provide the bean with information about the caller's identity and access to its EJB home object (local and remote) and properties. The bean can also use the JNDI naming context to access other beans and resource managers such as javax.sql.DataSource.

However, the CMP entity bean developer must ensure that ejbCreate( ) sets the CMP fields that correspond to the fields of the primary key. When a new CMP entity bean is created, the container will use the CMP fields in the bean class to instantiate and populate a primary key automatically. If the primary key is undefined, the container and database will work together to generate the primary key for the entity bean.

Once the bean's state has been populated and its ejbCreate( ) method has executed, the ejbPostCreate( ) method is invoked. This method gives the bean an opportunity to perform any postprocessing prior to servicing client requests. In CMP entity beans, ejbPostCreate( ) is used to manipulate container-managed relationship (CMR) fields. These CMR fields must not be modified by ejbCreate( ). The reason for this restriction has to do with referential integrity. The primary key for the entity bean may not be available until after ejbCreate( ) executes. The primary key is needed if the mapping for the relationship uses it as a foreign key, so assignment of relationships is postponed until ejbCreate( ) completes and the primary key becomes available. This is also true with autogenerated primary keys, which usually require that the insert be done before a primary key can be generated. In addition, referential integrity may specify non-null foreign keys in referencing tables, so the insert must take place first. In reality, the transaction does not complete until both ejbCreate( ) and ejbPostCreate( ) have executed, so the vendors are free to choose the best time for database inserts and linking of relationships.

The bean identity is not available during the call to ejbCreate( ), but it is available in ejbPostCreate( ). This means that the bean can access its own primary key and EJB object (local or remote) inside of ejbPostCreate( ). This can be useful for performing postprocessing prior to servicing business-method invocations.

Each ejbPostCreate( ) method must have the same parameters as the corresponding ejbCreate( ) method, as well as the same method name. For example, if the ShipBean class defines an ejbCreateByName(String name) method, it must also define a matching ejbPostCreateByName(String name) method. The ejbPostCreate( ) method returns void.

Matching the name and parameter lists of ejbCreate( ) and ejbPostCreate( ) methods is important for two reasons. First, it indicates which ejbPostCreate( ) method is associated with which ejbCreate( ) method. This ensures that the container calls the correct ejbPostCreate( ) method after ejbCreate( ) is done. Second, in CMP, it is possible that one of the parameters passed is not assigned to a CMP field. In this case, you would need to duplicate the parameters of the ejbCreate( ) method to have that information available in the ejbPostCreate( ) method. CMR fields are the primary reason for utilizing the ejbPostCreate( ) method in CMP, because of referential integrity.

ejbCreate( ) and ejbPostCreate( ) Sequence of Events

To understand how an entity bean instance gets up and running, we have to think of a entity bean in the context of its life cycle. Figure 10-1 shows the sequence of events during a portion of a CMP bean's life cycle, as defined by the EJB specification. Every EJB vendor must support this sequence of events.

The process begins when the client invokes one of the create( ) methods on the bean's EJB home. A create( ) method is invoked on the EJB home stub (step 1), which communicates the method to the EJB home across the network (step 2). The EJB home plucks a ShipBean instance from the pool and invokes its corresponding ejbCreate( ) method (step 3).

The create( ) and ejbCreate( ) methods are responsible for initializing the bean instance so that the container (CMP) or bean class (BMP) can insert a record into the database. In the case of the ShipBean, the minimal information required to add a new ship to the system is the ship's name and unique id. These persistent fields are set during the ejbCreate( ) method invocation (step 4).

In container-managed persistence, the container uses two of the bean's CMP fields (id and name), to insert a record into the database. Only the fields described as CMP fields in the deployment descriptor are accessed. Once the container has read the CMP fields from the bean instance (step 5), it will automatically insert a new record into the database using those fields (step 6).* How the data is written to the database is defined when the bean's fields are mapped at deployment time. In our example, a new record is inserted into the SHIP table.

* The specification does not actually require that the record be inserted into the database immediately after the ejbCreate( ) method is called (step 6). As an alternative, the record insert may be deferred until after the ejbPostCreate( ) method executes or even until the end of the transaction.

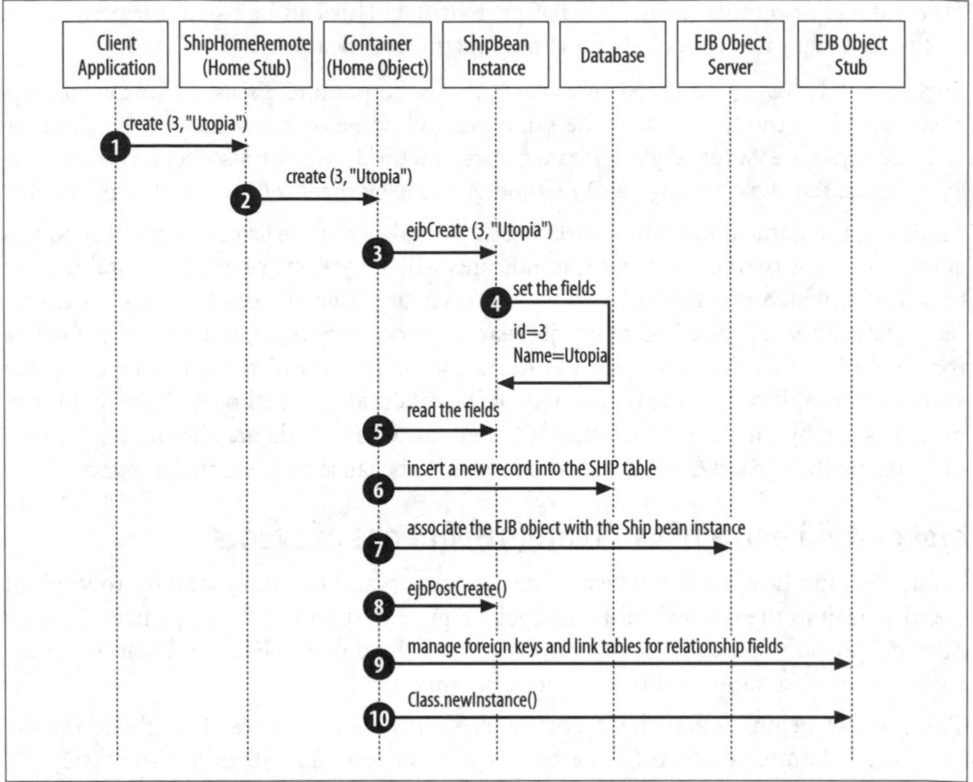

Figure 10-1. Event sequence for bean-instance creation

In bean-managed persistence, the bean class itself reads the fields and performs a database insert to add the bean's data to the database. This would take place in steps 5 and 6.

Once the record has been inserted into the database, the bean instance is ready to be assigned to an EJB object (step 7). Once the bean is assigned to an EJB object, the bean's identity is available. This is when `ejbPostCreate( )` is invoked (step 8).

In CMP entity beans, `ejbPostCreate( )` is used to manage the beans' container-managed relationship fields. This might involve setting the Cruise in the Ship EJB's `cruise` CMR field or some other relationship (step 9).

Finally, when the `ejbPostCreate( )` processing is complete, the bean is ready to service client requests. The EJB object stub is created and returned to the client application, which will use it to invoke business methods on the bean (step 10).

Using ejbLoad( ) and ejbStore( ) in Container-Managed Persistence

The process of ensuring that the database record and the entity bean instance are equivalent is called *synchronization*. In container-managed persistence, the bean's CMP fields are automatically synchronized with the database. Persistence in container-managed beans is fairly straightforward, so in most cases we will not need the `ejbLoad( )` and `ejbStore( )` methods.

Leveraging the `ejbLoad( )` and `ejbStore( )` callback methods in container-managed beans, however, can be useful if custom logic is needed when synchronizing CMP fields. Data intended for the database can be reformatted or compressed to conserve space; data just retrieved from the database can be used to calculate derived values for nonpersistent fields.

Imagine a hypothetical bean class that includes some binary value you want to store in the database. The binary value may be very large (an image, for example), so you may need to compress it before storing it away. Using the `ejbLoad( )` and `ejbStore( )` methods in a container-managed bean allows the bean instance to reformat the data as appropriate for the state of the bean and the structure of the database. Here's how this might work:

```
import java.util.zip.Inflater;
import java.util.zip.Deflater;

public abstract class HypotheticalBean implements javax.ejb.EntityBean {
    // Instance variable
    public byte [] inflatedImage;

    // CMP field methods
    public abstract void setImage(byte [] image);
    public abstract byte [] getImage( );

    // Business methods. Used by client.
    public byte [] getImageFile( ) {
        if(inflatedImage == null) {
            Inflater unzipper = new Inflater( );
            byte [] temp = getImage( );
            unzipper.setInput(temp);
            unzipper.inflate(inflatedImage);
        }
        return inflatedImage;
    }
    public void setImageFile(byte [] image) {
        inflatedImage = image;
    }

    // callback methods
    public void ejbLoad( ) {
        inflatedImage = null;
    }
```

```
        public void ejbStore() {
            if(inflatedImage != null) {
                Deflater zipper = new Deflater();
                zipper.setInput(inflatedImage);
                byte [] temp = new byte[inflatedImage.length];
                int size = zipper.deflate(temp);
                byte [] temp2 = new byte[size];
                System.arraycopy(temp, 0, temp2, 0, size);
                setImage(temp2);
            }
        }
    }
```

Just before the container synchronizes the state of entity bean with the database, it calls the `ejbStore()` method. This method uses the `java.util.zip` package to compress the image file, if it has been modified, before writing it to the database.

Just after the container updates the fields of the `HypotheticalBean` with fresh data from the database, it calls `ejbLoad()`, which reinitializes the `inflatedImage` instance variable to `null`. Decompression is preformed lazily, so it's done only when it is needed. Compression is performed by `ejbStore()` only if the image was accessed; otherwise, the image field is not modified.

Using ejbLoad() and ejbStore() in Bean-Managed Persistence

In bean-managed persistence, the `ejbLoad()` and `ejbStore()` methods are called by the container when it's time to read from or write to the database. The `ejbLoad()` method is invoked after the start of a transaction, but before the entity bean can service a method call. The `ejbStore()` method is usually called after the business method is called, but it must be called before the end of the transaction.

While the entity bean is responsible for reading and writing its state from and to the database, the container is responsible for managing the scope of the transaction. This means that the entity bean developer need not worry about committing operations on database-access APIs, provided the resource is managed by the container. The container will take care of committing the transaction and persisting the changes at the appropriate times.

If a BMP entity bean uses a resource that is not managed by the container system, the entity bean must manage the scope of the transaction manually, using operations specific to the API. Examples of how to use the `ejbLoad()` and `ejbStore()` methods in BMP are shown in detail in Chapter 9.

ejbPassivate() and ejbActivate()

The `ejbPassivate()` method notifies the bean developer that the entity bean instance is about to be pooled or otherwise disassociated from the entity bean identity. This gives the entity bean developer an opportunity to do some last-minute cleanup before the bean is placed in the pool, where it will be reused by some other EJB object. In real-world implementations, the `ejbPassivate()` method is rarely used, because most resources are obtained from the JNDI ENC and are managed automatically by the container.

The `ejbActivate()` method notifies the bean developer that the entity bean instance has just returned from the pool and is now associated with an EJB object and has been assigned an identity. This gives the entity bean developer an opportunity to prepare the entity bean for service, for example by obtaining some kind of resource connection.

As with the `ejbPassivate()` method, it's difficult to see why this method would be used in practice. It is best to secure resources lazily (i.e., as needed). The `ejbActivate()` method suggests that some kind of eager preparation can be accomplished, but this is rarely done in practice.

Even in EJB containers that do not pool entity bean instances, the value of `ejbActivate()` and `ejbPassivate()` is questionable. It's possible that an EJB container may choose to evict instances from memory between client invocations and create a new instance for each new transaction. While this may appear to hurt performance, it's a reasonable design, provided that the container system's Java Virtual Machine has an extremely efficient garbage collection and memory allocation strategy. Hotspot is an example of a JVM that has made some important advances in this area. Even in this case, however, `ejbActivate()` and `ejbPassivate()` provide little value because the `setEntityContext()` and `unsetEntityContext()` methods can accomplish the same thing.

One of the few practical reasons for using `ejbActivate()` is to reinitialize nonpersistent instance fields of the bean class that may have become "dirty" while the instance serviced another client.

Regardless of their general usefulness, these callback methods are at your disposal if you need them. In most cases, you are better off using `setEntityContext()` and `unsetEntityContext()`, since these methods will execute only once in the life cycle of a bean instance.

ejbRemove()

The component interfaces (remote, local, remote home, and local home) define remove methods that can be used to delete an entity from the system. When a client invokes one of the remove methods, as shown in the following code, the container must delete the entity's data from the database:

```
CustomerHomeRemote customerHome;
CustomerRemote customer;
```

```
customer.remove( );
// or
customerHome.remove(customer.getPrimaryKey( ));
```

The data deleted from the database includes all the CMP fields. So, for example, when you invoke a remove method on a Customer EJB, the corresponding record in the `CUSTOMER` table is deleted.

In CMP, the remove method also removes the link between the `CUSTOMER` record and the `ADDRESS` record. However, the `ADDRESS` record associated with the `CUSTOMER` record will not be automatically deleted. The address data will be deleted along with the customer data only if a *cascade delete* is specified. A cascade delete must be declared explicitly in the XML deployment descriptor, as explained in Chapter 7.

The `ejbRemove( )` method in container-managed persistence notifies the entity bean that it's about to be removed and its data is about to be deleted. This notification occurs after the client invokes one of the remove methods defined in a component interface but before the container actually deletes the data. It gives the bean developer a chance to do some last-minute cleanup before the entity is removed. Any cleanup operations that might ordinarily be done in the `ejbPassivate( )` method should also be done in the `ejbRemove( )` method, because the bean will be pooled after the `ejbRemove( )` method completes without having its `ejbPassivate( )` method invoked.

In bean-managed persistence, the bean developer is responsible for implementing the logic that deletes the entity bean's data from the database.

ejbHome( )

CMP and BMP entity beans can declare *home methods* that perform operations related to the EJB component but that are not specific to an entity bean instance. A home method must have a matching implementation in the bean class with the signature `ejbHome<METHOD-NAME>( )`.

For example, the Cruise EJB might define a home method that calculates the total revenue in bookings for a specific Cruise:

```
public interface CruiseHomeLocal extends javax.ejb.EJBLocalHome {

    public CruiseLocal create(String name, ShipLocal ship);
    public double totalReservationRevenue(CruiseLocal cruise);

}
```

Every home method declared by the home interfaces must have a corresponding `ejbHome<METHOD-NAME>( )` in the bean class. For example, the `CruiseBean` class would have an `ejbHomeTotalReservationRevenue( )` method, as shown in the following code:

```
public abstract class CruiseBean implements javax.ejb.EntityBean {
    public Integer ejbCreate(String name, ShipLocal ship) {
        setName(name);
```

```
        }
        ...
        public double ejbHomeTotalReservationRevenue(CruiseLocal cruise) {

            Set reservations = ejbSelectReservations(cruise);
            Iterator it = reservations.iterator( );
            double total = 0;
            while(it.hasNext( )) {
                ReservationLocal res = (ReservationLocal)it.next( );
                total += res.getAmount( );
            }
            return total;

        }

       public abstract ejbSelectReservations(CruiseLocal cruise);
       ...
    }
```

The ejbHome( ) methods execute without an identity within the instance pool. This is why ejbHomeTotalReservationRevenuc( ) rcquired that a CruiseLocal EJB object reference be passed in to the method. This makes sense once you realize that the caller is invoking the home method on the entity bean's EJB home object and not an entity bean reference directly. The EJB home (local or remote) is not specific to any one entity identity.

The bean developer may implement home methods in both bean-managed and container-managed persistence implementations. The ejbHome( ) methods of CMP entities typically rely on ejbSelect( ) methods, while the ejbHome( ) methods of BMP implementations frequently use direct database access and find methods to query data and apply changes.

EntityContext

The first method called by the container after a bean instance is created is setEntityContext( ). This method passes the bean instance a reference to its javax.ejb.EntityContext, which is really the instance's interface to the container.

The setEntityContext( ) method should be implemented by the entity bean developer so that it places the EntityContext reference in an instance field of the bean where it will be kept for the life of the instance. The definition of EntityContext is as follows:

```
public interface javax.ejb.EntityContext extends javax.ejb.EJBContext {
    public EJBLocalObject getEJBLocalObject( ) throws IllegalStateException
    public abstract EJBObject getEJBObject( ) throws IllegalStateException;
    public abstract Object getPrimaryKey( ) throws IllegalStateException;
}
```

As the bean instance is swapped from one EJB object to the next, the information obtainable from the EntityContext changes to reflect the EJB object to which the instance is assigned. This change is possible because the EntityContext is an interface, not a static class definition, so the container can implement the EntityContext with a concrete class that it controls. As the entity bean instance is swapped from one EJB object to another, the information made available through the EntityContext will also change.

The EntityContext.getEJBObject( ) method returns a remote reference to the bean instance's EJB object. The EntityContext.getEJBLocalObject( ) method, on the other hand, returns a local reference to the bean instance's EJB object.

Session beans also define the getEJBObject( ) and getEJBLocalObject( ) methods in the SessionContext interface; their behavior is exactly the same.

The EJB objects obtained from the EntityContext are the same kinds of references that might be used by an application client, in the case of a remote reference, or another co-located bean, in the case of a local reference. The getEJBObject( ) and getEJBLocalObject( ) methods allow the bean instance to get its own EJB object reference, which it can then pass to other beans. Here is an example:

```
public class A_Bean extends EntityBean {
    public EntityContext context;
    public void someMethod( ) {
        B_BeanRemote  b = ... // Get a remote reference to B_Bean.
        EJBObject obj = context.getEJBObject( );
        A_BeanRemote mySelf =  (A_BeanRemote)
            PortableRemoteObject.narrow(obj,A_BeanRemote.class);
        b.aMethod( mySelf );
    }
    ...
      }
```

It is illegal for a bean instance to pass a this reference to another bean; instead, it passes its remote or local EJB object reference, which the bean instance gets from its EntityContext.

The ability of a bean to obtain an EJB object reference to itself is also useful when establishing relationships with other beans in container-managed persistence. For example, the Customer EJB might implement a business method that allows it to assign itself a Reservation:

```
public abstract class CustomerBean implements javax.ejb.EntityBean {
    public EntityContext context;

    public void assignToReservation(ReservationLocal reservation) {
        EJBLocalObject localRef = context.getEJBLocalObject( );
        Collection customers = reservation.getCustomers( );
        customers.add(localRef);
    }
    ...
}
```

The EntityContext.getPrimaryKey( ) method allows a bean instance to get a copy of the primary key to which it is currently assigned. Use of this method outside of the ejbLoad( ) and ejbStore( ) methods of BMP entity beans is unusual, but the EntityContext makes the primary key available for those unusual circumstances when it is needed.

As the context in which the bean instance operates changes, some of the information made available through the EntityContext reference will be changed by the container. This is why the methods in the EntityContext throw the java.lang.IllegalStateException. The EntityContext is always available to the bean instance, but the instance is not always assigned to an EJB object. When the bean is between EJB objects (i.e., when it's in the pool), it has no EJB object or primary key to return. If the getEJBObject( ), getEJBLocalObject( ), or getPrimaryKey( ) methods are invoked when the bean is in the pool, they will throw an IllegalStateException. Appendix B provides tables of allowed operations for each bean type describing which EJBContext methods can be invoked at what times.

EJBContext

The EntityContext extends the javax.ejb.EJBContext class, which is also the base class for the SessionContext session beans use. EJBContext defines several methods that provide useful information to a bean at runtime.

Here is the definition of the EJBContext interface:

```
package javax.ejb;
public interface EJBContext {

    // EJB 2.1 only: TimerService
    public TimerService getTimerService( )
       throws java.lang.IllegalStateException;

    // EJB home methods
    public EJBHome getEJBHome( )
       java.lang.IllegalStateException;
    public EJBLocalHome getEJBLocalHome( )
       java.lang.IllegalStateException;

    // security methods
    public java.security.Principal getCallerPrincipal( );
    public boolean isCallerInRole(java.lang.String roleName);

    // transaction methods
    public javax.transaction.UserTransaction getUserTransaction( )
        throws java.lang.IllegalStateException;
    public boolean getRollbackOnly( )
        throws java.lang.IllegalStateException;
    public void setRollbackOnly( )
        throws java.lang.IllegalStateException;
```

```
    // deprecated methods
    public java.security.Identity getCallerIdentity( );
    public boolean isCallerInRole(java.security.Identity role);
    public java.util.Properties getEnvironment( );

}
```

The EJBContext.getTimerService( ) method (EJB 2.1 only) returns a reference to the container's Time Service, which allows the entity to set up notifications for itself of timed events. In other words, an entity can set alarms so that the container will call it when a specific date arrives, or some interval of time has passed. For example, an entity bean might set a timer as follows:

```
public class CustomerBean implements EntityBean, TimedObject {
    EntityContext ejbContext;
    ...
    public void scheduleAppointment(Date date, String description){
         TimerService timerService = ejbContext.getTimerServcie( );
         timerService.createTimer( date, description );
   }
   public void ejbTimeout(Timer timer){
       // do something when the timer goes off
   }
  ...
}
```

The scheduleAppointment( ) method is a business method that's made available to remote clients via the remote interface. A client can call this method passing in a date and description of an event, which are in turn used to create a timer; to register the entity for a timed event. In order for an entity to be notified of a timed event it must implement the javax.ejb.TimedObject interface, which defines one method: ejbTimeout( ). When the date of a timed event arrives, the Timer Service, which is part of the EJB container, will call the ejbTimeout( ) method. The entity can get details of the timed event from the javax.ejb.Timer object, including the description. The Timer Service is covered in detail in Chapter 13.

The EJBContext.getEJBHome( ) and EJBContext.getEJBLocalHome( ) methods return a reference to the bean's EJB home. This is useful if the bean needs to create or find entity beans of its own type. Access to the EJB home may be more useful in BMP entity beans than in CMP entity beans, which have select methods and CMR fields.

As an example, if all of the employees in Titan's system (including managers) are represented by BMP Employee beans, a manager who needs access to subordinate employees can use the getEJBLocalHome( ) method to get beans representing the appropriate employees:

```
public class EmployeeBean implements EntityBean {
    EntityContext ejbContext;
    ...
    public EmployeeLocal createSubordinate( ) {
        EmployeeLocal mySelf = (EmployeeLocal)ejbContext.getEJBLocalObject( );
```

```
            EmployeeHomeLocal home = (EmployeeHomeLocal)ejbContext.getEJBLocalHome( );
            EmployeeLocal subordinate = home.createSubordinateTo( mySelf );
            return subordinate;
        }
        ...
    }
```

The EJBContext.getCallerPrincipal( ) method is used to obtain the java.security.Principal object representing the client that is currently accessing the bean. The Principal object can, for example, be used by the BMP Ship EJB to track the identities of clients making updates:

```
    public class ShipBean implements EntityBean {
        String lastModifiedBy;
        EntityContext context;
        ...
        public void setTonnage(double tons) {
            tonnage = tons;
            Principal principal = context.getCallerPrincipal( );
            String modifiedBy = principal.getName( );
            ...
        }
        ...
    }
```

The EJBContext.isCallerInRole( ) method tells you whether the client accessing the bean is a member of a specific role, identified by a role name. This method is useful when more access control is needed than simple method-based access control can provide. In a banking system, for example, you might allow the Teller role to make most withdrawals but only the Manager role to make withdrawals of over $10,000. This kind of fine-grained access control cannot be addressed through EJB's security attributes because it involves a business logic problem. Therefore, we can use the isCallerInRole( ) method to augment the automatic access control provided by EJB. First, let's assume that all managers are also tellers. The business logic in the withdraw( ) method uses isCallerInRole( ) to make sure that only the Manager role can withdraw sums over $10,000.00:

```
    public class AccountBean implements EntityBean {
        int id;
        double balance;
        EntityContext context;

        public void withdraw(Double withdraw) throws AccessDeniedException {

            if (withdraw.doubleValue( ) > 10000) {
                boolean isManager = context.isCallerInRole("Manager");
                if (!isManager) {
                    // Only Managers can withdraw more than 10k.
                    throw new AccessDeniedException( );
                }
            }
```

```
            balance = balance - withdraw.doubleValue( );

        }
        ...
    }
```

The EJBContext contains some methods that were used in EJB 1.0 but were deprecated in EJB 1.1 and have been abandoned in EJB 2.0 and EJB 2.1. Support for these deprecated methods were optional for EJB 2.0 containers, they are not supported by EJB 2.1. EJB containers that do not support the deprecated security methods will throw a RuntimeException. The deprecated security methods are based on EJB 1.0's use of the Identity object instead of the Principal object. The semantics of the deprecated methods are basically the same but, because Identity is an abstract class, it has proven to be too difficult to use. Even if your EJB 2.0 vendor supports these deprecated methods, you should never use them for new entity beans. They should only be used if you are continuing to support legacy EJB 1.0 entities—a fairly rare occurence.

The getEnvironment() method has been replaced by the JNDI environment naming context, which is discussed later in this book. EJB 2.0 containers may optionally support this method for backward compatibly with legacy EJB 1.0 components, but EJB 2.1 containers do not support this method at all and will throw a RuntimeException if its called. The transactional methods—getUserTransaction( ), setRollbackOnly( ), and getRollbackOnly( )—are described in detail in Chapter 15.

The material on the EJBContext covered in this section applies equally well to session and message-driven beans. There are some exceptions, however, and these differences are covered in Chapter 11 and Chapter 12.

JNDI ENC

Starting with EJB 1.1, the bean-container contract for entity and stateful beans was expanded beyond the EJBContext using the Java Naming and Directory Interface (JNDI). A special JNDI name space, which is referred to as the *environment naming context* (ENC), was added to allow any enterprise bean to access environment entries, other beans, and resources (such as JDBC DataSource objects) specific to that enterprise bean.

The JNDI ENC continues to be an extremely important part of the bean-container contract. Although we used the JNDI ENC to access JDBC in the bean-managed persistence chapter (Chapter 9), it's not specific to entity beans. The JNDI ENC is used by session, entity, and message-driven beans alike. To avoid unnecessary duplication, a detailed discussion of this important facility is left for Chapter 11. What you learn about using the JNDI ENC in Chapter 11 applies equally well to session, entity, and message-driven beans.

The Life Cycle of an Entity Bean

To understand how to best develop entity beans, it is important to understand how the container manages them. The EJB specification defines just about every major event in an entity bean's life, from the time it is instantiated to the time it is garbage collected. This is called the *life cycle*, and it provides the bean developer and EJB vendors with all the information they need to develop beans and EJB servers that adhere to a consistent protocol. To understand the life cycle, we will follow an entity instance through several life-cycle events and describe how the container interacts with the entity bean during these events. Figure 10-2 illustrates the life cycle of an entity instance.

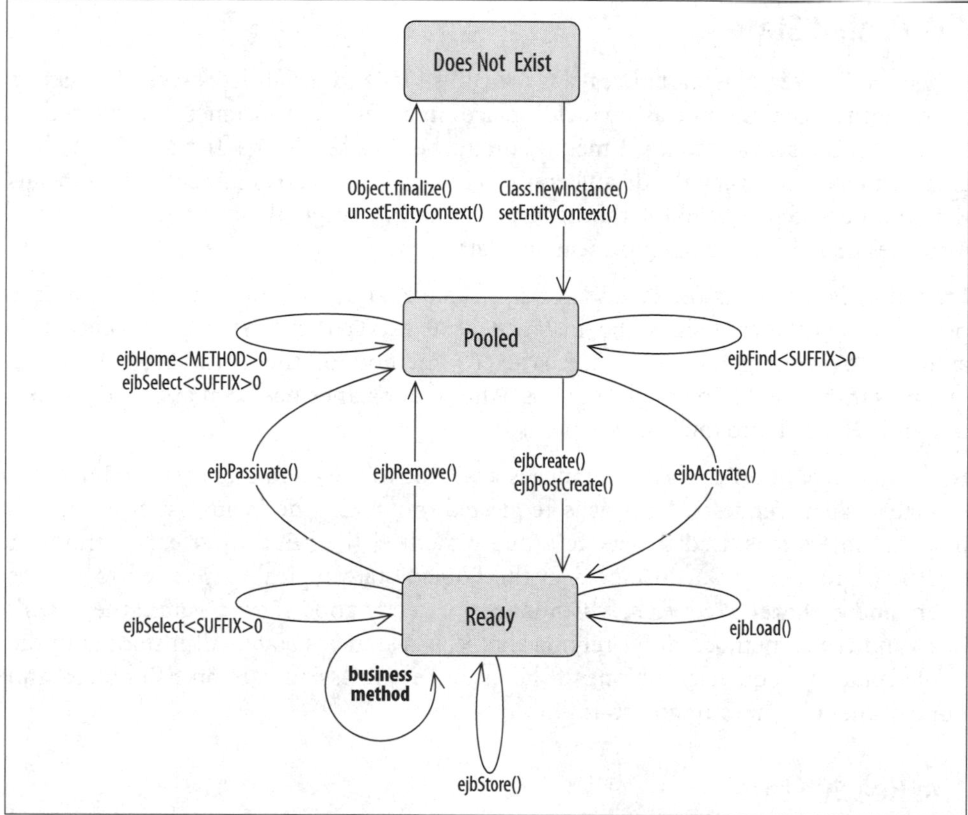

Figure 10-2. Entity bean life cycle

This section identifies the points at which the container calls each of the methods described in the `EntityBean` interface as well as the find methods and the select and home methods. Bean instances must implement the `EntityBean` interface, which means that invocations of the callback methods are invocations on the bean instance itself.

At each stage of the entity bean's life cycle, the bean container provides varying levels of access. For example, the `EntityContext.getPrimaryKey()` method will not work if it is invoked in the `ejbCreate()` method, but it does work when called in the `ejbPostCreate()` method. Other `EJBContext` methods have similar restrictions, as does the JNDI ENC.

Does Not Exist

The entity bean begins life as a collection of files. Included in that collection are the bean's deployment descriptor, component interfaces, and all the supporting classes generated at deployment time. At this stage, no instance of the bean exists.

The Pooled State

When the EJB server is started, it reads the EJB's files and instantiates several instances of the entity bean's bean class, which it places in a pool. The instances are created by calling the `Class.newInstance()` method on the bean class. The `newInstance()` method creates an instance using the default constructor, which has no arguments.* This means that the persistence fields of the bean instances are set at their default values; the instances themselves do not represent any data in the database.

Immediately following the creation of an instance, and just before it is placed in the pool, the container assigns the instance its `EntityContext`. The `EntityContext` is assigned by calling the `setEntityContext()` method of the `EntityBean` interface, which is implemented by the bean class. After the instance has been assigned its context, it is entered into the instance pool.

In the instance pool, the bean instance is available to the container as a candidate for servicing client requests. Until it is requested, however, the bean instance remains inactive unless it is used to service a query method (i.e., find or select method) or `ejbHome()` request. Bean instances in the Pooled state typically are used to service query and `ejbHome()` requests, which makes perfectly good sense because they aren't busy and these methods don't rely on the bean instance's state. All instances in the Pooled state are equivalent. None of the instances are assigned to an EJB object, and none of them has meaningful state.

The Ready State

When a bean instance is in the Ready state, it can accept client requests. A bean instance moves to the Ready state when the container assigns it to an EJB object.

* Constructors should never be defined in the bean class. The default no-argument constructor, which is implicit if no other constructors are declared, must be available to the container.

This occurs under two circumstances: when a new entity bean is being created, or when the container is activating an entity.

Transitioning from the Pooled state to the Ready state via creation

When a client application invokes a `create( )` method on an EJB home, several operations must take place before the EJB container can return a remote or local reference (EJB object) to the client. First, an EJB object must be created on the EJB server.* Once the EJB object is created, an entity bean instance is taken from the instance pool and assigned to the EJB object. Next, the `create( )` method, invoked by the client, is delegated to its corresponding `ejbCreate( )` method on the bean instance. After the `ejbCreate( )` method completes, a primary key is created.

When the `ejbCreate( )` method is done, the `ejbPostCreate( )` method on the entity bean instance is called. Finally, after the successful completion of the `ejbPostCreate( )` method, the home is allowed to return a remote or local reference—an EJB object—to the client. The bean instance and EJB object are now ready to service method requests from the client. This is one way that the bean instance can move from the Pooled state to the Ready state.

Transitioning from the Pooled state to the Ready state via a query method

When a query method is executed, each EJB object that is found as a result of the query will be realized by transitioning an instance from the Pooled state to the Ready state. When an entity bean is found, it is assigned to an EJB object and its EJB object reference is returned to the client. A found bean follows the same protocol as a passivated bean; it is activated when the client invokes a business method, and will move into the Ready state through activation, as described in the next section.

In many cases (depending on the EJB vendor), found entity beans don't actually migrate into the Ready state until they are accessed by the client. So, for example, if a find method returns a collection of entity beans, the entity beans may not be activated until they are obtained from the collection or accessed directly by the client. Resources are saved by activating entity beans lazily (as needed).

Transitioning from the Pooled state to the Ready state via activation

The activation process can also move an entity bean instance from the Pooled state to the Ready state. Activation facilitates resource management by allowing a few bean instances to service many EJB objects. Activation was explained in Chapter 3, but we will revisit the process here as it relates to the entity bean instance's life cycle. Activation presumes that the entity bean has previously been *passivated*. More is said

* This is only a conceptual model. In reality, an EJB container and the EJB object may be the same thing, or a single EJB object may provide a multiplexing service for all entities of the same type. The implementation details are not as important as understanding the life-cycle protocol.

about this state transition later; for now, suffice it to say that when a bean instance is passivated, it frees any resources that it does not need and leaves the EJB object for the instance pool. When the bean instance returns to the pool, the EJB object is left without an instance to which to delegate client requests. The EJB object maintains its stub connection on the client, so as far as the client is concerned, the entity bean hasn't changed. When the client invokes a business method on the EJB object, the EJB object must obtain a bean instance. This is accomplished by activating a bean instance.

When a bean instance is activated, it leaves the instance pool (the Pooled state) to be assigned to an EJB object. Once assigned to the proper EJB object, the `ejbActivate()` method is called—the instance's `EntityContext` can now provide information specific to the EJB object, but it cannot provide security or transactional information. The `ejbActivate()` callback method can be used in the bean instance to reobtain resources or perform any other necessary work before servicing the client.

When an entity bean instance is activated, nonpersistent instance fields of the bean instance may contain arbitrary (dirty) values and should be reinitialized in the `ejbActivate()` method.

In container-managed persistence, container-managed fields are automatically synchronized with the database after `ejbActivate()` is invoked and before a business method can be serviced by the bean instance. The order in which these things happen in CMP entity beans is:

1. `ejbActivate()` is invoked on the bean instance.
2. Persistence fields are synchronized automatically.
3. `ejbLoad()` notifies the bean that its persistence fields have been synchronized.
4. Business methods are invoked as needed.

In bean-managed persistence, persistence fields are synchronized by the `ejbLoad()` method after `ejbActivate()` has been called and before a business method can be invoked. Here is the order of operations in bean-managed persistence:

1. `ejbActivate()` is invoked on the bean instance.
2. `ejbLoad()` is called to let the bean synchronize its persistence fields.
3. Business methods are invoked as needed.

Transitioning from the Ready state to the Pooled state via passivation

A bean can move from the Ready state to the Pooled state via passivation, which is the process of disassociating a bean instance from an EJB object when it is not busy. After a bean instance has been assigned to an EJB object, the EJB container can passivate the instance at any time, provided that the instance is not currently executing a method. As part of the passivation process, the `ejbPassivate()` method is invoked on the bean instance. This callback method can be used by the instance to release any resources or perform other processing prior to leaving the EJB object. When `ejbPassivate()` has completed, the bean instance is disassociated from the EJB object server and returned to the instance pool. The bean instance is now back in the Pooled state.

A bean-managed entity instance should not try to save its state to the database in the `ejbPassivate()` method; this activity is reserved for the `ejbStore()` method. The container will invoke `ejbStore()` to synchronize the bean instance's state with the database prior to passivating the bean.

The most fundamental thing to remember is that, for entity beans, passivation is simply a notification that the instance is about to be disassociated from the EJB object. Unlike stateful session beans, an entity bean instance's fields are not serialized and held with the EJB object when the bean is passivated. Whatever values were held in the instance's nonpersistent fields when the entity bean was assigned to the EJB object will be carried with it to its next assignment.

Transitioning from the Ready state to the Pooled state via removal

A bean instance also moves from the Ready state to the Pooled state when it is removed. This occurs when the client application invokes one of the remove methods on the bean's EJB object or EJB home. With entity beans, invoking a remove method deletes the entity's data from the database. Once the entity's data has been deleted from the database, it is no longer a valid entity.

Once the `ejbRemove()` method has finished, the bean instance is moved back to the instance pool and out of the Ready state. It is important that the `ejbRemove()` method release any resources that would normally be released by `ejbPassivate()`, which is not called when a bean is removed. This can be done, if need be, by invoking the `ejbPassivate()` method within the `ejbRemove()` method body.

In bean-managed persistence, the `ejbRemove()` method is implemented by the entity bean developer and includes code to delete the entity bean's data from the database. The EJB container will invoke the `ejbRemove()` method in response to a client's invocation of the `remove()` method on one of the component interfaces.

In container-managed persistence, the `ejbRemove()` method notifies the entity bean instance that its data is about to be removed from the database. Immediately following the `ejbRemove()` call, the container deletes the entity bean's data.

In CMP the container also cleans up the entity bean's relationships with other entity beans in the database. If a cascade delete is specified, it removes each entity bean in the cascade delete relationships. This involves activating each entity bean and calling its `ejbActivate()` methods, loading each entity bean's state by calling its `ejbLoad()` method, calling the `ejbRemove()` on all of the entity beans in the cascade-delete relationship, and then deleting their data. This process can continue in a chain until all the cascade-delete operations of all the relationships have completed.

Life in the Ready State

A bean is in the Ready state when it is associated with an EJB object and is ready to service requests from the client. When the client invokes a business method, like `Ship.getName()`, on the bean's remote or local reference (EJB object), the method invocation is received by the EJB server and delegated to the bean instance. The instance performs the method and returns the results. As long as the bean instance is in the Ready state, it can service all the business methods invoked by the client. Business methods can be called zero or more times, in any order.

In addition to servicing business methods, an entity bean in the Ready state can execute select methods, which are called by the bean instance while servicing a business method.

The `ejbLoad()` and `ejbStore()` methods, which synchronize the bean instance's state with the database, can be called only when the bean is in the Ready state. These methods can be called in any order, depending on the vendor's implementation. Some vendors call `ejbLoad()` before every method invocation and `ejbStore()` after every method invocation, depending on the transactional context. Other vendors call these methods less frequently.

In bean-managed persistence, the `ejbLoad()` method should always use the `EntityContext.getPrimaryKey()` method to obtain data from the database and should not trust any primary key or other data that the bean has stored in its fields. (This is how we implemented it in the bean-managed version of the Ship bean in Chapter 9.) It should be assumed, however, that the state of the bean is valid when calling the `ejbStore()` method.

In container-managed persistence, the `ejbLoad()` method is always called immediately following the synchronization of the bean's container-managed fields with the database—in other words, right after the container updates the state of the bean instance with data from the database. This provides an opportunity to perform any calculations or reformat data before the instance can service business-method invocations from the client. The `ejbStore()` method is called just before the database is synchronized with the state of the bean instance—just before the container writes the container-managed fields to the database. This provides the CMP entity bean instance with an opportunity to change the data in the container-managed fields prior to their persistence to the database.

In bean-managed persistence, the `ejbLoad()` and `ejbStore()` methods are called when the container deems it appropriate to synchronize the bean's state with the database. These are the only callback methods that should be used to synchronize the bean's state with the database. Do not use `ejbActivate()`, `ejbPassivate()`, `setEntityContext()`, or `unsetEntityContext()` to access the database for the purpose of synchronization. You should use the `ejbCreate()` and `ejbRemove()` methods, however, to insert and delete (respectively) the entity's data into and from the database.

End of the Life Cycle

A bean instance's life cycle ends when the container decides to remove it from the pool and allow it to be garbage collected. This happens under a few different circumstances. If the container decides to reduce the number of instances in the pool—usually to conserve resources—it releases one or more bean instances and allows them to be garbage collected. The ability to adjust the size of the instance pool allows the EJB server to manage its resources (the number of threads, available memory, etc.) so that it can achieve the highest possible performance.

When an EJB server is shut down, most containers release all the bean instances so that they can be safely garbage collected. Some containers may also decide to release any instances that are behaving unfavorably or that have suffered from some kind of unrecoverable error that makes them unstable. For example, any time an entity bean instance throws a type of `RuntimeException` from any of its methods, the EJB container will evict that instance from memory and replace it with a stable instance from the instance pool.

When an entity bean instance leaves the instance pool to be garbage collected, the `unsetEntityContext()` method is invoked by the container to alert the bean instance that it is about be destroyed. This callback method lets the bean instance release any resources it maintains before being garbage collected. Once the bean's `unsetEntityContext()` method has been called, it is garbage collected.

The bean instance's `finalize()` method may or may not be invoked following the `unsetEntityContext()` method. A bean should not rely on its `finalize()` method, since each vendor handles evicting instances differently.

CHAPTER 11

Session Beans

Entity beans provide an object-oriented model that makes it easier for developers to create, modify, and delete data from the database. They allow developers to be more productive by encouraging reuse, thus reducing development costs. For example, once a bean has been defined to represent a concept like a Ship, that bean can be reused throughout a business system without redefining, recoding, or retesting the business logic and data access.

However, entity beans are not the entire story. We have seen another kind of enterprise bean: the *session bean*. Session beans fill the gaps left by entity beans. They are useful for describing interactions between other beans (taskflow) and for implementing particular tasks. Unlike entity beans, session beans do not represent shared data in the database, but they can access shared data. This means that we can use session beans to read, update, and insert data. For example, we might use a session bean to provide lists of information, such as a list of all available cabins. Sometimes we might generate the list by interacting with entity beans, like the cabin list we developed in the TravelAgent EJB in Chapter 4. More frequently, session beans will generate lists by accessing the database directly.

When do you use an entity bean and when do you use a session bean? As a rule of thumb, an entity bean should provide a safe and consistent interface to a set of shared data that defines a concept. This data may be updated frequently. Session beans access data that spans concepts, is not shared, and is usually read-only.

In addition to accessing data directly, session beans can represent *taskflow*. Taskflow means all the steps required to accomplish a particular task, such as booking passage on a ship or renting a video. Session beans frequently manage the interactions between entity beans, describing how they work together to accomplish a specific task. The relationship between session beans and entity beans is like the relationship between a script for a play and the actors that perform the play. Actors are pointless without a script; they may represent something, but they can't tell a story. Similarly, entities represented in a database aren't meaningful unless you can have interactions between entities. It makes no sense to have a database full of cabins, ships, customers, and such if we can't create interactions between them, such as booking a customer for a cruise.

Session beans are divided into two basic types: stateless and stateful. A *stateless* session bean is a collection of related services, each represented by a method; the bean maintains no state from one method invocation to the next. When you invoke a method on a stateless session bean, it executes the method and returns the result without knowing or caring what other requests have gone before or might follow. Think of a stateless session bean as a set of procedures or batch programs that execute a request based on some parameters and return a result.

A *stateful* session bean is an extension of the client application. It performs tasks on behalf of a client and maintains state related to that client. This state is called *conversational state* because it represents a continuing conversation between the stateful session bean and the client. Methods invoked on a stateful session bean can write and read data to and from this conversational state, which is shared among all methods in the bean. Stateful session beans tend to be specific to one scenario. They represent logic that might have been captured in the client application of a two-tier system.

Depending on the vendor, stateful session beans may have a timeout period. If the client fails to use the stateful bean before it times out, the bean instance is destroyed and the EJB object reference is invalidated. This prevents the stateful session bean from lingering long after a client has shut down or otherwise finished using it. After all, clients can crash, and users can walk away from their desks and forget what they're doing; we don't want stateful session beans associated with dead clients or forgetful users cluttering up our server forever. A client can also explicitly remove a stateful session bean by calling one of its remove methods.

Stateless session beans have longer lives because they do not retain any conversational state and are not dedicated to one client. As soon as a stateless session bean has finished a method invocation, it can be reassigned to service a new client. Stateless session beans may also have a timeout period and can be removed by the client, but the impact of a bean timeout or removal is different than with a stateful session bean. A timeout or remove operation simply invalidates the EJB object reference for that client; the bean instance is not destroyed and is free to service other client requests.

Whether they are stateful or stateless, session beans are not persistent like entity beans. In other words, session beans don't represent persistent date and are not saved to the database.

The Stateless Session Bean

A stateless session bean is very efficient and relatively easy to develop. A session bean can be swapped freely between EJB objects because it isn't dedicated to one client and doesn't maintain any conversational state. As soon as it is finished servicing a method invocation it can be swapped to another EJB object. Because it does not maintain conversational state, a stateless session bean does not require passivation or activation, further reducing the overhead of swapping. In short, stateless session beans are lightweight and fast.

Saying that a stateless session bean doesn't maintain any conversational state means that every method invocation is independent of previous invocations, and that everything the method needs to know has to be passed via the method's parameters. Since stateless session beans can't remember anything from one method invocation to the next, they must take care of an entire task in one method invocation. The only exception to this rule is information obtainable from the `SessionContext` and the JNDI ENC. Stateless session beans are EJB's version of the traditional transaction-processing applications, which are executed using a procedure call. The procedure executes from beginning to end and then returns the result. Once the procedure is done, nothing about the data that was manipulated or the details of the request are remembered.

These restrictions don't mean that a stateless session bean can't have instance variables or maintain any kind of internal state. Nothing prevents you from keeping a variable that tracks the number of times a bean has been called or that saves data for debugging. An instance variable can even hold a reference to a live resource, such as a URL connection for logging, verifying credit cards, or anything else that might be useful—the resource should be obtained from the JNDI ENC. However, it is important to remember that this state can never be visible to a client. A client can't assume that the same bean instance will service all of its requests. Instance variables may have different values in different bean instances, so their values can appear to change randomly as stateless session beans are swapped from one client to another. Therefore, any resources you reference in instance variables should be generic. For example, each bean instance might reasonably record debugging messages—that might be the only way to figure out what is happening on a large server with many bean instances. The client doesn't know or care where debugging output is going. However, it would clearly be inappropriate for a stateless bean to remember that it was in the process of making a reservation for Madame X—the next time it is called, it may be servicing another client entirely.

Stateless session beans can be used for report generation, batch processing, or some stateless services such as validating credit cards. Another good application might be a StockQuote EJB that returns a stock's current price. Any activity that can be accomplished in one method call is a good candidate for the high-performance stateless session bean.

The ProcessPayment EJB

Chapter 2 and Chapter 3 discussed the TravelAgent EJB, which has a business method called `bookPassage()` that uses the ProcessPayment EJB. The next section develops a complete definition of the TravelAgent EJB, including the logic of the bookPassage() method. At this point, however, we are primarily interested in the ProcessPayment EJB, which is a stateless bean the TravelAgent EJB uses to charge the customer for the price of the cruise. Charging customers is a common activity in Titan's business systems. Not only does the reservation system need to charge customers, but so do Titan's gift shops, boutiques, and other related businesses. Because many different systems charge customers for services, we've encapsulated the logic for charging customers in its own bean.

Payments are recorded in a special database table called PAYMENT. The PAYMENT data is batch processed for accounting purposes and is not normally used outside of accounting. In other words, the data is only inserted by Titan's system; it is not read, updated, or deleted. Because the process of making a charge can be completed in one method, and because the data is not updated frequently or shared, we will use a stateless session bean for processing payments. Several different forms of payment can be used: credit card, check, or cash. We will model these payment forms in our stateless ProcessPayment EJB.

The database table (PAYMENT)

The ProcessPayment EJB accesses an existing table in Titan's system called the PAYMENT table. Create a table in your database called PAYMENT with this definition:

```
CREATE TABLE PAYMENT
(
    customer_id     INTEGER,
    amount          DECIMAL(8,2),
    type            CHAR(10),
    check_bar_code  CHAR(50),
    check_number    INTEGER,
    credit_number   CHAR(20),
    credit_exp_date DATE
)
```

The remote interface (ProcessPaymentRemote)

A stateless session bean, like an entity bean, may have a local or remote interface, or both. The remote interface obviously needs a byCredit() method because the TravelAgent EJB uses it. We can also identify two other methods that we'll need: byCash() for customers paying cash and byCheck() for customers paying with a personal check. Here is a complete definition of the remote interface for the ProcessPayment EJB:

```
package com.titan.processpayment;

import java.rmi.RemoteException;
import com.titan.customer.CustomerRemote;

public interface ProcessPaymentRemote extends javax.ejb.EJBObject {

    public boolean byCheck(CustomerRemote customer, CheckDO check, double amount)
        throws RemoteException,PaymentException;
```

```
    public boolean byCash(CustomerRemote customer, double amount)
        throws RemoteException,PaymentException;

    public boolean byCredit(CustomerRemote customer, CreditCardDO card,
        double amount) throws RemoteException,PaymentException;
}
```

Remote interfaces in session beans follow the same rules as in entity beans. Here, we have defined the three business methods `byCheck()`, `byCash()`, and `byCredit()`, which take information relevant to the form of payment used and return a `boolean` value that indicates whether the payment succeeded. In addition to the required `RemoteException`, these methods can throw an application-specific exception, the `PaymentException`. The `PaymentException` is thrown if any problems occur while processing the payment, such as a low check number or an expired credit card. Notice, however, that nothing about the `ProcessPaymentRemote` interface is specific to the reservation system. It could be used just about anywhere in Titan's system. In addition, each method defined in the remote interface is completely independent of the others. All the data that is required to process a payment is obtained through the method's arguments.

As an extension of the `javax.ejb.EJBObject` interface, the remote interface of a session bean inherits the remote interface of an entity bean. However, the `getPrimaryKey()` method throws a `RemoteException`, since session beans do not have a primary key to return:

```
public interface javax.ejb.EJBObject extends java.rmi.Remote {
    public abstract EJBHome getEJBHome() throws RemoteException;
    public abstract Handle getHandle() throws RemoteException;
    public abstract Object getPrimaryKey() throws RemoteException;
    public abstract boolean isIdentical(EJBObject obj) throws RemoteException;
    public abstract void remove() throws RemoteException, RemoveException;
}
```

The `getHandle()` method returns a serializable `Handle` object, just like the `getHandle()` method in the entity bean. A stateless session bean can serialize and reuse this `Handle` at any time, as long as the stateless bean type is still available in the container that generated the `Handle`. You can obtain a remote reference to the bean from the `Handle` by invoking its `getEJBObject()` method:

```
public interface javax.ejb.Handle {
    public abstract EJBObject getEJBObject() throws RemoteException;
}
```

The ProcessPayment EJB has its own package, which means it has its own directory in our development tree, *dev/com/titan/processpayment*. That's where we'll store all the code and class files for this bean.

Dependent objects (CreditCardDO and CheckDO classes)

The ProcessPayment EJB's remote interface uses two classes that are particularly interesting, CreditCardDO and CheckDO:

```
/* CreditCardDO.java */
package com.titan.processpayment;

import java.util.Date;

public class CreditCardDO implements java.io.Serializable {
    final static public String MASTER_CARD = "MASTER_CARD";
    final static public String VISA = "VISA";
    final static public String AMERICAN_EXPRESS = "AMERICAN_EXPRESS";
    final static public String DISCOVER = "DISCOVER";
    final static public String DINERS_CARD = "DINERS_CARD";

    public String number;
    public Date expiration;
    public String type;

    public CreditCardDO(String nmbr, Date exp, String typ) {
        number = nmbr;
        expiration = exp;
        type = typ;
    }
}

/* CheckDO.java */
package com.titan.processpayment;

public class CheckDO implements java.io.Serializable {
    public String checkBarCode;
    public int checkNumber;

    public CheckDO(String barCode, int number) {
        checkBarCode = barCode;
        checkNumber = number;
    }
}
```

CreditCardDO and CheckDO are *dependent objects*, a concept we explored with the Address EJB in Chapter 6. They are simply serializable Java classes, not enterprise beans; they provide a convenient mechanism for transporting related data. CreditCardDO, for example, collects all the credit card data together in one class, making it easier to pass the information across the network as well as making our interfaces a little cleaner.

An application exception (PaymentException)

Any remote or local interface, whether it's for an entity bean or a session bean, can throw application exceptions. Application exceptions should describe a business logic problem—in this case, a problem making a payment. Application exceptions should be meaningful to the client, providing a brief and relevant identification of the error.

It is important to understand what exceptions to use and when to use them. The RemoteException indicates subsystem-level problems and is used by the RMI facility. Likewise, exceptions such as javax.naming.NamingException and java.sql.SQLException are thrown by other Java subsystems; usually these should not be thrown explicitly by your beans. You must use try/catch blocks to capture checked exceptions like these.

The EJBException indicates that the container ran into problems processing a local interface invocation. EJBException is unchecked, so you won't get a compile error if you don't catch it. However, under certain circumstances it is a good idea to catch EJBException, and in other circumstances it should be propagated.

When a bean method catches a checked exception from a subsystem (JDBC, JNDI, JMS, etc.), it should be rethrown as either an EJBException or an application exception. You would rethrow a checked exception as an EJBException if it represented a system-level problem; use an application exception if the original exception resulted from business logic problems. Your beans incorporate your business logic; if a problem occurs in the business logic, that problem should be represented by an application exception. When the enterprise bean throws an EJBException or some other type of RuntimeException, the exception is first processed by the container, which discards the bean instance and replaces it with another. After the container processes the exception, it propagates an exception to the client. For remote clients, the container throws a RemoteException; for local clients (co-located enterprise beans), the container rethrows the original EJBException or RuntimeException thrown by the bean instance.

The PaymentException describes a specific business problem, so it is an application exception. Application exceptions extend java.lang.Exception. Any instance variables you include in these exceptions should be serializable. Here is the definition of the PaymentException:

```
package com.titan.processpayment;

public class PaymentException extends java.lang.Exception {
    public PaymentException( ) {
        super( );
    }
    public PaymentException(String msg) {
        super(msg);
    }
}
```

The home interface (ProcessPaymentHomeRemote)

The home interface of a stateless session bean must declare a single create( ) method with no arguments. This is a requirement of the EJB specification. It is illegal to define `create()` methods with arguments, because stateless session beans do not maintain conversational state that needs to be initialized. There are no find methods in session beans either, because session beans do not represent data in the database. Unlike stateful session beans and entity beans, stateless session beans may not define any `create<SUFFIX>()` methods. This restriction has to do with the life cycle of stateless session beans, which is explained later in this chapter. Here is the definition of the remote home interface for the ProcessPayment EJB:

```
package com.titan.processpayment;

import java.rmi.RemoteException;
import javax.ejb.CreateException;

public interface ProcessPaymentHomeRemote extends javax.ejb.EJBHome {
    public ProcessPaymentRemote create( ) throws RemoteException, CreateException;
}
```

The `CreateException` is mandatory, as is the `RemoteException`. The `CreateException` can be thrown by the bean itself to indicate an application error in creating the bean. A `RemoteException` is thrown when other system errors occur—for example, when there is a problem with network communication or when an unchecked exception is thrown from the bean class.

The `ProcessPaymentHomeRemote` interface, as an extension of the `javax.ejb.EJBHome`, offers the same `EJBHome` methods as entity beans. The only difference is that `remove(Object primaryKey)` does not work, because session beans do not have primary keys; if this method is called, it throws a `RemoteException`. Here is the definition of the `javax.ejb.EJBHome` interface:

```
public interface javax.ejb.EJBHome extends java.rmi.Remote {
    public abstract HomeHandle getHomeHandle( ) throws RemoteException;
    public abstract EJBMetaData getEJBMetaData( ) throws RemoteException;
    public abstract void remove(Handle handle) throws RemoteException,
        RemoveException;
    public abstract void remove(Object primaryKey) throws RemoteException,
        RemoveException;
}
```

The home interface of a session bean can return the `EJBMetaData` for the bean, just like an entity bean. `EJBMetaData` is a serializable object that provides information about the bean's interfaces. The only difference between the `EJBMetaData` for a session bean and an entity bean is that calling `getPrimaryKeyClass()` on the session bean's `EJBMetaData` throws a `java.lang.RuntimeException`:

```
public interface javax.ejb.EJBMetaData {
    public abstract EJBHome getEJBHome( );
    public abstract Class getHomeInterfaceClass( );
    public abstract Class getPrimaryKeyClass( );
    public abstract Class getRemoteInterfaceClass( );
    public abstract boolean isSession( );
    public abstract boolean isStateless( );  // EJB 1.0 only
}
```

The bean class (ProcessPaymentBean)

The ProcessPayment EJB accesses data that is not generally shared by other parts of the system, so it is an excellent candidate for a stateless session bean. This bean really represents a set of independent operations—another indication that it is a good candidate for a stateless session bean. Here is the definition of the `ProcessPaymentBean` class:

```
package com.titan.processpayment;
import com.titan.customer.*;

import java.sql.*;
import java.rmi.RemoteException;
import javax.ejb.SessionContext;

import javax.naming.InitialContext;
import javax.sql.DataSource;
import javax.ejb.EJBException;
import javax.naming.NamingException;

public class ProcessPaymentBean implements javax.ejb.SessionBean {

    final public static String CASH = "CASH";
    final public static String CREDIT = "CREDIT";
    final public static String CHECK = "CHECK";

    public SessionContext context;

    public void ejbCreate( ) {
    }

    public boolean byCash(CustomerRemote customer, double amount)
        throws PaymentException{
        return process(getCustomerID(customer), amount, CASH, null, -1, null, null);
    }

    public boolean byCheck(CustomerRemote customer, CheckDO check, double amount)
        throws PaymentException{
        int minCheckNumber = getMinCheckNumber( );
        if (check.checkNumber > minCheckNumber) {
            return process(getCustomerID(customer), amount, CHECK,
                check.checkBarCode, check.checkNumber, null, null);
        }
        else {
            throw new PaymentException("Check number is too low.
                Must be at least "+minCheckNumber);
        }
    }
    public boolean byCredit(CustomerRemote customer, CreditCardDO card,
        double amount) throws PaymentException {
        if (card.expiration.before(new java.util.Date( ))) {
            throw new PaymentException("Expiration date has passed");
        }
```

```
        else {
            return process(getCustomerID(customer), amount, CREDIT, null,
            -1, card.number, new java.sql.Date(card.expiration.getTime( )));
        }
    }
    private boolean process(Integer customerID, double amount, String type,
        String checkBarCode, int checkNumber, String creditNumber,
        java.sql.Date creditExpDate) throws PaymentException {

        Connection con = null;

        PreparedStatement ps = null;

        try {
            con = getConnection( );
            ps = con.prepareStatement
                ("INSERT INTO payment (customer_id, amount, type,"+
                "check_bar_code,check_number,credit_number,"+
                "credit_exp_date) VALUES (?,?,?,?,?,?,?)");
            ps.setInt(1,customerID.intValue( ));
            ps.setDouble(2,amount);
            ps.setString(3,type);
            ps.setString(4,checkBarCode);
            ps.setInt(5,checkNumber);
            ps.setString(6,creditNumber);
            ps.setDate(7,creditExpDate);
            int retVal = ps.executeUpdate( );
            if (retVal!=1) {
                throw new EJBException("Payment insert failed");
            }
            return true;
        } catch(SQLException sql) {
            throw new EJBException(sql);
        } finally {
            try {
                if (ps != null) ps.close( );
                if (con!= null) con.close( );
            } catch(SQLException se) {
                se.printStackTrace( );
            }
        }
    }
    public void ejbActivate( ) {}
    public void ejbPassivate( ) {}
    public void ejbRemove( ) {}
    public void setSessionContext(SessionContext ctx) {
        context = ctx;
    }
    private Integer getCustomerID(CustomerRemote customer) {
        try {
            return (Integer)customer.getPrimaryKey( );
        } catch(RemoteException re) {
            throw new EJBException(re);
        }
```

```
        }
        private Connection getConnection( ) throws SQLException {
            // Implementations shown below
        }
        private int getMinCheckNumber( ) {
            // Implementations shown below
        }
    }
```

The three payment methods all use the private helper method process( ), which does the work of adding the payment to the database. This strategy reduces the possibility of programmer error and makes the bean easier to maintain. The process( ) method simply inserts the payment information into the PAYMENT table. The JDBC connection is obtained from the getConnection( ) method:

```
private Connection getConnection( ) throws SQLException {
    try {
        InitialContext jndiCntx = new InitialContext( );
        DataSource ds = (DataSource)
            jndiCntx.lookup("java:comp/env/jdbc/titanDB");
        return ds.getConnection( );
    } catch(NamingException ne) {
        throw new EJBException(ne);
    }
}
```

The byCheck( ) and byCredit( ) methods contain some logic to validate the data before processing it. byCredit( ) verifies that the credit card's expiration date does not precede the current date. If it does, a PaymentException is thrown. byCheck( ) verifies that the serial number of the check is above a certain minimum, which is determined by a property that is defined when the bean is deployed. If the check number is below this value, a PaymentException is thrown. The property is obtained from the getMinCheckNumber( ) method, which uses the JNDI ENC to read the value of the minCheckNumber property:

```
private int getMinCheckNumber( ) {
    try {
        InitialContext jndiCntx = new InitialContext( );
        Integer value = (Integer)
            jndiCntx.lookup("java:comp/env/minCheckNumber");
        return value.intValue( );
    } catch(NamingException ne) {
        throw new EJBException(ne);
    }
}
```

It is a good idea to capture thresholds and other limits in the bean's environment properties, rather than hardcoding them: it gives you greater flexibility. If, for example, Titan decided to raise the minimum check number, you would need to change the bean's deployment descriptor only, not the class definition. (You could also obtain this type of information directly from the database.)

Accessing environment properties (JNDI ENC)

In EJB, the bean container contract includes the JNDI environment naming context (JNDI ENC). The JNDI ENC is a JNDI namespace that is specific to each bean type. This namespace can be referenced from within any bean, not just entity beans, using the name `"java:comp/env"`. The enterprise naming context provides a flexible, yet standard mechanism for accessing properties, other beans, and resources from the container.

We've already seen the JNDI ENC several times. In Chapter 9, we used it to access a resource factory, the `DataSource`. The `ProcessPaymentBean` also uses the JNDI ENC to access a `DataSource` in the `getConnection( )` method. Furthermore, it uses the JNDI ENC to access an environment property in the `getMinCheckNumber( )` method. This section examines the use of the JNDI ENC to access environment properties.

Named properties can be declared and their values defined in a bean's deployment descriptor. The bean accesses these properties at runtime by using the JNDI ENC. Properties can be of type `String` or one of several primitive wrapper types, including `Integer`, `Long`, `Double`, `Float`, `Byte`, `Boolean`, and `Short`. By setting the values of the relevant properties, the bean deployer can change the bean's behavior without changing its code. As we've seen in the ProcessPayment EJB, we could change the minimum check number that we're willing to accept by modifying the `minCheckNumber` property at deployment.

Here's how to declare a named property:

```
<ejb-jar ...>
    <enterprise-beans>
        <session>
            <env-entry>
                <env-entry-name>minCheckNumber</env-entry-name>
                <env-entry-type>java.lang.Integer</env-entry-type>
                <env-entry-value>2000</env-entry-value>
            </env-entry>
            ...
        </session>
        ...
    </enterprise-beans>
    ...
</ejb-jar>
```

The ProcessPayment EJB's deployment descriptor

Deploying the ProcessPayment EJB presents no significant problems. It is essentially the same as deploying an entity bean, except that the ProcessPayment EJB has no primary key or persistence fields. Here is the XML deployment descriptor for the ProcessPayment EJB in EJB 2.1:

```
<?xml version="1.0" encoding="UTF-8" ?>
<ejb-jar
     xmlns="http://java.sun.com/xml/ns/j2ee"
```

```
 xmlns:xsi="http://www.w3.org/2001/XMLSchema-instance"
 xsi:schemaLocation="http://java.sun.com/xml/ns/j2ee
                     http://java.sun.com/xml/ns/j2ee/ejb-jar_2_1.xsd"
 version="2.1">
<enterprise-beans>
    <session>
        <description>
            A service that handles monetary payments.
        </description>
        <ejb-name>ProcessPaymentEJB</ejb-name>
        <home>
            com.titan.processpayment.ProcessPaymentHomeRemote
        </home>
        <remote>
            com.titan.processpayment.ProcessPaymentRemote
        </remote>
        <ejb-class>
            com.titan.processpayment.ProcessPaymentBean
        </ejb-class>
        <session-type>Stateless</session-type>
        <transaction-type>Container</transaction-type>
        <env-entry>
            <env-entry-name>minCheckNumber</env-entry-name>
            <env-entry-type>java.lang.Integer</env-entry-type>
            <env-entry-value>2000</env-entry-value>
        </env-entry>
        <resource-ref>
            <description>DataSource for the Titan database</description>
            <res-ref-name>jdbc/titanDB</res-ref-name>
            <res-type>javax.sql.DataSource</res-type>
            <res-auth>Container</res-auth>
        </resource-ref>
    </session>
</enterprise-beans>

<assembly-descriptor>
    <security-role>
        <description>
            This role represents everyone who is allowed full access
            to the ProcessPayment EJB.
        </description>
        <role-name>everyone</role-name>
    </security-role>

    <method-permission>
        <role-name>everyone</role-name>
        <method>
            <ejb-name>ProcessPaymentEJB</ejb-name>
            <method-name>*</method-name>
        </method>
    </method-permission>

    <container-transaction>
        <method>
```

```
                <ejb-name>ProcessPaymentEJB</ejb-name>
                <method-name>*</method-name>
            </method>
            <trans-attribute>Required</trans-attribute>
        </container-transaction>
    </assembly-descriptor>
</ejb-jar>
```

The deployment descriptor for EJB 2.0 is exactly the same, except it's based on a DTD instead of an XML Schema, so it uses a document declaration and has a simpler `<ejb-jar>` element.

```
<?xml version="1.0" encoding="UTF-8" ?>
<!DOCTYPE ejb-jar PUBLIC "-//Sun Microsystems, Inc.//DTD Enterprise
JavaBeans 2.0//EN" "http://java.sun.com/dtd/ejb-jar_2_0.dtd">

<ejb-jar>
    <enterprise-beans>
    ...
```

Exercise 11.1 in the Workbook shows how to deploy these examples.

Local component interfaces

Like entity beans, stateless session beans can define local component interfaces. Local interfaces allow other beans in the same container to use the stateless session bean more efficiently. The process of defining local interfaces for a stateless or stateful session bean is the same as for entity beans. The local interfaces extend `javax.ejb.EJBLocalObject` (for business methods) and `javax.ejb.EJBLocalHome` (for the home interfaces). These interfaces are then defined in the XML deployment descriptor in the `<local>` and `<local-home>` elements.

For the sake of brevity, we will not define local interfaces for either the stateless ProcessPayment EJB or the stateful TravelAgent EJB developed later in this chapter. Your experience creating local interfaces for entity beans in Chapter 5, Chapter 6, and Chapter 7 can be applied easily to any kind of session bean.

The Life Cycle of a Stateless Session Bean

The life cycle of a stateless session bean is very simple. It only has two states: *Does Not Exist* and *Method-Ready Pool*. The Method-Ready Pool is similar to the instance pool used for entity beans. This is an important difference between stateless and stateful session beans; stateless beans define instance pooling in their life cycle and stateful beans do not.* Figure 11-1 illustrates the states and transitions a stateless session bean instance goes through in its lifetime.

* Some vendors may *not* pool stateless instances, but may instead create and destroy instances with each method invocation. This is an implementation-specific decision that shouldn't affect the specified life cycle of the stateless bean instance.

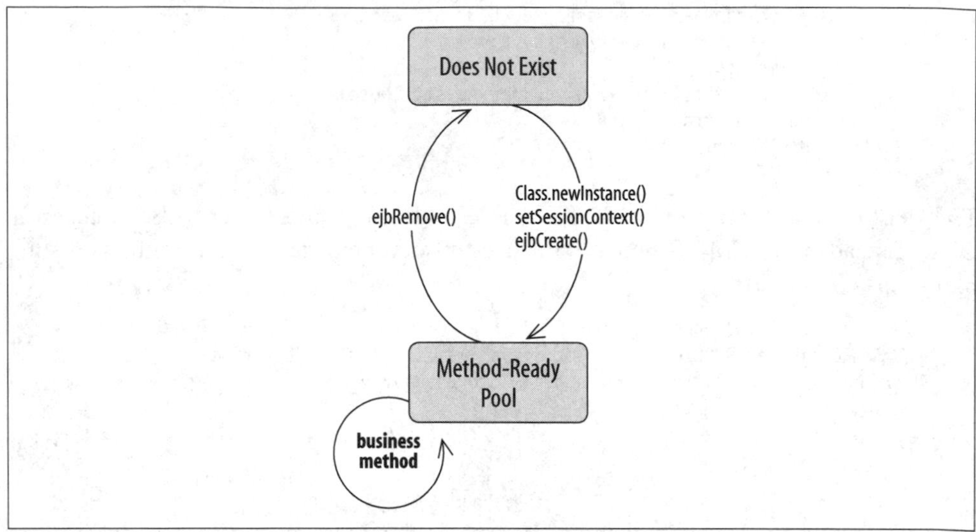

Figure 11-1. Stateless session bean life cycle

Does Not Exist

When a bean is in the Does Not Exist state, it is not an instance in the memory of the system. In other words, it has not been instantiated yet.

The Method-Ready Pool

Stateless bean instances enter the Method-Ready Pool as the container needs them. When the EJB server is first started, it may create a number of stateless bean instances and enter them into the Method-Ready Pool. (The actual behavior of the server depends on the implementation.) When the number of stateless instances servicing client requests is insufficient, more can be created and added to the pool.

Transitioning to the Method-Ready Pool

When an instance transitions from the Does Not Exist state to the Method-Ready Pool, three operations are performed on it. First, the bean instance is instantiated by invoking the `Class.newInstance()` method on the stateless bean class. Second, the bean instance's `setSessionContext(SessionContext context)` method is invoked. This is when the instance receives its reference to the `EJBContext`. The `SessionContext` reference may be stored in a nontransient instance field of the stateless session bean. Finally, the bean's no-argument `ejbCreate()` method is invoked. Remember that a stateless session bean has only one `ejbCreate()` method, which takes no arguments. `ejbCreate()` is invoked only once in the life cycle of the stateless session bean.

Entity, session, and message-driven beans must never define constructors. Take care of initialization within `ejbCreate( )` and other callback methods. The container instantiates instances of the bean class using `Class.newInstance( )`, which requires a no-argument constructor. If no constructors are defined, the no-augment constructor is implicit.

Stateless session beans are not subject to activation, so they can maintain open connections to resources for their entire life cycles.* The `ejbRemove( )` method should close any open resources before the stateless session bean is evicted from memory at the end of its life cycle. You'll read more about `ejbRemove( )` later in this section.

Life in the Method-Ready Pool

Once an instance is in the Method-Ready Pool, it is ready to service client requests. When a client invokes a business method on an EJB object, the method call is delegated to any available instance in the Method-Ready Pool. While the instance is executing the request, it is unavailable for use by other EJB objects. Once the instance has finished, it is immediately available to any EJB object that needs it. This is slightly different from the instance pool for entity beans described in Chapter 10. In the entity instance pool, a bean instance might be swapped in to service an EJB object for several method invocations. Stateless session instances are typically dedicated to an EJB object only for the duration of a single method call.

When an instance is swapped in, its `SessionContext` changes to reflect the context of the EJB object and the client invoking the method. The bean instance may be included in the transactional scope of the client's request and it may access `SessionContext` information specific to the client request: for example, the security and transactional methods. Once the instance has finished servicing the client, it is disassociated from the EJB object and returned to the Method-Ready Pool.

Stateless session beans are not subject to activation and never have their `ejbActivate( )` or `ejbPassivate( )` callback methods invoked. The reason is simple: stateless instances have no conversational state to be preserved. (*Stateful* session beans depend on activation, as we'll see later.)

Clients that need a remote or local reference to a stateless session bean begin by invoking the `create( )` method on the bean's EJB home:

```
Object ref = jndiConnection.lookup("ProcessPaymentHomeRemote");
ProcessPaymentHomeRemote home = (ProcessPaymentHomeRemote)
    PortableRemoteObject.narrow(ref,ProcessPaymentHomeRemote.class);

ProcessPaymentRemote pp = home.create( );
```

* The duration of a stateless bean instance's life is assumed to be very long. However, some EJB servers may actually destroy and create instances with every method invocation, making this strategy less attractive. Consult your vendor's documentation for details on how your EJB server handles stateless instances.

Unlike the entity bean and stateful session bean, invoking the `create()` method does not result in a call to the bean's `ejbCreate()` method. In stateless session beans, calling the EJB home's `create()` method results in the creation of an EJB object for the client, but that is all. `ejbCreate()` is invoked only once in the life cycle of an instance: when it is transitioning from the Does Not Exist state to the Method-Ready Pool. It is not reinvoked every time a client requests a remote reference to the bean. Stateless session beans are limited to a single no-argument `create()` method because there is no way for the container to anticipate which `create()` method the client will invoke.

Transitioning out of the Method-Ready Pool: The death of a stateless bean instance

Bean instances leave the Method-Ready Pool for the Does Not Exist state when the server no longer needs them; that is, when the server decides to reduce the total size of the Method-Ready Pool by evicting one or more instances from memory. The process begins by invoking the `ejbRemove()` method on the instance. At this time, the bean instance should perform any cleanup operations, such as closing open resources. As with `ejbCreate()`, `ejbRemove()` is invoked only once: when the bean is about to transition to the Does Not Exist state. When a client invokes one of a stateless session bean's remove methods, the bean's stub is invalidated, and the container is notified that the bean is no longer needed, but the bean itself is not removed. The container itself invokes `ejbRemove()` on the stateless instance at the end of the instance's life cycle—when it decides it no longer needs to maintain this instance in the pool. Again, this is different from both stateful session beans and entity beans, which suffer more destructive consequences when the client invokes a remove method. During the `ejbRemove()` method, the `SessionContext` and access to the JNDI ENC are still available to the bean instance. Following the execution of the `ejbRemove()` method, the bean is dereferenced and eventually garbage collected.

The Stateful Session Bean

Each stateful session bean is dedicated to one client for the life of the bean instance; it acts on behalf of that client as its agent. Stateful session beans are not swapped among EJB objects or kept in an instance pool like entity and stateless session bean instances. Once a stateful session bean is instantiated and assigned to an EJB object, it is dedicated to that EJB object for its entire life cycle.*

Stateful session beans maintain conversational state, which means that the instance variables of the bean class can maintain data specific to the client between method invocations. This makes it possible for methods to be interdependent, so that

* This is a conceptual model. Some EJB containers may actually use instance swapping with stateful session beans but make it appear as if the same instance is servicing all requests. Conceptually, however, the same stateful session bean instance services all requests.

changes made to the bean's state in one method call can affect the results of subsequent method invocations. Therefore, every method call from a client must be serviced by the same instance (at least conceptually), so the bean instance's state can be predicted from one method invocation to the next. In contrast, stateless session beans don't maintain client-specific data from one method call to the next, so any instance can be used to service any method call from any client.

Although stateful session beans maintain conversational state, they are not themselves persistent like entity beans. Entity beans represent data in the database; their persistence fields are written directly to the database. Stateful session beans can access the database but do not represent data in the database. In addition, stateful beans are not used concurrently like entity beans. If you have an entity EJB object that wraps an instance of the ship called *Paradise*, for example, all client requests for that ship will be coordinated through the same EJB object.* With stateful session beans, the EJB object is dedicated to one client—stateful session beans are not used concurrently.

Stateful session beans are often considered extensions of the client. This makes sense if you think of a client as being made up of operations and state. Each task may rely on some information gathered or changed by a previous operation. A GUI client is a perfect example: when you fill in the fields on a GUI client you are creating conversational state. Pressing a button executes an operation that might fill in more fields, based on the information you entered previously. The information in the fields is conversational state.

Stateful session beans allow you to encapsulate some of the business logic and conversational state of a client and move it to the server. Moving this logic to the server thins the client application and makes the system as a whole easier to manage. The stateful session bean acts as an agent for the client, managing processes or *taskflow* to accomplish a set of tasks; it manages the interactions of other beans in addition to direct data access over several operations to accomplish a complex set of tasks. By encapsulating and managing taskflow on behalf of the client, stateful beans present a simplified interface that hides the details of many interdependent operations on the database and other beans from the client.

Getting Set Up for the TravelAgent EJB

The TravelAgent EJB will make use of the Cabin, Cruise, Reservation, and Customer beans developed in Chapter 6 and Chapter 7. It will coordinate the interaction of these entity beans to book a passenger on a cruise. We'll modify the

* This is also a conceptual model. Some EJB containers may use separate EJB objects for concurrent access to the same entity, relying on the database to control concurrency. Conceptually, however, the end result is the same.

Reservation EJB that was used in Chapter 7 so that it can be created with all its relationships identified right away. To do so, we overload its ejbCreate( ) method:

```
public abstract class ReservationBean implements javax.ejb.EntityBean {

    public Integer ejbCreate(CustomerRemote customer, CruiseLocal cruise,
        CabinLocal cabin, double price, Date dateBooked) {

        setAmountPaid(price);
        setDate(dateBooked);
        return null;
    }
    public void ejbPostCreate(CustomerRemote customer, CruiseLocal cruise,
        CabinLocal cabin, double price, Date dateBooked)
        throws javax.ejb.CreateException {

        setCruise(cruise);

        // add Cabin to collection-based CMR field
        Set cabins = new HashSet( );
        cabins.add(cabin);
        this.setCabins(cabins);

        try {
            Integer primKey = (Integer)customer.getPrimaryKey( );
            javax.naming.Context jndiContext = new InitialContext( );
            CustomerHomeLocal home = (CustomerHomeLocal)
                jndiContext.lookup("java:comp/env/ejb/CustomerHomeLocal");
            CustomerLocal custL = home.findByPrimaryKey(primKey);

            // add Customer to collection-based CMR field
            Set customers = new HashSet( );
            customers.add(custL);
            this.setCustomers(customers);

        } catch (RemoteException re) {
            throw new CreateException("Invalid Customer");
        } catch (FinderException fe) {
            throw new CreateException("Invalid Customer");
        } catch (NamingException ne) {
            throw new CreateException("Invalid Customer");
        }
    }
```

Relationship fields use local EJB object references, so we must convert the CustomerRemote reference to a CustomerLocal reference in order to set the Reservation EJB's customer relationship field. To do this, you can either use the JNDI ENC to locate the local home interface and then execute the findByPrimaryKey( ) method, or implement an ejbSelect( ) method in the Reservation EJB to locate the CustomerLocal reference.

The TravelAgent EJB

The TravelAgent EJB, which we have already seen, is a stateful session bean that encapsulates the process of making a reservation on a cruise. We will develop this bean further to demonstrate how stateful session beans can be used as taskflow objects. We won't develop a local interface for the TravelAgent EJB, partly because it is designed to be used by remote clients (and therefore doesn't require local component interfaces), and partly because the rules for developing local interfaces for stateful session beans are the same as those for stateless session and entity beans.

The remote interface (TravelAgent)

In Chapter 4, we developed an early version of the `TravelAgentRemote` interface that contained a single business method, `listCabins()`. We are now going to remove the `listCabins()` method and redefine the TravelAgent EJB so that it behaves like a taskflow object. Later in this chapter, we will add a modified listing method for obtaining a more specific list of cabins for the user.

As a stateful session bean that models taskflow, the TravelAgent EJB manages the interactions between several other beans while maintaining conversational state. Here's the modified `TravelAgentRemote` interface:

```
package com.titan.travelagent;

import java.rmi.RemoteException;
import javax.ejb.FinderException;
import com.titan.processpayment.CreditCardDO;

public interface TravelAgentRemote extends javax.ejb.EJBObject {

    public void setCruiseID(Integer cruise)
        throws RemoteException, FinderException;

    public void setCabinID(Integer cabin)
        throws RemoteException, FinderException;

    public TicketDO bookPassage(CreditCardDO card, double price)
        throws RemoteException,IncompleteConversationalState;
}
```

The purpose of the TravelAgent EJB is to make cruise reservations. To accomplish this task, the bean needs to know which cruise, cabin, and customer make up the reservation. Therefore, the client using the TravelAgent EJB needs to gather this kind of information before making the booking. The `TravelAgentRemote` interface provides methods for setting the IDs of the cruise and cabin that the customer wants to book. We can assume that the cabin ID comes from a list and that the cruise ID comes from some other source. The customer is set in the `create()` method of the home interface—more about this later.

Once the customer, cruise, and cabin are chosen, the TravelAgent EJB is ready to process the reservation. This operation is performed by the `bookPassage( )` method, which needs the customer's credit card information and the price of the cruise. `bookPassage( )` is responsible for charging the customer's account, reserving the chosen cabin in the right ship on the right cruise, and generating a ticket for the customer. How this is accomplished is not important to us at this point; when we are developing the remote interface, we are concerned only with the business definition of the bean. We will discuss the implementation when we talk about the bean class.

Note that the `bookPassage( )` method throws an application-specific exception, `IncompleteConversationalState`. This exception is used to communicate business problems encountered while booking a customer on a cruise. The `IncompleteConversationalState` exception indicates that the TravelAgent EJB did not have enough information to process the booking. Here's the `IncompleteConversationalState` class:

```
package com.titan.travelagent;

public class IncompleteConversationalState extends java.lang.Exception {
    public IncompleteConversationalState(){super( );}
    public IncompleteConversationalState(String msg){super(msg);}
}
```

Dependent object (TicketDO)

Like the `CreditCardDO` and `CheckDO` classes used in the ProcessPayment EJB, the `TicketDO` class is defined as a pass-by-value object. One could argue that a ticket should be an entity bean since it is not dependent and may be accessed outside the context of the TravelAgent EJB. However, determining how a business object is used can also dictate whether it should be a bean or simply a class. The `TicketDO` object, for example, could be digitally signed and emailed to the client as proof of purchase. This would not be feasible if the `TicketDO` object were an entity bean, because enterprise beans are referenced only through their component interfaces and are never passed by value.

The constructor for TicketDO uses the local interfaces of creating a new `TicketDO` object:

```
package com.titan.travelagent;

import com.titan.cruise.CruiseLocal;
import com.titan.cabin.CabinLocal;
import com.titan.customer.CustomerRemote;

public class TicketDO implements java.io.Serializable {
    public Integer customerID;
    public Integer cruiseID;
    public Integer cabinID;
    public double price;
    public String description;
```

```
    public TicketDO(CustomerRemote customer, CruiseLocal cruise,
        CabinLocal cabin, double price) throws javax.ejb.FinderException,
        RemoteException, javax.naming.NamingException {

            description = customer.getFirstName( )+
                " " + customer.getLastName( ) +
                " has been booked for the "
                + cruise.getName( ) +
                " cruise on ship " +
                  cruise.getShip().getName( ) + ".\n" +
                " Your accommodations include " +
                  cabin.getName( ) +
                " a " + cabin.getBedCount( ) +
                " bed cabin on deck level " + cabin.getDeckLevel( ) +
                ".\n Total charge = " + price;
            customerID = (Integer)customer.getPrimaryKey( );
            cruiseID = (Integer)cruise.getPrimaryKey( );
            cabinID = (Integer)cabin.getPrimaryKey( );
            this.price = price;
        }

    public String toString( ) {
        return description;
    }
}
```

The home interface (TravelAgentHomeRemote)

Starting with the TravelAgentHomeRemote interface we developed in Chapter 4, we can modify the create( ) method to take a remote reference to the customer who is making the reservation:

```
package com.titan.travelagent;

import java.rmi.RemoteException;
import javax.ejb.CreateException;
import com.titan.customer.CustomerRemote;

public interface TravelAgentHomeRemote extends javax.ejb.EJBHome {
    public TravelAgentRemote create(CustomerRemote cust)
        throws RemoteException, CreateException;
}
```

The create( ) method in this home interface requires that a remote reference to a Customer EJB be used to create the TravelAgent EJB. Because there are no other create( ) methods, you cannot create a TravelAgent EJB if you do not know who the customer is. The Customer EJB reference provides the TravelAgent EJB with some of the conversational state it will need to process the bookPassage( ) method.

Taking a peek at the client view

Before settling on definitions for your component interfaces, it is a good idea to figure out how clients will use the bean. Imagine that the TravelAgent EJB is used by a Java application with GUI fields. These fields capture the customer's preference for the type of cruise and cabin. We start by examining the code used at the beginning of the reservation process:

```
Context jndiContext = getInitialContext( );
Object ref = jndiContext.lookup("CustomerHomeRemote");
CustomerHomeRemote customerHome =(CustomerHomeRemote)
    PortableRemoteObject.narrow(ref, CustomerHomeRemote.class);

String ln = tfLastName.getText( );
String fn = tfFirstName.getText( );
String mn = tfMiddleName.getText( );
CustomerRemote customer = customerHome.create(nextID, ln, fn, mn);

ref = jndiContext.lookup("TravelAgentHomeRemote");
TravelAgentHomeRemote home = (TravelAgentHomeRemote)
    PortableRemoteObject.narrow(ref, TravelAgentHomeRemote.class);

TravelAgentRemote agent = home.create(customer);
```

This code creates a new Customer EJB based on information the travel agent gathered over the phone. The CustomerRemote reference is then used to create a TravelAgent EJB. Next, we gather the cruise and cabin choices from another part of the applet:

```
Integer cruise_id = new Integer(textField_cruiseNumber.getText( ));

Integer cabin_id = new Integer( textField_cabinNumber.getText( ));

agent.setCruiseID(cruise_id);
agent.setCabinID(cabin_id);
```

The travel agent chooses the cruise and cabin the customer wishes to reserve. These IDs are set in the TravelAgent EJB, which maintains the conversational state for the whole process.

At the end of the process, the travel agent completes the reservation by processing the booking and generating a ticket. Because the TravelAgent EJB has maintained the conversational state, caching the customer, cabin, and cruise information, only the credit card and price are needed to complete the transaction:

```
String cardNumber = textField_cardNumber.getText( );
Date date = dateFormatter.parse(textField_cardExpiration.getText( ));
String cardBrand = textField_cardBrand.getText( );
CreditCardDO card = new CreditCardDO(cardNumber,date,cardBrand);
double price = double.valueOf(textField_cruisePrice.getText()).doubleValue( );
TicketDO ticket = agent.bookPassage(card,price);
PrintingService.print(ticket);
```

This summary of how the client will use the TravelAgent EJB confirms that our remote interface and home interface definitions are workable. We can now move ahead with development.

TravelAgentBean: The bean class

We can now implement all of the behavior expressed in the new remote interface and home interface for the TravelAgent EJB.* Here is a partial definition of the new `TravelAgentBean` class:

```
import com.titan.reservation.*;

import java.sql.*;
import javax.sql.DataSource;
import java.util.Vector;
import java.rmi.RemoteException;
import javax.naming.NamingException;
import javax.ejb.EJBException;
import com.titan.processpayment.*;
import com.titan.cruise.*;
import com.titan.customer.*;
import com.titan.cabin.*;

public class TravelAgentBean implements javax.ejb.SessionBean {

    public CustomerRemote customer;
    public CruiseLocal cruise;
    public CabinLocal cabin;

    public javax.ejb.SessionContext ejbContext;

    public javax.naming.Context jndiContext;

    public void ejbCreate(CustomerRemote cust) {
        customer = cust;
    }
    public void setCabinID(Integer cabinID) throws javax.ejb.FinderException {
        try {
            CabinHomeLocal home = (CabinHomeLocal)
                jndiContext.lookup("java:comp/env/ejb/CabinHomeLocal");

            cabin = home.findByPrimaryKey(cabinID);
        } catch(RemoteException re) {
            throw new EJBException(re);
        }
    }
    public void setCruiseID(Integer cruiseID) throws javax.ejb.FinderException {
        try {
```

* If you are modifying the bean developed in Chapter 4, remember to delete the `listCabin( )` method. We will add a new implementation of that method later in this chapter.

```
            CruiseHomeLocal home = (CruiseHomeLocal)
                jndiContext.lookup("java:comp/env/ejb/CruiseHomeLocal");

            cruise = home.findByPrimaryKey(cruiseID);
        } catch(RemoteException re) {
            throw new EJBException(re);
        }

    }
    public TicketDO bookPassage(CreditCardDO card, double price)
        throws IncompleteConversationalState {

        if (customer == null || cruise == null || cabin == null)
        {
            throw new IncompleteConversationalState( );
        }
        try {
            ReservationHomeLocal resHome = (ReservationHomeLocal)
                jndiContext.lookup("java:comp/env/ejb/ReservationHomeLocal");

            ReservationLocal reservation =
                resHome.create(customer, cruise, cabin, price, new Date( ));

            Object ref = jndiContext.lookup("java:comp/env/ejb/
                ProcessPaymentHomeRemote");

            ProcessPaymentHomeRemote ppHome = (ProcessPaymentHomeRemote)
                PortableRemoteObject.narrow (ref, ProcessPaymentHomeRemote.class);

            ProcessPaymentRemote process = ppHome.create( );
            process.byCredit(customer, card, price);

            TicketDO ticket = new TicketDO(customer, cruise, cabin, price);
            return ticket;
        } catch(Exception e) {
            throw new EJBException(e);
        }
    }
    public void ejbRemove( ) {}
    public void ejbActivate( ) {}
    public void ejbPassivate( ) {}

    public void setSessionContext(javax.ejb.SessionContext cntx)
    {

        ejbContext = cntx;
        try {
            jndiContext = new javax.naming.InitialContext( );
        } catch(NamingException ne) {
            throw new EJBException(ne);
        }
    }
}
```

This is a lot of code to digest, so we will approach it in small pieces. First, let's examine the ejbCreate( ) method:

```
public class TravelAgentBean implements javax.ejb.SessionBean {

    public CustomerRemote customer;
        ...

    public javax.ejb.SessionContext ejbContext;
    public javax.naming.Context jndiContext;

    public void ejbCreate(CustomerRemote cust) {
        customer = cust;
    }
```

When the bean is created, the remote reference to the Customer EJB is passed to the bean instance and maintained in the customer field. The customer field is part of the bean's conversational state. We could have obtained the customer's identity as an integer ID and constructed the remote reference to the Customer EJB in the ejbCreate( ) method. However, we passed the reference directly to demonstrate that remote references to beans can be passed from a client application to a bean. They can also be returned from the bean to the client and passed between beans on the same EJB server or between EJB servers.

References to the SessionContext and JNDI context are held in fields called ejbContext and jndiContext. The "ejb" and "jndi" prefixes help to avoid confusion between the different content types.

When a bean is passivated, the JNDI ENC must be maintained as part of the bean's conversational state. This means that the JNDI context should not be transient. Once a field is set to reference the JNDI ENC, the reference remains valid for the life of the bean. In the TravelAgentBean, we set the jndiContext field when the SessionContext is set, at the beginning of the bean's life cycle:

```
public void setSessionContext(javax.ejb.SessionContext cntx) {
    ejbContext = cntx;
    try {
        jndiContext = new InitialContext( );
    } catch(NamingException ne) {
        throw new EJBException(ne);
    }
}
```

The EJB container makes special accommodations for references to the SessionContext, the JNDI ENC, references to other beans (remote and home interface types), and the JTA UserTransaction type (discussed in Chapter 15). The container must maintain any instance fields that reference objects of these types as part of the conversational state, even if they are not serializable. All other fields must be serializable or null when the bean is passivated.

The TravelAgent EJB has methods for setting the desired cruise and cabin. These methods take Integer IDs as arguments and retrieve references to the appropriate Cruise or Cabin EJB from the appropriate home interface. These references are also part of the TravelAgent EJB's conversational state. Here's how setCabinID( ) and getCabinID( ) are defined:

```
public void setCabinID(Integer cabinID)
    throws javax.ejb.FinderException {
    try {
        CabinHomeLocal home = (CabinHomeLocal)
            jndiContext.lookup("java:comp/env/ejb/CabinHomeLocal");

        cabin = home.findByPrimaryKey(cabinID);
    } catch(RemoteException re) {
        throw new EJBException(re);
    }
}
public void setCruiseID(Integer cruiseID)
    throws javax.ejb.FinderException {
    try {
        CruiseHomeLocal home = (CruiseHomeLocal)
            jndiContext.lookup("java:comp/env/ejb/CruiseHomeLocal");

        cruise = home.findByPrimaryKey(cruiseID);
    } catch(RemoteException re) {
        throw new EJBException(re);
    }
}
```

It may seem strange that we set these values using Integer IDs, but we keep them in the conversational state as entity bean references. Using Integer IDs is simpler for the client, which does not work with their entity bean references. In the client code, we get the cabin and cruise IDs from text fields. Why make the client obtain a bean reference to the Cruise and Cabin EJBs when an ID is simpler? In addition, using the IDs is cheaper (i.e., requires less network traffic) than passing a remote reference. We need the EJB object references to these bean types in the bookPassage( ) method, so we use their IDs to obtain actual entity bean references. We could have waited until the bookPassage( ) method was invoked before reconstructing the remote references, but this strategy keeps the bookPassage( ) method simple.

JNDI ENC and EJB references

You can use the JNDI ENC to obtain a reference to the home interfaces of other beans. Using the ENC lets you avoid hardcoding vendor-specific JNDI properties into the bean. In other words, the JNDI ENC allows EJB references to be network and vendor independent.

In the TravelAgentBean, we used the JNDI ENC to acquire both the remote home interface of the ProcessPayment EJB and the local home interfaces of the Cruise and Cabin EJBs. The EJB specification recommends that all EJB references be bound to the "java:comp/env/ejb" context, which is the convention followed here. In the TravelAgent EJB, we append the name of the home object to "java:comp/env/ejb", giving a result like "java:comp/env/ejb/CruiseHomeLocal".

Remote EJB references in the JNDI ENC

The deployment descriptor provides a special set of tags for declaring remote EJB references. Here's how the <ejb-ref> tag and its subelements are used:

```
<ejb-ref>
    <ejb-ref-name>ejb/ProcessPaymentHomeRemote</ejb-ref-name>
    <ejb-ref-type>Session</ejb-ref-type>
    <home>
        com.titan.processpayment.ProcessPaymentHomeRemote
    </home>
    <remote>
       com.titan.processpayment.ProcessPaymentRemote
    </remote>
</ejb-ref>
```

These elements define a name for the bean within the ENC, declare the bean's type, and give the names of its remote and home interfaces. When a bean is deployed, the deployer maps the <ejb-ref> elements to actual beans in a way specific to the vendor. The <ejb-ref> elements can also be linked by the application assembler to beans in the same deployment (a subject covered in detail in Chapter 17). However, you should try to use local component interfaces for beans located in the same deployment and container.

Local EJB references in the JNDI ENC

The deployment descriptor also provides a special set of tags, the <ejb-local-ref> elements, to declare local EJB references: enterprise beans that are co-located in the same container and deployed in the same EJB JAR file. The <ejb-local-ref> elements are declared immediately after the <ejb-ref> elements:

```
<ejb-local-ref>
    <ejb-ref-name>ejb/CruiseHomeLocal</ejb-ref-name>
    <ejb-ref-type>Entity</ejb-ref-type>
    <local-home>
        com.titan.cruise.CruiseHomeLocal
    </local-home>
    <local>
        com.titan.cruise.CruiseLocal
    </local>
    <ejb-link>CruiseEJB</ejb-link>
</ejb-local-ref>
<ejb-local-ref>
    <ejb-ref-name>ejb/CabinHomeLocal</ejb-ref-name>
    <ejb-ref-type>Entity</ejb-ref-type>
    <local-home>
        com.titan.cabin.CabinHomeLocal
    </local-home>
```

```
    <local>
        com.titan.cabin.CabinLocal
    </local>
    <ejb-link>CabinEJB</ejb-link>
</ejb-local-ref>
```

The `<ejb-local-ref>` element defines a name for the bean within the ENC, declares the bean's type, and gives the names of its local component interfaces. These elements should be linked explicitly to other co-located beans using the `<ejb-link>` element, although linking them is not strictly required at this stage—the application assembler or deployer can do it later. The value of the `<ejb-link>` element within the `<ejb-local-ref>` must be the same as the `<ejb-name>` of the appropriate bean in the same JAR file.

At deployment time the EJB container's tools map the local references declared in the `<ejb-local-ref>` elements to entity beans that are co-located in the same container system.

The bookPassage( ) method

The last point of interest in our bean definition is the `bookPassage( )` method. This method makes use of the conversational state accumulated by the `ejbCreate( )`, `setCabinID( )`, and `setCruiseID( )` methods to process a reservation for a customer. Here's how the `bookPassage( )` method is defined:

```
public TicketDO bookPassage(CreditCardDO card, double price)
    throws IncompleteConversationalState {

    if (customer == null || cruise == null || cabin == null) {
        throw new IncompleteConversationalState( );
    }
    try {
        ReservationHomeLocal resHome = (ReservationHomeLocal)
            jndiContext.lookup("java:comp/env/ejb/ReservationHomeLocal");

        ReservationLocal reservation =
            resHome.create(customer, cruise, cabin, price, new Date( ));

        Object ref = jndiContext.lookup("java:comp/env/ejb/
            ProcessPaymentHomeRemote");

        ProcessPaymentHomeRemote ppHome = (ProcessPaymentHomeRemote)
            PortableRemoteObject.narrow(ref, ProcessPaymentHomeRemote.class);

        ProcessPaymentRemote process = ppHome.create( );
        process.byCredit(customer, card, price);

        TicketDO ticket = new TicketDO(customer,cruise,cabin,price);
        return ticket;
    } catch(Exception e) {
        throw new EJBException(e);
    }
}
```

This method deomonstrates the concept of taskflow. It uses several beans, including the Reservation, ProcessPayment, Customer, Cabin, and Cruise EJBs, to accomplish one task: booking a customer on a cruise. Deceptively simple, this method encapsulates several interactions that ordinarily might have been performed on the client. For the price of one `bookPassage()` call from the client, the TravelAgent EJB performs many operations:

1. Looks up and obtains a reference to the Reservation EJB's home.
2. Creates a new Reservation EJB.
3. Looks up and obtains a remote reference to the ProcessPayment EJB's home.
4. Creates a new ProcessPayment EJB.
5. Charges the customer's credit card using the ProcessPayment EJB.
6. Generates a new `TicketDO` with all the pertinent information describing the customer's purchase.

From a design standpoint, encapsulating the taskflow in a stateful session bean means a less complex interface for the client and more flexibility for implementing changes. We could easily change `bookPassage()` to check for overlapped booking (when a customer books passage on two cruises with overlapping dates). This type of enhancement does not change the remote interface, so the client application does not need modification. Encapsulating taskflow in stateful session beans allows the system to evolve without impacting clients.

In addition, the type of clients used can change. One of the biggest problems with two-tier architectures—besides scalability and transactional control—is that the business logic is intertwined with the client logic. As a result, it is difficult to reuse the business logic in a different kind of client. With stateful session beans this is not a problem, because stateful session beans are an extension of the client but are not bound to the client's presentation. Let's say that our first implementation of the reservation system used a Java applet with GUI widgets. The TravelAgent EJB would manage conversational state and perform all the business logic while the applet focused on the GUI presentation. If, at a later date, we decide to go to a thin client (HTML generated by a Java servlet, for example), we would simply reuse the TravelAgent EJB in the servlet. Because all the business logic is in the stateful session bean, the presentation (Java applet or servlet or something else) can change easily.

The TravelAgent EJB also provides transactional integrity for processing the customer's reservation. If any of the operations within the body of the `bookPassage()` method fails, all the operations are rolled back so that none of the changes are accepted. If the credit card cannot be charged by the ProcessPayment EJB, the newly created Reservation EJB and its associated record are not created. The transactional aspects of the TravelAgent EJB are explained in detail in Chapter 15.

The remote and local EJB references can be used within the same taskflow. For example, the `bookPassage()` method uses local references when accessing the Cruise and Cabin beans, but remote references when accessing the ProcessPayment and Customer EJBs. This usage is totally appropriate. The EJB container ensures that the transaction is atomic, i.e., that failures in either the remote or local EJB reference will affect the entire transaction.

Why use a Reservation entity bean?

If we have a Reservation EJB, why do we need a TravelAgent EJB? The TravelAgent EJB uses the Reservation EJB to create a reservation, but it also has to charge the customer and generate a ticket. These activities are not specific to the Reservation EJB, so they need to be captured in a stateful session bean that can manage taskflow and transactional scope. In addition, the TravelAgent EJB provides listing behavior, which spans concepts in Titan's system. It would have been inappropriate to include any of these other behaviors in the Reservation entity bean.

Listing behavior (listAvailableCabins( ))

As promised, we are going to bring back the cabin-listing behavior we played around with in Chapter 4. This time we are not going to use the Cabin EJB to get the list; instead, we will access the database directly. Accessing the database directly is a double-edged sword. On one hand, we don't want to access the database directly if entity beans exist that can access the same information. Entity beans provide a safe and consistent interface for a particular set of data. Once an entity bean has been tested and proven, it can be reused throughout the system, substantially reducing data-integrity problems. The Reservation EJB is an example of that kind of usage. Entity beans can also pull together disjointed data and apply additional business logic such as validation, limits, and security to ensure that data access follows the business rules.

But entity beans cannot define every possible data access needed, and they shouldn't. One of the biggest problems with entity beans is that they tend to become bloated over time. Huge entity beans containing dozens of methods are a sure sign of poor design. Entity beans should be focused on providing data access to a very limited, but conceptually bound, set of data. You should be able to update, read, and insert records or data. Data access that spans concepts, like listing behavior, should not be encapsulated in an entity bean.

Systems always need listing behavior to present clients with choices. In the reservation system, for example, customers need to choose a cabin from a list of available cabins. The word *available* is key to the definition of this behavior. The Cabin EJB can provide us with a list of cabins, but it does not know whether any given cabin is available. As you may recall, the Cabin-Reservation relationship we defined in Chapter 7 was *unidirectional*: the Reservation was aware of its Cabin relationships, but the reverse was not true. The question of whether a cabin is available is relevant to the process using it—in this case, the TravelAgent EJB—but may not be relevant to the cabin itself. As an analogy, an automobile entity would not care what road it is on; it is concerned only with characteristics that describe its state and behavior. An automobile-tracking system, on the other hand, would be concerned with the locations of individual automobiles.

To get availability information, we need to compare the list of cabins on our ship to the list of cabins that have already been reserved. The `listAvailableCabins()` method does exactly that. It uses an SQL query to produce a list of cabins that have not yet been reserved for the cruise chosen by the client:

```
public String [] listAvailableCabins(int bedCount)
    throws IncompleteConversationalState {
    if (cruise == null)
        throw new IncompleteConversationalState( );

    Connection con = null;
    PreparedStatement ps = null;;
    ResultSet result = null;
    try {
        Integer cruiseID = (Integer)cruise.getPrimaryKey( );
        Integer shipID = (Integer)cruise.getShip().getPrimaryKey( );
        con = getConnection( );
        ps = con.prepareStatement(
            "select ID, NAME, DECK_LEVEL  from CABIN "+
            "where SHIP_ID = ? and BED_COUNT = ? and ID NOT IN "+
            "(SELECT CABIN_ID FROM RESERVATION "+" WHERE CRUISE_ID = ?)");

        ps.setInt(1,shipID.intValue( ));
        ps.setInt(2, bedCount);
        ps.setInt(3,cruiseID.intValue( ));
        result = ps.executeQuery( );
        Vector vect = new Vector( );
        while(result.next( )) {
            StringBuffer buf = new StringBuffer( );
            buf.append(result.getString(1));
            buf.append(',');
            buf.append(result.getString(2));
            buf.append(',');
            buf.append(result.getString(3));
            vect.addElement(buf.toString( ));
        }
        String [] returnArray = new String[vect.size( )];
        vect.copyInto(returnArray);
        return returnArray;
    } catch (Exception e) {
        throw new EJBException(e);
    }
    finally {
        try {
            if (result != null) result.close( );
            if (ps != null) ps.close( );
            if (con!= null) con.close( );
        } catch(SQLException se){se.printStackTrace( );}
    }
}
```

As you can see, the SQL query is complex. It could have been defined using a method like `Cabin.findAvailableCabins(Cruise cruise)` in the Cabin EJB. However, this method would be difficult to implement because the Cabin EJB would need to access the Reservation EJB's data. It's also easy to imagine cluttering an entity bean with lots of fairly specific find methods that are tied to particular situations. Such clutter isn't necessary or desirable. To avoid adding find methods for every possible query, you can instead use direct database access as shown in the `listAvailableCabins( )` method. Direct database access generally has less impact on performance because the container does not have to manifest EJB object references, but it is also less reusable. When you are deciding whether to add a find method to an entity bean or to make a direct query in a session bean, keep in mind the tradeoff between reusability, performance, and clarity.

The `listAvailableCabins( )` method returns an array of `String` objects. We could have opted to return a collection of remote Cabin references, but we didn't because we want to keep the client application as lightweight as possible. A list of `String` objects is much more lightweight than a collection of remote references; this way, the client doesn't have to work with a group of stubs, each with its own connection to EJB objects on the server. By returning a lightweight `String` array, we reduce the number of stubs on the client, which keeps the client simple and conserves resources on the server.

To make this method work, you need to create a private `getConnection( )` method for obtaining a database connection. This method becomes part of the `TravelAgentBean`:

```
private Connection getConnection( ) throws SQLException {
    try {
        DataSource ds = (DataSource)jndiContext.lookup(
            "java:comp/env/jdbc/titanDB");
        return ds.getConnection( );
    } catch(NamingException ne) {
        throw new EJBException(ne);
    }
}
```

Change the remote interface for TravelAgent EJB to include the `listAvailableCabins( )` method:

```
package com.titan.travelagent;

import java.rmi.RemoteException;
import javax.ejb.FinderException;
import com.titan.processpayment.CreditCard;

public interface TravelAgentRemote extends javax.ejb.EJBObject {

    public void setCruiseID(Integer cruise) throws RemoteException, FinderException;

    public void setCabinID(Integer cabin) throws RemoteException, FinderException;
```

```
    public TicketDO bookPassage(CreditCardDO card, double price)
        throws RemoteException,IncompleteConversationalState;

    public String [] listAvailableCabins(int bedCount)
        throws RemoteException, IncompleteConversationalState;
}
```

The TravelAgent deployment descriptor

Here's an abbreviated version of the XML deployment descriptor used for the TravelAgent EJB. It defines not only the TravelAgent EJB, but also the Customer, Cruise, Cabin, and Reservation EJBs. The ProcessPayment EJB is not defined in this deployment descriptor because it is assumed to be deployed in a separate JAR file, or possibly even a separate EJB server on a different network node:

```
<?xml version="1.0" encoding="UTF-8" ?>
<ejb-jar
     xmlns="http://java.sun.com/xml/ns/j2ee"
     xmlns:xsi="http://www.w3.org/2001/XMLSchema-instance"
     xsi:schemaLocation="http://java.sun.com/xml/ns/j2ee
                         http://java.sun.com/xml/ns/j2ee/ejb-jar_2_1.xsd"
     version="2.1">
    <enterprise-beans>
        <session>
            <ejb-name>TravelAgentEJB</ejb-name>
            <home>com.titan.travelagent.TravelAgentHomeRemote</home>
            <remote>com.titan.travelagent.TravelAgentRemote</remote>
            <ejb-class>com.titan.travelagent.TravelAgentBean</ejb-class>
            <session-type>Stateful</session-type>
            <transaction-type>Container</transaction-type>

            <ejb-ref>
                <ejb-ref-name>ejb/ProcessPaymentHomeRemote</ejb-ref-name>
                <ejb-ref-type>Session</ejb-ref-type>
                <home>com.titan.processpayment.ProcessPaymentHomeRemote</home>
                <remote>com.titan.processpayment.ProcessPaymentRemote</remote>
            </ejb-ref>
            <ejb-local-ref>
                <ejb-ref-name>ejb/CabinHomeLocal</ejb-ref-name>
                <ejb-ref-type>Entity</ejb-ref-type>
                <local-home>com.titan.cabin.CabinHomeLocal</local-home>
                <local>com.titan.cabin.CabinLocal</local>
            </ejb-local-ref>
            <ejb-local-ref>
                <ejb-ref-name>ejb/CruiseHomeLocal</ejb-ref-name>
                <ejb-ref-type>Entity</ejb-ref-type>
                <local-home>com.titan.cruise.CruiseHomeLocal</local-home>
                <local>com.titan.cruise.CruiseLocal</local>
            </ejb-local-ref>
            <ejb-local-ref>
                <ejb-ref-name>ejb/ReservationHomeLocal</ejb-ref-name>
                <ejb-ref-type>Entity</ejb-ref-type>
                <local-home>com.titan.reservation.ReservationHomeLocal</local-home>
```

```
            <local>com.titan.reservation.ReservationLocal</local>
        </ejb-local-ref>

        <resource-ref>
            <description>DataSource for the Titan database</description>
            <res-ref-name>jdbc/titanDB</res-ref-name>
            <res-type>javax.sql.DataSource</res-type>
            <res-auth>Container</res-auth>
        </resource-ref>
    </session>
    <entity>
        <ejb-name>CabinEJB</ejb-name>
        <local-home>com.titan.cabin.CabinHomeLocal</local-home>
        <local>com.titan.cabin.CabinLocal</local>
        ...
    </entity>
    <entity>
        <ejb-name>CruiseEJB</ejb-name>
        <local-home>com.titan.cruise.CruiseHomeLocal</local-home>
        <local>com.titan.cruise.CruiseLocal</local>
        ...
    </entity>
    <entity>
        <ejb-name>ReservationEJB</ejb-name>
        <local-home>com.titan.reservation.ReservationHomeLocal</local-home>
        <local>com.titan.reservation.ReservationLocal</local>
        ...
    </entity>
 </enterprise-beans>

 <assembly-descriptor>
    <security-role>
        <description>This role represents everyone</description>
        <role-name>everyone</role-name>
    </security-role>

    <method-permission>
        <role-name>everyone</role-name>
        <method>
            <ejb-name>TravelAgentEJB</ejb-name>
            <method-name>*</method-name>
        </method>
    </method-permission>

    <container-transaction>
        <method>
            <ejb-name>TravelAgentEJB</ejb-name>
            <method-name>*</method-name>
        </method>
        <trans-attribute>Required</trans-attribute>
    </container-transaction>
 </assembly-descriptor>
</ejb-jar>
```

The deployment descriptor for EJB 2.0 is exactly the same, except it's based on a DTD instead of an XML Schema, so it uses a document declaration and has a simpler `<ejb-jar>` element.

```
<?xml version="1.0" encoding="UTF-8" ?>
<!DOCTYPE ejb-jar PUBLIC "-//Sun Microsystems, Inc.//DTD Enterprise
JavaBeans 2.0//EN" "http://java.sun.com/dtd/ejb-jar_2_0.dtd">

<ejb-jar>
    <enterprise-beans>
    ...
```

Once you have generated the deployment descriptor, *jar* the TravelAgent EJB and deploy it in your EJB server. You will also need to deploy the Reservation, Cruise, and Customer EJBs you downloaded earlier. Based on the business methods in the remote interface of the TravelAgent EJB and your past experiences with the Cabin, Ship, and ProcessPayment EJBs, you should be able to create your own client application to test this code.

Exercise 11.2 in the Workbook shows how to deploy the examples in this section.

The Life Cycle of a Stateful Session Bean

The biggest difference between the stateful session bean and the other bean types is that stateful session beans do not use instance pooling. Stateful session beans are dedicated to one client for their entire lives, so swapping or pooling of instances isn't possible.* When they are idle, stateful session bean instances are simply evicted from memory. The EJB object remains connected to the client, but the bean instance is dereferenced and garbage collected during inactive periods. This means that each stateful bean must be passivated before it is evicted in order to preserve the conversational state of the instance, and it must be activated to restore its state when the EJB object becomes active again.

The bean's perception of its life cycle depends on whether it implements a special interface called `javax.ejb.SessionSynchronization`. This interface defines an additional set of callback methods that notify the bean of its participation in transactions. A bean that implements `SessionSynchronization` can cache database data across several method calls before making an update. We have not discussed transactions in detail yet; we will consider this part of the bean's life cycle in Chapter 15. This section describes the life cycle of stateful session beans that do not implement the `SessionSynchronization` interface.

* Some vendors use pooling with stateful session beans, but that is a proprietary implementation and should not affect the specified life cycle of the stateful session bean.

The life cycle of a stateful session bean has three states: Does Not Exist, Method-Ready, and Passivated. This sounds a lot like a stateless session bean, but the Method-Ready state is significantly different from the Method-Ready Pool of stateless beans. Figure 11-2 shows the state diagram for stateful session beans.

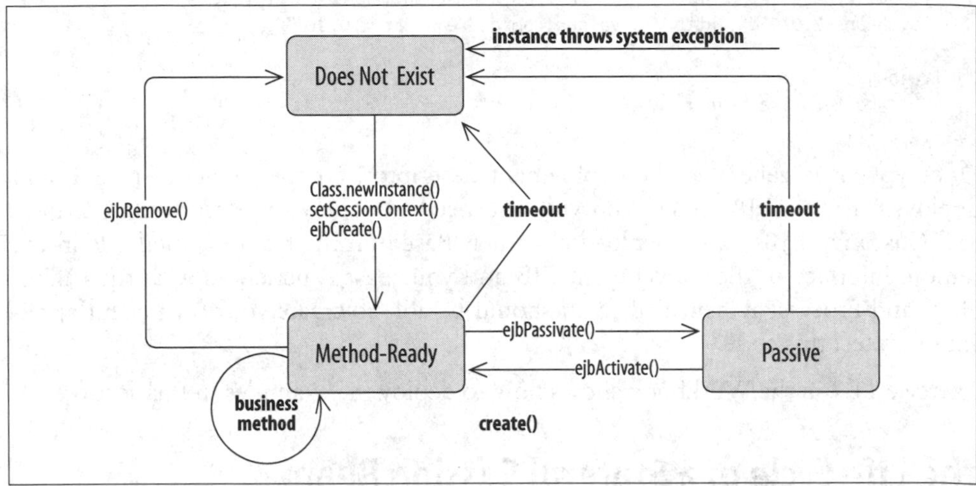

Figure 11-2. Stateful session bean life cycle

Does Not Exist State

A stateful bean instance in the Does Not Exist state has not been instantiated yet. It doesn't exist in the system's memory.

Method-Ready State

The Method-Ready state is the state in which the bean instance can service requests from its clients. This section explores the instance's transition into and out of the Method-Ready state.

Transitioning to the Method-Ready state

When a client invokes the `create()` method on an EJB home of a stateful session bean, the bean's life cycle begins. When the `create()` method is received by the container, the container invokes `newInstance()` on the bean class, creating a new instance of the bean. Next, the container invokes `setSessionContext()` on the instance, handing it its reference to the `SessionContext`, which it must maintain for life. At this point, the bean instance is assigned to its EJB object. Finally, the container invokes the `ejbCreate()` method on the instance that matches the `create()` method invoked by the client. Once `ejbCreate()` has completed, the container returns the EJB object's reference to the client. Note that there can be different, overloaded versions of `ejbCreate()`, unlike stateless session beans. The instance is now in the Method-Ready state and is ready to service business methods invoked by the client on the bean's remote reference.

Life in the Method-Ready state

While in the Method-Ready state, the bean instance is free to receive method invocations from the client, which may involve controlling the taskflow of other beans or accessing the database directly. During this time, the bean can maintain conversational state and open resources in its instance variables.

Transitioning out of the Method-Ready state

Bean instances leave the Method-Ready state to enter either the Passivated state or the Does Not Exist state. Depending on how the client uses the stateful bean, the EJB container's load, and the passivation algorithm used by the vendor, a bean instance may be passivated (and activated) several times in its life or not at all. If the bean is removed, it enters the Does Not Exist state. A client application can remove a bean by invoking one of the `remove( )` methods on the client API, or the container can choose to remove the bean.

The container can also move the bean instance from the Method-Ready state to the Does Not Exist state if the bean times out. Timeouts are declared at deployment time in a vendor-specific manner. When a timeout occurs in the Method-Ready state, the container may, but is not required to, call the `ejbRemove( )` method. A stateful bean cannot timeout while a transaction is in progress.

Passivated State

During the lifetime of a stateful session bean, there may be periods of inactivity when the bean instance is not servicing methods from the client. To conserve resources, the container can passivate the bean instance by preserving its conversational state and evicting the bean instance from memory. A bean's conversational state may consist of primitive values, objects that are serializable, and the following special types:

`javax.ejb.SessionContext`
`javax.ejb.EJBHome` (remote home interface types)
`javax.ejb.EJBObject` (remote interface types)
`javax.jta.UserTransaction` (bean transaction interface)
`javax.naming.Context` (only when it references the JNDI ENC)
`javax.ejb.EJBLocalHome` (local home interface types)
`javax.ejb.EJBLocalObject` (local interface types)
References to managed resource factories (e.g., `javax.sql.DataSource`)

The types in this list (and their subtypes) are handled specially by the passivation mechanism. They do not need to be serializable; they will be maintained through passivation and restored automatically when the bean instance is activated.

When a bean is about to be passivated, its `ejbPassivate( )` method is invoked, alerting the bean instance that it is about to enter the Passivated state. At this time, the bean instance should close any open resources and set all nontransient, nonserializable fields to `null`. This prevents problems from occurring when the bean is serialized. Transient fields are simply ignored.

How does the container store the bean's conversational state? It's largely up to the container. Containers can use standard Java serialization to preserve the bean instance, or some other mechanism that achieves the same result. Some vendors, for example, simply read the values of the fields and store them in a cache. The container is required to preserve remote references to other beans with the conversational state. When the bean is activated, the container must restore any bean references automatically. The container must also restore any references to the special types listed earlier.

When the client makes a request on an EJB object whose bean is passivated, the container activates the instance. This involves deserializing the bean instance and reconstructing the `SessionContext` reference, bean references, and managed resource factories held by the instance before it was passivated. When a bean's conversational state has been successfully restored, the `ejbActivate( )` method is invoked. The bean instance should open any resources that cannot be passivated and initialize the values of any transient fields within the `ejbActivate( )` method. Once `ejbActivate( )` is complete, the bean is back in the Method-Ready state and available to service client requests delegated by the EJB object.

The activation of a bean instance follows the rules of Java serialization, regardless of how the bean's state was actually stored. The exception to this is transient fields. In Java serialization, transient fields are set to their default values when an object is deserialized; primitive numbers become zero, Boolean fields `false`, and object references `null`. In EJB, transient fields can contain arbitrary values when the bean is activated. The values held by transient fields following activation are unpredictable across vendor implementations, so do not depend on them to be initialized. Instead, use `ejbActivate( )` to reset their values.

The container can also move the bean instance from the Passivated state to the Does Not Exist state if the bean times out. When a timeout occurs in the Passivated state, the `ejbRemove( )` method is not invoked.

System exceptions

Whenever a system exception is thrown by a bean method, the container invalidates the EJB object and destroys the bean instance. The bean instance moves directly to the Does Not Exist state and the `ejbRemove( )` method is *not* invoked.

A system exception is any unchecked exception, including `EJBException`. Checked exceptions thrown from subsystems are usually wrapped in an `EJBException` and rethrown as system exceptions. A checked exception thrown by a subsystem does not need to be handled this way if the bean can safely recover from the exception. In most cases, however, the subsystem exception should be rethrown as an `EJBException`.

CHAPTER 12

Message-Driven Beans

The Message-Driven Bean was introduced in EJB 2.0 to support the processing of asynchronous messages from a Java Message Service (JMS) provider. EJB 2.1 expanded the definition of the message-driven bean so that it can support any messaging system, not just JMS. This chapter examines both JMS-based message-driven beans, which all EJB 2.0 and EJB 2.1 vendors must support, as well as the expanded message-driven bean model available to EJB 2.1 developers.

JMS and Message-Driven Beans

All EJB 2.0 vendors must support a JMS provider. Most vendors have a JMS provider built in, but some may also support other JMS providers. EJB 2.1 vendors can support any JMS provider that complies with the J2EE Connector Architecture 1.5. However, regardless of whether your vendor has its own JMS provider, or allows you to integrate some other provider, a JMS provider is an absolute necessity for supporting message-driven beans. By forcing the adoption of JMS, Sun has guaranteed that EJB developers can expect to have a working JMS provider on which messages can be both sent and received.

JMS as a Resource

JMS is a vendor-neutral API that can be used to access enterprise messaging systems. Enterprise messaging systems (a.k.a. message-oriented middleware) facilitate the exchange of messages between software applications over a network. The role of JMS isn't unlike the role of JDBC: just as JDBC provides a common API for accessing many different relational databases, JMS provides vendor-independent access to enterprise messaging systems. Although messaging products aren't as familiar as database products, there's no shortage of messaging systems that support JMS, including IBM's MQSeries, BEA's WebLogic JMS service, Sun Microsystems' Sun ONE Message Queue, and Sonic's SonicMQ. Software applications that use the JMS API for sending or receiving messages are portable from one JMS vendor to another.

Applications that use JMS are called *JMS clients*, and the messaging system that handles routing and delivery of messages is called the *JMS provider*. A *JMS application* is a business system composed of many JMS clients and, generally, one JMS provider. A JMS client that sends a message is called a *producer*, while a JMS client that receives a message is called a *consumer*. A single JMS client can be both a producer and a consumer.

In EJB, enterprise beans of all types can use JMS to send messages. The messages are consumed by other Java applications or message-driven beans. JMS facilitates sending messages from enterprise beans using a *messaging service*, sometimes called a *message broker* or *router*. Message brokers have been around for a couple of decades—the oldest and most established is IBM's MQSeries—but JMS is fairly new, and specifically designed to deliver a variety of message types from one Java application to another.

Reimplementing the TravelAgent EJB with JMS

We can modify the TravelAgent EJB developed in Chapter 11 so that it uses JMS to alert some other Java application that a reservation has been made. The following code shows how to modify the bookPassage( ) method so that the TravelAgent EJB sends a simple text message based on a description obtained from the TicketDO object:

```
public TicketDO bookPassage(CreditCardDO card, double price)
    throws IncompleteConversationalState {

    if (customer == null || cruise == null || cabin == null) {
        throw new IncompleteConversationalState( );
    }
    try {
        ReservationHomeLocal resHome = (ReservationHomeLocal)
            jndiContext.lookup("java:comp/env/ejb/ReservationHomeLocal");

        ReservationLocal reservation =
            resHome.create(customer, cruise, cabin, price, new Date( ));

        Object ref = jndiContext.lookup
            ("java:comp/env/ejb/ProcessPaymentHomeRemote");

        ProcessPaymentHomeRemote ppHome = (ProcessPaymentHomeRemote)
            PortableRemoteObject.narrow(ref, ProcessPaymentHomeRemote.class);
        ProcessPaymentRemote process = ppHome.create( );
        process.byCredit(customer, card, price);

        TicketDO ticket = new TicketDO(customer,cruise,cabin,price);
        String ticketDescription = ticket.toString( );

        TopicConnectionFactory factory = (TopicConnectionFactory)
            jndiContext.lookup("java:comp/env/jms/TopicFactory");
```

```
            Topic topic = (Topic)
                jndiContext.lookup("java:comp/env/jms/TicketTopic");
            TopicConnection connect = factory.createTopicConnection( );
            TopicSession session = connect.createTopicSession(true,0);
            TopicPublisher publisher = session.createPublisher(topic);
            TextMessage textMsg = session.createTextMessage( );
            textMsg.setText(ticketDescription);
            publisher.publish(textMsg);
            connect.close( );

            return ticket;
        } catch(Exception e) {
            throw new EJBException(e);
        }
    }
```

While all the code we added may look a little overwhelming, the basics of JMS are not all that complicated.

TopicConnectionFactory and Topic

In order to send a JMS message, we need a connection to the JMS provider and a destination address for the message. A JMS connection factory makes the connection to the provider possible; the destination address is identified by a `Topic` object. Both the connection factory and the `Topic` object are obtained from the TravelAgent EJB's JNDI ENC:

```
TopicConnectionFactory factory = (TopicConnectionFactory)
    jndiContext.lookup("java:comp/env/jms/TopicFactory");
Topic topic = (Topic) jndiContext.lookup("java:comp/env/jms/TicketTopic");
```

The `TopicConnectionFactory` is similar to a `DataSource` in JDBC. Just as the `DataSource` provides a JDBC connection to a database, the `TopicConnectionFactory` provides a JMS connection to a message router.*

The `Topic` object itself represents a network-independent destination to which the message will be addressed. In JMS, messages aren't sent directly to applications; they're sent to topics or queues. A *topic* is analogous to an email list or newsgroup; any application with the proper credentials can receive messages from and send messages to a topic. When a JMS client receives messages from a topic, the client is said to *subscribe* to that topic. JMS decouples applications by allowing them to send messages to each other through a destination, which serves as virtual channel. A *queue* is another type of destination that we'll discuss in detail later.

* This analogy is not perfect. One might also say that the `TopicSession` is analogous to the `DataSource`, since both represent transaction-resources connections.

TopicConnection and TopicSession

The `TopicConnectionFactory` is used to create a `TopicConnection`, which is an actual connection to the JMS provider:

```
TopicConnection connect = factory.createTopicConnection( );
TopicSession session = connect.createTopicSession(true,0);
```

Once you have a `TopicConnection`, you can use it to create a `TopicSession`. A `TopicSession` allows you to group the actions of sending and receiving messages. In this case, you need only a single `TopicSession`. Using multiple `TopicSessions` is helpful if you wish to produce and consume messages in different threads. `Session` objects use a single-threaded model, which prohibits concurrent access to a single `Session` from multiple threads. The thread that creates a `TopicSession` is usually the thread that uses that `Session`'s producers and consumers (i.e., `TopicPublisher` and `TopicSubscriber` objects). If you wish to produce and consume messages using multithreading, you must create a different `Session` object for each thread.

The `createTopicSession( )` method has two parameters:

```
createTopicSession(boolean transacted, int acknowledgeMode)
```

According to the EJB specifications, these arguments are ignored at runtime because the EJB container manages the transaction and acknowledgment mode of any JMS resource obtained from the JNDI ENC. The specification recommends that developers use the arguments `true` for `transacted` and `0` for `acknowledgeMode`, but since they are supposed to be ignored, it should not matter what you use. Unfortunately, not all vendors adhere to this part of the specification. Some vendors ignore these parameters; others do not.

It's good programming practice to close a `TopicConnection` after it has been used:

```
TopicConnection connect = factory.createTopicConnection( );
...
connect.close( );
```

TopicPublisher

The `TopicSession` is used to create a `TopicPublisher`, which sends messages from the TravelAgent EJB to the destination specified by the `Topic` object. Any JMS clients that subscribe to that topic will receive a copy of the message:

```
TopicPublisher publisher = session.createPublisher(topic);

TextMessage textMsg = session.createTextMessage( );
textMsg.setText(ticketDescription);
publisher.publish(textMsg);
```

Message types

In JMS, a message is a Java object with two parts: a *header* and a *message body*. The header is composed of delivery information and metadata, while the message body carries the application data, which can take several forms: text, serializable objects, byte streams, etc. The JMS API defines several message types (TextMessage, MapMessage, ObjectMessage, and others) and provides methods for delivering messages to and receiving messages from other applications.

For example, we can change the TravelAgent EJB so that it sends a MapMessage instead of a TextMessage:

```
TicketDO ticket = new TicketDO(customer,cruise,cabin,price);
...
TopicPublisher publisher = session.createPublisher(topic);

MapMessage mapMsg = session.createMapMessage( );
mapMsg.setInt("CustomerID", ticket.customerID.intValue( ));
mapMsg.setInt("CruiseID", ticket.cruiseID.intValue( ));
mapMsg.setInt("CabinID", ticket.cabinID.intValue( ));
mapMsg.setDouble("Price", ticket.price);

publisher.publish(mapMsg);
```

The attributes of the MapMessage (CustomerID, CruiseID, CabinID, and Price) can be accessed by name from those JMS clients that receive it. As an alternative, the TravelAgent EJB could be modified to use the ObjectMessage type, which would allow us to send the entire TicketDO object as the message using Java serialization:

```
TicketDO ticket = new TicketDO(customer,cruise,cabin,price);
...
TopicPublisher publisher = session.createPublisher(topic);

ObjectMessage objectMsg = session.createObjectMessage( );
ObjectMsg.setObject(ticket);

publisher.publish(objectMsg);
```

In addition to the TextMessage, MapMessage, and ObjectMessage, JMS provides two other message types: StreamMessage and BytesMessage. StreamMessage can take the contents of an I/O stream as its payload. BytesMessage can take any array of bytes, which it treats as opaque data.

XML deployment descriptor

JMS resources must be declared in the bean's EJB deployment descriptor. The declaration is different in EJB 2.1 and EJB 2.0, so they are shown separately.

EJB 2.1: Declaring a JMS Resource

In EJB 2.1, a JMS resource is declared in a manner similar to the JDBC resource used by the Ship EJB in Chapter 9:

```
<enterprise-beans>
    <session>
        <ejb-name>TravelAgentBean</ejb-name>
```

```
    ...
    <resource-ref>
        <res-ref-name>jms/TopicFactory</res-ref-name>
        <res-type>javax.jms.TopicConnectionFactory</res-type>
        <res-auth>Container</res-auth>
    </resource-ref>
    <resource-ref>
        <res-ref-name>jdbc/titanDB</res-ref-name>
        <res-type>javax.sql.DataSource</res-type>
        <res-auth>Container</res-auth>
    </resource-ref>
    <message-destination-ref>
        <message-destination-ref-name>
             jms/TicketTopic
        </message-destination-ref-name>
        <message-destination-type>javax.jms.Topic</message-destination-type>
        <message-destination-usage>Produces</message-destination-usage>
    </message-destination-ref>
    ...
  </session>
</enterprise-beans>
```

The <resource-ref> for the JMS TopicConnectionFactory is similar to the <resource-ref> declaration for the JDBC DataSource: it declares the JNDI ENC name, interface type, and authorization protocol. In addition to the <resource-ref>, the TravelAgent EJB must also declare the <message-destination-ref>.

The <message-destination-ref> element is new in EJB 2.1. It describes the destination to which the EJB sends messages. The <message-destination-ref-name> declares the JNDI ENC name used to access the destination. The <message-destination-type> declares the type of destination (javax.jms.Topic or javax.jms.Queue) and the <message-destination-usage> tells whether the destination is used to send or receive messages; it can have one of the following values: Consumes, Produces, or ConsumesProduces. Consumes indicates that the JMS client only receives message from the destination, Produces indicates that it only sends messages to the destination, and ConsumesProduces indicates that the client uses the same destination to both send and receive messages. At deployment time, the deployer maps the JMS TopicConnectionFactory and Topic declared by the <resource-ref> and <message-destination-ref> elements to a JMS provider and a topic.

Although any EJB can send and receive messages, in most cases, it's best that only MDBs receive JMS messages. In this case, we declare the Topic used for sending a ticket message.

EJB 2.0: Declaring a JMS Resource

In EJB 2.0, a JMS resource is declared in a manner similar to the JDBC resource used by the Ship EJB in Chapter 9:

```
<enterprise-beans>
    <session>
```

```
        <ejb-name>TravelAgentBean</ejb-name>
        ...
        <resource-ref>
            <res-ref-name>jms/TopicFactory</res-ref-name>
            <res-type>javax.jms.TopicConnectionFactory</res-type>
            <res-auth>Container</res-auth>
        </resource-ref>
        <resource-ref>
            <res-ref-name>jdbc/titanDB</res-ref-name>
            <res-type>javax.sql.DataSource</res-type>
            <res-auth>Container</res-auth>
        </resource-ref>
        <resource-env-ref>
            <resource-env-ref-name>jms/TicketTopic</resource-env-ref-name>
            <resource-env-ref-type>javax.jms.Topic</resource-env-ref-type>
        </resource-env-ref>
        ...
    </session>
```

The `<resource-ref>` for the JMS `TopicConnectionFactory` is similar to the `<resource-ref>` declaration for the JDBC `DataSource`: it declares the JNDI ENC name, interface type, and authorization protocol. In addition to the `<resource-ref>`, the TravelAgent EJB must also declare the `<resource-env-ref>`, which lists any "administered objects" associated with a `<resource-ref>` entry. In this case, we declare the `Topic` used for sending a ticket message. At deployment time, the deployer maps the JMS `TopicConnectionFactory` and `Topic` declared by the `<resource-ref>` and `<resource-env-ref>` elements to a JMS factory and topic.

JMS Application Client

To get a better idea of how JMS is used, we can create a Java application whose sole purpose is receiving and processing reservation messages. This application is a simple JMS client that prints a description of each ticket as it receives the messages. We'll assume that the TravelAgent EJB is using the `TextMessage` to send a description of the ticket to the JMS clients. Here's how the JMS application client might look:

```
import javax.jms.Message;
import javax.jms.TextMessage;
import javax.jms.TopicConnectionFactory;
import javax.jms.TopicConnection;
import javax.jms.TopicSession;
import javax.jms.Topic;
import javax.jms.Session;
import javax.jms.TopicSubscriber;
import javax.jms.JMSException;
import javax.naming.InitialContext;

public class JmsClient_1 implements javax.jms.MessageListener {

    public static void main(String [] args) throws Exception {
```

```
        if(args.length != 2)
            throw new Exception("Wrong number of arguments");
        new JmsClient_1(args[0], args[1]);
        while(true){Thread.sleep(10000);}
    }

    public JmsClient_1(String factoryName, String topicName) throws Exception {

        InitialContext jndiContext = getInitialContext( );

        TopicConnectionFactory factory = (TopicConnectionFactory)
            jndiContext.lookup("TopicFactoryNameGoesHere");
        Topic topic = (Topic)jndiContext.lookup("TopicNameGoesHere");
        TopicConnection connect = factory.createTopicConnection( );
        TopicSession session =
            connect.createTopicSession(false,Session.AUTO_ACKNOWLEDGE);
        TopicSubscriber subscriber = session.createSubscriber(topic);
        subscriber.setMessageListener(this);

        connect.start( );
    }

    public void onMessage(Message message) {
        try {

            TextMessage textMsg = (TextMessage)message;
            String text = textMsg.getText( );
            System.out.println("\n RESERVATION RECIEVED:\n"+text);

        } catch(JMSException jmsE) {
            jmsE.printStackTrace( );
        }
    }

    public static InitialContext getInitialContext( ) {
        // create vendor-specific JNDI context here
    }
}
```

The constructor of `JmsClient_1` obtains the `TopicConnectionFactory` and `Topic` from the JNDI `InitialContext`. This context is created with vendor-specific properties so that the client can connect to the same JMS provider as the one used by the Travel-Agent EJB. For example, here's how the `getInitialContext( )` method for the WebLogic application server would be coded:*

```
public static InitialContext getInitialContext( ) {
    Properties env = new Properties( );
    env.put(Context.SECURITY_PRINCIPAL, "guest");
```

* JNDI also allows the properties to be set in a *jndi.properties* file, which contains the property values for the `InitialContext` and can be discovered dynamically at runtime. In this book, I chose to set the properties explicitly.

```
        env.put(Context.SECURITY_CREDENTIALS, "guest");
        env.put(Context.INITIAL_CONTEXT_FACTORY,
           "weblogic.jndi.WLInitialContextFactory");
        env.put(Context.PROVIDER_URL, "t3://localhost:7001");
        return new InitialContext(env);
    }
```

Once the client has the TopicConnectionFactory and Topic, it creates a TopicConnection and a TopicSession in the same way as the TravelAgent EJB. The main difference is that the TopicSession object is used to create a TopicSubscriber instead of a TopicPublisher. The TopicSubscriber is designed to process incoming messages that are published to its Topic:

```
TopicSession session =
    connect.createTopicSession(false,Session.AUTO_ACKNOWLEDGE);
TopicSubscriber subscriber = session.createSubscriber(topic);
subscriber.setMessageListener(this);
connect.start( );
```

The TopicSubscriber can receive messages directly, or it can delegate message processing to a javax.jms.MessageListener. We chose to have JmsClient_1 implement the MessageListener interface so that it can process the messages itself. MessageListener objects implement a single method, onMessage( ), which is invoked every time a new message is sent to the subscriber's topic. In this case, every time the TravelAgent EJB sends a reservation message to the topic, the JMS client's onMessage( ) method is invoked to receive and process a copy of the message:

```
public void onMessage(Message message) {
    try {
        TextMessage textMsg = (TextMessage)message;
        String text = textMsg.getText( );
        System.out.println("\n RESERVATION RECIEVED:\n"+text);
    } catch(JMSException jmsE) {
        jmsE.printStackTrace( );
    }
}
```

Exercise 12.1 in the Workbook shows how to deploy these examples in JBoss.

JMS Is Asynchronous

One of the principal advantages of JMS messaging is that it's *asynchronous*. In other words, a JMS client can send a message without having to wait for a reply. Contrast this flexibility with the synchronous messaging of Java RMI. Each time a client invokes a bean's method, it blocks the current thread until the method completes execution. This lock-step processing makes the client dependent on the availability of the EJB server, resulting in a tight coupling between the client and the enterprise bean. JMS clients send messages asynchronously to a destination (topic or queue), from which other JMS clients can also receive messages. When a JMS client sends a message, it doesn't wait for a reply; it sends the message to a router, which is responsible for forwarding the message to other clients. There's no effect on the client if one or more recipients are unavailable; it just goes ahead with its work. It's the router's responsibility to make sure that the message eventually reaches its destination. Clients sending messages are decoupled from the clients receiving them; senders are not dependent on the availability of receivers.

The limitations of RMI make JMS an attractive alternative for communicating with other applications. Using the standard JNDI environment-naming context, an enterprise bean can obtain a JMS connection to a JMS provider and use it to deliver asynchronous messages to other Java applications. For example, a TravelAgent session bean can use JMS to notify other applications that a reservation has been processed, as shown in Figure 12-1.

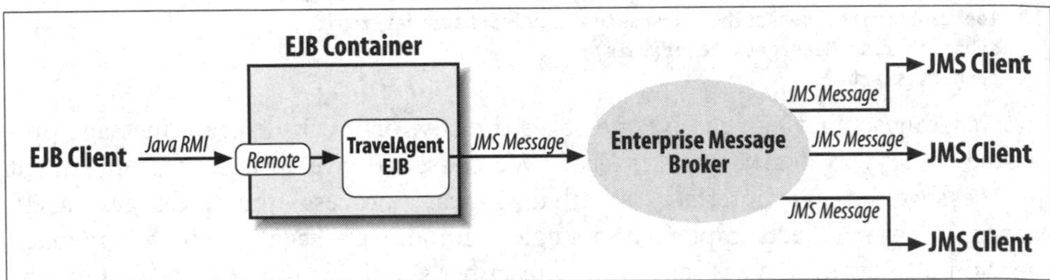

Figure 12-1. Using JMS with the TravelAgent EJB

In this case, the applications receiving JMS messages from the TravelAgent EJB may be message-driven beans, other Java applications in the enterprise, or applications in other organizations that benefit from being notified that a reservation has been processed. Examples might include business partners who share customer information or an internal marketing application that adds customers to a catalog mailing list.

Because messaging is inherently decoupled and asynchronous, the transactions and security contexts of the sender are not propagated to the receiver. For example, when the TravelAgent EJB sends the ticket message, the JMS provider may authenticate it, but the message's security context won't be propagated to the JMS client that received the message. When a JMS client receives the message from the TravelAgent EJB, the client has no idea about the security context under which the message was sent. This is how it should be, because the sender and receiver often operate in environments with different security domains.

Similarly, transactions are never propagated from the sender to the receiver. For one thing, the sender has no idea who the receivers of the message will be. If the message is sent to a topic, there could be one receiver or thousands; managing a distributed transaction under such ambiguous circumstances is not tenable. In addition, the clients receiving the message may not get it for a long time after it is sent; there may be a network problem, the client may be down, or there may be some other problem. Transactions are designed to be executed quickly because they lock up resources, and applications can't tolerate the possibility of a long transaction with an unpredictable end.

A JMS client can, however, have a distributed transaction with the JMS provider so that it manages the send or receive operation in the context of a transaction. For example, if the TravelAgent EJB's transaction fails for any reason, the JMS provider discards the ticket message sent by the TravelAgent EJB. Transactions and JMS are covered in more detail in Chapter 15.

JMS Messaging Models

JMS provides two types of messaging models: *publish-and-subscribe* and *point-to-point*. The JMS specification refers to these as *messaging domains*. In JMS terminology, publish-and-subscribe and point-to-point are frequently shortened to *pub/sub* and *p2p* (or *PTP*), respectively. This chapter uses both the long and short forms throughout.

In the simplest sense, publish-and-subscribe is intended for a one-to-many broadcast of messages, while point-to-point is intended for one-to-one delivery of messages (see Figure 12-2).

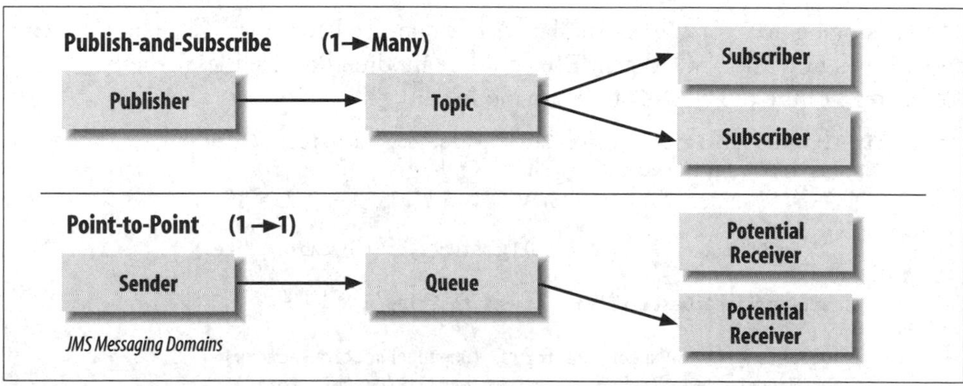

Figure 12-2. JMS messaging domains

Each messaging domain (i.e., pub/sub and p2p) has its own set of interfaces and classes for sending and receiving messages. This results in two different APIs, which share some common types. JMS 1.1, the most recent version (supported by EJB 2.1), introduced a Unified API that allows developers to use a single set of interfaces and classes for both messaging domains.

Publish-and-subscribe

In publish-and-subscribe messaging, one producer can send a message to many consumers through a virtual channel called a *topic*. Consumers can choose to *subscribe* to a topic. Any messages addressed to a topic are delivered to all the topic's consumers. The pub/sub messaging model is by and large a *push-based model*, in which messages are automatically broadcast to consumers without the consumers having to request or poll the topic for new messages.

In the pub/sub messaging model, the producer sending the message is not dependent on the consumers receiving the message. JMS clients that use pub/sub can establish durable subscriptions that allow consumers to disconnect and later reconnect and collect messages that were published while they were disconnected. The TravelAgent EJB in this chapter uses the pub/sub programming model with a `Topic` object as a destination.

Point-to-point. The point-to-point messaging model allows JMS clients to send and receive messages both synchronously and asynchronously via virtual channels known as *queues*. The p2p messaging model has traditionally been a *pull-* or *polling-based model*, in which messages are requested from the queue instead of being pushed to the client automatically.* A queue may have multiple receivers, but only one receiver may receive each message. As shown earlier in Figure 12-2, the JMS provider takes care of doling out the messages among JMS clients, ensuring that each message is consumed by only one JMS client. The JMS specification does not dictate the rules for distributing messages among multiple receivers.

The messaging API for p2p is similar to the one used for pub/sub. The following code shows how the TravelAgent EJB could be modified to use the queue-based p2p API instead of the topic-based pub/sub model:

```
public TicketDO bookPassage(CreditCardDO card, double price)
    throws IncompleteConversationalState {
        ...

        TicketDO ticket = new TicketDO(customer,cruise,cabin,price);

        String ticketDescription = ticket.toString( );

        QueueConnectionFactory factory = (QueueConnectionFactory)
            jndiContext.lookup("java:comp/env/jms/QueueFactory");
        Queue queue = (Queue)
            jndiContext.lookup("java:comp/env/jms/TicketQueue");
        QueueConnection connect = factory.createQueueConnection( );
        QueueSession session = connect.createQueueSession(true,0);
        QueueSender sender = session.createSender(queue);
        TextMessage textMsg = session.createTextMessage( );
        textMsg.setText(ticketDescription);
        sender.send(textMsg);
        connect.close( );
```

* The JMS specification does not specifically state how the p2p and pub/sub models must be implemented. Either model can use push or pull—but conceptually, pub/sub is push and p2p is pull.

```
            return ticket;
        } catch(Exception e) {
            throw new EJBException(e);
        }
    }
```

Which messaging model should you use?

The rationale behind the two models lies in the origin of the JMS specification. JMS started out as a way of providing a common API for accessing existing messaging systems. At the time of its conception, some messaging vendors had a p2p model and some had a pub/sub model. Hence, JMS needed to provide an API for both models to gain wide industry support.

Almost anything that can be done with the pub/sub model can be done with point-to-point, and vice versa. An analogy can be drawn to developers' programming language preferences. In theory, any application that can be written with Pascal can also be written with C. Anything that can be written in C++ can also be written in Java. In some cases, it comes down to a matter of preference, or which model you are already familiar with.

In most cases, the decision about which model to use depends on which model is a better fit for the application. With pub/sub, any number of subscribers can be listening on a topic, and they will all receive copies of the same message. The publisher may not care if everybody is listening, or even if nobody is listening. For example, consider a publisher that broadcasts stock quotes. If any particular subscriber is not currently connected and misses out on a great quote, the publisher is not concerned. In contrast, a point-to-point session is likely to be intended for a one-on-one conversation with a specific application at the other end. In this scenario, every message really matters. The range and variety of the data the messages represent can be a factor as well. Using pub/sub, messages are dispatched to the consumers based on filtering that is provided through the use of specific topics. Even when messaging is being used to establish a one-on-one conversation with another known application, it can be advantageous to use pub/sub with multiple topics to segregate different kinds of messages. Each kind of message can be dealt with separately through its own unique consumer and `onMessage()` listener.

Point-to-point is more convenient when you want a particular receiver to process a given message once. This is perhaps the most critical difference between the two models: p2p guarantees that only one consumer processes each message. This ability is extremely important when messages need to be processed separately but in tandem.

EJB 2.1: The Unified JMS API

Although the two messaging models (i.e., pub/sub and p2p) are distinct, JMS 1.1 provides a third *Unified API* that can be used for both pub/sub and p2p messaging.

It's important to understand that the Unified API does not represent a new messaging model. The publish/subscribe and point-to-point messaging models are the only two messaging models you have to choose from. The Unified API simply provides a third set of interfaces that allow developers to use the same API for both models. There is, however, another important advantage to the Unified API. It allows p2p and pub/sub messaging operations be part of the same transaction. In JMS 1.0.x, you could not use topic and queue-based APIs in the same transaction. The Unified API does away with this restriction.

Here's how the TravelAgent EJB could be modified to use the Unified API instead of the pub/sub or p2p models:

```
public TicketDO bookPassage(CreditCardDO card, double price)
    throws IncompleteConversationalState {
        ...

        TicketDO ticket = new TicketDO(customer,cruise,cabin,price);

        String ticketDescription = ticket.toString( );

        ConnectionFactory factory = (ConnectionFactory)
            jndiContext.lookup("java:comp/env/jms/ConnectionFactory");
        Destination destination= (Destination)
            jndiContext.lookup("java:comp/env/jms/TicketDestination");
        Connection connect = factory.createConnection( );
        Session session = connect.createSession(true,0);
        MessageProducer prodcuer = session.createProducer(destination);
        TextMessage textMsg = session.createTextMessage( );
        textMsg.setText(ticketDescription);
        producer.send(textMsg);
        connect.close( );

        return ticket;
    } catch(Exception e) {
        throw new EJBException(e);
    }
}
```

Entity and Session Beans Should Not Receive Messages

`JmsClient_1` was designed to consume messages produced by the TravelAgent EJB. Can another entity or session bean receive those messages also? The answer is yes, but it's a really bad idea.

Entity and session beans respond to Java RMI calls from EJB clients and cannot be programmed to respond to JMS messages as do message-driven beans. It's impossible to write a session or entity bean that is driven by incoming messages. It is possible to develop an entity or session bean that can consume a JMS message from a business method, but an EJB client must call the method first. For example, when the business method on the Hypothetical EJB is called, it sets up a JMS session and then attempts to read a message from a queue:

```
public class HypotheticalBean implements javax.ejb.SessionBean {
    InitialContext jndiContext;

    public String businessMethod( ) {

        try{

            QueueConnectionFactory factory = (QueueConnectionFactory)
                jndiContext.lookup("java:comp/env/jms/QueueFactory");
            Queue topic = (Queue)
                jndiContext.lookup("java:comp/env/jms/Queue");
            QueueConnection connect = factory.createQueueConnection( );
            QueueSession session = connect.createQueueSession(true,0);
            QueueReceiver receiver = session.createReceiver(queue);
            TextMessage textMsg = (TextMessage)receiver.receive( );

            connect.close( );

            return textMsg.getText( );

        } catch(Exception e) {
            throws new EJBException(e);
        }

    }
    ...
}
```

The `QueueReceiver`, which is a message consumer, is used to proactively fetch a message from the queue. While this operation has been programmed correctly, it is a dangerous because a call to the `QueueReceiver.receive( )` method blocks the thread until a message becomes available. If a message is never delivered, the thread is blocked indefinitely! If no one ever sends a message to the queue, the `QueueReceiver` just sits there waiting, forever.

To be fair, there are other `receive( )` methods that are less dangerous. For example, `receive(long timeout)` allows you to specify a time after which the `QueueReceiver` should stop blocking the thread and give up waiting for a message. There is also `receiveNoWait( )`, which checks for a message and returns `null` if there are none waiting, thus avoiding a prolonged thread block. However, this operation is still dangerous. There is no guarantee that the less risky `receive( )` methods will perform as expected, and the risk of programmer error (e.g., using the wrong `receive( )` method) is too great.

The moral of the story is simple: don't write convoluted code trying to force entity and session beans to receive messages. If you need to receive messages, use a message-driven bean; MDBs are specially designed to consume JMS messages.

Learning More About JMS

JMS (and enterprise messaging in general) represents a powerful paradigm in distributed computing. While this chapter has provided a brief overview of JMS, it has presented only enough material to prepare you for the discussion of message-driven beans in the next section. To understand JMS and how it is used, you will need to study it independently.* Taking the time to learn JMS is well worth the effort.

JMS-Based Message-Driven Beans

Message-driven beans (MDBs) are stateless, server-side, transaction-aware components for processing asynchronous messages delivered via the Java Message Service. While a message-driven bean is responsible for processing messages, its container manages the component's environment, including transactions, security, resources, concurrency, and message acknowledgment. It's particularly important to note that the container manages concurrency. The thread-safety provided by the container gives MDBs a significant advantage over traditional JMS clients, which must be custom-built to manage resources, transactions, and security in a multithreaded environment. An MDB can process hundreds of JMS messages concurrently because numerous instances of the MDB can execute concurrently in the container.

A message-driven bean is a complete enterprise bean, just like a session or entity bean, but there are some important differences. While a message-driven bean has a bean class and EJB deployment descriptor, it does not have EJB object or home interfaces. These interfaces are absent because the message-driven bean is not accessible via the Java RMI API; it responds only to asynchronous messages.

The ReservationProcessor EJB

The ReservationProcessor EJB is a message-driven bean that receives JMS messages notifying it of new reservations. The ReservationProcessor EJB is an automated version of the TravelAgent EJB that processes reservations sent via JMS. These messages might come from another application in the enterprise or from an application in some other organization—perhaps another travel agent. When the ReservationProcessor EJB receives a message, it creates a new Reservation EJB (adding it to the database), processes the payment using the ProcessPayment EJB, and sends out a ticket. This process is illustrated in Figure 12-3.

* For a detailed treatment of JMS, see *Java Message Service* by Richard Monson-Haefel and David Chappell (O'Reilly).

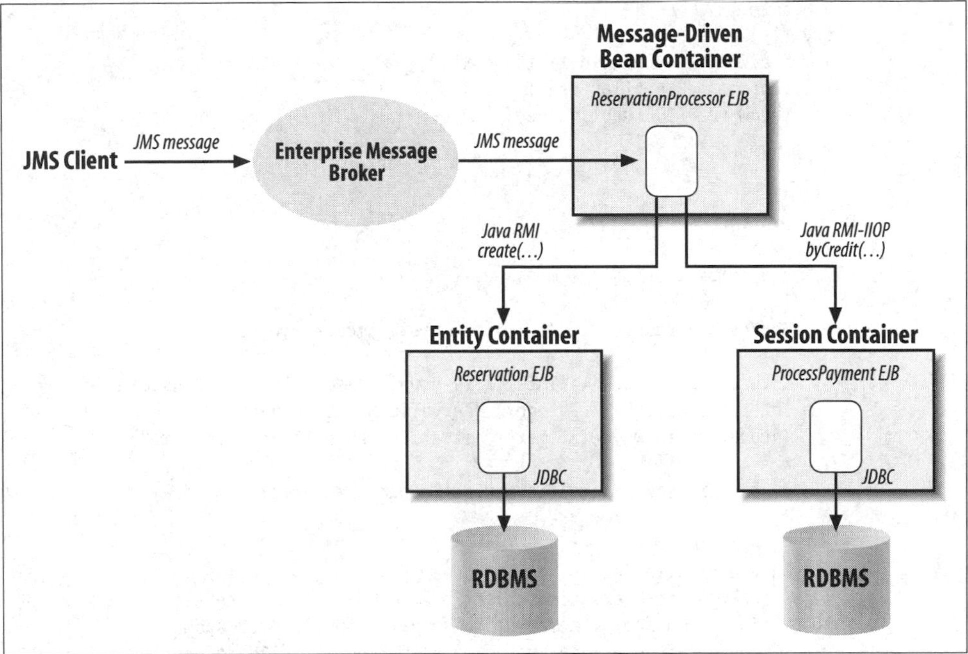

Figure 12-3. The ReservationProcessor EJB processing reservations

The ReservationProcessorBean Class

Here is a partial definition of the `ReservationProcessorBean` class. Some methods are left empty; they will be filled in later. Notice that the `onMessage( )` method contains the business logic; it is similar to the business logic developed in the `bookPassage( )` method of the TravelAgent EJB in Chapter 11. Here's the code:

```
package com.titan.reservationprocessor;

import javax.jms.Message;
import javax.jms.MapMessage;
import com.titan.customer.*;
import com.titan.cruise.*;
import com.titan.cabin.*;
import com.titan.reservation.*;
import com.titan.processpayment.*;
import com.titan.travelagent.*;
import java.util.Date;

public class ReservationProcessorBean implements javax.ejb.MessageDrivenBean,
    javax.jms.MessageListener {

    MessageDrivenContext ejbContext;
    Context jndiContext;

    public void setMessageDrivenContext(MessageDrivenContext mdc) {
```

```
        ejbContext = mdc;
        try {
            jndiContext = new InitialContext( );
        } catch(NamingException ne) {
            throw new EJBException(ne);
        }
    }

    public void ejbCreate( ) {}

    public void onMessage(Message message) {
        try {
            MapMessage reservationMsg = (MapMessage)message;

            Integer customerPk = (Integer)reservationMsg.getObject("CustomerID");
            Integer cruisePk = (Integer)reservationMsg.getObject("CruiseID");
            Integer cabinPk = (Integer)reservationMsg.getObject("CabinID");

            double price = reservationMsg.getDouble("Price");

            // get the credit card
            Date expirationDate =
                new Date(reservationMsg.getLong("CreditCardExpDate"));
            String cardNumber = reservationMsg.getString("CreditCardNum");
            String cardType = reservationMsg.getString("CreditCardType");
            CreditCardDO card = new CreditCardDO(cardNumber,
                expirationDate, cardType);

            CustomerRemote customer = getCustomer(customerPk);
            CruiseLocal cruise = getCruise(cruisePk);
            CabinLocal cabin = getCabin(cabinPk);

            ReservationHomeLocal resHome = (ReservationHomeLocal)
                jndiContext.lookup("java:comp/env/ejb/ReservationHomeLocal");
            ReservationLocal reservation =
                resHome.create(customer, cruise, cabin, price, new Date( ));
            Object ref = jndiContext.lookup
                ("java:comp/env/ejb/ProcessPaymentHomeRemote");
            ProcessPaymentHomeRemote ppHome = (ProcessPaymentHomeRemote)
                PortableRemoteObject.narrow(ref, ProcessPaymentHomeRemote.class);
            ProcessPaymentRemote process = ppHome.create( );
            process.byCredit(customer, card, price);

            TicketDO ticket = new TicketDO(customer,cruise,cabin,price);

            deliverTicket(reservationMsg, ticket);

        } catch(Exception e) {
            throw new EJBException(e);
        }
    }

    public void deliverTicket(MapMessage reservationMsg, TicketDO ticket) {
```

```
            // send it to the proper destination
        }
        public CustomerRemote getCustomer(Integer key)
            throws NamingException, RemoteException, FinderException {
            // get a remote reference to the Customer EJB
        }
        public CruiseLocal getCruise(Integer key)
            throws NamingException, FinderException {
            // get a local reference to the Cruise EJB
        }
        public CabinLocal getCabin(Integer key)
            throws NamingException, FinderException {
            // get a local reference to the Cabin EJB
        }

        public void ejbRemove( ) {
            try {
                jndiContext.close( );
                ejbContext = null;
            } catch(NamingException ne) { /* do nothing */ }
        }
    }
```

MessageDrivenBean interface

The message-driven bean class is required to implement the `javax.ejb.MessageDrivenBean` interface, which defines callback methods similar to those in entity and session beans. Here is the definition of the `MessageDrivenBean` interface:

```
package javax.ejb;

public interface MessageDrivenBean extends javax.ejb.EnterpriseBean {
    public void setMessageDrivenContext(MessageDrivenContext context)
        throws EJBException;
    public void ejbRemove( ) throws EJBException;
}
```

The `setMessageDrivenContext( )` method is called at the beginning of the MDB's life cycle and provides the MDB instance with a reference to its `MessageDrivenContext`:

```
MessageDrivenContext ejbContext;
Context jndiContext;

public void setMessageDrivenContext(MessageDrivenContext mdc) {
    ejbContext = mdc;
    try {
        jndiContext = new InitialContext( );
    } catch(NamingException ne) {
        throw new EJBException(ne);
    }
}
```

The `setMessageDrivenContext( )` method in the `ReservationProcessorBean` class sets the `ejbContext` instance field to the `MessageDrivenContext`, which was passed into the method. It also obtains a reference to the JNDI ENC, which it stores in the jndiContext. MDBs may have instance fields that are similar to a stateless session bean's instance fields. These instance fields are carried with the MDB instance for its lifetime and may be reused every time it processes a new message. Like stateless session beans, MDBs do not have conversational state and are not specific to a single JMS client; MDB instances process messages from many different clients. Instead, they are tied to the specific topic or queue from which they receive messages.

ejbRemove( ) provides the MDB instance with an opportunity to clean up any resources it stores in its instance fields. In this case, we use it to close the JNDI context and set the ejbContext field to null. These operations are not absolutely necessary, but they illustrate the kind of work that an ejbRemove( ) method might do. Note that ejbRemove( ) is called at the end of the MDB's life cycle, before it is garbage collected. It may not be called if the EJB server hosting the MDB fails or if an EJBException is thrown by the MDB instance in one of its other methods. When an EJBException (or any RuntimeException type) is thrown by any method in the MDB instance, the instance is immediately removed from memory and the transaction is rolled back.

MessageDrivenContext

The MessageDrivenContext simply extends the EJBContext; it does not add any new methods. The EJBContext is defined as:

```
package javax.ejb;
public interface EJBContext {

    // transaction methods
    public javax.transaction.UserTransaction getUserTransaction( )
        throws java.lang.IllegalStateException;
    public boolean getRollbackOnly( ) throws java.lang.IllegalStateException;
    public void setRollbackOnly( ) throws java.lang.IllegalStateException;

    // EJB home methods
    public EJBHome getEJBHome( );
    public EJBLocalHome getEJBLocalHome( );

    // security methods
    public java.security.Principal getCallerPrincipal( );
    public boolean isCallerInRole(java.lang.String roleName);

    // deprecated methods
    public java.security.Identity getCallerIdentity( );
    public boolean isCallerInRole(java.security.Identity role);
    public java.util.Properties getEnvironment( );

}
```

Only the transactional methods that MessageDrivenContext inherits from EJBContext are available to message-driven beans. The home methods—getEJBHome( ) and getEJBLocalHome()—throw a RuntimeException if invoked, because MDBs do not have home interfaces or EJB home objects. The security methods—getCallerPrincipal() and isCallerInRole()—also throw a RuntimeException if invoked on a MessageDrivenContext. When an MDB services a JMS message, there is no "caller," so there is no security context to be obtained from the caller. Remember that JMS is asynchronous and doesn't propagate the sender's security context to the receiver—that wouldn't make sense, since senders and receivers tend to operate in different environments.

MDBs usually execute in a container-initiated or bean-initiated transaction, so the transaction methods allow the MDB to manage its context. The transaction context is not propagated from the JMS sender; it is either initiated by the container or by the bean explicitly using javax.jta.UserTransaction. The transaction methods in the EJBContext are explained in more detail in Chapter 15.

Message-driven beans also have access to their own JNDI environment naming contexts (ENCs), which provide the MDB instances access to environment entries, other enterprise beans, and resources. For example, the ReservationProcessor EJB takes advantage of the JNDI ENC to obtain references to the Customer, Cruise, Cabin, Reservation, and ProcessPayment EJBs as well as a JMS QueueConnectionFactory and Queue for sending out tickets.

MessageListener interface

In addition to the MessageDrivenBean interface, MDBs implement the javax.jms.MessageListener interface, which defines the onMessage() method. This method processes the JMS messages received by a bean.

```
package javax.jms;
public interface MessageListener {
    public void onMessage(Message message);
}
```

It's interesting to consider why the MDB implements the MessageListener interface separately from the MessageDrivenBean interface. Why not just put the onMessage() method, MessageListener's only method, in the MessageDrivenBean interface so that there is only one interface for the MDB class to implement? This was the solution taken by an early, proposed version of EJB 2.0. However, the developers quickly realized that message-driven beans could, in the future, process messages from other types of systems, not just JMS. To make the MDB open to other messaging systems, it was decided that the MDB should implement the javax.jms.MessageListener interface separately, thus separating the concept of the message-driven bean from the types of messages it can process. It turns out that this was a good plan. As we'll see later in this chapter, EJB 2.1 lets you use MDBs with non-JMS messaging systems that use a different messaging interface.

Taskflow and integration for B2B (onMessage( ))

The onMessage( ) method is where all the business logic goes. As messages arrive, the container passes them to the MDB via the onMessage( ) method. When the method returns, the MDB is ready to process a new message. In the ReservationProcessor EJB, the onMessage( ) method extracts information about a reservation from a MapMessage and uses that information to create a reservation in the system:

```
public void onMessage(Message message) {
    try {
        MapMessage reservationMsg = (MapMessage)message;

        Integer customerPk = (Integer)reservationMsg.getObject("CustomerID");
        Integer cruisePk = (Integer)reservationMsg.getObject("CruiseID");
        Integer cabinPk = (Integer)reservationMsg.getObject("CabinID");

        double price = reservationMsg.getDouble("Price");

        // get the credit card

        Date expirationDate =
            new Date(reservationMsg.getLong("CreditCardExpDate"));
        String cardNumber = reservationMsg.getString("CreditCardNum");
        String cardType = reservationMsg.setString("CreditCardType");
        CreditCardDO card = new CreditCardDO(cardNumber,
            expirationDate, cardType);
```

JMS is frequently used as an integration point for business-to-business applications, so it's easy to imagine the reservation message coming from one of Titan's business partners (perhaps a third-party processor or branch travel agency).

The ReservationProcessor EJB needs to access the Customer, Cruise, and Cabin EJBs in order to process the reservation. The MapMessage contains the primary keys for these entities; the ReservationProcessor EJB uses helper methods (getCustomer( ), getCruise( ), and getCabin( )) to look up the entity beans and obtain EJB object references to them:

```
public void onMessage(Message message) {
    ...
    CustomerRemote customer = getCustomer(customerPk);
    CruiseLocal cruise = getCruise(cruisePk);
    CabinLocal cabin = getCabin(cabinPk);
    ...
}

public CustomerRemote getCustomer(Integer key)
    throws NamingException, RemoteException, FinderException {

    Object ref = jndiContext.lookup("java:comp/env/ejb/CustomerHomeRemote");
    CustomerHomeRemote home = (CustomerHomeRemote)
        PortableRemoteObject.narrow(ref, CustomerHomeRemote.class);
    CustomerRemote customer = home.findByPrimaryKey(key);
    return customer;
```

```
    }
    public CruiseLocal getCruise(Integer key)
        throws NamingException, FinderException {

        CruiseHomeLocal home = (CruiseHomeLocal)
            jndiContext.lookup("java:comp/env/ejb/CruiseHomeLocal");
        CruiseLocal cruise = home.findByPrimaryKey(key);
        return cruise;
    }
    public CabinLocal getCabin(Integer key)
        throws NamingException, FinderException{

        CabinHomeLocal home = (CabinHomeLocal)
            jndiContext.lookup("java:comp/env/ejb/CabinHomeLocal");
        CabinLocal cabin = home.findByPrimaryKey(key);
        return cabin;
    }
```

Once the information is extracted from the MapMessage, it is used to create a reservation and process the payment. This is basically the same taskflow that was used by the TravelAgent EJB in Chapter 11. A Reservation EJB is created that represents the reservation itself, and a ProcessPayment EJB is created to process the credit card payment:

```
ReservationHomeLocal resHome = (ReservationHomeLocal)
    jndiContext.lookup("java:comp/env/ejb/ReservationHomeLocal");
ReservationLocal reservation =
    resHome.create(customer, cruise, cabin, price, new Date( ));

Object ref = jndiContext.lookup("java:comp/env/ejb/ProcessPaymentHomeRemote");
ProcessPaymentHomeRemote ppHome = (ProcessPaymentHomeRemote)
    PortableRemoteObject.narrow (ref, ProcessPaymentHomeRemote.class);
ProcessPaymentRemote process = ppHome.create( );
process.byCredit(customer, card, price);
TicketDO ticket = new TicketDO(customer,cruise,cabin,price);
deliverTicket(reservationMsg, ticket);
```

Like a session bean, the MDB can access any other entity or session bean and use that bean to complete a task. An MDB can manage a process and interact with other beans as well as resources. For example, it is commonplace for an MDB to use JDBC to access a database based on the contents of the message it is processing.

Sending messages from a message-driven bean

An MDB can also send messages using JMS. The deliverTicket( ) method sends the ticket information to a destination defined by the sending JMS client:

```
public void deliverTicket(MapMessage reservationMsg, TicketDO ticket)
    throws NamingException, JMSException{

    Queue queue = (Queue)reservationMsg.getJMSReplyTo( );
    QueueConnectionFactory factory = (QueueConnectionFactory)
        jndiContext.lookup("java:comp/env/jms/QueueFactory");
```

```
        QueueConnection connect = factory.createQueueConnection( );
        QueueSession session = connect.createQueueSession(true,0);
        QueueSender sender = session.createSender(queue);
        ObjectMessage message = session.createObjectMessage( );
        message.setObject(ticket);
        sender.send(message);

        connect.close( );
    }
```

Every message type has two parts: a message header and a message body (a.k.a. the *payload*). The message header contains routing information and may also have properties for message filtering and other attributes. One of these attributes may be `JMSReplyTo`. The message's sender may set the `JMSReplyTo` attribute to any destination accessible to its JMS provider.* In the case of the reservation message, the sender set the `JMSReplyTo` attribute to the queue to which the resulting ticket should be sent. Another application can access this queue to read tickets and distribute them to customers or store the information in the sender's database.

You can also use the `JMSReplyTo` address to report business errors. For example, if the Cabin is already reserved, the ReservationProcessor EJB might send an error message to the `JMSReplyTo` queue explaining that the reservation could not be processed. Including this type of error handling is left as an exercise for the reader.

XML Deployment Descriptor

MDBs are described in EJB deployment descriptors the same as entity and session beans. They can be deployed alone, but it's more often deployed with the other enterprise beans that it references. For example, the ReservationProcessor EJB uses the local interfaces of the Customer, Cruise, and Cabin beans, so all four beans would have to be deployed in the same JAR.

EJB 2.1: Deployment descriptor for MDBs

The way EJB 2.1 defines the properties of message processing for MDB is significantly different than in EJB 2.0. EJB 2.0 defined a few JMS-specific elements, which have been abandoned in EJB 2.1 so that the MDB deployment descriptor can represent Connector-based MDBs as well as JMS-based MDBs. Since Connector-based MDBs don't necessarily use JMS as the message service, the `<activation-config>` element was introduced to describe the bean's messaging properties. The `<activation-config>` elements are shown in bold in the following listing.

* In EJB 2.0, if the destination identified by the `JMSReplyTo` attribute is of type `Queue`, the point-to-point (queue-based) messaging model must be used. If the destination type identified by the `JMSReplyTo` attribute is `Topic`, the publish-and-subscribe (topic-based) messaging model must be used. In EJB 2.1, you can use the Unified API for both publish-and-subscribe and point-to-point messaging.

```
<enterprise-beans>
    ...
    <message-driven>
        <ejb-name>ReservationProcessorEJB</ejb-name>
        <ejb-class>
            com.titan.reservationprocessor.ReservationProcessorBean
        </ejb-class>
        <messaging-type>javax.jms.MessageListener</messaging-type>
        <transaction-type>Container</transaction-type>
        <message-destination-type>
            javax.jms.Queue
        </message-destination-type>
        <activation-config>
           <activation-property>
               <activation-config-property-name>destinationType
               </activation-config-property-name>
               <activation-config-property-value>javax.jms.Queue
               </activation-config-property-value>
           <activation-property>
           <activation-property>
               <activation-config-property-name>messageSelector
               </activation-config-property-name>
               <activation-config-property-value>MessageFormat = 'Version 3.4'
               </activation-config-property-value>
           <activation-property>
           <activation-property>
               <activation-config-property-name>acknowledgeMode
               </activation-config-property-name>
               <activation-config-property-value>Auto-acknowledge
               </activation-config-property-value>
           <activation-property>
        </activation-config>
        <ejb-ref>
            <ejb-ref-name>ejb/ProcessPaymentHomeRemote</ejb-ref-name>
            <ejb-ref-type>Session</ejb-ref-type>
            <home>com.titan.processpayment.ProcessPaymentHomeRemote</home>
            <remote>com.titan.processpayment.ProcessPaymentRemote</remote>
        </ejb-ref>
        <ejb-ref>
            <ejb-ref-name>ejb/CustomerHomeRemote</ejb-ref-name>
            <ejb-ref-type>Entity</ejb-ref-type>
            <home>com.titan.customer.CustomerHomeRemote</home>
            <remote>com.titan.customer.CustomerRemote</remote>
        </ejb-ref>
        <ejb-local-ref>
            <ejb-ref-name>ejb/CruiseHomeLocal</ejb-ref-name>
            <ejb-ref-type>Entity</ejb-ref-type>
            <local-home>com.titan.cruise.CruiseHomeLocal</local-home>
            <local>com.titan.cruise.CruiseLocal</local>
        </ejb-local-ref>
        <ejb-local-ref>
            <ejb-ref-name>ejb/CabinHomeLocal</ejb-ref-name>
            <ejb-ref-type>Entity</ejb-ref-type>
            <local-home>com.titan.cabin.CabinHomeLocal</local-home>
```

```
            <local>com.titan.cabin.CabinLocal</local>
        </ejb-local-ref>
        <ejb-local-ref>
            <ejb-ref-name>ejb/ReservationHomeLocal</ejb-ref-name>
            <ejb-ref-type>Entity</ejb-ref-type>
            <local-home>com.titan.reservation.ReservationHomeLocal</local-home>
            <local>com.titan.reservation.ReservationLocal</local>
        </ejb-local-ref>
        <security-identity>
            <run-as>
                <role-name>everyone</role-name>
            </run-as>
        </security-identity>
        <resource-ref>
            <res-ref-name>jms/QueueFactory</res-ref-name>
            <res-type>javax.jms.QueueConnectionFactory</res-type>
            <res-auth>Container</res-auth>
        </resource-ref>
    </message-driven>
    ...
</enterprise-beans>
```

The property names and values used in the `<activation-config>` to describe the messaging service vary depending on the type of message service used, but EJB 2.1 defines a set of fixed properties for JMS-based message-driven beans. These properties are `acknowledgeMode`, `messageSelector`, `destinationType`, and `subscriptionDurablity`. These properties are also used by EJB 2.0 deployment descriptors, so we'll discuss them in the next section.

In addition to the `<activation-config>` element, EJB 2.1 introduces the `<messaging-type>` and `<message-destination-type>` elements. An MDB is declared in a `<message-driven>` element within the `<enterprise-beans>` element, alongside `<session>` and `<entity>` beans. Similar to `<session>` bean types, it defines an `<ejb-name>`, `<ejb-class>`, and `<transaction-type>`, but does not define component interfaces (local or remote). MDBs do not have remote or local interfaces, so these definitions aren't needed.

EJB 2.0: Deployment descriptor for MDBs

Here is the deployment descriptor for MDBs in EJB 2.0:

```
<enterprise-beans>
    ...
    <message-driven>
        <ejb-name>ReservationProcessorEJB</ejb-name>
        <ejb-class>
            com.titan.reservationprocessor.ReservationProcessorBean
        </ejb-class>
        <transaction-type>Container</transaction-type>
        <message-selector>MessageFormat = 'Version 3.4'</message-selector>
        <acknowledge-mode>Auto-acknowledge</acknowledge-mode>
```

```
        <message-driven-destination>
            <destination-type>javax.jms.Queue</destination-type>
        </message-driven-destination>
        <ejb-ref>
            <ejb-ref-name>ejb/ProcessPaymentHomeRemote</ejb-ref-name>
            <ejb-ref-type>Session</ejb-ref-type>
            <home>com.titan.processpayment.ProcessPaymentHomeRemote</home>
            <remote>com.titan.processpayment.ProcessPaymentRemote</remote>
        </ejb-ref>
        <ejb-ref>
            <ejb-ref-name>ejb/CustomerHomeRemote</ejb-ref-name>
            <ejb-ref-type>Entity</ejb-ref-type>
            <home>com.titan.customer.CustomerHomeRemote</home>
            <remote>com.titan.customer.CustomerRemote</remote>
        </ejb-ref>
        <ejb-local-ref>
            <ejb-ref-name>ejb/CruiseHomeLocal</ejb-ref-name>
            <ejb-ref-type>Entity</ejb-ref-type>
            <local-home>com.titan.cruise.CruiseHomeLocal</local-home>
            <local>com.titan.cruise.CruiseLocal</local>
        </ejb-local-ref>
        <ejb-local-ref>
            <ejb-ref-name>ejb/CabinHomeLocal</ejb-ref-name>
            <ejb-ref-type>Entity</ejb-ref-type>
            <local-home>com.titan.cabin.CabinHomeLocal</local-home>
            <local>com.titan.cabin.CabinLocal</local>
        </ejb-local-ref>
        <ejb-local-ref>
            <ejb-ref-name>ejb/ReservationHomeLocal</ejb-ref-name>
            <ejb-ref-type>Entity</ejb-ref-type>
            <local-home>com.titan.reservation.ReservationHomeLocal</local-home>
            <local>com.titan.reservation.ReservationLocal</local>
        </ejb-local-ref>
        <security-identity>
            <run-as>
                <role-name>everyone</role-name>
            </run-as>
        </security-identity>
        <resource-ref>
            <res-ref-name>jms/QueueFactory</res-ref-name>
            <res-type>javax.jms.QueueConnectionFactory</res-type>
            <res-auth>Container</res-auth>
        </resource-ref>
    </message-driven>
    ...
</enterprise-beans>
```

An MDB is declared in a <message-driven> element within the <enterprise-beans> element, alongside <session> and <entity> beans. Like session beans, an MDB defines an <ejb-name>, <ejb-class>, and <transaction-type>; unlike other kinds of beans, an MDB never defines local or remote component interfaces. MDBs do not have remote or local interfaces, so these definitions aren't needed.

Message selector

An MDB can declare a *message selector*. Message selectors allow an MDB to be more selective about the messages it receives from a particular topic or queue. Message selectors use Message properties as criteria in conditional expressions.* These conditional expressions use Boolean logic to declare which messages should be delivered. In EJB 2.1, a message selector is declared using standard property name, messageSelector, in an activation configuration element:

```
<activation-property>
   <activation-config-property-name>messageSelector
   </activation-config-property-name>
   <activation-config-property-value>MessageFormat = 'Version 3.4'
   </activation-config-property-value>
<activation-property>
```

In EJB 2.0, a message selector is declared using the <message-selector> element:

```
<message-selector>MessageFormat = 'Version 3.4'</message-selector>
```

Message selectors are based on message properties. Message properties are additional headers that can be assigned to a message; they allow vendors and developers to attach information to a message that isn't part of the message's body. The Message interface provides several methods for reading and writing properties. Properties can have a String value or one of several primitive values (boolean, byte, short, int, long, float, double). The naming of properties, together with their values and conversion rules, is strictly defined by JMS.

The ReservationProcessor EJB uses a message selector filter to select messages of a specific format. In this case the format is "Version 3.4"; this is a string Titan uses to identify messages of type MapMessage that contain the name values CustomerID, CruiseID, CabinID, CreditCard, and Price. In other words, adding a MessageFormat to each reservation message allows us to write MDBs that are designed to process different kinds of reservation messages. If a new business partner needs to use a different type of Message object, Titan would use a new message version and an MDB to process it.

Here's how a JMS producer would go about setting a MessageFormat property on a Message:

```
Message message = session.createMapMessage( );
message.setStringPropery("MessageFormat","Version 3.4");

// set the reservation named values

sender.send(message);
```

* Message selectors are also based on message headers, which are outside the scope of this chapter.

The message selectors are based on a subset of the SQL-92 conditional expression syntax that is used in the WHERE clauses of SQL statements. They can become fairly complex, including the use of literal values, Boolean expressions, unary operators, and so on.

Acknowledge mode

A JMS *acknowledgment* means that the JMS client notifies the JMS provider (message router) when a message is received. In EJB, it's the MDB container's responsibility to send an acknowledgment when it receives a message. Acknowledging a message tells the JMS provider that an MDB container has received and processed the message. Without an acknowledgment, the JMS provider does not know whether the MDB container has received the message, and unwanted redeliveries can cause problems. For example, once we have processed a reservation message using the ReservationProcessor EJB, we don't want to receive the same message again.

In EJB 2.1, the acknowledgment mode is set using the standard `acknowledgeMode` activation configuration property, as shown in the following XML snippet:

```
<activation-property>
    <activation-config-property-name>acknowledgeMode
    </activation-config-property-name>
    <activation-config-property-value>Auto-acknowledge
    </activation-config-property-value>
<activation-property>
```

In EJB 2.0, the acknowledgment mode is set using a special `<acknowledge-mode>` element, as shown in the following XML snippet:

```
<acknowledge-mode>Auto-acknowledge</acknowledge-mode>
```

Two values can be specified for acknowledgment mode: `Auto-acknowledge` and `Dups-ok-acknowledge`. `Auto-acknowledge` tells the container that it should send an acknowledgment to the JMS provider soon after the message is given to an MDB instance to process. `Dups-ok-acknowledge` tells the container that it doesn't have to send the acknowledgment immediately; any time after the message is given to the MDB instance will be fine. With `Dups-ok-acknowledge`, it's possible for the MDB container to delay acknowledgment so long that the JMS provider assumes that the message was not received and sends a "duplicate" message. Obviously, with `Dups-ok-acknowledge`, your MDBs must be able to handle duplicate messages correctly.

`Auto-acknowledge` avoids duplicate messages because the acknowledgment is sent immediately. Therefore, the JMS provider won't send a duplicate. Most MDBs use `Auto-acknowledge` to avoid processing the same message twice. `Dups-ok-acknowledge` exists because it can allow a JMS provider to optimize its use of the network. In practice, though, the overhead of an acknowledgment is so small, and the frequency of communication between the MDB container and JMS provider is so high, that `Dups-ok-acknowledge` doesn't have a big impact on performance.

Having said all of this, the acknowledgement mode is ignored most of the time—in fact, it is ignored unless the MDB executes with bean-managed transactions, or with the container-managed transaction attribute `NotSupported` (see Chapter 15). In all other cases, transactions are managed by the container, and acknowledgment takes place within the context of the transaction. If the transaction succeeds, the message is acknowledged. If the transaction fails, the message is not acknowledged. When using container-managed transactions with a `Required` transaction attribute, the acknowledgment mode is usually not specified; however, it is included in the deployment descriptor for the sake of discussion.

EJB 2.1: <messaging-type>

The `<messaging-type>` element declares the messaging interfaces used by the MDB:

```
<messaging-type>javax.jms.MessageListener</messaging-type>
```

For JMS-based MDBs, the messaging interface is always going to be `javax.jms.MessageListener`, but for other Connector-based MDBs it might be something completely different. If the `<messaging-type>` element is omitted, the type is assumed to be `javax.jms.MessageListener`.

EJB 2.1: <message-destination-type>

The `<message-destination-type>` element indicates the type of destination from which the MDB receives messages. The allowed values for JMS-based MDBs are `javax.jms.Queue` and `javax.jms.Topic`. A Connector-based MDB might use some other type. The value must always be a fully qualified class name.

In the ReservationProcessor EJB, this value is set to `javax.jms.Queue`, indicating that the MDB is getting its messages via the p2p messaging model from a queue:

```
<message-destination-type>
    javax.jms.Queue
</message-destination-type>
```

When the MDB is deployed, the deployer maps the MDB so that it listens to a real queue on the network.

You may have noticed that the `<message-destination-type>` and the `destinationType` configuration property specify the same thing. This seems redundant, and it is for JMS-based MDBs—but for Connector-based MDBs, it is not. That's because Connector-based MDBs have completely different activation configuration properties than a JMS-based MDB. It's important that the `<message-destination-type>` be specified for both JMS-based and Connector-based MDBs.

EJB 2.0: <message-driven-destination>

The `<message-driven-destination>` element indicates the type of destination from which the MDB receives messages. The allowed values for this element are `javax.jms.Queue` and `javax.jms.Topic`. In the ReservationProcessor EJB, this value is set to javax.jms.Queue, indicating that the MDB is getting its messages via the point-to-point messaging model from a queue:

```
<message-driven-destination>
    <destination-type>javax.jms.Queue</destination-type>
</message-driven-destination>
```

When the MDB is deployed, the deployer maps the MDB so that it listens to a real queue on the network.

Subscription durability

In EJB 2.1 and EJB 2.0, when a JMS-based MDB uses a javax.jms.Topic, the deployment descriptor must declare whether the subscription is Durable or NonDurable. A Durable subscription outlasts an MDB container's connection to the JMS provider, so if the EJB server suffers a partial failure, shuts down, or otherwise disconnects from the JMS provider, the messages that it would have received are not lost. The provider stores any messages that are delivered while the container is disconnected; the messages are delivered to the container (and from there, to the MDB) when the container reconnects. This behavior is commonly referred to as *store-and-forward messaging*. Durable MDBs are tolerant of disconnections, whether intentional or the result of a partial failure.

If the subscription is NonDurable, any messages the bean would have received while it was disconnected are lost. Developers use NonDurable subscriptions when it is not critical for all messages to be processed. Using a NonDurable subscription improves the performance of the JMS provider but significantly reduces the reliability of the MDBs.

In EJB 2.1, durability is declared using the standard subscriptionDurability activation configuration property:

```
<activation-property>
<activation-config-property-name>subscriptionDurability
</activation-config-property-name>
<activation-config-property-value>Durable
</activation-config-property-value>
<activation-property>
```

In EJB 2.0, durability is declared by the <subscription-durability> element within the <message-driven-destination> element:

```
<message-driven-destination>
    <destination-type>javax.jms.Topic</destination-type>
    <subscription-durability>Durable</subscription-durability>
</message-driven-destination>
```

When the destination type is javax.jms.Queue, as is the case in the ReservationProcessor EJB, durability is not a factor because of the nature of queue-based messaging systems. With a queue, messages may be consumed only once and remain in the queue until they are distributed to one of the queue's listeners.

The rest of the elements in both the EJB 2.1 and EJB 2.0 deployment descriptors should already be familiar. The <ejb-ref> element provides JNDI ENC bindings for a remote EJB home object, while the <ejb-local-ref> elements provide JNDI ENC bindings for local EJB home objects. Note that the <resource-ref> element that defined the JMS QueueConnectionFactory used by the ReservationProcessor EJB to send ticket messages is not accompanied by a <resource-env-ref> element. The queue to which the tickets are sent is obtained from the JMSReplyTo header of the MapMessage itself, and not from the JNDI ENC.

The ReservationProcessor Clients

In order to test the ReservationProcessor EJB, we need to develop two new client applications: one to send reservation messages and the other to consume ticket messages produced by the ReservationProcessor EJB.

The reservation message producer

The JmsClient_ReservationProducer sends 100 reservation requests very quickly. The speed with which it sends these messages forces many containers to use multiple MDB instances to process them. The code for JmsClient_ReservationProducer looks like this:

```
import javax.jms.Message;
import javax.jms.MapMessage;
import javax.jms.QueueConnectionFactory;
import javax.jms.QueueConnection;
import javax.jms.QueueSession;
import javax.jms.Session;
import javax.jms.Queue;
import javax.jms.QueueSender;
import javax.jms.JMSException;
import javax.naming.InitalContext;
import java.util.Date;

import com.titan.processpayment.CreditCardDO;

public class JmsClient_ReservationProducer {

    public static void main(String [] args) throws Exception {

        InitialContext jndiContext = getInitialContext( );

        QueueConnectionFactory factory = (QueueConnectionFactory)
            jndiContext.lookup("QueueFactoryNameGoesHere");

        Queue reservationQueue = (Queue)
            jndiContext.lookup("QueueNameGoesHere");

        QueueConnection connect = factory.createQueueConnection( );
```

```
            QueueSession session =
                connect.createQueueSession(false,Session.AUTO_ACKNOWLEDGE);

            QueueSender sender = session.createSender(reservationQueue);

            Integer cruiseID = new Integer(1);

            for(int i = 0; i < 100; i++){
                MapMessage message = session.createMapMessage( );
                message.setStringProperty("MessageFormat","Version 3.4");

                message.setInt("CruiseID",1);
                message.setInt("CustomerID",i%10);
                message.setInt("CabinID",i);
                message.setDouble("Price", (double)1000+i);

                // the card expires in about 30 days
                Date expirationDate = new Date(System.currentTimeMillis( )+43200000);
                message.setString("CreditCardNum", "923830283029");
                message.setLong("CreditCardExpDate", expirationDate.getTime( ));
                message.setString("CreditCardType", CreditCardDO.MASTER_CARD);

                sender.send(message);
            }
            connect.close( );
        }

        public static InitialContext getInitialContext( )
            throws JMSException {
            // create vendor-specific JNDI context here
        }
    }
```

Note that the `JmsClient_ReservationProducer` sets the `CustomerID`, `CruiseID`, and `CabinID` as primitive `int` values, but the `ReservationProcessorBean` reads these values as `java.lang.Integer` types. This is not a mistake. The `MapMessage` automatically converts any primitive to its proper wrapper if that primitive is read using `MapMessage.getObject( )`. So, for example, a named value that is loaded into a `MapMessage` using `setInt( )` can be read as an `Integer` using `getObject( )`. For example, the following code sets a value as a primitive `int` and then accesses it as a `java.long.Integer` object:

```
MapMessage mapMsg = session.createMapMessage( );

mapMsg.setInt("TheValue",3);

Integer myInteger = (Integer)mapMsg.getObject("TheValue");

if(myInteger.intValue( ) == 3 )
    // this will always be true
```

The ticket message consumer

The `JmsClient_TicketConsumer` is designed to consume all the ticket messages delivered by ReservationProcessor EJB instances to the queue. It consumes the messages and prints out the descriptions:

```
import javax.jms.Message;
import javax.jms.ObjectMessage;
import javax.jms.QueueConnectionFactory;
import javax.jms.QueueConnection;
import javax.jms.QueueSession;
import javax.jms.Session;
import javax.jms.Queue;
import javax.jms.QueueReceiver;
import javax.jms.JMSException;
import javax.naming.InitalContext;

import com.titan.travelagent.TicketDO;

public class JmsClient_TicketConsumer
    implements javax.jms.MessageListener {

    public static void main(String [] args) throws Exception {

        new JmsClient_TicketConsumer( );

        while(true){Thread.sleep(10000);}

    }

    public JmsClient_TicketConsumer( ) throws Exception {

        InitialContext jndiContext = getInitialContext( );

        QueueConnectionFactory factory = (QueueConnectionFactory)
            jndiContext.lookup("QueueFactoryNameGoesHere");
        Queue ticketQueue = (Queue)jndiContext.lookup("QueueNameGoesHere");
        QueueConnection connect = factory.createQueueConnection( );
        QueueSession session =
            connect.createQueueSession(false,Session.AUTO_ACKNOWLEDGE);
        QueueReceiver receiver = session.createReceiver(ticketQueue);

        receiver.setMessageListener(this);

        connect.start( );
    }

    public void onMessage(Message message) {
        try {
            ObjectMessage objMsg = (ObjectMessage)message;
            TicketDO ticket = (TicketDO)objMsg.getObject( );
            System.out.println("********************************");
            System.out.println(ticket);
            System.out.println("********************************");
```

```
            } catch(JMSException jmsE) {
                jmsE.printStackTrace( );
            }
        }
        public static InitialContext getInitialContext( ) throws JMSException {
            // create vendor-specific JNDI context here
        }
    }
```

To make the ReservationProcessor EJB work with the two client applications, `JmsClient_ReservationProducer` and `JmsClient_TicketConsumer`, you must configure your EJB container's JMS provider so that it has two queues: one for reservation messages and another for ticket messages.

Exercise 12.2 in the Workbook shows how to deploy these examples in the JBoss EJB container.

The Life Cycle of a Message-Driven Bean

Just as the entity and session beans have well-defined life cycles, so does the MDB bean. The MDB instance's life cycle has two states: *Does Not Exist* and *Method-Ready Pool*. The Method-Ready Pool is similar to the instance pool used for stateless session beans.* Figure 12-4 illustrates the states and transitions that an MDB instance goes through in its lifetime.

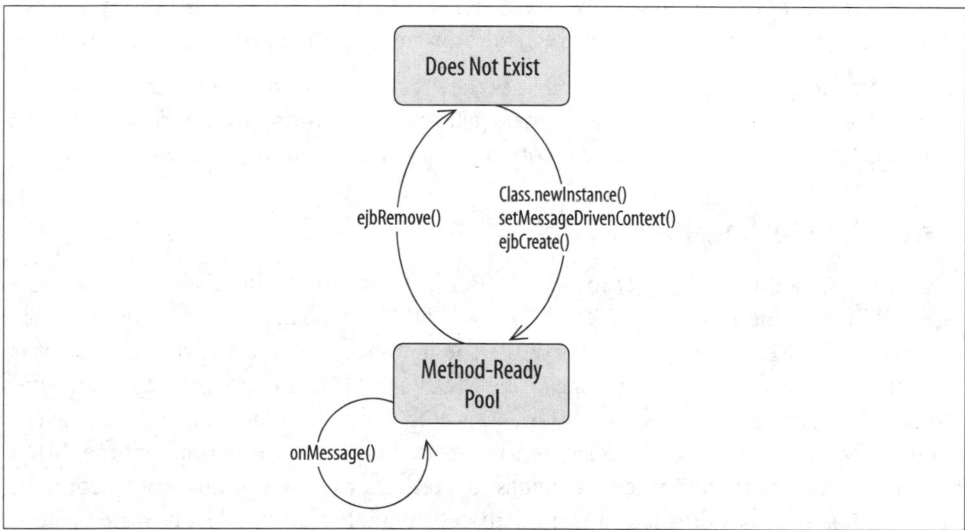

Figure 12-4. MDB life cycle

* Some vendors may *not* pool MDB instances, but may instead create and destroy instances with each new message. This is an implementation-specific decision that should not affect the specified life cycle of the stateless bean instance.

Does Not Exist

When an MDB instance is in the Does Not Exist state, it is not an instance in the memory of the system. In other words, it has not been instantiated yet.

The Method-Ready Pool

MDB instances enter the Method-Ready Pool as the container needs them. When the EJB server is first started, it may create a number of MDB instances and enter them into the Method-Ready Pool. (The actual behavior of the server depends on the implementation.) When the number of MDB instances handling incoming messages is insufficient, more can be created and added to the pool.

Transitioning to the Method-Ready Pool

When an instance transitions from the Does Not Exist state to the Method-Ready Pool, three operations are performed on it. First, the bean instance is instantiated when the container invokes the `Class.newInstance()` method on the MDB class. Second, the `setMessageDrivenContext()` method is invoked by the container providing the MDB instance with a reference to its `EJBContext`. The `MessageDrivenContext` reference may be stored in an instance field of the MDB.

Finally, the no-argument `ejbCreate()` method is invoked by the container on the bean instance. The MDB has only one `ejbCreate()` method, which takes no arguments. The `ejbCreate()` method is invoked only once in the life cycle of the MDB.

MDBs are not subject to activation, so they can maintain open connections to resources for their entire life cycles.* The `ejbRemove()` method should close any open resources before the MDB is evicted from memory at the end of its life cycle.

Life in the Method-Ready Pool

Once an instance is in the Method-Ready Pool, it is ready to handle incoming messages. When a message is delivered to an MDB, it is delegated to any available instance in the Method-Ready Pool. While the instance is executing the request, it is unavailable to process other messages. The MDB can handle many messages simultaneously, delegating the responsibility of handling each message to a different MDB instance. When a message is delegated to an instance by the container, the MDB instance's `MessageDrivenContext` changes to reflect the new transaction context. Once the instance has finished, it is immediately available to handle a new message.

* The duration of an MDB instance's life is assumed to be very long. However, some EJB servers may actually destroy and create instances with every new message, making this strategy less attractive. Consult your vendor's documentation for details on how your EJB server handles stateless instances.

Transitioning Out of the Method-Ready Pool: The Death of an MDB Instance

Bean instances leave the Method-Ready Pool for the Does Not Exist state when the server no longer needs them. This occurs when the server decides to reduce the total size of the Method-Ready Pool by evicting one or more instances from memory. The process begins by invoking the `ejbRemove( )` method on the instance. At this time, the bean instance should perform any necessary cleanup operations, such as closing open resources. The `ejbRemove( )` method is invoked only once in the life cycle of an MDB instance—when it is about to transition to the Does Not Exist state. During the `ejbRemove( )` method, the `MessageDrivenContext` and access to the JNDI ENC are still available to the bean instance. Following the execution of the `ejbRemove( )` method, the bean is dereferenced and eventually garbage collected.

Connector-Based Message-Driven Beans

Although the JMS-based MDB has proven very useful, it has limitations. Perhaps the most glaring limitation is that EJB vendors are only able to support a small number of JMS providers (usually only one). In fact, most EJB 2.0 vendors only support their own JMS provider, no others. Obviously, this limits your choices: if your company or a partner company uses a JMS provider that is not supported by your EJB vendor, you will not be able to process messages from that JMS provider.*

The root of the problem is complex and requires a fairly deep understanding of transaction management. In a nutshell, the delivery of the message by the JMS provider to the MDB, and all the work performed by the MDB (e.g., using JDBC, invoking methods on other beans, etc.), must be part of the same transaction, which is initiated by the EJB container. This requires that the EJB container have prior knowledge that message delivery is imminent, so that it can initiate a transaction before the message is actually delivered. Unfortunately, the JMS API doesn't support this kind of functionality. So an EJB 2.0 container requires special code to coordinate transactions with each JMS provider. Custom integration is expensive, so EJB 2.0 vendors generally choose to integrate with very few JMS providers.

Another limitation of MDBs in EJB 2.0 is that they only support the JMS programming model; no other messaging systems are supported. While JMS is very useful, it's not the only messaging system available. SOAP, email, CORBA Messaging, proprietary messaging systems used in ERP systems (SAP, PeopleSoft, etc.), and legacy messaging systems are examples of other non-JMS messaging systems.

* A workaround is to use a JMS Gateway, which routs messages from one JMS provider to another, but this is a custom solution outside the EJB specification.

EJB 2.1 supports an expanded, more open definition of message-driven beans that allows them to service any kind of messaging system from any vendor. The only requirement is that new types of message-driven beans implement the `javax.ejb.MessageDrivenBean` interface and adhere to the message-driven bean life cycle. While EJB 2.1 vendors can build custom code to support a new messaging system (something other than JMS), they must also support any message-driven bean type that's based on the J2EE Connector Architecture 1.5.

The J2EE Connector Architecture provides a standard Service Provider Interface (SPI) that allows any Enterprise Information System (EIS) to plug into any J2EE container system. Version 1.0 of the connector architecture applies only to request/reply resources in which the J2EE component (EJB or Servlet/JSP) initiates the request. The current version of the connector architecture (1.5), which is required by J2EE 1.4, is much more general, and can work with asynchronous messaging systems. In such systems, the J2EE component waits for messages to arrive, instead of initiating an interaction with an EIS; the EIS initiates the interaction by delivering a message.

J2EE Connectors 1.5 defines a messaging contract specifically tailored to message-driven beans. It defines the contracts between an EJB container and an asynchronous Connector so that message-driven beans automatically process incoming messages from the EIS. MDBs based on an asynchronous Connector implement the standard `javax.ejb.MessageDrivenBean` interface, as well as a specific messaging interface defined by the Connector itself. Instead of implementing the `javax.jms.MessageListener` interface, the MDB implements some other type of interface that is specific to the EIS.

For example, Chapter 3 introduced a hypothetical Email Connector that allows MDBs to process email—similar to how JMS-based MDBs process JMS messages. The Email Connector is purchased from Vendor X and delivered in a JAR file called a RAR (Resource ARchive). The RAR contains all the Connector code and deployment descriptors necessary to plug into the EJB container system. It also defines a messaging interface that the developer uses to create an Email MDB. Here is the hypothetical Email messaging interface that must be implemented by an Email MDB.

```
package com.vendorx.email;

public interface EmailListener {
    public void onMessage(javax.mail.Message message);
}
```

The bean class that implements this interface also implements the `javax.ejb.MessageDrivenBean` interface and is responsible for processing email messages delivered by the Email Connector. The following code shows a MDB that implements the `EmailListener` interface and processes email:

```
package com.titan.email;
public class EmailBean
  implements javax.ejb.MessageDrivenBean, com.vendorx.email.EmailListener {
```

```
        MessageDrivenContext ejbContext;
        public void setMessageDrivenContext(MessgeDrivenContext mdc){
            ejbContext = mdc;
        }
        public void ejbCreate(){}
        public void onMessage(javax.mail.Message message){
            javax.mail.internet.MimeMessage msg =
                (javax.mail.internet.MimeMessage) message;
            Address [] addresses = msg.getFrom();
            //  continue processing Email message
        }
        public void ejbRemove(){}
    }
```

In this example, the container calls `onMessage()` to deliver a JavaMail `Message` object, which represents an email message including MIME attachments. However, the messaging interfaces used by a Connector-based MDB don't have to use `onMessage()`. The method name and method signature can be whatever is appropriate to the EIS; it can even have a return types. For example, a Connector might be developed to handle request/reply style messaging for SOAP. This connector might use the `ReqRespListener` defined by the JAXM (Java API for XML Messaging), which is a SOAP messaging API defined by Sun Microsystems that is not a part of the J2EE platform:

```
package javax.xml.messaging;
import javax.xml.soap.SOAPMessage;

public interface ReqRespListener {
    public SOAPMessage onMessage(SOAPMessage message);
}
```

In this interface, `onMessage()` has a return type of `SOAPMessage`. This means the EJB container and Connector are responsible for coordinating the reply message back to the sender (or some destination defined in the deployment descriptor). In addition to supporting different method signatures, the messaging interface may have several methods for processing different kinds of messages using the same MDB.

There's no limit to the new kinds of message-driven beans that EJB 2.1 containers systems can support. The real beauty of all this is that Connector-based MDBs are completely portable across EJB 2.1 vendors—because all vendors must support them. If you use a Connector-based MDB with EJB 2.1 vendor A, and later change to EJB 2.1 vendor B, you can continue to use the same Connector-based MDB with no portability problems.

The activation configuration properties used with non-JMS-based MDBs depend on the type of Connector and its requirements. For example, the `<message-driven>` element of the deployment descriptor for the Email MDB might look something like this:

```
<enterprise-beans>
    ...
    <message-driven>
```

```
        <ejb-name>EmailEJB</ejb-name>
        <ejb-class>
            com.titan.email.EmailBean
        </ejb-class>
        <messaging-type>com.vendorx.email.EmailListener</messaging-type>
        <transaction-type>Bean</transaction-type>
        <activation-config>
           <activation-property>
               <activation-config-property-name>mailServer
               </activation-config-property-name>
               <activation-config-property-value>mail.ispx.com
               </activation-config-property-value>
           </activation-property>
           <activation-property>
               <activation-config-property-name>serverType
               </activation-config-property-name>
               <activation-config-property-value>POP3
               </activation-config-property-value>
           </activation-property>
           <activation-property>
               <activation-config-property-name>messageFilter
               </activation-config-property-name>
               <activation-config-property-value>to='submit@titan.com'
               </activation-config-property-value>
           </activation-property>
        </activation-config>
        <security-identity>
            <run-as>
                <role-name>Admin</role-name>
            </run-as>
        </security-identity>
    </message-driven>
    ...
</enterprise-beans>
```

Unfortunately, as of this writing there are no Connector-based MDBs commercially available, which is why all examples (like the Email EJB) are hypothetical. It's likely that new Connector-based MDBs will start popping up after EJB 2.1 servers have been around for a short while.

EJB 2.1: Message Linking

Message linking is a new feature to EJB 2.1 that allows the messages being sent by any enterprise bean to be routed to a specific message-driven bean in the same deployment. By using message linking, you can orchestrate a flow of messages between components in the same application. For example, in the beginning of this chapter, the TravelAgent EJB from Chapter 11 was re-implemented so that it sent a JMS message with the ticket information to a Topic destination. Here's a different implementation of the TravelAgent EJB's `bookPassage()` method, this time using an `ObjectMessage` type:

```
public TicketDO bookPassage(CreditCardDO card, double price)
    throws IncompleteConversationalState {

    if (customer == null || cruise == null || cabin == null) {
        throw new IncompleteConversationalState( );
    }
    try {
        ReservationHomeLocal resHome = (ReservationHomeLocal)
            jndiContext.lookup("java:comp/env/ejb/ReservationHomeLocal");
        ReservationLocal reservation =
            resHome.create(customer, cruise, cabin, price, new Date( ));
        Object ref = jndiContext.lookup
            ("java:comp/env/ejb/ProcessPaymentHomeRemote");
        ProcessPaymentHomeRemote ppHome = (ProcessPaymentHomeRemote)
            PortableRemoteObject.narrow(ref, ProcessPaymentHomeRemote.class);
        ProcessPaymentRemote process = ppHome.create( );
        process.byCredit(customer, card, price);

        TicketDO ticket = new TicketDO(customer,cruise,cabin,price);


        TopicConnectionFactory factory = (TopicConnectionFactory)
            jndiContext.lookup("java:comp/env/jms/TopicFactory");
        Topic topic = (Topic)
            jndiContext.lookup("java:comp/env/jms/TicketTopic");
        TopicConnection connect = factory.createTopicConnection( );
        TopicSession session = connect.createTopicSession(true,0);
        TopicPublisher publisher = session.createPublisher(topic);

        ObjectMessage objectMsg = session.createObjectMessage( );
        objectMsg.setObject(ticket);
        publisher.publish(objectMsg);
        connect.close( );

        return ticket;
    } catch(Exception e) {
        throw new EJBException(e);
    }
}
```

When we discussed this method earlier in the chapter, we never really mentioned where the ticket message was being sent. It could go to the reservation agent or some other department of Titan Cruises. However, message linking makes sure that the message goes directly to a message-driven bean that we deploy.

For example, we might deploy a message driven bean, the TicketDistributor EJB, that is responsible for distributing ticket information to several different targets such as legacy databases, partner organizations, marketing, etc. Figure 12-5 shows how the TicketDistributor EJB (an MDB) works with the TravelAgent EJB to distribute ticket information to several different targets.

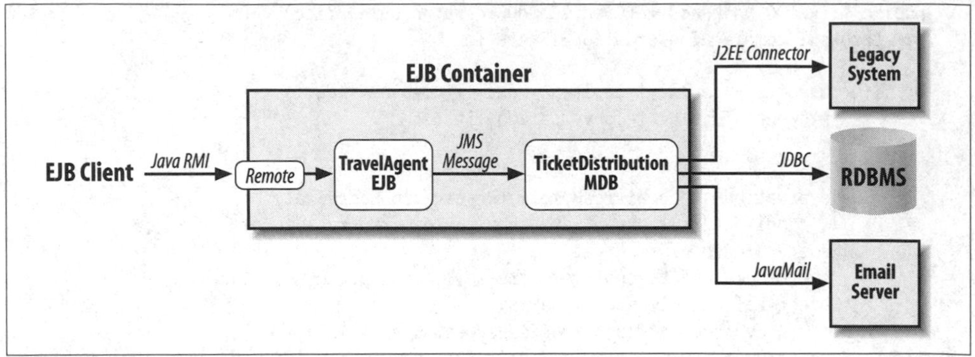

Figure 12-5. Message flow with message linking

The TicketDistributor distributes the ticket information to a variety of disparate targets, including a separate relational database using JDBC, a legacy system (e.g., IMS, CICS, etc.) using a J2EE Connector, and email using JavaMail. The TravelAgent EJB could have handled this type of distribution directly, but defining a separate MDB to do distribution provides more flexibility and better performance.

The TicketDistributor MDB is more flexible because the routing for the message can be changed without modifying the TravelAgent EJB. The TravelAgent EJB always sends messages to the same JMS topic; it's the responsibility of the TicketDistributor to distribute the ticket information to other sources. The TicketDistributor also improves performance, because the TicketAgent doesn't have to wait on the various targets (a separate database, legacy system, and email) to accept and process the message before finishing the reservation. The TicketAgent just sends the ticket information and forgets about it. It's the responsibility of the TicketDistribution MDB to distribute the ticket information to the appropriate parities. In addition, the TravelAgent EJB doesn't have to coordinate a distributed transaction across different resources, which can create significant bottlenecks and affect throughput.

In order to link the outgoing messages sent by the TravelAgent EJB with the incoming messages consumed and processed by the TicketDistribution MDB, we need to define `<message-destination-link>` elements in the deployment descriptor. The `<message-destination-link>` element is defined by the `<message-destination-ref>` element of the TravelAgent EJB. The TicketDistributor EJB also declares the `<message-destination-link>` element. Both elements reference the same logical destination declared in the assembly descriptor:

```
<ejb-jar ...>

  <enterprise-beans>
    ...
    <session>
        <ejb-name>TravelAgentBean</ejb-name>
        ...
        <resource-ref>
```

```
            <res-ref-name>jms/TopicFactory</res-ref-name>
            <res-type>javax.jms.TopicConnectionFactory</res-type>
            <res-auth>Container</res-auth>
        </resource-ref>
        <message-destination-ref>
            <message-destination-ref-name>
                   jms/TicketTopic
            </message-destination-ref-name>
            <message-destination-type>javax.jms.Topic</message-destination-type>
            <message-destination-usage>Produces</message-destination-usage>
            <message-destination-link>
                 Distributor
            </message-destination-link>
        </message-destination-ref>
        ...
    </session>
    <message-driven>
        <ejb-name>TicketDistributorEJB</ejb-name>
        <ejb-class>
            com.titan.distributor.TicketDistributorBean
        </ejb-class>
        <messaging-type>javax.jms.MessageListener</messaging-type>
        <transaction-type>Bean</transaction-type>
        <message-destination-type>
            javax.jms.Topic
        </message-destination-type>
        <message-destination-link>
            Distributor
        </message-destination-link>
        ...
    </message-driven>
    ...
  </enterprise-beans>
  <assembly-descriptor>
    ...
    <message-destination>
       <message-destination-name>Distributor</message-destination-name>
    </message-destination>
    ...
  </assembly-descriptor>
</ejb-jar>
```

As you know, a `<message-destination-ref>` element declares the destination to which an enterprise beans sends or receives messages. When the `<message-destination-ref>` includes a `<message-destination-link>` element, it means that message senders and receivers will be sharing a logical destination described in the assembly-descriptor. In the example above, the TravelAgent EJB's `<message-destination-ref>` declares a `<message-destination-link>`, which points to the `<message-destination>` element in the `<assembly-descriptor>` that has the name `Distributor`. The `<message-destination-link>` defined by the TicketDistributor MDB points to the same `<message-destination>` element. This means the messages sent by the TravelAgent EJB to the `Distributor` message destination will go to the TicketDistributor MDB.

Message-driven beans always consume messages from the destination defined by the <message-destination-link> element defined directly under the <message-bean> element. However, they can also produce messages that are sent to a logical message destination if they use the message API described by their own <message-destination-ref> element. The following listing shows that the TicketDistributor consumes messages from the Distributor destination, but also uses the JMS to send messages to a completely different destination, called Partner:

```
<ejb-jar ...>

  <enterprise-beans>
      ...
       <message-driven>
      <ejb-name>TicketDistributorEJB</ejb-name>
      <ejb-class>
          com.titan.distributor.TicketDistributorBean
      </ejb-class>
      <messaging-type>javax.jms.MessageListener</messaging-type>
      <transaction-type>Bean</transaction-type>
      <message-destination-type>
        javax.jms.Topic
      </message-destination-type>
      <message-destination-link>
         Distributor
      </message-destination-link>
         ...
      <message-destination-ref>
          <message-destination-ref-name>
                 jms/PartnerCompany
          </message-destination-ref-name>
          <message-destination-type>javax.jms.Topic</message-destination-type>
          <message-destination-usage>Produces</message-destination-usage>
          <message-destination-link>
              Partner
           </message-destination-link>
        </message-destination-ref>
        ...
    </message-driven>
     ...
  </enterprise-beans>
  <assembly-descriptor>
    ...
    <message-destination>
       <message-destination-name>Distributor</message-destination-name>
    </message-destination>
    <message-destination>
       <message-destination-name>Partner</message-destination-name>
    </message-destination>
    ...
  </assembly-descriptor>
</ejb-jar>
```

At deployment time, each of the `<message-destination>` elements are mapped to a real messaging destination in the target environment. In most cases, this will be a JMS topic or queue, but it could be a destination of some other type of messaging system.

The J2EE application server doesn't have to route the messages through an actual destination. It can asynchronously send them from the sender to the receiver; in this case, from the TravelAgent EJB to the TicketDistributor MDB. However, if the application server handles message delivery itself, rather than going through a messaging provider, it must follow the semantics of the messaging system. For JMS, transactions, persistence, durability, security, and acknowledgments should be handled correctly whether the message is sent directly from one component to another, or via a JMS provider.

Although any enterprise bean can consume (receive) messages from a logical destination as well as produce (send) messages, only MDBs should consume messages. The reasons for this limitation were discussed earlier in this chapter (see "Entity and Session Beans Should Not Receive Messages").

CHAPTER 13

Timer Service

Business systems frequently use scheduling systems to run programs at specified times. Scheduling systems typically run applications that generate reports, reformat data, or do audit work at night. In other cases, scheduling systems provide callback APIs that can alert subsystems of events such as due dates, deadlines, etc. Scheduling systems often run *batch jobs* (a.k.a. *scheduled jobs*), which perform routine work automatically at a prescribed time. Users in the Unix world frequently run scheduled jobs using *cron*, a simple but useful scheduling system that runs programs listed in a configuration file. Other job-scheduling systems include the OMG's COS Timer Event Service, which is a CORBA API for timed events, as well as commercial products.

Regardless of the software, scheduling systems are used in many different scenarios:

- In a credit card processing system, credit card charges are processed in batches so that all the charges made for an entire day are settled together instead of separately. This work is scheduled to be done in the evening to reduce the impact of processing on the system.
- In a hospital or clinical system, Electronic Data Interface (EDI) software is used to send medical claims to various HMOs. Each HMO has its own processing requirements, but they are all routine, so jobs are scheduled to gather claim data, put it in the proper format, and transfer it to the HMO.
- In just about any company, managers need specific reports run on a regular basis. A scheduling system can be configured to run those reports automatically and deliver them via email to managers.

Scheduling systems are also common in *workflow applications*, which are systems that manage document processing that typically spans days or months, and involves many systems and lots of human intervention. In workflow applications, scheduling is employed for auditing tasks that periodically take inventory of the state of an application, invoice, sales order, etc., in order to ensure everything is proceeding as scheduled. The scheduling system maintains timers and delivers events to alert applications and components when a specified date and time is reached, or when some period has expired. Here are some examples of workflow scheduling:

- In a mortgage system, a lot of tasks have to be completed (i.e., appraisal, rate lock-in, closing appointment, etc.) before the mortgage can be closed. Timers can be set on mortgage applications to perform periodic audits that ensure everything is proceeding on schedule.
- In a healthcare claims processing system, claims must be processed within 90 days according to terms negotiated by in-network physicians and clinics. Each claim could have a timer set to go off seven days before the deadline.
- In a stockbroker system, buy-at-limit orders can be created for a specific number of shares, but only at a specified price or lower. These buy-at-limit orders typically have a time limit. If the stock price falls below the specified price before the time limit, the buy-at-limit order is carried out. If the stock price does not fall below the specified price before the time limit, the timer expires and the buy-at-limit order is canceled.

In the EJB world, there has been a general interest in scheduling systems that can work directly with enterprise beans. However, prior to EJB 2.1, there has been no standard J2EE scheduling system. Enterprise JavaBeans 2.1 introduces a standardized but limited scheduling system called the *Timer Service*.

The Java 2 Platform, Standard Edition includes the class `java.util.Timer`, which allows threads to schedule tasks for future execution in a background thread. This facility is useful for a variety of applications, but it's too limited to be used in enterprise computing. Note, however, that the scheduling semantics of `java.util.Timer` are similar to those of the EJB Timer Service.

The Timer Service is a facility of the EJB container system that provides a timed-event API, which can be used to schedule timers for specified dates, periods, and intervals. A timer is associated with the enterprise bean that set it, and calls that bean's `ejbTimeout()` method when it goes off. The rest of this chapter describes the EJB Timer Service API and its use with entity, stateless session, and message-driven beans, as well as providing some criticism of and suggested improvements for the Timer Service.

Titan's Maintenance Timer

Titan Cruises has a policy of performing regular maintenance on its ships. For example, the engines require extensive and varied maintenance activities throughout the year, as does navigation equipment, communications, sewer and water systems, etc. In fact, there are literally thousands of maintenance functions to be performed on a ship throughout the year. To manage all these items, Titan uses the EJB Timer Service to alert the proper maintenance crews when an item needs to be serviced. In this chapter, we modify the Ship EJB to manage its own maintenance schedule. Titan's Health and Safety department can use business methods on the Ship EJB to schedule and cancel maintenance items, and the Ship EJB will take care of alerting the correct maintenance crew when an item needs to be serviced.

Timer Service API

The Timer Service enables an enterprise bean to be notified when a specific date has arrived, when some period of time has elapsed, or at recurring intervals. To use the Timer Service, an enterprise bean must implement the `javax.ejb.TimedObject` interface, which defines a single callback method, `ejbTimeout( )`:

```
package javax.ejb;

public interface TimedObject {
    public void ejbTimeout(Timer timer) ;
}
```

When the scheduled time is reached or the specified interval has elapsed, the container system invokes the enterprise bean's `ejbTimeout( )` method. The enterprise bean can then perform any processing it needs to respond to the timeout, such as run reports, audit records, modify the states of other beans, etc. For example, the Ship EJB can be modified to implement the `TimedObject` interface, as shown:

```
public abstract class ShipBean
      implements javax.ejb.EntityBean, javax.ejb.TimedObject {
    javax.ejb.EntityContext ejbContext;
    public void setEntityContext(javax.ejb.EntityContext ctxt){
         ejbContext = ctxt;
    }
    public void ejbTimeout(javax.ejb.Timer timer) {
       // business logic for timer goes here
    }
    public Integer ejbCreate(Integer primaryKey,String name,double tonnage) {
        setId(primaryKey);
        setName(name);
        setTonnage(tonnage);
        return null;
    }
    public void ejbPostCreate(Integer primaryKey,String name,double tonnage) {}
    public abstract void setId(Integer id);
    public abstract Integer getId( );
    public abstract void setName(String name);
    public abstract String getName( );
    public abstract void setTonnage(double tonnage);
    public abstract double getTonnage( );
    public void unsetEntityContext( ){}
    public void ejbActivate( ){}
```

```
        public void ejbPassivate( ){}
        public void ejbLoad( ){}
        public void ejbStore( ){}
        public void ejbRemove( ){}
    }
```

An enterprise bean schedules itself for a timed notification using a reference to the `TimerService`, which it obtains from the `EJBContext`. The `TimerService` allows a bean to register itself for notification on a specific date, after some period of time, or at recurring intervals. The following code shows how a bean would register for notification exactly 30 days from now:

```
// Create a Calendar object that represents the time 30 days from now.
Calendar time = Calendar.getInstance( );  // the current time.
time.add(Calendar.DATE, 30); // add 30 days to the current time.
Date date = time.getTime( );

// Create a timer that will go off 30 days from now.
EJBContext ejbContext = // ...: get EJBContext object from somewhere.
TimerService timerService = ejbContext.getTimerService( );
timerService.createTimer( date,  null);
```

This example creates a `Calendar` object that represents the current time, then increments this object by 30 days so that it represents the time 30 days from now. The code obtains a reference to the container's `TimerService` and calls the `TimerService.createTimer( )` method, passing it the `java.util.Date` value of the `Calendar` object, thus creating a timer that will go off after 30 days.

We can add a method, `scheduleMaintenance( )`, to the Ship EJB that allows a client to schedule a maintenance item. When the method is called, the client passes in a description of the maintenance item and the date on which it is to be performed. For example, a client could schedule a maintenance item for the cruise ship Valhalla on April 2, 2004, as shown in the following code snippet:

```
InitialContext jndiCntxt = new InitialContext( );
ShipHomeRemote shipHome =
  (ShipHomeRemote) jndiCntxt.lookup("java:comp/env/ejb/ShipHomeRemote");
ShipRemote ship = shipHome.findByName("Valhalla");
Calendar april2nd = Calendar.getInstance( );
april2nd.set(2004, Calendar.APRIL, 2);
String description = "Stress Test: Test Drive Shafts A & B ...";
ship.scheduleMaintenance( description, april2nd.getTime() );
```

The `ShipBean` implements the `scheduleMaintenance( )` method and takes care of scheduling the event using the Timer Service, as shown below:

```
public abstract class ShipBean
      implements javax.ejb.EntityBean, javax.ejb.TimedObject {
    javax.ejb.EntityContext ejbContext;
    public void setEntityContext(javax.ejb.EntityContext ctxt){
         ejbContext = ctxt;
    }
```

```
    public void scheduleMaintenance(String description, Date dateOfTest){
        TimerService timerService = ejbContext.getTimerService( );
        timerService.createTimer( dateOf, description);
    }
    public void ejbTimeout(javax.ejb.Timer timer) {
       // business logic for timer goes here
    }
    ...
}
```

As you can see, the Ship EJB is responsible for obtaining a reference to the Timer Service and scheduling its own events. When April 2, 2004, rolls around, the Timer Service calls the `ejbTimeout( )` method on the Ship EJB representing the Valhalla. When the `ejbTimeout( )` method is called, the Ship EJB sends a JMS message containing the description of the test to the Health and Safety department at Titan Cruises, alerting them that a stress test is required. Here's how the implementation of `ejbTimeout( )` looks:

```
public abstract class ShipBean
      implements javax.ejb.EntityBean, javax.ejb.TimedObject {
    javax.ejb.EntityContext ejbContext;
    public void setEntityContext(javax.ejb.EntityContext ctxt){
         ejbContext = ctxt;
    }
    public void scheduleMaintenance(String description, Date dateOfTest){
        TimerService timerService = ejbContext.getTimerService( );
        timerService.createTimer( dateOf, description);
    }
    public void ejbTimeout(javax.ejb.Timer timer) {
      try{
        String description = (String)timer.getInfo( );

        InitialContext jndiContext = new InitialContext( );
        TopicConnectionFactory factory = (TopicConnectionFactory)
        jndiContext.lookup("java:comp/env/jms/TopicFactory");

        Topic topic = (Topic)
        jndiContext.lookup("java:comp/env/jms/MaintenanceTopic");

        TopicConnection connect = factory.createTopicConnection( );
        TopicSession session = connect.createTopicSession(true,0);
        TopicPublisher publisher = session.createPublisher(topic);

        TextMessage textMsg = session.createTextMessage( );
         textMsg.setText(description);
        publisher.publish(textMsg);
        connect.close( );
      }catch(Exception e){
        throw new EJBException(e);
      }
    }
        ....
}
```

The TimerService Interface

The TimerService interface provides an enterprise bean with access to the EJB container's Timer Service so that new timers can be created and existing timers can be listed. The TimerService interface is a part of the javax.ejb package in EJB 2.1 and has the following definition:

```
package javax.ejb;
import java.util.Date;
import java.io.Serializable;
public interface TimerService {

   // Create a single-action timer that expires on a specified date.
   public Timer createTimer(Date expiration, Serializable info)
      throws IllegalArgumentException,IllegalStateException,EJBException;
   // Create a single-action timer that expires after a specified duration.
   public Timer createTimer(long duration, Serializable info)
      throws IllegalArgumentException,IllegalStateException,EJBException;
   // Create an interval timer that starts on a specified date.
   public Timer createTimer(
      Date initialExpiration, long intervalDuration, Serializable info)
      throws IllegalArgumentException,IllegalStateException,EJBException;
   // Create an interval timer that starts after a specified durration.
   public Timer createTimer(
      long initialDuration, long intervalDuration, Serializable info)
      throws IllegalArgumentException,IllegalStateException,EJBException;
  //  Get all the active timers associated with this bean
   public java.util.Collection getTimers()
      throws IllegalStateException,EJBException;
}
```

Each of the four TimerService.createTimer() methods establishes a timer with a different type of configuration. There are essentially two types of timers: *single-action* and *interval*. A single-action timer expires once, while an interval timer expires many times, at specified intervals. When a timer expires, the Timer Service calls the bean's ejbTimeout() method.

Here's how each of the four createTimer() methods works. At this point, we are only discussing the expiration and duration parameters and their uses. The Serializable info parameter is discussed later in this chapter.

createTimer(Date expiration, Serializable info)
: Creates a single-action timer that expires once. The timer expires on the date set for the expiration parameter. Here's how to set a timer that expires on July 4, 2004:

```
Calendar july4th = Calendar.getInstance();
july4th.set(2004, Calendar.JULY, 4);
timerService.createTimer(july4th.getTime(), null);
```

`createTimer(long duration, Serializable info)`

Creates a single-action timer that only expires once. The timer expires after `duration` time (measured in milliseconds) has elapsed. Here's how to set a timer that expires in 90 days:

```
long ninetyDays = 1000 * 60 * 60 * 24 * 90; //  90 days
timerService.createTimer(ninetyDays, null);
```

`createTimer(Date initialExpiration, long intervalDuration, Serializable info)`

Creates an interval timer that expires many times. The timer first expires on the date set for the `initialExpiration` parameter. After the first expiration, subsequent expirations occur at intervals equal to the `intervalDuration` parameter (in milliseconds). Here's how to set a timer that expires on July 4, 2004 and continues to expire every three days after that date:

```
Calendar july4th = Calendar.getInstance( );
july4th.set(2004, Calendar.JULY, 4);
long threeDaysInMillis = 1000 * 60 * 60 * 24 * 3; // 3 days
timerService.createTimer(july4th.getTime( ), threeDaysInMillis, null);
```

`createTimer(long initialDuration, long intervalDuration, Serializable info)`

Creates an interval timer that expires many times. The timer first expires after the period given by `initialDuration` has elapsed. After the first expiration, subsequent expirations occur at intervals given by the `intervalDuration` parameter. Both `initialDuration` and `intervalDuration` are in milliseconds. Here's how to set a timer that expires in 10 minutes and continues to expire every hour thereafter:

```
long tenMinutes = 1000 * 60 * 10;  // 10 minutes
long oneHour = 1000 * 60 * 60; // 1 hour
timerService.createTimer(tenMinutes, oneHour, null);
```

When a timer is created, the Timer Service makes it persistent in some type of secondary storage, so it will survive system failures. If the server goes down, the timers are still active when the server comes back up. While the specification isn't clear, it's assumed that any timers that expire while the system is down will go off when it comes back up again. If an interval timer expires many times while the server is down, it may go off multiple times when the system comes up again. Consult your vendors' documentation to learn how they handle expired timers following a system failure.

The `TimerService.getTimers( )` method returns all the timers that have been set for a particular enterprise bean. For example, if this method is called on the EJB representing the cruise ship Valhalla, it returns only the timers that are set for the Valhalla, not timers set for other ships. The `getTimers( )` method returns a `java.util.Collection`, an unordered collection of zero or more `javax.ejb.Timer` objects. Each `Timer` object represents a different timed event that has been scheduled for the bean using the Timer Service.

The `getTimers( )` method is often used to manage existing timers. A bean can look through the `Collection` of `Timer` objects and cancel any timers that are no longer valid or need to be rescheduled. For example, the Ship EJB defines the clearSchedule( ) method, which allows a client to cancel all of the timers on a specific ship. Here's the implementation of clearSchedule( ):

```
public abstract class ShipBean
      implements javax.ejb.EntityBean, javax.ejb.TimedObject {
    javax.ejb.EntityContext ejbContext;
    public void setEntityContext(javax.ejb.EntityContext ctxt){
         ejbContext = ctxt;
    }
    public void clearSchedule( ){
        TimerService timerService = ejbContext.getTimerService( );
        java.util.Iterator timers = timerService.getTimers().iterator( );
        while( timers.hasNext( ) ){
                javax.ejb.Timer timer = (javax.ejb.Timer) timers.next( );
                timer.cancel( );
        }
    }
    public void scheduleMaintenance(String description, Date dateOfTest){
        // code for scheduling timer goes here
    }
    public void ejbTimeout(javax.ejb.Timer timer) {
       // business logic for timer goes here
    }
    ...
}
```

The logic here is simple. After getting a reference to the TimerService, we get an iterator that contains all of the Timers. Then we work through the iterator, cancelling each timer as we go. The Timer objects implement a cancel( ) method, which removes the timed event from the Timer Service so that it never expires.

Exceptions

The TimerService.getTimers( ) method can throw an IllegalStateException or an EJBException. All of the createTimer( ) methods declare these two exceptions, plus a third exception, the IllegalArgumentException. The reasons that the TimerService methods would throw these exceptions are:

java.lang.IllegalArgumentException
: The duration and expiration parameters must have valid values. This exception is thrown if a negative number is used for one of the duration parameters or a null value is used for the expiration parameter, which is of type java.util.Date.

java.lang.IllegalStateException
: This exception is thrown if the enterprise bean attempts to invoke one of the TimerService methods from a method where it's not allowed. Each enterprise bean type (i.e., entity, stateless session, and message-driven) defines its own set of allowed operations. However, in general the TimerService methods can be invoked from anywhere except the EJBContext methods (i.e., setEntityContext( ), setSessionContext( ), and setMessageDrivenContext( )).

`javax.ejb.EJBException`
: This exception is thrown when some type of system-level exception occurs in the Timer Service.

The Timer

A `Timer` is an object that implements the `javax.ejb.Timer` interface. It represents a timed event that has been scheduled for an enterprise bean using the Timer Service. `Timer` objects are returned by the `TimerService.createTimer( )` and `TimerService.getTimers( )` methods, and a `Timer` is the only parameter of the `TimedObject.ejbTimeout( )` method. The `Timer` interface is:

```
package javax.ejb;

public interface Timer {

    // Cause the timer and all its associated expiration
    // notifications to be canceled
    public void cancel( )
         throws IllegalStateException,NoSuchObjectLocalException,EJBException;

    // Get the information associated with the timer at the time of creation.
    public java.io.Serializable getInfo( )
         throws IllegalStateException,NoSuchObjectLocalException,EJBException;

    // Get the point in time at which the next timer
    // expiration is scheduled to occur.
    public java.util.Date getNextTimeout( )
         throws IllegalStateException,NoSuchObjectLocalException,EJBException;

    // Get the number of milliseconds that will elapse
    // before the next scheduled timer expiration
    public long getTimeRemaining( )
         throws IllegalStateException,NoSuchObjectLocalException,EJBException;

    //Get a serializable handle to the timer.
    public TimerHandle getHandle( )
         throws IllegalStateException,NoSuchObjectLocalException,EJBException;
}
```

A `Timer` instance represents exactly one timed event and can be used to cancel the timer, obtain a serializable handle, obtain the application data associated with the timer, and find out when the timer's next scheduled expiration will occur.

Cancelling timers

The previous section used the `Timer.cancel( )` method. It's used to cancel a specific timer: remove the timed event from the Timer Service so that it never expires. It is useful if a particular timer needs to be removed completely or simply rescheduled. To reschedule a timed event, cancel the timer and create a new one. For example, when one of the ship's components fails and is replaced, that component must have its maintenance rescheduled: it doesn't make sense to perform a yearly overhaul on an engine in June if it was replaced in May. The scheduleMaintenance( ) method can be modified so that it can add a new maintenance item or replace an existing one by canceling it and adding the new one.

```
public abstract class ShipBean
    implements javax.ejb.EntityBean, javax.ejb.TimedObject {
  javax.ejb.EntityContext ejbContext;
  public void setEntityContext(javax.ejb.EntityContext ctxt){
       ejbContext = ctxt;
  }
  public void scheduleMaintenance(String description, Date dateOfTest){
      TimerService timerService = ejbContext.getTimerService( );
      java.util.Iterator timers = timerService.getTimers().iterator( );
      while( timers.hasNext() ){
              javax.ejb.Timer timer = (javax.ejb.Timer) timers.next( );
              String timerDesc = (String) timer.getInfo( );
              if( description.equals( timerDesc)){
                   timer.cancel( );
              }
      }
      timerService.createTimer( dateOf, description);
  }
  public void ejbTimeout(javax.ejb.Timer timer) {
     // business logic for timer goes here
  }
  ...
```

The scheduleMaintenance( ) method first obtains a Collection of all timers defined for the Ship. It then compares the description of each timer to the description passed into the method. If there is a match, it means a timer for that maintenance item was already scheduled and should be canceled. After the while loop, the new Timer is added to the Timer Service.

Identifying timers

Of course, comparing descriptions is a fairly unreliable way of identifying timers, since descriptions tend to vary over time. What is really needed is a far more robust information object that can contain both a description and a precise identifier.

All of the TimeService.createTimer( ) methods declare an info object as their last parameter. The info object is application data that is stored with by the Timer Service and delivered to the enterprise bean when its ejbTimeout( ) method is called. The serializable object used as the info parameter can be anything, as long it implements the java.io.Serializable interface and follows the rules of serialization.* The info object can be put to many uses, but one obvious use is to associate the timer with some sort of identifier.

* In the most basic cases, all an object needs to do to be serializable is implement the java.io.Serializable interface and make sure any nonserializable fields (e.g., JDBC connection handle) are marked as transient.

To get the info object from a timer, call the timer's getInfo( ) method. This method returns a serializable object, which you'll have to cast to an appropriate type. So far, we've been using strings as info objects, but there are much more elaborate (and reliable) possibilities. For example, rather than compare maintenance descriptions to find duplicate timers, Titan decided to use unique Maintenance Item Numbers (MINs). MINs and maintenance descriptions can be combined into a new MaintenanceItem object:

```
public class MaintenanceItem implements java.io.Serializable {
    private long maintenanceItemNumber;
    private String description;
    public MaintenanceItem(long min, String desc){
        maintenanceItemNumber = min;
        description = desc;
    }
    public long getMIN( ){
        return maintenanceItemNumber;
    }
    public String getDescription( ){
        return description;
    }
}
```

Using the MaintenanceItem type, we can modify the scheduleMaintenance( ) method to be more precise, as shown below (changes are in bold):

```
public abstract class ShipBean
      implements javax.ejb.EntityBean, javax.ejb.TimedObject {
    javax.ejb.EntityContext ejbContext;
    public void setEntityContext(javax.ejb.EntityContext ctxt){
         ejbContext = ctxt;
    }
    public void scheduleMaintenance(
      MaintenanceItem maintenanceItem, Date dateOfTest){
        TimerService timerService = ejbContext.getTimerService( );
        java.util.Iterator timers = timerService.getTimers().iterator( );
        while( timers.hasNext( ) ){
                javax.ejb.Timer timer = (javax.ejb.Timer) timers.next( );
                MaintenanceItem timerMainItem = (MaintenanceItem) timer.getInfo( );
                if( maintenanceItem.getMIN() == timerMainItem.getMIN( )){
                     timer.cancel( );
                   }
        }
        timerService.createTimer( dateOf, maintenanceItem);
    }
    public void ejbTimeout(javax.ejb.Timer timer) {
       // business logic for timer goes here
    }
    ...
```

The MaintenanceInfo class contains information about the maintenance work that is to be done and is sent to the maintenance system using JMS. When one of the timers expires, the Timer Service calls the ejbTimeout( ) method on the Ship EJB. When the ejbTimeout() method is called, the info object is obtained from the Timer object and used to determine which timer logic should be executed.

Exercise 13.1 in the Workbook shows how to deploy these examples in JBoss.

Retrieving other information from timers

The Timer.getNextTimeout() method simply returns the date—represented by a java.util.Date instance—on which the timer will expire next. If the timer is a single-action timer, the Date returned is the time at which the timer will expire. If, however, the timer is an interval timer, the Date returned is the time remaining until the next expiration. Oddly, there is no way to determine subsequent expirations or the interval at which an interval timer is configured. The best way to handle this is to put that information into your info object.

The Timer.getTimeRemaining() method returns the number of milliseconds before the timer will next expire. Like the getNextTimeout() method, this method only provides information about the next expiration.

The TimerHandle object

The Timer.getHandle() method returns a TimerHandle. The TimerHandle is similar to the javax.ejb.Handle and javax.ejb.HomeHandle discussed in Chapter 5. It's a reference that can be saved to a file or some other resource, then used later to regain access to the Timer. The TimerHandle interface is simple:

```
package javax.ejb;
public interface TimerHandle extends java.io.Serializable {
    public Timer getTimer() throws NoSuchObjectLocalException, EJBException;
}
```

The TimerHandle is only valid as long as the timer has not expired (if it's a single-action timer) or been canceled. If the timer no longer exists, calling the TimerHandle.getTimer() method throws a javax.ejb.NoSuchObjectException.

TimerHandle objects are local, which means they cannot be used outside the container system that generated them. Passing the TimerHandle as an argument to a remote or endpoint interface method is illegal. However, a TimerHandle can be passed between local enterprise beans using their local interface, because local enterprise beans must be co-located in the same container system.

Exceptions

All the methods defined in the Timer interface declare two exceptions:

javax.ejb.NoSuchObjectLocalException
: This exception is thrown if you invoke any method on an expired single-action timer or a canceled timer.

javax.ejb.EJBException
: This exception is thrown when some type of system level exception occurs in the Timer Service.

Transactions

When a bean calls `createTimer()`, the operation is performed in the scope of the current transaction. If the transaction rolls back, the timer is undone: it's not created (or, more precisely, uncreated). For example, if the Ship EJB's `scheduleMaintenance()` method has a transaction attribute of `RequiresNew`, a new transaction will be created when the method is called. If an exception is thrown by the method, the transaction rolls back and the new timer event is not created.

In most cases, the `ejbTimeout()` method on beans should have a transaction attribute of `RequiresNew`. This ensures that the work performed by the `ejbTimeout()` method is in the scope of container-initiated transactions. Transactions are covered in more detail in Chapter 16.

Entity Bean Timers

Entity beans set timers on a specific type of entity bean (e.g., Ship, Customer, Reservation, etc.) with a specific primary key. When a timer goes off, the container uses the primary key associated with the timer to load the entity bean with proper data. Once the entity bean is in the ready state—its data is loaded and it's ready to service requests—the `ejbTimeout()` method is invoked. The container associates the primary key with the timer implicitly.

Using timers with entity beans allows entity beans to manage their own timed events. As we've seen, it makes sense for a Ship to manage its own maintenance schedule. The maintenance schedule is unique for each ship and required in order to keep the ship sailing, so it could be considered intrinsic to the definition of a ship. If, however, the timed event is not a part of the entity's definition, it's best to put the timer into a taskflow bean (i.e., stateless session or message-driven) that represents the scenario, instead of placing the logic in the entity bean. This avoids *entity bloat*, in which an entity bean's definition becomes huge from attempting to manage every possible application of the entity bean. It's the same reason we move taskflow logic out of entity beans and into session beans.

A serious concern with entity beans is the possibility of *timer attack*, which occurs when too many timers expire at the same time. A timer attack is not caused by malicious intent, but rather poor design. For example, if all the Customer beans in Titan system had timers set to expire five days before a cruise (perhaps to send email reminders to customers), it's possible that thousands of timers would expire simultaneously. This scenario could lead to a timer attack. A timer attack causes congestion and competition for resources that can overwhelm the EJB server to the point where it cannot handle other requests. The timer attack can be exacerbated by timer rollbacks, which occur when a timer fails to execute properly. As timers fight for resources and fail, they are re-executed, prolonging the strain on the system. Good design and intelligent containers are the only safeguard against a timer attack. Be aware of the types of timers you are creating and the possibility of many timers executing simultaneously.

The entity bean can access the `TimerService` from the `EntityContext` in any business method or callback method, except the `seEntityContext()` method. The timers associated with an entity bean are canceled automatically when the entity is removed, so there is no need to explicitly cancel timers in the `ejbRemove()` method.

When an entity bean implements the `TimedObject` interface, its life cycle changes to accommodate timed events. When a bean's timer expires, the container transitions a bean instance to the Ready state, calling its `ejbActivate()` and then `ejbLoad()` methods after loading the bean's persistent fields. When the `ejbTimeout()` method returns, the container calls the bean's `ejbStore()` method, stores changes to the database, calls the bean's `ejbPassivate()` method, and returns the bean to the Pooled state. Figure 13-1 shows the life cycle of the entity bean that implements the `TimedObject` interface.

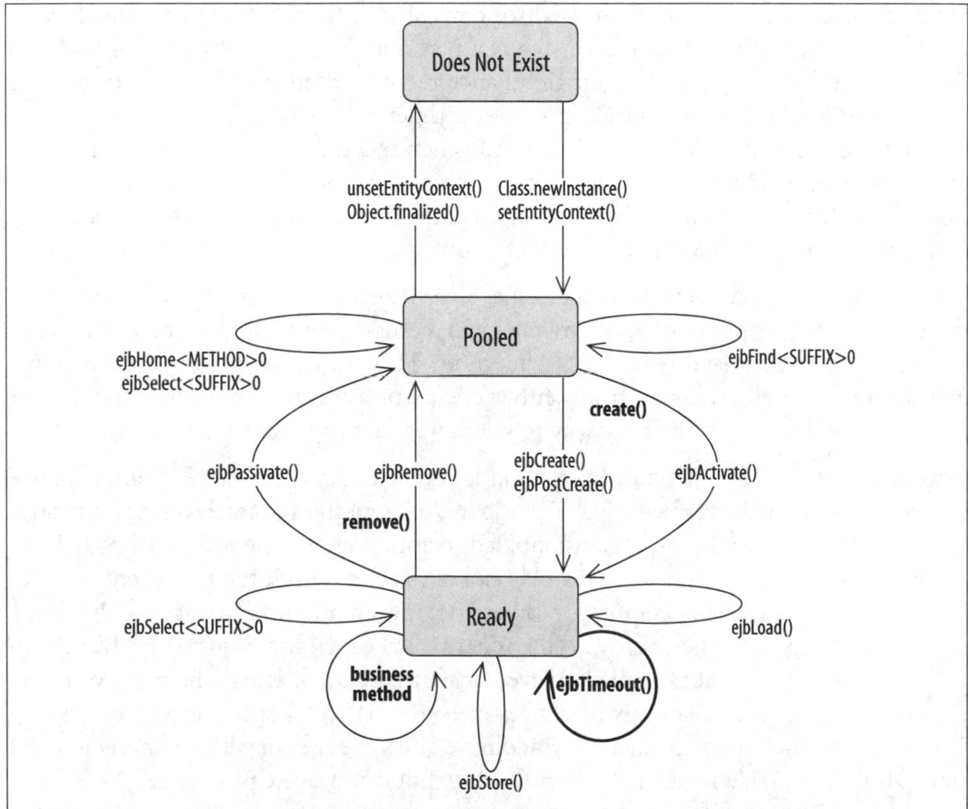

Figure 13-1. Entity bean life cycle with TimedObject

Stateless Session Bean Timers

Stateless session bean timers can be used for *auditing* or *batch processing*. As an auditing agent, a stateless session timer can monitor the state of the system to ensure that tasks are being completed and that data is consistent. This type of work spans entities and possibly data sources. Such EJBs can also perform batch processing work such as database clean up, transfer of records, etc. Stateless session bean timers can also be deployed as agents that perform some type of intelligent work on behalf of the organization they serve. An agent can be thought of as an extension of an audit: it monitors the system but it also fixes problems automatically.

While entity timers are associated with a specific entity bean and primary key, stateless session bean timers are associated only with a specific type of session bean. When a timer for a stateless session bean goes off, the container selects an instance of that stateless bean type from the instance pool and calls its `ejbTimeout( )` method. This makes sense, because all stateless session beans in the instance pool are logically equivalent. Any instance can serve any client, including the container itself.

Stateless session timers are often used to manage taskflow or when the timed event applies to a collection of entities instead of just one. For example, stateless session timers might be used to audit all maintenance records to ensure that they meet state and federal guidelines: at specific intervals, a timer notifies the bean to look up the maintenance records from all the Ships and generate a report. In contrast, a timer for an entity bean helps that entity manage its own state. A stateless session timer can also be used to do something like send notifications to all the passengers for a particular cruise, thus avoiding the timer attack problem.

The stateless session bean can access the `TimerService` from the `SessionContext` in the `ejbCreate( )`, `ejbRemove( )`, or any business method, but it cannot access the timer service from the `setSessionContext( )` method. This means a client must call some method on a stateless session bean (either create, or a business method) in order for a timer to be set. This is the only way to guarantee that the timer is set.

Setting a timer on the `ejbCreate( )` method is problematic. First, there is no guarantee that `ejbCreate( )` will ever be called. The `ejbCreate( )` method's stateless session bean is called sometime after the bean is instantiated, before it enters the Method Ready Pool. However, a container might not create a pool of instances until the first client accesses that bean, so if a client (remote or otherwise) never attempts to access the bean, `ejbCreate( )` may never be called and the timer will never be set. Another problem with using `ejbCreate( )` is that it's called on every instance before it enters the pool; you have to prevent subsequent instances (instances created after the first instance) from setting the timer—the first instance created would have already done this. It's tempting to use a static variable to avoid recreating timers (below), but it can cause problems.

```
public class StatelessTimerBean
    implements javax.ejb.SessionBean, javax.ejb.TimedObject {

    static boolean isTimerSet = false;
```

```
public void ejbCreate( ){
    if( isTimerSet == false) {
        TimerService timerService = ejbContext.getTimerService( );
        InitialContext jndiContext = new InitialContext( );
        Long expirationDate = (Long)
          jndiContext.lookup("java:comp/env/expirationDate");
        timerService.createTimer(expirationDate.longValue( ), null );
        isTimerSet = true;
    }
}
```

While this may seem like a good solution, it only works when your application is deployed within a single server with one VM and one classloader. If you are using a clustered system, a single server with multiple VMs, or multiple classloaders (very common), it won't work because bean instances that are not instantiated in the same VM with the same classloader will not have access to the same static variable. In this scenario, it's easy to end up with multiple timers doing the same thing. An alternative is to have `ejbCreate( )` access and remove all preexisting timers to see if the timer is already established, but this can affect performance because it's likely that new instances will be created and added to the pool many times, resulting in many calls to `ejbCreate( )` and therefore many calls to `TimerService.getTimers( )`. Also, there is no requirement that the timer service work across a cluster, so timers set on one node in a cluster may not be visible to timers set on some other node in the cluster.

With stateless session beans, you should never use the `ejbRemove( )` method to cancel or create timers. The `ejbRemove( )` method is called on individual instances before they are evicted from memory. It is not called in response to client calls to the remote or local remove method. Also, the `ejbRemove( )` method doesn't correspond to an undeployment of a bean; it's only specific to a single instance. As a result, you cannot determine anything meaningful about the EJB as a whole from a call to the `ejbRemove( )` method and you should not use it to create or cancel timers.

When a stateless session bean implements the `javax.ejb.TimedObject` interface, its life cycle changes to include the servicing of timed events. The Timer Service pulls an instance of the bean from the instance pool when a timer expires; if there are no instances in the pool, the container creates one. Figure 13-2 shows the life cycle of a stateless session bean that implements the `TimedOut` interface.

Using a Stateless Session Timer

The InactiveCustomer EJB is a stateless session timer that periodically cleans inactive customer records from the database. It activates every 30 days and deletes records for customers who were created between 4 and 5 months ago, and who have never booked a cruise. Titan discovered that it accumulated a lot of these inactive customer records because customers would occasionally book a cruise, then cancel the reservation, and never return for more business. Once it's deployed and activated, the InactiveCustomer EJB continues to work automatically until canceled. It's

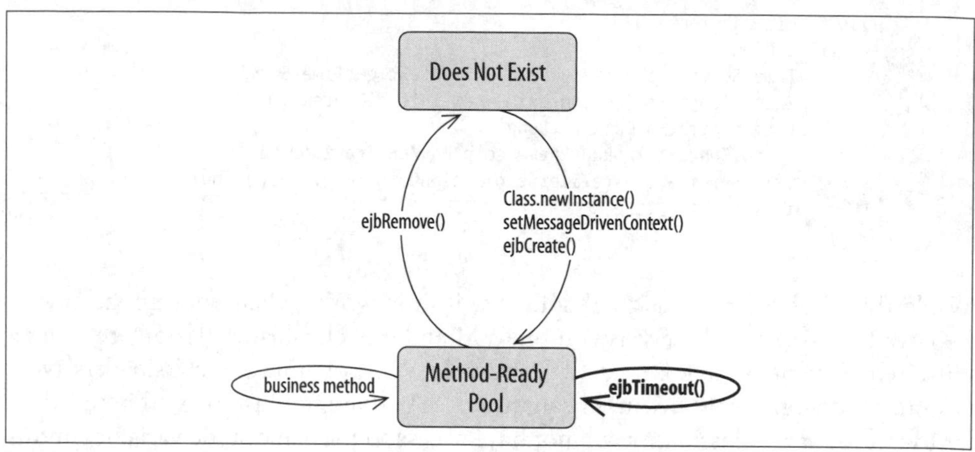

Figure 13-2. Stateless session bean life cycle with TimedObject

a schedule-and-forget-it type of agent. Here's the bean class definition for the InactiveCustomer EJB:

```
public class InactiveCustomerBean
    implements javax.ejb.SessionBean, javax.ejb.TimedObject {

    final long THIRTY_DAYS  = 1000 * 60 * 60 * 24 * 30;// Thirty Days in Milliseconds

    SessionContext ejbContext;
    public void setSessionContext(javax.ejb.SessionContext cntx){
        ejbContext = cntx;
    }
    public void ejbCreate( ){}

    public void schedule(Date begin){
         TimerService timerService = ejbContext.getTimerService( );
         TimerService.createTimer(begin, THIRTY_DAYS);
    }
    public void ejbTimeout( ) throws EJBException {
    try{
        Calendar calendar = Calendar.getInstance( );
        calendar.add(Calendar.DATE, -120);
        Date date_120daysAgo = calendar.getTime( );

        calendar = Calendar.getInstance( );
        calendar.add(Calendar.DATE, -150);
        Date date_150daysAgo = calendar.getTime( );

        InitialContext jndiEnc = new InitialContext( );
        CustomerHomeLocal home = (CustomerHomeLocal)
          jndiEnc.lookup("java:comp/env/ejb/CustomerHomeLocal");
        Iterator customers = home.findCustomersWithNoReservations().iterator( );
        while(customers.hasNext( )){
            CustomerLocal customer = (CustomerLocal)customers.next( );
            Date dateCreated = customer.getDateCreated( )
```

```
            if( dateCreated.after(date_150daysAgo) &&
                dateCreated.before(date_120daysAgo)){
                 customer.remove( );
            }
        }
     }catch(Exception e){ // exception handle logic goes here }
    }
    public void ejbActivate( ){}
    public void ejbPassivate( ){}
    public void ejbRemove( ){}
}
```

The InactiveCustomer EJB has a single business method, `schedule( )`, that starts the timer, setting it to expire first on the given date, and every 30 days thereafter. In order for the InactiveCustomer EJB to function, a client application must call `schedule( )` and pass in a start date. It's probably best to develop a strategy similar to this one, in which the timer is scheduled only after an explicit call is made by a client, rather than attempting to design a stateless session bean timer that somehow automatically schedules itself when it's deployed. The following code shows how an InvalidCustomer EJB is scheduled by a client:

```
InvalidCustomerHomeRemote invalidCustomer =
  jndiEnc.lookup("java:comp/env/ejb/InvalidCustomerHomeRemote");
invalidCustomer.schedule( new Date( ) );
```

The `ejbTimeout( )` method is hardcoded to fetch all the customers created between four and five months ago who never made reservations. These customers are removed from the system.

There are a number of improvements that could be made to this strategy. For example, the time window could be configured in the deployment descriptor or passed into the bean by the client. In addition, the `schedule( )` method should remove any existing timers so that we don't schedule multiple timers for the same task. These types of changes are left as an exercise for you to develop if you are interested.

Message-Driven Bean Timers

Message-driven bean timers are similar to stateless session bean timers in several ways: timers are associated only with the type of bean. When a timer expires, a message-driven bean instance is selected from a pool to execute the `ejbTimeout( )` method. In addition, message-driven beans can be used for performing audits or other types of batch jobs. The primary difference between a message-driven bean timer and a stateless session bean timer is the way in which they're initiated: timers are created in response to an incoming message or, if the container supports it, from a configuration file.

In order to initialize a message-driven bean timer from an incoming message, simply put the call to the `TimerService.createTimer( )` method in the message-handling method. For a JMS-based message-driven bean, the method call goes in the onMessage( ) method:

```
public class JmsTimerBean
    implements javax.ejb.MessageDrivenBean, javax.ejb.TimedObject {

    public void onMessage(Message message){
        MapMessage mapMessage = (MapMessage)message;
        long expirationDate = mapMessage.getLong("expirationDate");

        TimerService timerService = ejbContext.getTimerService( );
        timerService.createTimer(expirationDate, null );
    }

    public void ejbTimeout( ){
        // put timeout logic hear
    }
```

The incoming JMS message should contain information about the timer: the beginning (start) date, duration, or even the serializable info object. Combining JMS with the Timer Service can offer some powerful design options for implementing audits, batch processing, and agent-like solutions.

Although it's not standardized, it is possible that vendors will allow message-driven bean timers to be configured at deployment time. This would require a proprietary solution, since standard configuration options for message-driven bean timers do not exist. The advantage of configured timers is that they do not require a client to initiate some action to start the timer. When the bean is deployed, its timer is set automatically. This capability makes message-driven bean timers more like Unix cron jobs, which are preconfigured and then run. Consult your vendor to see if they offer a proprietary configuration for message-driven bean timers.

As was the case for stateless session beans, the TimedObject interface changes the life cycle of the message-driven bean slightly (see Figure 13-3). When a timed event occurs, the container must pull a message-driven bean instance from the pool. If there are no instances in the pool, then an instance must be moved from the Does Not Exist state to the Method Ready Pool before it can receive the timed event.

Problems with the Timer Service

The Timer Service is an excellent addition to the EJB platform, but it's limited. A lot can be learned from cron, the Unix scheduling utility that's been around for years. Here are some proposals for improving the service. If you are only interested in learning how timers work now, as opposed to how they may be improved, feel free to skip the rest of this chapter—it's not required reading. That said, understanding how timers can be improved helps you understand their limitations. If you have some time and want to expand your understanding of timers, keep reading.

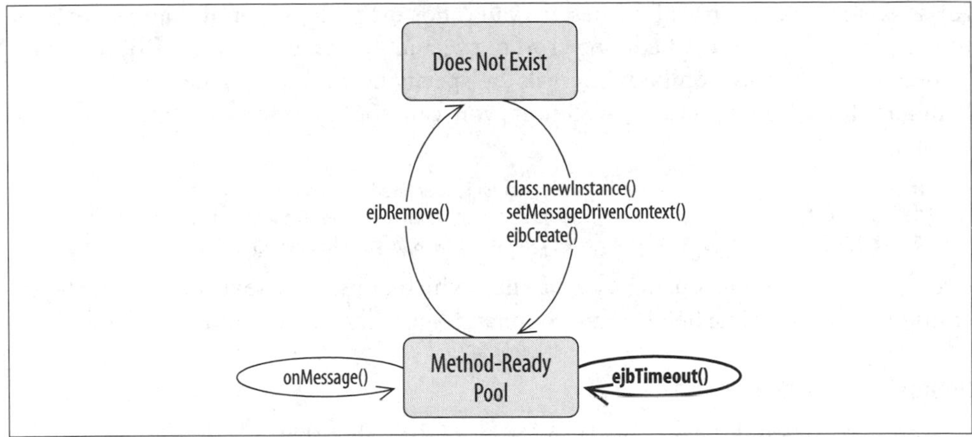

Figure 13-3. Message-driven bean life cycle with TimedObject

A very little bit about cron

Cron is a Unix program that allows you to schedule scripts (similar to batch files in DOS), commands, and other programs to run at specified dates and times. Unlike the EJB Timer Service, cron allows for flexible calendar-based scheduling. Cron jobs (anything cron runs is called a *job*) can be scheduled to run at intervals, including a specific minute of the hour, hour of the day, day of the week, day of the month, and month of the year.

For example, you can schedule a cron job to run every Friday at 12:15 p.m., or every hour, or the first day of every month. While this level of refinement may sound complicated, it is actually very easy to specify. Cron uses a simple text format of five fields of integer values, separated by spaces or tabs, to describe the intervals at which scripts should be run. Figure 13-4 shows the field positions and their meanings.

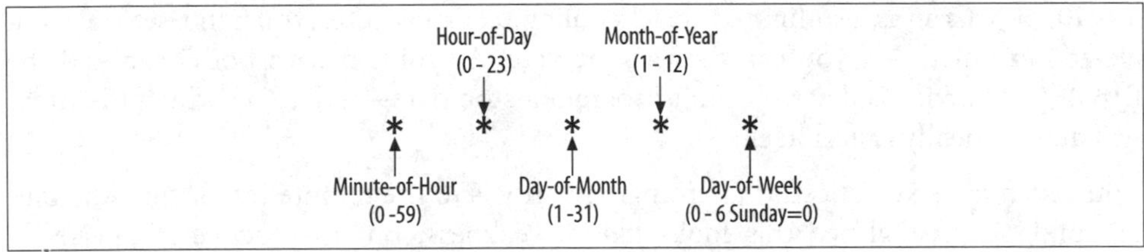

Figure 13-4. Cron date and time format

The order of the fields is significant, since each specifies a different calendar designator: minute, hour, day, month, and day of the week. The following examples show how to schedule cron jobs:

```
20    *   *   *   *    --->  20 minutes after every hour. (00:20, 01:20, etc.)
 5   22   *   *   *    --->  Every day at 10:05 p.m.
 0    8   1   *   *    --->  First day of every month at 8:00 a.m.
 0    8   4   7   *    --->  The fourth of July at 8:00 a.m.
15   12   *   *   5    --->  Every Friday at 12:15 p.m.
```

An asterisk indicates that all values are valid. For example, if you use an asterisk for the minute field, you're scheduling cron to execute the job every minute of the hour. You can define more complex intervals by specifying multiple values, separated by commas, for a single field. In addition, you can specify ranges of time using the hyphen:

```
0  8   *   *   1,3,5   --->   Every Monday, Wednesday, and Friday at 8:00 a.m.
0  8   1,15   *   *    --->   The first and 15th of every month at 8:00 a.m.
0  8-17    *   *   1-5 --->   Every hour from 8 a.m. through 5 p.m., Mon-Fri.
```

Cron jobs are scheduled using *crontab* files, which are simply text files in which you configure the date/time fields and a command—usually a command to run a script.

Improving the Timer Service

The cron date/time format provides a lot more flexibility than is currently offered by the EJB Timer Service. The Timer Service requires you to designate intervals in exact milliseconds, which is a bit awkward to work with (you have to convert days, hours, and minutes to milliseconds), but more importantly, it's not flexible enough for many real-world scheduling needs. For example, there is no way to schedule a timer to expire on the first and 15th of every month, or every hour between 8 a.m. and 5 p.m., Monday through Friday. You can derive some of the more complex intervals, but only at the cost of adding logic to your bean code to calculate them, and in more complicated scenarios, you'll need multiple timers for the same task.

Cron is not perfect either. Scheduling jobs is like setting a timer on a VCR: everything is scheduled according to the clock and calendar. You can specify that cron run a job at specific times of the day on specific days of the year, but you can't have it run a job at relative intervals from an arbitrary starting point. For example, cron's date/time format doesn't let you schedule a job to run every 10 minutes, starting now. You have to schedule it to run at specific minutes of the hour (e.g., 0, 10, 20, 30, 40, 50). Cron is also limited to scheduling recurring jobs; you can't set up a single-action timer, and you can't set a start date. A problem with both cron and the EJB Timer Service is that you can't program a stop date—a date on which the timer will automatically cancel itself.

You also may have noticed that cron granularity is to the minute rather than the millisecond. At first glance this looks like a weakness, but in practice it's perfectly acceptable. For calendar-driven scheduling, more precision simply isn't very useful.

The Timer Service interface would be improved if it could handle a cron-like date/time format, with a start date and end date. Rather than discard the current `createTimer()` calls (which are useful, especially for single-action timers and arbitrary millisecond intervals), it would be preferable simply to add a new method with cron-like semantics. Instead of using 0–6 to designate the day of the week, it would be better to use the values `Sun`, `Mon`, `Tue`, `Wed`, `Thu`, `Fri`, and `Sat` (as in the Linux version of cron). For example, code to schedule a timer that would run every weekday at 11:00 p.m. starting October 1, 2003, and ending May 31, 2004, would look like this:

```
TimerService timerService = ejbContext.getTimerService( );
Calendar start = Calendar.getInstance( ).set(2003, Calendar.OCTOBER, 1);
Calendar end = Calendar.getInstance( ).set(2004, Calendar.MAY, 31);

String dateTimeString = "23   *   *   *  Mon-Fri";
timerService.createTimer(dateTimeString, start, end, null);
```

This proposed change to the Timer Service retains the millisecond-based `createTimer( )` methods, because they are very useful. While cron-like configuration is powerful, it's not a silver bullet. If you need to schedule a timer to go off every 30 seconds starting now (or any arbitrary point in time), you need to use one of the existing `createTimer( )` methods. True millisecond accuracy is difficult; first of all, normal processing and thread contention tend to delay response time, and secondly, a server clock must be properly synchronized with the correct time (i.e., UTC)* to the millisecond, and most are not.

Message-driven bean timers: Standard configuration properties

There is enormous potential for using message-driven beans as cron-like jobs that are configured at deployment and run automatically. Unfortunately, there is no standard way to configure a message-driven bean timer at deployment time. Some vendors may support this, while others do not. Preconfigured message-driven bean timers are going to be in high demand by developers who want to schedule message-driven beans to perform work at specific dates and times. Without support for deployment-time configuration, the only reliable way to program an enterprise bean timer is to have a client call a method or send a JMS message. This is not an acceptable solution. Developers need deployment-time configuration and it should be added to the next version of the specification.

Building on the cron-like semantics proposed in the previous subsection, it would be easy to devise standard activation properties for configuring message-driven bean timers at deployment time. For example, the following code configures a message-driven bean, the Audit EJB, to run at 11 p.m., Monday through Friday, starting October 1, 2003, and ending May 31, 2004 (start and end dates are not required):

```
<activation-config>
  <description>Run Monday through Friday at 11:00 p.m.
               Starting on Oct 1st,2003 until May 31st, 2004</description>
  <activation-config-property>
```

* Coordinated Universal Time (UTC) is the international standard reference time. Servers can be coordinated with UTC using the Network Time Protocol (NTP) and public time servers. Coordinated Universal Time is abbreviated UTC as a compromise among standardizing nations. A full explanation is provided by the National Institute of Standards and Technology's FAQ on UTC at *http://www.boulder.nist.gov/timefreq/general/misc.htm#Anchor-14550*.

```
      <activation-config-property-name>dateTimeFields
      </activation-config-property-name>
      <activation-config-property-value> 23    *    *    *    Mon-Fri
      </activation-config-property-value>
    </activation-config-property>
    <activation-config-property>
      <activation-config-property-name>startDate</activation-config-property-name>
      <activation-config-property-value>October 1, 2003
      </activation-config-property-value>
    </activation-config-property>
    <activation-config-property>
      <activation-config-property-name>endDate</activation-config-property-name>
      <activation-config-property-value>May 31, 2004
      </activation-config-property-value>
    </activation-config-property>
  </activation-config>
```

This type of configuration would be fairly easy for providers to implement if they supported enhanced cron-like semantics. In addition, you could configure message-driven beans to use the millisecond-based timers EJB 2.1 already supports.

Other problems with Timer API

The semantics of the `Timer` object convey little information about the object itself. There is no way to determine whether a timer is a single-action timer or an interval timer. If it's an interval timer, there is no way to determine the configured interval, or whether the timer has executed its first expiration. To solve these problems, additional methods should be added to the Timer interface that provide this information. As a stopgap, it's a good idea to place this information in the `info` object so it can be accessed by applications that need it.

Final Words

Whether the changes outlined in this chapter are adopted is a matter for the EJB expert group, which should be responsive to the EJB developer community. It's likely that others will find ways to improve on these proposed changes. Regardless of the outcome, the limited semantics of the Timer Service and the lack of support for configurable message-driven bean timers are problems. As you develop timers, you will quickly discover the need for a much richer way of describing expirations, and some way to configure timers at deployment time, rather than having to use a client application to initiate a scheduled event.

CHAPTER 14

EJB 2.1: Web Service Standards

Web services have taken the enterprise computing industry by storm in the past couple of years, and for good reason. They present the opportunity for real interoperability across hardware, operating systems, programming languages, and applications. Based on XML, SOAP, and WSDL standards, web services have enjoyed widespread adoption by pretty much all the major enterprise players, including Microsoft, IBM, BEA, Oracle, Hewlett Packard, and others. Sun Microsystems has integrated web services into the J2EE platform; specifically, Sun and the Java Community Process have introduced several web service APIs, including JAX-RPC (Java API for XML-based RPC), SAAJ (SOAP with Attachments API for Java), and JAXR (Java API for XML Registries). These web service APIs have been integrated into J2EE 1.4 and are supported by EJB 2.1.

This chapter provides an overview of the technologies that are the foundation of web services: XML Schema and Namespaces, SOAP 1.1, and WSDL 1.1. Chapter 15 provides an overview of JAX-RPC, the most important web services API.

Web Services Overview

The term *web service* means different things to different people, but thankfully the definition is fairly straightforward for EJB developers because the J2EE platform has adopted a rather narrow view of web services. Specifically, a web service is a remote application described using WSDL (Web Service Description Language) and accessed using SOAP (Simple Object Access Protocol) according to the rules defined by the WS-I Basic Profile 1.0. The WS-I (Web Services Integration Organization) is group of vendors (Microsoft, IBM, BEA, Sun Microsystems, Oracle, HP, and others) that have banded together to ensure web services are interoperable across all platforms. To do this, they have created a recommendation called the Basic Profile 1.0, which defines a set of rules for using XML, SOAP, and WSDL together to create interoperable web services.

In order to understand SOAP and WSDL, you must understand XML Schema and XML Namespaces. The rest of this chapter conducts a whirlwind tour of XML, SOAP, and WSDL. Although it's not the purpose of this book to cover these subjects in depth, you should be able to understand the basics. For more in-depth coverage, you can turn to *J2EE Web Services* (Addison-Wesley) by the author of this book, Richard Monson-Haefel, or *Java Web Services* by David A. Chappell and Tyler Jewell (O'Reilly).

XML Schema and XML Namespaces

We'll start with the basics of XML Schemas and XML Namespaces. It's assumed that you already understand how to use basic XML elements and attributes. If you don't, you should probably read a primer on XML before proceeding. I recommend the book *Learning XML* by Erik T. Ray (O'Reilly). If you already understand how XML Schema and XML Namespaces work, skip ahead to the section on SOAP.

XML Schema

An *XML Schema* is similar in purpose to a *DTD* (Document Type Definition), which validates the structure of an XML document. To illustrate some of the basic concepts of XML Schema, let's start with an XML document with address information:

```
<?xml version='1.0' encoding='UTF-8' standalone='yes'?>
<address>
  <street>3243 West 1st Ave.</street>
  <city>Madison</city>
  <state>WI</state>
  <zip>53591</zip>
</address>
```

In order to ensure that the XML document contains the proper type of elements and data, the Address information must be evaluated for *correctness*. There are two ways that the correctness of an XML document can be measured: if it is *well formed* and if it is *valid*. To be well formed, an XML document must obey the syntactic rules of the XML markup language: it must use proper attribute declarations, the correct characters to denote the start and end of elements, and so on. Most XML parsers based on standards like SAX and DOM detect documents that aren't well formed automatically.

In addition to being well formed, it's sometimes important to check that the document uses the right types of elements and attributes in the correct order and structure. A document that meets these criteria is called valid. However, the criteria for validity have nothing to do with XML itself; they have more to do with application in which the document is used. For example, the Address document would not be valid if it didn't include the Zip code or state elements. In order to validate an XML document, you need a way to represent these application-specific constraints.

The XML Schema for the Address XML document looks like this:

```
<?xml version='1.0' encoding='UTF-8' ?>
<schema xmlns="http://www.w3.org/2001/XMLSchema"
    xmlns:titan="http://www.titan.com/Reservation"
    targetNamespace="http://www.titan.com/Reservation">

  <element name="address" type="titan:AddressType"/>

  <complexType name="AddressType">
    <sequence>
      <element name="street" type="string"/>
      <element name="city" type="string"/>
      <element name="state" type="string"/>
      <element name="zip" type="string"/>
    </sequence>
  </complexType>

</schema>
```

The first thing to focus on in this XML Schema is the `<complexType>` element, which declares a type of element in much the same way that a Java class declares a type of object. The `<complexType>` element explicitly declares the names, types, and order of elements that an `AddressType` element may contain. In this case, it may contain five elements of type `string` in the following order: `street`, `city`, `state`, and `zip`. Validation is pretty strict, so any XML document that claims conformance with this XML Schema must contain exactly the right elements with the right data types, in the correct order.

There are about two dozen simple data types that are automatically supported by XML Schema, called *built-in types*. Built-in types are a part of the XML Schema language and are automatically supported by any XML Schema–compliant parser. Table 14-1 shows a short list of some of the built-in types. It also shows Java types that correspond to each built-in type. (Table 14-1 presents only a subset of all the XML Schema (XSD) built-in types, but it's more than enough for this book.)

Table 14-1. XML Schema built-in types and their corresponding Java types

XML Schema built-in type	Java primitive type
byte	byte
boolean	boolean
short	short
int	int
long	long
float	float
double	double
string	java.lang.String
dateTime	java.util.Calendar
integer	java.math.BigInteger
decimal	java.math.BigDecimal

By default, each element declared by a <complexType> must occur once in an XML document, but you can specify that an element is optional or that it must occur more than once by using the occurrence attributes. For example, we can say that the street element must occur once but may occur two times:

```
<complexType name="AddressType">
  <sequence>
    <element name="street" type="string" maxOccurs="2" minOccurs="1" />
    <element name="city" type="string"/>
    <element name="state" type="string"/>
    <element name="zip" type="string"/>
  </sequence>
</complexType>
```

By default, the maxOccurs and minOccurs attributes are always 1, indicating that the element must occur exactly once. Setting the maxOccurs to "2" allows an XML document to have two street elements or just one. You can also set the maxOccurs to "unbounded", which means the element may occur as many times as needed. Setting minOccurs to "0" means the element is optional and can be omitted.

The <element> declarations are nested under a <sequence> element, which indicates that the elements must occur in the order they are declared. You can also nest the elements under an <all> declaration, which allows the elements to appear in any order. The following shows the AddressType declared with an <all> element instead of a <sequence> element:

```
<complexType name="AddressType">
    <all>
      <element name="street" type="string" maxOccurs="2" minOccurs="1" />
      <element name="city" type="string"/>
      <element name="state" type="string"/>
      <element name="zip" type="string"/>
    </all>
</complexType>
```

In addition to declaring elements of XSD built-in types, you can declare elements based on complex types. This is similar to how Java class types declare fields that are other Java class types. For example, we can define a CustomerType that makes use of the AddressType:

```
<?xml version='1.0' encoding='UTF-8' ?>
<schema xmlns="http://www.w3.org/2001/XMLSchema"
    xmlns:titan="http://www.titan.com/Reservation"
    targetNamespace="http://www.titan.com/Reservation">

  <element name="customer" type="titan:CustomerType"/>

<complexType name="CustomerType">
    <sequence>
      <element name="last-name" type="string"/>
      <element name="first-name" type="string"/>
      <element name="address" type="titan:AddressType"/>
```

```
    </sequence>
  </complexType>
<complexType name="AddressType">
    <sequence>
      <element name="street" type="string" />
      <element name="city" type="string"/>
      <element name="state" type="string"/>
      <element name="zip" type="string"/>
    </sequence>
 </complexType>

</schema>
```

This XSD tells us that an element of `CustomerType` must contain a `<last-name>` and `<first-name>` element of built-in type `string`, and an element of type `AddressType`. This is pretty straightforward, except for the `titan:` prefix on `AddressType`. That prefix identifies the XML Namespace of the `AddressType`; we'll discuss namespaces later in the chapter. For now, just think of it as declaring that the `AddressType` is a custom type defined by Titan Cruises; it's not a standard XSD built-in type. An XML document that conforms to the Customer XSD would look like this:

```
<?xml version='1.0' encoding='UTF-8' ?>
<customer>
  <last-name>Jones</last-name>
  <first-name>Sara</first-name>
  <address>
    <street>3243 West 1st Ave.</street>
    <city>Madison</city>
    <state>WI</state>
    <zip>53591</zip>
  </address>
</customer>
```

Building on what you've learned so far, we can create a Reservation schema, using the `CustomerType` and the `AddressType`, and a new `CreditCardType`:

```
<?xml version='1.0' encoding='UTF-8' ?>
<schema xmlns="http://www.w3.org/2001/XMLSchema"
    xmlns:titan="http://www.titan.com/Reservation"
    targetNamespace="http://www.titan.com/Reservation">

  <element name="reservation" type="titan:ReservationType"/>

  <complexType name="ReservationType">
    <sequence>
      <element name="customer" type="titan:CustomerType"/>
      <element name="cruise-id" type="int"/>
      <element name="cabin-id" type="int"/>
      <element name="price-paid" type="double"/>
    </sequence>
  </complexType>
  <complexType name="CustomerType">
    <sequence>
```

```
      <element name="last-name" type="string"/>
      <element name="first-name" type="string"/>
      <element name="address" type="titan:AddressType"/>
      <element name="credit-card" type="titan:CreditCardType"/>
    </sequence>
  </complexType>
  <complexType name="CreditCardType">
    <sequence>
      <element name="exp-date" type="dateTime"/>
      <element name="number" type="string"/>
      <element name="name" type="string"/>
      <element name="organization" type="string"/>
    </sequence>
  </complexType>
  <complexType name="AddressType">
    <sequence>
      <element name="street" type="string"/>
      <element name="city" type="string"/>
      <element name="state" type="string"/>
      <element name="zip" type="string"/>
    </sequence>
  </complexType>
</schema>
```

An XML document that conforms to the Reservation XSD would include information describing the customer (name and address), credit card information, and the identity of the cruise and cabin that is being reserved. This document might be sent to Titan Cruises from a travel agency that cannot access the TravelAgent EJB to make reservations. Here's an XML document that conforms to the Reservation XSD:

```
<?xml version='1.0' encoding='UTF-8' ?>
<reservation>
  <customer>
    <last-name>Jones</last-name>
    <first-name>Sara</first-name>
    <address>
      <street>3243 West 1st Ave.</street>
      <city>Madison</city>
      <state>WI</state>
      <zip>53591</zip>
    </address>
    <credit-card>
      <exp-date>09-2005</exp-date>
      <number>0394029302894028930</number>
      <name>Sara Jones</name>
      <organization>VISA</organization>
    </credit-card>
  </customer>
  <cruise-id>123</cruise-id>
  <cabin-id>333</cabin-id>
  <price-paid>6234.55</price-paid>
</reservation>
```

At runtime, the XML parser compares the document to its Schema, ensuring that the document conforms to the rules set down by the Schema. If the document doesn't adhere to the Schema, it is considered invalid, and the parser produces error messages. An XML Schema checks that XML documents received by your system are properly structured, so you won't encounter errors while parsing the documents and extracting the data. For example, if someone sent your application a Reservation document that omitted the credit-card element, the XML parser could reject the document as invalid before your code even sees it: you don't have to worry about errors in your code caused by missing information in the document.

This brief overview represents only the tip of the iceberg. XML Schema is a very rich XML typing system and can only be given sufficient attention in a text dedicated to the subject. For an in-depth and insightful coverage of XML Schema, read *XML Schema: The W3C's Object-Oriented Descriptions for XML* by Eric van der Vlist (O'Reilly) or read the XML Schema specification, starting with the primer at the W3C (World Wide Web Consortium) web site (*http://www.w3.org/TR/xmlschema-0/*).

XML Namespaces

The Reservation schema defines an *XML markup language* that describes the structure of a specific kind of XML document. Just as a Class is a type of Java object, an XML markup language, defined by an XML Schema, is a type of XML document. In some cases, it's convenient to combine two or more XML markup languages into a single document, so that the elements from each markup language can be validated separately using different XML Schemas. This is especially useful when you want to reuse a markup language in many difference contexts. For example, the `AddressType` defined in the previous section is useful in a variety of contexts, not just the Reservation XSD, so it could be defined as a separate markup language in its own XML Schema.

```
<?xml version='1.0' encoding='UTF-8' ?>
<schema xmlns="http://www.w3.org/2001/XMLSchema"
    targetNamespace="http://www.titan.com/Address">

  <complexType name="AddressType">
    <sequence>
      <element name="street" type="string"/>
      <element name="city" type="string"/>
      <element name="state" type="string"/>
      <element name="zip" type="string"/>
    </sequence>
  </complexType>
</schema>
```

In order to use different markup languages in the same XML document, you must clearly identify the markup language to which each element belongs. Here is an XML document for a reservation, but this time we are using XML Namespaces to separate the address information from the reservation information:

```
<?xml version='1.0' encoding='UTF-8' ?>
<res:reservation xmlns:res="http://www.titan.com/Reservation" >
  <res:customer>
    <res:last-name>Jones</res:last-name>
    <res:first-name>Sara</res:first-name>

    <addr:address xmlns:addr="http://www.titan.com/Address">
      <addr:street>3243 West 1st Ave.</addr:street>
      <addr:city>Madison</addr:city>
      <addr:state>WI</addr:state>
      <addr:zip>53591</addr:zip>
    </addr:address>

    <res:credit-card>
      <res:exp-date>09-2005</res:exp-date>
      <res:number>0394029302894028930</res:number>
      <res:name>Sara Jones</res:name>
      <res:organization>VISA</res:organization>
    </res:credit-card>
  </res:customer>
  <res:cruise-id>123</res:cruise-id>
  <res:cabin-id>333</res:cabin-id>
  <res:price-paid>6234.55</res:price-paid>
</res:reservation>
```

All the elements for the address information are prefixed with characters `addr:`, and all the reservation elements are prefixed with `res:`. These prefixes allow parsers to identify and separate the elements that belong to the Address markup from those that belong to the Reservation markup. As a result, the address elements can be validated against the Address XSD while the reservation elements are validated against the Reservation XSD. The prefixes are assigned using XML Namespace declarations, which are shown in bold in the previous listing. An XML Namespace declaration follows this format:

```
xmlns:prefix="URI"
```

The prefix can be anything you like, as long as it does not include blanks or any special characters. We use prefixes that are abbreviations for the name of the markup language: `res` stands for Reservation XSD and `addr` stands for Address XSD. This is the convention that most XML documents follow, but it's not a requirement; you could use prefixes like `foo` or `bar` or anything else you fancy.

While the prefix can be any arbitrary token, the URI must be very specific. A URI (Universal Resource Identifier) is an identifier that is a superset of the URL (Universal Resource Locator) that you use every day to look up web pages. In most cases, people use the stricter URL format for XML Namespaces because URLs are familiar and easy to understand. The URI used in the XML Namespace declaration identifies the exact markup language that is employed. It doesn't have to point at a web page or an XML document; it just needs to be unique to that markup language. For example, the XML Namespace used by the Address markup is different from the URL used for the Reservation markup.

```
xmlns:addr="http://www.titan.com/Address"
xmlns:res="http://www.titan.com/Reservation"
```

The URI in the XML Namespace declaration should match the target namespace declared by an XML Schema. Here is the Address XSD with the target namespace declaration shown in bold. The URL value of the `targetNamespace` attribute is identical to the URL assigned to the `add:` prefix in the reservation document, shown earlier.

```
<?xml version='1.0' encoding='UTF-8' ?>
<schema xmlns="http://www.w3.org/2001/XMLSchema"
    targetNamespace="http://www.titan.com/Address">

  <complexType name="AddressType">
    <sequence>
      <element name="street" type="string"/>
      <element name="city" type="string"/>
      <element name="state" type="string"/>
      <element name="zip" type="string"/>
    </sequence>
  </complexType>
</schema>
```

The `targetNamespace` attribute identifies the unique URI of the markup language; it is the permanent identifier for that XML Schema. Whenever elements from the Address XSD are used in some other document, the document must use an XML Namespace declaration to identify those elements as belonging to the Address markup language.

Prefixing every element in an XML document with its namespace identifier is a bit tedious, so XML Namespace allows you to declare a default namespace that applies to all elements that are not prefixed. The default namespace is simply an XML Namespace declaration that has no prefix (`xmlns="`*`URL`*`"`). For example, we can use a default name in the reservation document for all Reservation elements:

```
<?xml version='1.0' encoding='UTF-8' ?>
<reservation xmlns="http://www.titan.com/Reservation" >
  <customer>
    <last-name>Jones</last-name>
    <first-name>Sara</first-name>

    <addr:address xmlns:addr="http://www.titan.com/Address">
      <addr:street>3243 West 1st Ave.</addr:street>
      <addr:city>Madison</addr:city>
      <addr:state>WI</addr:state>
      <addr:zip>53591</addr:zip>
    </addr:address>

    <credit-card>
      <exp-date>09-2005</exp-date>
      <number>0394029302894028930</number>
      <name>Sara Jones</name>
```

```
      <organization>VISA</organization>
    </credit-card>
  </customer>
  <cruise-id>123</cruise-id>
  <cabin-id>333</cabin-id>
  <price-paid>6234.55</price-paid>
</reservation>
```

None of the Reservation elements names are prefixed. Any nonprefixed element belongs to the default namespace. The Address elements do not belong to the Reservation namespace, so they are prefixed to indicate which namespace they belong to. The default namespace declaration has *scope*; in other words, it applies to the element in which it is declared (if that element has no namespace prefix), and to all nonprefixed elements nested under that element. We can use the scoping rules of namespace to further simplify the Reservation document by allowing the Address elements to override the default namespace with their own default namespace.

```
<?xml version='1.0' encoding='UTF-8' ?>
<reservation xmlns="http://www.titan.com/Reservation" >
  <customer>
    <last-name>Jones</last-name>
    <first-name>Sara</first-name>

    <address xmlns="http://www.titan.com/Address">
      <street>3243 West 1st Ave.</street>
      <city>Madison</city>
      <state>WI</state>
      <zip>53591</zip>
    </address>

    <credit-card>
      <exp-date>09-2005</exp-date>
      <number>0394029302894028930</number>
      <name>Sara Jones</name>
      <organization>VISA</organization>
    </credit-card>
  </customer>
  <cruise-id>123</cruise-id>
  <cabin-id>333</cabin-id>
  <price-paid>6234.55</price-paid>
</reservation>
```

The Reservation default namespace applies to the `<reservation>` element and all of its children except for the Address elements. The `<address>` element and its children have defined their own default namespace, which overrides the default namespace of the `<reservation>` element.

Default namespaces do not apply to attributes. As a result, any attributes used in an XML document should be prefixed with a namespace identifier. The only exceptions to this rule are attributes defined by the XML language itself, such as the `xmlns` attribute, which establishes an XML Namespace declaration. This attribute doesn't need to be prefixed because it is part of XML language.

XML Namespaces are just URIs that uniquely identify a namespace, but do not actually point at a resource. In other words, you don't normally use the URI of a XML Namespace to look something up. It's usually just an identifier. However, you might want to indicate the location of the XML Schema associated with an XML Namespace so that a parser can upload it and use it in validation. This is accomplished using the `schemaLocation` attribute:

```
<?xml version='1.0' encoding='UTF-8' ?>
<reservation xmlns="http://www.titan.com/Reservation"
             xmlns:xsi="http://www.w3.org/2001/XMLSchema-Instance"
             xsi:schemaLocation="http://www.titan.com/Reservation
                                 http://www.titan.com/schemas/reservation.xsd">
  <customer>
    <last-name>Jones</last-name>
    <first-name>Sara</first-name>

    <address xmlns="http://www.titan.com/Address"
             xsi:schemaLocation="http://www.titan.com/Address
                                 http://www.titan.com/schemas/address.xsd">
      <street>3243 West 1st Ave.</street>
      <city>Madison</city>
      <state>WI</state>
      <zip>53591</zip>
    </address>

    <credit-card>
      <exp-date>09-2005</exp-date>
      <number>0394029302894028930</number>
      <name>Sara Jones</name>
      <organization>VISA</organization>
    </credit-card>
  </customer>
  <cruise-id>123</cruise-id>
  <cabin-id>333</cabin-id>
  <price-paid>6234.55</price-paid>
</reservation>
```

The `schemaLocation` attribute provides a list of values as Namespace-Location value pairs. The first value is the URI of the XML Namespace; the second is the physical location (URL) of the XML Schema. The following `schemaLocation` attribute states that all elements belonging to the Reservation Namespace (*http://www.titan.com/Reservation*) can be validated against a XML Schema located at the URL *http://www.titan.com/reservation.xsd*:

```
xsi:schemaLocation="http://www.titan.com/Reservation
                    http://www.titan.com/schemas/reservation.xsd">
```

The `schemaLocation` attribute is not a part of the XML language, so we'll actually need to prefix it with the appropriate namespace in order to use it. The XML Schema specification defines a special namespace that can be used for `schemaLocation` (as well as other attributes). That namespace is `http://www.w3.org/2001/XMLSchema-Instance`. In order to properly declare the `schemaLocation` attribute, declare its XML namespace and prefix it with the identifier for that namespace as shown in the following snippet:

```
<?xml version='1.0' encoding='UTF-8' ?>
<reservation xmlns="http://www.titan.com/Reservation"
                         xmlns:xsi="http://www.w3.org/2001/XMLSchema-Instance"
                         xsi:schemaLocation="http://www.titan.com/Reservation
                                             http://www.titan.com/schemas/reservation.xsd">
```

A namespace declaration only needs to be defined once; it applies to all elements nested under the element in which it's declared. The convention is to use the prefix `xsi` for the XML Schema Instance namespace (*http://www.w3.org/2001/XMLSchema-Instance*).

XML Schemas also use XML Namespaces. Let's look at XML Schema for the Address markup language with a new focus on the use of XML Namespaces:

```
<?xml version='1.0' encoding='UTF-8' ?>
<schema
   xmlns="http://www.w3.org/2001/XMLSchema"
   targetNamespace="http://www.titan.com/Address"
   xmlns:addr="http://www.titan.com/Address" >

  <element name="address" type="addr:AddressType"/>

  <complexType name="AddressType">
    <sequence>
      <element name="street" type="string"/>
      <element name="city" type="string"/>
      <element name="state" type="string"/>
      <element name="zip" type="string"/>
    </sequence>
  </complexType>
```

In this file, namespaces are used in three separate declarations. The first namespace declaration states that the default namespace is `http://www.w3c.org/2001/XMLSchema`, which is the namespace of the XML Schema specification. This declaration makes it easier to read the XSD because most of the elements do not need to be prefixed. The second declaration states that the target namespace of the XML Schema is the namespace of the Address markup. This tells us that all the types and elements defined in this XSD belong to that namespace. Finally, the third namespace declaration assigns the prefix `addr` to the target namespace so that types can be referenced exactly. For example, the top level `<element>` definition uses the name `addr:AddressType` to say that the element is of type `AddressType`, belonging to the namespace *http://www.titan.com/Address*.

Why do you have to declare a prefix for the target namespace? The reason is clearer when you examine the XSD for the Reservation XSD:

```
<?xml version='1.0' encoding='UTF-8' ?>
<schema
```

```
    xmlns="http://www.w3.org/2001/XMLSchema"
    xmlns:xsi="http://www.w3.org/2001/XMLSchema-Instance"
    xmlns:addr="http://www.titan.com/Address"
    xmlns:res="http://www.titan.com/Reservation"
    targetNamespace="http://www.titan.com/Reservation">

  <import namespace="http://www.titan.com/Address"
               xsi:schemaLocation="http://www.titan.com/Address.xsd" />

  <element name="reservation" type="res:ReservationType"/>

  <complexType name="ReservationType">
    <sequence>
      <element name="customer" type="res:CustomerType"/>
      <element name="cruise-id" type="int"/>
      <element name="cabin-id" type="int"/>
      <element name="price-paid" type="double"/>
    </sequence>
  </complexType>
  <complexType name="CustomerType">
    <sequence>
      <element name="last-name" type="string"/>
      <element name="first-name" type="string"/>
      <element name="address" type="addr:AddressType"/>
      <element name="credit-card" type="res:CreditCardType"/>
    </sequence>
  </complexType>
  <complexType name="CreditCardType">
    <sequence>
      <element name="exp-date" type="dateTime"/>
      <element name="number" type="string"/>
      <element name="name" type="string"/>
      <element name="organization" type="string"/>
    </sequence>
  </complexType>
</schema>
```

The Reservation XSD imports the Address XSD so that the `AddressType` can be used to define the `CustomerType`. You can see the use of namespaces in the definition of the `CustomerType`, which references types from both the Reservation and Address namespace, prefixed by addr and res:

```
<?xml version='1.0' encoding='UTF-8' ?>
<schema
    xmlns="http://www.w3.org/2001/XMLSchema"
    xmlns:xsi="http://www.w3.org/2001/XMLSchema-Instance"
    xmlns:addr="http://www.titan.com/Address"
    xmlns:res="http://www.titan.com/Reservation"
    targetNamespace="http://www.titan.com/Reservation">
...
 <complexType name="CustomerType">
    <sequence>
      <element name="last-name" type="string"/>
      <element name="first-name" type="string"/>
```

```
        <element name="address" type="addr:AddressType"/>
        <element name="credit-card" type="res:CreditCardType"/>
      </sequence>
    </complexType>
```

Assigning a prefix to the Reservation namespace allowed us to distinguish between elements that are defined as Reservation types (e.g., `credit-card`) and elements that are defined as Address types (e.g., `address`). All the `type` attributes that reference built-in types `string` and `int` also belong to the XML Schema namespace, so we don't need to prefix them. We could, though, for clarity. That is, we'd replace `string` and `int` with `xsd:string` and `xsd:int`. The prefix `xsd` references the XML Schema namespace; using it allows us to identify built-in types defined as XML Schema more clearly. It's not a problem that the default namespace is the same as the namespace prefixed by `xsd`. By convention, the `xsd` prefix is the one used in most XML schemas.

SOAP 1.1

SOAP 1.1 is simply a distributed object protocol like DCOM, CORBA IIOP, and Java RMI-JRMP. The most significant difference between SOAP 1.1 and other distributed object protocols is that SOAP 1.1 is based on XML.

EJB 2.1 and the J2EE 1.4 platform are standardized on SOAP 1.1. At the time of this writing, SOAP 1.2 (the latest version of SOAP) has just been released, but it is not supported by J2EE 1.4/EJB 2.1. From this point forward, we'll only talk about SOAP 1.1, which we'll simply call SOAP.

SOAP is defined by its own XML Schema and relies heavily on the use of XML Namespaces. Every SOAP message that is sent across the wire is an XML document that consists of standard SOAP elements and application data. The use of namespaces differentiates the standard SOAP elements from the application data. Here's a SOAP request message that might be sent from a client to a server:

```
<?xml version='1.0' encoding='UTF-8' ?>
<env:Envelope  xmlns:env="http://schemas.xmlsoap.org/soap/envelope/">
   <env:Header />
   <env:Body>
       <reservation xmlns="http://www.titan.com/Reservation>
             <customer>
                      <!-- customer info goes here -->
             </customer>
             <cruise-id>123</cruise-id>
             <cabin-id>333</cabin-id>
             <price-paid>6234.55</price-paid>
       </reservation>
   </env:Body>
</env:Envelope>
```

The standard SOAP elements are shown in bold while the application data, the Reservation XML document fragment, is shown in regular text. SOAP's primary purpose is to establish a standard XML framework for packaging application data that is exchanged between different software platforms, such as Java and Perl, or Java and .NET. To do this, SOAP defines a set of elements, each of which is designed to carry different data. The `<Envelope>` element is the root of the SOAP message; all other elements are contained by it. Within the `<Envelope>` element are two direct children: the `<Header>` element and the `<Body>` element.

The `<Header>` element is generally used for carrying infrastructure data such as security tokens, transaction IDs, routing information, and so on. In the previous example, the `<Header>` element is empty, which is not unusual for basic web services. In many cases, we are only interested in exchanging information and not in more advanced issues, such as those relating to security and transactions. Although the `<Body>` element is required, the `<Header>` element is not. From this point forward, the `<Header>` element will be omitted from examples.

The `<Body>` element carries the application information that is being exchanged. In the previous example, the `<Body>` element contains a `<reservation>` element, which is the application data. It's an XML document fragment based on the Reservation XSD developed earlier in this chapter. It's called a "fragment" because it's embedded inside a SOAP message, rather than standing alone.

SOAP Messaging Modes

The SOAP message we just looked at is a Document/Literal message, which means that the message carries an XML document fragment that may be validated against an XML Schema.

The `schemaLocation` attribute could have been included; it's omitted because we assume that the receiver is already familiar with the schema used for that type of SOAP message.

The other messaging mode allowed by the WS-I Basic Profile 1.0 and supported by EJB 2.1 is RPC/Literal. RPC/Literal represents SOAP messages as RPC calls, with parameters and return values, rather than arbitrary XML document fragments. The following Java interface defines a single method called `makeReservation( )`:

```
public interface TravelAgent extends java.rmi.Remote {
    public void makeReservation(int cruiseID, int cabinID,
                                int customerId, double price)
    throws java.rmi.RemoteException;
}
```

The `makeReservation( )` method can be modeled as a SOAP message using the RPC/Literal messaging style:

```
<env:Envelope
    xmlns:env="http://schemas.xmlsoap.org/soap/envelope/"
```

```
 xmlns:titan="http://www.titan.com/TravelAgent"/>
 <env:Body>
    <titan:makeReservation xmlns="http://www.titan.com/TravelAgent" >
          <cruiseId>23</cruiseId>
          <cabinId>144</cabinId>
          <customerId>9393</cusotmerId>
          <price>5677.88</price>
    </titan:makeReservation>
 </env:Body>
</env:Envelope
```

The first element within the `<Body>` identifies the web service operation being invoked. In this case, it's the `makeReservation` operation. Directly under the `<titan:makeReservation>` element are the parameters of the RPC call, each of which is represented by an element with a value.

EJB 2.1, but not the WS-I Basic Profile 1.0, supports the RPC/Encoded mode of SOAP messaging. Most SOAP applications used RPC/Encoded when web services were first created. However, the web services industry has moved toward Document/Literal and RPC/Literal, primarily because interoperability between platforms using RPC/Encoded proved to be less than perfect, and sometimes downright difficult. While RPC/Encoded SOAP messages rely on SOAP defined types for Arrays, Enumeration, Union, Lists, and the like, RPC/Literal and Document/Literal depend only on XML Schema for their data types, which seems to provide a better system for interoperability across programming languages. Although EJB 2.1 supports RPC/Encoded messaging, it's really not a very good option to use in web services. RPC/Encoded messaging will not be addressed in this book.

Exchanging SOAP Messages with HTTP

SOAP messages are *network protocol–agnostic*, which means that a SOAP message is not aware of or dependent on the type of network or protocol used to carry it. That said, SOAP is primarily exchanged using HTTP. The reason for using HTTP is simple. Most Internet products, including web servers, application servers, and wireless devices, are designed to handle the HTTP protocol. The widespread support for HTTP provides an instant infrastructure for SOAP messaging. The fact that SOAP can leverage the ubiquity of HTTP is one of the reasons it has become so popular so quickly.

Another advantage of using HTTP is that SOAP messages can slip through firewalls without any hassles. If you have ever tried to support internal or external customers who are separated from you by a firewall (yours or theirs), you know the headaches a firewall can create. Unless you have direct control over the firewall, your chances of communicating with arbitrary clients using anything but HTTP or SMTP (email) are slim to none. However, because SOAP can be transmitted with HTTP, it slips through the firewall unnoticed. This ability makes life a lot simpler for the application developer, but it's a point of contention with the security folks. Understandably, the security community is a bit irked about the idea of application developers circumventing their defenses. Using HTTP to carry an application protocol like SOAP is commonly called *HTTP tunneling*. In the past, support for tunneling by vendors of other distributed object protocols (CORBA IIOP, DCOM, and so on) was sporadic and proprietary, making interoperability extremely difficult. With SOAP, tunneling over HTTP is built into the SOAP 1.1 specification—which means interoperability is no longer a problem. As just about every application server vendor rapidly adopts SOAP, SOAP-HTTP tunneling is becoming ubiquitous.

You can use SOAP 1.1 with other protocols, such as SMTP, FTP, and even raw TCP/IP, but HTTP is the only protocol for which a binding is currently specified. As a result, EJB 2.1 and J2EE 1.4 require support for SOAP 1.1 over HTTP 1.1, but not other protocols.

Now You See It, Now You Don't

All this talk about SOAP is designed to give you a better idea of what is going on under the hood, but in practice, you are unlikely to interact with the protocol directly. Like most protocols, SOAP is designed to be produced and consumed by software and is usually encapsulated by a developer API. In EJB 2.1, the API you will use to exchange SOAP messages is JAX-RPC (Java API for XML-based RPC), which hides the details of SOAP messaging so you can focus on developing and invoking web services. While using JAX-RPC, you will rarely have to deal with the SOAP protocol, which is nice because it makes you a lot more productive. JAX-RPC is covered in Chapter 15.

WSDL 1.1

WSDL (Web Service Description Language) is an XML markup language used to describe a web service. WSDL is programming language–, platform-, and protocol-agnostic. The fact that WSDL is protocol-agnostic means it can describe web services that use protocols other than SOAP and HTTP. This ability makes WSDL very flexible, but it has the nasty side effect of making WSDL abstract and difficult to understand. Fortunately, the WS-I Basic Profile 1.0 endorses only SOAP 1.1 over HTTP, so we'll discuss WSDL as if that's the only combination of protocols supported.

Imagine that you want to develop a web service component that implements the following interface:

```
public interface TravelAgent extends java.rmi.Remote {
    public String makeReservation(int cruiseID, int cabinID,
                                  int customerId, double price)
    throws java.rmi.RemoteException;
}
```

Any application should be able to invoke this method using SOAP, regardless of the language in which it was written or the platform on which it is running. Since other programming languages don't understand Java, we have to describe the web service in a language they do understand: XML. Using XML, and specifically the WSDL markup language, we can describe the type of SOAP messages that must be sent to invoke the `makeReservation( )` method. A WSDL document that describes the `makeReservation( )` method might look like this:

```
<?xml version="1.0"?>
<definitions name="TravelAgent"
   xmlns="http://schemas.xmlsoap.org/wsdl/"
   xmlns:soap="http://schemas.xmlsoap.org/wsdl/soap/"
   xmlns:xsd="http://www.w3.org/2001/XMLSchema"
   xmlns:titan="http://www.titan.com/TravelAgent"
   targetNamespace="http://www.titan.com/TravelAgent">

<!-- message elements describe the paramters and return values -->
<message name="RequestMessage">
   <part name="cruiseId"   type="xsd:int" />
   <part name="cabinId"    type="xsd:int" />
   <part name="customerId" type="xsd:int" />
   <part name="price"      type="xsd:double" />
</message>
<message name="ResponseMessage">
   <part name="reservationId" type="xsd:string" />
</message>

<!-- portType element describes the abstract interface of a web service -->
<portType name="TravelAgent">
  <operation name="makeReservation">
     <input message="titan:RequestMessage"/>
     <output message="titan:ResponseMessage"/>
  </operation>
</portType>

<!-- binding element tells us which protocols and encoding styles are used  -->
<binding name="TravelAgentBinding" type="titan:TravelAgent">
   <soap:binding style="rpc"
                 transport="http://schemas.xmlsoap.org/soap/http"/>
   <operation name="makeReservation">
      <soap:operation soapAction="" />
      <input>
        <soap:body use="literal"
              namespace="http://www.titan.com/TravelAgent"/>
      </input>
      <output>
        <soap:body use="literal"
              namespace="http://www.titan.com/TravelAgent"/>
      </output>
   </operation>
</binding>

<!-- service element tells us the Internet address of a web service -->
<service name="TravelAgentService">
  <port name="TravelAgentPort" binding="titan:TravelAgentBinding">
```

```
    <soap:address location="http://www.titan.com/webservices/TravelAgent" />
  </port>
</service>

</definitions>
```

If you find the previous WSDL listing indecipherable, don't despair. Most people can't understand a WSDL document the first time they see one. Like many things that are complicated, the best approach to understanding WSDL is to study it in pieces. And fortunately, modern web services platforms like Axis generate (and read) WSDL for you. WSDL should be something you only need to look at when things break. At this point, things still break fairly often, so it's helpful to be familiar with WSDL: it will show you what the server expects when a method is called. But don't think that you'll be called on to write a WSDL document by yourself.

The <definitions> Element

The root element of a WSDL document is the `<definitions>` element. Usually, a WSDL document declares all the XML namespaces used in the root element. In the previous example, the `<definitions>` element makes four XML Namespace declarations:

```
<?xml version="1.0"?>
<definitions name="TravelAgent"
   xmlns="http://schemas.xmlsoap.org/wsdl/"
   xmlns:soap="http://schemas.xmlsoap.org/wsdl/soap/"
   xmlns:xsd="http://www.w3.org/2001/XMLSchema"
   xmlns:titan="http://www.titan.com/TravelAgent"
   targetNamespace="http://www.titan.com/TravelAgent">
```

The default namespace (`xmlns="http://schemas.xmlsoap.org/wsdl/"`) is the WSDL namespace. The `xsd` prefix is assigned to the XML Schema namespace. It is used primarily to identify simple data types such as `xsd:string`, `xsd:int`, and `xsd:dateTime` in `<message>` elements:

```
<message name="RequestMessage">
   <part name="cruiseId"   type="xsd:int" />
   <part name="cabinId"    type="xsd:int" />
   <part name="customerId" type="xsd:int" />
   <part name="price"      type="xsd:double" />
</message>
<message name="ResponseMessage">
   <part name="reservationId" type="xsd:string" />
</message>
```

The `titan` prefix is assigned to a Titan Cruise URL, which indicates that it's an XML Namespace that belongs to Titan Cruises. This namespace is also the value of the `targetNamespace` attribute. This attribute is similar to the one used in XML Schemas. For example, the `<portType>` references `<message>` elements, and the `<binding>` element references a `<portType>` using the target namespace:

```
<!-- message elements describe the paramters and return values -->
<message name="RequestMessage">
```

```
    <part name="cruiseId"   type="xsd:int" />
    <part name="cabinId"    type="xsd:int" />
    <part name="customerId" type="xsd:int" />
    <part name="price"      type="xsd:double" />
</message>
<message name="ResponseMessage">
    <part name="reservationId" type="xsd:string" />
</message>

<!-- portType element describes the abstract interface of a web service -->
<portType name="TravelAgent">
  <operation name="makeReservation">
     <input message="titan:RequestMessage"/>
     <output message="titan:ResponseMessage"/>
  </operation>
</portType>

<!-- binding element tells us which protocols and encoding styles are used  -->
<binding name="TravelAgentBinding" type="titan:TravelAgent">
   ...
</binding>
```

As you can see, the different WSDL types reference each other by name, and a named WSDL type automatically takes on the namespace declared by the targetNamespace attribute.

The <portType> and <message> Elements

The <message> and <portType> elements are the immediate children of the <definitions> element. Here's what they look like:

```
<!-- message elements describe the paramters and return values -->
<message name="RequestMessage">
   <part name="cruiseId"   type="xsd:int" />
   <part name="cabinId"    type="xsd:int" />
   <part name="customerId" type="xsd:int" />
   <part name="price"      type="xsd:double" />
</message>
<message name="ResponseMessage">
   <part name="reservationId" type="xsd:string" />
</message>

<!-- portType element describes the abstract interface of a web service -->
<portType name="TravelAgent">
  <operation name="makeReservation">
     <input message="titan:RequestMessage"/>
     <output message="titan:ResponseMessage"/>
  </operation>
</portType>
```

The <portType> element describes the web service operations (Java methods) that are available. An operation can have *input*, *output*, and *fault* messages. An *input* message describes the type of SOAP message a client should send to the web service. An *output* message describes the type of SOAP message a client should expect to get back. A *fault* message (not shown in the example) describes any SOAP error messages that the web service might send back to the client. A fault message is similar to a Java exception.

JAX-RPC, and therefore EJB 2.1, supports two styles of web service messaging: *request-response* and *one-way*. You know you are dealing with request-response if the `<operation>` element contains a single `<input>` element, followed by a single `<output>` element, and, optionally, zero or more `<fault>` elements. The TravelAgent `<portType>` is an example of the request-response messaging style:

```
<!-- portType element describes the abstract interface of a web service -->
<portType name="TravelAgent">
  <operation name="makeReservation">
     <input message="titan:RequestMessage"/>
     <output message="titan:ResponseMessage"/>
  </operation>
</portType>
```

The one-way message style, on the other hand, is implied by the presence of a single `<input>` element but no `<output>` or `<fault>` messages. Here is a web service that supports one-way messaging:

```
<!-- portType element describes the abstract interface of a web service -->
<portType name="ReservationProcessor">
  <operation name="submitReservation">
     <input message="titan:ReservationMessage"/>
  </operation>
</portType>
```

The request-response style of messaging is the kind you expect in RPC programming: you send a message and get a response. The one-way style tends to be used for asynchronous messaging; you send a message but do not expect a response. In addition, one-way messaging is frequently used to deliver XML documents, like Reservation, rather than parameters and return values. However, both request-response and one-way messaging styles can be used with either RPC or document-style messaging.

WSDL also supports two other messaging styles: *notification* (a single `<output>` and no `<input>`) and *solicitation* (a single `<output>` followed by a single `<input>`). While WSDL makes these messaging styles available, they are not supported by the WS-I Basic Profile 1.0 or JAX-RPC.

The <types> Element

If your service needs any custom types, they are defined in the `<types>` element, which is the first child of the `<definitions>` element. The complete WSDL document shown earlier did not include a `<types>` element because it didn't define any new types (it used XML Schema built-in types). The `<types>` element allows us to declare more complex XML types. For example, instead of declaring each of the parameters of the makeReservation operation as individual parts, they can be combined into a single structure that serves as the parameter of the operation:

```
<?xml version="1.0"?>
<definitions name="TravelAgent"
   xmlns="http://schemas.xmlsoap.org/wsdl/"
   xmlns:soap="http://schemas.xmlsoap.org/wsdl/soap/"
   xmlns:xsd="http://www.w3.org/2001/XMLSchema"
   xmlns:titan="http://www.titan.com/TravelAgent"
   targetNamespace="http://www.titan.com/TravelAgent">

<!-- types element describes complex XML data types -->
<types>
  <xsd:schema
    targetNamespace="http://www.titan.com/TravelAgent">

    <xsd:complexType name="ReservationType">
      <xsd:sequence>
        <xsd:element name="cruiseId" type="xsd:int"/>
        <xsd:element name="cabinId" type="xsd:int"/>
        <xsd:element name="customerId" type="xsd:int"/>
        <xsd:element name="price-paid" type="xsd:double"/>
      </xsd:sequence>
    </xsd:complexType>
  </xsd:schema>
</types>

<!-- message elements describe the paramters and return values -->
<message name="RequestMessage">
   <part name="reservation" type="titan:ReservationType" />
</message>
<message name="ResponseMessage">
   <part name="reservationId" type="xsd:string" />
</message>
```

The <types> element is frequently used with document-oriented messaging. For example, the following WSDL binding defines an XML Schema for the Reservation markup so that Reservation documents can be submitted to Titan as one-way messages. The schema is embedded within the WSDL document, as the content of the <types> element.

```
<?xml version="1.0"?>
<definitions name="Reservation"
   xmlns="http://schemas.xmlsoap.org/wsdl/"
   xmlns:soap="http://schemas.xmlsoap.org/wsdl/soap/"
   xmlns:xsd="http://www.w3.org/2001/XMLSchema"
   xmlns:titan="http://www.titan.com/Reservation"
   targetNamespace="http://www.titan.com/Reservation">

<!-- types element describes complex XML data types -->
<types>
  <xsd:schema
    targetNamespace="http://www.titan.com/Reservation">

  <xsd:element name="reservation" type="titan:ReservationType"/>
```

```
  <xsd:complexType name="ReservationType">
    <xsd:sequence>
      <xsd:element name="customer" type="titan:CustomerType"/>
      <xsd:element name="cruise-id" type="xsd:int"/>
      <xsd:element name="cabin-id" type="xsd:int"/>
      <xsd:element name="price-paid" type="xsd:double"/>
    </xsd:sequence>
  </xsd:complexType>
  <xsd:complexType name="CustomerType">
    <xsd:sequence>
      <xsd:element name="last-name" type="xsd:string"/>
      <xsd:element name="first-name" type="xsd:string"/>
      <xsd:element name="address" type="titan:AddressType"/>
      <xsd:element name="credit-card" type="titan:CreditCardType"/>
    </xsd:sequence>
  </xsd:complexType>
  <xsd:complexType name="CreditCardType">
    <xsd:sequence>
      <xsd:element name="exp-date" type="xsd:dateTime"/>
      <xsd:element name="number" type="xsd:string"/>
      <xsd:element name="name" type="xsd:string"/>
      <xsd:element name="organization" type="xsd:string"/>
    </xsd:sequence>
  </xsd:complexType>
  <xsd:complexType name="AddressType">
    <xsd:sequence>
      <xsd:element name="street" type="xsd:string"/>
      <xsd:element name="city" type="xsd:string"/>
      <xsd:element name="state" type="xsd:string"/>
      <xsd:element name="zip" type="xsd:string"/>
    </xsd:sequence>
  </xsd:complexType>
 </xsd:schema>
</types>

<!-- message elements describe the paramters and return values -->
<message name="ReservationMessage">
   <part name="inmessage" element="titan:reservation" />
</message>
<!-- portType element describes the abstract interface of a web service -->
<portType name="ReservationProcessor">
  <operation name="submitReservation">
     <input message="titan:ReservationMessage"/>
  </operation>
</portType>
<!-- binding tells us which protocols and encoding styles are used  -->
<binding name="ReservationProcessorBinding" type="titan:ReservationProcessor">
   <soap:binding style="document"
                 transport="http://schemas.xmlsoap.org/soap/http"/>
   <operation name="submitReservation">
      <soap:operation soapAction="" />
      <input>
        <soap:body use="literal"/>
      </input>
```

```
    </operation>
  </binding>
  <!-- service tells us the Internet address of a web service -->
  <service name="ReservationProcessorService">
    <port name="ReservationProcessorPort" binding="titan:ReservationProcessorBinding">
       <soap:address location="http://www.titan.com/webservices/Reservation" />
    </port>
  </service>

  </definitions>
```

The <binding> and <service> elements

In addition to the <portType> and <message> elements, a WSDL document also defines <binding> and <service> elements. These elements are used by JAX-RPC to generate marshalling and network communication code used to send and receive messages.

The <binding> element describes the type of encoding used to send and receive messages as well as the protocol on which the SOAP messages are carried. The <binding> definition for the TravelAgent port type looks like this:

```
<!-- binding element tells us which protocols and encoding styles are used  -->
<binding name="TravelAgentBinding" type="titan:TravelAgent">
   <soap:binding style="rpc"
                 transport="http://schemas.xmlsoap.org/soap/http"/>
   <operation name="makeReservation">
      <soap:operation soapAction="" />
      <input>
        <soap:body use="literal"
              namespace="http://www.titan.com/TravelAgent"/>
      </input>
      <output>
        <soap:body use="literal"
              namespace="http://www.titan.com/TravelAgent"/>
      </output>
   </operation>
</binding>
```

A binding element is always interlaced with protocol-specific elements—usually, the elements describe the SOAP protocol binding. (In fact, this is the only binding that is allowed by the WS-I Basic Profile 1.0.) Because J2EE web services must support SOAP with attachments, the MIME binding is also supported when attachments (images, documents, and so on) are sent with SOAP messages. However, that subject is a bit involved and is outside the scope of this book.

The <binding> element contains <operation>, <input>, <output>, and <fault> elements, similar to the <portType> element. In fact, a binding is specific to a particular <portType>: its <operation>, <input>, and <output> elements describe the implementation details of the corresponding <portType>. The previous example used the HTTP protocol with RPC/Literal–style messaging. The WSDL binding for Document/Literal style messaging would be different:

```
<!-- binding element tells us which protocols and encoding styles are used  -->
<binding name="TravelAgentBinding" type="titan:TravelAgent">
   <soap:binding style="document"
                 transport="http://schemas.xmlsoap.org/soap/http"/>
   <operation name="submitReservation">
      <soap:operation soapAction="" />
      <input>
        <soap:body use="literal/"/>
      </input>
   </operation>
</binding>
```

The <binding> element describes a one-way web service that accepts an XML document fragment. The <portType> associated with this <binding> also defines a single input message (consistent with one-way messaging) within an operation called submitReservation:

```
<!-- portType element describes the abstract interface of a web service -->
<portType name="ReservationProcessor">
  <operation name="submitReservation">
     <input message="titan:ReservationMessage"/>
  </operation>
</portType>
```

UDDI 2.0

UDDI (Universal Description, Discovery and Integration) is a specification that describes a standard for publishing and discovering web services on the Internet. It's essentially a repository with a rigid data structure that describes companies and the web services that they provide. UDDI is not as fundamental to web services and XML, SOAP, and WSDL, but it is considered a basic constituent of web services in J2EE.

The analogy normally used to describe UDDI is that it provides electronic White, Yellow, and Green pages for companies and their web services. You can look up companies by name or identifier (White pages) or by business or product category (Yellow pages). You can also discover information about web services hosted by a company by examining the technical entities of a UDDI registry (Green pages). In other words, UDDI is an electronic directory that allows organizations to advertise their business and web services and to locate other organizations and web services.

Not only does a UDDI registry provide information about web services and their hosts, a UDDI repository is itself a web service. You can search, access, add, update, and delete information in a UDDI registry using a set of standard SOAP messages. All UDDI registry products must support the standard UDDI data structures and SOAP messages, which means you can access any UDDI-compliant registry using the same standard set of SOAP messages.

Although organizations can set up private UDDI registries, there is a free UDDI registry anyone can use, called the UBR (Universal Business Registry). This registry is accessed at one of four sites hosted by Microsoft, IBM, SAP, and NTT. If you publish information about your company in any one of these sites, the data will be replicated to the each of the other four. You can find out more about the UBR and the sites that host it at *http://www.uddi.org*.

From Standards to Implementation

Understanding the fundamental web service standards (XML, SOAP, and WSDL) is essential to becoming a competent web services developer. However, you'll also need to understand how to implement web services in software. There are numerous web service platforms that allow you to build production systems based on the web service standards, including .NET, Perl, Apache Axis, and J2EE. The focus of this book is obviously the J2EE platform, and specifically support for web services in EJB. The next chapter explains how JAX-RPC is used to support web services in Enterprise JavaBeans.

CHAPTER 15

EJB 2.1 and Web Services

Support for web services in EJB 2.1 is based on the web services for the J2EE 1.1 (WS-J2EE) specification. This specification includes the Java API for XML-based RPC (JAX-RPC), SOAP with Attachments API for Java (SAAJ), and the Java API for XML Registries (JAXR). JAX-RPC is basically Java RMI over SOAP; SAAJ is an API for manipulating the structure of a SOAP message; and JAXR allows you to access web service registries, usually UDDI (Universal Description, Discovery and Integration).

While this chapter and the one before it provide you with a launching pad for learning about web services in J2EE (specifically EJB), the subject is too huge to cover in a book about EJB. In order to cover J2EE web services comprehensively we would have needed another 500 pages—since you'll need to lift this book to read it, I wrote a lighter approach to the subject. This chapter provides you with an introduction to JAX-RPC, but it should not be considered a comprehensive guide to the API.

If you are interested in learning more about the standard web services technologies (XML, SOAP 1.1, WSDL, and UDDI) and J2EE APIs (JAX-RPC, SAAJ, and JAXR), you might want to read *J2EE Web Services* (Addison-Wesley) by the author of this book, for a complete and thorough coverage of these topics.

The main purpose of JAX-RPC is to describe the relationship between WSDL 1.1, XML, SOAP 1.1, and Java. JAX-RPC provides EJB with a client-side programming model for accessing remote web services, as well as a server-side programming model for deploying EJBs as web services.

Accessing Web Services with JAX-RPC

JAX-RPC provides a client-side programming model based on Java RMI that allows you to access web services on other platforms from your EJBs. In other words, by using JAX-RPC, EJBs can access web services across the network hosted on Java and non-Java platforms (Perl, .NET, C++, and so on) alike. There are three APIs for accessing web services: generated stubs, dynamic proxies, and the DII (Dynamic Invocation Interface). Of these three APIs, the one you are most likely to use is the Generated Stubs programming model, which is the primary focus of this chapter.

Generated stubs are based on the classic Java RMI programming model, where the client accesses a remote service via a Java RMI remote interface implemented by a network stub. The stub translates calls made on the remote interface into network messages sent to the remote service. It's pretty much the same as using an EJB remote reference, except the protocol is SOAP over HTTP rather than CORBA IIOP. Figure 15-1 illustrates the RMI loop executed with a JAX-RPC generated stub.

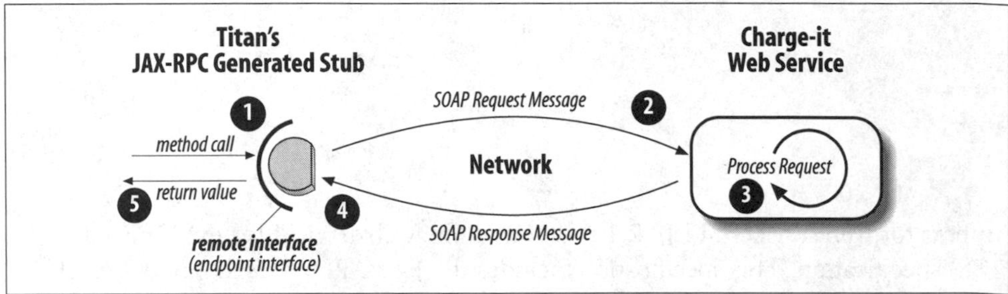

Figure 15-1. The JAX-RPC RMI Loop

The RMI loop in JAX-RPC is basically the same as any other RMI loop. In step 1, the client invokes a method on the JAX-RPC generated stub. The method invocation is transformed into a SOAP message that is sent to the server in step 2. In step 3 the web service process the request and send the results back as a SOAP response message in step 4. In step 5, the SOAP response messages is transformed into either a return value or an exception (if it was a SOAP Fault) and returned to the client.

Generating JAX-RPC Stubs from WSDL

Generated stubs get their name because the remote interface, called an *endpoint interface*, and the network stub are generated at deployment time. A JAX-RPC–compliant compiler generates the endpoint interface and stub from a WSDL document. The WSDL `<portType>` is used to create an endpoint interface, while the WSDL `<binding>` and `<port>` definitions are used to create the stub. The WSDL document is provided by the organization that hosts the web service. The JAX-RPC compiler reads the WSDL document and translates it into an endpoint interface and stub that you can use at runtime to send and receive SOAP messages.

Imagine that Titan Cruises subcontracts a company, Charge-It, Inc., to process payments made by customers using credit cards. Charge-It runs a system based on .NET and exposes its credit card processing application to clients via a web service. The web service is described by a WSDL document. The WSDL document for Charge-It's web service looks like this:

```
<?xml version="1.0" encoding="UTF-8"?>
<definitions xmlns="http://schemas.xmlsoap.org/wsdl/"
    xmlns:wsdl="http://schemas.xmlsoap.org/wsdl/"
    xmlns:xsd="http://www.w3.org/2001/XMLSchema"
```

```
    xmlns:soap="http://schemas.xmlsoap.org/wsdl/soap/"
    xmlns:tns="http://charge-it.com/Processor"
    targetNamespace="http://charge-it.com/Processor">

<message name="chargeRequest">
  <part name="name" type="xsd:string"/>
  <part name="number" type="xsd:string"/>
  <part name="exp-date" type="xsd:dateTime"/>
  <part name="card-type" type="xsd:string"/>
  <part name="amount" type="xsd:float"/>
</message>
<message name="chargeResponse">
  <part name="return" type="xsd:int"/>
</message>
<portType name="Processor">
  <operation name="charge">
    <input message="tns:chargeRequest"/>
    <output message="tns:chargeResponse"/>
  </operation>
</portType>
<binding name="ProcessorSoapBinding" type="tns:Processor">
  <soap:binding style="rpc"
      transport="http://schemas.xmlsoap.org/soap/http"/>
  <operation name="charge">
    <soap:operation soapAction="" style="rpc"/>
    <input>
      <soap:body use="literal"
          namespace="http://charge-it.com/Processor"/>
    </input>
    <output>
      <soap:body use="literal"
          namespace="http://charge-it.com/Processor"/>
    </output>
  </operation>
</binding>
<service name="ProcessorService">
   <port name="ProcessorPort" binding="tns:ProcessorSoapBinding">
      <soap:address
       location="http://www.charge-it.com/ProcessorService"/>
   </port>
</service>
</definitions>
```

The endpoint interface is based on the WSDL <portType> and its corresponding <message> definitions. Based on these definitions, a JAX-RPC compiler would generate the following interface:

```
package com.charge_it;

public interface Processor extends java.rmi.Remote {
    public int charge(String name, String number, java.util.Calendar expDate,
                      String cardType, float amount)
    throws java.rmi.RemoteException;
}
```

An endpoint interface is a Java RMI remote interface that extends the `java.rmi.Remote` type. Its methods must throw the `java.rmi.RemoteException` and, optionally, application exceptions. The interface name, method names, parameters, and exceptions are all derived from the WSDL document. Figure 15-2 shows the mapping between the <portType> and <message> definitions and the endpoint interface.

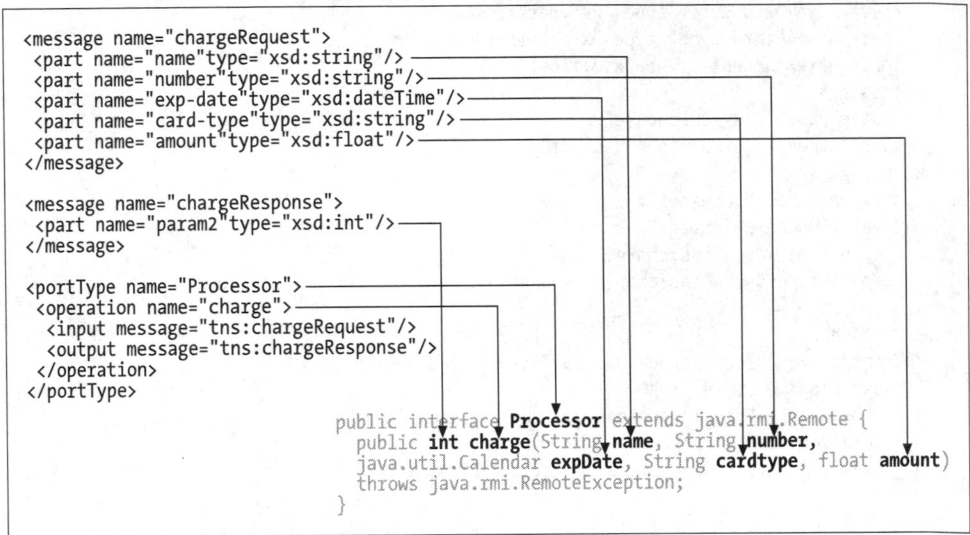

Figure 15-2. Mapping a WSDL <portType> to a JAX-RPC endpoint interface

The name of the endpoint interface comes from the name of the <portType>, which is `Processor`. The methods defined by the endpoint interface are derived from the <operation> elements declared by the WSDL <portType>. In this case, there is one <operation> element, which maps a single method, `charge()`. The parameters of the `charge()` method are derived from <operation> element's input message. For each <part> element of the input message, there will be a corresponding parameter in the `charge()` method. The output message, in this case, declares a single <part> element, which maps to the return type of the `charge()` method.

The JAX-RPC specification defines an exact mapping between many of the XML Schema built-in types and Java. This is how the XML Schema types declared by the WSDL <part> elements are mapped to the parameters and the return type of an endpoint method. Table 15-1 shows the mapping between XML Schema built-in types and Java primitives and classes.

Table 15-1. XML Schema built-in types and their corresponding Java types

XML Schema built-in type	Java type
xsd:byte	byte
xsd:boolean	boolean
xsd:short	short

Table 15-1. XML Schema built-in types and their corresponding Java types (continued)

XML Schema built-in type	Java type
xsd:int	int
xsd:long	long
xsd:float	float
xsd:double	double
xsd:string	java.lang.String
xsd:dateTime	java.util.Calendar
xsd:integer	java.math.BigInteger
xsd:decimal	java.math.BigDecimal
xsd:QName	java.xml.namespace.QName
xsd:base64Binary	byte [ ]
xsd:hexBinary	byte [ ]

JAX-RPC also maps *nillable* types (types that can be null), based on XML Schema built-in types, to Java primitive wrappers. For example, a nillable `xsd:int` type would map to a `java.lang.Integer` type and a nillable `xsd:double` would map to a `java.lang.Long` type.

In addition, JAX-RPC defines a mapping between complex types defined in the WSDL <types> element and Java bean classes. Complex types are addressed later in this chapter.

The stub, which implements the endpoint interface, is generated from the `<binding>` and `<port>` definitions. The JAX-RPC compiler translates the messaging style specified by the `<binding>` definition into a marshalling algorithm for converting method calls made on the endpoint stub into SOAP request and reply messages. Charge-It's WSDL document defines the following `<binding>` element:

```
<binding name="ProcessorSoapBinding" type="tns:Processor">
  <soap:binding style="rpc"
      transport="http://schemas.xmlsoap.org/soap/http"/>
  <operation name="charge">
    <soap:operation soapAction="" style="rpc"/>
    <input>
      <soap:body use="literal"
          namespace="http://charge-it.com/Processor"/>
    </input>
    <output>
      <soap:body use="literal"
          namespace="http://charge-it.com/Processor"/>
    </output>
  </operation>
</binding>
```

According to the `<binding>` element, the web service employs RPC/Literal SOAP 1.1 messages with a request-response style operation. When the JAX-RPC compiler reads this <binding>, it generates a corresponding stub that implements the endpoint interface. The stub is responsible for converting method calls made on the endpoint interface into SOAP messages sent to the web service. It's also responsible for converting SOAP response messages sent back to the stub into a return value—or, if it's a SOAP fault message, into an exception thrown by the endpoint method.

The stub is also based on a particular <port> definition, which declares the Internet address where the web service is located. The Charge-It WSDL document defines the following <port> element:

```
<service name="ProcessorService">
   <port name="ProcessorPort" binding="tns:ProcessorSoapBinding">
      <soap:address
       location="http://www.charge-it.com/ProcessorService"/>
   </port>
</service>
```

Based on this <port> definition, the JAX-RPC compiler generates the stub that exchanges SOAP messages with the URL indicated by the address attribute (`http://www.charge-it.com/ProcessorService`). Figure 15-3 illustrates how the Processor endpoint interface and stub are used to access the Charge-It credit card processing web service.

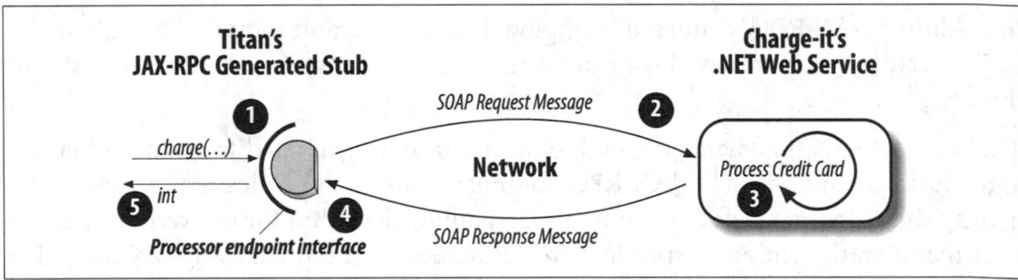

Figure 15-3. The JAX-RPC RMI loop for the Charge-It web service

In addition to the endpoint interface and its stub, the JAX-RPC compiler also creates a Service interface, which is used to get an instance of the generated stub at runtime. The Service interface is based on the <service> element of the WSDL document and declares methods for obtaining a live endpoint stub. Here's the definition of the `ProcessorService` interface generated from Charge-It's WSDL document:

```
package com.charge_it;

public interface ProcessorService extends javax.xml.rpc.Service {
   public com.charge_it.Processor getProcessorPort( )
      throws javax.xml.rpc.ServiceException;
   public java.lang.String getProcessorPortAddress( );
   public com.charge_it.Processor getProcessorPort(java.net.URL portAddress)
      throws javax.xml.rpc.ServiceException;
}
```

The getProcessorPort( ) method returns a live endpoint stub that is ready to invoke methods on the web service. The getProcessPortAddress( ) method returns the URL that the stub accesses by default. The getProcessorPort(URL) method allows you to create an endpoint stub that accesses a URL that is different from the default URL defined in the WSDL document.

The JAX-RPC compiler also generates a class that implements the Service interface. This class is tightly bound to the EJB Container system and manufactures endpoint stubs at runtime.

Using JAX-RPC Generated Stubs

Just like other resources (JDBC, JMS, and so on) the JAX-RPC Service is bound to a specific namespace in the JNDI ENC at deployment time. To get a reference to a stub at runtime, therefore, the EJB requests a specific JAX-RPC Service from the JNDI ENC. The stub is then used to execute operations on the remote web service.

To illustrate how stubs are used by EJBs, we will modify the bookPassage( ) method of the TravelAgentBean defined in Chapter 11. Instead of using the ProcessPayment EJB to process credit cards, the TravelAgent EJB will use the Charge-It's Processor web service. The following code shows the changes to the TravelAgentBean class:

```
package com.titan.travelagent;
import com.charge_it.ProcessorService;
import com.charge_it.Processor;
...
public class TravelAgentBean implements javax.ejb.SessionBean {
    public CustomerRemote customer;
    public CruiseLocal cruise;
    public CabinLocal cabin;
    public javax.naming.Context jndiContext;
    ...
    public TicketDO bookPassage(CreditCardDO card, double price)
        throws IncompleteConversationalState {

        if (customer == null || cruise == null || cabin == null)
        {
            throw new IncompleteConversationalState( );
        }
        try {
            ReservationHomeLocal resHome = (ReservationHomeLocal)
                jndiContext.lookup("java:comp/env/ejb/ReservationHomeLocal");

            ReservationLocal reservation =
                resHome.create(customer, cruise, cabin, price, new Date( ));

            ProcessorService webService = (ProcessorService) jndiContext.lookup(
                "java:comp/env/service/ChargeItProcessorService");

            Processor endpointStub = webService.getProcessorPort( );
```

```
            String customerName = customer.getFirstName( )+" "+
                                  customer.getLastName( );
            java.util.Calandar expDate = new Calandar(card.date);

            endpointStub.charge(customerName, card.number,
                                expDate, card.type, price);

            TicketDO ticket = new TicketDO(customer, cruise, cabin, price);
            return ticket;
        } catch(Exception e) {
            throw new EJBException(e);
        }
    }
    ...
}
```

As you can see, the EJB uses the JAX-RPC endpoint stub much like it would any other resource. It obtains a reference to a resource factory from the JNDI ENC, uses that to obtain the stub, and uses the stub to invoke operations on the web service—in this case, Charge-It's Processor web service.

The stub, however, presents some problems in a transactional environment. If the stub encounters a networking problem or SOAP processing error, it throws a `JAXRPCException`, which is caught and rethrown as an `EJBException`, causing the entire transaction to roll back. However, if an error occurs after the web service has executed but before the EJB method successfully returns, a partial rollback occurs: the reservation would be rolled back, but the charge made using the Charge-It web service would not.

The <service-ref> Deployment Element

EJB 2.1 includes a new element, `<service-ref>`, which binds a JAX-RPC Service to the JNDI ENC. The modified TravelAgent EJB declares a `<service-ref>` element that looks like this:

```
<?xml version='1.0' encoding='UTF-8' ?>
<ejb-jar
 xmlns="http://java.sun.com/xml/ns/j2ee"
 xmlns:xsi="http://www.w3.org/2001/XMLSchema-instance"
 xmlns:chargeIt="http://charge-it.com/Processor"
 xsi:schemaLocation="http://java.sun.com/xml/ns/j2ee
                     http://java.sun.com/xml/ns/j2ee/ejb-jar_2_1.xsd"
 version="2.1">
   <enterprise-beans>
     <session>
       <ejb-name>TravelAgentEJB</ejb-name>
       ...
       <service-ref>
         <service-ref-name>service/ChargeItProcessorService</service-ref-name>
         <service-interface>com.charge_it.ProcessorService</service-interface>
         <wsdl-file>META-INF/wsdl/ChargeItProcessor.wsdl</wsdl-file>
```

```
            <jaxrpc-mapping-file>META-INF/mapping.xml</jaxrpc-mapping-file>
            <service-qname>chargeIt:ProcessorService</service-qname>
          </service-ref>
        ...
      </session>
    </enterprise-beans>
    ...
  </ejb-jar>
```

The `<service-ref-name>` element declares the name of the JAX-RPC Service in the JNDI ENC—it's always relative to the `"java:comp/env"` context. The `<service-interface>` identifies the JAX-RPC Service interface, which is implemented by a JAX-RPC service object. The `<wsdl-file>` identifies the location of the WSDL document that describes the Charge-It web service. The WSDL document must be packaged in the same EJB-JAR file as the EJB that is making the web service call. The path is always relative to the root of the EJB-JAR file. In this case, a copy of the Charge-It WSDL document, `ChargeItProcessor.wsdl`, is stored in the *META-INF* directory of the EJB-JAR file. The `<jaxrpc-mapping-file>` identifies the location of the JAX-RPC mapping file relative to the root of the EJB-JAR file. In this case, it's also located in the *META-INF* directory. (The *JAX-RPC mapping file* is an additional deployment file that helps the EJB container system understand the mapping between the WSDL document and the endpoint service interfaces.) The `<service-qname>` identifies the fully qualified XML name of the WSDL `<service>` definition to which this reference pertains. The qualified service name is relative to the WSDL document identified by the `<wsdl-file>` element.

The JAX-RPC Mapping File

A JAX-RPC mapping file is required if an EJB is to use JAX-RPC to access web services. The mapping file conforms to a specific XML Schema defined by the Web Services for J2EE 1.1 specification. This file helps the deployment tools and EJB container understand the relationship between a JAX-RPC service and endpoint interfaces, and their corresponding WSDL document, allowing the deployment tools to generate a proper stub: one that uses the correct protocols and messaging modes.

At a bare minimum, the JAX-RPC mapping file must specify the mapping between the WSDL XML namespace of a `<service>` element and a Java package name. Example 15-1 is a perfectly legal JAX-RPC mapping file for the `<service-ref>` used by the TravelAgent EJB.

Example 15-1. EJB 2.1: Lightweight JAX-RPC mapping file

```
<?xml version='1.0' encoding='UTF-8' ?>
<java-wsdl-mapping
  xmlns="http://java.sun.com/xml/ns/j2ee"
  xmlns:xsi="http://www.w3.org/2001/XMLSchema-instance"
  xsi:schemaLocation="http://java.sun.com/xml/ns/j2ee
            http://www.ibm.com/webservices/xsd/j2ee_jaxrpc_mapping_1_1.xsd"
version="1.1">
```

Example 15-1. EJB 2.1: Lightweight JAX-RPC mapping file (continued)

```
  <package-mapping>
    <package-type>com.charge_it</package-type>
    <namespaceURI>http://charge-it.com/Processor</namespaceURI>
  </package-mapping>
</java-wsdl-mapping>
```

The JAX-RPC mapping shown in the previous listing is as simple as it gets. Only under very specific conditions can a JAX-RPC mapping file be this simple; the TravelAgent EJB happens to use a web service that qualifies. Here's a brief list of the attributes a WSDL document must have in order to qualify for a package-only JAX-RPC mapping file:

1. It has only one `<service>` element, which contains one `<port>` element.
2. The `<service>`, `<binding>`, `<portType>`, and all custom XML types (`complexType` and `simpleType`) have unique names.
3. The `<binding>` definition uses the RPC messaging style (`style="rpc"`) and SOAP 1.1 Encoding (`encodingStyle="http://schemas.xmlsoap.org/soap/encoding/"`) for all input, output, and fault message parts.
4. No header blocks or header faults are specified in the `<binding>` definition; the `parts` attribute of input and output elements must be omitted or, if the parts attribute is declared, it must list all parts.
5. Each `<operation>` within a `<portType>` definition must:
    - Have a unique name.
    - Include exactly one `<input>` element, zero or one `<output>` elements, and zero or more `<fault>` elements.
    - Omit the `parameterOrder` attribute. If the `parameterOrder` is declared, the `<operation>` must specify all parts from the input message in the order they are originally declared in the corresponding `<message>` definition.
6. A fault `<message>` definition has one part named `"message"` of type `"xsd:string"`.
7. The input `<message>` definition may declare zero or more `<part>` elements, and the output `<message>` definition may declare zero or one `<part>` elements.
8. Every `<part>` definition is defined with a `name` attribute and a `type` attribute; the `element` attribute is not used. The `type` attribute may be one of the following:
    - A standard XML Schema built-in type
    - An XML Schema–based complex type, which uses either the `xsd:sequence` or `xsd:all` compositor and can be easily mapped to Java beans according to the JAX-RPC specifications
    - A WSDL-restricted SOAP Encoded array

The *ChargeItProcessor.wsdl* document meets all these requirements; as a result, it only needs to have a package mapping. It's not difficult to create WSDL documents that meet these requirements; however, if you are attempting to access a web service defined by someone else, you're likely to run into WSDL documents that do not adhere to the criteria for a lightweight mapping file. In that case, you'll have to create a heavyweight mapping file. Example 15-2 is a heavyweight mapping file for the *ChargeItProcessor.wsdl* document.

Example 15-2. Heavyweight JAX-RPC mapping file

```
<?xml version='1.0' encoding='UTF-8' ?>
<java-wsdl-mapping
  xmlns="http://java.sun.com/xml/ns/j2ee"
  xmlns:chargeIt="http://charge-it.com/Processor"
  xmlns:xsi="http://www.w3.org/2001/XMLSchema-instance"
  xmlns:xsd="http://www.w3.org/2001/XMLSchema"
  xsi:schemaLocation="http://java.sun.com/xml/ns/j2ee
           http://www.ibm.com/webservices/xsd/j2ee_jaxrpc_mapping_1_1.xsd"
  version="1.1">

  <package-mapping>
   <package-type>com.charge_it</package-type>
   <namespaceURI>http://charge-it.com/Processor</namespaceURI>
  </package-mapping>
  <service-interface-mapping>
    <service-interface>com.charge_it.ProcessorService</service-interface>
    <wsdl-service-name>chargeIt:ProcessorService</wsdl-service-name>
    <port-mapping>
      <port-name>chargeIt:ProcessorPort</port-name>
      <java-port-name>ProcessorPort</java-port-name>
    </port-mapping>
  </service-interface-mapping>
  <service-endpoint-interface-mapping>
    <service-endpoint-interface>com.charge_it.Processor
    </service-endpoint-interface>
    <wsdl-port-type>chargeIt:Processor</wsdl-port-type>
    <wsdl-binding>chargeIt:ProcessorSoapBinding</wsdl-binding>
    <service-endpoint-method-mapping>
      <java-method-name>charge</java-method-name>
      <wsdl-operation>chargeIt:charge</wsdl-operation>
      <method-param-parts-mapping>
        <param-position>0</param-position>
        <param-type>java.lang.String</param-type>
        <wsdl-message-mapping>
          <wsdl-message>chargeIt:chargeRequest</wsdl-message>
          <wsdl-message-part-name>name</wsdl-message-part-name>
          <parameter-mode>IN</parameter-mode>
        </wsdl-message-mapping>
      </method-param-parts-mapping>
      <method-param-parts-mapping>
        <param-position>1</param-position>
        <param-type>java.lang.String</param-type>
        <wsdl-message-mapping>
          <wsdl-message>chargeIt:chargeRequest</wsdl-message>
          <wsdl-message-part-name>number</wsdl-message-part-name>
```

Example 15-2. Heavyweight JAX-RPC mapping file (continued)

```
          <parameter-mode>IN</parameter-mode>
        </wsdl-message-mapping>
      </method-param-parts-mapping>
      <method-param-parts-mapping>
        <param-position>2</param-position>
        <param-type>java.util.Calandar</param-type>
        <wsdl-message-mapping>
          <wsdl-message>chargeIt:chargeRequest</wsdl-message>
          <wsdl-message-part-name>exp-date</wsdl-message-part-name>
          <parameter-mode>IN</parameter-mode>
        </wsdl-message-mapping>
      </method-param-parts-mapping>
      <method-param-parts-mapping>
        <param-position>3</param-position>
        <param-type>java.lang.String</param-type>
        <wsdl-message-mapping>
          <wsdl-message>chargeIt:chargeRequest</wsdl-message>
          <wsdl-message-part-name>card-type</wsdl-message-part-name>
          <parameter-mode>IN</parameter-mode>
        </wsdl-message-mapping>
      </method-param-parts-mapping>
      <method-param-parts-mapping>
        <param-position>4</param-position>
        <param-type>float</param-type>
        <wsdl-message-mapping>
          <wsdl-message>chargeIt:chargeRequest</wsdl-message>
          <wsdl-message-part-name>amount</wsdl-message-part-name>
          <parameter-mode>IN</parameter-mode>
        </wsdl-message-mapping>
      </method-param-parts-mapping>
      <wsdl-return-value-mapping>
        <method-return-value>int</method-return-value>
        <wsdl-message>chargeIt:chargeResponse</wsdl-message>
        <wsdl-message-part-name>return</wsdl-message-part-name>
      </wsdl-return-value-mapping>
    </service-endpoint-method-mapping>
  </service-endpoint-interface-mapping>
</java-wsdl-mapping>
```

The complete JAX-RPC mapping file is too complicated to discuss in detail. Suffice it to say, the heavyweight mapping file is complex and provides elements for mapping every aspect of the service and endpoint interfaces to a WSDL document. The service interface is mapped to a WSDL `<service>` element, the endpoint interface is mapped to a WSDL `<portType>`, each method is mapped to a WSDL `<operation>`, and every parameter and return value is mapped to a specific WSDL `<part>` of a specific WSDL `<message>` definition.

It seems to me that a JAX-RPC compiler should be able to interpret a far broader set of WSDL definitions than the very narrow criteria required for a lightweight mapping. The Web Services for J2EE specification requires a complete mapping for any

JAX-RPC resource that strays even a little from the minimum criteria for a lightweight mapping. In my opinion, the criteria should be broadened. Only the nonconforming aspects of the WSDL document should be mapped; conforming elements should not require documentation in the mapping file.

Exercise 15.1 in the Workbook shows how to deploy these examples.

EJB Endpoints

An EJB *endpoint* is a stateless session bean that serves as a web service. Basically, the endpoint exposes a stateless session bean through a new component interface, called the *endpoint interface*; remote clients use SOAP 1.1 to access the methods defined in this interface. Because an EJB endpoint is simply a SOAP-accessible stateless session bean, it has the same advantages as other EJBs. An EJB endpoint runs in the EJB container that automatically manages transactions and security and provides access to other EJBs and resources via the JNDI ENC.

To illustrate how an EJB endpoint is developed, we'll create a new version of the TravelAgent EJB. The revised TravelAgent will use the same logic as the TravelAgent EJB developed in Chapter 11 and the ReservationProcessor developed in Chapter 12, but it will be deployed as a stateless session bean with an endpoint interface. The TravelAgent endpoint is based on the WSDL document shown earlier in this chapter.

The WSDL Document

Every EJB endpoint must have a WSDL document that describes the web service. The `<portType>` declared by the WSDL document must be aligned with the endpoint interface of the web service. In other words, the mapping between the WSDL `<portType>` and the endpoint interface must be correct according to the JAX-RPC specification. One way to accomplish this is to create the WSDL document first, and then use it to generate the endpoint interface:

```
<?xml version="1.0"?>
<definitions name="TravelAgent"
   xmlns="http://schemas.xmlsoap.org/wsdl/"
   xmlns:soap="http://schemas.xmlsoap.org/wsdl/soap/"
   xmlns:xsd="http://www.w3.org/2001/XMLSchema"
   xmlns:titan="http://www.titan.com/TravelAgent"
   targetNamespace="http://www.titan.com/TravelAgent">

<!-- message elements describe the parameters and return values -->
<message name="RequestMessage">
   <part name="cruiseId"   type="xsd:int" />
   <part name="cabinId"    type="xsd:int" />
   <part name="customerId" type="xsd:int" />
   <part name="price"      type="xsd:double" />
</message>
<message name="ResponseMessage">
```

```
    <part name="reservationId" type="xsd:string" />
</message>

<!-- portType element describes the abstract interface of a web service -->
<portType name="TravelAgentEndpoint">
  <operation name="makeReservation">
     <input message="titan:RequestMessage"/>
     <output message="titan:ResponseMessage"/>
  </operation>
</portType>

<!-- binding element tells us which protocols and encoding styles are used  -->
<binding name="TravelAgentBinding" type="titan:TravelAgentEndpoint">
   <soap:binding style="rpc"
                 transport="http://schemas.xmlsoap.org/soap/http"/>
   <operation name="makeReservation">
      <soap:operation soapAction="" />
      <input>
        <soap:body use="literal"
              namespace="http://www.titan.com/TravelAgent"/>
      </input>
      <output>
        <soap:body use="literal"
              namespace="http://www.titan.com/TravelAgent"/>
      </output>
   </operation>
</binding>

<!-- service element tells us the Internet address of a web service -->
<service name="TravelAgentService">
  <port name="TravelAgentPort" binding="titan:TravelAgentBinding">
     <soap:address location="http://www.titan.com/webservices/TravelAgent" />
  </port>
</service>

</definitions>
```

The Endpoint Interface

Based on this WSDL document, we can generate a JAX-RPC endpoint interface, which will be implemented by our EJB endpoint. The endpoint interface is generated from the <portType> and <message> definitions (and <types>, if present). The endpoint interface looks like this:

```
package com.titan.webservice;

public interface TravelAgentEndpoint extends java.rmi.Remote {
    public java.lang.String makeReservation(int cruiseId, int cabinId,
                                            int customerId, double price)
    throws java.rmi.RemoteException;
}
```

The endpoint interface defines the business methods that will be accessible as SOAP operations. The interface extends `java.rmi.Remote`—there is no EJBObject interface—and defines one or more business methods, each of which must throw a `java.rmi.RemoteException`. The types that can be used as parameters and return types are the same types that can be used with JAX-RPC generated endpoints (see Table 15-1). You can also use simple Java bean types for holding complex data.

No Home Interface

An EJB endpoint does not define a home interface; there is no EJB home object for creating or locating EJB endpoints. An EJB endpoint cannot be created or located; it's a truly stateless service, both semantically and physically. The only time an EJB would have a home interface is if the EJB defined remote or local interfaces in addition to the endpoint interface. In other words, a single EJB can be local, remote, and an endpoint.

The Stateless Bean Class

The bean class defined for the TravelAgent endpoint must implement the methods defined by the endpoint interface. A stateless bean class can implement the endpoint interface directly—something that's not recommended for the local or remote interfaces. That's because the endpoint interface is a direct descendent of `java.rmi.Remote`, and doesn't define any `EJBObject` methods. Here's the new definition for the TravelAgent bean class:

```
package com.titan.webservice;
import com.titan.reservation.*;
import com.titan.cruise.*;
import com.titan.customer.*;
import com.titan.cabin.*;
import com.titan.processpayment.*;
import java.rmi.RemoteException;
import javax.rmi.PortableRemoteObject;
import javax.naming.NamingException;
import javax.ejb.EJBException;
import java.util.Date;
import java.util.Calendar;

public class TravelAgentBean
    implements TravelAgentEndpoint, javax.ejb.SessionBean {
    public javax.naming.Context jndiContext;

    public void ejbCreate() {}

    public String makeReservation(int cruiseId, int cabinId,
                                  int customerId, double price){
      try {
            CruiseLocal cruise = this.getCruise(cruiseId);
            CabinLocal cabin = this.getCabin(cabinId);
```

```
            CustomerRemote customer = this.getCustomer(customerId);
            CreditCardDO card = this.getCreditCard(customerId);

            ReservationHomeLocal resHome = (ReservationHomeLocal)
                jndiContext.lookup("java:comp/env/ejb/ReservationHomeLocal");
            ReservationLocal reservation =
                resHome.create(customer, cruise, cabin, price, new Date( ));
            Object ref = jndiContext.lookup(
                     "java:comp/env/ejb/ProcessPaymentHomeRemote");
            ProcessPaymentHomeRemote ppHome = (ProcessPaymentHomeRemote)
            PortableRemoteObject.narrow(ref, ProcessPaymentHomeRemote.class);

            ProcessPaymentRemote process = ppHome.create( );
            process.byCredit(customer, card, price);

            return reservation.getPrimaryKey().toString( );

        } catch(Exception e) {
            throw new EJBException(e);
        }
    }

    public CustomerRemote getCustomer(int customer_id) throws Exception {
        Integer customerID = new Integer(customer_id);
        CustomerHomeRemote home = (CustomerHomeRemote)
                jndiContext.lookup("java:comp/env/ejb/CustomerHomeRemote");

        return home.findByPrimaryKey(customerID);
    }
    public CreditCardDO getCreditCard(int customer_id) throws Exception{
        Integer customerID = new Integer(customer_id);
        CustomerHomeLocal home = (CustomerHomeLocal)
                jndiContext.lookup("java:comp/env/ejb/CustomerHomeLocal");

        CustomerLocal customer = home.findByPrimaryKey(customerID);
        CreditCardLocal card = customer.getCreditCard( );
        return new CreditCardDO(card.getNumber(),card.getExpirationDate( ),
                               card.getCreditOrganization( ));
    }
    public CabinLocal getCabin(int cabin_id) throws Exception {
        Integer cabinID = new Integer(cabin_id);
        CabinHomeLocal home = (CabinHomeLocal)
             jndiContext.lookup("java:comp/env/ejb/CabinHomeLocal");

        return home.findByPrimaryKey(cabinID);
    }
    public CruiseLocal getCruise(int cruise_id) throws Exception {
        Integer cruiseID = new Integer(cruise_id);
        CruiseHomeLocal home = (CruiseHomeLocal)
               jndiContext.lookup("java:comp/env/ejb/CruiseHomeLocal");

        return home.findByPrimaryKey(cruiseID);
    }
    public void ejbRemove( ) {}
```

```
    public void ejbActivate( ) {}
    public void ejbPassivate( ) {}
    public void setSessionContext(javax.ejb.SessionContext cntx){
        try {
            jndiContext = new javax.naming.InitialContext( );
        }catch(NamingException ne) {
            throw new EJBException(ne);
        }
    }
}
```

The TravelAgentBean class is not that different from the TravelAgent EJB developed earlier in this chapter (the version that uses the Charge-It credit card processing web service). The primary difference is that it responds to web service calls, rather than remote or local calls.

The Deployment Files

The TravelAgent endpoint requires four deployment files: a standard *ejb-jar.xml* deployment descriptor, a WSDL file, a JAX-RPC mapping file, and a *webservices.xml* file.

ejb-jar.xml file

An EJB endpoint is deployed using the same ejb-jar.xml elements as a regular stateless session bean. The endpoint declares a single component interface element, the <service-endpoint>. This element can be used only with stateless session beans that are deployed as EJB endpoints. A single EJB can actually support remote, local, and endpoint interfaces simultaneously. Here, we'll keep it simple and limit the TravelAgent endpoint to web services. Other than the <service-endpoint> element, the rest of the deployment descriptor is pretty much the same as a regular stateless session bean:

```
<?xml version='1.0' encoding='UTF-8' standalone='yes'?>
<ejb-jar
     xmlns="http://java.sun.com/xml/ns/j2ee"
     xmlns:xsi="http://www.w3.org/2001/XMLSchema-instance"
     xsi:schemaLocation="http://java.sun.com/xml/ns/j2ee
                         http://java.sun.com/xml/ns/j2ee/ejb-jar_2_1.xsd"
     version="2.1">
    <enterprise-beans>
        <session>
            <description>
                A Web Service reservation service
            </description>
            <ejb-name>TravelAgentEjbEndpoint</ejb-name>
            <service-endpoint>
                 com.titan.webservice.TravelAgentEndpoint
            </service-endpoint>
            <ejb-class>
                com.titan.webservice.TravelAgentBean
            </ejb-class>
```

```
            <session-type>Stateless</session-type>
            <transaction-type>Container</transaction-type>
            <ejb-ref>
                <ejb-ref-name>ejb/ProcessPaymentHomeRemote</ejb-ref-name>
                <ejb-ref-type>Session</ejb-ref-type>
                <home>com.titan.processpayment.ProcessPaymentHomeRemote</home>
                <remote>com.titan.processpayment.ProcessPaymentRemote</remote>
            </ejb-ref>
            ...
        </session>
        ...
    </enterprise-beans>
    <assembly-descriptor>
        ...
    </assembly-descriptor>
</ejb-jar>
```

The value for the <ejb-name> element can be anything you choose; in this book, we use the suffix "Endpoint" to denote an EJB endpoint component.

You cannot declare the transaction attribute of any method of an endpoint as *mandatory*, because doing so implies that the Enterprise Bean method must be enrolled in the calling client's transaction. Since transaction propagation is not standardized in web services, it's assumed that the client will not be propagating a transaction.

WSDL file

The WSDL file used to generate the endpoint interface must be packaged with the EJB endpoint. Normally, the WSDL document is placed in the *META-INF* directory of the JAR file, but it can go anywhere as long as it's in the same JAR file as the EJB endpoint.

JAX-RPC mapping file

EJB endpoints, like JAX-RPC generated stubs, require you to define a JAX-RPC mapping file. The mapping file can have any name, but it should be descriptive, and the file type should be XML. It's common to name this file *mapping.xml* or *travelagent_mapping.xml*, or something along those lines. Here's a lightweight JAX-RPC mapping file for the TravelAgent endpoint:

```
<?xml version='1.0' encoding='UTF-8' ?>
<java-wsdl-mapping
  xmlns="http://java.sun.com/xml/ns/j2ee"
  xmlns:xsi="http://www.w3.org/2001/XMLSchema-instance"
  xsi:schemaLocation="http://java.sun.com/xml/ns/j2ee
              http://www.ibm.com/webservices/xsd/j2ee_jaxrpc_mapping_1_1.xsd"
  version="1.1">
  <package-mapping>
    <package-type>com.titan.webservice</package-type>
    <namespaceURI>http://www.titan.com/TravelAgent</namespaceURI>
  </package-mapping>
</java-wsdl-mapping>
```

The JAX-RPC mapping file was covered earlier in this chapter, in the section entitled "The JAX-RPC Mapping File." Basically, this deployment descriptor maps a Java package to the XML Namespace of the WSDL `<port>` and other elements, helping the container to understand which packaged classes are associated with which WSDL definitions.

webservices.xml file

The *webservices.xml* file is the baling wire that ties the separate deployment files together. It defines the relationships between the *ejb-jar.xml*, the WSDL file, and the JAX-RPC mapping file:

```
<?xml version='1.0' encoding='UTF-8' ?>
<webservices
   xmlns="http://java.sun.com/xml/ns/j2ee"
   xmlns:xsi="http://www.w3.org/2001/XMLSchema-instance"
   xmlns:titan="http://www.titan.com/TravelAgent"
   xsi:schemaLocation="http://java.sun.com/xml/ns/j2ee
                http://www.ibm.com/webservices/xsd/j2ee_web_services_1_1.xsd"
   version="1.1">

      <webservice-description>
         <webservice-description-name>TravelAgentService
         </webservice-description-name>
         <wsdl-file>/META-INF/travelagent.wsdl</wsdl-file>
         <jaxrpc-mapping-file>/META-INF/travelagent_mapping.xml
         </jaxrpc-mapping-file>
         <port-component>
            <port-component-name>TravelAgentEndpoint</port-component-name>
            <wsdl-port>titan:TravelAgentPort</wsdl-port>
            <service-endpoint-interface>
               com.titan.webservice.TravelAgentEndpoint
            </service-endpoint-interface>
            <service-impl-bean>
               <ejb-link>TravelAgentEjbEndpoint</ejb-link>
            </service-impl-bean>
         </port-component>
      </webservice-description>
</webservices>
```

The `<webservice-description>` element describes an EJB endpoint: there may be one or more of these elements in a single *webservices.xml* file.* The `<webservice-description-name>` is a unique name assigned to the web service description. It can be anything you like. The `<wsdl-file>` element points to the WSDL document of the EJB endpoint. Each EJB endpoint has exactly one WSDL document, which is usually located in the *META-INF* directory of the EJB-JAR file. When the EJB endpoint

* The `<webservice-description>` element can also describe a JAX-RPC service endpoint, which is a servlet-based web service that is outside the scope of this book.

is deployed, your deployment tool will probably provide you with the option of copying the WSDL document to some type of public URL or registry so that others can discover the web service. The `<jaxrpc-mapping-file>` element indicates the location of the JAX-RPC mapping file that is associated with the EJB endpoint and the WSDL document. It, too, is usually located in the *META-INF* directory of the EJB JAR file.

The `<port-component>` element maps a stateless session bean declared in the *ejb-jar.xml* file to a specific `<port>` in the WSDL document. The `<port-component-name>` is the logical name you assign the EJB endpoint. It can be anything. The `<wsdl-port>` element maps the EJB endpoint deployment information to a specific WSDL `<port>` element in the WSDL document. The `<service-endpoint-interface>` is the fully qualified name of the endpoint interface—it must be the same interface declared by the `<service-endpoint>` element for the EJB in the *ejb-jar.xml* file. The `<service-impl-bean>` and its `<ejb-link>` element link the `<port-component>` to a specific EJB in the *ejb-jar.xml*. The value of the `<ejb-link>` must match the value of the `<ejb-name>` in the *ejb-jar.xml* file.

CHAPTER 16
Transactions

ACID Transactions

To understand how transactions work, we will revisit the TravelAgent EJB, the stateful session bean developed in Chapter 11 that encapsulates the process of making a cruise reservation for a customer. The TravelAgent EJB's `bookPassage( )` method looks like this:

```
public TicketDO bookPassage(CreditCardDO card, double price)
    throws IncompleteConversationalState {

    if (customer == null || cruise == null || cabin == null) {
        throw new IncompleteConversationalState( );
    }
    try {
        ReservationHomeLocal resHome = (ReservationHomeLocal)
            jndiContext.lookup("java:comp/env/ejb/ReservationHomeLocal");
        ReservationLocal reservation =
            resHome.create(customer, cruise, cabin, price);
        Object ref = jndiContext.lookup
            ("java:comp/env/ejb/ProcessPaymentHomeRemote");
        ProcessPaymentHomeRemote ppHome = (ProcessPaymentHomeRemote)
            PortableRemoteObject.narrow(ref, ProcessPaymentHomeRemote.class);
        ProcessPaymentRemote process = ppHome.create( );
        process.byCredit(customer, card, price);

        TicketDO ticket = new TicketDO(customer,cruise,cabin,price);

        return ticket;
    } catch(Exception e) {
        throw new EJBException(e);
    }
}
```

The TravelAgent EJB is a fairly simple session bean, and its use of other EJBs is typical of business-object design and taskflow. Unfortunately, good business-object design is not enough to make these EJBs useful in an industrial-strength application.

The problem is not with the definition of the EJBs or the taskflow; the problem is that a good design does not, in and of itself, guarantee that the TravelAgent EJB's `bookPassage()` method represents a good *transaction*. To understand why, we will take a closer look at what a transaction is and what criteria a transaction must meet to be considered reliable.

In business, a transaction usually involves an exchange between two parties. When you purchase an ice cream cone, you exchange money for food; when you work for a company, you exchange skill and time for money (which you use to buy more ice cream). When you are involved in these exchanges, you monitor the outcome to ensure that you don't get "ripped off." If you give the ice cream vendor a $20 bill, you don't want him to drive off without giving you your change; likewise, you want to make sure that your paycheck reflects all the hours you worked. By monitoring these commercial exchanges, you are attempting to ensure the reliability of the transactions; you are making sure that each transaction meets everyone's expectations.

In business software, a transaction embodies the concept of a commercial exchange. A business system transaction (transaction for short) is the execution of a *unit-of-work* that accesses one or more shared resources, usually databases. A unit-of-work is a set of activities that relate to each other and must be completed together. The reservation process is a unit-of-work made up of several activities: recording a reservation, debiting a credit card, and generating a ticket together make up a unit-of-work.

The object of a transaction is to execute a unit-of-work that results in a reliable exchange. Here are some types of business systems that employ transactions:

ATM
: The ATM (automatic teller machine) you use to deposit, withdraw, and transfer funds executes these units-of-work as transactions. In an ATM withdrawal, for example, the ATM checks to make sure you don't overdraw and then debits your account and spits out some money.

Online book order
: You've probably purchased many of your Java books—maybe even this book—from an online bookseller. This type of purchase is also a unit-of-work that takes place as a transaction. In an online book purchase, you submit your credit card number, it is validated, and a charge is made for price of the book. Then an order to ship you the book is sent to the bookseller's warehouse.

Medical system
: In a medical system, important data—some of it critical—is recorded about patients every day, including information about clinical visits, medical procedures, prescriptions, and drug allergies. The doctor prescribes the drug, then the system checks for allergies, contraindications, and appropriate dosages. If all tests pass, the drug can be administered. These tasks make up a unit-of-work. A unit-of-work in a medical system may not be financial, but it's just as important. Failure to identify a drug allergy in a patient could be fatal.

As you can see, transactions are often complex and usually involve the manipulation of a lot of data. Mistakes in data can cost money, or even a life. Transactions must therefore preserve data integrity, which means that the transaction must work perfectly every time or not be executed at all. This is a pretty tall order. As difficult as this requirement is, however, when it comes to commerce, there is no room for error. Units-of-work involving money or anything of value always require the utmost reliability, because errors impact the revenues and the well-being of the parties involved.

To give you an idea of the accuracy required by transactions, think about what would happen if a transactional system suffered from seemingly infrequent errors. ATMs provide customers with convenient access to their bank accounts and represent a significant percentage of the total transactions in personal banking. The transactions handled by ATMs are simple but numerous, providing us with a great example of why transactions must be error-proof. Let's say that a bank has 100 ATMs in a metropolitan area, and each ATM processes 300 transactions (deposits, withdrawals, or transfers) a day, for a total of 30,000 transactions per day. If each transaction, on average, involves the deposit, withdrawal, or transfer of about $100, about 3 million dollars will move through the ATM system per day. In the course of a year, that's a little over a billion dollars:

365 days × 100 ATMs × 300 transactions × $100.00 = $1,095,000,000.00

How well do the ATMs have to perform to be considered reliable? For the sake of argument, let's say that ATMs execute transactions correctly 99.99% of the time. This seems to be more than adequate: after all, only one out of every ten thousand transactions executes incorrectly. But over the course of a year, if you do the math, that could result in over $100,000 in errors!

$1,095,000,000.00 × .01% = $109,500.00

Obviously, this example is an oversimplification of the problem, but it illustrates that even a small percentage of errors is unacceptable in high-volume or mission-critical systems. For this reason, experts have identified four characteristics of a transaction that must be met for a system to be considered safe. Transactions must be *atomic*, *consistent*, *isolated*, and *durable* (ACID)—the four horsemen of transaction services. Here's what each term means:

Atomic
: An atomic transaction must execute completely or not at all. This means that every task within a unit-of-work must execute without error. If any of the tasks fails, the entire unit-of-work or transaction is aborted, meaning that any changes to the data are undone. If all the tasks execute successfully, the transaction is committed, which means that the changes to the data are made permanent or durable.

Consistent
: Consistency is a transactional characteristic that must be enforced by both the transactional system and the application developer. Consistency refers to the

integrity of the underlying data store. The transactional system fulfills its obligation for consistency by ensuring that a transaction is atomic, isolated, and durable. The application developer must ensure that the database has appropriate constraints (primary keys, referential integrity, and so forth) and that the unit-of-work, the business logic, doesn't result in inconsistent data (i.e., data that is not in harmony with the real world it represents). In an account transfer, for example, a debit to one account must equal the credit to another account.

Isolated

A transaction must be allowed to execute without interference from other processes or transactions. In other words, the data that a transaction accesses cannot be affected by any other part of the system until the transaction or unit-of-work is completed.

Durable

Durability means that all the data changes made during the course of a transaction must be written to some type of physical storage before the transaction is successfully completed. This ensures that the changes are not lost if the system crashes.

To get a better idea of what these principles mean, we will examine the TravelAgent EJB in terms of the four ACID properties.

Is the TravelAgent EJB Atomic?

Our first measure of the TravelAgent EJB's reliability is its atomicity: does it ensure that the transaction executes completely or not at all? What we are really concerned with are the critical tasks that change or create information. In the `bookPassage()` method, a Reservation EJB is created, the ProcessPayment EJB debits a credit card, and a `TicketDO` object is created. All of these tasks must be successful for the entire transaction to be successful.

To understand the importance of the atomic characteristic, imagine what would happen if even one of the subtasks failed to execute. If, for example, the creation of a Reservation EJB failed but all other tasks succeeded, your customer would probably end up getting bumped from the cruise or sharing the cabin with a stranger. As far as the travel agent is concerned, the `bookPassage()` method executed successfully because a `TicketDO` was generated. If a ticket is generated without the creation of a reservation, the state of the business system becomes inconsistent with reality, because the customer paid for a ticket but the reservation was not recorded. Likewise, if the ProcessPayment EJB fails to charge the customer's credit card, the customer gets a free cruise. He may be happy, but management won't be. Finally, if the `TicketDO` is never created, the customer will have no record of the transaction and probably will not be allowed onto the ship.

So the only way `bookPassage()` can be completed is if all the critical tasks execute successfully. If something goes wrong, the entire process must be aborted. Aborting a transaction requires more than simply not finishing the tasks; in addition, all the tasks that did execute within the transaction must be undone. If, for example, the creation of the Reservation EJB and `ProcessPayment.byCredit()` method succeeded but the creation of the `TicketDO` failed, throwing an exception from the constructor, the reservation record and payment records must not be added to the database.

Is the TravelAgent EJB Consistent?

In order for a transaction to be consistent, the business system must make sense after the transaction has completed. In other words, the *state* of the business system must be consistent with the reality of the business. This requires that the transaction enforce the atomic, isolated, and durable characteristics of the transaction, and it also requires diligent enforcement of integrity constraints by the application developer. If, for example, the application developer fails to include the credit card charge operation in the `bookPassage()` method, the customer will be issued a ticket but will never be charged. The data will be inconsistent with the expectation of the business—a customer should be charged for passage.

In addition, the database must be set up to enforce integrity constraints. For example, it should not be possible for a record to be added to the `RESERVATION` table unless the `CABIN_ID`, `CRUISE_ID`, and `CUSTOMER_ID` foreign keys map to corresponding records in the `CABIN`, `CRUISE`, and `CUSTOMER` tables, respectively. If a `CUSTOMER_ID` that does not map to a `CUSTOMER` record is used, referential integrity should cause the database to throw an error message.

Is the TravelAgent EJB Isolated?

If you are familiar with the concept of thread synchronization in Java or row-locking schemes in relational databases, isolation will be a familiar concept. To be isolated, a transaction must protect the data it is accessing from other transactions. This is necessary to prevent other transactions from interacting with data that is in transition. In the TravelAgent EJB, the transaction is isolated to prevent other transactions from modifying the EJBs that are being updated. Imagine the problems that would arise if separate transactions were allowed to change any entity bean at any time—transactions would walk all over each other. You could easily have several customers book the same cabin because their travel agents happened to make their reservations at the same time.

The isolation of data accessed by EJBs does not mean that the entire application shuts down during a transaction. Only those entity beans and data directly affected by the transaction are isolated. In the TravelAgent EJB, for example, the transaction isolates only the Reservation EJB created. There can be many Reservation EJBs in existence; there's no reason these other EJBs can't be accessed by other transactions.

Is the TravelAgent EJB Durable?

To be durable, the `bookPassage()` method must write all changes and new data to a permanent data store before it can be considered successful. While this may seem like a no-brainer, often it is not what happens in real life. In the name of efficiency, changes are often maintained in memory for long periods of time before being saved on a disk drive. The idea is to reduce disk accesses—which slow systems down—and only periodically write the cumulative effect of data changes. While this approach is great for performance, it is also dangerous because data can be lost when the system goes down and memory is wiped out. Durability requires the system to save all updates made within a transaction as the transaction successfully completes, thus protecting the integrity of the data.

In the TravelAgent EJB, this means that the new `RESERVATION` and `PAYMENT` records inserted are made persistent before the transaction can complete successfully. Only when the data is made durable are those specific records accessible through their respective EJBs from other transactions. Hence, durability also plays a role in isolation. A transaction is not finished until the data is successfully recorded.

Ensuring that transactions adhere to the ACID principles requires careful design. The system has to monitor the progress of a transaction to ensure that it does all its work, that the data is changed correctly, that transactions do not interfere with each other, and that the changes can survive a system crash. Engineering all this functionality into a system is a lot of work, and not something you would want to reinvent for every business system on which you work. Fortunately, EJB is designed to support transactions automatically, making the development of transactional systems easier. The rest of this chapter examines how EJB supports transactions implicitly (through declarative transaction attributes) and explicitly (through the Java Transaction API).

Declarative Transaction Management

One of the primary advantages of Enterprise JavaBeans is that it allows for *declarative transaction management*. Without this feature, transactions must be controlled using explicit transaction demarcation, which involves the use of fairly complex APIs like the OMG's Object Transaction Service (OTS) or its Java implementation, the Java Transaction Service (JTS). At best, explicit demarcation is difficult to use, particularly if you are new to transactional systems. In addition, explicit transaction demarcation requires that the transactional code be written within the business logic, which reduces the clarity of the code and, more importantly, creates inflexible distributed objects. Once transaction demarcation is hardcoded into the business object, changes in transaction behavior require changes to the business logic itself. We talk more about explicit transaction management and EJB later in this chapter.

With declarative transaction management, the transactional behavior of EJBs can be controlled using the *deployment descriptor*, which sets transaction attributes for individual enterprise bean methods. This means that the transactional behavior of an EJB can be changed without changing the EJB's business logic. In addition, an EJB deployed in one application can be defined with different transactional behavior than the same EJB deployed in a different application. Declarative transaction management reduces the complexity of transactions for EJB developers and application developers and makes it easier to create robust transactional applications.

Transaction Scope

Transaction scope is a crucial concept for understanding transactions. In this context, transaction scope means those EJBs—both session and entity—that are participating in a particular transaction. In the `bookPassage()` method of the TravelAgent EJB, all the EJBs involved are part of the same transaction scope. The scope of the transaction starts when a client invokes the TravelAgent EJB's `bookPassage()` method. Once the transaction scope has started, it is *propagated* to both the newly created Reservation EJB and the ProcessPayment EJB.

As you know, a transaction is a unit-of-work made up of one or more tasks. In a transaction, all the tasks that make up the unit-of-work must succeed for the entire transaction to succeed; in other words, the transaction must be atomic. If any task fails, the updates made by all the other tasks in the transaction will be rolled back or undone. In EJB, tasks are expressed as enterprise bean methods, and a unit-of-work consists of every enterprise bean method invoked in a transaction. The scope of a transaction includes every EJB that participates in the unit-of-work.

It is easy to trace the scope of a transaction by following the thread of execution. If the invocation of the `bookPassage()` method begins a transaction, then logically, the transaction ends when the method completes. The scope of the `bookPassage()` transaction would include the TravelAgent, Reservation, and ProcessPayment EJBs—every EJB touched by the `bookPassage()` method. A transaction is propagated to an EJB when that EJB's method is invoked and included in the scope of that transaction.

A transaction can end if an exception is thrown while the `bookPassage()` method is executing. The exception can be thrown from one of the other EJBs or from the `bookPassage()` method itself. An exception may or may not cause a rollback, depending on its type. We'll discuss exceptions and transactions in more detail later.

The thread of execution is not the only factor that determines whether an EJB is included in the scope of a transaction; the EJB's transaction attributes also play a role. Determining whether an EJB participates in the transaction scope of any unit-of-work is accomplished implicitly, using the EJB's transaction attributes, or explicitly, using the Java Transaction API (JTA).

Transaction Attributes

As an application developer, you don't normally need to control transactions explicitly when using an EJB server. EJB servers can manage transactions implicitly, based on the transaction attributes established at deployment time. When an EJB is deployed, you can set its runtime transaction attribute in the deployment descriptor to one of several values. Here are the XML attribute values used to specify transaction attributes:

```
NotSupported
Supports
Required
RequiresNew
Mandatory
Never
```

You can set a transaction attribute for the entire EJB (in which case it applies to all methods) or you can set different transaction attributes for individual methods. The former method is much simpler and less error-prone, but setting attributes at the method level offers more flexibility. The code in the following sections shows how to set the default transaction attribute of an EJB in the EJB's deployment descriptor.

Setting a transaction attribute

In the XML deployment descriptor, a `<container-transaction>` element specifies the transaction attributes for the EJBs described in the deployment descriptor:

```
<ejb-jar ...>
    ...
    <assembly-descriptor>
        ...
        <container-transaction>
            <method>
                <ejb-name>TravelAgentEJB</ejb-name>
                <method-name> * </method-name>
            </method>
            <trans-attribute>Required</trans-attribute>
        </container-transaction>
        <container-transaction>
            <method>
                <ejb-name>TravelAgentEJB</ejb-name>
                <method-name>listAvailableCabins</method-name>
            </method>
            <trans-attribute>Supports</trans-attribute>
        </container-transaction>
        ...
    </assembly-descriptor>
    ...
</ejb-jar>
```

This deployment descriptor specifies the transaction attributes for the TravelAgent EJB. Each `<container-transaction>` element specifies a method and that method's transaction attribute. The first `<container-transaction>` element specifies that all methods have a transaction attribute of `Required` by default; the * is a wildcard that indicates all the methods of the TravelAgent EJB. The second `<container-transaction>` element overrides the default setting to specify that the `listAvailableCabins()` method has a `Supports` transaction attribute. Note that we have to specify which EJB we are referring to with the `<ejb-name>` element; an XML deployment descriptor can cover many EJBs.

Transaction attributes defined

Here are the definitions of the transaction attributes listed earlier. In a few of the definitions, the client transaction is described as *suspended*. This means the transaction is not propagated to the enterprise bean method being invoked; propagation of the transaction is temporarily halted until the enterprise bean method returns. To make things easier, we will talk about attribute types as if they were bean types: for example, we'll say a "`Required` EJB" as shorthand for "an enterprise bean with the `Required` transaction attribute." The attributes are:

`NotSupported`

Invoking a method on an EJB with this transaction attribute suspends the transaction until the method is completed. This means that the transaction scope is not propagated to the `NotSupported` EJB or any of the EJBs it calls. Once the method on the `NotSupported` EJB is done, the original transaction resumes its execution.

Figure 16-1 shows that a `NotSupported` EJB does not propagate the client transaction when one of its methods is invoked.

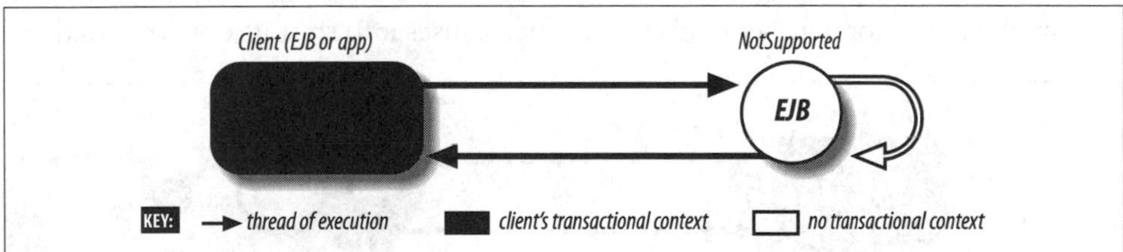

Figure 16-1. NotSupported attribute

`Supports`

This attribute means that the enterprise bean method will be included in the transaction scope if it is invoked within a transaction. In other words, if the EJB or client that invokes the `Supports` EJB is part of a transaction scope, the `Supports` EJB and all EJBs accessed by it become part of the original transaction. However, the `Supports` EJB doesn't have to be part of a transaction and can interact with clients and other EJBs that are not included in a transaction scope.

Figure 16-2 (a) shows the `Supports` EJB being invoked by a transactional client and propagating the transaction. Figure 16-2 (b) shows the `Supports` EJB being invoked by a nontransactional client.

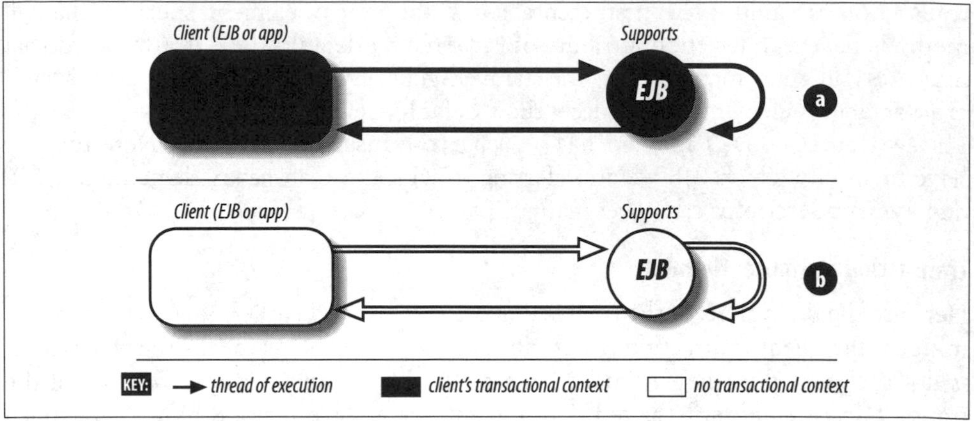

Figure 16-2. Supports attribute

`Required`

This attribute means that the enterprise bean method must be invoked within the scope of a transaction. If the calling client or EJB is part of a transaction, the `Required` EJB is automatically included in its transaction scope. If, however, the calling client or EJB is not involved in a transaction, the `Required` EJB starts its own new transaction. The new transaction's scope covers only the `Required` EJB and all other EJBs accessed by it. Once the method invoked on the `Required` EJB is done, the new transaction's scope ends.

Figure 16-3 (a) shows the `Required` EJB being invoked by a transactional client and propagating the transaction. Figure 16-3 (b) shows the `Required` EJB being invoked by a nontransactional client, which causes it to start its own transaction.

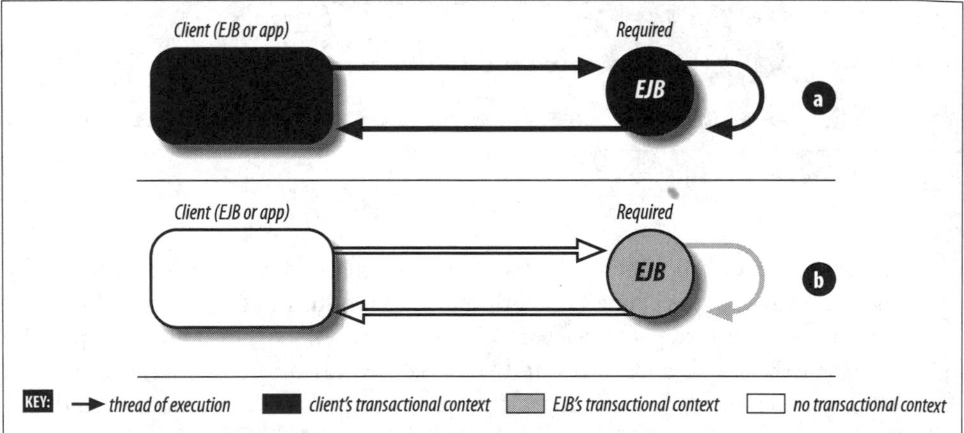

Figure 16-3. Required attribute

`RequiresNew`

This attribute means that a new transaction is always started. Regardless of whether the calling client or EJB is part of a transaction, a method with the `RequiresNew` attribute begins a new transaction when invoked. If the calling client is already involved in a transaction, that transaction is suspended until the `RequiresNew` EJB's method call returns. The new transaction's scope covers only the `RequiresNew` EJB and all the EJBs accessed by it. Once the method invoked on the `RequiresNew` EJB is done, the new transaction's scope ends and the original transaction resumes.

Figure 16-4 (a) shows the `RequiresNew` EJB being invoked by a transactional client. The client's transaction is suspended while the EJB executes under its own transaction. Figure 16-4 (b) shows the `RequiresNew` EJB being invoked by a nontransactional client; the `RequiresNew` EJB executes under its own transaction.

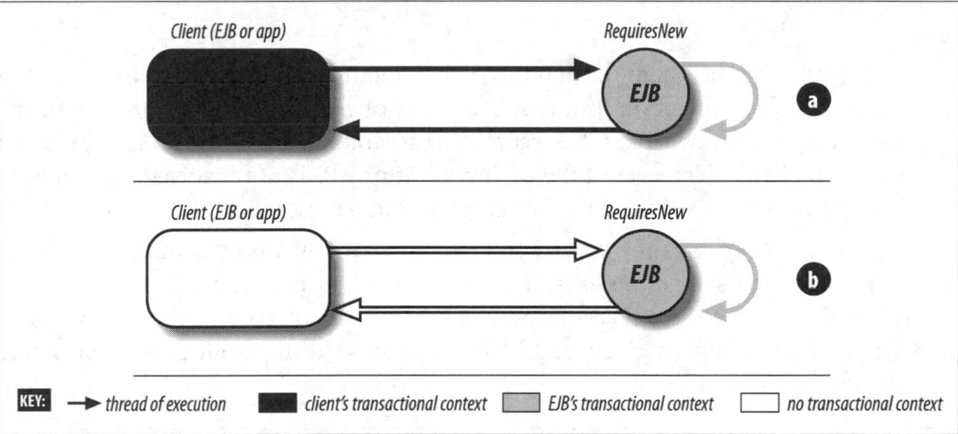

Figure 16-4. RequiresNew attribute

`Mandatory`

This attribute means that the enterprise bean method must always be made part of the transaction scope of the calling client. The EJB may not start its own transaction; the transaction must be propagated from the client. If the calling client is not part of a transaction, the invocation will fail, throwing a `javax.transaction.TransactionRequiredException` to remote clients or a `javax.ejb.TransactionRequiredLocalException` to local EJB clients.

Figure 16-5 (a) shows the `Mandatory` EJB being invoked by a transactional client and propagating the transaction. Figure 16-5 (b) shows the `Mandatory` EJB being invoked by a nontransactional client; the method throws a `TransactionRequiredException` to remote clients or a `TransactionRequredLocalException` to local EJB clients, because there is no transaction scope.

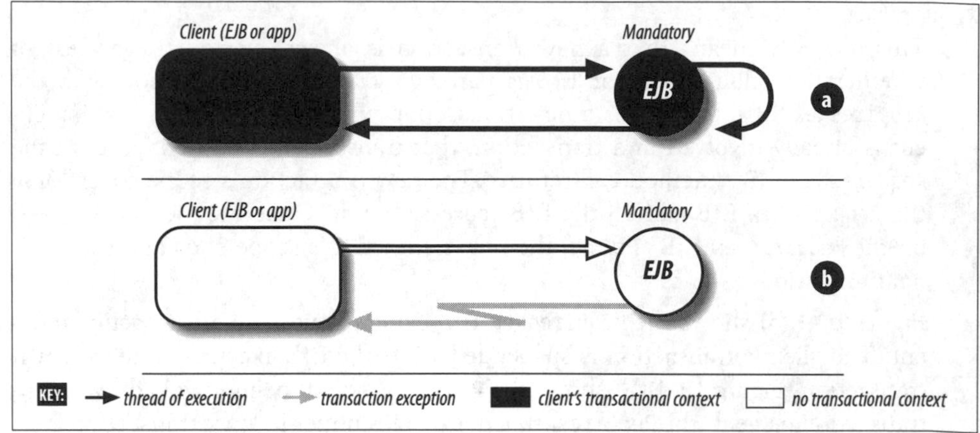

Figure 16-5. Mandatory attribute

`Never`

This attribute means that the enterprise bean method must not be invoked within the scope of a transaction. If the calling client or EJB is part of a transaction, the `Never` EJB will throw a `RemoteException` to remote clients or an `EJBException` to local EJB clients. However, if the calling client or EJB is not involved in a transaction, the `Never` EJB will execute normally without a transaction.

Figure 16-6 (a) shows the `Never` EJB being invoked by a nontransactional client. Figure 16-6 (b) shows the `Never` EJB being invoked by transactional client; the method throws a `RemoteException` to remote clients or an `EJBException` to local EJB clients, because a client or EJB that is included in a transaction can never invoke the method.

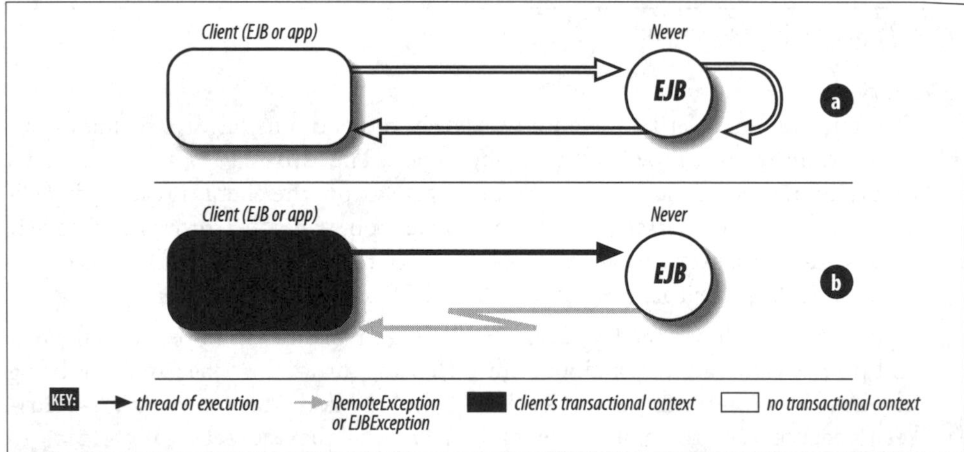

Figure 16-6. Never attribute

Container-managed persistence and transaction attributes

The EJB specification strongly advises that CMP entity beans use only the `Required`, `RequiresNew`, and `Mandatory` transaction attributes. This restriction ensures that all database access occurs in the context of a transaction, which is important when the container is automatically managing persistence. While the specification requires that these three transaction attributes be supported for CMP, support for the `Never`, `Supports`, and `NotSupported` transaction attributes is optional. If a vendor wishes to support these attributes (which allow the bean to execute without a transaction) they may do so, but it's not recommended. Consult your vendor's documentation to determine if they support the optional transaction attributes. This book recommends that you use only `Required`, `RequiresNew`, or `Mandatory` with EJB container-managed persistence entity beans.

Message-driven beans and transaction attributes

Message-driven beans may declare only the `NotSupported` or `Required` transaction attributes. The other transaction attributes don't make sense in message-driven beans because they apply to client-initiated transactions. The `Supports`, `RequiresNew`, `Mandatory`, and `Never` attributes are all relative to the transaction context of the client. For example, the `Mandatory` attribute requires the client to have a transaction in progress before calling the enterprise bean. This is meaningless for a message-driven bean, which is decoupled from the client.

The `NotSupported` transaction attribute indicates that the message will be processed without a transaction. The `Required` transaction attribute indicates that the message will be processed with a container-initiated transaction.

EJB endpoints and transaction attributes

The `Mandatory` transaction attribute cannot be used with EJB endpoints, because an EJB endpoint does not propagate a client transaction. Perhaps when web service transactions become standardized this will change, but for now using `Mandatory` with an EJB endpoint method is prohibited.

Transaction Propagation

To illustrate the impact of transaction attributes, we'll look once again at the `bookPassage( )` method of the TravelAgent EJB. In order for `bookPassage( )` to execute as a successful transaction, both the creation of the Reservation EJB and the charge to the customer must be successful. This means both operations must be included in the same transaction. If either operation fails, the entire transaction fails. We could have specified the `Required` transaction attribute as the default for all the EJBs involved, because that attribute enforces our desired policy that all EJBs must execute within a transaction and thus ensures data consistency.

As a transaction monitor, an EJB server watches each method call in the transaction. If any of the updates fail, all the updates to all the EJBs will be reversed or *rolled back*. A rollback is like an undo command. If you have worked with relational databases, the concept of a rollback should be familiar to you. Once an update is executed, you can either commit the update or roll it back. A commit makes the changes requested by the update permanent; a rollback aborts the update and leaves the database in its original state. Making EJBs transactional provides the same kind of rollback/commit control. For example, if the Reservation EJB cannot be created, the charge made by the ProcessPayment EJB is rolled back. Transactions make updates an all-or-nothing proposition. This ensures that the unit-of-work, like the bookPassage( ) method, executes as intended, and it prevents inconsistent data from being written to databases.

In cases in which the container implicitly manages the transaction, the commit and rollback decisions are handled automatically. When transactions are managed explicitly within an enterprise bean or by the client, the responsibility falls on the enterprise bean or application developer to commit or roll back a transaction. Explicit demarcation of transactions is covered in detail later in this chapter.

Let's assume that the TravelAgent EJB is created and used on a client as follows:

```
TravelAgent agent = agentHome.create(customer);
agent.setCabinID(cabin_id);
agent.setCruiseID(cruise_id);
try {
    agent.bookPassage(card,price);
} catch(Exception e) {
    System.out.println("Transaction failed!");
}
```

Furthermore, let's assume that the bookPassage( ) method has been given the transaction attribute RequiresNew. In this case, the client that invokes the bookPassage( ) method is not itself part of a transaction. When bookPassage( ) is invoked on the TravelAgent EJB, a new transaction is created, as dictated by the RequiresNew attribute. This means the TravelAgent EJB registers itself with the EJB server's transaction manager, which will manage the transaction automatically. The transaction manager coordinates transactions, propagating the transaction scope from one EJB to the next to ensure that all EJBs touched by a transaction are included in the transaction's unit-of-work. That way, the transaction manager can monitor the updates made by each enterprise bean and decide, based on the success of those updates, whether to commit all changes made by all enterprise beans to the database or roll them all back. If a *system exception* is thrown by the bookPassage( ) method, the transaction is automatically rolled back. We talk more about exceptions later in this chapter.

When the byCredit( ) method is invoked within the bookPassage( ) method, the ProcessPayment EJB registers with the transaction manager under the transactional context that was created for the TravelAgent EJB; the transactional context is propagated to the ProcessPayment EJB. When the new Reservation EJB is created, it is also registered with the transaction manager under the same transaction. When all the EJBs are registered and their updates are made, the transaction manager checks to ensure that their updates will work. If all the updates will work, the transaction manager allows the changes to become permanent. If one of the EJBs reports an error or fails, any changes made by either the ProcessPayment or Reservation EJB are rolled back by the transaction manager. Figure 16-7 illustrates the propagation and management of the TravelAgent EJB's transactional context.

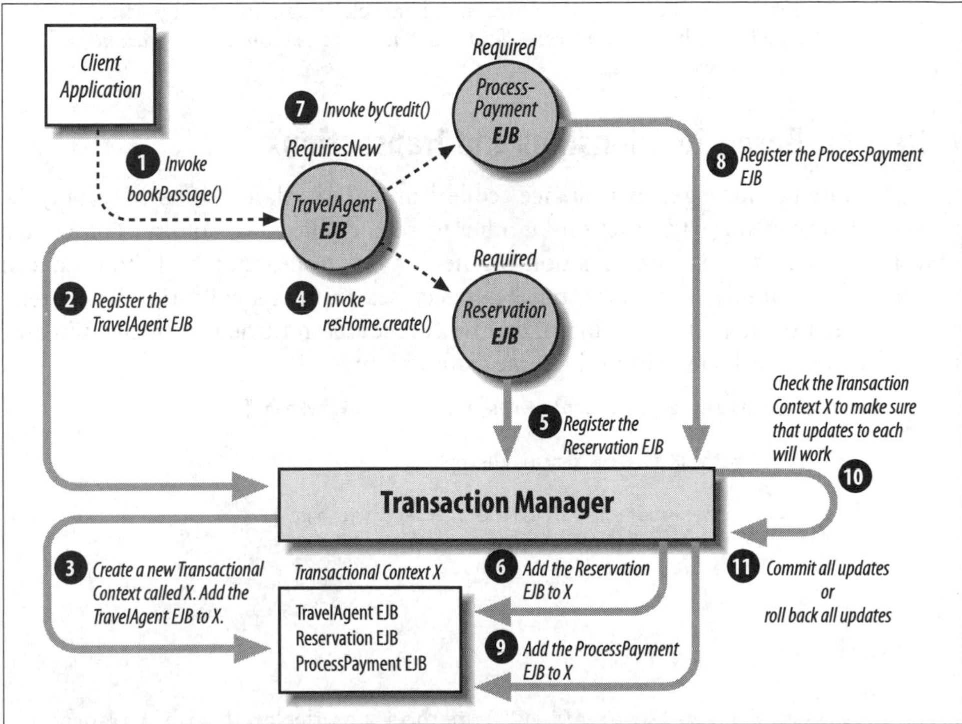

Figure 16-7. Managing the TravelAgent EJB's transactional context

In addition to managing transactions in its own environment, an EJB server can coordinate with other transactional systems. If, for example, the ProcessPayment EJB actually came from a different EJB server than the TravelAgent EJB, the two EJB servers would cooperate to manage the transaction as one unit-of-work. This is called a *distributed transaction*.* A distributed transaction requires what is called a *two-phase commit* (2-PC or TPC). 2-PC allows transactions to be managed across different servers and resources (e.g., databases and JMS providers). The details of a 2-PC are beyond the scope of this book, but a system that supports it will not require any extra

* Not all EJB servers support distributed transactions.

operations by an EJB or application developer. If distributed transactions are supported, the protocol for propagating transactions, as discussed earlier, will be supported. In other words, as an application or EJB developer, you should not notice a difference between local and distributed transactions.

There are a number of books on transaction processing and 2-PC. Perhaps the best books on the subject are *Principles of Transaction Processing* (Morgan Kaufmann 1997) and *Transaction Processing: Concepts and Techniques* (Morgan Kaufmann 1993). A much lighter resource is the series of "XA Exposed" articles (I, II, and III) by Mike Spielle, which you can find at *http://jroller.com/page/pyrasun/?anchor=xa_exposed*.

Collection-Based Relationships and Transactions

In EJB container-managed persistence, collection-based relationships may only be accessed within a single transaction. In other words, it's illegal to obtain a `Collection` object from a collection-based relationship field in one transaction and then use it in another. For example, if an enterprise bean accesses another's collection-based relationship field through its local interface, the `Collection` returned from the accessor method can be used only within the same transaction:

```
public class HypotheticalBean implements javax.ejb.EntityBean {

    public void methodX(CustomerLocal customer) {

        Collection reservations = customer.getReservations( );
        Iterator iterator = reservations.iterator;
        while(iterator.hasNext( )){
            ...
        }
    }
}
```

If the Customer EJB's `getReservations( )` method was declared with a transaction attribute of `RequiresNew`, attempting to invoke any methods on the `Collection`, including the `iterator( )` method, will result in a `java.lang.IllegalStateException`. This exception is thrown because the `Collection` object was created within the scope of the `getReservations( )` transaction, not in the scope of `methodX( )`'s transaction. The transaction context of `methodX( )` is different from the transaction context of the `getReservations( )` method.

The `Collection` from an entity bean can be used by another co-located bean only if it is obtained and accessed in the same transaction context. As long as the Customer EJB's `getReservations( )` method propagates the transaction context of `methodX( )`, the `Collection` can be used without any problems. This can be accomplished by changing the `getReservations( )` method so that it declares its transaction attribute as `Required` or `Mandatory`.

Isolation and Database Locking

Transaction isolation (the "I" in ACID) is a critical part of any transactional system. This section explains isolation conditions, database locking, and transaction isolation levels. These concepts are important when deploying any transactional system.

Dirty, Repeatable, and Phantom Reads

Transaction isolation is defined in terms of isolation conditions called *dirty reads*, *repeatable reads*, and *phantom reads*. These conditions describe what can happen when two or more transactions operate on the same data.* To illustrate these conditions, let's think about two separate client applications using their own instances of the TravelAgent EJB to access the same data—specifically, a cabin record with the primary key of 99. These examples revolve around the `RESERVATION` table, which is accessed by both the `bookPassage( )` method (through the Reservation EJB) and the `listAvailableCabins( )` method (through JDBC). (It might be a good idea to go back to Chapter 11 and review how the `RESERVATION` table is accessed through these methods. This will help you to understand how two transactions executed by two different clients can impact each other.) Assume that both methods have a transaction attribute of `Required`.

Dirty reads

A *dirty read* occurs when a transaction reads uncommitted changes made by a previous transaction. If the first transaction is rolled back, the data read by the second transaction becomes invalid because the rollback undoes the changes. The second transaction will not be aware that the data it has read has become invalid. Here's a scenario showing how a dirty read can occur (illustrated in Figure 16-8):

1. Time 10:00:00: Client 1 executes the `TravelAgent.bookPassage( )` method. Along with the Customer and Cruise EJBs, Client 1 had previously chosen Cabin 99 to be included in the reservation.
2. Time 10:00:01: Client 1's TravelAgent EJB creates a Reservation EJB within the `bookPassage( )` method. The Reservation EJB's `create( )` method inserts a record into the `RESERVATION` table, which reserves Cabin 99.
3. Time 10:00:02: Client 2 executes `TravelAgent.listAvailableCabins( )`. Client 1 has reserved Cabin 99, so it is not in the list of available cabins that is returned from this method.
4. Time 10:00:03: Client 1's TravelAgent EJB executes the `ProcessPayment.byCredit( )` method within the `bookPassage( )` method. The `byCredit( )` method throws an exception because the expiration date on the credit card has passed.

* Isolation conditions are covered in detail by the ANSI SQL-92 Specification, Document Number: ANSI X3.135-1992 (R1998).

5. Time 10:00:04: The exception thrown by the ProcessPayment EJB causes the entire `bookPassage()` transaction to be rolled back. As a result, the record inserted into the `RESERVATION` table when the Reservation EJB was created is not made durable (i.e., it is removed). Cabin 99 is now available.

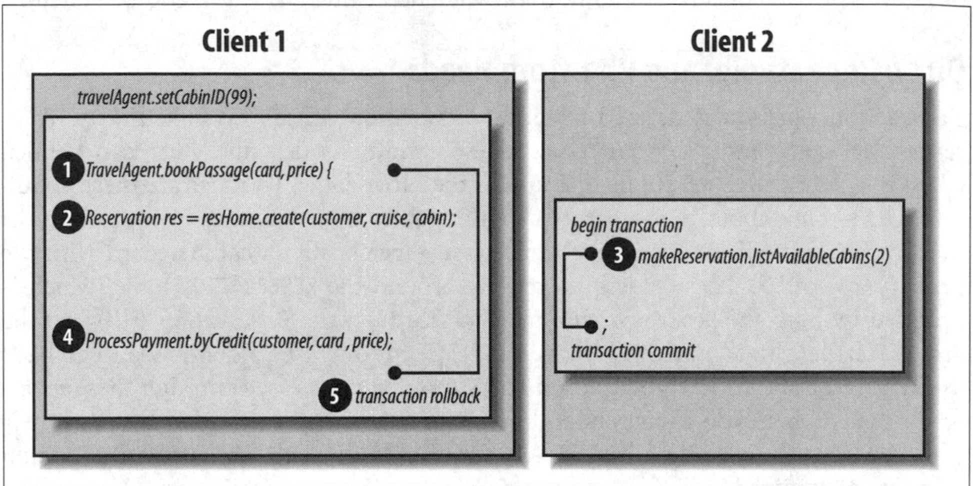

Figure 16-8. A dirty read

Client 2 is now using an invalid list of available cabins because Cabin 99 is available but is not included in the list. This omission would be serious if Cabin 99 was the last available cabin, because Client 2 would inaccurately report that the cruise was booked. The customer would presumably try to book a cruise on a competing cruise line.

Repeatable reads

A *repeatable read* occurs when the data read is guaranteed to look the same if read again during the same transaction. Repeatable reads are guaranteed in one of two ways: either the data read is locked against changes or the data read is a snapshot that doesn't reflect changes. If the data is locked, it cannot be changed by any other transaction until the current transaction ends. If the data is a snapshot, other transactions can change the data, but these changes will not be seen by this transaction if the read is repeated. Here's an example of a repeatable read (illustrated in Figure 16-9):

1. Time 10:00:00: Client 1 begins an explicit `javax.transaction.UserTransaction`.
2. Time 10:00:01: Client 1 executes `TravelAgent.listAvailableCabins(2)`, asking for a list of available cabins that have two beds. Cabin 99 is in the list of available cabins.
3. Time 10:00:02: Client 2 is working with an interface that manages Cabin EJBs. Client 2 attempts to change the bed count on Cabin 99 from 2 to 3.
4. Time 10:00:03: Client 1 re-executes `TravelAgent.listAvailableCabins(2)`. Cabin 99 is still in the list of available cabins.

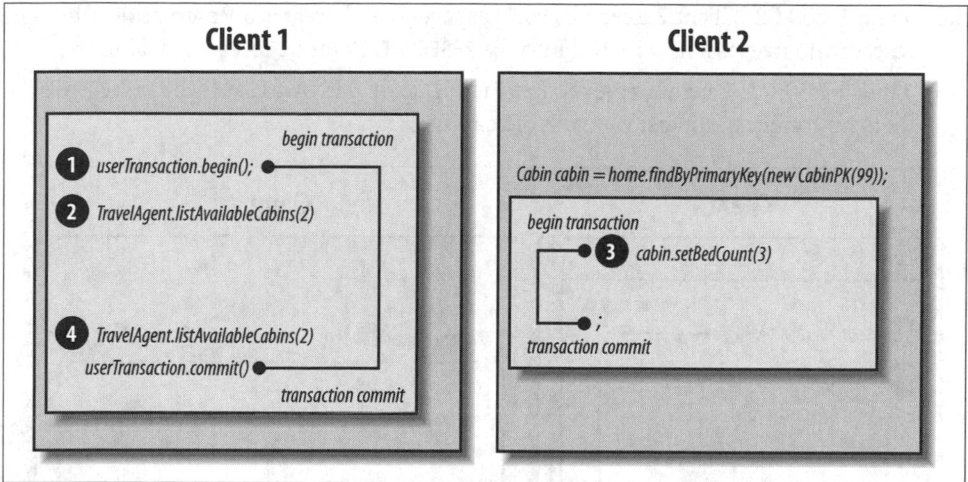

Figure 16-9. Repeatable read

This example is somewhat unusual because it uses `javax.transaction.UserTransaction`. This class is covered in more detail later in this chapter; essentially, it allows a client application to control the scope of a transaction explicitly. In this case, Client 1 places transaction boundaries around both calls to `listAvailableCabins()`, so that they are a part of the same transaction. If Client 1 didn't do this, the two `listAvailableCabins()` methods would have executed as separate transactions and our repeatable read condition would not have occurred.

Although Client 2 attempted to change the bed count for Cabin 99 to 3, Cabin 99 still shows up in the Client 1 call to `listAvailableCabins()` when a bed count of 2 is requested. Either Client 2 was prevented from making the change (because of a lock) or Client 2 was able to make the change, but Client 1 is working with a snapshot of the data that doesn't reflect that change.

A *nonrepeatable read* is when the data retrieved in a subsequent read within the same transaction can return different results. In other words, the subsequent read can see the changes made by other transactions.

Phantom reads

A *phantom read* occurs when new records added to the database are detectable by transactions that started prior to the insert. Queries will include records added by other transactions after their transaction has started. Here's a scenario that includes a phantom read (illustrated in Figure 16-10):

1. Time 10:00:00: Client 1 begins an explicit `javax.transaction.UserTransaction`.
2. Time 10:00:01: Client 1 executes `TravelAgent.listAvailableCabins(2)`, asking for a list of available cabins that have two beds. Cabin 99 is in the list of available cabins.

3. Time 10:00:02: Client 2 executes `bookPassage()` and creates a Reservation EJB. The reservation inserts a new record into the `RESERVATION` table, reserving Cabin 99.
4. Time 10:00:03: Client 1 re-executes `TravelAgent.listAvailableCabins(2)`. Cabin 99 is no longer in the list of available cabins.

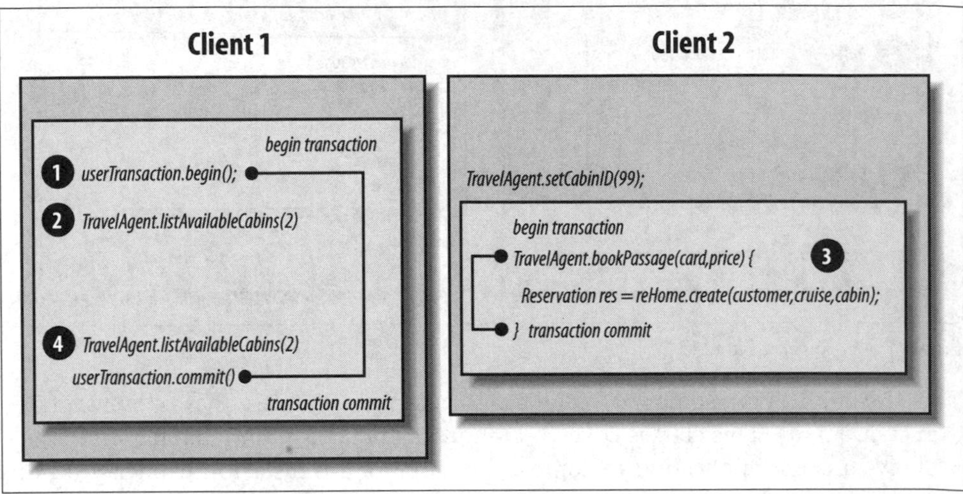

Figure 16-10. Phantom read

Client 1 places transaction boundaries around both calls to `listAvailableCabins()`, so that they are part of the same transaction. In this case, the reservation was made between the `listAvailableCabins()` queries in the same transaction. Therefore, the record inserted in the `RESERVATION` table did not exist when the first `listAvailableCabins()` method was invoked, but it did exist and was visible when the second `listAvailableCabins()` method was invoked. The record inserted is called a *phantom record.*

Database Locks

Databases, especially relational databases, normally use several different locking techniques. The most common are *read locks*, *write locks*, and *exclusive write locks*. (I've taken the liberty of adding "snapshots," although this isn't a formal term.) These locking mechanisms control how transactions access data concurrently. Locking mechanisms impact the read conditions just described. These types of locks are simple concepts that are not directly addressed in the EJB specification. Database vendors implement these locks differently, so you should understand how your database addresses these locking mechanisms to best predict how the isolation levels described in this section will work.

The four types of locks are:

Read locks
: Read locks prevent other transactions from changing data read during a transaction until the transaction ends, thus preventing nonrepeatable reads. Other transactions can read the data but not write to it. The current transaction is also prohibited from making changes. Whether a read lock locks only the records read, a block of records, or a whole table depends on the database being used.

Write locks
: Write locks are used for updates. A write lock prevents other transactions from changing the data until the current transaction is complete but allows dirty reads by other transactions and by the current transaction itself. In other words, the transaction can read its own uncommitted changes.

Exclusive write locks
: Exclusive write locks are used for updates. An exclusive write lock prevents other transactions from reading or changing the data until the current transaction is complete. An exclusive write lock prevents dirty reads by other transactions. Other transactions are not allowed to read the data while it is exclusively locked. Some databases do not allow transactions to read their own data while it is exclusively locked.

Snapshots
: Some databases get around locking by providing every transaction with its own snapshot of the data. A snapshot is a frozen view of the data that is taken when the transaction begins. Snapshots can prevent dirty reads, nonrepeatable reads, and phantom reads. They can be problematic because the data is not real-time; it is old the instant the snapshot is taken.

Transaction Isolation Levels

Transaction isolation is defined in terms of the isolation conditions (dirty reads, repeatable reads, and phantom reads). Isolation levels are commonly used in database systems to describe how locking is applied to data within a transaction.* The following terms are used to discuss isolation levels:

Read Uncommitted
: The transaction can read uncommitted data (i.e., data changed by a different transaction that is still in progress). Dirty reads, nonrepeatable reads, and phantom reads can occur. Bean methods with this isolation level can read uncommitted changes.

* Isolation conditions are covered in detail by ANSI SQL-92 Specification, Document Number: ANSI X3.135-1992 (R1998).

Read Committed

The transaction cannot read uncommitted data; data that is being changed by a different transaction cannot be read. Dirty reads are prevented; nonrepeatable reads and phantom reads can occur. Bean methods with this isolation level cannot read uncommitted data.

Repeatable Read

The transaction cannot change data that is being read by a different transaction. Dirty reads and nonrepeatable reads are prevented; phantom reads can occur. Bean methods with this isolation level have the same restrictions as Read Committed and can execute only repeatable reads.

Serializable

The transaction has exclusive read and update privileges to data; different transactions can neither read nor write to the same data. Dirty reads, nonrepeatable reads, and phantom reads are prevented. This isolation level is the most restrictive.

These isolation levels are the same as those defined for JDBC. Specifically, they map to the static final variables in the `java.sql.Connection` class. The behavior modeled by the isolation levels in the connection class is the same as the behavior described here.

The exact behavior of these isolation levels depends largely on the locking mechanism used by the underlying database or resource. How the isolation levels work depends in large part on how your database supports them.

In EJB, the deployer sets transaction isolation levels in a vendor-specific way if the container manages the transaction. The EJB developer sets the transaction isolation level if the enterprise bean manages its own transactions. Up to this point, we have discussed only container-managed transactions; we will discuss bean-managed transactions later in this chapter.

Balancing Performance Against Consistency

Generally speaking, as the isolation levels become more restrictive, the performance of the system decreases because more restrictive isolation levels prevent transactions from accessing the same data. If isolation levels are very restrictive, like Serializable, then all transactions, even simple reads, must wait in line to execute. This can result in a system that is very slow. EJB systems that process a large number of concurrent transactions and need to be very fast will therefore avoid the Serializable isolation level where it is not necessary.

Isolation levels, however, also enforce consistency of data. More restrictive isolation levels help ensure that invalid data is not used for performing updates. The old adage "garbage in, garbage out" applies. The Serializable isolation level ensures that data is never accessed concurrently by transactions, thus ensuring that the data is always consistent.

Choosing the correct isolation level requires some research about the database you are using and how it handles locking. You must also balance the performance needs of your system against consistency. This is not a cut-and-dried process, because different applications use data differently.

Although there are only three ships in Titan's system, the entity beans that represent them are included in most of Titan's transactions. This means that many, possibly hundreds, of transactions will be accessing these Ship EJBs at the same time. Access to Ship EJBs needs to be fast or a bottleneck will occur, so we do not want to use a restrictive isolation level. At the same time, the ship data also needs to be consistent; otherwise, hundreds of transactions will be using invalid data. Therefore, we need to use a strong isolation level when making changes to ship information. To accommodate these conflicting requirements, we can apply different isolation levels to different methods.

Most transactions use the Ship EJB's get methods to obtain information. This is *read-only* behavior, so the isolation level for the get methods can be very low—such as Read Uncommitted. The set methods of the Ship EJB are almost never used; the name of the ship probably will not change for years. However, the data changed by the set methods must be isolated to prevent dirty reads by other transactions, so we will use the most restrictive isolation level, Serializable, on the ship's set methods. By using different isolation levels on different business methods, we can balance consistency against performance.

Controlling isolation levels

Different EJB servers allow different levels of granularity for isolation levels; some servers defer this responsibility to the database. Most EJB servers control the isolation level through the resource access API (e.g., JDBC and JMS) and may allow different resources to have different isolation levels, but will generally require that access to the same resource within a single transaction use a consistent isolation level. Consult your vendor's documentation to find out the level of control your server offers.

Bean-managed transactions in session beans and message-driven beans, however, allow you to specify the transaction isolation level using the database's API. The JDBC API, for example, provides a mechanism for specifying the isolation level of the database connection. For example:

```
DataSource source = (javax.sql.DataSource)
    jndiCntxt.lookup("java:comp/env/jdbc/titanDB");

Connection con = source.getConnection( );
con.setTransactionIsolation(Connection.TRANSACTION_SERIALIZABLE);
```

You can have different isolation levels for different resources within the same transaction, but all enterprise beans that use the same resource in a transaction should use the same isolation level.

Nontransactional Beans

Beans outside of a transaction's scope normally provide some kind of stateless service that does not manipulate data in a data store. While these types of enterprise beans may be necessary as utilities during a transaction, they do not need to meet the ACID requirements. Consider a nontransactional stateless session bean, the Quote EJB, that provides live stock quotes. This EJB may respond to a request from an EJB involved in a stock purchase transaction. The success or failure of the stock purchase, as a transaction, will not impact the state or operations of the Quote EJB, so it does not need to be part of the transaction. Beans that are involved in transactions are subjected to the isolated ACID property, which means that their services *cannot* be shared during the life of the transaction. Making an enterprise bean transactional can be expensive at runtime. Declaring an EJB to be nontransactional (i.e., `NotSupported`) leaves it out of the transaction scope, which may improve the performance and availability of that service.

Explicit Transaction Management

Although this section covers JTA, it is strongly recommended that you do not attempt to manage transactions explicitly. Through transaction attributes, Enterprise JavaBeans provides a comprehensive and simple mechanism for delimiting transactions at the method level and propagating transactions automatically. Only developers with a thorough understanding of transactional systems should attempt to use JTA with EJB.

EJB provides implicit transaction management on the method level: we can define transactions that are delimited by the scope of the method being executed. This is one of the primary advantages of EJB over cruder distributed object implementations: it reduces complexity and therefore programmer error. In addition, declarative transaction demarcation, as used in EJB, separates the transactional behavior from the business logic; a change to transactional behavior does not require changes to the business logic. In rare situations, however, it may be necessary to take control of transactions explicitly.

Explicit management of transactions is normally accomplished using the OMG's Object Transaction Service (OTS) or the Java implementation of OTS, the Java Transaction Service (JTS). OTS and JTS provide APIs that allow developers to work with transaction managers and resources (e.g., databases and JMS providers) directly. While the JTS implementation of OTS is robust and complete, it is not the easiest API to work with; it requires clean and intentional control over the bounds of enrollment in transactions.

Enterprise JavaBeans supports a much simpler API, the Java Transaction API (JTA), for working with transactions. This API is implemented by the `javax.transaction` package. JTA actually consists of two components: a high-level transactional client interface and a low-level X/Open XA interface. We are concerned with the high-level client interface, since it is accessible to enterprise beans and is also recommended for client applications. The low-level XA interface is used by the EJB server and container to coordinate transactions with resources such as databases.

Your use of explicit transaction management will probably focus on one simple interface: `javax.transaction.UserTransaction`. `UserTransaction` allows you to manage the scope of a transaction explicitly. Here's how explicit demarcation might be used in an EJB or client application:

```
Object ref = getInitialContext( ).lookup("TravelAgentHomeRemote");
TravelAgentHome home = (TravelAgentHome)
    PortableRemoteObject.narrow(ref, TravelAgentHome.class);

TravelAgent tr1 = home.create(customer);
tr1.setCruiseID(cruiseID);
tr1.setCabinID(cabin_1);
TravelAgent tr2 = home.create(customer);
tr2.setCruiseID(cruiseID);
tr2.setCabinID(cabin_2);

javax.transaction.UserTransaction tran = ...; // Get the UserTransaction.
tran.begin( );
tr1.bookPassage(visaCard,price);
tr2.bookPassage(visaCard,price);
tran.commit( );
```

The client application needs to book two cabins for the same customer—in this case, the customer is purchasing a cabin for himself and his children. The customer does not want to book either cabin unless he can get both, so the client application is designed to include both bookings in the same transaction. Explicitly marking the transaction's boundaries through the use of the `javax.transaction.UserTransaction` object does this. Each enterprise bean method invoked by the current thread between the `UserTransaction.begin( )` and `UserTransaction.commit( )` methods is included in the same transaction scope, according to the transaction attributes of the enterprise bean methods invoked.

Obviously, this example is contrived, but the point it makes is clear. Transactions can be controlled directly, instead of depending on method scope to delimit them. The advantage of using explicit transaction demarcation is that it gives the client control over the bounds of a transaction. The client, in this case, may be a client application or another enterprise bean.* In either case, the same `javax.transaction.UserTransaction` is used, but it is obtained from different sources depending on whether it is needed on the client or in an enterprise bean.

* Only beans declared as managing their own transactions (bean-managed transaction beans) can use the `UserTransaction` interface.

Java 2 Enterprise Edition (J2EE) specifies how a client application can obtain a `UserTransaction` object using JNDI. Here's how a client obtains a `UserTransaction` object if the EJB container is part of a J2EE system (J2EE and its relationship with EJB is covered in more detail in Chapter 18):

```
Context jndiCntx = new InitialContext( );
UserTransaction tran = (UserTransaction)
    jndiCntx.lookup("java:comp/UserTransaction");
utx.begin( );
...
utx.commit( );
```

Enterprise beans can also manage transactions explicitly. Only session beans and message-driven beans with the `<transaction-type>` value of `Bean` can manage their own transactions. Enterprise beans that manage their own transactions are frequently referred to as bean-managed transaction (BMT) beans. Entity beans can never be BMT beans. BMT beans do not declare transaction attributes for their methods. Here's how a session bean declares that it will manage transactions explicitly:

```
<ejb-jar>
    <enterprise-beans>
    ...
        <session>
        ...
        <transaction-type>Bean</transaction-type>
        ...
```

To manage its own transaction, an enterprise bean needs to obtain a `UserTransaction` object. An enterprise bean obtains a reference to the `UserTransaction` from the `EJBContext`:

```
public class HypotheticalBean extends SessionBean {
    SessionContext ejbContext;

    public void someMethod( ) {
        try {
            UserTransaction ut = ejbContext.getUserTransaction( );
            ut.begin( );

            // Do some work.

            ut.commit( );
    } catch(IllegalStateException ise) {...}
        catch(SystemException se) {...}
        catch(TransactionRolledbackException tre) {...}
        catch(HeuristicRollbackException hre) {...}
        catch(HeuristicMixedException hme) {...}
```

An enterprise bean can also access the `UserTransaction` from the JNDI ENC. The enterprise bean performs the lookup using the `"java:comp/env/UserTransaction"` context:

```
InitialContext jndiCntx = new InitialContext( );
UserTransaction tran = (UserTransaction)
    jndiCntx.lookup("java:comp/env/UserTransaction");
```

Transaction Propagation in Bean-Managed Transactions

With stateless session beans, transactions that are managed using `UserTransaction` must be started and completed within the same method. In other words, `UserTransaction` transactions cannot be started in one method and ended in another. This makes sense because stateless session bean instances are shared across many clients; while one stateless instance may service a client's first request, a completely different instance may service a subsequent request by the same client. With stateful session beans, however, a transaction can begin in one method and be committed in another because a stateful session bean is used by only one client. Therefore, a stateful session bean can associate itself with a transaction across several different client-invoked methods. As an example, imagine the TravelAgent EJB as a BMT bean. In the following code, the transaction is started in the `setCruiseID( )` method and completed in the `bookPassage( )` method. This allows the TravelAgent EJB's methods to be associated with the same transaction. The definition of the `TravelAgentBean` class looks like this:

```
import com.titan.reservation.*;

import java.sql.*;
import javax.sql.DataSource;
import java.util.Vector;
import java.rmi.RemoteException;
import javax.naming.NamingException;
import javax.ejb.EJBException;

public class TravelAgentBean implements javax.ejb.SessionBean {
    ...
    public void setCruiseID(Integer cruiseID)
        throws javax.ejb.FinderException {
        try {
            ejbContext.getUserTransaction().begin( );
            CruiseHomeLocal home = (CruiseHomeLocal)
                jndiContext.lookup("java:comp/env/ejb/CruiseHome");

            cruise = home.findByPrimaryKey(cruiseID);
        } catch(RemoteException re) {
            throw new EJBException(re);
        }

    }
    public TicketDO bookPassage(CreditCardDO card, double price)
        throws IncompleteConversationalState {

        try {
            if (ejbContext.getUserTransaction().getStatus( ) !=
                javax.transaction.Status.STATUS_ACTIVE) {

                throw new EJBException("Transaction is not active");
            }
```

```
        } catch(javax.transaction.SystemException se) {
            throw new EJBException(se);
        }

        if (customer == null || cruise == null || cabin == null)
        {
            throw new IncompleteConversationalState( );
        }
        try {
            ReservationHomeLocal resHome = (ReservationHomeLocal)
                jndiContext.lookup("java:comp/env/ejb/ReservationHomeLocal");

            ReservationLocal reservation =
                resHome.create(customer, cruise, cabin, price);

            Object ref =
                jndiContext.lookup("java:comp/env/ejb/ProcessPaymentHomeRemote");

            ProcessPaymentHomeRemote ppHome = (ProcessPaymentHomeRemote)
                PortableRemoteObject.narrow(ref, ProcessPaymentHomeRemote.class);

            ProcessPaymentRemote process = ppHome.create( );
            process.byCredit(customer, card, price);

            TicketDO ticket = new TicketDO(customer,cruise,cabin,price);

            ejbContext.getUserTransaction().commit( );

            return ticket;
        } catch(Exception e) {
            throw new EJBException(e);
        }
    }
    ...
}
```

Repeated calls to the `EJBContext.getUserTransaction( )` method return a reference to the same `UserTransaction` object. The container is required to retain the association between the transaction and the stateful bean instance across multiple client calls until the transaction terminates.

In the `bookPassage( )` method, we can check the status of the transaction to ensure that it is still active. If the transaction is no longer active, we throw an exception. The use of `getStatus( )` is covered in more detail later in this chapter.

When a client that is already involved in a transaction invokes a bean-managed transaction method, the client's transaction is suspended until the method returns. This suspension occurs regardless of whether the BMT bean explicitly started its own transaction within the method or the transaction was started in a previous method invocation. The client transaction is always suspended until the BMT method returns.

Transaction control across methods is strongly discouraged because it can result in improperly managed transactions and long-lived transactions that lock up resources.

Message-driven beans and bean-managed transactions

Message-driven beans also have the option of managing their own transactions. In the case of MDBs, the scope of the transaction must begin and end within the `onMessage( )` method—it is not possible for a bean-managed transaction to span `onMessage( )` calls.

You can transform the ReservationProcessor EJB you created in Chapter 12 into a BMT bean simply by changing its `<transaction-type>` value to `Bean`:

```
<ejb-jar>
    <enterprise-beans>
    ...
        <message-driven>
        ...
          <transaction-type>Bean</transaction-type>
        ...
```

In this case, the `ReservationProcessorBean` class would be modified to use `javax.transaction.UserTransaction` to mark the beginning and end of the transaction:

```
public class ReservationProcessorBean implements javax.ejb.MessageDrivenBean,
    javax.jms.MessageListener {

     MessageDrivenContext ejbContext;
    Context jndiContext;

    public void onMessage(Message message) {
        try {

            ejbContext.getUserTransaction().begin( );

            MapMessage reservationMsg = (MapMessage)message;

            Integer customerPk = (Integer)reservationMsg.getObject("CustomerID");
            Integer cruisePk = (Integer)reservationMsg.getObject("CruiseID");
            Integer cabinPk = (Integer)reservationMsg.getObject("CabinID");
            double price = reservationMsg.getDouble("Price");

            //get the credit card
            Date expirationDate =
                new Date(reservationMsg.getLong("CreditCardExpDate"));
            String cardNumber = reservationMsg.getString("CreditCardNum");
            String cardType = reservationMsg.getString("CreditCardType");

            CreditCardDO card =
                new CreditCardDO(cardNumber,expirationDate,cardType);
            CustomerRemote customer = getCustomer(customerPk);
```

```
            CruiseLocal cruise = getCruise(cruisePk);
            CabinLocal cabin = getCabin(cabinPk);

            ReservationHomeLocal resHome = (ReservationHomeLocal)
                jndiContext.lookup("java:comp/env/ejb/ReservationHomeLocal");
            ReservationLocal reservation =
                resHome.create(customer,cruise,cabin,price,new Date( ));

            Object ref =
                jndiContext.lookup("java:comp/env/ejb/ProcessPaymentHomeRemote");
            ProcessPaymentHomeRemote ppHome = (ProcessPaymentHomeRemote)
                PortableRemoteObject.narrow(ref,ProcessPaymentHomeRemote.class);
            ProcessPaymentRemote process = ppHome.create( );

            process.byCredit(customer,card,price);
            TicketDO ticket = new TicketDO(customer,cruise,cabin,price);
            deliverTicket(reservationMsg,ticket);

            ejbContext.getUserTransaction.commit( );

        } catch(Exception e) {
            throw new EJBException(e);
        }
    }
    ...
```

It is important to understand that in a BMT, the message consumed by the MDB is not part of the transaction. When an MDB uses container-managed transactions, the message it is handling is a part of the transaction, so if the transaction is rolled back, the consumption of the message is also rolled back, forcing the JMS provider to redeliver the message. But with bean-managed transactions, the message is not part of the transaction, so if the BMT transaction is rolled back, the JMS provider will not be aware of the transaction's failure. However, all is not lost, because the JMS provider can still rely on message acknowledgment to determine if the message was successfully delivered.

The EJB container will acknowledge the message if the `onMessage( )` method returns successfully. If, however, a `RuntimeException` is thrown by the `onMessage( )` method, the container will not acknowledge the message and the JMS provider will suspect a problem and probably attempt to redeliver the message. If redelivery of a message is important when a transaction fails, your best course of action is to ensure that the `onMessage( )` method throws an `EJBException`, so that the container will *not* acknowledge the message received from the JMS provider.

Vendors use proprietary (declarative) mechanisms to specify the number of times to redeliver messages to BMT/`NotSupported` MDBs that "fail" to acknowledge receipt. The JMS-MDB provider may provide a "dead message" area into which such messages will be placed if they cannot be successfully processed according to the retry count. Administrators can monitor the dead message area, and delivered messages can be detected and handled manually.

Although the message is not part of the transaction, everything else between the `UserTransaction.begin()` and `UserTransaction.commit()` methods is part of the same transaction. This includes creating a new Reservation EJB and processing the credit card using the ProcessPayment EJB. If a transaction failure occurs, these operations will be rolled back. The transaction also includes the use of the JMS API in the `deliverTicket()` method to send the ticket message. If a transaction failure occurs, the ticket message will not be sent.

Heuristic Decisions

Transactions are normally controlled by a *transaction manager* (often the EJB server) that manages the ACID characteristics across several enterprise beans, databases, and servers. The transaction manager uses a two-phase commit (2-PC) to manage transactions. 2-PC is a protocol for managing transactions that commits updates in two stages. 2-PC is complex, but basically it requires that servers and databases cooperate through an intermediary—the transaction manager—in order to ensure that all the data is made durable together. Some EJB servers support 2-PC, while others do not, and the value of this transaction mechanism is a source of some debate. The important point to remember is that a transaction manager controls the transaction; based on the results of a poll against the resources (databases, JMS providers, and other resources), it decides whether all the updates should be committed or rolled back. A *heuristic decision* takes place when one of the resources makes a unilateral decision to commit or roll back without permission from the transaction manager. When a heuristic decision has been made, the atomicity of the transaction is lost and data-integrity errors can occur.

`UserTransaction`, discussed in the next section, throws a few different exceptions related to heuristic decisions; these are included in the following discussion.

UserTransaction

EJB servers are required to support `UserTransaction`, but not required to support the rest of JTA, nor are they required to use JTS for their transaction service. The `UserTransaction` is defined as:

```
public interface javax.transaction.UserTransaction {

    public abstract void begin( ) throws IllegalStateException, SystemException;
    public abstract void commit( ) throws IllegalStateException, SystemException,
        TransactionRolledbackException, HeuristicRollbackException,
        HeuristicMixedException;
    public abstract int getStatus( );
    public abstract void rollback( ) throws IllegalStateException, SecurityException,
        SystemException;
    public abstract void setRollbackOnly( ) throws IllegalStateException,
        SystemException;
    public abstract void setTransactionTimeout(int seconds) throws SystemException;

}
```

Here's what the methods defined in this interface do:

`begin()`
: Invoking the `begin()` method creates a new transaction. The thread that executes the `begin()` method is immediately associated with the new transaction, which is then propagated to any EJB that supports existing transactions. The `begin()` method can throw one of two checked exceptions. An `IllegalStateException` is thrown when `begin()` is called by a thread that is already associated with a transaction. You must complete any transactions associated with that thread before beginning a new transaction. A `SystemException` is thrown if the transaction manager (i.e., the EJB server) encounters an unexpected error condition.

`commit()`
: The `commit()` method completes the transaction that is associated with the current thread. When `commit()` is executed, the current thread is no longer associated with a transaction. This method can throw several checked exceptions. An `IllegalStateException` is thrown if the current thread is not associated with a transaction. A `SystemException` is thrown if the transaction manager (the EJB server) encounters an unexpected error condition. A `TransactionRolledbackException` is thrown when the entire transaction is rolled back instead of committed; this can happen if one of the resources was unable to perform an update or if the `UserTransaction.rollBackOnly()` method was called. A `HeuristicRollbackException` indicates that heuristic decisions were made by one or more resources to roll back the transaction. A `HeuristicMixedException` indicates that heuristic decisions were made by resources to both roll back and commit the transaction; that is, some resources decided to roll back while others decided to commit.

`rollback()`
: The `rollback()` method is invoked to roll back the transaction and undo updates. The `rollback()` method can throw one of three different checked exceptions. A `SecurityException` is thrown if the thread using the `UserTransaction` object is not allowed to roll back the transaction. An `IllegalStateException` is thrown if the current thread is not associated with a transaction. A `SystemException` is thrown if the transaction manager (the EJB server) encounters an unexpected error condition.

`setRollbackOnly()`
: The `setRollbackOnly()` method is invoked to mark the transaction for rollback. This means that, whether or not the updates executed within the transaction succeed, the transaction must be rolled back when completed. This method can be invoked by any BMT EJB participating in the transaction or by the client application. The `setRollBackOnly()` method can throw one of two checked exceptions: an `IllegalStateException` is thrown if the current thread is not

associated with a transaction; a `SystemException` is thrown if the transaction manager (the EJB server) encounters an unexpected error condition.

`setTransactionTimeout(int seconds)`
: The `setTransactionTimeout(int seconds)` method sets the lifespan of a transaction; i.e., how long it will live before timing out. The transaction must complete before the transaction timeout is reached. If this method is not called, the transaction manager (EJB server) automatically sets the timeout. If this method is invoked with a value of `0` seconds, the default timeout of the transaction manager will be used. This method must be invoked after the `begin( )` method. A `SystemException` is thrown if the transaction manager (EJB server) encounters an unexpected error condition.

`getStatus( )`
: The `getStatus( )` method returns an integer that can be compared to constants defined in the `javax.transaction.Status` interface. A sophisticated programmer can use this method to determine the status of a transaction associated with a `UserTransaction` object. A `SystemException` is thrown if the transaction manager (EJB server) encounters an unexpected error condition.

Status

`Status` is a simple interface that contains no methods, only constants. Its sole purpose is to provide a set of constants that describe the current status of a transactional object—in this case, the `UserTransaction`:

```
interface javax.transaction.Status
{
    public final static int STATUS_ACTIVE;
    public final static int STATUS_COMMITTED;
    public final static int STATUS_COMMITTING;
    public final static int STATUS_MARKED_ROLLBACK;
    public final static int STATUS_NO_TRANSACTION;
    public final static int STATUS_PREPARED;
    public final static int STATUS_PREPARING;
    public final static int STATUS_ROLLEDBACK;
    public final static int STATUS_ROLLING_BACK;
    public final static int STATUS_UNKNOWN;
}
```

The value returned by `getStatus( )` tells the client using the `UserTransaction` the status of a transaction. Here's what the constants mean:

`STATUS_ACTIVE`
: An active transaction is associated with the `UserTransaction` object. This status is returned after a transaction has been started and prior to a transaction manager beginning a two-phase commit. (Transactions that have been suspended are still considered active.)

`STATUS_COMMITTED`
: A transaction is associated with the `UserTransaction` object; the transaction has been committed. It is likely that heuristic decisions have been made; otherwise, the transaction would have been destroyed and the `STATUS_NO_TRANSACTION` constant would have been returned instead.

`STATUS_COMMITTING`
: A transaction is associated with the `UserTransaction` object; the transaction is in the process of committing. The `UserTransaction` object returns this status if the transaction manager has decided to commit but has not yet completed the process.

`STATUS_MARKED_ROLLBACK`
: A transaction is associated with the `UserTransaction` object; the transaction has been marked for rollback, perhaps as a result of a `UserTransaction.setRollbackOnly()` operation invoked somewhere else in the application.

`STATUS_NO_TRANSACTION`
: No transaction is currently associated with the `UserTransaction` object. This occurs after a transaction has completed or if no transaction has been created. This value is returned rather than throwing an `IllegalStateException`.

`STATUS_PREPARED`
: A transaction is associated with the `UserTransaction` object. The transaction has been prepared, which means that the first phase of the two-phase commit process has completed.

`STATUS_PREPARING`
: A transaction is associated with the `UserTransaction` object; the transaction is in the process of preparing, which means that the transaction manager is in the middle of executing the first phase of the two-phase commit.

`STATUS_ROLLEDBACK`
: A transaction is associated with the `UserTransaction` object; the outcome of the transaction has been identified as a rollback. It is likely that heuristic decisions have been made; otherwise, the transaction would have been destroyed and the `STATUS_NO_TRANSACTION` constant would have been returned.

`STATUS_ROLLING_BACK`
: A transaction is associated with the `UserTransaction` object; the transaction is in the process of rolling back.

`STATUS_UNKNOWN`
: A transaction is associated with the `UserTransaction` object; its current status cannot be determined. This is a transient condition and subsequent invocations will ultimately return a different status.

EJBContext Rollback Methods

Only BMT beans have access to the `UserTransaction` from the `EJBContext` and JNDI ENC. Container-managed transaction (CMT) beans cannot use the `UserTransaction`. CMT beans use the `setRollbackOnly()` and `getRollbackOnly()` methods of the `EJBContext` to interact with the current transaction instead.

The `setRollbackOnly()` method gives an enterprise bean the power to veto a transaction. This power can be used if the enterprise bean detects a condition that would cause inconsistent data to be committed when the transaction completes. Once an enterprise bean invokes the `setRollbackOnly()` method, the current transaction is marked for rollback and cannot be committed by any other participant in the transaction—including the container.

The `getRollbackOnly()` method returns `true` if the current transaction has been marked for rollback. This information can be used to avoid executing work that would not be committed anyway. If, for example, an exception is thrown and captured within an enterprise bean method, `getRollbackOnly()` can be used to determine whether the exception caused the current transaction to be rolled back. If it did, there is no sense in continuing the processing. If it did not, the EJB has an opportunity to correct the problem and retry the task that failed. Only expert EJB developers should attempt to retry tasks within a transaction. Alternatively, if the exception did not cause a rollback (`getRollbackOnly()` returns `false`), a rollback can be forced using the `setRollbackOnly()` method.

BMT beans must *not* use the `setRollbackOnly()` and `getRollbackOnly()` methods of the `EJBContext`. BMT beans should use the `getStatus()` and `rollback()` methods on the `UserTransaction` object to check for rollback and force a rollback, respectively.

Exceptions and Transactions

Exceptions have a large impact on the outcome of transactions.

System Exceptions Versus Application Exceptions

System exceptions are `java.lang.RuntimeException` and its subtypes, including `EJBException`. An *application exception* is any exception that does *not* extend `java.lang.RuntimeException` or `java.rmi.RemoteException`.

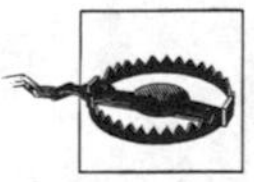

An application exception must never extend the `RuntimeException`, the `RemoteException`, or one of their subtypes.

Transactions are *automatically* rolled back if a system exception is thrown from an enterprise bean method. Transactions are *not* automatically rolled back if an application exception is thrown. If you remember these two rules, you will be well prepared to deal with exceptions and transactions in EJB. The bookPassage( ) method illustrates how to use application exceptions:

```
public TicketDO bookPassage(CreditCardDO card, double price)
    throws IncompleteConversationalState {

    if (customer == null || cruise == null || cabin == null) {
        throw new IncompleteConversationalState( );
    }
    try {
        ReservationHomeLocal resHome = (ReservationHomeLocal)
            jndiContext.lookup("java:comp/env/ejb/ReservationHomeLocal");

        ReservationLocal reservation =
            resHome.create(customer, cruise, cabin, price);

        Object ref =
            jndiContext.lookup("java:comp/env/ejb/ProcessPaymentHomeRemote");

        ProcessPaymentHomeRemote ppHome = (ProcessPaymentHomeRemote)
            PortableRemoteObject.narrow(ref, ProcessPaymentHomeRemote.class);

        ProcessPaymentRemote process = ppHome.create( );
        process.byCredit(customer, card, price);

        TicketDO ticket = new TicketDO(customer,cruise,cabin,price);

        return ticket;
    } catch(Exception e) {
        throw new EJBException(e);
    }
}
```

System exceptions

System exceptions include RuntimeException and its subclasses. The EJBException is a subclass of the RuntimeException, so it is considered a system exception.

System exceptions always cause a transaction to roll back when they are thrown from an enterprise bean method. Any RuntimeException (EJBException, NullPointerException, IndexOutOfBoundsException, and so on) thrown within the bookPassage( ) method is handled by the container automatically and results in a transaction rollback. In Java, RuntimeException types do not need to be declared in the throws clause of the method signature or handled using try/catch blocks; they are automatically thrown from the method.

The container handles system exceptions automatically; it will always:

- Roll back the transaction.
- Log the exception to alert the system administrator.
- Discard the EJB instance.

When a system exception is thrown from the callback methods (`ejbLoad( )`, `ejbActivate( )`, and so on) are treated the same as exceptions thrown from business methods.

While EJB requires system exceptions must be logged, it does not specify how exceptions should be logged or the format of the log file. The exact mechanism for recording exceptions and reporting them to the system administrator is left to the vendor.

When a system exception occurs, the EJB instance is discarded, which means that it is dereferenced and garbage collected. The container assumes that the EJB instance may have corrupt variables or otherwise be unstable and is therefore unsafe to use.

The impact of discarding an EJB instance depends on the enterprise bean's type. In the case of stateless session beans and entity beans, the client does not notice that the instance was discarded. These instance types are not dedicated to a particular client; they are swapped in and out of an instance pool, so any instance can service a new request. With stateful session beans, however, the impact on the client is severe. Stateful session beans are dedicated to a single client and maintain conversational state. Discarding a stateful bean instance destroys the instance's conversational state and invalidates the client's reference to the EJB. When stateful session instances are discarded, subsequent invocations of the EJB's methods by the client result in a `NoSuchObjectException`, a subclass of the `RemoteException`.*

With message-driven beans, a system exception thrown by the `onMessage( )` method or one of the callback methods (`ejbCreate( )` or `ejbRemove( )`) will cause the bean instance to be discarded. If the MDB was a BMT bean, the message it was handling may or may not be redelivered, depending on when the EJB container acknowledges delivery. In the case of container-managed transactions, the container will roll back the transaction, so the message will not be acknowledged and may be redelivered.

In session and entity beans, when a system exception occurs and the instance is discarded, a `RemoteException` is always thrown to remote clients—that is, clients using the beans' remote component interfaces. If the client started the transaction, which was then propagated to the EJB, a system exception (thrown by the enterprise bean method) will be caught by the container and rethrown as a `javax.transaction.TransactionRolledbackException`. The `TransactionRolledbackException` is a subtype of the `RemoteException`; it is a more explicit indication to the client that a rollback occurred.

In EJB session and entity beans, when a system exception occurs and the instance is discarded, an `EJBException` is always thrown to any local enterprise bean clients (i.e., clients using the enterprise bean's local component interfaces). If the client started the transaction and it was then propagated to the EJB, a system exception (thrown by the enterprise bean method) will be caught by the container and rethrown as a `javax.ejb.TransactionRolledbackLocalException`. The `TransactionRolledbackLocalException` is a

* Although the instance is always discarded with a `RuntimeException`, the impact on the remote reference may vary depending on the vendor.

subtype of the `EJBException`; it is a more explicit indication to the client that a rollback occurred. In all other cases, whether the EJB is container-managed or bean-managed, a `RuntimeException` thrown from within the enterprise bean method will be caught by the container and rethrown as an `EJBException`.

An `EJBException` should generally be thrown when a subsystem throws an exception, such as JDBC throwing a `SQLException` or JMS throwing a `JMSException`. In some cases, however, the bean developer may attempt to handle the exception and retry an operation rather then throw an `EJBException`. This should be done only when the exceptions thrown by the subsystem and their repercussions on the transaction are well understood. As a rule of thumb, rethrow subsystem exceptions as `EJBExceptions` and allow the EJB container to roll back the transaction and discard the bean instance.

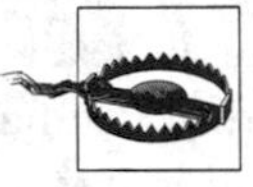

The callback methods defined in the `javax.ejb.EntityBean` and `javax.ejb.SessionBean` interfaces declare the `java.rmi.RemoteException` in their `throws` clauses. This is left over from EJB 1.0 and has been deprecated since EJB 1.1. You should never throw `RemoteExceptions` from callback methods or any other bean class methods.

Application exceptions

An *application exception* is normally thrown in response to a business-logic error, as opposed to a system error. Application exceptions are always delivered directly to the client, without being repackaged as `RemoteException` or `EJBException` types. They do not typically cause transactions to roll back; the client usually has an opportunity to recover after an application exception is thrown. For example, the `bookPassage()` method throws an application exception called `IncompleteConversationalState`; this is an application exception because it does not extend `RuntimeException` or `RemoteException`. The `IncompleteConversationalState` exception is thrown if one of the arguments passed into the `bookPassage()` method is `null`. (Application errors are frequently used to report validation errors like this.) In this case, the exception is thrown before tasks are started and is clearly not the result of a subsystem failure (e.g., JDBC, JMS, Java RMI, JNDI).

Because it is an application exception, throwing an `IncompleteConversationalState` exception does not result in a transaction rollback. The exception is thrown before any work is done, avoiding unnecessary processing by the `bookPassage()` method and providing the client (the enterprise bean or application that invoked the `bookPassage()` method) with an opportunity to recover and possibly retry the method call with valid arguments.

Business methods defined in the remote and local interfaces can throw any kind of application exception. These application exceptions must be declared in the method signatures of the remote and local interfaces and in the corresponding methods in the enterprise EJB classes.

The EJB create, find, and remove methods can also throw several exceptions defined in the `javax.ejb` package: `CreateException`, `DuplicateKeyException`, `FinderException`, `ObjectNotFoundException`, and `RemoveException`. These exceptions are considered application exceptions: they are delivered to the client as-is, without being repackaged as `RemoteExceptions`. Furthermore, these exceptions don't necessarily cause a transaction to roll back, giving the client the opportunity to retry the operation. These exceptions may be thrown by the EJBs themselves; in the case of container-managed persistence, the container can also throw any of these exceptions while handling the EJB's create, find, or remove methods (`ejbCreate()`, `ejbFind()`, and `ejbRemove()`). The container might, for example, throw a `CreateException` if it encounters a bad argument while attempting to insert a record for a container-managed EJB. You can always choose to throw a standard application exception from the appropriate method regardless of how persistence is managed.

Here is a detailed explanation of the five standard application exceptions and the situations in which they are thrown:

`CreateException`
: `CreateException` is thrown by the `create()` method in the remote interface. The container can throw this exception if the container is managing persistence, or it can be thrown explicitly by the EJB developer in the `ejbCreate()` or `ejbPostCreate()` methods. It indicates that an application error (invalid arguments, etc.) occurred while the EJB was being created. If the container throws this exception, it may or may not roll back the transaction. Explicit transaction methods must be used to determine the outcome. Bean developers should roll back the transaction before throwing this exception only if data integrity is a concern.

`DuplicateKeyException`
: `DuplicateKeyException` is a subtype of `CreateException`; it is thrown by the `create()` method in the remote interface. The container can throw this exception if the container is managing persistence, or it can be thrown explicitly by the EJB developer in the `ejbCreate()` method. It indicates that an EJB with the same primary key already exists in the database. The EJB provider or container typically does not roll the transaction back before throwing this exception.

`FinderException`
: `FinderException` is thrown by the find methods in the home interface. The container can throw this exception if the container is managing persistence, or it can be thrown explicitly by the EJB developer in the `ejbFind()` methods. It indicates that an application error (invalid arguments, etc.) occurred while the container was attempting to find the EJBs. Do not use this method to indicate that entities were not found. Multi-entity find methods return an empty collection if no entities were found; single-entity find methods throw an `ObjectNotFoundException` to indicate that no object was found. The EJB provider or container typically does not roll the transaction back before throwing this exception.

`ObjectNotFoundException`

`ObjectNotFoundException` is thrown from a single-entity find method to indicate the container could not find the requested entity. This exception can be thrown either by the container (if the container is managing persistence) or explicitly by the EJB developer in the `ejbFind()` methods. It shouldn't be thrown to indicate a business-logic error (invalid arguments, etc.). Use the `FinderException` to indicate business-logic errors in single-entity find methods. The `ObjectNotFoundException` is thrown by single-entity find methods only to indicate that the entity requested was not found. Find methods that return multiple entities should return an empty collection if nothing is found. The EJB provider or container typically does not roll the transaction back before throwing this exception.

`RemoveException`

The `RemoveException` is thrown from the `remove()` methods in the remote and home interfaces. The container can throw this exception if the container is managing persistence, or it can be thrown explicitly by the EJB developer in the `ejbRemove()` method. It indicates that an application error has occurred while the EJB was being removed. The transaction may or may not have been rolled back by the container before throwing this exception. Explicit transaction methods must be used to determine the outcome. Bean developers should roll back the transaction before throwing the exception only if data integrity is a concern.

Table 16-1 summarizes the interactions between different types of exceptions and transactions in session and entity beans.

Table 16-1. Exception summary for session and entity beans

Transaction scope	Transaction type attributes	Exception thrown	Container's action	Client's view
Client-initiated transaction. The transaction is started by the client (application or EJB) and propagated to the enterprise bean method.	`transaction-type = Container` `transaction-attribute = Required| Mandatory| Supports`	Application exception	If the EJB invoked `setRollbackOnly()`, mark the client's transaction for rollback. Rethrow the application exception.	Receives the application exception. The client's transaction may or may not have been marked for rollback.
		System exception	Mark the client's transaction for rollback. Log the error. Discard the instance. Rethrow the JTA `TransactionRolledbackException` to remote clients or the `javax.ejb.TransactionRolledbackLocalException` to EJB local clients.	Remote clients receive the JTA `TransactionRolledbackException`; local clients receive the `javax.ejb.TransactionRolledbackLocalException`. The client's transaction has been rolled back.

Table 16-1. Exception summary for session and entity beans (continued)

Transaction scope	Transaction type attributes	Exception thrown	Container's action	Client's view
Container-managed transaction. The transaction started when the EJB's method was invoked and will end when the method completes.	`transaction-type = Container` `transaction-attribute = Required | RequiresNew`	Application exception	If the EJB invoked `setRollbackOnly()`, roll back the transaction and rethrow the application exception. If the EJB did not explicitly roll back the transaction, attempt to commit the transaction and rethrow the application exception.	Receives the application exception. The EJB's transaction may or may not have been rolled back. The client's transaction is not affected.
		System exception	Roll back the transaction. Log the error. Discard the instance. Rethrow the `RemoteException` to remote clients or the `EJBException` to EJB local clients.	Remote clients receive the `RemoteException`; local EJB clients receive the `EJBException`. The EJB's transaction was rolled back. The client's transaction may marked for rollback, depending on the vendor.
The bean is not part of a transaction. The EJB was invoked but doesn't propagate the client's transaction and doesn't start its own transaction.	`transaction-type = Container` `transaction-attribute = Never | NotSupported | Supports |`	Application exception	Rethrow the application exception.	Receives the application exception. The client's transaction is not affected.
		System exception	Log the error. Discard the instance. Rethrow the `RemoteException` to remote clients or the `EJBException` to EJB local clients.	Remote clients receive the `RemoteException`; local EJB clients receive the `EJBException`. The client's transaction may or may not be marked for rollback, depending on the vendor.
Bean-managed transaction. The stateful or stateless session EJB uses the `EJBContext` to explicitly manage its own transaction.	`transaction-type = Bean` `transaction-attribute =` Bean-managed transaction EJBs do not use transaction attributes.	Application exception	Rethrow the application exception.	Receives the application exception. The client's transaction is not affected.

Table 16-1. Exception summary for session and entity beans (continued)

Transaction scope	Transaction type attributes	Exception thrown	Container's action	Client's view
		System exception	Roll back the transaction. Log the error. Discard the instance. Rethrow the `RemoteException` to remote clients or the `EJBException` to EJB local clients.	Remote clients receive the `RemoteException`; local EJB clients receive the `EJBException`. The client's transaction is not affected.

Table 16-2 summarizes the interactions between different types of exceptions and transactions in message-driven beans.

Table 16-2. Exception summary for message-driven beans

Transaction scope	Transaction type attributes	Exception thrown	Container's action
Container-initiated transaction. The transaction started before the `onMessage( )` method was invoked and will end when the method completes.	`transaction-type = Container` `transaction-attribute = Required`	System exception	Roll back the transaction. Log the error. Discard the instance.
Container-initiated transaction. No transaction was started.	`transaction-type = Container` `transaction-attribute = NotSupported`	System exception	Log the error. Discard the instance.
Bean-managed transaction. The message-driven bean uses the `EJBContext` to explicitly manage its own transaction.	`transaction-type = Bean` `transaction-attribute` = Bean-managed transaction EJBs do not use transaction attributes.	System exception	Roll back the transaction. Log the error. Discard the instance.

Transactional Stateful Session Beans

Session beans can interact directly with the database as easily as they can manage the taskflow of other enterprise beans. The ProcessPayment EJB, for example, makes inserts into the `PAYMENT` table when the `byCredit()` method is invoked, and the TravelAgent EJB queries the database directly when the `listAvailableCabins()` method is invoked. Stateless session beans such as the ProcessPayment EJB have no conversational state, so each method invocation must make changes to the database immediately. With stateful session beans, however, we may not want to make changes to the database until the transaction is complete. Remember, a stateful session bean can be one of many participants in a transaction, so it may be advisable to postpone database updates until the entire transaction is committed or to avoid updates if it is rolled back.

There are several different scenarios in which a stateful session bean might cache changes before applying them to the database. For example, think of a shopping cart implemented by a stateful session bean that accumulates several items for purchase. If the stateful bean implements `SessionSynchronization`, it can cache the items and write them to the database only when the transaction is complete.

The `javax.ejb.SessionSynchronization` interface allows a session bean to receive additional notification of the session's involvement in transactions. The addition of these transaction callback methods by the `SessionSynchronization` interface expands the EJB's awareness of its life cycle to include a new state, the *Transactional Method-Ready state*. This third state, although not discussed in Chapter 11, is always a part of the life cycle of a transactional stateful session bean. Implementing the `SessionSynchronization` interface simply makes it visible to the EJB. Figure 16-11 shows the stateful session bean with the additional state.

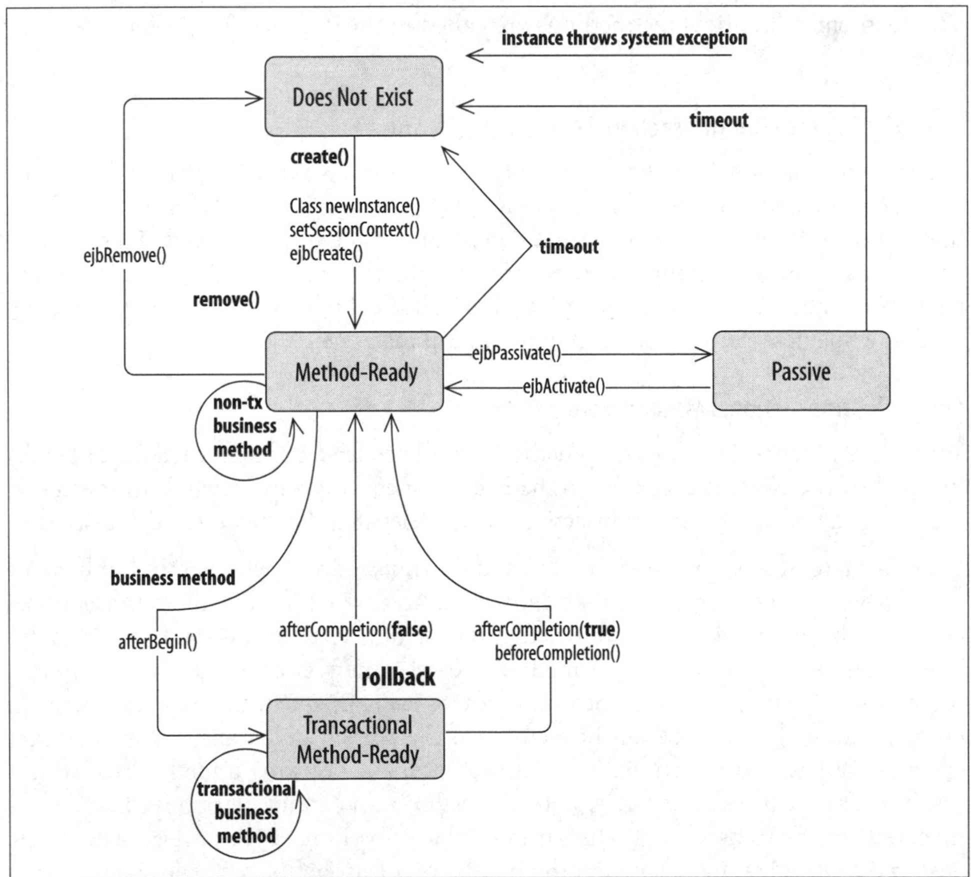

Figure 16-11. Life cycle of a stateful session bean

The SessionSynchronization interface is defined:

```
package javax.ejb;

public interface javax.ejb.SessionSynchronization {
    public abstract void afterBegin( ) throws RemoteException;
    public abstract void beforeCompletion( ) throws RemoteException;
    public abstract void afterCompletion(boolean committed) throws RemoteException;
}
```

When a method of the SessionSynchronization bean is invoked outside of a transaction scope, the method executes in the Method-Ready state, as discussed in Chapter 11. However, when a method is invoked within a transaction scope (or creates a new transaction), the EJB moves into the Transactional Method-Ready state.

The Transactional Method-Ready State

The SessionSynchronization methods are called in the Transactional Method-Ready state.

Transitioning into the Transactional Method-Ready state

When a transactional method is invoked on a SessionSynchronization bean, the stateful bean becomes part of the transaction, causing the afterBegin( ) callback method defined in the SessionSynchronization interface to be invoked. This method should take care of reading any data from the database and storing the data in the bean's instance fields. The afterBegin( ) method is called before the EJB object delegates the business-method invocation to the EJB instance.

Life in the Transactional Method-Ready state

When the afterBegin( ) callback method completes, the business method originally invoked by the client is executed on the EJB instance. Any subsequent business methods invoked within the same transaction will be delegated directly to the EJB instance.

Once a stateful session bean is a part of a transaction—whether it implements SessionSynchronization or not—it cannot be accessed by any other transactional context. This is true regardless of whether the client tries to access the EJB with a different context or the EJB's own method creates a new context. If, for example, a method with a transaction attribute of RequiresNew is invoked, the new transactional context causes an error to be thrown. Since the NotSupported and Never attributes specify a different transactional context (no context), invoking a method with these attributes also causes an error. A stateful session bean cannot be removed while it is involved in a transaction. This means that invoking ejbRemove( ) while the SessionSynchronization bean is in the middle of a transaction will cause an error to be thrown.

At some point, the transaction in which the `SessionSynchronization` bean has been enrolled will come to an end. If the transaction is committed, the `SessionSynchronization` bean will be notified through its `beforeCompletion()` method. At this time, the EJB should write its cached data to the database. If the transaction is rolled back, the `beforeCompletion()` method will not be invoked, avoiding the pointless effort of writing changes that won't be committed to the database.

The `afterCompletion()` method is always invoked, whether the transaction ended successfully with a commit or unsuccessfully with a rollback. If the transaction was a success—which means that `beforeCompletion()` was invoked—the `committed` parameter of the `afterCompletion()` method will be `true`. If the transaction was unsuccessful, `committed` will be `false`.

It may be desirable to reset the stateful session bean's instance variables to some initial state if the `afterCompletion()` method indicates that the transaction was rolled back.

CHAPTER 17

J2EE

The specification for the Java 2 Enterprise Edition (J2EE) defines a platform for developing web-enabled applications that includes Enterprise JavaBeans, servlets, and JavaServer Pages (JSP). J2EE products are application servers that provide a complete implementation of the EJB, servlet, and JSP technologies. In addition, J2EE outlines how these technologies work together to provide a complete solution for developing applications. To help you understand J2EE, we must introduce servlets and JSP and explain the synergy between these technologies and Enterprise JavaBeans.

At the risk of spoiling the story, J2EE provides two kinds of "glue" to make it easier for components to interact. First, the JNDI *enviroment naming context* (ENC) is used to standardize the way components look up resources they need. We discussed the ENC in the context of enterprise beans; in this chapter, we will look briefly at how servlets, JSPs, and even some clients can use the ENC to find resources. Second, the use of *deployment descriptors*—in particular, the use of XML to define a language for deployment descriptors—is extended to servlets and JSP. Java servlets and JSP pages can be packaged with deployment descriptors that define their relationships to their environment. Deployment descriptors are also used to define entire assemblies of many components into applications.

Servlets

The servlet specification defines a server-side component model that can be implemented by web server vendors. *Servlets* provide a simple but powerful API for generating web pages dynamically. (Although servlets can be used for many different request-response protocols, they are predominantly used to process HTTP requests for web pages.)

Servlets are developed in the same fashion as enterprise beans; they are Java classes that extend a base component class and have a deployment descriptor. Once a servlet is developed and packaged in a JAR file, it can be deployed in a web server. When a servlet is deployed, it is assigned to handle requests for a specific web page or to assist other servlets in handling page requests. The following servlet, for example, might be assigned to handle any request for the *helloworld.html* page on a web server:

```
import javax.servlet.*;
import javax.servlet.http.*;

public class HelloWorld extends HttpServlet {

    protected void doGet(HttpServletRequest req, HttpServletResponse response)
        throws ServletException,java.io.IOException {

    try {
        ServletOutputStream writer = response.getWriter( );
        writer.println("<HTML><BODY>");
        writer.println("<h1>Hello World!!</h1>");
        writer.println("</BODY></HTML>");
    } catch(Exception e) {
        // handle exception
    }
    ...
}
```

When a browser sends a request for the page to the web server, the server delegates the request to the appropriate servlet instance by invoking the servlet's `doGet( )` method.* The servlet is provided with information about the request in the `HttpServletRequest` object and can use the `HttpServletResponse` object to reply to the request. This simple servlet sends a short HTML document (including the text "Hello World") back to the browser, which displays it. Figure 17-1 illustrates how a request is sent by a browser and serviced by a servlet running in a web server.

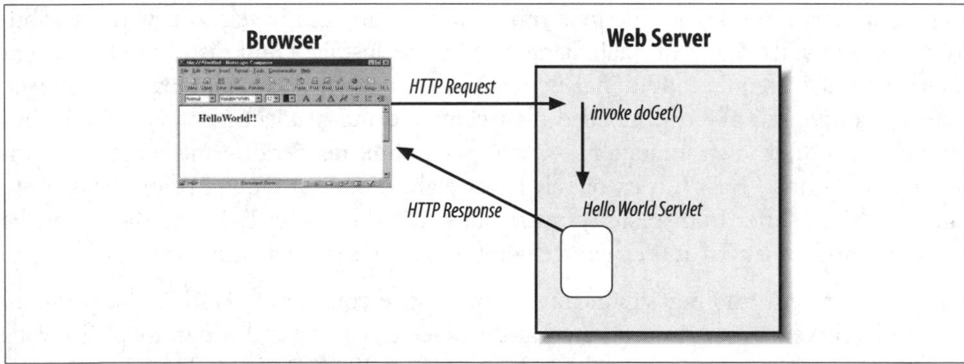

Figure 17-1. Servlet servicing an HTTP request

Servlets are similar to session beans because they both perform a service and can directly access backend resources (e.g., databases) through JDBC, but they do not

* HttpServlets also have a `doPost( )` method that handles requests for forms.

represent persistent data. Servlets do not, however, have support for container-managed transactions and are not composed of business methods. Servlets deal with very specific (usually HTTP) requests and respond by writing to an output stream.

The servlet specification is extensive and robust but also simple and elegant. Learn more about servlets by reading *Java Servlet Programming* by Jason Hunter (O'Reilly).

JavaServer Pages

JavaServer Pages is an extension of the servlet component model that simplifies the process of generating HTML dynamically. JSP essentially allows you to incorporate Java directly into an HTML page as a scripting language. In J2EE, the Java code in a JSP page can access the JNDI ENC, just like the code in a servlet. In fact, JSP pages (text documents) are translated and compiled into Java servlets, which are then run in a web server just like any other servlet—some servers do the compilation automatically at runtime. You can also use JSP to generate XML documents dynamically. If you want to learn more about JSP, take a look at *JavaServer Pages* by Hans Bergsten (O'Reilly).

Web Components and EJB

Together, servlets and JSP provide a powerful platform for generating web pages dynamically. Servlets and JSP, which are collectively called *web components*, can access resources like JDBC and enterprise beans. Because web components can access databases using JDBC, they allow an enterprise to expose its business systems to the Web through an HTML interface. HTML interfaces have several advantages over more conventional client interfaces. The most important advantages have to do with distribution and firewalls. Conventional clients need to be installed and distributed on client machines: they require additional work for deployment and maintenance. Applets, which are dynamically downloaded, can eliminate the headache of installation, but applets have their own limitations—such as sandbox restrictions and lengthy downloads. In contrast, HTML is extremely lightweight, does not require prior installation, and does not suffer from security restrictions. In addition, HTML interfaces can be modified and enhanced at their source without having to update the clients.

Firewalls present another significant problem in e-commerce. HTTP, the protocol over which web pages are requested and delivered, can pass through most firewalls without a problem, but protocols such as IIOP or JRMP cannot. This limitation is extremely important. It means that a client usually cannot access a server using IIOP or JRMP without modifications to the firewall. And the firewall is usually not under the control of the groups who need the application to run. HTTP does not suffer from this limitation, since practically all firewalls allow HTTP to pass unhindered.

The problems with distribution and firewalls have led most of the EJB industry to adopt an architecture based on web components (servlets/JSP) and Enterprise

JavaBeans. Web components provide the presentation logic for generating web pages; EJB supplies a middle tier for business logic. Web components access enterprise beans using the same API as application clients. Each technology is doing what it does best: servlets and JSP are excellent components for generating dynamic HTML, while EJB is an excellent platform for business logic. Figure 17-2 illustrates how the architecture works.

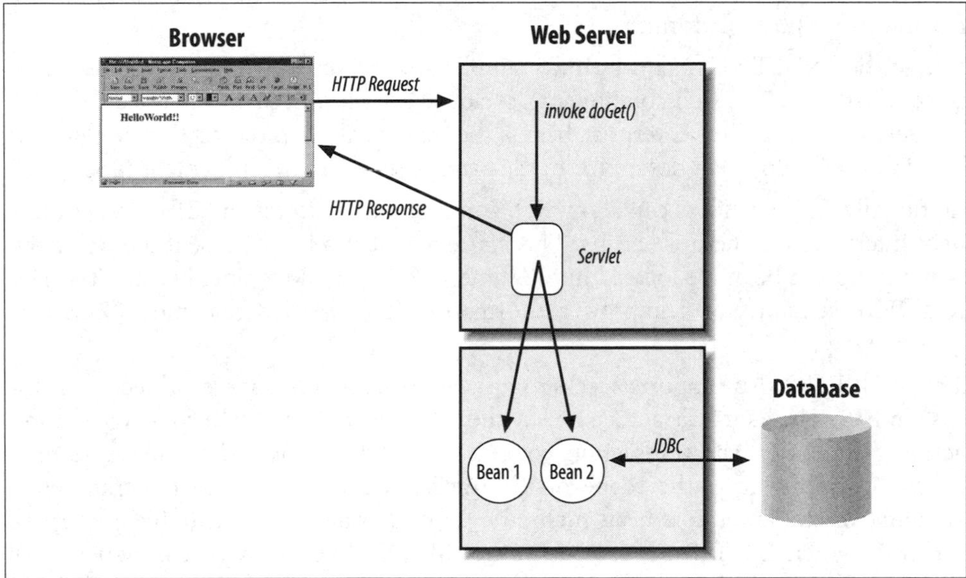

Figure 17-2. Using servlets/JSP and EJB together

This web component-EJB architecture is so widely accepted that it begs the question, "Should there be a united platform?" The J2EE specification answers this question. J2EE defines a single application server platform that focuses on the interaction between servlets, JSP, and EJB. J2EE is important because it provides a specification for the interaction of web components with enterprise beans, making solutions more portable across vendors that support both component models.

Filling in the Gaps

The J2EE specification attempts to fill the gaps between the web components and Enterprise JavaBeans by defining how these technologies come together to form a complete platform. One of the ways in which J2EE adds value is by creating a consistent programming model across web components and enterprise beans through the use of the JNDI ENC and XML deployment descriptors. A servlet in J2EE can access JDBC `DataSource` objects, environment entries, and references to enterprise beans through a JNDI ENC in exactly the same way that enterprise beans use the JNDI ENC. To support the JNDI ENC, web components have their own XML deployment descriptor that declares elements for the JNDI ENC (`<ejb-ref>`, `<resource-ref>`, `<env-entry>`) as well as security roles and other elements specific to web components. In J2EE, web components are packaged along with their XML deployment descriptors and deployed in JAR files with the extension *.war*, which stands for *web archive*. A *.war* file can contain several servlets and JSP documents that share an XML deployment descriptor. The use of the JNDI ENC, deployment descriptors, and JAR files in web components makes them consistent with the EJB programming model and unifies the entire J2EE platform.

Use of the JNDI ENC makes it much simpler for web components to access Enterprise JavaBeans. The web component developer does not need to be concerned with the network location of enterprise beans; the server will map the `<ejb-ref>` elements listed in the deployment descriptor to the enterprise beans at deployment time.

Optionally, J2EE vendors can allow web components to access the EJB local component interfaces of enterprise beans. This strategy makes a lot of sense if the web component and the bean are located in the same Java Virtual Machine, because the Java RMI-IIOP semantics can improve performance. It's expected that most J2EE vendors will support this option.

The JNDI ENC also supports access to a `javax.jta.UserTransaction` object, as is the case in EJB. The `UserTransaction` object allows the web component to manage transactions explicitly. The transaction context must be propagated to any enterprise beans accessed within the scope of the transaction (according to the transaction attribute of the enterprise bean method). J2EE also defines an *.ear* file (*enterprise archive*), which is a JAR file for packaging EJB JAR files and web component JAR files (*.war* files) together into one complete deployment, called a *J2EE application*. A J2EE application has its own XML deployment descriptor that points to the EJB and web component JAR files (called *modules*) as well as other elements such as icons, descriptions, and the like. When a J2EE application is created, interdependencies such as `<ejb-ref>` and `<ejb-local-ref>` elements can be resolved and security roles can be edited to provide a unified view of the entire web application. Figure 17-3 illustrates the file structure of a J2EE archive file.

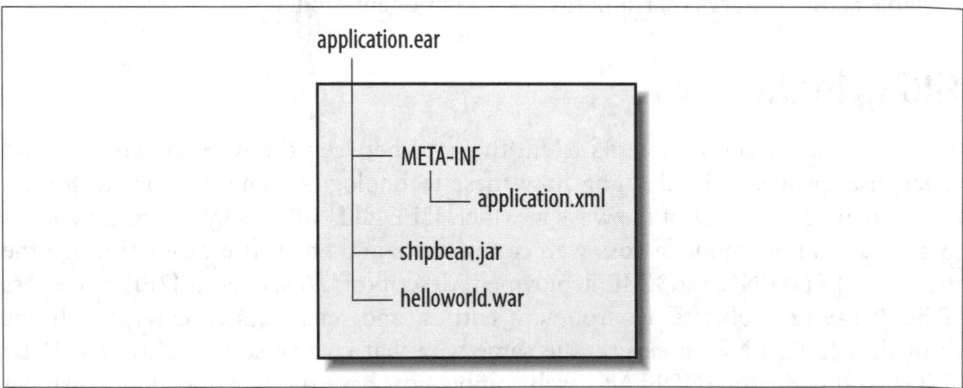

Figure 17-3. Contents of a J2EE .ear file

J2EE Application Client Components

In addition to integrating web and enterprise bean components, J2EE introduces a new component model: the *application client component*. An application client component is a Java application that resides on a client machine and accesses enterprise bean components on the J2EE server. Client components also have access to a JNDI ENC that operates the same way as the JNDI ENC for web and enterprise bean components. The client component includes an XML deployment descriptor that declares the `<env-entry>`, `<ejb-ref>`, and `<resource-ref>` elements of the JNDI ENC in addition to a `<description>`, `<display-name>`, and `<icon>` that can be used to represent the component in a deployment tool.

A client component is simply a Java program that uses the JNDI ENC to access environment properties, enterprise beans, and resources (JDBC, JavaMail, and so on) made available by the J2EE server. Client components reside on the client machine, not the J2EE server. Here is an extremely simple component:

```
public class MyJ2eeClient {

    public static void main(String [] args) {

        InitialContext jndiCntx = new InitialContext( );

        Object ref = jndiCntx.lookup("java:comp/env/ejb/ShipBean");
        ShipHome home = (ShipHome)
            PortableRemoteObject.narrow(ref,ShipHome.class);

        Ship ship = home.findByPrimaryKey(new ShipPK(1));
        String name = ship.getName( );
        System.out.println(name);

    }
}
```

`MyJ2eeClient` illustrates how a client component is written. Notice that the client component did not need to use a network-specific JNDI `InitialContext`. In other words, we did not have to specify the service provider in order to connect to the J2EE server. This is the real power of the J2EE application client component: *location transparency*. The client component does not need to know the exact location of the Ship EJB or choose a specific JNDI service provider; the JNDI ENC takes care of locating the enterprise bean.

When application components are developed, an XML deployment descriptor is created that specifies the JNDI ENC entries. At deployment time, a vendor-specific J2EE tool generates the class files needed to deploy the component on client machines. A client component is packaged into a JAR file with its XML deployment descriptor and can be included in a J2EE application. Once a client component is included in the J2EE application deployment descriptor, it can be packaged in the *.ear* file with the other components, as Figure 17-4 illustrates.

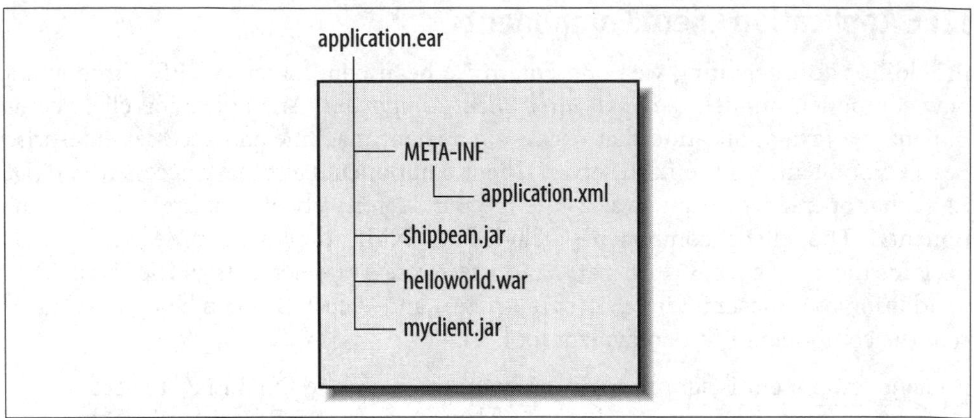

Figure 17-4. Contents of a J2EE .ear file with application component

Guaranteed Services

The J2EE specifications require application servers to support a specific set of protocols and Java enterprise extensions, ensuring a consistent platform for deploying J2EE applications. J2EE application servers must provide the following "standard" services:

Java Virtual Machine
: J2EE 1.4 products must support Java 2, SDK 1.4. J2EE 1.3 products must support Java 2, SDK 1.3.

Enterprise JavaBeans
: J2EE 1.4 products must support EJB 2.1. J2EE 1.3 products must support EJB 2.0.

Servlets
: J2EE 1.4 products must support Servlets 2.4. J2EE 1.3 products must support Servlets 2.3.

JavaServer Pages
: J2EE 1.4 products must support JSP 2.0. J2EE 1.3 products must support JSP 1.2.

HTTP and HTTPS
: Web components in a J2EE server service both HTTP and HTTPS requests. The J2EE product must be capable of advertising HTTP 1.0 and HTTPS (HTTP 1.0 over SSL 3.0) on ports 80 and 443, respectively. Components must have full access to HTTP/HTTPS client APIs.

Java RMI-IIOP
: Support for Java RMI-IIOP is required. However, the vendor may also use other protocols, as long as they are compatible with Java RMI-IIOP semantics.

Java RMI-JRMP.
: J2EE components can be native Java RMI (JRMP) clients.

JavaIDL
: Web components and enterprise beans must be able to access CORBA services hosted outside the J2EE environment using JavaIDL, a standard part of the Java 2 platform.

JDBC

J2EE 1.4 requires support for JDBC 3.0. J2EE 1.3 requires support for the JDBC 2.0 and some parts of the JDBC 2.0 Extension.

Java Naming and Directory Interface (JNDI) 1.2

Web and enterprise bean components must have access to the JNDI ENC, to access things like the `EJBHome` objects, JTA `UserTransaction` objects, JDBC `DataSource` objects, Java Message Service `ConnectionFactory` objects, and JAX-RPC `ConnectionFactory` objects.

JavaMail and JAF

J2EE 1.4 products must support JavaMail 1.3, including access to a message store. J2EE 1.3 products must support JavaMail 1.2. Both platforms must support JAF (Java Activation Framework) 1.0; it's needed to support different MIME types and required for support of JavaMail.

Java Message Service (JMS)

J2EE 1.4 products must support JMS 1.1. J2EE 1.3 products must support JMS 1.0.2. J2EE products must provide support for both point-to-point (p2p) and publish-and-subscribe (pub/sub) messaging models. J2EE 1.4 must also support the Unified messaging model.

Java API for XML Parsing (JAXP)

J2EE 1.4 products must support JAXP 1.2, which includes XML Schema validation, while J2EE 1.3 products must support JAXP 1.1.

J2EE Connector Architecture (J2CA)

J2EE 1.4 products must support J2CA 1.5, which includes asynchronous messaging. J2EE 1.3 products must support J2CA 1.0.

Java Authentication and Authorization Service (JAAS)

J2EE 1.4 and 1.3 products must support the use of JAAS 1.0, as described in the J2CA specifications.

Java Transaction API 1.0.1

J2EE 1.4 and 1.3 products must support JTA 1.0 and must have access to the `UserTransaction` objects via the JNDI ENC.

Web Services for J2EE (WS-J2EE)

J2EE 1.4 must support Web Services for J2EE 1.1 The specification includes JAX-RPC 1.1, JAXR 1.0, and SAAJ 1.2.

Java Logging API

J2EE 1.4 products must support the logging of events using the `java.util.logging` package, which is part of the J2SDK 1.4 core.

J2EE Management API

J2EE 1.4 products must support the J2EE Management API 1.0, including support for some features of JMX 1.2.

J2EE Deployment API

J2EE 1.4 products must support the J2EE Deployment API 1.1. Vendors must support the plug-in component for tool vendors.

Java Authorization Service Provider Contract (JACC)
J2EE 1.4 must support the JACC 1.0, which defines a contract between a J2EE application server and an authorization policy provider.

Fitting the Pieces Together

To illustrate how a J2EE platform might function, imagine using a J2EE server in Titan's reservation system. To build this system, we would use the TravelAgent, Cabin, ProcessPayment, Customer, and other enterprise beans we defined in this book, along with web components that would provide an HTML interface. The web components would access the enterprise beans in the same way that any Java client would, using the enterprise beans' remote and home interfaces. The web components would generate HTML to represent the reservation system.

Figure 17-5 shows a web page generated by a servlet or JSP page for the Titan reservation system. This web page was generated by web components on the J2EE server. When this page appears, the person using the reservation system has been guided through a login page, a customer selection page, and a cruise selection page, and is about to choose an available cabin for a reservation.

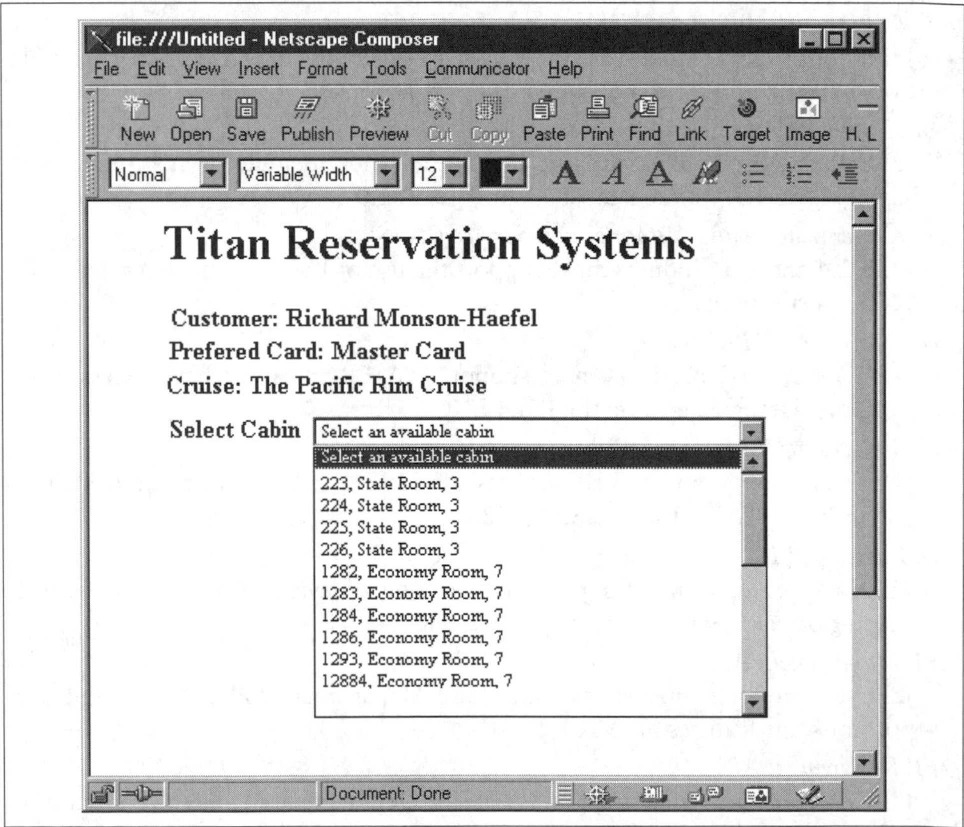

Figure 17-5. HTML interface to the Titan reservation system

The list of available cabins is obtained from the TravelAgent EJB, whose `listAvailableCabins( )` method is invoked by the servlet that generated the web page. The list of cabins creates an HTML list box in a web page that is loaded into the user's browser. When the user chooses a cabin and submits the selection, an HTTP request is sent to the J2EE server. The J2EE server receives the request and delegates it to the `ReservationServlet`, which invokes the `TravelAgent.bookPassage( )` method to do the actual reservation. The ticket information returned by the `bookPassage( )` method is then used to create another web page, which is sent back to the user's browser. Figure 17-6 shows how the different components work together to process the request.

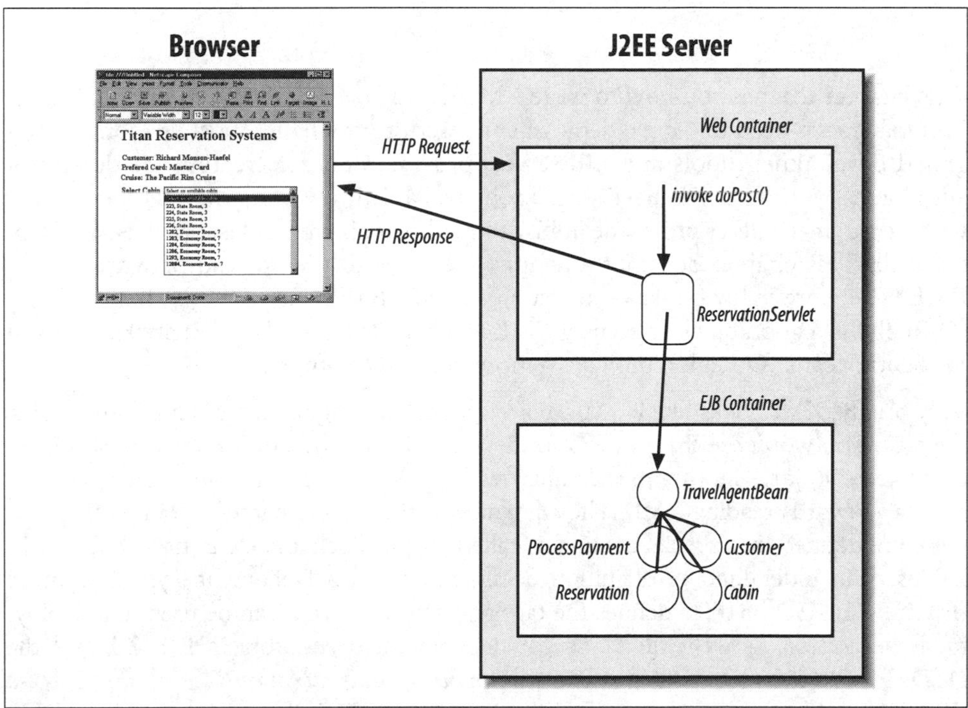

Figure 17-6. J2EE Titan reservation system

CHAPTER 18
XML Deployment Descriptors

This chapter teaches you how to write XML deployment descriptors for your beans. You may never need to write a deployment descriptor by hand: most vendors of integrated development tools and EJB servers provide tools for creating the descriptor automatically. Even if you have such a tool available, however, you must be familiar with deployment descriptors: the ability to read a deployment descriptor is an essential skill. This chapter does not attempt to teach you how to read or write correct XML. There are many books on the subject: *XML Pocket Reference* by Bob Eckstein (O'Reilly) is a good quick reference; *XML in a Nutshell*, by Elliotte Rusty Harold and W. Scott Means (O'Reilly), provides a more detailed treatment.

Very briefly, XML looks like HTML, but with different tag names and attributes inside the tags. You won't see `<h1>` and `<p>` inside a deployment descriptor; instead, you'll see tags like `<ejb-jar>`. But if you're familiar with the structure of HTML, you're most of the way towards reading XML. The tag names and attribute names for an XML document are defined by a special document called an XML Schema Definition (XSD). (EJB 2.0 used an older kind of definition document called a Document Type Definition (DTD)). An XSD or DTD defines the tags and attributes that can be used in a deployment descriptor, as well; the XSDs for deployment descriptors in EJB 2.1 and the DTDs for EJB 2.0 are available online at *http://java.sun.com/xml/ns/j2ee/ejb-jar_2_1.xsd* (EJB 2.1) and *http://java.sun.com/dtd/ejb-jar_2_0.dtd* (EJB 2.0).

There are other important differences between XML and HTML. XML is much more strict; many things that are acceptable in HTML are errors in XML. This should not make a difference if you're just reading a deployment descriptor, but if you're writing one, be careful. Two differences are particularly important. First, XML is case-sensitive: you cannot mix uppercase and lowercase in your tag names. HTML does not care about the difference between `<h1>` and `<H1>`, but XML does. All the tags and attributes used in deployment descriptors are lowercase. Second, XML will not forgive you if you fail to supply closing tags. In HTML, you can write `<p>...<p>` without ever putting in a `</p>` to end the first paragraph. But XML never allows you to be sloppy. Whenever you have an opening tag, you must also supply a closing tag.

That's about it. These few paragraphs don't qualify as a real introduction to XML, but the basic ideas are very simple, and they are all you need to get going.

The ejb-jar File

The JAR file format is a platform-independent format for compressing, packaging, and delivering several files together. Based on the Zip file format and the ZLIB compression standards, the JAR (Java archive) packages and tool were originally developed to make downloads of Java applets more efficient. As a packaging mechanism, however, the JAR file format is a convenient way to "shrink-wrap" components and other software for delivery to third parties. The original JavaBeans component architecture depends on JAR files for packaging, as does Enterprise JavaBeans. The goal in using the JAR file format is to package all the classes and interfaces associated with one or more beans, including the deployment descriptor, into one file.

The JAR file is created using a vendor-specific tool, or using the *jar* utility that is part of the Java 2, Standard Edition development kit. An *ejb-jar* file contains:

- The XML deployment descriptors
- The bean classes
- The remote and home interfaces
- The primary key class
- Dependent classes and interfaces

All of the XML deployment descriptors (*ejb-jar.xml*, *webservices.xml*, WSDL, JAX-RPC Mapping) should be located in the *META-INF* directory and must contain all the deployment information for all the beans in the *ejb-jar* file. For each bean declared in the XML deployment descriptor, the *ejb-jar* file must contain its bean class, remote and home interfaces, and dependent classes and interfaces. Dependent classes and interfaces are usually things like application-specific exceptions, business interfaces, and other supertypes, and dependent objects that are used by the bean. In the *ejb-jar* file for the TravelAgent bean, for example, we would include the `IncompleteConversationalState` application exception and the `Ticket` and `CreditCard` classes, as well as the remote and home interfaces to other beans referenced by the TravelAgent bean, such as the Customer and ProcessPayment beans.*

You can use the *jar* utility from the command line to package a bean in a JAR file. Here's an example of how the *jar* utility was used to package the Cabin EJB in Chapter 4:

```
\dev % jar cf cabin.jar com/titan/cabin/*.class META-INF/ejb-jar.xml

F:\..\dev>jar cf cabin.jar com\titan\cabin\*.class META-INF\ejb-jar.xml
```

* The EJB 1.1 specification also allows remote and home interfaces of referenced beans to be named in the manifest's `Class-Path` attribute, instead of including them in the JAR file. Use of the `Class-Path` entry in the JAR's manifest is addressed in more detail in the Java 2, Standard Edition specification.

You might have to create the *META-INF* directory first, and copy *ejb-jar.xml* into that directory. The c option tells the *jar* utility to create a new JAR file that contains the files indicated in subsequent parameters. It also tells the *jar* utility to stream the resulting JAR file to standard output. The f option tells *jar* to redirect the standard output to a new file named in the second parameter (*cabin.jar*). It is important to get the order of the option letters and the command-line parameters to match. You can learn more about the *jar* utility and the java.util.zip package in *Java in a Nutshell* by David Flanagan or *Learning Java* by Pat Niemeyer and Jonathan Knudsen, both published by O'Reilly.

The *jar* utility creates the file *cabin.jar* in the *dev* directory. If you are interested in looking at the contents of the JAR file, you can use any standard ZIP application (WinZip, PKZIP, etc.) or the command jar tvf cabin.jar.

The Contents of a Deployment Descriptor

We've discussed XML deployment descriptors throughout this book—you probably know enough to write deployment descriptors on your own. However, it is still worthwhile to take a tour through a complete descriptor. Example 18-1 is a complete deployment descriptor for the Cabin EJB, which we created in Chapter 4. Other than the type of schema used (XSD or DTD) and the fact that EJB 2.1 uses XML namespaces, the elements are the same in EJB 2.1 and 2.0. The Cabin EJB's deployment descriptor contains most of the tags that are needed to describe entity beans; session and message-driven beans are not much different. The differences between the versions are small but significant. We'll use this deployment descriptor to guide our discussion in the following sections.

Example 18-1. Cabin EJB deployment descriptor

```
<?xml version="1.0" encoding="UTF-8"?>
...
<ejb-jar ...>
    <enterprise-beans>
        <entity>
            <description>
                This Cabin enterprise bean entity represents a cabin
                on a cruise ship.
            </description>
            <ejb-name>CabinEJB</ejb-name>
            <home>com.titan.cabin.CabinHomeRemote</home>
            <remote>com.titan.cabin.CabinRemote</remote>
            <local-home>com.titan.cabin.CabinHomeLocal</local-home>
            <local>com.titan.cabin.CabinLocal</local>
            <ejb-class>com.titan.cabin.CabinBean</ejb-class>
            <persistence-type>Container</persistence-type>
            <prim-key-class>com.titan.cabin.CabinPK</prim-key-class>
            <reentrant>False</reentrant>
            <cmp-version>2.x</cmp-version>
```

Example 18-1. Cabin EJB deployment descriptor (continued)

```
            <abstract-schema-name>Cabin</abstract-schema-name>
            <cmp-field><field-name>id</field-name></cmp-field>
            <cmp-field><field-name>name</field-name></cmp-field>
            <cmp-field><field-name>deckLevel</field-name></cmp-field>
            <cmp-field><field-name>shipId</field-name></cmp-field>
            <cmp-field><field-name>bedCount</field-name></cmp-field>
            <primkey-field>id</primkey-field>
        </entity>
    </enterprise-beans>

    <assembly-descriptor>
        <security-role>
            <description>
                This role represents everyone who is allowed full access
                to the Cabin EJB.
            </description>
            <role-name>everyone</role-name>
        </security-role>

        <method-permission>
            <role-name>everyone</role-name>
            <method>
                <ejb-name>CabinEJB</ejb-name>
                <method-name>*</method-name>
            </method>
        </method-permission>

        <container-transaction>
            <method>
                <ejb-name>CabinEJB</ejb-name>
                <method-name>*</method-name>
            </method>
            <trans-attribute>Required</trans-attribute>
        </container-transaction>
    </assembly-descriptor>
</ejb-jar>
```

The Document Header and Schema Declarations

An XML document may start with a tag that specifies the version of XML in use:

```
<?xml version="1.0" encoding="UTF-8"?>
```

This tag identifies the document as an XML document that adheres to Version 1.0 of the XML specification and uses the UTF-8 character encoding. EJB vendors usually support this character encoding.

In EJB 2.1, the element following the XML header (the `<ejb-jar>` element) is the root element of the deployment descriptor. This element declares the document's XML namespace and the location of the XML schema that can be used to validate its contents. A complete <ejb-jar> element looks like this:

```
<?xml version="1.0" encoding="UTF-8"?>
<ejb-jar xmlns="http://java.sun.com/xml/ns/j2ee"
      xmlns:xsi="http://www.w3.org/2001/XMLSchema-instance"
      xsi:schemaLocation="http://java.sun.com/xml/ns/j2ee
          http://java.sun.com/xml/ns/j2ee/ejb-jar_2_1.xsd"
      version="2.1">
...
</ejb-jar>
```

In EJB 2.0, a DOCTYPE element follows the document header and specifies the DTD that defines the document's contents:

```
<?xml version="1.0" encoding="UTF-8"?>
<!DOCTYPE ejb-jar PUBLIC "-//Sun Microsystems, Inc.//DTD Enterprise
JavaBeans 2.0//EN" "http://java.sun.com/dtd/ejb-jar_2_0.dtd">
<ejb-jar>
...
</ejb-jar>
```

In both EJB 2.1 and 2.0, the schema definition provides a URL from which you (or, more importantly, tools processing the deployment descriptor) can download the schema used to validate the XML document; this means that the EJB server deploying the bean can download the XSD or DTD and use it to prove that your deployment descriptor is correct (i.e., that it is organized correctly and uses the right tag names, and that all the tags and attributes have the appropriate parameters).

The Descriptor's Body

The body of any XML document begins and ends with the tag for the document's root element. For an EJB deployment descriptor, the root element is named <ejb-jar>, and looks like this (EJB 2.1 includes XML namespace and schemaLocation attributes not shown):

```
<ejb-jar ...>
... other elements ...
</ejb-jar>
```

All other elements must be nested within the <ejb-jar> element. You can place the following kinds of elements within <ejb-jar>:

<description> *(optional)*

The <description> element provides a description of the deployment descriptor. This element can be used in many contexts within a deployment descriptor: to describe the descriptor as a whole, to describe particular beans, to describe particular security roles, and so on. The Cabin EJB deployment descriptor doesn't use a <description> element for the deployment descriptor as a whole, but it does provide a description for the Cabin EJB itself.

`<display-name>` *(optional)*

Tools (such as a deployment wizard) that are working with the deployment descriptor use the `<display-name>` element to provide a convenient visual label for the entire JAR file and for individual bean components.

`<small-icon>` *and* `<large-icon>` *(optional)*

These elements point to files within the JAR file that provide icons a deployment wizard or some other tool can use to represent the JAR file. Icons must be image files in either the JPEG or GIF format. Small icons must be 16 × 16 pixels; large icons must be 32 × 32 pixels. These icon elements are also used in the `<entity>`, `<session>`, and `<message-driven>` elements to represent individual enterprise bean components.

`<enterprise-beans>` *(one required)*

The `<enterprise-beans>` element contains descriptions of one or more enterprise beans that are contained in the JAR file. A deployment descriptor may have only one `<enterprise-beans>` element. Within this element, `<entity>`, `<session>`, and `<message-driven>` elements describe the individual beans.

`<relationships>` *(optional)*

The `<relationships>` element describes the container-managed relationships of entity beans declared in the deployment descriptor. The `<relationships>` element contains a number of other elements that describe the participants, direction, and cardinality of each relationship.

`<assembly-descriptor>` *(optional)*

The application assembler or bean developer adds an `<assembly-descriptor>` element to the deployment descriptor to define how the enterprise beans are used in an actual application. The `<assembly-descriptor>` contains a number of elements that define the security roles used to access the bean, the method permissions that govern which roles can call different methods, and the transaction attributes.

`<ejb-client-jar>` *(optional)*

The `<ejb-client-jar>` element provides the path of the client JAR, which normally contains all the classes (including stubs, remote and home interface classes, and so on) the client will need in order to access the beans defined in the deployment descriptor. How client JAR files are organized and delivered to the client is not specified—consult your vendor's documentation.

These elements are quite simple, with the exception of the `<enterprise-beans>` and `<assembly-descriptor>` elements. These two elements contain a lot of nested material. We'll look at the `<enterprise-beans>` element first.

Describing Enterprise Beans

The enterprise beans contained in a JAR file are laid out within the deployment descriptor's <enterprise-beans> element. So far, we have talked about deployment descriptors for a single enterprise bean, but it is possible to package several enterprise beans in a JAR file and describe them all within a single deployment descriptor. We could, for example, have deployed the TravelAgent, ProcessPayment, Cruise, Customer, Reservation, and ReservationProcessor EJBs in the same JAR file. The deployment descriptor would look something like this:

```
<?xml version="1.0" encoding="UTF-8"?>
...
<ejb-jar...>
    <description>
        This Deployment includes all the beans needed to make a reservation:
        TravelAgent, ProcessPayment, Reservation, Customer, Cruise, and Cabin.
    </description>
    <enterprise-beans>
        <session>
            <ejb-name>TravelAgentEJB</ejb-name>
            <remote>com.titan.travelagent.TravelAgentRemote</remote>
            ...
        </session>
        <entity>
            <ejb-name>CustomerEJB</ejb-name>
            <remote>com.titan.customer.CustomerRemote</remote>
            ...
        </entity>
        <session>
            <ejb-name>ProcessPaymentEJB</ejb-name>
            <remote>com.titan.processpayment.ProcessPaymentRemote</remote>
            ...
        </session>
        <message-driven>
            <ejb-name>ReservationProcessorEJB</ejb-name>
            ...
        </message-driven>
        ...
    </enterprise-beans>
    <relationships>
        ...
    </relationships>
    <assembly-descriptor>
        ...
    </assembly-descriptor>
    ...
</ejb-jar>
```

In this descriptor, the <enterprise-beans> element contains two <session> elements, one <entity> element, and a <message-driven> element describing the enterprise beans. Other elements within the <entity>, <session>, and <message-driven>

elements provide detailed information about the enterprise beans; as you can see, the `<ejb-name>` element defines the enterprise bean's name. We will discuss all the things that can go into a bean's description later.

When CMP entity beans are deployed, all the beans that have relationships must be deployed in the same EJB-JAR file, using the same deployment descriptor. The relationships are expressed in the `<relationships>` element, which follows the `<enterprise-beans>` element.

All types of EJBs share assembly information, which is defined in the `<assembly-descriptor>` element that follows the `<relationships>` element (if it's present). In other words, beans can share security and transactional declarations, making it simpler to deploy them consistently. For example, deployment is easier if the same logical security roles control access to all the beans, and it is easiest to guarantee that the roles are defined consistently if they are defined in one place. This strategy also makes it easier to ensure that the transaction attributes are applied consistently to all the beans, because you can declare them all at once.

Session and Entity Beans

The `<session>` and `<entity>` elements, which describe session and entity beans, usually contain many nested elements. The lists of allowable subelements are similar, so we'll discuss the `<session>` and `<entity>` elements together.

Like the `<ejb-jar>` element, a `<session>` or `<entity>` element can optionally contain `<description>`, `<display-name>`, `<small-icon>`, and `<large-icon>` elements. These are fairly self-explanatory and, in any case, have the same meanings as when they appear in the `<ejb-jar>` element. The `<description>` lets you provide a comment that describes the enterprise bean; the `<display-name>` is used by deployment tools to represent the enterprise bean; and the two icon elements are used to represent the enterprise bean in visual environments. The icon elements must point to JPEG or GIF images within the JAR file. The other elements are more interesting:

`<ejb-name>` *(one required)*
: Specifies the name of the enterprise bean component. It is used in the `<methodx>` element to scope method declarations to the correct enterprise bean. Throughout this book, we use a name of the form "NameEJB" as the `<ejb-name>` for an enterprise bean. Other common conventions use names of the form "NameBean" or "TheName".

`<home>` *(optional)*
: Specifies the fully qualified class name of the enterprise bean's remote home interface.

`<remote>` *(optional)*
: Specifies the fully qualified class name of the enterprise bean's remote interface.

`<local-home>` *(optional)*
: Specifies the fully qualified class name of the enterprise bean's local home interface.

`<local>` *(optional)*
: Specifies the fully qualified class name of the enterprise bean's local interface.

`<service-endpoint>` *(EJB 2.1 only; optional)*
: Identifies the JAX-RPC endpoint interface used with stateless session beans that are deployed as EJB Endpoints. Web services and EJB are covered in detail in Chapters 14 and 15.

`<ejb-class>` *(one required)*
: Specifies the fully qualified class name of the bean class.

`<session-type>` *(one required; session beans only)*
: Declares that a session bean is either stateful or stateless. This element can have one of two values: `Stateful` or `Stateless`.

`<primkey-field>` *(optional; entity beans only)*
: Specifies the primary key field for entity beans that use container-managed persistence. This element's value is the name of the field that is used as the primary key. It is not used if the bean has a compound primary key or if the entity bean manages its own persistence. In the Cabin EJB, the `<primkey-field>` is the `id` CMP field. This element is discussed in more detail in the "Specifying Primary Keys" section, later in this chapter.

`<prim-key-class>` *(one required; entity beans only)*
: Specifies the class of the primary key for entity beans. This element's value is the fully qualified name of the primary key class; it makes no difference whether you are using a custom compound primary key or a simple `<primkey-field>` such as an `Integer`, `String`, `Date`, etc. If you defer definition of the primary key class to the deployer, specify the type as `java.lang.Object` in this element.

`<persistence-type>` *(one required; entity beans only)*
: Declares that the entity bean uses either container-managed persistence or bean-managed persistence. This element can have one of two values: `Container` or `Bean`.

`<reentrant>` *(one required; entity beans only)*
: Declares that the bean either allows loopbacks (reentrant invocations) or does not. This element can have one of two values: `True` or `False`. `True` means that the bean allows loopbacks; `False` means that the bean throws an exception if a loopback occurs.

`<cmp-version>` *(optional; entity beans only)*
: Describes the version of container-managed persistence for which the entity bean is deployed. EJB containers must support EJB 2.1 CMP, EJB 2.0 CMP, and even EJB 1.1 CMP for backward compatibility. This element may have one of two values: `2.x` for EJB 2.1 and EJB 2.0 or `1.x` for EJB 1.1.

`<abstract-schema-name>` *(optional; entity beans only)*
: Uniquely identifies entity beans in a JAR file so that EJB QL statements can reference them. This method is described in more detail in the section "Declaring EJB QL Elements."

`<cmp-field>` *(zero or more; entity beans only)*
: Used in entity beans with container-managed persistence. A `<cmp-field>` element must exist for each container-managed field in the bean class. Each `<cmp-field>` element may include a `<description>` element and must include a `<field-name>` element. The `<description>` is an optional comment describing the field. The `<field-name>` is required and must be the name of one of the bean's CMP fields. It must match the method name of the abstract accessor method (e.g., `deckLevel` for `getDeckLevel()/setDeckLevel()`). The following portion of a descriptor shows several `<cmp-field>` declarations for the Cabin EJB:

```
<cmp-field>
    <description>This is the primary key</description>
    <field-name>id</field-name>
</cmp-field>
<cmp-field>
    <field-name>name</field-name>
</cmp-field>
<cmp-field>
    <field-name>deckLevel</field-name>
</cmp-field>
<cmp-field>
    <field-name>shipId</field-name>
</cmp-field>
<cmp-field>
    <field-name>bedCount</field-name>
</cmp-field>
```

`<env-entry>` *(zero or more)*
: Declares an environment entry that is available through the JNDI ENC. The use of environment entries in a bean and a deployment descriptor is discussed further in the "Environment Entries" section.

`<ejb-ref>` *(zero or more)*
: Declares a remote enterprise bean reference that is available through the JNDI ENC. The mechanism for making bean references available through the ENC is described in more detail later, in the "References to Other Beans" section.

`<ejb-local-ref>` *(zero or more)*
: Declares a local enterprise bean reference that is available through the JNDI ENC. The mechanism for making bean references available through the ENC is described in more detail later, in the "References to Other Beans" section.

`<security-role-ref>` *(zero or more)*
: Used to declare security roles in the deployment descriptor and map them into the security roles in effect for the bean's runtime environment. This method is described in more detail in the "Security Roles" section.

<security-identity> *(optional)*
: Specifies security identity under which a method will run. This element is described in more detail in the "Specifying Security Roles and Method Permissions" section.

<resource-ref> *(zero or more)*
: Declares a reference to a connection factory that is available through the JNDI ENC. An example of a resource factory is the javax.sql.DataSource, which is used to obtain a connection to a database. This element is discussed in detail in the "References to External Resources" section later in this chapter.

<resource-env-ref> *(zero or more)*
: Describes additional "administered objects" required by the resource. The <resource-env-ref> element and administered objects are explained in more detail in the "References to External Resources" section later in this chapter.

<message-destination-ref> *(EJB 2.1 only: optional)*
: The <message-destination-ref> element is new in EJB 2.1. It describes the type of destination the EJB will send messages to. The <message-destination-ref-name> declares the JNDI ENC lookup name used by the EJB to access the destination.

<transaction-type> *(one required; session beans only)*
: Declares either that a session bean manages its own transactions or that the container manages its transactions. This element can have one of two values: Bean or Container. A bean that manages its own transactions will not have container-transaction declarations in the <assembly-descriptor> section of the deployment descriptor.

<query> *(zero or more; entity beans only)*
: Contains an EJB QL statement that is bound to a find or a select method. The EJB QL statement defines how the find or select method should execute at runtime. This element is described in more detail later in the "Declaring EJB QL Elements" section later in this chapter.

Message-Driven Beans

The <message-driven> element describes message-driven bean deployments. <message-driven> elements occur after <entity> and <session> elements within the <enterprise-bean> element. Like the <entity> and <session> elements, the <message-driven> element can optionally have <description>, <display-name>, <small-icon>, and <large-icon> elements. These elements are used primarily by visual deployment tools to represent the message-driven bean. The <message-driven> element also requires the declaration of the <ejb-name>, <ejb-class>, <transaction-type>, and <security-id-entity> elements. In addition, it contains the standard JNDI ENC elements <env-entry>, <ejb-ref>, <ejb-local-ref>, <resource-ref>, and <resource-env-ref>. These are fairly self-explanatory and have the same meaning as they did in the <entity> and <session> elements.

The elements specific to the message-driven bean are different in EJB 2.1 and EJB 2.0.

EJB 2.1 elements

EJB 2.0 defined a few JMS specific elements, which have been abandoned in EJB 2.1 so that the MDB deployment descriptor can represent JMS-based MDBs as well as Connector-based MDBs. The MDB elements and properties are covered in detail in Chapter 12.

`<messaging-type>`
: Declares the messaging interfaces used by the MDB. For JMS-based MDBs, the messaging interface is always going to be `javax.jms.MessageListener`, but for other J2EE Connector-based MDBs it might be something different. If this element is omitted, the type is assumed to be `javax.jms.MessageListener`.

`<message-destination-type>`
: Designates the type of destination from which the MDB receives messages. The allowed values for JMS-based MDBs are `javax.jms.Queue` and `javax.jms.Topic`. A J2EE Connector-based MDB might use some other type.

`<activation-config>`
: Describes the messaging properties of the MDB. The property names and values used in `<activation-config>` depend on the type of message service used, but EJB 2.1 defines a set of fixed properties for JMS-based message-driven beans, including:

  `acknowledgeMode`
  : The container considers this property only if the message-driven bean uses bean-managed transactions; with container-managed transactions, it is ignored. It determines which type of acknowledgment it uses; its value can be either `Auto-acknowledge` or `Dups-ok-acknowledge`. The first value acknowledges messages immediately; the second can delay acknowledgment to benefit performance but may result in duplicate or redelivered messages.

  `messageSelector`
  : Message selectors allow an MDB to be more selective about the messages it receives from a particular topic or queue. Message selectors use `Message` properties as criteria in conditional expressions.* These conditional expressions use Boolean logic to declare which messages should be delivered to a client. The syntax of message selectors can cause problems with XML processing. See the "CDATA Sections" sidebar later in this chapter.

  `destinationType`
  : The `<message-destination-type>` and the `destinationType` activation configuration property are redundant for JMS-based MDBs—but not for other

* Message selectors are also based on message headers, which are outside the scope of this chapter.

types of J2EE Connector-based MDBs. That's because the activation configuration properties of Connector-based MDBs and JMS-based MDBs are completely different. It's important that the `<message-destination-type>` be specified for both JMS-based and Connector-based MDBs.

`subscriptionDurablity`
: When a JMS-based MDB uses a `javax.jms.Topic`, the subscription must be declared to be either `Durable` or `NonDurable`. A `Durable` subscription outlasts an MDB container's connection to the JMS provider; if the EJB server suffers a partial failure, shuts down, or otherwise disconnects from the JMS provider, the messages that it would have received are not lost. A `NonDurable` subscription means that any messages the bean would have received while it was disconnected are lost.

EJB 2.0 elements

EJB 2.0 supports only one type of Message Driven Bean, the JMS-based MDB. Since only one messaging API is supported, EJB 2.0 defined JMS-specific elements, which were replaced in EJB 2.1 with JMS-specific properties.

`<message-selector>`
: Message selectors allow an MDB to be more selective about the messages it receives from a particular topic or queue. Message selectors use `Message` properties as criteria in conditional expressions. These conditional expressions use Boolean logic to declare which messages should be delivered to a client. The syntax of message selectors can cause problems with XML processing. See the "CDATA Sections" sidebar later in this chapter.

`<acknowledge-mode>`
: The container considers this element only if the message-driven bean uses bean-managed transactions; with container-managed transactions, it is ignored. It determines which type of acknowledgment it uses; its value can be either `Auto-acknowledge` or `Dups-ok-acknowledge`. The first acknowledges messages immediately; the second can delay acknowledgment to benefit performance, but may result in duplicate or redelivered messages.

`<message-driven-destination>`
: This element designates the type of destination to which the MDB subscribes or listens. The allowed values for this element are `javax.jms.Queue` and `javax.jms.Topic`.

`<subscription-durability>`
: When a MDB uses a `javax.jms.Topic`, the subscription must be declared to be either `Durable` or `NonDurable`. A `Durable` subscription outlasts an MDB container's connection to the JMS provider; if the EJB server suffers a partial failure, shuts down, or otherwise disconnects from the JMS provider, the messages that it would have received are not lost. A `NonDurable` subscription means that any messages the bean would have received while it was disconnected are lost.

CDATA Sections

The <message-selector> elements used by message-driven beans and the <ejb-ql> elements often require the use of characters that have special meanings in XML, like < and >. These characters cause parsing errors unless *CDATA sections* are used.

The CDATA section takes the form `<![CDATA[ literal-text ]]>`. When an XML processor encounters a CDATA section, it does not attempt to parse the contents enclosed by the CDATA section.

Here's how to use a CDATA section in a <message-selector> element:

```
<message-selector>

<![CDATA[
    TotalCharge >500.00 AND ((TotalCharge /ItemCount)>=75.00)
    AND State IN ('MN','WI','MI','OH')";]]>
</message-selector>
```

Here's how to use a CDATA section in an <ejb-ql> element:

```
<query>
    <query-method>
        ...
    </query-method>
    <ejb-ql>
        <![CDATA[
            SELECT OBJECT(r ) FROM Reservation r
            WHERE r.amountPaid  > 300.00
        ]]>
    </ejb-ql>
 </query>
```

Specifying Primary Keys

If a single field in the bean can serve naturally as a unique identifier, you can use that field as the primary key. Optionally, a custom primary key can be used as a compound primary key. In the Cabin EJB, for example, the primary key type could be the `CabinPK`, which is mapped to the bean class fields `id` and `name`, as shown here (the `CabinBean` is using bean-managed persistence to better illustrate):

```
public class CabinBean implements javax.ejb.EntityBean {

    public int id;
    public String name;
    public int deckLevel;
    public int ship;
    public int bedCount;

    public CabinPK ejbCreate(int id, String name) {
        this.id = id;
        this.name = name;
```

```
        return null;
    }
    ...
}
```

In Chapter 4, we used the appropriate primitive wrapper, `java.lang.Integer`, instead of the custom `CabinPK` class, and defined the `CabinBean` as:

```
public class CabinBean implements javax.ejb.EntityBean {

    public int id;
    public String name;
    public int deckLevel;
    public int ship;
    public int bedCount;

    public Integer ejbCreate(int id) {
        this.id = id;
        return null;
    }
    ...
}
```

This simplifies things a lot. Instead of taking the time to define a custom primary key like `CabinPK`, we simply use the appropriate wrapper. To do this, we need to add a `<primkey-field>` element to the Cabin EJB's deployment descriptor, so it knows which field to use as the primary key. We also need to change the `<prim-key-class>` element to state that the `Integer` class is being used to represent the primary key. Here's how the Cabin EJB's deployment descriptor would need to change to use `Integer` as the primary key field:

```
<entity>
    <description>
        This Cabin enterprise bean entity represents a cabin on
        a cruise ship.
    </description>
    <ejb-name>CabinEJB</ejb-name>
    <home>com.titan.cabin.CabinHome</home>
    <remote>com.titan.cabin.Cabin</remote>
    <ejb-class>com.titan.cabin.CabinBean</ejb-class>
    <persistence-type>Bean</persistence-type>
    <prim-key-class>java.lang.Integer</prim-key-class>
    <reentrant>False</reentrant>

    <cmp-field><field-name>id</field-name></cmp-field>
    <cmp-field><field-name>name</field-name></cmp-field>
    <cmp-field><field-name>deckLevel</field-name></cmp-field>
    <cmp-field><field-name>ship</field-name></cmp-field>
    <cmp-field><field-name>bedCount</field-name></cmp-field>
    <primkey-field>id</primkey-field>
</entity>
```

Simple primary key fields are not limited to the primitive wrapper classes (Byte, Boolean, Integer, and so on); any container-managed field can be used as a primary key, as long as it is serializable. String types are probably the most common, but other types, such as java.lang.StringBuffer, java.util.Date, or even java.util.Hashtable are also valid. Custom types can also be primary keys, provided they are serializable. Use common sense when choosing a primary key: since it is used as an index to the data in the database, it should be lightweight.

Deferring primary key definition

Container-managed persistence makes it possible for the bean developer to defer defining the primary key, leaving key definition to the bean deployer. This feature might be needed if, for example, the primary key is generated by the database and is not a container-managed field in the bean class. Containers that have a tight integration with database or legacy systems that automatically generate primary keys might use this approach. It is also an attractive approach for vendors that sell shrink-wrapped beans, because it makes the bean more portable. Here's how an entity bean using container-managed persistence defers the definition of the primary key to the deployer:

```
// bean class for bean that uses a deferred primary key
public class HypotheticalBean implements javax.ejb.EntityBean {
    ...
    public java.lang.Object ejbCreate( ) {
        ...
        return null;
    }
    ...
}

// home interface for bean with deferred primary key
public interface HypotheticalHome extends javax.ejb.EJBHome {
    public Hypothetical create( ) throws ...;
    public Hypothetical findByPrimaryKey(java.lang.Object key) throws ...;
}
```

Here's the relevant portion of the deployment descriptor:

```
// primkey-field declaration for the Hypothetical bean
...
<entity>
    <ejb-name>HypotheticalEJB</ejb-name>
    ...
    <persistence-type>Container</persistence-type>
    <prim-key-class>java.lang.Object</prim-key-class>
    <reentrant>False</reentrant>
    <cmp-field><field-name>creationDate</field-name></cmp-field>
    ...
</entity>
```

Because the primary key is of type java.lang.Object, the client application's interaction with the bean's key is limited to the Object type and its methods.

Environment Entries

A deployment descriptor can define *environment entries*, values similar to properties the bean can read when it is running. The bean can use environment entries to customize its behavior, find out about how it is deployed, and so on.

The <env-entry> element is used to define environment entries. This element contains the subelements <description> (optional), <env-entry-name> (required), <env-entry-type> (required), and <env-entry-value> (optional). Here is a typical <env-entry> declaration:

```
<env-entry>
    <env-entry-name>minCheckNumber</env-entry-name>
    <env-entry-type>java.lang.Integer</env-entry-type>
    <env-entry-value>2000</env-entry-value>
</env-entry>
```

The <env-entry-name> is relative to the "java:comp/env" context. For example, the minCheckNumber entry can be accessed using the path "java:comp/env/minCheckNumber" in a JNDI ENC lookup:

```
InitialContext jndiContext = new InitialContext( );
Integer miniumValue = (Integer)
   jndiContext.lookup("java:comp/env/minCheckNumber");
```

The <env-entry-type> can be of type String or one of several primitive wrapper types, including Integer, Long, Double, Float, Byte, Boolean, and Short.

The <env-entry-value> is optional. The value can be specified by the bean developer or deferred to the application assembler or deployer.

References to Other Beans

In EJB, references to other beans can be local or remote. In EJB 2.1 you can also reference a web Service object that provides access to an EJB endpoint (see Chapter 15 to learn more about EJB endpoints).

Remote references

The <env-ref> element defines references to other beans within the JNDI ENC. This makes it much easier for beans to reference other beans; a bean can use JNDI to look up a reference to the home interface for any bean in which it is interested.

The <env-ref> element contains the subelements <description> (optional), <ejb-ref-name> (required), <ejb-ref-type> (required), <remote> (required), <home> (required), and <ejb-link> (optional). Here is a typical <env-ref> declaration:

```
<ejb-ref>
    <ejb-ref-name>ejb/ProcessPaymentHomeRemote</ejb-ref-name>
    <ejb-ref-type>Session</ejb-ref-type>
    <home>com.titan.processpayment.ProcessPaymentHomeRemote</home>
    <remote>com.titan.processpayment.ProcessPaymentHomeRemote</remote>
</ejb-ref>
```

The <ejb-ref-name> is relative to the "java:comp/env" context. It is recommended but not required that the name be placed under a subcontext of ejb/. Following this convention, the path used to access the ProcessPayment EJB's home would be "java:comp/env/ejb/ProcessPaymentHomeRemote". Here's how a client bean would use this context to look up a reference to the ProcessPayment EJB:

```
InitialContext jndiContext = new InititalContext();
Object ref = jndiContext.lookup("java:comp/env/ejb/ProcessPaymentHomeRemote");
ProcessPaymentHomeRemote home = (ProcessPaymentHomeRemote)
    PortableRemoteObject.narrow(ref, ProcessPaymentHomeRemote.class);
```

The <ejb-ref-type> can have one of two values, Entity or Session, according to whether it is an entity or a session bean.

The <home> element specifies the fully qualified class name of the bean's home interface; the <remote> element specifies the fully qualified class name of the bean's remote interface.

If the bean referenced by the <ejb-ref> element is deployed in the same deployment descriptor (i.e., it is defined under the same <ejb-jar> element), the <ejb-ref> element can be linked to the bean's declaration using the <ejb-link> element. If, for example, the TravelAgent bean uses a reference to the ProcessPayment EJB that is declared in the same deployment descriptor, the <ejb-ref> elements for the TravelAgent bean can use an <ejb-link> element to map its <ejb-ref> elements to the ProcessPayment EJB. The <ejb-link> value must match one of the <ejb-name> values declared in the same deployment descriptor. Here's a portion of a deployment descriptor that uses the <ejb-link> element:

```
<ejb-jar>
    <enterprise-beans>
        <session>
            <ejb-name>TravelAgentEJB</ejb-name>
            <remote>com.titan.travelagent.TravelAgentRemote</remote>
            ...
            <ejb-ref>
                <ejb-ref-name>ejb/ProcessPaymentHome</ejb-ref-name>
                <ejb-ref-type>Session</ejb-ref-type>
                <home>com.titan.processpayment.ProcessPaymentHomeRemote</home>
                <remote>com.titan.processpayment.ProcessPaymentRemote</remote>
                <ejb-link>ProcessPaymentEJB</ejb-link>
            </ejb-ref>
            ...
        </session>

        <session>
            <ejb-name>ProcessPaymentEJB</ejb-name>
            <remote>com.titan.processpayment.ProcessPaymentRemote</remote>
            ...
        </session>
        ...
    </enterprise-beans>
    ...
</ejb-jar>
```

In most cases, you are better off using the `<ejb-local-ref>` element to obtain references to beans in the same JAR file, unless the referenced enterprise bean does not have a set of local component interfaces. If that's the situation, use the `<ejb-link>` element with the `<ejb-ref>` element to get a remote reference to the enterprise bean.

Local references

The deployment descriptor also provides a special set of tags, the `<ejb-local-ref>` elements, to declare local EJB references, i.e., references to enterprise beans that are co-located in the same container and deployed in the same EJB JAR file. The `<ejb-local-ref>` elements are declared immediately after the `<ejb-ref>` elements:

```
<ejb-local-ref>
    <ejb-ref-name>ejb/CruiseHomeLocal</ejb-ref-name>
    <ejb-ref-type>Entity</ejb-ref-type>
    <local-home>com.titan.cruise.CruiseHomeLocal</local-home>
    <local>com.titan.cruise.CruiseLocal</local>
    <ejb-link>CruiseEJB</ejb-link>
</ejb-local-ref>
<ejb-local-ref>
    <ejb-ref-name>ejb/CabinHomeLocal</ejb-ref-name>
    <ejb-ref-type>Entity</ejb-ref-type>
    <local-home>com.titan.cabin.CabinHomeLocal</local-home>
    <local>com.titan.cabin.CabinLocal</local>
    <ejb-link>CabinEJB</ejb-link>
</ejb-local-ref>
```

The `<ejb-local-ref>` element defines a name for the bean within the ENC, declares the bean's type, and gives the names of its local component interfaces. These elements should be linked explicitly to other co-located beans using the `<ejb-link>` element, but it's not required—the application assembler or deployer can do it later. The value of the `<ejb-link>` element within the `<ejb-local-ref>` must equal the `<ejb-name>` of the appropriate bean in the same JAR file.

At deployment time, the EJB container's tools map the local references declared in the `<ejb-local-ref>` elements to entity beans that are co-located in the same container system.

Enterprise beans declared in the `<ejb-local-ref>` elements are local enterprise beans and so do not require the use of the `PortableRemoteObject.narrow( )` method to narrow the reference. Instead, you can use a simple native cast operation:

```
InitialContext jndiContext = new InititalContext( );
CabinHome home = (CabinHome)
    jndiContext.lookup("java:comp/env/ejb/CabinHomeLocal");
```

References to External Resources

Enterprise beans also use the JNDI ENC to look up external resources, such as database connections, that they need to access. The mechanism for doing this is similar to the mechanism used for referencing other beans and environment entries: the external resources are mapped into a name within the JNDI ENC namespace. For external resources, the mapping is performed by the <resource-ref> element.

The <resource-ref> element contains the <description> (optional), <res-ref-name> (required), <res-type> (required), and <res-auth> (required) subelements.

Here is a <resource-ref> declaration used for a DataSource connection factory:

```
<resource-ref>
    <description>DataSource for the Titan database</description>
    <res-ref-name>jdbc/titanDB</res-ref-name>
    <res-type>javax.sql.DataSource</res-type>
    <res-auth>Container</res-auth>
</resource-ref>
```

The <res-ref-name> is relative to the "java:comp/env" context. Although not a requirement, it is a good idea to place connection factories under a subcontext that describes the resource type. For example:

- jdbc/ for a JDBC DataSource factory
- jms/ for a JMS QueueConnectionFactory or TopicConnectionFactory factory
- mail/ for a JavaMail session factory
- url/ for a javax.net.URL factory

Here is how a bean would use JNDI to look up a resource—in this case, a DataSource:

```
InitialContext jndiContext = new InitialContext( );
DataSource source = (DataSource)
    jndiContext.lookup("java:comp/env/jdbc/titanDB");
```

The <res-type> element declares the fully qualified class name of the connection factory. In this example, the <res-type> is javax.sql.DataSource.

The <res-auth> element tells the server who is responsible for authentication. It can have one of two values: Container or Application. If Container is specified, the container will automatically perform authentication (sign-on or login) to use the resource, as specified at deployment time. If Application is specified, the bean itself must perform authentication before using the resource. Here's how a bean might sign on to a connection factory when Application is specified for <res-auth>:

```
InitialContext jndiContext = new InitialContext( );
DataSource source = (DataSource)
    jndiContext.lookup("java:comp/env/jdbc/titanDB");

String loginName = ejbContext.getCallerPrincipal().getName( );
String password = ...; // get password from somewhere

// use login name and password to obtain a database connection
java.sql.Connection con = source.getConnection(loginName, password);
```

Additional administered objects

In addition to the resource factory described in the <resource-ref> element, some resources may have other administered objects that need to be obtained from the JNDI ENC. An *administered object* is a resource that is configured at deployment time and managed by the EJB container at runtime. For example, to use JMS, the bean developer must obtain both a JMS factory object and a destination object:

```
TopicConnectionFactory factory = (TopicConnectionFactory)
    jndiContext.lookup("java:comp/env/jms/TopicFactory");

Topic topic = (Topic)
    jndiContext.lookup("java:comp/env/ejb/TicketTopic");
```

Both the JMS factory and destination are administered objects that must be obtained from the JNDI ENC. The <resource-ref> element declares the JMS factory, while the <resource-env-ref> element declares the destination:

```
<resource-ref>
    <res-ref-name>jms/TopicFactory</res-ref-name>
    <res-type>javax.jms.TopicConnectionFactory</res-type>
    <res-auth>Container</res-auth>
</resource-ref>
<resource-ref>
    <res-ref-name>jdbc/titanDB</res-ref-name>
    <res-type>javax.sql.DataSource</res-type>
    <res-auth>Container</res-auth>
</resource-ref>
<resource-env-ref>
    <resource-env-ref-name>jms/TicketTopic</resource-env-ref-name>
    <resource-env-ref-type>javax.jms.Topic</resource-env-ref-type>
</resource-env-ref>
```

At deployment time, the deployer maps the JMS `TopicConnectionFactory` or `QueueConnectionFactory` and the `Topic` or `Queue` declared by the <resource-ref> and <resource-env-ref> elements to a JMS factory and topic.

Shareable resources

When several enterprise beans in a unit-of-work or transaction all use the same resource, you will want to configure your EJB server to share that resource. Sharing a resource means that each enterprise bean will use the same connection to access the resource (e.g., database or JMS provider), a strategy that is more efficient than using separate resource connections.

In the TravelAgent EJB, the `bookPassage( )` method uses the ProcessPayment EJB and the Reservation EJB to book a passenger on a cruise. If the enterprise beans use the same database, they should share their resource connection for efficiency. Enterprise JavaBeans containers share resources by default, but resource sharing can be turned on or off explicitly with the <resource-ref> element:

```
<resource-ref>
    <res-ref-name>jdbc/titanDB</res-ref-name>
    <res-type>javax.sql.DataSource</res-type>
    <res-auth>Container</res-auth>
   <res-sharing-scope>Shareable</res-sharing-scope>
</resource-ref>
```

`<res-sharing-scope>` is an optional element that may be declared as either `Shareable`, indicating that connections should be shared in local transactions, or `Unshareable`, indicating that they should not. If it is not specified, the default is `Shareable`.

Occasionally, advanced developers may run into situations where resource sharing is not desirable, and having the option to turn off resource sharing is beneficial. Unless you have a good reason for turning off resource sharing, I recommend that you use `Shareable` resources.

The <service-ref> Deployment Element (EJB 2.1)

EJB 2.1 includes a new element, `<service-ref>`, that is used to bind a JAX-RPC Service to the JNDI ENC. The modified TravelAgent EJB declares a `<service-ref>` element that looks like this:

```
<ejb-jar
 xmlns="http://java.sun.com/xml/ns/j2ee"
 xmlns:xsi="http://www.w3.org/2001/XMLSchema-instance"
 xmlns:chargeIt="http://charge-it.com/Processor"
 xsi:schemaLocation="http://java.sun.com/xml/ns/j2ee
                     http://java.sun.com/xml/ns/j2ee/ejb-jar_2_1.xsd"
 version="2.1">
   <enterprise-beans>
     <session>
       <ejb-name>TravelAgentEJB</ejb-name>
       ...
       <service-ref>
         <service-ref-name>service/ChargeItProcessorService</service-ref-name>
         <service-interface>com.charge_it.ProcessorService</service-interface>
         <wsdl-file>META-INF/wsdl/ChargeItProcessor.wsdl</wsdl-file>
         <jaxrpc-mapping-file>META-INF/mapping.xml</jaxrpc-mapping-file>
         <service-qname>chargeIt:ProcessorService</service-qname>
       </service-ref>
      ...
    </session>
  </enterprise-beans>
  ...
</ejb-jar>
```

The `<service-ref-name>` element declares the JNDI ENC lookup name of the JAX-RPC Service: it is always relative to the `"java:comp/env"` context. For more details about various web service deployment descriptors, see Chapter 15.

Security Roles

The <security-role-ref> element defines the security roles that are used by a bean and maps them into the security roles that are in effect for the runtime environment. It can contain three subelements: an optional <description>, a <role-name> (required), and an optional <role-link>.

Here's how security roles are defined. When a role name is used in the EJBContext.isCallerInRole(String roleName) method, the role name must be statically defined (it cannot be derived at runtime) and it must be declared in the deployment descriptor using the <security-role-ref> element:

```
<-- security-role-ref declaration for Account bean -->
<entity>
    <ejb-name>AccountEJB</ejb-name>
    ...
    <security-role-ref>
        <description>
            The caller must be a member of this role in
            order to withdraw over $10,000
        </description>
        <role-name>Manager</role-name>
        <role-link>Administrator</role-link>
    </security-role-ref>
    ...
</entity>
```

The <role-name> defined in the deployment descriptor must match the role name used in the EJBContext.isCallerInRole( ) method. Here is how the role name is used in the bean's code:

```
// Account bean uses the isCallerInRole( ) method
public class AccountBean implements EntityBean {
    int id;
    double balance;
    EntityContext context;

    public void withdraw(Double withdraw) throws AccessDeniedException {

        if (withdraw.doubleValue( ) > 10000) {
            boolean isManager = context.isCallerInRole("Manager");
            if (!isManager) {
                // only Managers can withdraw more than 10k
                throw new AccessDeniedException( );
            }
        }
        balance = balance - withdraw.doubleValue( );
    }
    ...
}
```

The <role-link> element is optional; it can be used to map the role name used in the bean to a logical role defined in a <security-role> element in the <assembly-descriptor>

section of the deployment descriptor. If no <role-link> is specified, the deployer must map the <security-role-ref> to an existing security role in the target environment.

Declaring EJB QL Elements

EJB QL statements are declared in <query> elements in an entity bean's deployment descriptor. In the following listing, you can see that findByName() and ejbSelectShips() methods were declared in the <query> elements of the Cruise EJB deployment descriptor:

```
<ejb-jar>
    <enterprise-beans>
        <entity>
            <ejb-name>ShipEJB</ejb-name>
            ...
            <abstract-schema-name>Ship</abstract-schema-name>
            ...
        </entity>
        <entity>
            <ejb-name>CruiseEJB</ejb-name>
            ...
            <reentrant>False</reentrant>
            <abstract-schema-name>Cruise</abstract-schema-name>
            <cmp-version>2.x</cmp-version>
            <cmp-field>
                <field-name>name</field-name>
            </cmp-field>
            <primkey-field>id</primkey-field>
            <query>
                <query-method>
                    <method-name>findByName</method-name>
                    <method-params>
                  <mehod-param>java.lang.String</method-param>
                    </method-params>
                </query-method>
                <ejb-ql>
                  SELECT OBJECT(c) FROM Cruise c WHERE c.name = ?1
                </ejb-ql>
            </query>
            <query>
                <query-method>
                    <method-name>ejbSelectShips</method-name>
                    <method-params></method-params>
                </query-method>
                <result-type-mapping>Remote</result-type-mapping>
                <ejb-ql>
                    SELECT OBJECT(s) FROM Ship AS s
                </ejb-ql>
            </query>
        </entity>
    </enterprise-beans>
</ejb-jar>
```

The <query> element contains two primary elements; the <query-method> element identifies the find method of the remote or local home interface, and the <ejb-ql> element declares the EJB QL statement. The <query> element binds the EJB QL statement to the proper find method. The syntax of EJB QL may cause problems for the XML parser; you may need to wrap the query in a CDATA section. See the sidebar "CDATA Sections" for more details.

When two find methods in the local and remote home interfaces have the same method name and parameters, the query declaration applies to both methods. The container returns the proper type for each query method: queries that use the remote home return one or more remote EJB objects, and queries that use the local home return one or more local EJB objects. This feature allows you to define the behavior of both the local and remote home find methods using a single <query> element—which is convenient if you want local clients to have access to the same find methods as remote clients.

The <result-type-mapping> element can be used to declare whether a select method should return local or remote EJB objects. The value `Local` indicates that a method should return local EJB objects; `Remote` indicates remote EJB objects. If the <result-type-mapping> element is not declared, the default is `Local`. In the <query> element for the `ejbSelectShips()` method, the <result-type-mapping> is declared as `Remote`, which means the query should return remote EJB object types (i.e., remote references to the Ship EJB).

Every entity bean that is referenced in an EJB QL statement must have an *abstract schema name*, which is declared by the <abstract-schema-name> element. No two entity beans may have the same abstract schema name. In the entity element that describes the Cruise EJB, the abstract schema name is `Cruise`, while the Ship EJB's abstract schema name is `Ship`. The <ejb-ql> element contains an EJB QL statement that uses this identifier in its `FROM` clause.

In Chapter 7, you learned that the abstract persistence schema of an entity bean is defined by its <cmp-field> and <cmr-field> elements. The abstract schema name is also an important part of the abstract persistence schema. EJB QL statements are always expressed in terms of the abstract persistence schemas of entity beans. EJB QL uses the abstract schema names to identify entity bean types, the container-managed persistence (CMP) fields to identify specific entity bean data, and the container-managed relationship (CMR) fields to create paths for navigating from one entity bean to another.

Describing Relationships

CMP entity bean classes are defined using abstract accessor methods that represent virtual persistence and relationship fields. As discussed in Chapters 6, 7, and 8, the fields themselves are not declared in the entity classes. Instead, the characteristics of these fields are described in the bean's deployment descriptor. The *abstract persistence schema* is the set of XML elements in the deployment descriptor that describe the relationship and persistence fields. By combining the abstract persistence schema with the abstract programming model (i.e., the abstract accessor methods) and a little help from the deployer, the container tool has enough information to map the entity and its relationships with other entity beans.

The relationships between entity beans are described in the `<relationships>` section of the XML deployment descriptor. The `<relationships>` section falls between the `<enterprise-beans>` and `<assembly-descriptor>` sections. Within the `<relationships>` element, each entity-to-entity relationship is defined in a separate `<ejb-relation>` element:

```
<ejb-jar>
    <enterprise-beans>
    ...
    </enterprise-beans>
    <relationships>
        <ejb-relation>
        ...
        </ejb-relation>
        <ejb-relation>
        ...
        </ejb-relation>
    </relationships>
    <assembly-descriptor>
    ...
    </assembly-descriptor>
</ejb-jar>
```

Defining relationship fields requires that an `<ejb-relation>` element be added to the XML deployment descriptor for each entity-to-entity relationship. These `<ejb-relation>` elements complement the abstract programming model. For each pair of abstract accessor methods that define a relationship field, there is an `<ejb-relation>` element in the deployment descriptor. EJB requires that the entity beans in a relationship be defined in the same XML deployment descriptor.

Here is a partial listing of the deployment descriptor for the Customer and Address EJBs, emphasizing the elements that define the relationship:

```
<ejb-jar>
    ...
    <enterprise-beans>
        <entity>
            <ejb-name>CustomerEJB</ejb-name>
            <local-home>com.titan.customer.CusomterLocalHome</local-home>
            <local>com.titan.customer.CustomerLocal</local>
            ...
        </entity>
        <entity>
            <ejb-name>AddressEJB</ejb-name>
```

```
            <local-home>com.titan.address.AddressLocalHome</local-home>
            <local>com.titan.address.AddressLocal</local>
            ...
        </entity>
        ...
    </enterprise-beans>

    <relationships>
        <ejb-relation>
            <ejb-relation-name>Customer-Address</ejb-relation-name>
            <ejb-relationship-role>
                <ejb-relationship-role-name>
                    Customer-has-an-Address
                </ejb-relationship-role-name>
                <multiplicity>One</multiplicity>
                <relationship-role-source>
                    <ejb-name>CustomerEJB</ejb-name>
                </relationship-role-source>
                <cmr-field>
                    <cmr-field-name>homeAddress</cmr-field-name>
                </cmr-field>
            </ejb-relationship-role>
            <ejb-relationship-role>
                <ejb-relationship-role-name>
                    Address-belongs-to-Customer
                </ejb-relationship-role-name>
                <multiplicity>One</multiplicity>
                <relationship-role-source>
                    <ejb-name>AddressEJB</ejb-name>
                </relationship-role-source>
            </ejb-relationship-role>
        </ejb-relation>
    </relationships>
</ejb-jar>
```

All relationships between the Customer EJB and other entity beans, such as the CreditCard, Address, and Phone EJBs, require that we define an `<ejb-relation>` element to complement the abstract accessor methods. Every relationship may have a relationship name, which is declared in the `<ejb-relation-name>` element. This name is intended for people reading the deployment descriptor or for deployment tools, but it is not required.

Every `<ejb-relation>` element has exactly two `<ejb-relationship-role>` elements, one for each participant in the relationship. In the previous example, the first `<ejb-relationship-role>` declares the Customer EJB's role in the relationship. We know this because the `<relationship-role-source>` element specifies the `<ejb-name>` as `CustomerEJB`, which is the `<ejb-name>` used in the Customer EJB's original declaration in the `<enterprise-beans>` section. The `<relationship-role-source>` element's `<ejb-name>` must always match an `<ejb-name>` element in the `<enterprise-beans>` section.

The <ejb-relationship-role> element also declares the cardinality, or *multiplicity*, of the role. The <multiplicity> element can be either One or Many. In this case, the Customer EJB's <multiplicity> element has a value of One, which means that every Address EJB has a relationship with exactly one Customer EJB. The Address EJB's <multiplicity> element also specifies One, which means that every Customer EJB has a relationship with exactly one Address EJB. If the Customer EJB had a relationship with many Address EJBs, the Address EJB's <multiplicity> element would be set to Many.

If the bean described by the <ejb-relationship-role> element maintains a reference to the other bean in the relationship, that reference must be declared as a container-managed relationship field in the <cmr-field> element. The <cmr-field> element is declared under the <ejb-relationship-role> element:

```
<ejb-relationship-role>
    <ejb-relationship-role-name>
        Customer-has-an-Address
    </ejb-relationship-role-name>
    <multiplicity>One</multiplicity>
    <relationship-role-source>
        <ejb-name>CustomerEJB</ejb-name>
    </relationship-role-source>
    <cmr-field>
        <cmr-field-name>homeAddress</cmr-field-name>
    </cmr-field>
</ejb-relationship-role>
```

EJB requires that the <cmr-field-name> begin with a lowercase letter. For every relationship field defined by a <cmr-field> element, the bean class must include a pair of matching abstract accessor methods. One method in this pair must be defined with the method name set*<cmr-field-name>*( ), and the first letter of the <cmr-field-name> must be changed to uppercase. The other method is defined as get*<cmr-field-name>*( ), also with the first letter of the <cmr-field-name> in uppercase. In this example, the <cmr-field-name> is homeAddress, which corresponds to the getHomeAddress( ) and setHomeAddress( ) methods defined in the CustomerBean class:

```
// bean class code
public abstract void setHomeAddress(AddressLocal address);
public abstract AddressLocal getHomeAddress( );

// XML deployment descriptor declaration
<cmr-field>
    <cmr-field-name>homeAddress</cmr-field-name>
</cmr-field>
```

The <cascade-delete> element requests cascade deletion; it can be used with one-to-one or one-to-many relationships. It is always declared as an empty element: <cascade-delete/>. <cascade-delete> indicates that the lifetime of one entity bean in a particular relationship depends upon the lifetime the other entity bean in the relationship. Here's how to modify the relationship declaration for the Customer and Address EJBs to obtain a cascade delete:

```
<relationships>
    <ejb-relation>
        <ejb-relationship-role>
            <multiplicity>One</multiplicity>
            <role-source>
                <ejb-name>CustomerEJB</ejb-name>
            </role-source>
            <cmr-field>
                <cmr-field-name>homeAddress</cmr-field-name>
            </cmr-field>
        </ejb-relationship-role>
        <ejb-relationship-role>
            <multiplicity>One</multiplicity>
            <cascade-delete/>
            <role-source>
                <dependent-name>Address</dependent-name>
            </role-source>
        </ejb-relationship-role>
    </ejb-relation>
</relationships>
```

With this declaration, the Address EJB will be deleted automatically when the Customer EJB that refers to it is deleted.

Describing Bean Assembly

At this point, we have said just about all that can be said about the bean itself. We are now ready to describe how the beans are assembled into an application. That is, we are ready to talk about the other major element inside the `<ejb-jar>` element: the `<assembly-descriptor>`.

The `<assembly-descriptor>` element is optional, though it is difficult to imagine a bean being deployed successfully without one. When we say that the `<assembly-descriptor>` is optional, we really mean that a developer whose only role is to create enterprise beans (for example, someone who is developing beans for use by another party and who has no role in deploying the beans) can omit this part of the deployment descriptor. The descriptor is valid without it—but someone will almost certainly have to fill in the assembly information before the bean can be deployed.

The `<assembly-descriptor>` serves three purposes: it describes the transaction attributes of the bean's methods; it describes the logical security roles that are used in the method permissions; and it specifies the method permissions (i.e., which roles are allowed to call each of the methods). To this end, an `<assembly-descriptor>` can contain three kinds of elements, each of which is fairly complex in its own right. These are:

`<container-transaction>` *(zero or more)*
: This element declares which transaction attributes apply to which methods. It contains an optional `<description>` element, one or more `<method>` elements, and

exactly one <trans-attribute> element. Entity beans must have <container-transaction> declarations for all remote and home interface methods. Session beans that manage their own transactions will not have <container-transaction> declarations. This element is discussed in more detail in the next section.

<security-role> *(zero or more)*
: This element defines the security roles that are used to access the bean. These security roles are used in the <method-permission> element. A <security-role> element contains an optional description and one <role-name>. This element and the <method-permission> element are described in more detail in the "Specifying Security Roles and Method Permissions" section.

<method-permission> *(zero or more)*
: This element specifies which security roles are allowed to call one or more of a bean's methods. It contains an optional <description> element, one or more <role-name> elements, and one or more <method> elements. It is discussed in more detail in the "Specifying Security Roles and Method Permissions" section, along with the <security-role> element.

The <container-transaction> and <method-permission> elements both rely on the ability to identify particular methods. This can be a complicated affair, given features of the Java language such as method overloading. The <method> element is used within these tags to identify methods; it is described at length in the "Identifying Specific Methods" section.

Specifying a Bean's Transaction Attributes

The <container-transaction> elements are used to declare the transaction attributes for all the beans defined in the deployment descriptor. A <container-transaction> element maps one or more bean methods to a single transaction attribute, so each <container-transaction> specifies one transaction attribute and one or more bean methods.

The <container-transaction> element includes a single <trans-attribute> element, which can have one of six values: NotSupported, Supports, Required, RequiresNew, Mandatory, and Never. These are the transaction attributes we discussed in Chapter 14. In addition to <trans-attribute>, the <container-transaction> element includes one or more <method> elements.

The <method> element itself contains at least two subelements: an <ejb-name> element, which specifies the name of the bean, and a <method-name> element, which specifies a subset of the bean's methods. The value of the <method-name> can be a method name or an asterisk (*), which acts as wildcard for all the bean's methods. A lot more complexity is involved in handling overloading and other special cases, but we'll discuss the rest later.

To see how the <container-transaction> element is typically used, let's look again at the Cabin EJB. Assume that we want to give the transaction attribute Mandatory to the create( ) method; all other methods use the Required attribute:

```
<container-transaction>
    <method>
        <ejb-name>CabinEJB</ejb-name>
        <method-name>*</method-name>
    </method>
    <trans-attribute>Required</trans-attribute>
</container-transaction>
<container-transaction>
    <method>
        <ejb-name>CabinEJB</ejb-name>
        <method-name>create</method-name>
    </method>
    <trans-attribute>Mandatory</trans-attribute>
</container-transaction>
```

In the first <container-transaction>, we have a single <method> element that uses the wildcard character (*) to refer to all of the Cabin EJB's methods. We set the transaction attribute for these methods to Required. Then, we have a second <container-transaction> element that specifies a single method of the Cabin EJB: create( ). We set the transaction attribute for this method to Mandatory. This setting overrides the wildcard setting; in <container-transaction> elements, specific method declarations always override more general declarations.

For entity beans, the following methods must be assigned transaction attributes:

- All business methods defined in the remote interface (and all superinterfaces)
- Create methods defined in the home interface
- Find methods defined in the home interface
- Home methods defined in the home interface
- Remove methods defined in the EJBHome and EJBObject interfaces

And for session beans, the following methods must be assigned transactional attributes:

- All business methods defined in the remote interface (and all superinterfaces)

For session beans, only the business methods have transaction attributes; the create and remove methods in session beans do not have transaction attributes.

The ejbSelect( ) methods do not have their own transaction attributes. ejbSelect( ) methods always propagate the transaction of the methods that call them.

Specifying Security Roles and Method Permissions

Two elements define logical security roles and specify which roles can call particular bean methods. The <security-role> can contain an optional <description>, plus a single <role-name> that provides the name. An <assembly-descriptor> can contain any number of <security-role> elements.

It is important to realize that the security role names are not derived from a specific security realm. These security role names are logical; they are simply labels that can be mapped to real security roles in the target environment at deployment time. For example, the following <security-role> declarations define two roles—everyone and administrator:

```
<security-role>
    <description>
        This role represents everyone who is allowed read/write access
        to existing Cabin EJBs.
    </description>
    <role-name>everyone</role-name>
</security-role>
<security-role>
    <description>
        This role represents an administrator or manager who is allowed
        to create new Cabin EJBs. This role may also be a member
        of the everyone role.
    </description>
    <role-name>administrator</role-name>
</security-role>
```

These role names might not exist in the environment in which the beans will be deployed. There's nothing inherent in everyone that gives it fewer (or greater) privileges than an administrator. It is up to the deployer to map one or more roles from the target environment to the logical roles in the deployment descriptor. For example, the deployer may find that the target environment has two roles, DBA (database administrator) and CSR (customer service representative), which map to the administrator and everyone roles defined in the <security-role> element.

Assigning roles to methods

Security roles would not be worth much if you couldn't specify what the roles were allowed to do. That's where the <method-permission> element comes in. This element maps the security roles to methods in the remote and home interfaces of the bean. A <method-permission> is a flexible declaration that allows a many-to-many relationship between methods and roles. It contains an optional <description>, one or more <method> elements, and one or more <role-name> elements. The names specified in the <role-name> elements correspond to the roles that appear in the <security-role> elements.

Here's one way to set method permissions for the Cabin EJB:

```
<method-permission>
    <role-name>administrator</role-name>
    <method>
        <ejb-name>CabinEJB</ejb-name>
```

```
            <method-name>*</method-name>
        </method>
    </method-permission>
    <method-permission>
        <role-name>everyone</role-name>
        <method>
            <ejb-name>CabinEJB</ejb-name>
            <method-name>getDeckLevel</method-name>
        </method>
    </method-permission>
```

In this example, the administrator role has access to all methods in the Cabin EJB. The everyone role has access only to the getDeckLevel( ) method—it cannot access any of the other methods of the Cabin EJB. Note that the specific method permissions are combined to form a union. The getDeckLevel( ) method, for example, is accessible by both the administrator and everyone roles. Once again, we still do not know what administrator and everyone mean. The person deploying the bean, who must map these logical security roles to real security roles defined in the target environment, defines them.

All the methods defined in the remote or home interface and all superinterfaces, including the methods defined in the EJBObject and EJBHome interfaces, can be assigned security roles in the <method-permission> elements. Any method that is excluded will not be accessible by any security role.

Unchecked methods

A set of methods can be designated as *unchecked*, which means that security permissions are not checked before the method is invoked. Any client can invoke an unchecked method, no matter what role it is using.

To designate a method or methods as unchecked, use the <method-permission> element and replace the <role-name> element with an empty <unchecked> element:

```
<method-permission>
    <unchecked/>
    <method>
        <ejb-name>CabinEJB</ejb-name>
        <method-name>*</method-name>
    </method>
    <method>
        <ejb-name>CustomerEJB</ejb-name>
        <method-name>findByPrimaryKey</method-name>
    </method>
</method-permission>
<method-permission>
    <role-name>administrator</role-name>
    <method>
        <ejb-name>CabinEJB</ejb-name>
        <method-name>*</method-name>
    </method>
</method-permission>
```

This declaration tells us that all the methods of the Cabin EJB, as well as the Customer EJB's `findByPrimaryKey()` method, are unchecked. Although the second `<method-permission>` element gives the administrator permission to access all the Cabin EJB's methods, this declaration is overridden by the unchecked method permission. Unchecked method permissions always override all other method permissions.

The runAs security identity

In addition to specifying the `Principals` that have access to an enterprise bean's methods, the deployer can also specify the *runAs* `Principal` for the entire enterprise bean. The runAs security identity was originally specified in EJB 1.0, but was abandoned in EJB 1.1. It has been reintroduced in EJB 2.0 and modified so that it is easier for vendors to implement.

While the `<method-permission>` elements specify which `Principals` have access to the bean's methods, the `<security-identity>` element specifies the `Principal` under which the method will run. In other words, the runAs `Principal` is used as the enterprise bean's identity when it tries to invoke methods on other beans—and this identity isn't necessarily the same as the identity that's currently accessing the bean. For example, the following deployment descriptor elements declare that the `create()` method can be accessed only by `JimSmith`, but that the Cabin EJB always runs under the `Administrator` security identity:

```
<enterprise-beans>
...
    <entity>
        <ejb-name>EmployeeService</ejb-name>
        ...
        <security-identity>
            <run-as>
                <role-name>Administrator</role-name>
            </run-as>
        </security-identity>
        ...
    </entity>
...
</enterprise-beans>
<assembly-descriptor>
    <security-role>
        <role-name>Administrator</role-name>
    </security-role>
    <security-role>
        <role-name>JimSmith</role-name>
    </security-role>
    ...
    <method-permission>
        <role-name>JimSmith</role-name>
        <method>
            <ejb-name>CabinEJB</ejb-name>
            <method-name>create</method-name>
```

```
            </method>
        </method-permission>
        ...
    </assembly-descriptor>
```

To specify that an enterprise bean will execute under the caller's identity, the `<security-identity>` role contains a single empty element, `<use-caller-identity/>`. The following declarations specify that the Cabin EJB always executes under the caller's identity, so if Jim Smith invokes the `create()` method, the bean will run under the `JimSmith` security identity:

```
<enterprise-beans>
...
    <entity>
        <ejb-name>EmployeeService</ejb-name>
        ...
        <security-identity>
            <use-caller-identity/>
        </security-identity>
        ...
    </entity>
...
</enterprise-beans>
```

The use of `<security-identity>` applies to entity and stateless session beans. Message-driven beans have only a runAs identity; they never execute under the caller identity, because there is no "caller." The messages that a message-driven bean processes are not considered calls, and the clients that send them are not associated with the messages. With no caller identity to propagate, message-driven beans must always have a runAs security identity specified.

Exclude list

The last element of the `<assembly-descriptor>` is the optional `<exclude-list>` element. The `<exclude-list>` element contains a `<description>` and a set of `<method>` elements. Every method listed in the `<exclude-list>` should be considered uncallable, which means that the deployer needs to set up security permissions for those methods so that all calls, from any client, are rejected. Remote clients should receive a `java.rmi.remoteException` and local clients should receive a `javax.ejb.AccessLocalException`:

```
<ejb-jar>
    <enterprise-beans>
        <entity>
            <ejb-name>CabinEJB</ejb-name>
        </entity>
    </enterprise-beans>
    <assembly-descriptor>
        <exclude-list>
            <method>
                <ejb-name>CabinEJB</ejb-name>
```

```
                <method-name>getDeckLevel</method-name>
            </method>
            <method>
                ...
            </method>
        </exclude-list>
    </assembly-descriptor>
</ejb-jar>
```

Identifying Specific Methods

The <method> element is used by the <method-permission> and <container-transaction> elements to specify a specific group of methods in a particular bean. The <method> element always contains an <ejb-name> element that specifies the bean's name and a <method-name> element that specifies the method. It may also include a <description> element, <method-params> elements that specify which method parameters will be used to resolve overloaded methods, and a <method-intf> element that specifies whether the method belongs to the bean's home, remote, local home, or local interface. This last element takes care of the possibility that the same method name might be used in more than one interface.

Wildcard declarations

The method name in a <method> element can be a simple wildcard (*). A wildcard applies to all methods of the bean's home and remote interfaces. For example:

```
<method>
    <ejb-name>CabinEJB</ejb-name>
    <method-name>*</method-name>
</method>
```

Although it's tempting to combine the wildcard with other characters, don't. The value get*, for example, is illegal. The asterisk character can be used only by itself.

Named method declarations

Named declarations apply to all methods defined in the bean's remote and home interfaces that have the specified name. For example:

```
<method>
    <ejb-name>CabinEJB</ejb-name>
    <method-name>create</method-name>
</method>
<method>
    <ejb-name>CabinEJB</ejb-name>
    <method-name>getDeckLevel</method-name>
</method>
```

These declarations apply to all methods with the given name in both interfaces. They do not distinguish between overloaded methods. For example, if the home interface for the Cabin EJB is modified so that it has three overloaded create( ) methods, as shown here, the previous <method> declaration would apply to all three methods:

```
public interface CabinHome javax.ejb.EJBHome {
    public Cabin create( ) throws CreateException, RemoteException;
    public Cabin create(int id) throws CreateException, RemoteException;
    public Cabin create(int id, Ship ship, double [][] matrix)
        throws CreateException, RemoteException;
    ...
}
```

Specific method declarations

Specific method declarations use the <method-params> element to pinpoint a specific method by listing its parameters, allowing you to differentiate between overloaded methods. The <method-params> element contains zero or more <method-param> elements that correspond, in order, to each parameter type (including multidimensional arrays) declared in the method. To specify a method with no arguments, use a <method-params> element with no <method-param> elements nested within it.

For example, let's look again at our Cabin EJB, to which we have added some overloaded create( ) methods. Here are three <method> elements, each of which unambiguously specifies one of the create( ) methods by listing its parameters:

```
<method>
    <description>Method: public Cabin create(); </description>
    <ejb-name>CabinEJB</ejb-name>
    <method-name>create</method-name>
    <method-params></method-params>
</method>
<method>
    <description>Method: public Cabin create(int id);</description>
    <ejb-name>CabinEJB</ejb-name>
    <method-name>create</method-name>
    <method-params>
          <method-param>int</method-param>
    </method-params>
</method>
<method>
    <description>
         Method: public Cabin create(int id, Ship ship, double [][] matrix);
    </description>
    <ejb-name>CabinEJB</ejb-name>
    <method-name>create</method-name>
    <method-params>
          <method-param>int</method-param>
          <method-param>com.titan.ship.Ship</method-param>
          <method-param>double [][]</method-param>
    </method-params>
</method>
```

Remote/home/local differentiation

There's one problem left. The same method name can be used in the home interface, the local home interface, the remote interface, and the local interface. To resolve this ambiguity, add the `<method-intf>` element to a method declaration as a modifier. Four values are allowed for a `<method-intf>` element: `Remote`, `Home`, `LocalHome`, `Local`, and `ServiceEndpoint`.

In practice, it is unlikely that a good developer would use the same method names in both home and remote interfaces: it would lead to unnecessarily confusing code. However, you would expect to see the same names in the local, remote, and possibly endpoint interfaces, or the home and local home interfaces. It is also likely that you will need the `<method-intf>` element in a wildcarded declaration. For example, the following declaration specifies all the methods in the remote interface of the Cabin EJB:

```
<method>
    <ejb-name>CabinEJB</ejb-name>
    <method-name>*</method-name>
    <method-intf>Remote</method-intf>
</method>
```

All these styles of method declarations can be used in any combination, within any element that uses the `<method>` element. The `<method-permission>` elements are combined to form a union of role-to-method permissions. For example, in the following listing the first `<method-permission>` element declares that the `administrator` has access to the Cabin EJB's home methods (create and find methods). The second `<method-permission>` specifies that everyone has access to the `findByPrimaryKey( )` method. This means both roles (everyone and `administrator`) have access to the `findByPrimaryKey( )` method:

```
<method-permission>
    <role-name>administrator</role-name>
    <method>
        <ejb-name>CabinEJB</ejb-name>
        <method-name>*</method-name>
        <method-intf>Home</method_intf>
    </method>
</method-permission>
<method-permission>
    <role-name>everyone</role-name>
    <method>
        <ejb-name>CabinEJB</ejb-name>
        <method-name>findByPrimaryKey</method-name>
    </method>
</method-permission>
```

CHAPTER 19

EJB Design in the Real World

EJB changed rapidly over the past couple of years. Best practices for using EJBs "in the real world" are only now beginning to be documented, and there are already entire books on how to use EJBs. We cannot hope to cover everything in a single chapter. However, we can hit the important topics in designing EJBs for use in real-world business applications.

This chapter covers:

- The questions you need to ask about your EJB container and database selections *before* you begin designing your EJBs.
- A step-by-step how-to for designing EJBs from functional requirements to completed EJB design, including the identification of potential base classes and EJB-helper classes.
- Alternatives to EJB. There are places where Enterprise JavaBeans are not the best choice. The last section in this chapter helps you identify those places and introduces some alternatives.

Pre-Design: Containers and Databases

Before you begin designing your application, it is essential that you consider the execution environment in which your code is run. The execution environment includes your:

Hardware platform
Operating system
Java Virtual Machine (JVM) implementation
Application server (EJB container)
Database server

Each of these elements has a direct effect on your application design's success. We won't talk about hardware and operating systems (about which you may have little choice, anyway), and we'll stay away from arguments about who has a better JVM.

We'll focus on the last two issues; they have the greatest effect on EJB application architecture.

Container Capabilities

Which EJB container you choose has a significant effect on your application's implementation and design. Regardless of your application's functional requirements, spend some time familiarizing yourself with how your application server works. Ideally, you'd develop that familiarity *before* choosing your application server.

When learning your container's capabilities, you are trying to find out how the application server's vendor has implemented its key features. Here are the primary areas on which to focus:

What version of the EJB specification does it implement?
: A container that implements the latest (2.1) EJB specification will offer more features (non-JMS MDBs, for example). However, a container that implements the older (2.0) specification will be more mature.

What vendor-specific functionality or extensions does it implement?
: Almost all EJB containers introduce some vendor-specific features. If you choose to use vendor-specific features, your application will be tied to that vendor's container. Switching to another vendor later may be costly. While this is often unavoidable (several popular development tools, for example, tie you closely to a vendor's implementation), there are tools such as XDoclet* that help to alleviate some of the risk.

How does the container's design or implementation affect performance?
: Because every vendor's implementation of the EJB spec is unique, containers from different vendors will perform differently. If possible, research the performance of your various container options specifically for the functionality you need before choosing.

Most vendors do a good job of implementing the specification, and it's relatively easy to move from one vendor to another. But don't walk into the EJB arena with your eyes closed. Ask the same kinds of questions that you would ask for any other major software purchase, and you'll be okay.

Database Capabilities

While we place a lot of emphasis on the EJB container, the database server is just as influential on the overall system. Although the EJB container isolates you from the database, the database is still there, and every data-related function depends on it.

* XDoclet is an open source Java tool that allows for attribute-driven development. See *http://xdoclet.sourceforge.net/* for more information.

The most critical function of a database is to ensure that data is available and consistent. Availability and consistency are qualities that depend on how your application uses transactions and how the database implements transactions.* When investigating how your database implements transactions, your primary concern should be the database's locking, isolation levels, and other resource management. Here are some questions to ask:

What transaction isolation levels does the database support?
: While most databases support the four isolation levels discussed in Chapter 16 (read uncommitted, read committed, repeatable read, and serializable), there are some that do not. For example, PostgreSQL 7.3.x† offers only read committed and serializable.

What are the lock types and lock scopes? What factors influence them?
: Lock scope is the number of rows that are protected when a lock is enacted. Depending on the vendor, the database may lock only the rows used by the transaction, blocks of rows (pages) that contain the rows used, or the entire table. The more rows are protected, the more likely it is that another process won't be able to access the data it needs. If such contention occurs, the other process will either fail or wait until the lock is released.

  As for what factors influence lock types and lock scopes, the database may "promote" locks under certain situations, such as if a query cannot use an index. This could mean that a nonexclusive write lock becomes an exclusive write lock or that a row-specific lock becomes a table-wide lock, should an index on that table not be usable in the write.

How are database resources handled within a transaction?
: During a transaction, especially a multi-step transaction, the database has certain resources that it must manage; a good example is the number of open cursors involved in executing the transaction. Depending on how the database handles reclaiming those open cursors, a series of database operations that work fine outside a transaction may not work at all when included in a transaction because needed cursors are left committed until after the end of the last operation. In this case, large, multi-step, iterative processes ("batch" processes) can hit the maximum number of open cursors and fail. Knowing how your database manages resources like open cursors can help you plan your transaction structure to ensure success.

Obviously, there is more involved in the selection of a database server for your application/system than we've described here. However, these issues all have direct ramifications on your EJB application.

* Transactions are discussed in Chapter 16.

† The most recent version of PostgreSQL at the time this was written.

Design

In this section, we go through the process of designing several EJBs. While the design process of an EJB application is 95% identical to the design process for a non-EJB application (maybe even 99% identical), there are some steps in this process that require special attention.

To discuss design, we need to change our thinking a bit. Throughout this book, we have focused the details of EJBs and how their individual components work. In this section, we consider the Titan EJB application as a system meeting a business need, and not simply as a collection of fine-grained components. We will look at the design of such a system from the ground up, taking the application—as a whole—rather than continuing to view only the EJB components themselves (though we'll obviously pay special attention to those components, since this is a book on EJBs). Let's start by looking at its requirements.

At a high level, the application will be used by:

- Travel agents to sell reservations
- The general public to view cruise details
- Cruise administrators to manage the application's ship and cruise data

The application will be accessed via three mechanisms. The first two mechanisms are for "person" users (as opposed to "system" users, described below):

- Web interface (general public, travel agents, and cruise administrators)
- Standalone Java application (travel agents)

The third access mechanism is for systems that need direct access to the business layer. For our application, this includes access by:

- External travel agency systems (which includes both travel agents not working for Titan and reservation distribution services that act as clearing houses for cruise line availability)
- Ship provisioning companies that need to know physical specifications for Titan's ships in order to provide auto-ordering of provisions (ship capacity, fuel type, and so on)

All three communications mechanisms (web client, standalone application, and business-to-business) must allow only secure actions to be executed by the users. Connectivity to the external travel agencies and to the ship provisioning vendors is not guaranteed, so the communication mechanism will need to handle disconnects. Finally, we want to generate reservation confirmations and other forms in PDF format. Figure 19-1 is a system diagram for our requirements so far.

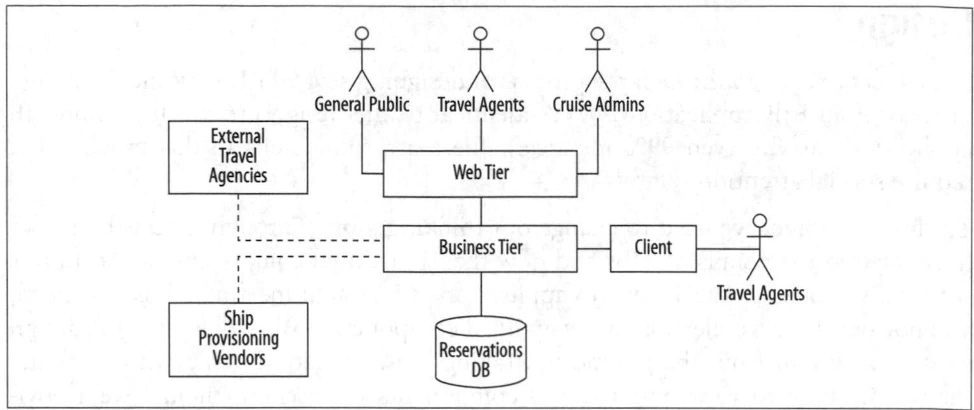

Figure 19-1. Application system diagram

Business Entity Identification

Now that we know our application's requirements, at least at a high level, we can identify the key business entities the application needs to represent. This is generally a lengthy process, and we will only go over some of the results here. While in our example this is presented as a step-by-step, one-time process, it is really iterative. You will probably take a first stab at identifying business entities, and then go through the process again and again before having a final list of all your business entities.

Here are some of the business entities for the Titan application:

Reservation
: Reservations are created by Travel Agents and belong to a Customer. They are associated with a Cruise and zero or more Cabins. A Reservation has a financial subtotal.

Travel Agent
: Travel Agents create and update Reservations and view Cruise information. Travel Agents are a kind of Person.

Customer
: A Customer is also a kind of Person. Customers have zero or more Reservations.

Ship
: A Ship has zero or more Cabins and belongs to zero or more Cruises.

Cruise
: A Cruise has a Ship and a date period and is associated with zero or more Reservations.

Cabin
: A Cabin belongs to a Ship and is associated with zero or more Reservations. All associated Reservations must have a Cruise with a Ship that matches the Ship for the Cabin on the Reservation.

There's more structure to this list than is immediately apparent. It follows a number of guidelines that help reveal the important aspects of each entity:

Capitalization
: Business entities are capitalized, while simpler pieces of information (date period, subtotal) are not.

"Kind of," "belongs," "has," "is associated with"
: These phrases indicate fundamental connections between two entities. We have guessed at specific connection types for now, though the reality may change as we proceed. "Kind of" may indicate inheritance. "Has" and "have" may indicate that an entity is the parent in a parent/child relationship, while "belongs" may indicate that the entity is a child of another entity. "Is associated with" is a relationship too, but with a weaker sense of ownership (i.e., not parent-child).

Concrete verbs
: There are three concrete verbs (*create*, *update*, and *view*), all in the description of the Travel Agent business entity. These verbs indicate processes or significant responsibilities handled by the entity.

Since we focus on the components that will end up being EJBs, our functional analysis is complete: selecting business entities is the most important part of the EJB design process.*

The next step is to look at the technical architecture and its implications for our entities. We'll get to that in just a moment. First, let's take a moment to diagram our business entities using UML so that we have a clear understanding of their relationships. While the textual descriptions help define the business relationships, a UML diagram depicts them more exactly. Figure 19-2 is a UML diagram of our business entities and their relationships.

The UML diagram introduces a Person entity from which we will derive both the TravelAgent and Customer entities. We've also introduced a mapping entity for mapping Reservation entities to Cabin entities. Otherwise, the UML diagram states exactly what we described earlier in the text.

The next step is to consider which entities to implement as EJBs, and what types of EJBs to use. But first, it will help to understand the architecture of the system as aspects of that technical architecture will have direct implications on our entity implementation choices.

* Business entity identification is part of a complete functional analysis. There is a great deal more involved in functional analysis for an application: user interface comps, lists of fields or attributes for each entity, and nonfunctional requirements (the number of users, usage patterns, and so on) are all examples of additional items you may need to include in a functional analysis in order to design the complete application.

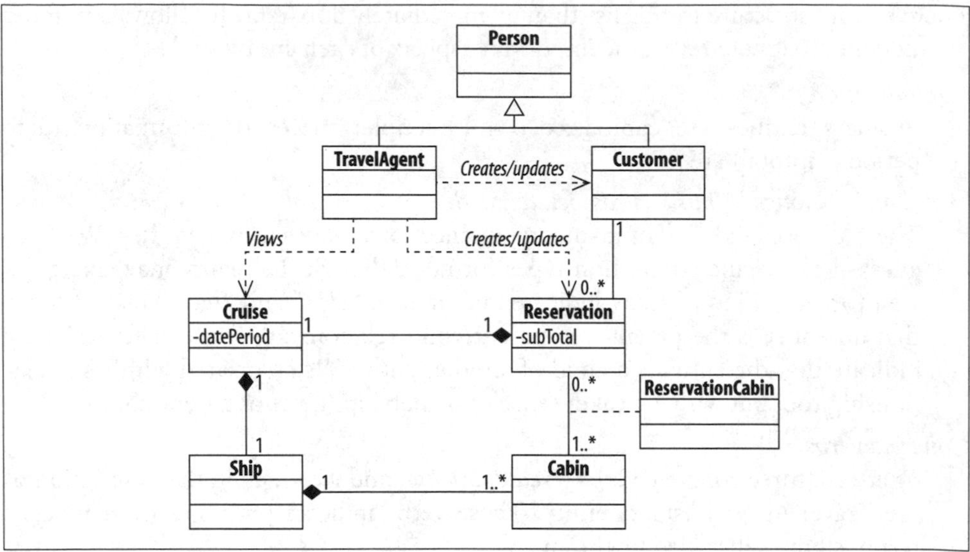

Figure 19-2. UML diagram of the application's business entities

Technical Architecture

Earlier, we depicted our system in a high-level diagram (Figure 19-1). This diagram depicts relationships among various entities and our system, but not much more. What else do we know about the various interactions of these entities and our Titan application?

1. We know that connectivity between the external travel agencies and our system is not guaranteed. Since we are working with a Java implementation of this system, we may want to consider JMS as the communication mechanism between our system and theirs.
2. Furthermore, we know that communication between our application and external travel agencies will be two-way (our application must be able to accept reservation requests), but communication between our application and the shop provision entities need only be one way (we will tell them how many people are attending a cruise, for example).
3. From our initial description we can infer that making reservations is transactional and involves the following steps:
    - Reserve a Cabin for use by a Customer.
    - Reduce the total number of Cabins by one.
    - Increase the total number of Customers for whom the provisioning vendor must provide food.

These steps could involve up to three different database tables. At a minimum, this might involve the following database objects and systems:

- One to store Reservations.
- One to store Cabin availability.
- One to store Customer information for provisioning.

While the complexity of these operations is not clearly defined, we can assume that reservations systems and the management of cruise and ship data are probably of moderate to high complexity. When combined with the need for transactional enforcement and the fact that only certain users will be able to execute certain actions (implied), using EJBs to represent the entities is appropriate.

4. We know that customers and travel agents will be able to access the Titan application over the web. This indicates that part of our system will involve controlling a user interface. EJBs are not well suited to user-interface work, so we'll include the use of servlets and JSPs in our system view.
5. We also know that travel agents will be able to further access the system via a standalone Java application, indicating that some of the communications with the business tier of our application might not come via the Web.

Using this information, our technical system diagram can be amended as shown in Figure 19-3.

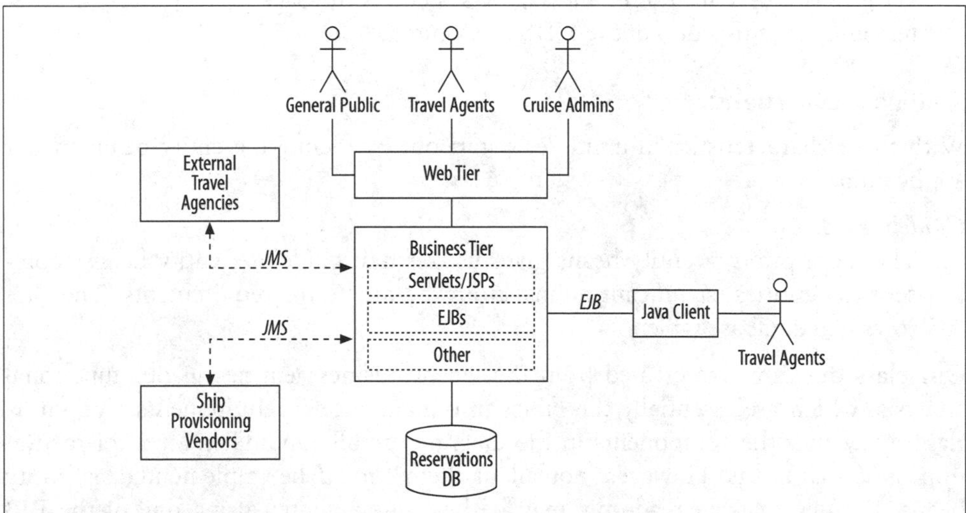

Figure 19-3. Amended system diagram

While it may not look like it at first, we've gotten much closer to identifying our EJBs. Between the new architecture diagram and our business entity UML diagram, we have all we need to move forward.

EJB Identification

Not all of our business entities will turn out to be EJBs, so the next step in our design process is to identify which of them *should*. Our understanding of the application's technical architecture helps. This is not a simple or well-defined process, like completing a jigsaw puzzle or building a bridge. For all but the simplest of applications, the process of identifying EJBs in the application's technical architecture presents ambiguity and conflicting requirements. It's not easy to make the right choices. Fortunately, there are several rules of thumb that will help guide the process.

Let's quickly review the EJB types:

Entity beans
: Represent records persisted in a database. Entity beans can often be used to represent the nouns or *things* from our functional description. If a business entity has a real-world counterpart, it is probably an entity bean.

Session beans
: Manage processes or tasks, often calling other EJBs and non-EJB business objects. Represent *taskflows*. They are invoked locally or via RMI, both synchronous mechanisms.

Message-driven beans
: Manage processes or tasks, like session beans, but are invoked *asynchronously*, via JMS or possibly another messaging system. A message is received by the system and some function of the MDB is executed.

Identifying entity beans

With these characteristics in mind, let's start out by identifying entity beans in our application.

Guideline #1
: The description of entity beans gives us our first guideline: entity beans represent the entities (significant nouns) from the functional requirements. They are rows in a database table.

Our class diagram was created from the list of business entities in our functional analysis, which are essentially the *things* in our functional requirements. We know right away that the components in the diagram are all candidates for implementation as entity beans. However, not all of them *should* be implemented as entity beans. Entities that are read-only may be best implemented using one of the EJB alternatives, such as JDBC or JDO. Read-only entity beans can take advantage of caching and other vendor-specific optimizations that your container may offer, but they really don't need the transaction enforcement that EJB provides.

Other factors to bear in mind when making this decision are your team's skill set, the performance ramifications of the options, and the relative amount of functionality implemented in the options.

You should also avoid logical inheritance with entity beans, in which one entity bean, `Customer`, is a subclass of another entity bean, `Person`, and could be cast to the parent's type. While inheritance works all right for sharing common EJB implementation code between different EJBs (see the "Base and Utility Classes" section below), never try to implement logical inheritance with entity beans. The most important reason to avoid logical inheritance derives from the fact that entity beans correspond to rows in a database table, and inheritance, as an object-oriented concept, is foreign to the database world. You can't define tables `CUSTOMER` and `TRAVEL_AGENT` to inherit the attributes of a third `PERSON` table. Moving back to our entity beans, our best option is to remove the inheritance relationship and replace it with a composition relationship, which is functionally equivalent. Which brings us to the next guideline.

Guideline #2

Guideline #2 involves using composition between entity beans instead of logical inheritance. This means the `Customer` and `TravelAgent` entity beans will have a corresponding `Person` entity bean. Figure 19-4 shows the updated class diagram.

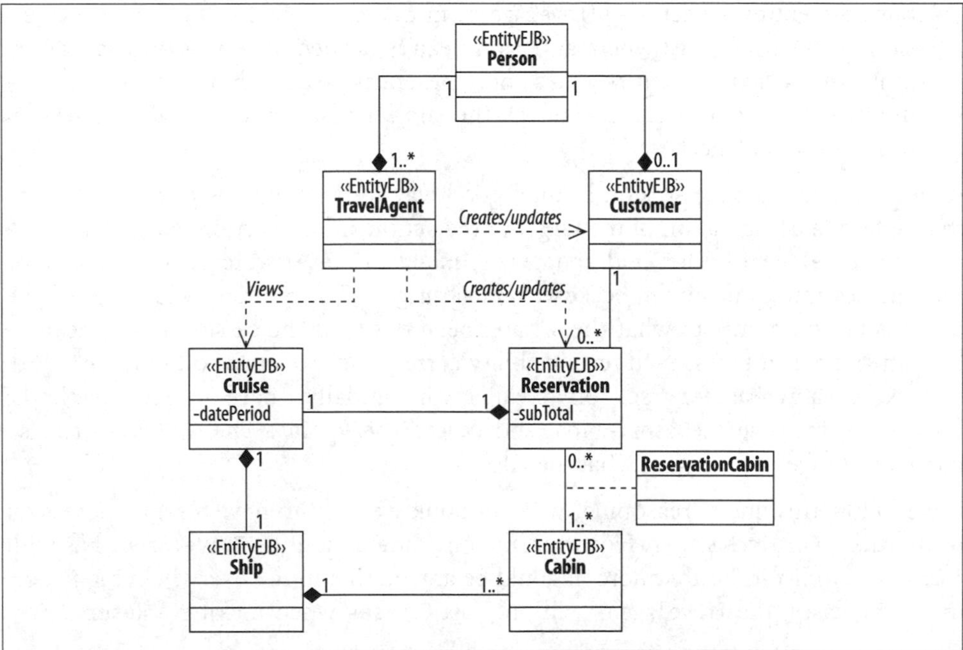

Figure 19-4. Updated class diagram

Identifying session beans

While entity beans are the *things* in our application, session beans implement *task-flow*. They are the processors and workhorses; they *do* stuff. We will identify them by considering the work that our application must do, and a good starting place is the responsibilities depicted in the class diagram.

Looking over the class diagram, we see `TravelAgent` has the following responsibilities:

- Views Cruises
- Creates and updates Reservations
- Creates and updates Customers

In any application, functionality seems to clump around one or more entities. Such a grouping of responsibilities often indicates that a session bean is needed. And this gives us the next guideline.

Guideline #3

> Each session bean encapsulates access to data that spans concepts as identified in the functional requirements analysis and initial technical architecture. So, when we see the clumping, as we do with `TravelAgent` in our class diagram, we know that a new session bean needs to be added to the design. However, the business entity (or actor)—`TravelAgent`, in this case—will not become the session bean. It indicates where a session bean is needed. The session bean represents the *action* the entity takes, not the entity itself. Think of the entity—implemented as an entity bean—as the subject of a sentence and the session bean as the sentence's verb.*

As for the name for the session bean, a good way to think of it is to create a name that reflects a combination of the target of the action and the action itself. For example, the `TravelAgent` creates and updates or "manages" `Reservations`, so a good name for our session bean might be `ReservationManager`. The primary objective of the name is to communicate what the session bean does. As the session bean encapsulates the responsibilities, each responsibility corresponds to a method in the EJB. So, our `ReservationManager` session bean will initially have three methods: `bookReservation`, `updateReservation`, and `cancelReservation`. These names are also named intuitively, to suggest what they do.

If we follow this line of reasoning, we may think we need to have a separate session bean called a `CruiseManager`. However, the only interaction the `TravelAgent` has with a `Cruise` is to list it. Furthermore, it could be argued that in the overwhelming majority of the cases, the `TravelAgent` will only list `Cruises` when making a `Reservation`.

* To extend the metaphor, the direct objects of the sentence will be the other entity beans (or possibly even session beans) that will be used by the session bean when it executes. This approach is the starting point from which we evolve the Session Façade design pattern, in which session beans encapsulate a taskflow that uses one or more components.

For these reasons, it might make more sense to combine the Cruise functionality and simply add a new listCruises method to the ReservationManager.

The listCruises method stands apart from the other methods a bit, both in effect (it reads data while the other methods write data) and in direct object (it returns a collection of cruises while the other methods manipulate a single reservation). This suggests Guideline #4.

Guideline #4

If a given session bean has a method that's *almost always* called in the context of another session bean's function(s), combine the session beans or move the method.

We have now accounted for all the responsibilities depicted in the class diagram, but we haven't accounted for all the functionality specified in the functional requirements. Creating the initial class diagram from the business entities initially misses functionality that has no "source" entity. For example, we've focused only on the reservations and the actions and entities around them. However, a reservation involves a Cruise that has certain characteristics. Some part of our application must be available to administer these Cruises. Cruises are made up of Cabins and Ships. Our administration functionality should focus on the management of all three entities: Cruise, Ship, and Cabin.

Our application revolves around travel agency functionality, but without the configuration of the cruises themselves, the travel agency functionality (creation of reservations, and so on) would be meaningless. Let's add a general session bean around this and other (to be determined) configuration chores. While we may need to break this into multiple session beans later, we can start with one called ConfigurationManager.

Here too, we want to give it methods based on the functionality it encapsulates. Since no taskflows are detailed above, we will assume that all three items need to be created, updated, and deactivated. Thus, these actions (for the three entities) become nine initial methods:

- addCruise
- updateCruise
- cancelCruise
- addShip
- updateShip
- inactivateShip
- addCabin
- updateCabin
- inactivateCabin*

* Most developers would expect to see "deleted" instead of "inactivated," but we have found that it is more prudent not to let the business tier delete configuration data (and possibly all application data). Instead, data should be deactivated by the business tier, and deleted only during archival or export to a data warehouse, according to an agreed upon process.

We can now expand our entity diagram into the class diagram of Figure 19-5.

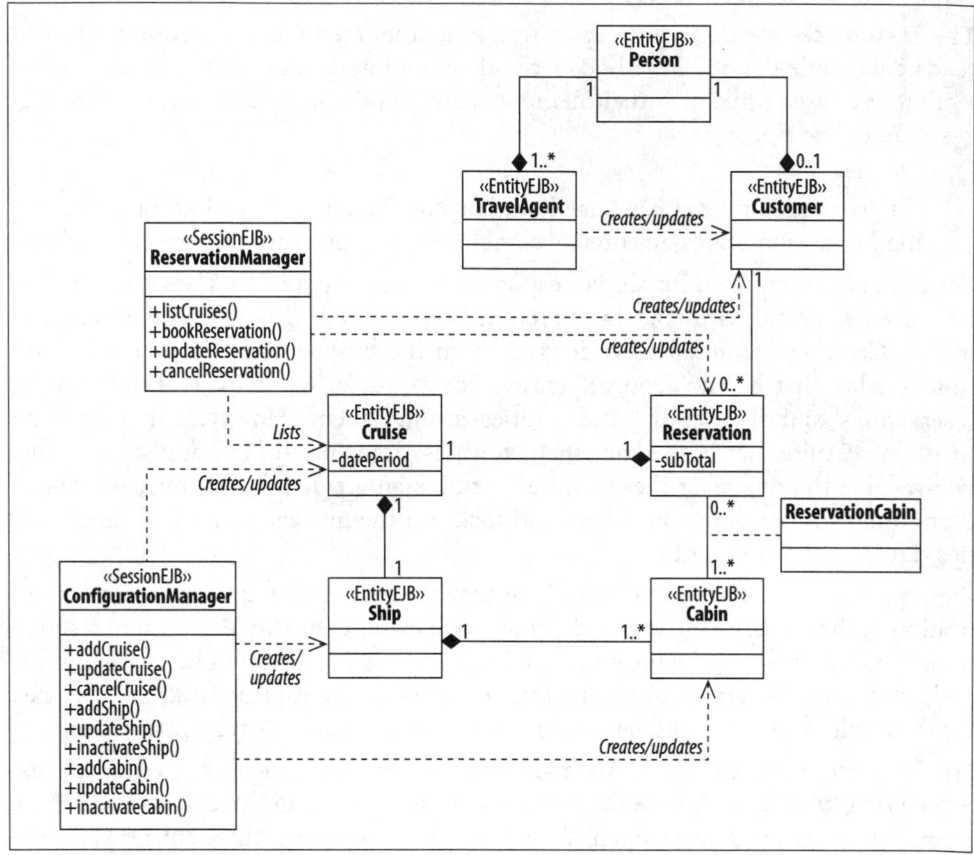

Figure 19-5. Entity diagram expanded into a class diagram

Identifying message-driven beans

Now we need to look for the message-driven beans in the application. As our review of the EJB types reminds us, message-driven beans (MDBs) implement *taskflows* like session beans but can be invoked *asynchronously*. Roughly put, they are transactional message handlers.*

Guideline #5

> Each message-driven bean encapsulates related functionality that must be invoked in a transactional manner when an asynchronous message is received. So, in order to tell where we might want to use message-driven beans—the same as with session beans—we look for groups of functionality. However, for MDBs the functionality is usually initiated with the reception of an asynchronous message.

* EJB qualities such as object distribution and role-based security enforcement are irrelevant in this context, because the MDB has no connection to the message sender.

Here's where our system architecture diagram helps us. There are two places where messaging takes place between our system and another (ostensibly external) system:

- Between external travel agencies and the Titan application
- Between ship provisioning vendors and the Titan application

As you can see from our functional requirements and the technical architecture diagram, our system *receives* messages only from external travel agencies, so we'll focus on the travel agent functionality.

Since we've not been told anything to the contrary, we assume that external travel agent systems function like ours. Thus, ours should include all the functionality incorporated into `ReservationManager`. Additionally, the external travel agencies need some way to retrieve a list of ships and their cabins. This listing ability is included because the external travel agency systems can only communicate via messaging. This suggests that one or more MDBs could be used to implement this functionality.

For the Titan application, we will have two MDBs:

ReservationListener
: The ReservationListener creates, updates, or cancels one or more reservation in response to a reservation function message.

QueryListener
: The QueryListener retrieves cruise and ship data in response to a query message.

> **The Naming of MDBs**
>
> MDB names, like session bean names, should suggest what the component does. A rule of thumb is to combine a description of the kind of messages that the MDB receives with the word "Listener." "Processor" is a common alternative to "Listener," but it is less definitive and thus easier to confuse.

Compare the responsibilities of `ReservationListener` with those of `ReservationManager`. The cruise-listing behavior and the reservation-specific behavior are implemented in separate MDBs. Why? Guideline #4 tells us that if we are only going to execute a given piece of functionality in the context of a given process, we should combine that function with the others. This guideline is appropriate for session beans. To add another method to a session bean does not introduce any complexity to the bean. It's just another method. However, in JMS-based MDB, you have only one `onMessage` function. While you can certainly have many different types of messages coming into the queue on which the MDB is listening, each message type must be processed separately. Each message type adds another significant condition to the MDB's processing logic. Furthermore, the functionality represented by the various messages for the `ReservationListener` will be largely the same, but messages representing queries for cruise information might be different.

While we're talking about JMS-based MDB, it makes sense to discuss the importance of message design. When a message listener is invoked, the only information it has is the message that it has been passed. In many cases, the message listener needs specific business information to do its work, and that information is packaged in the message.

Exactly how it is packaged depends on which message type you choose: `javax.jms.Message` or its subinterfaces (`BytesMessage`, `MapMessage`, `ObjectMessage`, `StreamMessage`, and `TextMessage`). A general rule of thumb is to use `ObjectMessage` for messaging between systems that are guaranteed to be Java-based and to use `TextMessage` for messaging between potentially non-Java systems. Because `ObjectMessage` carries a full Java object, the data inside it is already structured for easy access by the MDB, whereas all but the simplest data embedded in a `TextMessage` (and the other types to varying extents) will generally have to be processed before it can be used (by a `StringTokenizer`, an XML parser, `Integer.parseInt`, or something similar).

On the upside, `TextMessage` (and maybe `BytesMessage`) is the most universal message type—every messaging system knows how to send and receive simple text (and also binary data). That said, you should investigate message types and their trade-offs before making final decisions.

Because we need to accept messages from the greatest variety of external travel agency systems, we will use `TextMessage` messages carrying XML payloads. While it requires a heavy XML parser when processing messages, it provides interoperability benefits that fit our needs.

We've now identified all of the EJBs in our sample application. Figure 19-6 is an updated class diagram.

EJB Details

Now that we have identified the EJBs in our application along with some of their methods, we are about two-thirds done with our design. So far, much of the design has flowed almost naturally from our business and technical requirements. The remaining third of the design is more difficult and requires some hard decisions.

Much of the remaining design work centers on determining each bean's sub-type and interface type (remote or local). Our application has the following EJBs:

Entity beans
: Cabin, Cruise, Customer, Person, Reservation, Ship, TravelAgent

Session beans
: ConfigurationManager, ReservationManager

Message-driven beans
: QueryListener, ReservationListener

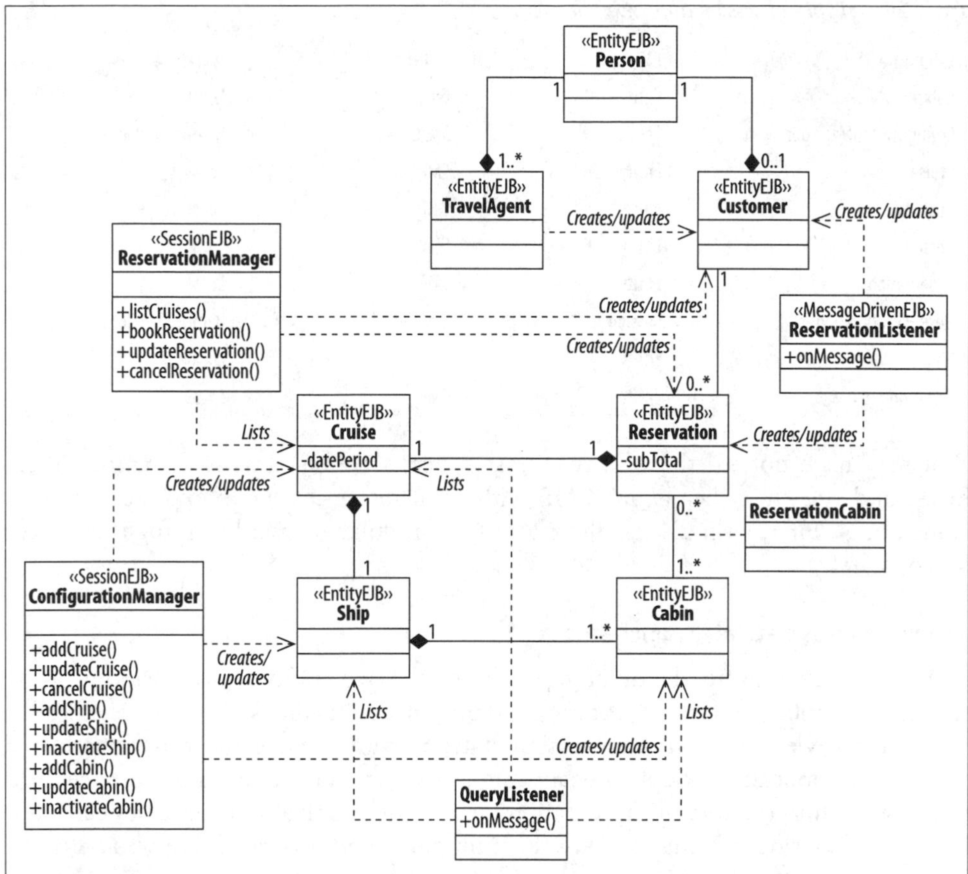

Figure 19-6. Updated class diagram

We can ignore the MDBs, because they do not have sub-types or interface types—other than `javax.jms.MessageListener`. However, we must determine the sub-type and interface type for the remaining EJBs. The attributes are critical to your application's design, as they dictate the overall usage and implementation of your core business components. For example, implementing an EJB with a remote interface requires that all invocations of that EJB must catch a `RemoteException`. It is not impossible to change these attributes later in your application's lifetime, but it can be difficult. For example, if we change an EJB from a remote interface to a local interface, we need to review and possibly remove all the code that was catching `RemoteException`s.

With this in mind, let's determine the sub-type and interface type of our session and entity beans. We start by listing the decisions, and then discuss the reasoning in the following sections. After reviewing the business and technical requirements, we implement the EJBs as indicated in Table 19-1.

Table 19-1. Types of session and entity beans

EJB name	EJB type	EJB sub-type	Interface type
Cabin	Entity	CMP	Local
ConfigurationManager	Session	Stateless	Remote and local
Cruise	Entity	CMP	Local
Customer	Entity	CMP	Local
Person	Entity	CMP	Local
Reservation	Entity	CMP	Local
ReservationManager	Session	Stateless	Remote and local
Ship	Entity	CMP	Local
TravelAgent	Entity	CMP	Local

You may have noticed that the two session beans are stateless with remote interfaces, and the entity beans are CMP with local interfaces. Let's explore how this came about. First, we'll discuss the reasons a particular session bean might be stateless or stateful.

Stateless versus stateful session beans

As their names indicate, the difference between the two sub-types of session beans is the maintenance of state. A common source of confusion is that we use similar words when we talk about web session state, as with servlets and other aspects of web-based applications. Session bean state is taskflow-related and should have little or no relation to the web or presentation tiers of your application. Session bean state is a way of sharing information between multiple methods of the same session bean. For example, the stateful version of `ReservationManager` contains the current `Customer`, so that it is not passed into the `bookReservation`, `updateReservation`, and `cancelReservation` methods (Figure 19-7).

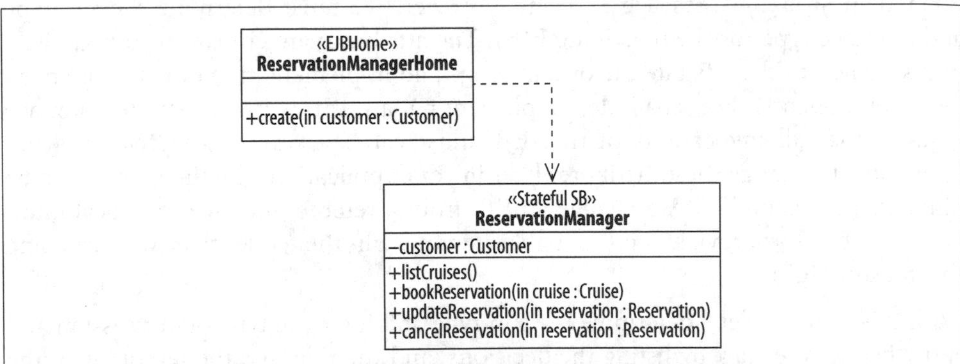

Figure 19-7. Stateful version of ReservationManager

Contrast that with the stateless version of ReservationManager, in which the current Customer is a parameter for those methods (Figure 19-8).

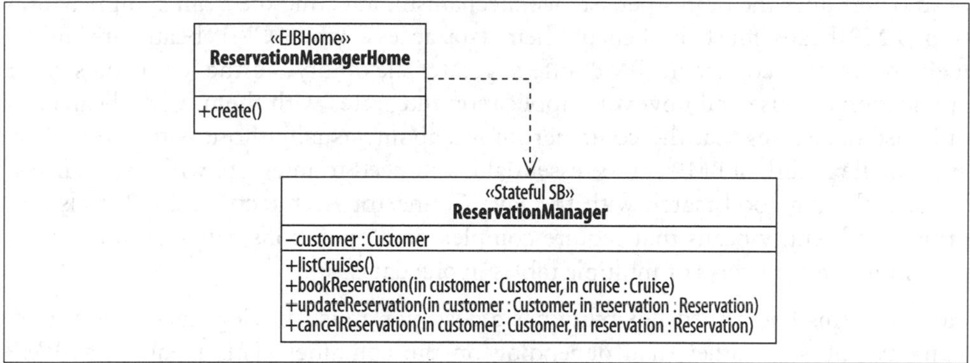

Figure 19-8. Stateless version of ReservationManager

The stateful session bean appears more elegant when we need to call bookReservation, updateReservation, or cancelReservation multiple times. However, that elegance has a cost. Stateful session beans are slower and more resource intensive than stateless session beans. This makes the choice of stateful session beans a trade-off rather than a pure benefit.

Perhaps you're thinking, "That's a pretty balanced trade-off." Unfortunately, stateful session beans are not as useful as they first appear. Remember that stateful session beans share information between multiple methods of the same session bean. But the methods in the session bean's interface are coarse-grained enough that the application should only be calling one at any given time. Why would your code call bookReservation and then cancelReservation?

In our example, we wouldn't. However, you will encounter situations where you will need to execute multiple methods on the same EJB. In that case, you should apply the Session Façade design pattern.* In essence, the Session Façade pattern manages a taskflow, and it can manage information just as a stateful session bean does. Even better, it offers the same transaction and security management between multiple EJBs. Thus, stateless session beans with the Session Façade pattern are preferable to stateful session beans.

* There are four design patterns that will often be used in the design of EJB applications: Session Façade, Data Access Object, Transfer Object, and Business Delegate. We will not cover these in detail in this chapter. For more information, see the Design Patterns section of the Sun Microsystems site at *http://java.sun.com/blueprints/corej2eepatterns/Patterns/*.

Container-managed versus bean-managed persistence

The decision to use containter-managed or bean-managed persistence for an entity bean determines the bean's persistence mechanism, affecting the bean's implementation. BMP beans must implement their data access, while CMP beans are implemented by the container. BMP offers greater flexibility in the datastores your application can use and how your application integrates with them. CMP beans can only use datastores that the container knows about, usually those with JDBC drivers. The flexibility of BMP can be essential if you need to integrate with external systems, making a good match with the Java Connector Architecture. BMP is also an option with entity beans that require complex data operations, such as those spanning multiple datastores or multiple tables in one datastore.

However, this heightened flexibility has a cost: you must develop data access functionality yourself, rather than depending on the container. This means that BMP beans require more effort to develop and maintain. CMP beans are virtually guaranteed to integrate flawlessly with the container, while BMP beans may contain code that is not EJB safe. BMP beans that integrate with external systems should hide the operational and semantic differences between EJB and the external system's technology. Otherwise, the external system may cause all kinds of potentially serious side effects, some subtle and unpredictable. Also, BMP code may not be portable—which makes sense for code that is specifically written for complex data operations or integration with external systems.

CMP beans don't have these issues. Here are some considerations about CMP:

- CMP is easy to build and maintain. It requires only the creation and maintenance of deployment descriptors and the rest of the abstract persistence mechanism.
- CMP can persist to any JDBC-capable datastore, which is sufficient for most applications.
- CMP and CMR are fully capable of implementing simple to moderately complex data operations, which will generally cover most of your needs.
- CMP is fully integrated into the container, so there is less concern about dangerous code or unpredictable external systems. This also allows you to take advantage of vendor-specific features more easily.

Don't use BMP beans unless the requirements supporting them are strong and clear-cut. If you are using BMP beans to integrate with external datastores, locate or create as much documentation as possible.

Local versus remote interfaces

Don't use remote interfaces unless you really have to: it can't be emphasized enough. Distributing your EJBs adds a whole layer of complication that is often unnecessary. There are the basic, only somewhat irritating issues, such as handling `RemoteExceptions` in your client code, and there are the complex, intractable issues, such as loss of performance and reliability when your components must operate across a network. One big complication is that remote interfaces (and the implementation they present) are often difficult to change, because the remote interface will be used by other systems or applications that may be resistant to change.

Our application clearly needs to be distributed: it must support the standalone Java client that our internal travel agents will use. In your application, take a long, hard look at any requirements that push you in the direction of distributed components. Approach such requirements as with BMP:

- Understand the requirements in detail and validate them.
- Determine whether the requirements truly merit being implemented as distributed EJBs.
- Document the detailed requirements before initiating development in order to ensure agreement and to prevent scope creep.

If, after this process, you determine that you need distributed functionality, your next task is to identify which EJBs should be implemented with remote interfaces and which should stay as local interfaces. In our application, travel agents will use the standalone client to access the full range of application functionality. We already know that session beans are the workhorses of our application—which is why we have exposed the session beans via remote interfaces.

However, none of our entity beans use remote interfaces. Why not? Remember that session beans encapsulate taskflows that manage entity beans, especially when we make good use of the Session Façade pattern. If our session beans are well designed, there should be no need to access entity beans remotely. Also, recall that CMR requires the dependent entities have local interfaces. So we avoid remote interfaces for entity beans.

In that case, how do we pass the entity data, such as cruise information, across the remote interface? Good answers to this question are provided in the "Returning Entity Data from EJBs" section below. The Transfer Object pattern is preferable to the other approaches when working with remote interfaces. Transfer Objects complement the strict interface of EJB components, and most EJB applications will have Java clients.

In the EJB list above, we chose to implement both remote and local interfaces for our session beans. While this does result in slightly more code to build and maintain, it is a good idea to use the local interfaces in the code that runs inside the application server, such as servlets or JSPs. The small duplication is worth avoiding the remote interface.

Thus, our interface recommendations are:

- Use remote interfaces only if you must, and only for session beans.
- Insist that entity beans have only local interfaces.
- Implement local interfaces for session beans if there will be code calling them from inside your application server.

Fleshing Out the Design

Now that you've determined the major aspects of your EJBs, all that remains is to complete the design down to the class and method level. This is the same task you would do for any application, so we will not cover it here. However, this stage can undo or compromise a good EJB design if it is executed poorly. This section discusses the two most critical lessons we have learned to keep an EJB design in good shape.

Minimize transaction scope

As you flesh out your EJBs, especially session beans, make sure that your transactions have the smallest scope possible. By scope, we mean the number of operations executed and the number of components used. Operations executed inside a transactional context require more container management than nontransactional operations, and this management generally results in limitations and performance costs. The limitations depend on the container, database, and other transactional components of your application. Exceeding these limitations can create problems that depend greatly on the execution environment and the exact processing being done.

This variability often makes diagnosis and troubleshooting of transactional problems difficult, so the best approach is to minimize transactional scope during design or early in coding. Here is how to identify possible transaction resource problems:

1. Understand the transactional capabilities and constraints of your EJB container, your database, and other subsystems. You should be concerned with what resources are limited during a transaction. Remember to check both the vendor documentation and any specification documentation.
2. Identify the complex taskflows in your application. Focus on functionality that iterates through EJBs, aggregates through data, or chains EJBs (where one EJB calls another, which calls another, and so on) inside a single transaction.*
3. Estimate the amount of processing that the taskflows will perform. Consider the data entities used in the taskflows, and determine the maximum number of each entity that your application will support.† This knowledge can help you determine how many EJBs will be used. Also, consider non-EJB resources, such as database cursors. Combine this data with the steps and dependencies of each taskflow to produce a list of resources used.
4. Compare the list of resources used by each taskflow to the relevant setting or constraint. For example, the total number of EJB instances is limited by the `max-beans-in-pool` deployment descriptor setting. Where the resources used could exceed the available resources, you will need to minimize the transactional scope.

* Remember that the transaction scope is propagated to all EJBs touched by the thread of execution, except for those EJB methods that have `NotSupported` or `RequiresNew` specified for their transaction attributes in the deployment descriptor.

† This kind of information is also necessary for accurate database sizing.

Repeat this evaluation if you make significant changes to your EJBs, especially after revisions that affect your session beans.

Don't confuse EJB types

This may seem like a no-brainer, but don't try to make one EJB type behave like another. If you've been paying attention throughout this book (you have, haven't you?), the differences between EJB types should be pretty clear in your head. Session and message-driven beans manage processes (synchronously and asynchronously, respectively), entity beans persist data, and everyone is happy. That's great! There are two possible wrinkles:

- Not everyone has read this book; some people will have different understandings of how to design EJBs.
- Your application will evolve, and the changes may alter your EJB design.

As a consequence, you may find some of the following in your application:

- A custom JMS listener that calls a session bean.
- Session beans presenting getters/setters for individual data items.
- Entity beans containing complex business logic.*

These are all *bad things*.† If you see these or any similar misconceptions about what each kind of EJB does, do everything you can to fix them ASAP. Depending on the exact circumstances, the consequences may be minor—an additional class or two requiring creation and maintenance—or they may make the EJB nonfunctional or impossible to maintain.

Special Circumstances

Any application will have features that are best implemented by combining two or more technologies. We'll look at several scenarios where EJB technology may need to be combined with other technologies and give some approaches to melding them successfully.

Returning entity data from EJBs

In all but the simplest applications, you will need to return data from your EJBs. This data will be used by other components, other tiers of the application, and maybe

* We once saw a BMP entity bean designed to retrieve and manage a hierarchical collection, a tree, of key-value pairs. The entity bean contained data elements from the key table and the value table, all held in multiple instances of the same kind of entity bean. The entity bean contained the necessary logic to populate, traverse, and persist the entire tree of data.

† Can you identify the kinds of EJBs the examples should be? Hint: a message-driven bean, an entity bean, and a session bean.

even other systems. While EJBs, specifically entity beans, could fulfill this need, there are several reasons why entity beans should not be used outside the EJB container (see the "Local versus remote interfaces" section, above).

The Transfer Object pattern is one solution to this problem. It provides lightweight objects specifically for sending data outside the EJB container. We can also use some other approaches to represent an entity's data, such as an array of `String`s, a `Map` of field-value pairs, a JDBC `ResultSet`, or XML. These approaches are generally more loosely coupled than Transfer Objects, providing greater flexibility with commensurate costs. Here's a quick summary of the pros and cons of each approach:

Transfer objects
: The available data is set in code, which makes for a strict interface. The remote client must be Java-based.

Array of Strings
: There is no metadata, so the data order of the array must be known ahead of time, which makes for a unintuitive interface. The remote client does not need to be Java-based.

Map of field-value pairs
: The field names in the `Map` provide some metadata, so data ordering is not a constraint. No type information is provided, so that must be specified or not needed. (For example, by assuming everything is a string.) This may handicap the interface for some complex business taskflows, but it is sufficient for most situations. The remote client must be Java-based.

JDBC ResultSet
: This provides full metadata, making it useful for even the most complex taskflows. On the downside, the remote client must be Java-based.

XML
: XML can express multiple levels of metadata and relationship complexity. Thus, it can be equivalent to the `Map` approach, equivalent to the `ResultSet` approach, or even express a complete entity hierarchy. The remote client does not need to be Java-based, but XML imposes some performance penalties. It is not very size-efficient, resulting in higher memory usage and slower network transmission, and it must be parsed to be programmatically accessed.

You have lots of freedom in how you choose to implement these approaches. For example, you could implement a `Map`-like structure using arrays of `String`s to get the benefits of the former while remaining platform-agnostic. However, the benefits of that approach may be offset by the effort needed to build it.

One drawback to these approaches is that the data is a snapshot. If the underlying data changes, none of these structures will know. Therefore, it's possible that changes to the underlying data could render the data contained in these structures incorrect. This risk can be mitigated by the following data latency strategies:

- Use the data only during a limited lifetime, say, during a single UI request. Then discard it.
- Always validate your business preconditions and process inputs before executing a taskflow. Do not blindly execute business logic. That way, you can always ensure that the right thing happens.
- Buy or build a caching framework that integrates with your EJB code or your EJB container.

Of course, all of these strategies have downsides. You will need to balance the trade-offs of entity beans, these "snapshot" approaches, and the above data latency strategies against your requirements.

Sequential processing with EJBs

Many applications, especially those focused on business operations, require sequential ("batch") processing, such as for an end-of-day process. In these kinds of taskflows, a series of well-defined steps are executed, and many of these steps involve processing a collection of entities. For example, our travel agent application might have an end-of-day process wherein it iterates through all the Customers and generates an invoice record for any new Reservations. Another step might populate reporting tables in a database. There are many other possible steps.

EJB makes implementing these features both easier and more difficult. It is easier because of the transactional enforcement and the logical assignment of responsibilities. After all, the application will make multiple changes in each step (at least one to each entity), and wrapping the changes in a transaction might save us from having to keep track of which entities we've processed and which we haven't. It makes sense to put any processing logic in one place, such as a session bean.

On the other hand, sequential processing can be challenging because of EJB's performance and resource overhead, and the constraints of transaction enforcement (see the "Minimize transaction scope" section, above). The more steps involved in your taskflow, the more likely you will be to exceed your system's capabilities. The same is true as more EJBs (entity or session) are used in the taskflow: each additional EJB slows the processing that much more, perhaps unacceptably. Additionally, a gargantuan transaction that takes a long time to complete can have extreme concurrency ramifications.

The bottom line is EJB alone will probably not be successful here. A framework must be developed that incorporates EJB but is not limited by EJB. The heart of the framework is a process controller that knows how to execute a series of steps, each in its own transaction. Part of the process controller is implemented as a session bean. Then you can group the logical tasks of the business process into separate transactional steps. Each of these steps is implemented as a plain Java class that in turn calls the best feasible technology, and each class is called by the process controller. For example, aggregating reporting data in a database might be best implemented as a database stored procedure. Figure 19-9 illustrates a rough UML diagram of the framework.

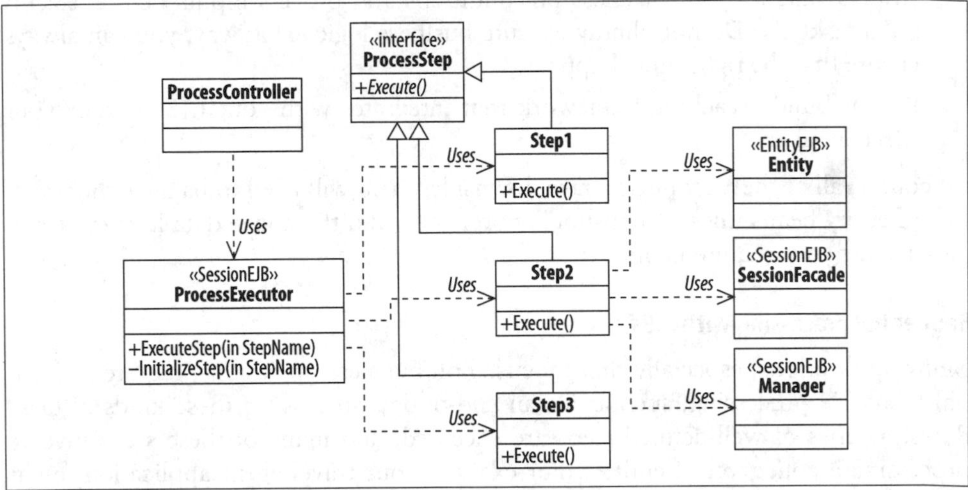

Figure 19-9. Rough UML diagram of the framework

In short, the sequential processing in your application will probably require some creative integration of EJB and other technologies. Be willing to explore different technologies to serve your needs.

Exceptions

Exceptions are fundamental to error notification and management in Java. Understanding exceptions and how to handle them is even more important in EJB because exceptions have a significant effect on transaction control. Be sure to review the section on exceptions and transactions in Chapter 16.

Exception design for EJBs is essentially the same as general exception design. The most noticeable difference is that EJB distinguishes between application and system exceptions rather than checked and unchecked exceptions. System exceptions are the same as unchecked exceptions (`java.lang.RuntimeException` and its subclasses), and application exceptions are checked exceptions—with one exclusion. That exclusion is `java.rmi.RemoteException` and its subclasses, which is used to indicate an underlying problem with a remote EJB call, such as a communication failure. As such, `RemoteException` appears in each EJB method in the interface, but not in the corresponding implementation.

There is an informal category of checked exceptions that deserve special treatment. We call them *subsystem exceptions*. As the name indicates, subsystem exceptions are checked exceptions thrown by a subsystem of the JVM or a resource, such as JDBC or JMS. For example, `IOException` is thrown by the I/O subsystem; `JMSException` is thrown by JMS; `SQLException` is thrown by JDBC, and so on. When one EJB calls another (by its remote interface), you treat `RemoteException` as a subsystem exception.

Here are the fundamental steps in exception design:

1. Determine what application exceptions are needed.
2. Design an exception hierarchy for the application exceptions.
3. Wrap subsystem exceptions.
4. Everything else will be system exceptions.

Identifying application exceptions

The first step is to determine the application exceptions. Application exceptions encapsulate business errors that prevent the completion of a taskflow. The user should be notified, or the application should attempt to recover from the error, or both. The essential criterion is that the error needs to be propagated several layers (at least) up the application call stack. For example, the Titan application would throw an application exception if a reservation could not be completed because the desired cruise was sold out, and this exception would cause the user interface to display an error message. Avoid scenarios where application exceptions are used as costly `if-then` statements or other forms of flow control. Exceptions are *exceptional*.*

Application exceptions can often be identified almost straight from your business requirements, so if the requirements are fully defined, much of the work in this step is already done. The trick is to make sure your exceptions focus on error conditions. Some developers have used exceptions for user interface control, which is bad. For example, if a query for cabin information from the Titan application had no results, it is better to return an empty `Collection` than throw an exception. Exceptions should be reserved for errors, and other mechanisms should be employed for controlling user interaction.

Design the exception hierarchy

After you have determined what application exceptions you need, incorporate them into a class hierarchy. A hierarchy provides at least two benefits:

- Common functionality can be implemented in superclasses.
- A package-specific superclass can be used in throws clauses instead of listing multiple subclasses. For example, the signature can show `InventoryException` instead of `CabinSoldOutException`, `DeckSoldOutException`, and `CruiseSoldOutException`.

* Because throwing exceptions is costly, your application should take reasonable steps to avoid predictable exceptions. In other words, be sure to check the preconditions at the beginning of all taskflows and methods. This also avoids performing part of a taskflow only to have to roll it back, which is a waste of time and resources. For example, check if the cruise is sold out before attempting to create a reservation. While the cruise might sell out in the split second between the check and the creation, it's unlikely 99% of the time.

Here are some specific steps to assist in creating the hierarchy:

1. Always have a base class, probably abstract, to contain general exception functionality. This can be called `AbstractException`.
2. `AbstractException` should also contain code and attributes for passing at least two error codes: one for user notification and another for developer notification. The codes should correspond to entries in a resource bundle or other text localization mechanism. Short, mnemonic textual codes ("AVAILABLE_INVENTORY_EXCEEDED") rather than numeric or otherwise cryptic codes ("I-01765") are preferable.
3. Create a subclass of `AbstractException` for each major package, e.g., `InventoryException`, `GuestException`.
4. Package-specific exceptions can be subclassed as necessary to indicate particular error conditions. As mentioned above, `CabinSoldOutException`, `DeckSoldOutException`, and `CruiseSoldOutException` are possible subclasses of `InventoryException`. Use as many subclasses as you need.
5. When designing the EJB interfaces, start out by listing all exceptions that each method can throw. A rule of thumb is that if three or more exceptions thrown by a method are subclasses of the same package-level exception, replace them with the package-level exception.

Wrap subsystem exceptions

Subsystem exceptions should not appear in your EJB method signatures. The EJB interface presents functionality and data from a business perspective, while subsystems are implementation-specific. If you cannot recover from a subsystem exception inside your EJB, *always* catch and rethrow it wrapped in an `EJBException`.

```
try {
    ...
} catch ( SQLException se ) {
   throw new EJBException("SQLException caught during processing: " +
                          se.getMessage(), se);
} catch ( RemoteException re ) {
   throw new EJBException("RemoteException caught during processing: "
                          + re.getMessage(), re);
}
```

Base and Utility Classes

As you design your EJBs, you will begin to spot areas of common functionality. For example, since several classes and functions deal with reservations in the Titan application, several of the implementations may require the use of `startDate` and `endDate` parameters. They may even be of similar type (i.e., `java.util.Date` or something similar). As another example, suppose the DBA for your application's database decides that there will be a timestamp column named `LAST_MODIFIED` in all database tables.

Every single entity bean in your application will support this field. Furthermore, the implementation of this field will have to remain consistent across all implementations of all entity beans in order to be of use.

As a final example, consider the EJB implementation interfaces `javax.ejb.EntityBean`, `javax.ejb.SessionBean`, and `javax.ejb.MessageDrivenBean`. All require that our EJBs implement various container callback methods, regardless of whether they are actually implemented or not. For example, stateless session beans require but do not use `ejbActivate( )` and `ejbPassivate( )`.

Each one of these situations adds some amount of code to every EJB; code which must be written and maintained. To avoid this development overhead, consider implementing this functionality in either *base classes* or *utility classes*, as appropriate. While it might not make sense to build a unique base class for two separate EJBs, if you have 10, suddenly the time investment in building the base class more than pays for itself.

As discussed here, a *base class* is generally declared abstract and inherited by your EJBs. They implement methods needed by all or several EJBs. A *utility class* implements generalized, frequently used structures or functionality. Utility classes are often used across several packages and really can't be assigned to a specific domain area.

Base classes

We will create base classes for our EJBs that contain empty implementations of the container callback methods as well as methods for getting and setting the EJB context. Since the specific set of callback methods and the EJB context class depend on the type of EJB, we will create three base classes: `AbstractEntityBean`, `AbstractSessionBean`, and `AbstractMessageDrivenBean`. In addition, we will add support for the `LAST_MODIFIED` timestamp column, as it is a common feature in EJB applications. This step requires that we incorporate two abstract methods (`getLastModified( )` and `setLastModified( )`) into the `AbstractEntityBean` class.

This is the code for `AbstractEntityBean`:

```
package com.titan.common;

import javax.ejb.EntityContext;
import javax.ejb.EntityBean;
import java.sql.Timestamp;

public abstract class AbstractEntityBean implements EntityBean {

   private EntityContext entityContext = null;

   public void setEntityContext(EntityContext context) {
      entityContext = context;
   }
```

```
    public EntityContext getEntityContext( ) {
       if ( null == entityContext ) {
          throw new IllegalStateException("The entity context has " +
                                          "not been set.");
       }
       return entityContext;
    }

    public void unsetEntityContext( ) {
       entityContext = null;
    }

    public void ejbActivate( ) {
    }

    public void ejbPassivate( ) {
    }

    public void ejbLoad( ) {
    }

    public void ejbStore( ) {
    }

    public void ejbRemove( ) {
    }

    public abstract Timestamp getLastModified( );

    public abstract void setLastModified(Timestamp lastModified);

}
```

This is the code for `AbstractSessionBean`:

```
package com.titan.common;

import javax.ejb.SessionBean;
import javax.ejb.SessionContext;

public abstract class AbstractSessionBean implements SessionBean {

   private SessionContext sessionContext;

   public void setSessionContext(SessionContext context) {
      sessionContext = context;
   }

   public SessionContext getSessionContext( ) {
      if ( null == sessionContext ) {
         throw new IllegalStateException("The session context has " +
                                         "not been set.");
      }
```

```
            return sessionContext;
        }

        public void unsetSessionContext( ) {
            sessionContext = null;
        }

        public void ejbActivate( ) {
        }

        public void ejbPassivate( ) {
        }

        public void ejbCreate( ) {
        }

        public void ejbRemove( ) {
        }
    }
```

And here's the code for AbstractMessageDrivenBean:

```
package com.titan.common;

import javax.ejb.MessageDrivenBean;
import javax.ejb.MessageDrivenContext;

public abstract class AbstractMessageDrivenBean implements MessageDrivenBean {

    private MessageDrivenContext messageContext;

    public void setMessageDrivenContext(MessageDrivenContext context) {
        messageContext = context;
    }

    public MessageDrivenContext getMessageDrivenContext( ) {
        if ( null == messageContext ) {
            throw new IllegalStateException("The message context has " +
                                             "not been set.");
        }

        return messageContext;
    }

    public void unsetMessageDrivenContext( ) {
        messageContext = null;
    }

    public void ejbCreate( ) {
    }

    public void ejbRemove( ) {
    }
}
```

Empty implementations of ejbCreate( ) have been provided for the session and message-driven bean base classes. We did not provide an ejbCreate( ) for the entity bean base class because each entity bean's ejbCreate( ) must return that bean's primary key type.

Our bean implementation classes will now extend the appropriate base class, like so:

```
public abstract class CabinBean extends AbstractEntityBean {
    ...
}

public class ReservationProcessorBean extends AbstractMessageDrivenBean implements
javax.jms.MessageListener {
    ...
}

public class TravelAgentBean extends AbstractSessionBean {
    ...
}
```

MDBs must still implement the javax.jms.MessageListener interface.

With these changes, we have decreased the amount of code we have to write and maintain. During the implementation phase, you will probably find additional code that can be moved into the base classes.

Using base classes in this way presents three pitfalls:

- If you only have a few EJBs, you will spend more time creating and using the base classes than you will save.
- You will gain no benefit if you have to override more than a few methods in the base classes. This is especially likely with the container callback methods when you are creating stateful session beans.
- You will not be able to inherit functionality from another class. If you need to do so, you will have to decide whether to copy the base class methods to your EJB or to access the other class's functionality in another manner, such as composition.*

Utility classes

Now that we have taken care of the base classes, let's turn to the *utility classes*. Utility classes are hard to define precisely, because they include generalized data-holding classes, such as a DateRange class that encapsulates a start date and an end date, and non-data classes that contain infrastructure-related, library-like, and convenience methods. Examples of non-data classes include a StringUtils class containing String manipulation functionality, an ObjectUtils class containing various equality and

* I have never seen a case where an EJB should subclass a class other than with a base class, and a requirement like that is suspicious.

comparison convenience methods, or a DatabaseUtils class containing primary key generation and database connection functionality. Data-holding classes can be more ambiguous. Determining whether they are utility classes or domain-specific types will depend on your particular application and design. For example, a Money class that combines an amount and a currency could be considered a generalized, cross-package class or a finance-specific class.

The primary benefit of utility classes is reducing code duplication, which makes it easier to fix or improve your application without risking shotgun surgery.* Utility classes can also increase code readability.

You will discover candidate utility classes as you implement your design. The biggest sign that you might need a utility class is code duplication. If your code performs the same or very similar logic multiple times, or if two or more classes always accompany each other in methods or method signatures, you have a possible utility class (more correctly, a possible utility method or a possible utility class). Here's a method that might belong in a utility class:

```
public static boolean isEmpty(String str) {
   return ((str == null) || (str.trim( ).equals("")));
}
```

The isEmpty method is very simple, but implementing it in a utility class is worthwhile if you check for null or empty Strings often enough—say, when validating method arguments. I would put this method in a StringUtils class.

Here's an example of a data-holding utility class: suppose you have a series of classes with method signatures that require both a currency and an amount parameter every time:

```
public Ticket bookPassage(CreditCard card, double price, Integer currency)
```

If you created a Money class, the modified method from the TravelAgent session bean would look like this:

```
public Ticket bookPassage(CreditCard card, Money amount)
```

A DateRange utility class is a common requirement in handling reservations. For example, say that we had added startDate and endDate virtual persistence fields to the Cruise EJB:

```
public Date getStartDate( );
public void setStartDate(Date start);

public Date getEndDate( );
public void setEndDate(Date end);
```

* *Shotgun surgery* takes place "...when every time you make a kind of change, you have to make a lot of little changes to a lot of different classes." (From *Refactoring: Improving the Design of Existing Code* by Martin Fowler, published by Addison-Wesley.)

Because travel agents will want to search for cruises by these fields, we have added a `listMatchingCruises` method to the `TravelAgent` EJB:

```
public Collection listMatchingCruises(Date start, Date end) throws RemoteException;
```

After a `DateRange` class is created, this method changes to:

```
public Collection listMatchingCruises(DateRange range) throws RemoteException;
```

While reduced duplication is the most obvious benefit to implementing utility classes, an additional benefit is that reduced duplication makes the interface more coherent: it's easier to understand a method signature with a date range than a method signature with separate parameters for the start and end dates. Likewise, it's easier to understand a `Money` parameter than separate price and currency parameters. Everyone who touches the revised `bookPassage` and `listMatchingCruises` methods—their developers, the developers of any client code, or some college intern tasked with maintaining the code a year or two down the line—will have a more intuitive grasp of what those methods expect.

Unfortunately, knowing when to implement this type of refactoring comes with experience. Fortunately, there is an excellent book on refactoring: Martin Fowler's *Refactoring: Improving the Design of Existing Code* (Addison-Wesley). Take a look for other ways to identify candidates for utility classes (and for other ways to refactor your code).

Should You Use EJBs?

This book assumes that you've already made the decision to use EJBs. However, there are several instances where EJBs are not the best solution to a problem. It makes sense, therefore to review where EJBs are strong and then discuss situations in which EJBs don't make as much sense. There are several situations—even some enterprise database-centric applications—in which EJBs are simply not the best choice. At the end of this section, we'll look at some of the alternative approaches and where they might fit.

When to Use EJBs

Here's a list of situations where EJBs are strong; we haven't distinguished between different types of EJBs.

Single and multisystem business transactions
: The ability to maintain transactional integrity for complex business entities is one of an EJB's key strengths. EJBs aren't alone in providing straightforward transactional control over a single data repository. However, EJBs shine where multiple resources (relational databases, messaging systems, etc.) are involved because they allow transactions to spread across as many different resources as you like, so long as the resources support distributed transactions.

Distributed functionality

Business services often live on a remote server. For example, a business enterprise will have many different systems, ranging in degrees of inflexibility and entrenchment. One of these systems may need to access another; EJBs, which are inherently distributed, are often the simplest way to distribute remote services. EJB also allows you to provide business services to remote clients more easily than some alternatives. Remote access through components is easier to maintain than direct database access, because the component code can shield the client from database schema changes.

Portable components (not classes)

Until recently, if you wanted to share your business services with another application developer, you were forced to share classes or at least packages. Java did not allow for the easy creation of enterprise components, reusable software building blocks that can be assembled with other components to form an application. EJBs allow you to package your business logic into a tidy, distributable unit that can be shared in a loosely coupled fashion. The user of your component need only tweak a descriptor file for her environment.

Applications relying on asynchronous messaging

EJBs (specifically MDBs) provide a strong technology for handling asynchronous communication such as JMS-based messaging or web services.

Security roles

If your application's business operations can be mapped to specific business roles in your enterprise, then EJBs may be a good choice. So much is made of the transaction management capability of EJBs that their deployment-descriptor–based security management features are overlooked. This capability is very powerful; if your application's users fit into distinct roles and the rules for those roles dictate which users can write what data, EJBs are a good choice.

When Not to Use EJBs

There are several situations in building a software application—even an "enterprise" software application—in which using EJBs may actually be a barrier to meeting your business goals. The following list represents places where you might not want to use EJBs:

Read-mostly applications

If your application requires only (or even mostly) database reads (as opposed to writes), then the added complexity and performance overhead of EJBs may be unwarranted. If your application is only reading and presenting data, you should go with straight JDBC (see below) or another persistence mechanism. That said, if your application's writes (database update and inserts) require transactional support (especially if those transactions go over multiple systems), then EJBs may be the way to go—at least for the write portion of the application.

Applications requiring thread control

If your application design requires extensive use of threads, then the EJB spec actually prevents you from using EJBs (although some EJB container vendors may provide nonportable ways around this restriction). Container systems manage resources, transactions, security, and other qualities of service using threads; threads you create are outside of the container's control and can potentially cause system failures. Also, EJB containers may distribute EJBs across multiple JVMs, preventing the synchronization of threads.

Performance

Because EJBs do so much more than plain Java classes, they are slower than plain Java classes. The EJB container has to do a lot: maintain transactional integrity, manage bean instances and the bean pools, enforce security roles, manage resources and resource pools, coordinate distributed operations, synchronize shared services (if the vendor offers clustering capabilities), and so on. The security and transactional management operations can have a significant impact on the performance of method calls (on both local and remote interfaces). If you require real-time or near-real-time performance characteristics, EJB may not be your best choice.

Alternatives to EJB

There are several alternatives to EJB; some of them are growing in popularity and maturity. EJBs still rank as the de facto standard for enterprise transactional needs, but some of the alternatives, like JDO, are also available.

JDBC

The first (and likely most common) alternative to using EJB is to write straight JDBC functions. While EJB provides you with many niceties, there are situations in which JDBC makes more sense. The simplest case is when your application is only reading (and not writing) data from a database table in a row-column format (list displays, for example). In this scenario, using EJB would not only be more complex but also quite a bit slower than straight JDBC.

If you are writing only simple rows of data without parent-child or foreign key relationships it may be better to use JDBC—especially if your application is built for a single user working with a single database or multiple users using a single database with little chance of contention while writing (relatively rare writes). This case is a little more ambiguous, because you are writing as well as reading data. But if the way you're using the database is simple, JDBC may end up being easier.

However, there is one scenario in which people often go with JDBC when EJB might make their lives easier. Say that you have no need of transactional support and the data with which you are interacting does not involve parent-child or foreign key relationships, but you still need to represent that data as an object (potentially in relation to other objects that also represent data). To be more specific, suppose your application handles only contact management. The application may not write data very often and there may be little need for the transactional support or security provided by EJB. However, your application needs to represent contacts (and their affiliated phone numbers, addresses, and so on) as business objects. The ease with which EJB can help you represent this data as business objects, specifically as entity beans, may save a great deal of time.

The situations in which straight JDBC is preferable to EJB are not concrete. You should use straight JDBC when the need for speed outweighs the need for transactional support or security provided by EJB. Here's a simple example that uses JDBC:

```
import java.sql.*;

public class JDBCExample {

 public static void main(java.lang.String[] args) {
   try {
     // Load driver
     Class.forName("sun.jdbc.odbc.JdbcOdbcDriver");
   }
   catch (ClassNotFoundException e) {
     System.out.println("Cannot load driver.");
     return;
   }

   try {
     // Connect to database.
     Connection con = DriverManager.getConnection("jdbc:odbc:contactdb",
            "", "");

     // Create SQL Statement and execute.
     Statement stmt = con.createStatement(  );
     ResultSet rs = stmt.executeQuery("SELECT name FROM contacts");

     // Display the SQL Results.
     while(rs.next( )) {
       System.out.println(rs.getString("name"));
     }

     // Release database resources.
     rs.close( );
     stmt.close( );
     con.close( );

     }
     catch (SQLException se) {
       // Display error message upon exception.
       System.out.println("SQL Exception: " + se.getMessage(  ));
       se.printStackTrace(System.out);
      }
    }
}
```

JDBC is very straightforward; it allows you to access your data repository directly. However, you must understand a fair amount of the underlying mechanics in order to use it (SQL, database connection properties, and so on). Now, in a "real" application using JDBC, you centralize most of this code into a few classes, but you still must write all the SQL yourself.

Java Data Objects

Java Data Objects or JDO is a recent Sun specification for database persistence and access with Java. According to the JDO specification (JSR 12), its objectives are:

> ...first, to provide application programmers a transparent Java-centric view of persistent information, including enterprise data and locally stored data; and second, to enable pluggable implementations of data stores into application servers.

This description sounds very similar to the objectives laid out for JDBC or EJB. Why another specification to allow for database connectivity and use? For one thing, after setting up a mapping file, you need not deal with database information again; you can access data as you would access Java objects. You can edit and delete data using a "persistence manager" (more on this in a moment) that insulates you from having to deal directly with the SQL involved.

But EJB does these things as well. Once you have set up your EJB and created a suitable descriptor file, you deal with the data through the use of the objects representing the data (as opposed to through result sets as in JDBC, for example). However, JDO allows for a simpler mapping (JDO mapping files are simpler than EJB descriptor files); in addition, there's no mucking about with remote and home interfaces. JDO classes look like any other classes.

There are six basic steps to using JDO in your applications:

1. Create a Java class that represents the underlying database business entity.
2. Create a metadata file containing information about the fields of your Java class. This metadata file can contain data about your already existing database, or not. If it does not, you can run a schema builder that looks at this object and generates the SQL for the database generation.
3. Compile your Java to a `.class` file.
4. Run the JDO enhancer against your metadata file. The enhancer grabs your class name from the metadata file and uses it to grab the compiled `.class` file. The enhancer then modifies the `.class` file—at the bytecode level—to implement JDO's `PresistenceCapable` interface.*

* The use of an implementation-specific JDO enhancer to modify your compiled class at the bytecode level is still debated often in the JDO community. The specification does not force this implementation. You can also simply modify your Java class to implement the `PersistenceCapable` interface yourself.

5. Run the JDO schema builder* against your metadata file and the (now modified) `.class` file for your Java class. The schema builder generates DDL SQL that you can use to create the database objects required for your newly modified JDO class. (Optional)
6. Create an application that uses your Java class. This application will use the `PersistenceManagerFactory` and `PersistenceManager` classes from your JDO implementation. These two classes are your handlers for interacting with your newly created class file.

The best way to demonstrate this process is through a brief example. We'll create a very simple `Contact` class and uses JDO to persist it to a database. We use the LIBeLIS LiDO JDO implementation (community edition). In this implementation, the generation of a database schema involves the use of a separate application from the JDO enhancer:

```
package com.oreilly.ejb.jdoexample;

public class SimpleContact {
    public String name;
    public String ssn;

    public AddressImpl(String pName, String pSsn){
        this.name = pName;
                this.ssn = pSsn;
    }

    public String getName( ) {
        return this.name;
    }

    public String getSsn( ) {
        return this.ssn;
    }

    public void setName(String pName) {
        this.name = pName;
    }

    public void setSsn(String pSsn) {
        this.ssn = pSsn;
    }
}
```

The `SimpleContact` class contains no details on how the information will be persisted to the database, nor the fact that it will implement the `PersistenceCapable` interface.

* In some JDO implementations, the schema builder is just a side effect of the enhancer. In these implementations, you must specify a command-line parameter to tell the enhancer to generate schema generation SQL (rather than run a separate schema builder application).

Next, we create a metadata file for SimpleContact, called *SimpleContact.jdo*:

```
<?xml version="1.0" encoding="UTF-8"?>
<!DOCTYPE jdo SYSTEM "file:/c:/work/jdo.dtd">
<jdo>
   <package name="com.oreilly.ejb.jdoexample">
      <class name="SimpleContact" identity-type="datastore">
      </class>
   </package>
</jdo>
```

This code is pretty straightforward. The metadata points to the location of the JDO DTD (which you can get from your implementation), the package name for your class, and the name of the class itself.

We'll assume you compile your *SimpleContact.java* file to *SimpleContact.class*. Now you must "enhance" the *SimpleContact.class* file so that it implements the JDO PersistenceCapable interface like so:

```
java com.libelis.lido.Enhance -metadata SimpleContact.jdo
```

This command reads the *SimpleContact.jdo* file, uses it to find *SimpleContact.class*, and modifies its bytecodes to implement the JDO PersistenceCapable interface. Next, you can build a schema like this:*

```
java com.libelis.lido.ds.jdbc.DefineSchema
     -driver org.gjt.mm.mysql.Driver
     -database jdbc:mysql://localhost/jdoexample
     -metadata metadata.jdo
```

This generates a series of SQL files (not shown) that you can use to generate the database for your SimpleContact data. All that's left is to create an application that allows you to use your new persistent object. The following class allows you add a new SimpleContact instance to the database:

```
package com.oreilly.ejb.jdoexample;

import javax.jdo.PersistenceManagerFactory;
import javax.jdo.PersistenceManager;
import javax.jdo.Transaction;

public class Test1 {
    public static final String DBURL = "jdbc:mysql://localhost/jdoexample";
    public static final String DBDRIVER = "org.gjt.mm.mysql.Driver";

    public static void main(String[] args) {
        try {
            // Use a factory class to generate PersistenceManager.
            // You are using the LIBeLIS JDO implementation
            // of the PersistenceManagerFactory and PersistenceManager
```

* There are several details carefully ignored here so as not to interfere with the JDO example. For example, we will not cover the setup of the MySQL JDBC driver or MySQL itself.

```
            // classes.
            PersistenceManagerFactory pmf = (PersistenceManagerFactory)
              Class.forName("com.libelis.lido.PersistenceManagerFactory")
                   .newInstance( );
            pmf.setConnectionURL(DBURL);
            pmf.setConnectionDriverName(DBDRIVER);
            PersistenceManager pm = pmf.getPersistenceManager( );

            // Grab the current transaction.
            Transaction t = pm.currentTransaction( );

            // Start a new transaction
            t.begin( );

            SimpleContact a =
            new SimpleContact("Gern Blanston", "222334444");
            pm.makePersistent(a);
            // Commit the transaction.
            // All changes made between the begin and
            // commit are persisted to the DB.
            t.commit( );

            pm.close( );
        } catch (Exception e) {
            e.printStackTrace( );
        }
    }
}
```

You start by instantiating a `PersistenceManagerFactory`, which then generates a `PersistenceManager` for your use. Finally, you create an instance of our `SimpleContact` class and then tell the `PersistenceManager` to write it (by committing the transaction begun earlier.

There is much more to JDO than this very simple example demonstrates (such as editing, deleting, and querying using the JDO query language). For more information about JDO, see *Java Data Objects*, by David Jordan and Craig Russell (O'Reilly). JDO is worth investigating, especially if you have no need for the extra transactional and security features provided by EJB.

While JDO is an alternative to EJB, the context in which it is used must be seriously considered. EJB is designed for high-traffic transaction-centric systems. These types of applications are not a very good fit for JDO because it doesn't have the enterprise level support for transactions, security, clustering and sessions that EJB does. Smaller systems can frequently be built using JDO, but really big systems are best left to EJB.

Others

There are, of course, other alternatives to EJB than straight JDBC and JDO. Here are a few worth reviewing for suitability, should you determine that your application does not require EJB or that certain requirements (speed, for example) demand an alternative approach.

Castor JDO[*] *(http://www.exolab.org)*
: While Castor JDO contains the word "JDO," Exolabs built it independently from Sun's specification. Like JDO, its primary function is to perform data binding. Castor generates Java class source files from an XML schema document that describes the XML data model of an object. You can instantiate objects of these classes directly from XML documents, if those documents conform to the original XML schema. However, the conversion of an XML document into an object instance is only half of what Castor provides; it can also turn an object instance back into an XML document. Conversion from object to XML document is called *marshalling*, and it's Castor's original focus. In addition, Castor has the ability to map objects to database tables through mapping files very similar to those for JDO.

Hibernate (http://www.hibernate.org)
: Hibernate is another Java class-to-database table mapping project. While JDO is designed for mapping Java objects to relational or object-oriented data stores, Hibernate is specifically designed for object relational (OR) mapping. It allows you to create straight Java classes and a database-mapping file (by hand or automatically, using XDoclet tags or something similar). The mechanics of interacting with the database are similar to those of JDO, but with slightly different manager objects (sessions and connections instead of managers, etc.). This is gross oversimplification of all that Hibernate will do, but suffice it to say that Hibernate is functionally equivalent to something like JDO, which maps Java objects to database entities through an XML mapping file and handles the persistence machinery for you. Take a look at Hibernate instead of EJB if you are considering JDO, as the two are similar and fit in similar situations.

Prevayler (http://www.prevayler.org)
: Prevayler approached data binding from a very different perspective, one that does not rely on mappings. Prevayler is all about speed. It uses a fairly old idea: keep all your data in RAM throughout the life of your application and write your data en masse to the database from time to time. This approach makes accessing database information much faster (mostly because you are accessing RAM instead of the database after your data is loaded into memory). Where would it make sense to use Prevayler? The most effective target for something like Prevayler is a single-user database application when storage of database changes can be

[*] Castor JDO was developed and useful before Sun's JDO spec. There is some debate as to whether "JDO" should be used with Castor or not, but this seems too contrived to some extent to build support for Sun's JDO. While Castor JDO is still useful, the debate as to whether it constitutes "real" JDO has led to a decline in its acceptance in some circles.

non-realtime. It is also appropriate for read-only "static" systems in which the data is mostly unchanging.

As you can see, there are several alternatives to EJB. If your application doesn't need the complexity or some of the features of EJB, take a look around. Data persistence with Java has been around for some time and there is a wide assortment of approaches.

Wrapping Up

The main purpose of this book is to teach you how to use the Enterprise JavaBeans components and APIs as opposed to design and architecture of enterprise systems. Although this chapter has focused on design considerations and alternatives to EJB,it is not a comprehensive or complete treatment of architecture or design—that requires an entire book dedicated to that subject.

There are a number of books that we feel complement this chapter and will extend your understanding of design and architecture of EJB and J2EE systems. Chief among them is *Core J2EE Patterns: Best Practices and Design Strategies*, Second Edition by Deepak Alur, et al. (Addison-Wesley), and *Patterns of Enterprise Application Architecture* by Martin Fowler (Addison-Wesley). These books are excellent resources for a more in-depth understanding of design and architecture issues. That said, these books provide only shallow or no discussion of the EJB APIs, life cycles, deployment and components. To master those topics, critical during development, you'll need this book.

PART II

JBoss Workbook

Introduction

This workbook is designed to be a companion for O'Reilly's *Enterprise JavaBeans,* Fourth Edition, by Richard Monson-Haefel, for users of JBoss™, an open-source J2EE™ application server. The goal of this workbook is to provide step-by-step instructions for installing, configuring, and using JBoss, and for deploying and running the examples from *Enterprise JavaBeans*.

This workbook is based on the production release of JBoss 4.0 and includes all the EJB 2.0 examples from the *Enterprise JavaBeans*, Fourth Edition book. All the examples in this workbook will work properly with JBoss 4.0 and above, but not with earlier versions of JBoss.

Contents of the JBoss Workbook

The workbook is divided into three sections:

JBoss Installation and Configuration
: Walks you through downloading, installing, and configuring JBoss. Also provides a brief overview of the structure of the JBoss installation.

Exercises
: Contains step-by-step instructions for downloading, building, and running the example programs in *Enterprise JavaBeans*, Fourth Edition (for brevity, this workbook calls it "the EJB book"). The text also walks through the various deployment descriptors and source code to point out JBoss features and concerns.

Appendix
: Provides useful information that did not fit neatly in the other sections, including a collection of XML snippets for configuring a few popular JDBC drivers from various database vendors.

The workbook text for each exercise depends on the amount of configuration required for the example program, but generally also include s instructions on:

- Compiling and building the example code
- Deploying the EJB components to the application server
- Running the example programs and evaluating the results

The exercises were designed to be built and executed in order. Every effort was made to remove any dependencies between exercises by including all components each one needs in the directory for that exercise, but some dependencies still exist. The workbook text will guide you through these where they arise.

Also note that this workbook is not intended to be a course on database configuration or design. The exercises have been designed to work out-of-the-box with the open-source database Hypersonic SQL, which is shipped with JBoss, and the application server creates all database tables automatically, at run time.

Online Resources

This workbook is designed for use with the EJB book and with downloadable example code, both available from our web site:

http://www.oreilly.com/catalog/entjbeans4/workbooks/index.html

We will post any errata here, and any updates required to support changes in specifications or products. This site also contains links to many popular EJB-related sites on the Internet.

We hope you find this workbook useful in your study of Enterprise JavaBeans and the JBoss open source J2EE implementation. Comments, suggestions, and error reports on the text of this workbook or the downloaded example files are welcome and appreciated. Please post on the JBoss Forum:

http://www.jboss.org/index.html?module=bb&op=viewforum&f=152

In order to obtain more information about JBoss or the JBoss project, visit the project's web site:

http://www.jboss.org/

There you will find links to detailed JBoss documentation, online forums, and events happening in the JBoss community. You will also be able to obtain detailed information on JBoss training, support, and consulting services.

JBoss, Inc. has also produced books on JBoss and other J2EE standards, among them *JBoss Administration and Development* by Marc Fleury and Scott Stark, and *JMX: Managing J2EE with Java Management Extensions* by Marc Fleury and Juha Lindfors.

Acknowledgments

We would like to thank Marc Fleury, the founder of JBoss, for recommending us for this book and Richard Monson-Haefel for accepting the recommendation. We would also like to thank Greg Nyberg, the author of the WebLogic edition in this series of workbooks. The example programs he provided in his workbook were a great starting place for us and made our lives much easier.

Special thanks also go out to those who reviewed and critiqued this work: the members of JBoss Inc., Daniel Ruflé, and Thomas Laresch. We would like to publicly recognize the series editor, Brian Christeson, for his courage and bravery for digging so deeply in this book and relentlessly hunting down our anglish misthakes (especially Sacha's Franco-British dialect).

Finally, Bill would like to thank his wife for putting up with all his whining and complaining, and Sacha promises Sophie that he will no longer use the writing of this workbook as an excuse for being late for any of their rendezvous.

WORKBOOK 1

JBoss Installation and Configuration

This chapter guides you through the steps required to install a fully working JBoss server. Along the way, you will learn about JBoss 4.0's microkernel architecture, and the last section will show you how to install the code for the forthcoming exercises. If you need more detailed information about JBoss configuration, visit the JBoss web site, *http://www.jboss.org*, where you will find comprehensive online documentation.

About JBoss

JBoss is a collaborative effort of a worldwide group of developers to create an open source application server based on the Java 2 Platform, Enterprise Edition (J2EE). With more than five million downloads in the last two years, JBoss is the leading J2EE application server.

JBoss implements the full J2EE stack of services:

- EJB (Enterprise JavaBeans)
- JMS (Java Message Service)
- JTS/JTA (Java Transaction Service/Java Transaction API)
- Servlets and JSP (JavaServer Pages)
- JNDI (Java Naming and Directory Interface)

It also provides advanced features such as clustering, JMX, web services, and IIOP (Internet Inter-ORB Protocol) integration.

Because JBoss code is licensed under the LGPL (GNU Lesser General Public License, see *http://www.gnu.org/copyleft/lesser.txt*), you can use it freely, at no cost, in any commercial application, or redistribute it as is.

Installing JBoss Application Server

Before going any further, make sure you have the J2SE JDK 1.4 or higher installed and correctly configured.

To download the JBoss binaries, go to the JBoss web site at *http://www.jboss.org* and follow the Downloads link. There you will find all current binaries in both *zip* and *tar.gz* archive formats. Download the package that best meets your needs.

Extract the downloaded archive in the directory of your choice. Under Windows, you can use the *WinZip* utility to extract the archive content. Under Unix, you can use the following commands:

```
$ gunzip jboss-4.0.tar.gz
$ tar xf jboss-4.0.tar
```

Then change to the *$JBOSS_HOME/bin* directory and launch the run script that matches your OS:

Unix:

```
$ run.sh
```

Windows:

```
C:\jboss-4.0\bin>run.bat
```

That's it! You now have a fully working JBoss server!

Discovering the JBoss Directory Structure

Installing JBoss creates the directory structure shown in Figure W-1.

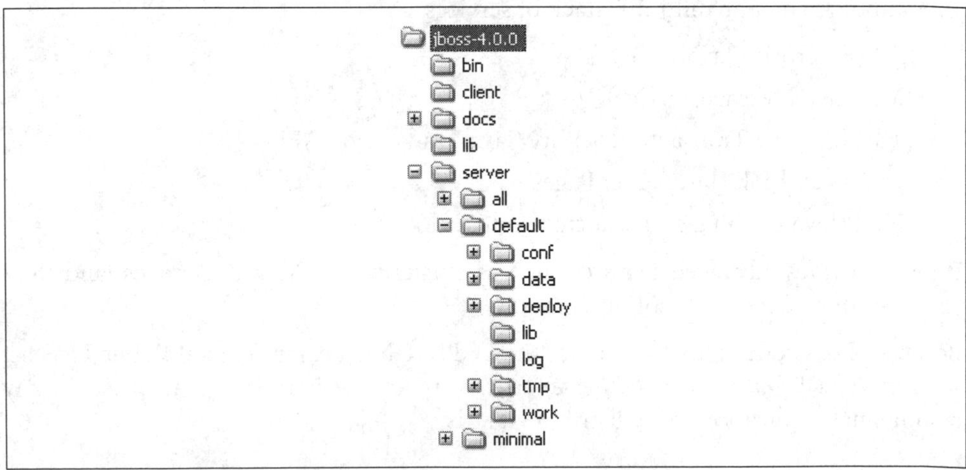

Figure W-1. JBoss directory structure

Table W-1 describes the purposes of the various directories.

Table W-1. JBoss directories

Directory	Description
bin	Scripts to start and shut down JBoss.
client	Client-side Java libraries (JARs) required to communicate with JBoss.
docs	Sample configuration files (for database configuration, etc.)
docs/dtd	DTDs (Document Type Definitions) for the various XML files used in JBoss.
lib	JARs loaded at startup by JBoss and shared by all JBoss configurations. (You won't put your own libraries here.)
server	Various JBoss configurations. (Each configuration must be in a different subdirectory. The name of the subdirectory represents the name of the configuration. As distributed, JBoss contains three configurations: minimal, default, and all.)
server/all	JBoss's complete configuration; starts all services, including clustering and IIOP.
server/minimal	JBoss's minimal configuration; starts only very basic services; cannot be used to deploy EJBs.
server/default	JBoss's default configuration; used when no configuration name is specified on JBoss command line.
server/default/conf	JBoss's configuration files. (You will learn more about the content of this directory in the next section.)
server/default/data	JBoss's database files (embedded database or JBossMQ, for example).
server/default/deploy	JBoss's hot-deployment directory. (Any file or directory dropped in this directory is automatically deployed in JBoss: EJBs, WARs, EARs, and even services.)
server/default/lib	JARs that JBoss loads at startup when starting this particular configuration. (The all and minimal configurations also have this directory and the next two.)
server/default/log	JBoss's logfiles.
server/default/tmp	JBoss's temporary files.

If you want to define your own configuration, create a new sub-directory under the *server* directory containing the appropriate files. To start JBoss with a given configuration, use the `-c` parameter on the command line:

Windows:

```
C:\jboss-4.0\bin> run.bat -c config-name
```

Unix:

```
$ ./run.sh -c config-name
```

JBoss Configuration Files

As the previous section described, JBoss's *server* directory can contain any number of directories, each representing a different JBoss configuration.

The *server/config-name/conf* directory contains JBoss's configuration files. The purpose of the various files is discussed in Table W-2.

Table W-2. JBoss configuration files

File	Description
jacorb.properties	JBoss IIOP configuration.
jbossmq-state.xml	JBossMQ (JMS implementation) user configuration.
jboss-service.xml	Definition of JBoss's services launched at startup (class loaders, JNDI, deployers, etc.).
log4j.xml	Log4J logging configuration.
login-config.xml	JBoss security configuration (JBossSX).
standardjaws.xml	Default configuration for JBoss's legacy CMP 1.1 engine; contains JDBC-to-SQL mapping information for various databases, default CMP settings, logging configuration, etc.
standardjboss.xml	Default container configuration.
standardjbosscmp-jdbc.xml	Same as *standardjaws.xml* except that it is used for JBoss's CMP 2.0 engine.

Deployment in JBoss

The deployment process in JBoss is straightforward. In each configuration, JBoss constantly scans a specific directory for changes: *$JBOSS_HOME/server/config-name/deploy*. This directory is generally referred to informally as the *deploy directory*.

You can copy to this directory:

- Any JAR library (the classes it contains are automatically added to the JBoss classpath)
- An EJB JAR
- A WAR (Web Application aRrchive)
- An EAR (Enterprise Application aRchive)
- An XML file containing JBoss MBean definitions
- A directory ending in *.jar*, *.war*, or *.ear* and containing respectively the extracted content of an EJB JAR, a WAR, or an EAR

To *redeploy* any of the above files (JAR, WAR, EAR, XML, etc.), simply overwrite it with a more recent version. JBoss will detect the change by comparing the files' timestamps, undeploy the previous files, and deploy their replacements. To redeploy a directory, update its modification timestamp by using a command-line utility such as *touch*. To *undeploy* a file, just remove it from the deploy directory.

A Quick Look at JBoss Internals

Since Version 3.0, JBoss has been built around a few very powerful concepts that allow users to customize and fine-tune their servers for very specific needs, not limited to J2EE. This flexibility allows JBoss to be used in very different environments, ranging from embedded systems to very large server clusters. The next few sections comment on some of these concepts briefly.

Microkernel Architecture

JBoss is based on a microkernel design in which components can be plugged at runtime to extend its behavior.

This design fits particularly well with the J2EE platform, which is essentially a service-based platform. The platform contains services for persistence, transactions, security, naming, messaging, logging, and so on.

Other application servers are generally built as monolithic applications containing all services of the J2EE platform at all times. JBoss takes a radically different approach: each of the services is hot-deployed as a component running on top of a very compact core, called the *JBoss Server Spine* (Figure W-2). Furthermore, users are encouraged to implement their own services to run on top of JBoss.

Consequently, the JBoss application server is not limited to J2EE applications, and indeed is frequently used to build any kind of application requiring a strong and reliable base. For this reason, the JBoss core is also known as the *WebOS*.

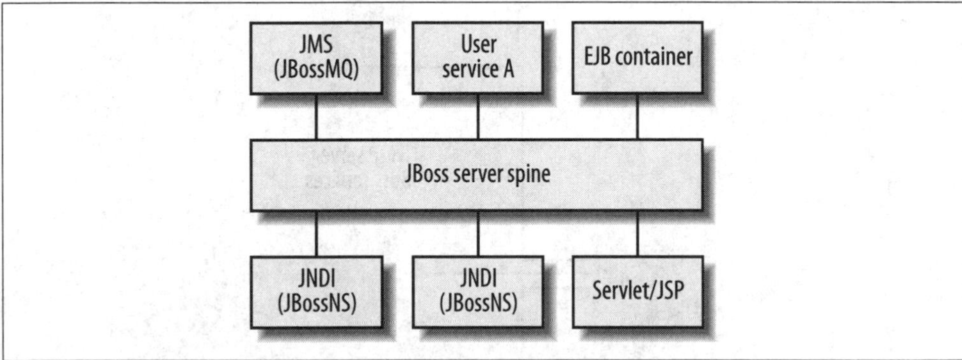

Figure W-2. JBoss Server Spine with some hot-deployed services

JBoss Server Spine itself is based on Sun's Java Management eXtensions (JMX) specification, making any deployed component automatically manageable in a standard fashion. In the JMX terminology, a service deployed in JBoss is called an a *managed bean* (MBean).

More information about the JMX specification can be found at the Sun web site, *http://java.sun.com/products/JavaManagement/*.

Hot Deployment

Since Release 2.0, JBoss has been famous for being the first J2EE-based application server to support hot deployment and redeployment of applications (EJB JAR, WAR, and EAR), while many application servers required a restart to update an application.

Thanks to its microkernel architecture and revolutionary Java class loader, JBoss 3.0 and later releases push this logic further. Not only can they hot-deploy and -redeploy applications, but they can hot-(re)deploy any service and keep track of dependencies between services. These features make JBoss usable in very demanding environments such as telecommunications systems.

Net Boot

JBoss is able to boot itself and your applications from any network location just by pointing the JBoss Server Spine to a simple URL. This allows you to manage the entire configuration of a cluster of JBoss nodes from one central web server. This impressive flexibility makes deployment of new servers very easy (Figure W-3).

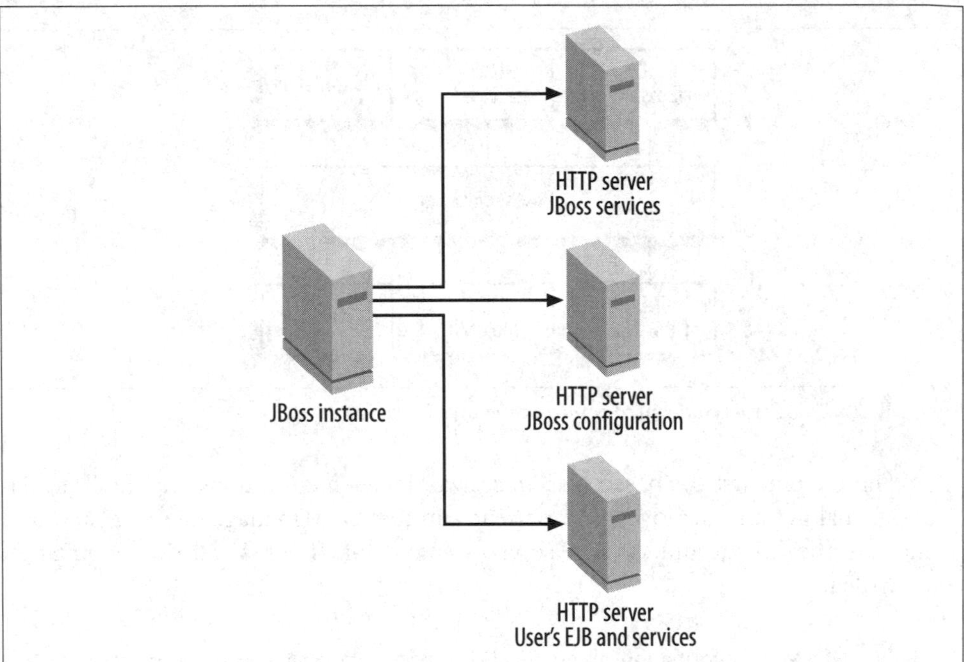

Figure W-3. A JBoss instance bootstrapping from three distinct netboot servers

JBoss's bootstrap code is approximately 50K, which makes it suitable for many embedded systems.

Detached Invokers

JBoss completely detaches the protocol handlers on which invocations are received from the target service that eventually serves the requests. Consequently, when a new handler (called an *invoker* in JBoss) for a given protocol is deployed in JBoss, all existing services and applications can automatically be reached through this new invocation transport. Figure W-4 shows detached invokers.

JBoss 4.0 currently supports the following kinds of invokers:

- RMI
- RMI over HTTP
- IIOP
- JMS
- SOAP
- HA-RMI (Clustering over RMI)

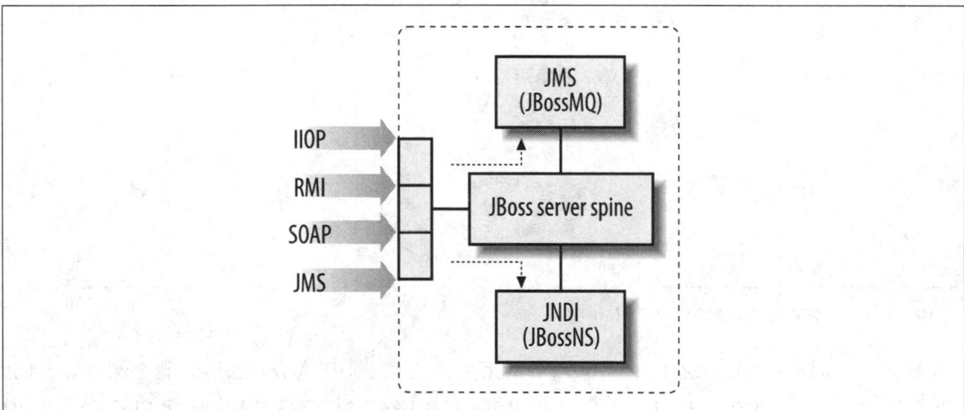

Figure W-4. Detached invokers

Exercise Code Setup and Configuration

You can download the example code for the exercises from *http://www.oreilly.com/catalog/entjbeans4/workbooks/index.html*. Exercises that require a database will use JBoss's default embedded database. Consequently, no additional database setup is required. This workbook includes an Appendix that shows you how to configure JBoss to use a different database, if you want to.

Exercises Directory Structure

The example code is organized as a set of directories, one for each exercise (Figure W-5). You'll find the code of each exercise in the *src/main* subdirectory and the configuration files in *src/resources*.

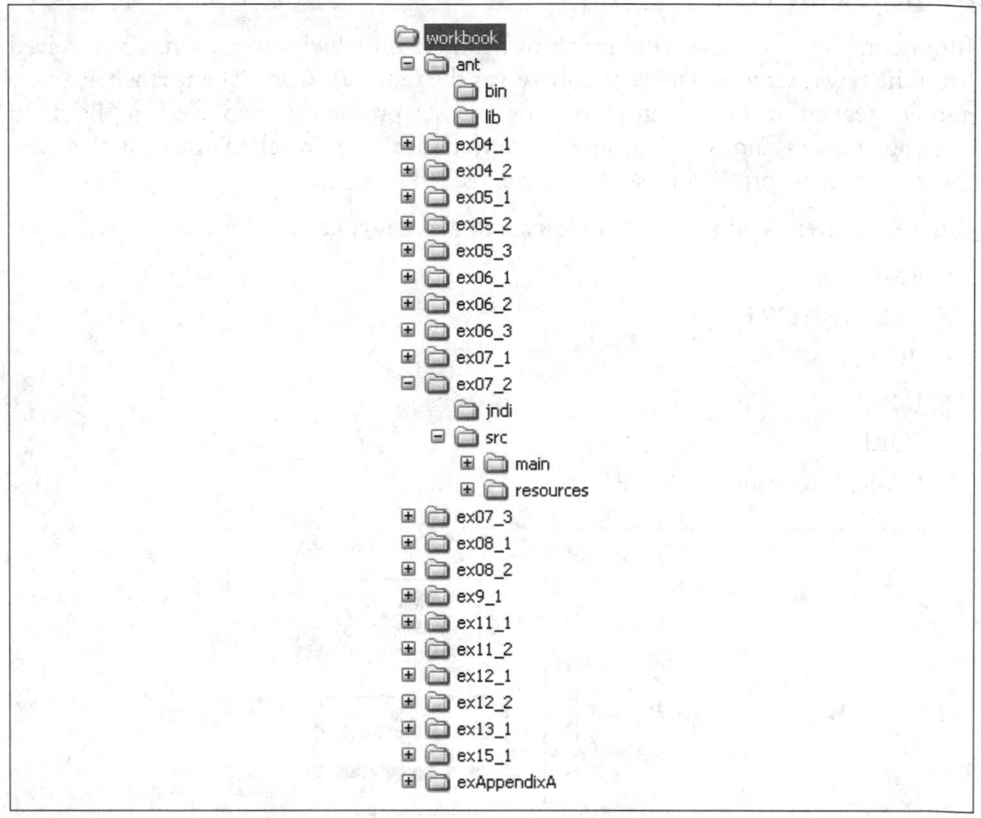

Figure W-5. Exercises directory structure

To build and run the exercises, you'll use the *Ant* tool. A *build.xml* is provided for each exercise. It contains the Ant configuration needed to compile the classes, build the EJB JAR, deploy it to JBoss, and run the client test applications. For this reason, the Ant tool is provided with the exercises and can be found in the *ant* directory.

You can find out more about Ant at the Apache Jakarta web site *http://jakarta.apache.org/ant/*.

Environment Setup

For the Ant scripts to work correctly, first set some environment variables in the shells you will use to run the exercises:

- The `JAVA_HOME` environment variable must point to where your JDK is installed.
- The `JBOSS_HOME` environment variable must point to where JBoss is installed.
- The directory containing the Ant scripts must be in your path.

Depending on your platform, you'll have to execute commands like these:

Windows:

```
C:\workbook\ex04_1> set JAVA_HOME=C:\jdk1.4.2
C:\workbook\ex04_1> set JBOSS_HOME=C:\jboss-4.0
C:\workbook\ex04_1> set PATH=..\ant\bin;%PATH%
```

Unix:

```
$ export JAVA_HOME=/usr/local/jdk1.4.2
$ export JBOSS_HOME=/usr/local/jboss-4.0
$ export PATH=../ant/bin:$PATH
```

In each chapter, you'll find detailed instructions on how to build, deploy, and run the exercises using Ant.

WORKBOOK 2

Exercises for Chapter 4

Exercise 4.1: A Simple Entity Bean

The Cabin EJB demonstrates basic CMP 2.0 capability for a simple entity bean mapped to a single table. The following sections outline the steps necessary to build, deploy, and execute the Cabin EJB example. Please note that because you're using JBoss's default embedded database, you don't need to configure the database or create tables. The code you'll see here mirrors the example code provided in Chapter 4 of the EJB book.

Start Up JBoss

Start up JBoss as described in the *JBoss Installation and Configuration* chapter at the beginning of this workbook.

Initialize the Database

The database table for this exercise will automatically be created in JBoss's default database, HypersonicSQL, when the EJB JAR is deployed.

Build and Deploy the Example Programs

Perform the following steps:

1. Open a command prompt or shell terminal and change to the *ex04_1* directory created by the extraction process.
2. Set the `JAVA_HOME` and `JBOSS_HOME` environment variables to point to where your JDK and JBoss 4.0 are installed. Examples:

   Windows:

   ```
   C:\workbook\ex04_1> set JAVA_HOME=C:\jdk1.4.2
   C:\workbook\ex04_1> set JBOSS_HOME=C:\jboss-4.0
   ```

   Unix:

   ```
   $ export JAVA_HOME=/usr/local/jdk1.4.2
   $ export JBOSS_HOME=/usr/local/jboss-4.0
   ```

3. Add ant to your execution path. Ant is the build utility

   Windows:

   ```
   C:\workbook\ex04_1> set PATH=..\ant\bin;%PATH%
   ```

   Unix:

   ```
   $ export PATH=../ant/bin:$PATH
   ```

4. Perform the build by typing ant. Ant uses *build.xml* to figure out what to compile and how to build your JARs.

If you need to learn more about the Ant utility, visit the Ant project at the Jakarta web site at *http://jakarta.apache.org/ant/index.html*.

Ant compiles the Java source code, builds the EJB JAR, and deploys the JAR simply by copying it to JBoss's *deploy* directory. If you are watching the JBoss console window, you will notice that JBoss automatically discovers the EJB JAR once it has been copied into the *deploy* directory, and automatically deploys the bean.

Another particularly interesting thing about building EJB JARs is that there is no special EJB compilation step. Unlike other servers, JBoss does not generate code for client stubs. Instead, it has a lightweight mechanism that creates client proxies when the EJB JAR is deployed, accelerating the development and deployment cycle.

Deconstructing build.xml

The *build.xml* file provided for each workbook exercise gives the Ant utility information about how to compile and deploy your Java programs and EJBs. The following build tasks can be executed by typing `ant taskname` :

- The default task (just typing ant without a task name) compiles the code, builds the EJB JAR, and deploys the JAR into JBoss. The deployment procedure is just a simple copy into the JBoss *deploy* directory.
- `ant compile` compiles all the Java source files.
- `ant clean` removes all *.class* and *.jar* files from the working directory and undeploys the JAR from JBoss by deleting the file from JBoss's *deploy* directory.
- `ant clean.db` provides you with a clean copy of the HypersonicSQL database used throughout the exercises. This task works only with HypersonicSQL.
- `run.client_xxx` runs a specific example program. Each exercise in this book will have a `run.client` rule for each example program.

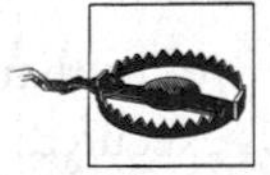

`clean.db` can be used only when JBoss is not running.

Here's a breakdown of what is contained in *build.xml*.

```
<project name="JBoss" default="ejbjar" basedir=".">
```

The default attribute defines the default target that ant will run if you type only ant on the command line. The basedir attribute tells Ant what directory to run the build in:

```
<property environment="env"/>
<property name="src.dir" value="${basedir}/src/main"/>
<property name="src.resources" value="${basedir}/src/resources"/>
<property name="jboss.home" value="${env.JBOSS_HOME}"/>
<property name="build.dir" value="${basedir}/build"/>
<property name="build.classes.dir" value="${build.dir}/classes"/>
```

All the properties defined above are variables that Ant will use throughout the build process. You can see that the JBOSS_HOME environment variable is pulled from the system environment and other directory paths defined:

```
<path id="classpath">
     <fileset dir="${jboss.home}/client">
         <include name="**/*.jar"/>
     </fileset>
  <pathelement location="${build.classes.dir}"/>
  <pathelement location="${basedir}/jndi"/>
</path>
```

To compile and run the example applications in this workbook, add all the JARS in *$JBOSS_HOME/client* to the Java classpath. Also notice that *build.xml* inserts the *${basedir}/jndi* directory into the classpath. A *jndi.properties* file in this directory enables the example programs to find and connect to JBoss's JNDI server:

```
<property name="build.classpath" refid="classpath"/>

<target name="prepare" >
  <mkdir dir="${build.dir}"/>
  <mkdir dir="${build.classes.dir}"/>
</target>
```

The prepare target creates the directories where the Java compiler will place compiled classes:

```
<target name="compile" depends="prepare">
  <javac srcdir="${src.dir}"
         destdir="${build.classes.dir}"
         debug="on"
         deprecation="on"
         optimize="off"
         includes="**">
          <classpath refid="classpath"/>
  </javac>
</target>
```

The compile target compiles all the Java files under the *src/main* directory. Notice that it depends on the prepare target; prepare will run before the compile target is executed:

```
<target name="ejbjar" depends="compile">
  <jar jarfile="build/titan.jar">
    <fileset dir="${build.classes.dir}">
         <include name="com/titan/cabin/*.class"/>
```

```
    </fileset>
    <fileset dir="${src.resources}/">
        <include name="**/*.xml"/>
    </fileset>
  </jar>
  <copy file="build/titan.jar"
        todir="${jboss.home}/server/default/deploy"/>
</target>
```

The ejbjar target creates the EJB JAR file and deploys it to JBoss simply by copying it to JBoss's *deploy* directory:

```
<target name="run.client_41a" depends="ejbjar">
  <java classname="com.titan.clients.Client_1" fork="yes" dir=".">
    <classpath refid="classpath"/>
  </java>
</target>

<target name="run.client_41b" depends="ejbjar">
  <java classname="com.titan.clients.Client_2" fork="yes" dir=".">
    <classpath refid="classpath"/>
  </java>
</target>
```

The run.client_xxx targets are used to run the example programs in this chapter:

```
<target name="clean.db">
  <delete dir="${jboss.home}/server/default/db/hypersonic"/>
</target>
```

The clean.db target cleans the default database used by JBoss for the example programs in this book. Remember, you can only use it when JBoss is not running:

```
<target name="clean">
  <delete dir="${build.dir}"/>
  <delete file="${jboss.home}/server/default/deploy/titan.jar"/>
</target>
</project>
```

The clean target removes compiled classes and undeploys the EJB JAR from JBoss by deleting the JAR file in the *deploy* directory.

Examine the JBoss-Specific Files

You do not need any JBoss-specific files to write a simple EJB. For an entity bean as simple as the Cabin EJB, JBoss creates the appropriate database tables within its embedded database Hypersonic SQL by examining the *ejb-jar.xml* deployment descriptor.

In later chapters, you will learn how to map entity beans to different data sources and pre-existing database tables using JBoss-specific CMP deployment descriptors.

By default, JBoss uses the <ejb-name> from the bean's *ejb-jar.xml* deployment descriptor for the JNDI binding of the bean's home interface. If you do not like this default, you can override it in a *jboss.xml* file. Clients use this name to look up an EJB's home interface. For this example, CabinEJB is bound to CabinHomeRemote.

jboss.xml

```
<jboss>
  <enterprise-beans>
    <entity>
      <ejb-name>CabinEJB</ejb-name>
      <jndi-name>CabinHomeRemote</jndi-name>
    </entity>
  </enterprise-beans>
</jboss>
```

Examine and Run the Client Applications

Two example programs implement the sample clients provided in the EJB book:

Client_1.java
: Creates a single Cabin bean, populates each of its attributes, then queries the created bean with the primary key.

Client_2.java
: Creates 99 additional Cabins with a variety of different data that will be used in subsequent exercises.

Client_1.java

```
package com.titan.clients;

import com.titan.cabin.CabinHomeRemote;
import com.titan.cabin.CabinRemote;

import javax.naming.InitialContext;
import javax.naming.Context;
import javax.naming.NamingException;
import javax.rmi.PortableRemoteObject;
import java.rmi.RemoteException;

public class Client_1
{
   public static void main(String [] args)
   {
      try
      {
         Context jndiContext = getInitialContext();
         Object ref = jndiContext.lookup("CabinHomeRemote");
         CabinHomeRemote home = (CabinHomeRemote)
            PortableRemoteObject.narrow(ref,CabinHomeRemote.class);
         CabinRemote cabin_1 = home.create(new Integer(1));
```

```
            cabin_1.setName("Master Suite");
            cabin_1.setDeckLevel(1);
            cabin_1.setShipId(1);
            cabin_1.setBedCount(3);

            Integer pk = new Integer(1);

            CabinRemote cabin_2 = home.findByPrimaryKey(pk);
            System.out.println(cabin_2.getName());
            System.out.println(cabin_2.getDeckLevel());
            System.out.println(cabin_2.getShipId());
            System.out.println(cabin_2.getBedCount());

         }
         catch (java.rmi.RemoteException re){re.printStackTrace();}
         catch (javax.naming.NamingException ne){ne.printStackTrace();}
         catch (javax.ejb.CreateException ce){ce.printStackTrace();}
         catch (javax.ejb.FinderException fe){fe.printStackTrace();}
      }

      public static Context getInitialContext()
         throws javax.naming.NamingException
      {
         return new InitialContext();
      }
   }
```

The `getInitialContext()` method creates an `InitialContext` with no properties. Because no properties are set, the Java library that implements `InitialContext` searches the classpath for the file *jndi.properties*. Each example program in this workbook will have a *jndi* directory that contains a *jndi.properties* file. You will be executing all example programs through Ant, and it will set the classpath appropriately to refer to this properties file.

Run the *Client_1* application by invoking `ant run.client_41a` at the command prompt. Remember to set your `JBOSS_HOME` and `PATH` environment variables.

The output of *Client_1* should look something like this:

```
C:\workbook\ex04_1>ant run.client_41a
Buildfile: build.xml

prepare:

compile:

ejbjar:

run.client_41a:
     [java] Master Suite
     [java] 1
     [java] 1
     [java] 3
```

Client_1 adds a row to the database representing the Cabin bean and does not delete it at the conclusion of the program. You cannot run this program more than once unless you stop JBoss, clean the database by invoking the Ant task `clean.db` and restarting JBoss. Otherwise, you will get the following error:

```
run.client_41a:
     [java] javax.ejb.DuplicateKeyException: Entity with primary key 1 already exists
     [java]     at org.jboss.ejb.plugins.cmp.jdbc.JDBCCreateEntityCommand.
execute(JDBCCreateEntityCommand.java:160)
     [java]     at org.jboss.ejb.plugins.cmp.jdbc.JDBCStoreManager.
createEntity(JDBCStoreManager.java:633)
     [java]     at org.jboss.ejb.plugins.CMPPersistenceManager.
createEntity(CMPPersistenceManager.java:253)
     [java]     at org.jboss.resource.connectionmanager.CachedConnectionInterceptor.
createEntity(CachedConnectionInterce
...
     [java]     at org.jboss.invocation.InvokerInterceptor.invoke(InvokerInterceptor.
java:92)
     [java]     at org.jboss.proxy.TransactionInterceptor.
invoke(TransactionInterceptor.java:77)
     [java]     at org.jboss.proxy.SecurityInterceptor.invoke(SecurityInterceptor.
java:80)
     [java]     at org.jboss.proxy.ejb.HomeInterceptor.invoke(HomeInterceptor.java:
175)
     [java]     at org.jboss.proxy.ClientContainer.invoke(ClientContainer.java:82)
     [java]     at $Proxy0.create(Unknown Source)
     [java]     at com.titan.clients.Client_1.main(Client_1.java:22)
```

Run the *Client_2* application by invoking `ant run.client_41b` at the command prompt. Remember to set your `JBOSS_HOME` and `PATH` environment variables.

The output of *Client_2* should look something like this:

```
run.client_41b:
     [java] PK=1, Ship=1, Deck=1, BedCount=3, Name=Master Suite
     [java] PK=2, Ship=1, Deck=1, BedCount=2, Name=Suite 100
     [java] PK=3, Ship=1, Deck=1, BedCount=3, Name=Suite 101
     [java] PK=4, Ship=1, Deck=1, BedCount=2, Name=Suite 102
     [java] PK=5, Ship=1, Deck=1, BedCount=3, Name=Suite 103
     [java] PK=6, Ship=1, Deck=1, BedCount=2, Name=Suite 104
     [java] PK=7, Ship=1, Deck=1, BedCount=3, Name=Suite 105
     [java] PK=8, Ship=1, Deck=1, BedCount=2, Name=Suite 106
     ...
     [java] PK=90, Ship=3, Deck=3, BedCount=3, Name=Suite 309
     [java] PK=91, Ship=3, Deck=4, BedCount=2, Name=Suite 400
     [java] PK=92, Ship=3, Deck=4, BedCount=3, Name=Suite 401
     [java] PK=93, Ship=3, Deck=4, BedCount=2, Name=Suite 402
     [java] PK=94, Ship=3, Deck=4, BedCount=3, Name=Suite 403
     [java] PK=95, Ship=3, Deck=4, BedCount=2, Name=Suite 404
     [java] PK=96, Ship=3, Deck=4, BedCount=3, Name=Suite 405
     [java] PK=97, Ship=3, Deck=4, BedCount=2, Name=Suite 406
     [java] PK=98, Ship=3, Deck=4, BedCount=3, Name=Suite 407
     [java] PK=99, Ship=3, Deck=4, BedCount=2, Name=Suite 408
     [java] PK=100, Ship=3, Deck=4, BedCount=3, Name=Suite 409
```

Like *Client_1*, this example creates rows in the database and does not delete them when it finishes. *Client_2* can be executed only once without causing DuplicateKey exceptions.

Managing Entity Beans

Every EJB in JBoss is deployed and managed as a JMX MBean. You can view and manage EJBs deployed within JBoss through your web browser by accessing the JMX management console available at *http://localhost:8080/jmx-console/* (Figure W-6).

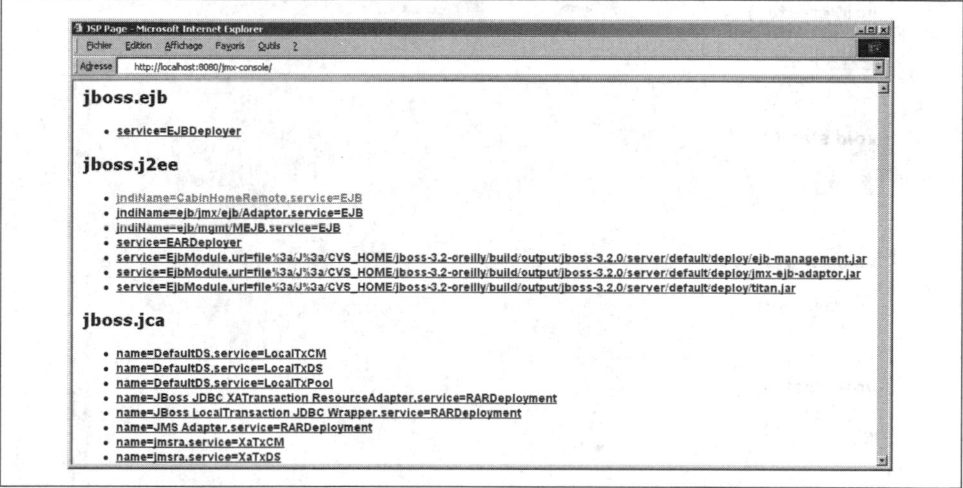

Figure W-6. The JMX management console

Click on the *jndiName=CabinHomeRemote,service=EJB* link shown in Figure W-6. Entity beans have two management functions. You can flush the entity bean's cache or view the number of cached objects for it. To flush, click on the flushCache button. To view the number of cached beans, click on the getCacheSize button (Figure W-7).

Exercise 4.2: A Simple Session Bean

In this exercise, you will create and build the TravelAgent EJB. This simple bean illustrates the use of a stateless session bean and mirrors the code shown in Chapter 4 of the EJB section of this book.

Start Up JBoss

If you already have JBoss running, there is no reason to restart it. Otherwise, start it up as instructed in the *JBoss Installation and Configuration* chapter.

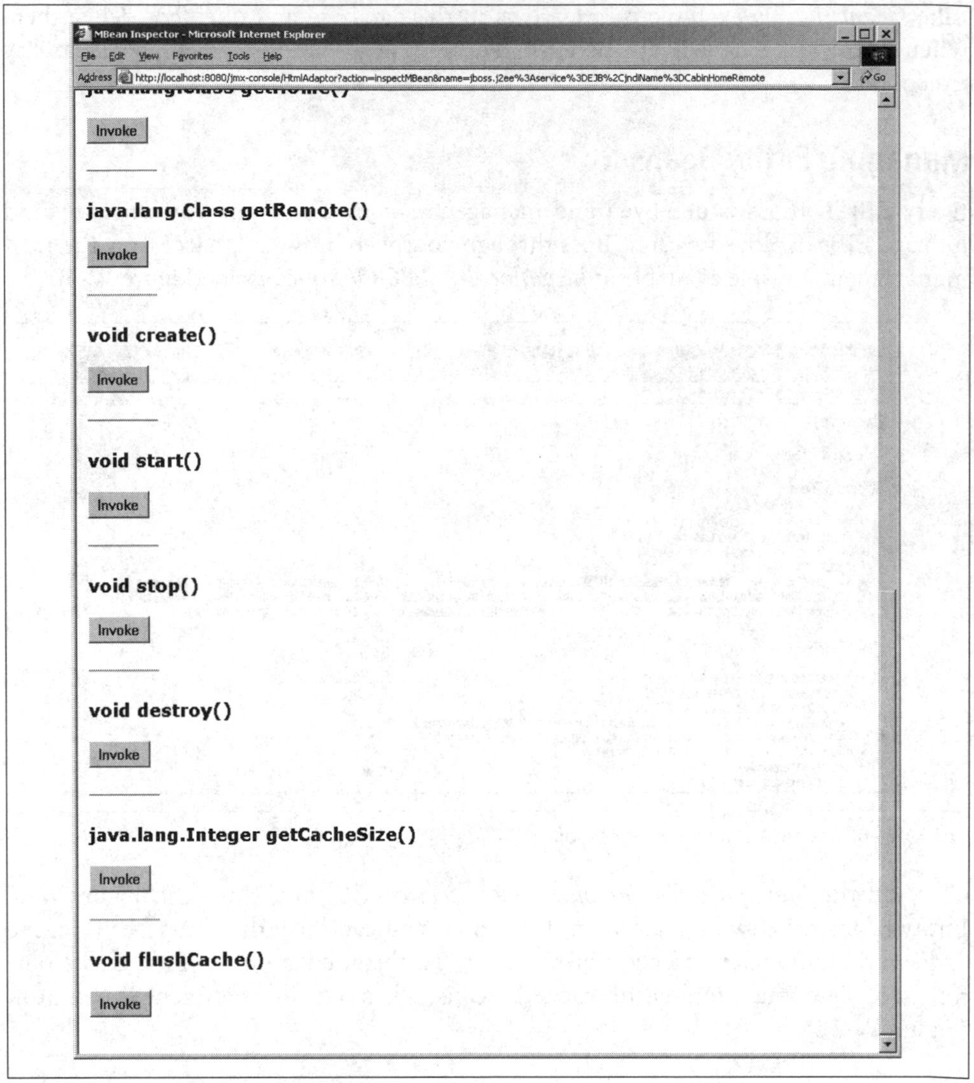

Figure W-7. Managing entity beans from the console

Initialize the Database

The database should contain the 100 rows created by a successful execution of the test programs from the previous exercise, *Client_1* and *Client_2*.

Build and Deploy the Example Programs

Perform the following steps:

1. Open a command prompt or shell terminal and change to the *ex04_2* directory created by the extraction process.
2. Set the JAVA_HOME and JBOSS_HOME environment variables to point to where your JDK and JBoss 4.0 are installed. Examples:

   Windows:

   ```
   C:\workbook\ex04_2> set JAVA_HOME=C:\jdk1.4.2
   C:\workbook\ex04_2> set JBOSS_HOME=C:\jboss-4.0
   ```

   Unix:

   ```
   $ export JAVA_HOME=/usr/local/jdk1.4.2
   $ export JBOSS_HOME=/usr/local/jboss-4.0
   ```

3. Add ant to your execution path. Ant is the build utility.

   Windows:

   ```
   C:\workbook\ex04_2> set PATH=..\ant\bin;%PATH%
   ```

   Unix:

   ```
   $ export PATH=../ant/bin:$PATH
   ```

4. Perform the build by typing ant.

As in the last exercise, you will see *titan.jar* rebuilt, copied to the JBoss *deploy* directory, and redeployed by the application server.

Examine the JBoss-Specific Files

In this example, the *jboss.xml* deployment descriptor overrides the default JNDI binding for the deployed EJBs. CabinEJB is bound to CabinHomeRemote and TravelAgentEJB is bound to TravelAgentHomeRemote.

jboss.xml

```
<jboss>
  <enterprise-beans>
    <entity>
      <ejb-name>CabinEJB</ejb-name>
      <jndi-name>CabinHomeRemote</jndi-name>
    </entity>
    <session>
      <ejb-name>TravelAgentEJB</ejb-name>
      <jndi-name>TravelAgentHomeRemote</jndi-name>
      <ejb-ref>
        <ejb-ref-name>ejb/CabinHomeRemote</ejb-ref-name>
        <jndi-name>CabinHomeRemote</jndi-name>
      </ejb-ref>
    </session>
  </enterprise-beans>
</jboss>
```

The EJB book describes how you must use `<ejb-ref>` declarations when one EJB references another. The TravelAgent EJB references the Cabin entity bean, so the following XML is required in *ejb-jar.xml*.

ejb-jar.xml

```
<ejb-ref>
  <ejb-ref-name>ejb/CabinHomeRemote</ejb-ref-name>
  <ejb-ref-type>Entity</ejb-ref-type>
  <home>com.titan.cabin.CabinHomeRemote</home>
  <remote>com.titan.cabin.CabinRemote</remote>
</ejb-ref>
```

If you have a `<ejb-ref-name>` declared in your *ejb-jar.xml* file, you must have a corresponding `<ejb-ref>` declaration in your *jboss.xml* file that maps the portable JNDI name used by the TravelAgent EJB to the real JNDI name of the Cabin EJB.

jboss.xml

```
<jboss>
  <enterprise-beans>
    <entity>
      <ejb-name>CabinEJB</ejb-name>
      <jndi-name>CabinHomeRemote</jndi-name>
    </entity>
    <session>
      <ejb-name>TravelAgentEJB</ejb-name>
      <jndi-name>TravelAgentHomeRemote</jndi-name>
      <ejb-ref>
       <ejb-ref-name>ejb/CabinHomeRemote</ejb-ref-name>
       <jndi-name>CabinHomeRemote</jndi-name>
      </ejb-ref>
    </session>
  </enterprise-beans>
</jboss>
```

Examine and Run the Client Application

The example program in this section invokes the TravelAgent EJB to list cabins that meet certain criteria.

Client_3.java

```
...
Context jndiContext = getInitialContext();

Object ref = jndiContext.lookup("TravelAgentHomeRemote");
TravelAgentHomeRemote home = (TravelAgentHomeRemote)
   PortableRemoteObject.narrow(ref,TravelAgentHomeRemote.class);
```

```
TravelAgentRemote travelAgent = home.create();

// Get a list of all cabins on ship 1 with a bed count of 3.
String list [] = travelAgent.listCabins(SHIP_ID,BED_COUNT);

for(int i = 0; i < list.length; i++)
{
   System.out.println(list[i]);
}
...
```

The client code does a JNDI lookup for the TravelAgent home and does a simple `create()` method invocation to obtain a reference to a TravelAgent EJB. The client then calls `listCabins()` and receives a list of cabin names that meet the provided criteria.

Let's examine a little of the code in TravelAgent EJB's `listCabins()` method to see how it works.

TravelAgentBean.java

```
public String [] listCabins(int shipID, int bedCount)
{
   try
   {
      javax.naming.Context jndiContext = new InitialContext();
       Object obj =
             jndiContext.lookup("java:comp/env/ejb/CabinHomeRemote");


       CabinHomeRemote home =
   ...
```

When a deployed EJB in JBoss wants to access JNDI, all that's needed is a simple `new InitialContext()`. JBoss will automatically create an optimized, in-process reference to the JNDI server running inside the application server, to avoid the overhead of a distributed network call when accessing it. The rest of `listCabins()` is pretty straightforward, so you can just go on to running the client application.

Run the *Client_3* application by invoking `ant run.client_42` at the command prompt. Remember to set your `JBOSS_HOME` and `PATH` environment variables.

The output of *Client_3* should look something like this:

```
C:\workbook\ex04_2>ant run.client_42
Buildfile: build.xml

prepare:

compile:

ejbjar:
```

```
run.client_42:
     [java] 1,Master Suite,1
     [java] 3,Suite 101,1
     [java] 5,Suite 103,1
     [java] 7,Suite 105,1
     [java] 9,Suite 107,1
     [java] 12,Suite 201,2
     [java] 14,Suite 203,2
     [java] 16,Suite 205,2
     [java] 18,Suite 207,2
     [java] 20,Suite 209,2
     [java] 22,Suite 301,3
     [java] 24,Suite 303,3
     [java] 26,Suite 305,3
     [java] 28,Suite 307,3
     [java] 30,Suite 309,3
```

WORKBOOK 3

Exercises for Chapter 5

Exercise 5.1: The Remote Component Interfaces

The example programs in Exercise 5.1 dive into some of the features of the home interface of an EJB, including the use of the `remove()` method. They also show you how to obtain and use various metadata available through an EJB's API.

Start Up JBoss

If you already have JBoss running, there is no reason to restart it. Otherwise, start it up as instructed in the *JBoss Installation and Configuration* chapter at the beginning of this workbook.

Initialize the Database

The database should contain the 100 rows created by a successful execution of the test programs from Exercise 4.1.

Build and Deploy the Example Programs

Perform the following steps:

1. Open a command prompt or shell terminal and change to the *ex05_1* directory created by the extraction process.
2. Set the `JAVA_HOME` and `JBOSS_HOME` environment variables to point to where your JDK and JBoss 4.0 are installed. Examples:

   Windows:

   ```
   C:\workbook\ex05_1> set JAVA_HOME=C:\jdk1.4.2
   C:\workbook\ex05_1> set JBOSS_HOME=C:\jboss-4.0
   ```

   Unix:

   ```
   $ export JAVA_HOME=/usr/local/jdk1.4.2
   $ export JBOSS_HOME=/usr/local/jboss-4.0
   ```

3. Add ant to your execution path.

   Windows:

   ```
   C:\workbook\ex05_1> set PATH=..\ant\bin;%PATH%
   ```

   Unix:

   ```
   $ export PATH=../ant/bin:$PATH
   ```

4. Perform the build by typing `ant`.

As in the last exercise, you will see *titan.jar* rebuilt, copied to the JBoss *deploy* directory, and redeployed by the application server.

Examine the JBoss-Specific Files

There are no new JBoss configuration files or components in this exercise.

Examine and Run the Client Applications

Two example programs illustrate the concepts explained in the EJB book:

Client_51a.java
: Illustrates the use of the `remove()` method on the Cabin EJB home interface.

Client _51b.java
: Illustrates the use of bean metadata methods.

The example code for *Client_51a* and *Client_51b* is pulled directly from the EJB book. There is no need to go into this code here because the EJB book already does a very good job of that.

Run *Client_51a* by invoking `ant run.client_51a` at the command prompt. Remember to set your `JBOSS_HOME` and `PATH` environment variables. Run *Client_51b* the same way: `ant run.client_51b`. The output of *Client_51a* should be exactly as described in the EJB book. The output of *Client_51b* is as follows:

```
C:\workbook\ex05_1>ant run.client_51b
Buildfile: build.xml

prepare:

compile:

run.client_51b:
     [java] com.titan.cabin.CabinHomeRemote
     [java] com.titan.cabin.CabinRemote
     [java] java.lang.Integer
     [java] false
     [java] Master Suite
```

Note that if you try to run *Client_51a* more than once, an exception will tell you that the entity you're attempting to remove does not exist.

```
[java] java.rmi.NoSuchObjectException: Entity not found: primaryKey=30
```

Exercise 5.2: The EJBObject, Handle, and Primary Key

The example programs in Exercise 5.2 explore the APIs available through the `EJBObject` and `EJBMetaData` interfaces. They also reveal how to use `Handle` and `HomeHandle` as persistent references to EJB objects and homes.

Start Up JBoss

If you already have JBoss running, there is no reason to restart it. Otherwise, start it up as instructed in the *JBoss Installation and Configuration* chapter at the beginning of this workbook.

Initialize the Database

The database should contain the 100 rows created by a successful execution of the test programs from Exercise 4.1; otherwise, this example will not work properly.

Build and Deploy the Example Programs

In the *ex05_2* directory, build and deploy the examples as you did for Exercise 5.1.

Examine the JBoss-Specific Files

There are no new JBoss configuration files or components in this exercise.

Examine and Run the Client Applications

Three example programs illustrate the concepts explained in the EJB book:

Client_52a.java
: Shows the use of `EJBObject` to retrieve an EJB's home interface.

Client _52b.java
: Shows how to use `isIdentical()` to determine whether two EJB references are to the same object.

Client _52c.java
: Shows how to use EJB handles as persistent bean references.

The example code is pulled directly from the EJB book and embellished somewhat to expand on introduced concepts. The EJB book does a pretty good job of explaining the concepts illustrated in the example programs, so further explanation of the code is not needed in this workbook.

Run *Client_52a*, *Client_52b*, and *Client_52c* by invoking the appropriate Ant task as you did in previous examples: `run.client_52a`, `run.client_52b`, and `run.client_52c`. Remember to set your `JBOSS_HOME` and `PATH` environment variables.

Exercise 5.3: The Local Component Interfaces

The example program in Exercise 5.3 explores the use of local interfaces. The Cabin entity bean you created in Exercise 4.1 will be expanded to provide a local interface for use in the TravelAgent stateless session bean. This exercise also describes how to modify your EJB deployment descriptors to enable local interfaces.

Start Up JBoss

If you already have JBoss running, there is no reason to restart it. Otherwise, start it up as instructed in the *JBoss Installation and Configuration* chapter.

Initialize the Database

The database should contain the 100 rows created by a successful execution of the test programs from Exercise 4.1.

Build and Deploy the Example Programs

In the *ex05_3* directory, build and deploy the examples as you did for Exercise 5.1.

Examine the JBoss-Specific Files

JBoss has a minor restriction. It requires that you use `<ejb-link>` when you want your bean to reference a local bean through an `<ejb-local-ref>` tag.

ejb-jar.xml

```
<ejb-jar>
 <enterprise-beans>
    ...
    <session>
     <ejb-name>TravelAgentEJB</ejb-name>
     <home>com.titan.travelagent.TravelAgentHomeRemote</home>
     <remote>com.titan.travelagent.TravelAgentRemote</remote>
     <ejb-class>com.titan.travelagent.TravelAgentBean</ejb-class>
     <session-type>Stateless</session-type>
     <transaction-type>Container</transaction-type>
```

```
    <ejb-local-ref>
      <ejb-ref-name>ejb/CabinHomeLocal</ejb-ref-name>
      <ejb-ref-type>Entity</ejb-ref-type>
      <local-home>com.titan.cabin.CabinHomeLocal</local-home>
      <local>com.titan.cabin.CabinLocal</local>
     <!-- ejb-link is required by jboss for local-refs. -->
     <ejb-link>CabinEJB</ejb-link>
    </ejb-local-ref>
    ...
</ejb-jar>
```

If you examine the *jboss.xml* file for Exercise 5.3, you'll see that you must also declare the JNDI binding for the remote home interface. The Cabin EJB's local home interface doesn't need a binding in *jboss.xml*, though, because the binding information is contained in the `<ejb-link>` tag instead. JBoss will register both `CabinHomeRemote` and `CabinHomeLocal` into the JNDI tree.

jboss.xml

```
<jboss>
  <enterprise-beans>
    <entity>
      <ejb-name>CabinEJB</ejb-name>
      <jndi-name>CabinHomeRemote</jndi-name>
      <local-jndi-name>CabinHomeLocal</local-jndi-name>
    </entity>
```

`TravelAgentEJB` only tells JBoss under which JNDI name it should be bound:

```
    <session>
       <ejb-name>TravelAgentEJB</ejb-name>
       <jndi-name>TravelAgentHomeRemote</jndi-name>
    </entity>
  </enterprise-beans>
</jboss>
```

Examine and Run the Client Applications

The example code for *Client_53* is exactly the same as *Client_3* from Exercise 4.2.

Run *Client_53* by invoking the appropriate Ant task, as you did in previous examples: `run.client_53`. Remember to set your `JBOSS_HOME` and `PATH` environment variables.

The output should look something like this:

```
C:\workbook\ex05_3>ant run.client_53
Buildfile: build.xml

prepare:

compile:

ejbjar:
```

```
run.client_53:
     [java] 1,Master Suite,1
     [java] 3,Suite 101,1
     [java] 5,Suite 103,1
     [java] 7,Suite 105,1
     [java] 9,Suite 107,1
     [java] 12,Suite 201,2
     [java] 14,Suite 203,2
     [java] 16,Suite 205,2
     [java] 18,Suite 207,2
     [java] 20,Suite 209,2
     [java] 22,Suite 301,3
     [java] 24,Suite 303,3
     [java] 26,Suite 305,3
     [java] 28,Suite 307,3
```

WORKBOOK 4

Exercises for Chapter 6

Exercise 6.1: Basic Persistence in CMP 2.0

This exercise begins walking you through the intricacies of CMP 2.0. In this chapter, you will learn more detailed JBoss CMP 2.0 configuration mechanisms by creating the Customer EJB described in the EJB book.

Start Up JBoss

If you already have JBoss running, there is no reason to restart it. Otherwise, start it up as instructed in the *JBoss Installation and Configuration* chapter.

Initialize the Database

The database table for this exercise will automatically be created in JBoss's default database, HypersonicSQL, when the EJB JAR is deployed.

Build and Deploy the Example Programs

Perform the following steps:

1. Open a command prompt or shell terminal and change to the *ex06_1* directory created by the extraction process
2. Set the `JAVA_HOME` and `JBOSS_HOME` environment variables to point to where your JDK and JBoss 4.0 are installed. Examples:

   Windows:

   ```
   C:\workbook\ex06_1> set JAVA_HOME=C:\jdk1.4.2
   C:\workbook\ex06_1> set JBOSS_HOME=C:\jboss-4.0
   ```

   Unix:

   ```
   $ export JAVA_HOME=/usr/local/jdk1.4.2
   $ export JBOSS_HOME=/usr/local/jboss-4.0
   ```

3. Add ant to your execution path.

   Windows:

   ```
   C:\workbook\ex06_1> set PATH=..\ant\bin;%PATH%
   ```

   Unix:

   ```
   $ export PATH=../ant/bin:$PATH
   ```

4. Perform the build by typing ant.

As in the last exercise, you will see *titan.jar* rebuilt, copied to the JBoss *deploy* directory, and redeployed by the application server.

Examine the JBoss-Specific Files

In this section, we introduce a new JBoss CMP 2.0 deployment descriptor, *jbosscmp-jdbc.xml*. This file provides more detailed control of your bean's database mapping as well as more advanced performance-tuning options.

jbosscmp-jdbc.xml

```
<jbosscmp-jdbc>

   <defaults>
      <datasource>java:/DefaultDS</datasource>
      <datasource-mapping>Hypersonic SQL</datasource-mapping>
      <create-table>true</create-table>
      <remove-table>true</remove-table>
   </defaults>

   <enterprise-beans>
      <entity>
         <ejb-name>CustomerEJB</ejb-name>
         <table-name>Customer</table-name>
         <cmp-field>
            <field-name>id</field-name>
            <column-name>ID</column-name>
         </cmp-field>
         <cmp-field>
            <field-name>lastName</field-name>
            <column-name>LAST_NAME</column-name>
         </cmp-field>
         <cmp-field>
            <field-name>firstName</field-name>
            <column-name>FIRST_NAME</column-name>
         </cmp-field>
         <cmp-field>
            <field-name>hasGoodCredit</field-name>
            <column-name>HAS_GOOD_CREDIT</column-name>
         </cmp-field>
      </entity>
   </enterprise-beans>
</jbosscmp-jdbc>
```

The <defaults> section

The <datasource> configuration variable tells JBoss's CMP engine what database connection pool to use for the entity beans defined in this JAR.

```
<datasource>java:/DefaultDS</datasource>
```

It is currently configured to use the default data source defined in *$JBOSS_HOME/server/default/deploy/hsqldb-service.xml*, but you can change it to your own defined data sources. The workbook's Appendix goes into more detail on how to configure your own data sources.

This variable describes the database mapping that CMP should use:

```
<datasource-mapping>Hypersonic SQL</datasource-mapping>
```

Here are some other mappings you could use (this list is not exhaustive):

```
<datasource-mapping>Oracle8</datasource-mapping>
<datasource-mapping>Oracle7</datasource-mapping>
<datasource-mapping>MS SQLSERVER</datasource-mapping>
<datasource-mapping>MS SQLSERVER2000</datasource-mapping>
```

For other available supported database mappings, please review JBoss's advanced documentation on its web site at *http://www.jboss.org*.

When the <create-table> configuration variable is set to true, JBoss creates the database tables for each entity bean defined in the deployment descriptor unless these tables already exist. This create action is triggered when the EJB JAR is deployed:

```
<create-table>true</create-table>
```

When the <remove-table> configuration variable is set to true, JBoss drops the database tables for each entity bean defined in the deployment descriptor. This remove action is triggered when the EJB JAR is redeployed or undeployed:

```
<remove-table>true</remove-table>
```

The <enterprise-beans> section

There's an XML fragment <entity></entity> for each entity bean defined in this EJB JAR. The <ejb-name> variable defines the entity bean that is described in that section:

```
<ejb-name>CustomerEJB</ejb-name>
```

The <table-name> variable defines what database table this entity bean should map to:

```
<table-name>Customer</table-name>
```

Each <cmp-field> section describes the mapping between an entity bean's fields and the corresponding columns of the database table. The <field-name> tag is the entity bean field's name, while the <column-name> defines the table column's name:

```
<cmp-field>
     <field-name>id</field-name>
     <column-name>ID</column-name>
  </cmp-field>
```

Examine and Run the Client Applications

There is only one client application for this exercise, *Client_61*. It is modeled after the example in the EJB book. It creates Customer EJBs in the database based on the command-line parameters.

To run the client, first set your JBOSS_HOME and PATH environment variables appropriately. Then invoke the provided wrapper script to execute the program. For each customer, you must supply on the command line a set of values for primary key, first name, and last name, as shown here:

```
Client_61 777 Bill Burke 888 Sacha Labourey
```

The output of this execution should be:

```
C:\workbook\ex06_1>client_61 777 Bill Burke 888 Sacha Labourey
Buildfile: build.xml

prepare:

compile:

ejbjar:

run.client_61:
     [java] 777 = Bill Burke
     [java] 888 = Sacha Labourey
```

When it finishes, the example program removes the created beans, so no data remains in the database.

Exercise 6.2: Dependent Value Classes in CMP 2.0

The example programs in Exercise 6.2 explore using a dependent value class to combine multiple CMP fields into a single serializable object that can be passed in and out of entity-bean methods.

Start Up JBoss

If you already have JBoss running, there is no reason to restart it.

Initialize the Database

No database initialization is needed.

Build and Deploy the Example Programs

Perform the following steps:

1. Open a command prompt or shell terminal and change to the *ex06_2* directory created by the extraction process
2. Set the JAVA_HOME and JBOSS_HOME environment variables to point to where your JDK and JBoss 4.0 are installed. Examples:

   Windows:

   ```
   C:\workbook\ex06_2> set JAVA_HOME=C:\jdk1.4.2
   C:\workbook\ex06_2> set JBOSS_HOME=C:\jboss-4.0
   ```

   Unix:

   ```
   $ export JAVA_HOME=/usr/local/jdk1.4.2
   $ export JBOSS_HOME=/usr/local/jboss-4.0
   ```

3. Add ant to your execution path.

   Windows:

   ```
   C:\workbook\ex06_2> set PATH=..\ant\bin;%PATH%
   ```

   Unix:

   ```
   $ export PATH=../ant/bin:$PATH
   ```

4. Perform the build by typing ant.

As in the last exercise, you will see *titan.jar* rebuilt, copied to the JBoss *deploy* directory, and redeployed by the application server.

Examine the JBoss-Specific Files

There are no new JBoss configuration files or components in this exercise.

Examine and Run the Client Applications

The example program, *Client_62*, shows how the Name dependent value class is used with the Customer EJB. The example code is pulled directly from the EJB book and embellished somewhat to expand on introduced concepts. The EJB book does a pretty good job of explaining the concepts illustrated in *Client_62*, so further explanation of the code is not needed in this workbook.

The client application uses the new getName() and setName() methods of the Customer EJB to initialize, modify, and display a newly created Customer bean using the Name dependent value class. This test bean is then removed from the database before the application finishes.

To run *Client_62*, invoke the Ant task run.client_62. Remember to set your JBOSS_HOME and PATH environment variables. The output should look something like this:

```
C:\workbook\ex06_2>ant run.client_62
Buildfile: build.xml

prepare:
```

```
compile:

ejbjar:

run.client_62:
     [java] 1 = Richard Monson
     [java] 1 = Richard Monson-Haefel
```

Exercise 6.3: A Simple Relationship in CMP 2.0

The example program in Exercise 6.3 shows how to implement a simple CMP relationship between the Customer EJB and the Address EJB. The client again uses dependent value classes, to pass address information along to the Customer EJB.

Build and Deploy the Example Programs

Perform the following steps:

1. Open a command prompt or shell terminal and change to the *ex06_3* directory created by the extraction process.
2. Set the JAVA_HOME and JBOSS_HOME environment variables to point to where your JDK and JBoss 4.0 are installed. Examples:

   Windows:
   ```
   C:\workbook\ex06_3> set JAVA_HOME=C:\jdk1.4.2
   C:\workbook\ex06_3> set JBOSS_HOME=C:\jboss-4.0
   ```
   Unix:
   ```
   $ export JAVA_HOME=/usr/local/jdk1.4.2
   $ export JBOSS_HOME=/usr/local/jboss-4.0
   ```
3. Add ant to your execution path.

   Windows:
   ```
   C:\workbook\ex06_3> set PATH=..\ant\bin;%PATH%
   ```
   Unix:
   ```
   $ export PATH=../ant/bin:$PATH
   ```
4. Perform the build by typing ant.

As in the last exercise, you will see *titan.jar* rebuilt, copied to the JBoss *deploy* directory, and redeployed by the application server.

Examine the JBoss-Specific Files

The Customer-Address relationship in this example can be mapped to a database table by defining the mapping in *jbosscmp-jdbc.xml*.

jbosscmp-jdbc.xml

```
<jbosscmp-jdbc>
...
</enterprise-beans>
```

```
<relationships>
   <ejb-relation>
      <ejb-relation-name>Customer-Address</ejb-relation-name>
      <foreign-key-mapping/>
      <ejb-relationship-role>
         <ejb-relationship-role-name>Customer-has-a-Address
            </ejb-relationship-role-name>
         <key-fields/>
      </ejb-relationship-role>
      <ejb-relationship-role>
         <ejb-relationship-role-name>Address-belongs-to-Customer
            </ejb-relationship-role-name>
         <key-fields>
            <key-field>
               <field-name>id</field-name>
               <column-name>HOME_ADDRESS</column-name>
            </key-field>
          </key-fields>
       </ejb-relationship-role>
    </ejb-relation>
</relationships>
</jbosscmp-jdbc>
```

To define the mapping of a relationship to a database table, you must define `<key-fields>`. The `<field-name>` tag must be the primary key field of the entity bean in the relationship. Thus above, the `id` `<field-name>` corresponds to the Address EJB's primary key field. You can define the `<column-name>` field to be whatever the column name is in the database. Based on the mappings defined in this file, the Customer table would look like this:

```
CREATE TABLE CUSTOMER
(ID INTEGER NOT NULL,
LAST_NAME VARCHAR(256),
FIRST_NAME VARCHAR(256),
HAS_GOOD_CREDIT BIT NOT NULL,
HOME_ADDRESS INTEGER,
CONSTRAINT PK_CUSTOMER PRIMARY KEY (ID))
```

For details on more complex optimizations and database-to-relationship mappings, please see the JBoss CMP 2.0 documentation available at *http://www.jboss.org*.

Examine and Run the Client Applications

The example program, *Client_63*, shows how to create a Customer EJB and set the Address relation on that customer.

AddressBean.java

```
public abstract class AddressBean implements javax.ejb.EntityBean
{
   private static final int IDGEN_START =
                                (int)System.currentTimeMillis();
   private static int idgen = IDGEN_START;
```

```
    public Integer ejbCreateAddress (String street, String city,
                                     String state,  String zip )
       throws CreateException
    {
       setId(new Integer(idgen++));
       setStreet(street);
       setCity(city);
       setState(state);
       setZip(zip);
       return null;
    }
    ...
}
```

JBoss CMP does have automatic primary-key generation. For this and subsequent examples, though, a very crude ID generator has been created to provide a more predictable mechanism for creating keys. The code just takes the current time in milliseconds at the load of the bean and increments it by one at every `ejbCreate()`. Crude, workable for these examples, but not recommended for real applications.

In order to run *Client_63*, invoke the Ant task `run.client_63`. Remember to set your `JBOSS_HOME` and `PATH` environment variables.

The output should look something like this:

```
C:\workbook\ex06_3>ant run.client_63
Buildfile: build.xml

prepare:

compile:

ejbjar:

run.client_63:
     [java] Creating Customer 1..
     [java] Creating AddressDO data object..
     [java] Setting Address in Customer 1...
     [java] Acquiring Address data object from Customer 1...
     [java] Customer 1 Address data:
     [java] 1010 Colorado
     [java] Austin,TX 78701
     [java] Creating new AddressDO data object..
     [java] Setting new Address in Customer 1...
     [java] Customer 1 Address data:
     [java] 1600 Pennsylvania Avenue NW
     [java] DC,WA 20500
     [java] Removing Customer 1...
```

WORKBOOK 5

Exercises for Chapter 7

Exercise 7.1: Entity Relationships in CMP 2.0, Part 1

This exercise walks you through implementing a complex set of interrelated entity beans defined in Chapter 7 of the EJB book.

Start Up JBoss

If JBoss is not running, start it up. If it's already running, there's no reason to restart it.

Initialize the Database

The database table for this exercise will automatically be created in JBoss's default database, HypersonicSQL, when the EJB JAR is deployed.

Build and Deploy the Example Programs

Perform the following steps:

1. Open a command prompt or shell terminal and change to the *ex07_1* directory created by the extraction process
2. Set the JAVA_HOME and JBOSS_HOME environment variables to point to where your JDK and JBoss 4.0 are installed. Examples:

   Windows:

   ```
   C:\workbook\ex07_1> set JAVA_HOME=C:\jdk1.4.2
   C:\workbook\ex07_1> set JBOSS_HOME=C:\jboss-4.0
   ```

   Unix:

   ```
   $ export JAVA_HOME=/usr/local/jdk1.4.2
   $ export JBOSS_HOME=/usr/local/jboss-4.0
   ```

3. Add `ant` to your execution path.

   Windows:

   ```
   C:\workbook\ex07_1> set PATH=..\ant\bin;%PATH%
   ```

   Unix:

   ```
   $ export PATH=../ant/bin:$PATH
   ```

4. Perform the build by typing `ant`.

As in the last exercise, you will see *titan.jar* rebuilt, copied to the JBoss *deploy* directory, and redeployed by the application server.

Examine the JBoss-Specific Files

This chapter introduces no new features in JBoss-specific files. Please review Exercise 6.1 to understand the JBoss-specific files in this example. Also, this chapter implements nonperformance-tuned entity beans and relies on the CMP 2.0 engine to create all database tables. To learn about JBoss's extensive configuration options, please review the advanced CMP 2.0 documentation at *http://www.jboss.org*.

Examine and Run the Client Applications

From this chapter on, we no longer use remote entity bean interfaces (so the example code matches the code illustrated in the EJB section of this book). Accordingly, the Customer EJB switches to local-only interfaces:

- `CustomerHomeRemote` becomes `CustomerHomeLocal`.
- `CustomerRemote` becomes `CustomerLocal`.
- Bean interface methods no longer throw `RemoteExceptions`.
- The *ejb-jar.xml* descriptor changes to use local interfaces. Thus:

  ```
  <ejb-name>CustomerEJB</ejb-name>
  <home>com.titan.customer.CustomerHomeRemote</home>
  <remote>com.titan.customer.CustomerRemote</remote>
  <ejb-class>com.titan.customer.CustomerBean</ejb-class>
  ```

  changes to:

  ```
  <ejb-name>CustomerEJB</ejb-name>
  <local-home>com.titan.customer.CustomerHomeLocal</local-home>
  <local>com.titan.customer.CustomerLocal</local>
  <ejb-class>com.titan.customer.CustomerBean</ejb-class>
  ```

- The JNDI binding in *jboss.xml* changes as well. Thus:

  ```
  <entity>
    <ejb-name>CustomerEJB</ejb-name>
    <jndi-name>CustomerHomeRemote</jndi-name>
  </entity>
  ```

  changes to:

  ```
  <entity>
    <ejb-name>CustomerEJB</ejb-name>
    <local-jndi-name>CustomerHomeLocal</local-jndi-name>
  </entity>
  ```

Because interfaces are now local, the example programs no longer need to use dependent value classes to set up relationships like Customer-Address. This change simplifies the code and allows you to pass local entity beans such as Address, Credit Card, and Phone to Customer EJB methods directly.

Another consequence is that remote clients can no longer invoke business logic on the entity beans implemented in this chapter. Instead, you'll implement all example business logic in the methods of a stateless session bean. Also, EJB containers don't allow the manipulation of a relationship collection (including iteration through the collection) outside the context of a transaction. In JBoss, all bean methods are `Required` by default, so all example test code will run within a transaction. Chapter 16 in the EJB book discusses transactions in more detail.

To execute these examples from the command line, implement separate, distinct remote clients that get a reference to the stateless test bean and invoke the appropriate test method.

Client_71a

The *Client_71a* example program reveals the unidirectional relationship between Customer and Address. The business logic for this example is implemented in `com.titan.test.Test71Bean` in the `test71a()` method.

In `test71a()`, output is written to the `PrintWriter` created below. The method finishes by extracting a `String` from the `PrintWriter` and passing it back to the remote client for display:

```
public String test71a() throws RemoteException
{
   String output = null;
   StringWriter writer = new StringWriter();
   PrintWriter out = new PrintWriter(writer);
   try
   {
```

The first part of `test71a()` simply fetches the home interfaces of Customer and Address from JNDI. It then creates both a Customer and an Address:

```
InitialContext jndiContext = getInitialContext();
Object obj = jndiContext.lookup("CustomerHomeLocal");
CustomerHomeLocal customerhome = (CustomerHomeLocal)obj;

obj = jndiContext.lookup("AddressHomeLocal");
AddressHomeLocal addresshome = (AddressHomeLocal)obj;

out.println("Creating Customer 71");

Integer primaryKey = new Integer(71);
CustomerLocal customer = customerhome.create(primaryKey);
customer.setName( new Name("Smith","John") );
```

```
AddressLocal addr = customer.getHomeAddress();

if (addr==null)
{
   out.println("Address reference is NULL, Creating one and
            setting in Customer..");
   addr = addresshome.createAddress("333 North Washington"
                                     ,"Minneapolis"
                                     ,"MN","55401");
```

A call to customer.setHomeAddress() sets up the relationship:

```
   customer.setHomeAddress(addr);
 }
 ...
```

Next, modify the address directly with new information. Calling the Address object's set methods is the correct way to modify a unidirectional relationship that has already been set up.

```
addr.setStreet("445 East Lake Street");
addr.setCity("Wayzata");
addr.setState("MN");
addr.setZip("55432");
...
```

The next bit of code shows the *wrong* way to modify a unidirectional relationship that's already been created. Instead of modifying the existing Address entity, it creates a new one. Passing the new one to customer.setHomeAddress() orphans the old one, which thereafter just sits there in the database, unused and forgotten. The result is a database "leak:"

```
addr = addresshome.createAddress("700 Main Street"
                                  ,"St. Paul","MN","55302");
...
customer.setHomeAddress(addr);
```

Two different relationships can share the same entity. This code shares a single address between the Home Address and Billing Address relationships:

```
addr = customer.getHomeAddress();
...
customer.setBillingAddress(addr);

AddressLocal billAddr = customer.getBillingAddress();
AddressLocal homeAddr = customer.getHomeAddress();
```

The Billing Address and Home Address now refer to the same bean:

```
if (billAddr.isIdentical(homeAddr))
{
   out.println("Billing and Home are the same!");
}
else
{
   out.println("Billing and Home are NOT the same!
            BUG IN JBOSS!");
```

```
        }
    }
      catch (Exception ex)
      {
         ex.printStackTrace(out);
      }
```

Finally, test71a() closes the PrintWriter, extracts the output string, and returns it to the client for display:

```
      out.close();
      output = writer.toString();

      return output;
   }
```

In order to run *Client_71a,* invoke the Ant task run.client_71a. Remember to set your JBOSS_HOME and PATH environment variables. The output should look something like this:

```
C:\workbook\ex07_1>ant run.client_71a
Buildfile: build.xml

prepare:

compile:

run.client_71a:
     [java] Creating Customer 71
     [java] Address reference is NULL, Creating one and setting in Customer..
     [java] Address Info: 333 North Washington Minneapolis, MN 55401
     [java] Modifying Address through address reference
     [java] Address Info: 445 East Lake Street Wayzata, MN 55432
     [java] Creating New Address and calling setHomeAddress
     [java] Address Info: 700 Main Street St. Paul, MN 55302
     [java] Retrieving Address reference from Customer via getHomeAddress
     [java] Address Info: 700 Main Street St. Paul, MN 55302
     [java] Setting Billing address to be the same as Home address.
     [java] Testing that Billing and Home Address are the same Entity.
     [java] Billing and Home are the same!
```

Client_71b

The *Client_71b* program illustrates a simple one-to-one bidirectional relationship between a Customer bean and a Credit Card bean. The business logic for this example is implemented in com.titan.test.Test71Bean, in the test71b() method. Examine the code for this example.

You use the default JNDI context to obtain references to the local home interfaces of the Customer and Credit Card EJBs. The code also creates an instance of a Customer EJB:

```
// obtain CustomerHome
InitialContext jndiContext = getInitialContext();
```

```
Object obj = jndiContext.lookup("CustomerHomeLocal");
CustomerHomeLocal customerhome = (CustomerHomeLocal)obj;

obj = jndiContext.lookup("CreditCardHomeLocal");
CreditCardHomeLocal cardhome = (CreditCardHomeLocal)obj;
Integer primaryKey = new Integer(71);
CustomerLocal customer = customerhome.create(primaryKey);
customer.setName( new Name("Smith","John") );
```

Next, create an instance of a Credit Card. Notice that you don't need to pass in a primary key; the crude algorithm introduced in Exercise 6.3 generates one automatically:

```
// set Credit Card info
Calendar now = Calendar.getInstance();
CreditCardLocal card = cardhome.create(now.getTime(),
                "370000000000001", "John Smith", "O'Reilly");
```

Then you establish the one-to-one bidirectional relationship between Customer and Credit Card simply by calling the Customer EJB's `setCreditCard()` method:

```
customer.setCreditCard(card);
```

The following code illustrates the bidirectional nature of the relationship by navigating from a Credit Card to a Customer and vice versa:

```
String cardname = customer.getCreditCard().getNameOnCard();
out.println("customer.getCreditCard().getNameOnCard()="
            + cardname);

Name name = card.getCustomer().getName();
String custfullname = name.getFirstName() + " " +
                      name.getLastName();
out.println("card.getCustomer().getName()="+custfullname);
```

Finally, the code illustrates how to destroy the relationship between the Customer and Credit Card beans:

```
card.setCustomer(null);

CreditCardLocal newcardref = customer.getCreditCard();
if (newcardref == null)
{
   out.println
      ("Card is properly unlinked from customer bean");
}
else
{
   out.println("Whoops, customer still thinks it has a
               card!  BUG IN JBOSS!");
}
```

In order to run *Client_71b*, invoke the Ant task `run.client_71b`. Remember to set your `JBOSS_HOME` and `PATH` environment variables. The output should look something like this:

```
C:\workbook\ex07_1>ant run.client_71b
Buildfile: build.xml
```

```
prepare:

compile:

run.client_71b:
     [java] Finding Customer 71
     [java] Creating CreditCard
     [java] Linking CreditCard and Customer
     [java] Testing both directions on relationship
     [java] customer.getCreditCard().getNameOnCard()=John Smith
     [java] card.getCustomer().getName()=John Smith
     [java] Unlink the beans using CreditCard, test Customer side
     [java] Card is properly unlinked from customer bean
     [java]
```

Client_71c

The *Client_71c* program illustrates the proper use of a one-to-many unidirectional relationship between customers and their phone numbers. The business logic for this example is implemented in `com.titan.test.Test71Bean`, in the `test71c()` method.

First, the test code locates the Customer home interface through JNDI, then finds the Customer that needs new phone numbers:

```
// obtain CustomerHome
InitialContext jndiContext = getInitialContext();
Object obj = jndiContext.lookup("CustomerHomeLocal");
CustomerHomeLocal home = (CustomerHomeLocal)obj;

// Find Customer 71
Integer primaryKey = new Integer(71);
CustomerLocal customer = home.findByPrimaryKey(primaryKey);
```

The next bit of code invokes the Customer helper method `addPhoneNumber()` to relate two phone numbers to the customer and outputs the contents of the customer-phone relationship after each addition:

```
// Display current phone numbers and types
out.println("Starting contents of phone list:");
ArrayList vv = customer.getPhoneList();
for (int jj=0; jj<vv.size(); jj++)
{
   String ss = (String)(vv.get(jj));
   out.println(ss);
}

// add a new phone number
out.println("Adding a new type 1 phone number..");
customer.addPhoneNumber("612-555-1212",(byte)1);

out.println("New contents of phone list:");
vv = customer.getPhoneList();
for (int jj=0; jj<vv.size(); jj++)
{
```

```
        String ss = (String)(vv.get(jj));
        out.println(ss);
    }

    // add a new phone number
    out.println("Adding a new type 2 phone number..");
    customer.addPhoneNumber("800-333-3333",(byte)2);
    out.println("New contents of phone list:");
    vv = customer.getPhoneList();
    for (int jj=0; jj<vv.size(); jj++)
    {
        String ss = (String)(vv.get(jj));
        out.println(ss);
    }
```

This code uses the `updatePhoneNumber()` helper method to modify an existing phone number:

```
    // update a phone number
    out.println("Updating type 1 phone numbers..");
    customer.updatePhoneNumber("763-555-1212",(byte)1);

    out.println("New contents of phone list:");
    vv = customer.getPhoneList();
    for (int jj=0; jj<vv.size(); jj++)
    {
        String ss = (String)(vv.get(jj));
        out.println(ss);
    }
```

Finally, this code illustrates how to remove a member of a one-to-many unidirectional relationship:

```
    // delete a phone number
    out.println("Removing type 1 phone numbers from this
                 Customer..");
    customer.removePhoneNumber((byte)1);

    out.println("Final contents of phone list:");
    vv = customer.getPhoneList();
    for (int jj=0; jj<vv.size(); jj++)
        {
        String ss = (String)(vv.get(jj));
        out.println(ss);
    }
```

Note that the phone entity hasn't been destroyed. It's still in the database; it's just no longer related to this customer bean.

In order to run *Client_71c*, invoke the Ant task `run.client_71c`. Remember to set your `JBOSS_HOME` and `PATH` environment variables. The output should look something like this:

```
C:\workbook\ex07_1>ant run.client_71c
Buildfile: build.xml
```

```
prepare:

compile:

run.client_71c:
     [java] Starting contents of phone list:
     [java] Adding a new type 1 phone number..
     [java] New contents of phone list:
     [java] Type=1  Number=612-555-1212
     [java] Adding a new type 2 phone number..
     [java] New contents of phone list:
     [java] Type=1  Number=612-555-1212
     [java] Type=2  Number=800-333-3333
     [java] Updating type 1 phone numbers..
     [java] New contents of phone list:
     [java] Type=1  Number=763-555-1212
     [java] Type=2  Number=800-333-3333
     [java] Removing type 1 phone numbers from this Customer..
     [java] Final contents of phone list:
     [java] Type=2  Number=800-333-3333
```

Exercise 7.2: Entity Relationships in CMP 2.0, Part 2

The example programs in Exercise 7.2 illustrate the remaining four types of entity-bean relationship:

- Many-to-one unidirectional (Cruise-Ship)
- One-to-many bidirectional (Cruise-Reservation)
- Many-to-many bidirectional (Customer-Reservation)
- Many-to-many unidirectional (Cabin-Reservation)

Start Up JBoss

If you already have JBoss running, there is no reason to restart it.

Initialize the Database

No database is initialization needed; JBoss will create the needed tables at bean deployment.

Build and Deploy the Example Programs

Perform the following steps:

1. Open a command prompt or shell terminal and change to the *ex07_2* directory created by the extraction process

2. Set the JAVA_HOME and JBOSS_HOME environment variables to point to where your JDK and JBoss 4.0 are installed. Examples:

   Windows:

   ```
   C:\workbook\ex07_2> set JAVA_HOME=C:\jdk1.4.2
   C:\workbook\ex07_2> set JBOSS_HOME=C:\jboss-4.0
   ```

   Unix:

   ```
   $ export JAVA_HOME=/usr/local/jdk1.4.2
   $ export JBOSS_HOME=/usr/local/jboss-4.0
   ```

3. Add *ant* to your execution path.

   Windows:

   ```
   C:\workbook\ex07_2> set PATH=..\ant\bin;%PATH%
   ```

   Unix:

   ```
   $ export PATH=../ant/bin:$PATH
   ```

4. Perform the build by typing `ant`.

As in the last exercise, you will see *titan.jar* rebuilt, copied to the JBoss *deploy* directory, and redeployed by the application server.

Examine the JBoss-Specific Files

No new concepts are introduced in the JBoss-specific deployment descriptors.

Examine and Run the Client Applications

This exercise uses six example programs to demonstrate the various relationships described in the corresponding chapter of the EJB book. Note that you can rerun any of these examples as many times as you like because they clean up after themselves by removing all the entities they create.

Client_72a
: Demonstrates the many-to-one unidirectional Cruise-Ship relationship, as well as the sharing of a reference between different beans.

Client_72b
: Demonstrates the one-to-many bidirectional Cruise-Reservation relationship and how to use set methods to modify reservations that are associated with a cruise.

Client_72c
: Expands on the Cruise-Reservation relationship, using the `addAll()` method to modify the reservations associated with a cruise.

Client_72d
: Demonstrates the many-to-many bidirectional Customer-Reservation relationship.

Client_72e
: Continues the demonstration of the Customer-Reservation relationship by showing how to use `setCustomers()` to modify the Customers for a Reservation.

Client_72f
: Demonstrates the many-to-many unidirectional Cabin-Reservation relationship.

Client_72a

The business logic for this example is implemented in `com.titan.test.Test72Bean`, in the `test72a()` method. *Client_72a* models the many-to-one unidirectional Cruise-Ship relationships shown in Figure 7-12 of the EJB section of this book.

First, this code creates the relationships described in the top half of the figure. Cruises 1 to 3 embark on Ship A; Cruises 4 to 6 set sail on Ship B.

```
cruises[0] = cruisehome.create("Cruise 1", shipA);
cruises[1] = cruisehome.create("Cruise 2", shipA);
cruises[2] = cruisehome.create("Cruise 3", shipA);
cruises[3] = cruisehome.create("Cruise 4", shipB);
cruises[4] = cruisehome.create("Cruise 5", shipB);
cruises[5] = cruisehome.create("Cruise 6", shipB);
```

Next, the code switches Cruise 4 so that it is now handled by Ship A instead of Ship B. This relationship change is illustrated in the bottom half of Figure 7-12:

```
ShipLocal newship = cruises[0].getShip();
cruises[3].setShip(newship);
```

In order to run *Client_72a*, invoke the Ant task `run.client_72a`. Remember to set your `JBOSS_HOME` and `PATH` environment variables. The output should look something like this:

```
C:\workbook\ex07_2>ant run.client_72a
Buildfile: build.xml

prepare:

compile:

run.client_72a:
     [java] Creating Ships
     [java] PK=1001 name=Ship A tonnage=30000.0
     [java] PK=1002 name=Ship B tonnage=40000.0
     [java] Creating Cruises
     [java] Cruise 1 is using Ship A
     [java] Cruise 2 is using Ship A
     [java] Cruise 3 is using Ship A
     [java] Cruise 4 is using Ship B
     [java] Cruise 5 is using Ship B
     [java] Cruise 6 is using Ship B
     [java] Changing Cruise 4 to use same ship as Cruise 1
     [java] Cruise 1 is using Ship A
     [java] Cruise 2 is using Ship A
     [java] Cruise 3 is using Ship A
     [java] Cruise 4 is using Ship A
     [java] Cruise 5 is using Ship B
     [java] Cruise 6 is using Ship B
     [java] Removing created beans
```

Client_72b

The business logic for this example is implemented in `com.titan.test.Test72Bean`, in the `test72b()` method. *Client_72b* models the one-to-many bidirectional Cruise-Reservation relationships shown in Figure 7-14 of the EJB section of this book.

First, this code creates the relationships described in the top half of the figure. Reservations 1 to 3 are for Cruise A; Reservations 4 to 6 are for Cruise B:

```
for (int i = 0; i < 6; i++)
{
   CruiseLocal cruise = (i < 3) ? cruiseA : cruiseB;
   reservations[i] = reservationhome.create(cruise,new ArrayList());
   reservations[i].setDate(date.getTime());
   reservations[i].setAmountPaid((i + 1) * 1000.0);
   date.add(Calendar.DAY_OF_MONTH, 7);
}
```

Next, the code sets the reservations of Cruise B to be the reservations of Cruise A. Those relationships actually move from A to B. Afterward, Cruise A and Reservations 1–3 no longer have any Cruise-Reservation relationships, as you see in the bottom half of Figure 7-14:

```
Collection a_reservations = cruiseA.getReservations();
cruiseB.setReservations( a_reservations );
```

To run *Client_72b*, invoke the Ant task `run.client_72b`. Remember to set your `JBOSS_HOME` and `PATH` environment variables. The output will look something like this:

```
C:\workbook\ex07_2>ant run.client_72b
Buildfile: build.xml

prepare:

compile:

run.client_72b:
     [java] Creating Cruises
     [java] name=Cruise A
     [java] name=Cruise B
     [java] Creating Reservations
     [java] Reservation date=11/01/2002 is for Cruise A
     [java] Reservation date=11/08/2002 is for Cruise A
     [java] Reservation date=11/15/2002 is for Cruise A
     [java] Reservation date=11/22/2002 is for Cruise B
     [java] Reservation date=11/29/2002 is for Cruise B
     [java] Reservation date=12/06/2002 is for Cruise B
     [java] Testing CruiseB.setReservations(CruiseA.getReservations() )
     [java] Reservation date=11/01/2002 is for Cruise B
     [java] Reservation date=11/08/2002 is for Cruise B
     [java] Reservation date=11/15/2002 is for Cruise B
     [java] Reservation date=11/22/2002 is for No Cruise!
     [java] Reservation date=11/29/2002 is for No Cruise!
     [java] Reservation date=12/06/2002 is for No Cruise!
     [java] Removing created beans.
```

Client_72c

The business logic for this example is implemented in com.titan.test.Test72Bean, in the test72c() method. *Client_72c* explores the use of Collection.addAll() in the Cruise-Reservation one-to-many bidirectional relationship shown in Figure 7-15 of the EJB section.

First, this code creates the relationships described in the top half of the figure. Reservations 1 to 3 are for Cruise A; Reservations 4 to 6 are for Cruise B:

```
for (int i = 0; i < 6; i++)
{
   CruiseLocal cruise = (i < 3) ? cruiseA : cruiseB;
   reservations[i] = reservationhome.create(cruise,new ArrayList());
   reservations[i].setDate(date.getTime());
   reservations[i].setAmountPaid((i + 1) * 1000.0);
   date.add(Calendar.DAY_OF_MONTH, 7);
}
```

Then the code changes all reservations of Cruise A to be for Cruise B instead. The result of this action can be seen in the bottom half of Figure 7-15:

```
Collection a_reservations = cruiseA.getReservations();
Collection b_reservations = cruiseB.getReservations();
b_reservations.addAll(a_reservations);
```

In order to run *Client_72c,* invoke the Ant task run.client_72c. Remember to set your JBOSS_HOME and PATH environment variables. The output should look something like this:

```
C:\workbook\ex07_2>ant run.client_72c
Buildfile: build.xml

prepare:

compile:

run.client_72c:
     [java] Creating Cruises
     [java] name=Cruise A
     [java] name=Cruise B
     [java] Creating Reservations
     [java] Reservation date=11/01/2002 is for Cruise A
     [java] Reservation date=11/08/2002 is for Cruise A
     [java] Reservation date=11/15/2002 is for Cruise A
     [java] Reservation date=11/22/2002 is for Cruise B
     [java] Reservation date=11/29/2002 is for Cruise B
     [java] Reservation date=12/06/2002 is for Cruise B
     [java] Testing using b_res.addAll(a_res) to combine reservations
     [java] Reservation date=11/01/2002 is for Cruise B
     [java] Reservation date=11/08/2002 is for Cruise B
     [java] Reservation date=11/15/2002 is for Cruise B
     [java] Reservation date=11/22/2002 is for Cruise B
     [java] Reservation date=11/29/2002 is for Cruise B
     [java] Reservation date=12/06/2002 is for Cruise B
```

Client_72d

The business logic for this example is implemented in `com.titan.test.Test72Bean`, in the `test72d()` method. *Client_72d* explores the use of `Collection.addAll()` in the Customer-Reservation many-to-many bidirectional relationship shown in Figure 7-17 of the EJB section.

First, two sets of customers are created:

```
Set lowcustomers = new HashSet();
Set highcustomers = new HashSet();
CustomerLocal[] allCustomers = new CustomerLocal[6];
for (int kk=0; kk<6; kk++)
{
   CustomerLocal cust = customerhome.create(new Integer(kk));
   allCustomers[kk] = cust;
   cust.setName(new Name("Customer "+kk,""));
   if (kk<=2)
   {
      lowcustomers.add(cust);
   }
   else
   {
      highcustomers.add(cust);
   }
   out.println(cust.getName().getLastName());
}
```

Next, the code creates six reservations and relates them to one of the customer sets, as shown in the top half of Figure 7-17. Customers 1 to 3 have Reservation A; Customers 4 to 6 have Reservation B.

```
reservations[0] = reservationhome.create(cruiseA, lowcustomers);
reservations[0].setDate(date.getTime());
reservations[0].setAmountPaid(4000.0);
date.add(Calendar.DAY_OF_MONTH, 7);

reservations[1] = reservationhome.create(cruiseA, highcustomers);
reservations[1].setDate(date.getTime());
reservations[1].setAmountPaid(5000.0);
```

Finally, the code uses `addAll()` to relate Customers 4 to 6 with Reservation A. They now have a reservation for both Cruise A and Cruise B. The bottom half of Figure 7-17 illustrates this result:

```
Set customers_a = reservations[0].getCustomers();
Set customers_b = reservations[1].getCustomers();
customers_a.addAll(customers_b);
```

In order to run *Client_72d*, invoke the Ant task `run.client_72d`. Remember to set your `JBOSS_HOME` and `PATH` environment variables. The output should look something like this:

```
C:\workbook\ex07_2>ant run.client_72d
Buildfile: build.xml
```

```
prepare:

compile:

run.client_72d:
     [java] cruise.getName()=Cruise A
     [java] ship.getName()=Ship A
     [java] cruise.getShip().getName()=Ship A
     [java] Creating Customers 1-6
     [java] Customer 0
     [java] Customer 1
     [java] Customer 2
     [java] Customer 3
     [java] Customer 4
     [java] Customer 5
     [java] Creating Reservations 1 and 2, each with 3 customers
     [java] Reservation date=11/01/2002 is for Cruise A with customers Customer 2
Customer 1 Customer 0
     [java] Reservation date=11/08/2002 is for Cruise A with customers Customer 5
Customer 4 Customer 3
     [java] Performing customers_a.addAll(customers_b) test
     [java] Reservation date=11/01/2002 is for Cruise A with customers Customer 2
Customer 1 Customer 0 Customer 5 Custo
mer 4 Customer 3
     [java] Reservation date=11/08/2002 is for Cruise A with customers Customer 5
Customer 4 Customer 3
     [java] Removing created beans
```

Client_72e

The business logic for this example is implemented in `com.titan.test.Test72Bean`, in the `test72e()` method. *Client_72e* explores the use of `setCustomers()` to share an entire collection, in the Customer-Reservation many-to-many bidirectional relationship shown in Figure 7-18 of the EJB section.

First, four sets of customers are created:

```
Set customers13 = new HashSet();
Set customers24 = new HashSet();
Set customers35 = new HashSet();
Set customers46 = new HashSet();
CustomerLocal[] allCustomers = new CustomerLocal[6];
for (int kk=0; kk<6; kk++)
{
   CustomerLocal cust = customerhome.create(new Integer(kk));
   allCustomers[kk] = cust;
   cust.setName(new Name("Customer "+kk,""));
   if (kk<=2)             { customers13.add(cust); }
   if (kk>=1 && kk<=3) { customers24.add(cust); }
   if (kk>=2 && kk<=4) { customers35.add(cust); }
   if (kk>=3)             { customers46.add(cust); }
}
```

Next, the code sets up the relationships between Customers and Reservations shown in the top half of Figure 7-18:

```
reservations[0] = reservationhome.create(cruiseA, customers13);
reservations[0].setDate(date.getTime());
reservations[0].setAmountPaid(4000.0);
date.add(Calendar.DAY_OF_MONTH, 7);

reservations[1] = reservationhome.create(cruiseA, customers24);
reservations[1].setDate(date.getTime());
reservations[1].setAmountPaid(5000.0);
date.add(Calendar.DAY_OF_MONTH, 7);

reservations[2] = reservationhome.create(cruiseA, customers35);
reservations[2].setDate(date.getTime());
reservations[2].setAmountPaid(6000.0);
date.add(Calendar.DAY_OF_MONTH, 7);

reservations[3] = reservationhome.create(cruiseA, customers46);
reservations[3].setDate(date.getTime());
reservations[3].setAmountPaid(7000.0);
```

Finally, the code sets up the relationships shown in the bottom half of the figure:

```
Set customers_a = reservations[0].getCustomers();
 reservations[3].setCustomers(customers_a);
```

In order to run *Client_72e*, invoke the Ant task `run.client_72e`. Remember to set your `JBOSS_HOME` and `PATH` environment variables. The output should look something like this:

```
C:\workbook\ex07_2>ant run.client_72e
Buildfile: build.xml

prepare:

compile:

run.client_72e:
     [java] Creating a Ship and Cruise
     [java] cruise.getName()=Cruise A
     [java] ship.getName()=Ship A
     [java] cruise.getShip().getName()=Ship A
     [java] Creating Customers 1-6
     [java] Creating Reservations 1-4 using three customers each
     [java] Reservation date=11/01/2002 is for Cruise A with customers Customer 2
Customer 1 Customer 0
     [java] Reservation date=11/08/2002 is for Cruise A with customers Customer 3
Customer 2 Customer 1
     [java] Reservation date=11/15/2002 is for Cruise A with customers Customer 4
Customer 3 Customer 2
     [java] Reservation date=11/22/2002 is for Cruise A with customers Customer 5
Customer 4 Customer 3
     [java] Performing reservationD.setCustomers(customersA) test
```

```
    [java] Reservation date=11/01/2002 is for Cruise A with customers Customer 2
Customer 1 Customer 0
    [java] Reservation date=11/08/2002 is for Cruise A with customers Customer 3
Customer 2 Customer 1
    [java] Reservation date=11/15/2002 is for Cruise A with customers Customer 4
Customer 3 Customer 2
    [java] Reservation date=11/22/2002 is for Cruise A with customers Customer 2
Customer 1 Customer 0
    [java] Removing created beans.
```

Client_72f

The business logic for this example is implemented in `com.titan.test.Test72Bean`, in the `test72f()` method. *Client_72f* demonstrates removing beans in the many-to-many unidirectional Cabin-Reservation relationship, as shown in Figure 7-20 of the EJB section.

First, four sets of cabins are created:

```
Set cabins13 = new HashSet();
Set cabins24 = new HashSet();
Set cabins35 = new HashSet();
Set cabins46 = new HashSet();
CabinLocal[] allCabins = new CabinLocal[6];
for (int kk=0; kk<6; kk++)
{
   CabinLocal cabin = cabinhome.create(new Integer(kk));
   allCabins[kk] = cabin;
   cabin.setName("Cabin "+kk);
   if (kk<=2)             { cabins13.add(cabin); }
   if (kk>=1 && kk<=3) { cabins24.add(cabin); }
   if (kk>=2 && kk<=4) { cabins35.add(cabin); }
   if (kk>=3)             { cabins46.add(cabin); }
   out.println(cabin.getName());
}
```

Next, the code creates the initial relationships between Reservations and Cabins, shown in the top half of Figure 7-20:

```
reservations[0] = reservationhome.create(cruiseA, null);
reservations[0].setCabins(cabins13);
reservations[0].setDate(date.getTime());
reservations[0].setAmountPaid(4000.0);
date.add(Calendar.DAY_OF_MONTH, 7);

reservations[1] = reservationhome.create(cruiseA, null);
reservations[1].setCabins(cabins24);
reservations[1].setDate(date.getTime());
reservations[1].setAmountPaid(5000.0);
date.add(Calendar.DAY_OF_MONTH, 7);

reservations[2] = reservationhome.create(cruiseA, null);
reservations[2].setCabins(cabins35);
reservations[2].setDate(date.getTime());
```

```
reservations[2].setAmountPaid(6000.0);
date.add(Calendar.DAY_OF_MONTH, 7);

reservations[3] = reservationhome.create(cruiseA, null);
reservations[3].setCabins(cabins46);
reservations[3].setDate(date.getTime());
reservations[3].setAmountPaid(7000.0);
```

Finally, the code removes some of the relationships, as shown in the bottom half of the figure:

```
Set cabins_a = reservations[0].getCabins();
Iterator iterator = cabins_a.iterator();
while (iterator.hasNext())
{
   CabinLocal cc = (CabinLocal)iterator.next();
   out.println("Removing "+cc.getName()+" from cabins_a");
   iterator.remove();
}
```

In order to run *Client_72f*, invoke the Ant task `run.client_72f`. Remember to set your `JBOSS_HOME` and `PATH` environment variables. The output should look something like this:

```
C:\workbook\ex07_2>ant run.client_72f
Buildfile: build.xml

prepare:

compile:

run.client_72f:
     [java] Creating a Ship and Cruise
     [java] cruise.getName()=Cruise A
     [java] ship.getName()=Ship A
     [java] cruise.getShip().getName()=Ship A
     [java] Creating Cabins 1-6
     [java] Cabin 0
     [java] Cabin 1
     [java] Cabin 2
     [java] Cabin 3
     [java] Cabin 4
     [java] Cabin 5
     [java] Creating Reservations 1-4 using three cabins each
     [java] Reservation date=11/01/2002 is for Cruise A with cabins Cabin 2 Cabin 1
Cabin 0
     [java] Reservation date=11/08/2002 is for Cruise A with cabins Cabin 3 Cabin 2
Cabin 1
     [java] Reservation date=11/15/2002 is for Cruise A with cabins Cabin 4 Cabin 3
Cabin 2
     [java] Reservation date=11/22/2002 is for Cruise A with cabins Cabin 5 Cabin 4
Cabin 3
     [java] Performing cabins_a collection iterator.remove() test
     [java] Removing Cabin 2 from cabins_a
```

```
     [java] Removing Cabin 1 from cabins_a
     [java] Removing Cabin 0 from cabins_a
     [java] Reservation date=11/01/2002 is for Cruise A with cabins
     [java] Reservation date=11/08/2002 is for Cruise A with cabins Cabin 3 Cabin 2
Cabin 1
     [java] Reservation date=11/15/2002 is for Cruise A with cabins Cabin 4 Cabin 3
Cabin 2
     [java] Reservation date=11/22/2002 is for Cruise A with cabins Cabin 5 Cabin 4
Cabin 3
     [java] Removing created beans
```

Exercise 7.3: Cascade Deletes in CMP 2.0

This very short exercise demonstrates the use of the automatic cascade-delete feature of CMP 2.0 containers. It does this with an example Customer bean and some other beans related to it.

Build and Deploy the Example Programs

Perform the following steps:

1. Open a command prompt or shell terminal and change to the *ex07_3* directory created by the extraction process.
2. Set the `JAVA_HOME` and `JBOSS_HOME` environment variables to point to where your JDK and JBoss 4.0 are installed. Examples:

   Windows:
   ```
   C:\workbook\ex07_3> set JAVA_HOME=C:\jdk1.4.2
   C:\workbook\ex07_3> set JBOSS_HOME=C:\jboss-4.0
   ```
   Unix:
   ```
   $ export JAVA_HOME=/usr/local/jdk1.4.2
   $ export JBOSS_HOME=/usr/local/jboss-4.0
   ```
3. Add ant to your execution path.

   Windows:
   ```
   C:\workbook\ex07_3> set PATH=..\ant\bin;%PATH%
   ```
   Unix:
   ```
   $ export PATH=../ant/bin:$PATH
   ```
4. Perform the build by typing `ant`.

As in the last exercise, you will see *titan.jar* rebuilt, copied to the JBoss *deploy* directory, and redeployed by the application server.

Examine the JBoss-Specific Files

There are no new JBoss configuration files or components in this exercise.

Examine and Run the Client Applications

Client_73 is a simple example to demonstrate cascade-delete. The example code is pretty straightforward and needs no explanation.

In order to run *Client_73*, invoke the Ant task `run.client_73`. Remember to set your `JBOSS_HOME` and `PATH` environment variables. The output should look something like this:

```
C:\workbook\ex07_3>ant run.client_73
Buildfile: build.xml

prepare:

compile:

run.client_73:
     [java] Creating Customer 10078, Addresses, Credit Card, Phones
     [java] Creating CreditCard
     [java] customer.getCreditCard().getName()=Ringo Star
     [java] Creating Address
     [java] Address Info: 780 Main Street Beverly Hills, CA 90210
     [java] Creating Phones
     [java] Adding a new type 1 phone number..
     [java] Adding a new type 2 phone number.
     [java] New contents of phone list:
     [java] Type=1  Number=612-555-1212
     [java] Type=2  Number=888-555-1212
     [java] Removing Customer EJB only
```

WORKBOOK 6

Exercises for Chapter 8

Exercise 8.1: Simple EJB QL Statements

The exercises in this section reveal some of the basic aspects of EJB QL programming and functionality. You'll explore basic finder methods, `ejbSelect` methods, and the use of the `IN` operation in EJB QL queries.

Start Up JBoss

If you already have JBoss running, there is no reason to restart it.

Build and Deploy the Example Programs

Perform the following steps:

1. Open a command prompt or shell terminal and change to the *ex08_1* directory created by the extraction process
2. Set the `JAVA_HOME` and `JBOSS_HOME` environment variables to point to where your JDK and JBoss 4.0 are installed. Examples:

   Windows:

   ```
   C:\workbook\ex08_1> set JAVA_HOME=C:\jdk1.4.2
   C:\workbook\ex08_1> set JBOSS_HOME=C:\jboss-4.0
   ```

   Unix:

   ```
   $ export JAVA_HOME=/usr/local/jdk1.4.2
   $ export JBOSS_HOME=/usr/local/jboss-4.0
   ```

3. Add `ant` to your execution path.

   Windows:

   ```
   C:\workbook\ex08_1> set PATH=..\ant\bin;%PATH%
   ```

   Unix:

   ```
   $ export PATH=../ant/bin:$PATH
   ```

4. Perform the build by typing `ant`.

As in the last exercise, you will see *titan.jar* rebuilt, copied to the JBoss *deploy* directory, and redeployed by the application server.

Examine the JBoss-Specific Files

This exercise introduces no new features in JBoss-specific files. If you think you need to, review Exercise 6.1 of this workbook to understand the JBoss-specific files in this example.

Initialize the Database

The database tables for this exercise will automatically be created in JBoss's default database, HypersonicSQL, when the EJB JAR is deployed. To initialize all the tables in this example, though, you must perform the Ant task `run.initialize`:

```
C:\workbook\ex08_1>ant run.initialize
Buildfile: build.xml

prepare:

compile:

run.initialize:
   [java] added Bill Burke
   [java] added Sacha Labourey
   [java] added Marc Fleury
   [java] added Jane Swift
   [java] added Nomar Garciaparra
```

As in the preceding exercise, all business logic is implemented within a stateless session bean. If you would like to see the database initialization code, take a look at `com.titan.test.Test81Bean`'s `initialize()` method, which creates all the entity beans for this exercise.

Examine and Run the Client Applications

Each example method of `Test81Bean` implements the example code fragments shown in the EJB book. Each `Test81Bean` method is invoked by a small, simple client application.

Client_81a

The *Client_81a* program demonstrates a few simple finder methods that are exposed through the Customer home interface:

```
public interface CustomerHomeLocal extends javax.ejb.EJBLocalHome
{
   ...
   public CustomerLocal findByName(String lastName,
                                   String firstName)
      throws FinderException;
```

```
    public Collection findByGoodCredit()
        throws FinderException;
    ...
}
```

The Customer EJB's deployment descriptor defines these finder methods as follows:

```
<query>
    <query-method>
        <method-name>findByName</method-name>
        <method-params>
            <method-param>java.lang.String</method-param>
            <method-param>java.lang.String</method-param>
        </method-params>
    </query-method>
    <ejb-ql>
        SELECT OBJECT(c) FROM Customer c
        WHERE c.lastName = ?1 AND c.firstName = ?2
    </ejb-ql>
</query>
<query>
    <query-method>
        <method-name>findByGoodCredit</method-name>
        <method-params/>
    </query-method>
    <ejb-ql>
        SELECT OBJECT(c) FROM Customer c
        WHERE c.hasGoodCredit = TRUE
    </ejb-ql>
</query>
```

The example also demonstrates a few ejbSelect methods, defined in the Address EJB's deployment descriptor as follows:

```
<query>
    <query-method>
        <method-name>ejbSelectZipCodes</method-name>
        <method-params>
            <method-param>java.lang.String</method-param>
        </method-params>
    </query-method>
    <ejb-ql>
        SELECT a.zip FROM Address AS a
        WHERE a.state = ?1
    </ejb-ql>
</query>
<query>
    <query-method>
        <method-name>ejbSelectAll</method-name>
        <method-params/>
    </query-method>
    <ejb-ql>
        SELECT OBJECT(a) FROM Address AS a
    </ejb-ql>
</query>
```

```
<query>
   <query-method>
      <method-name>ejbSelectCustomer</method-name>
      <method-params>
        <method-param>com.titan.address.AddressLocal</method-param>
      </method-params>
    </query-method>
    <ejb-ql>
        SELECT OBJECT(C) FROM Customer AS c
        WHERE c.homeAddress = ?1
    </ejb-ql>
</query>
```

Because ejbSelect methods are private to the entity bean class, the Address home interface needs custom home methods to wrap and invoke the private ejbSelect methods.

```
public interface AddressHomeLocal extends javax.ejb.EJBLocalHome
{
   ...
   public Collection queryZipCodes(String state)
      throws FinderException;

   public Collection queryAll()
      throws FinderException;

   public CustomerLocal queryCustomer(AddressLocal addr)
      throws FinderException;
}
```

These custom home methods need corresponding ejbHome methods defined in the Address bean class. All they do is delegate to the ejbSelect methods they wrap.

```
public abstract class AddressBean implements javax.ejb.EntityBean
{
   ...
   public abstract Collection ejbSelectZipCodes(String state)
      throws FinderException;

   public abstract Collection ejbSelectAll()
      throws FinderException;

   public abstract CustomerLocal ejbSelectCustomer
      (AddressLocal addr)
      throws FinderException;

   public Collection ejbHomeQueryZipCodes(String state)
      throws FinderException
   {
      return ejbSelectZipCodes(state);
   }

   public Collection ejbHomeQueryAll()
      throws FinderException
```

```
    {
       return ejbSelectAll();
    }

    public CustomerLocal ejbHomeQueryCustomer(AddressLocal addr)
       throws FinderException
    {
       return ejbSelectCustomer(addr);
    }
    ...
}
```

Custom home methods are described briefly in Chapter 5 of the EJB book and in more detail in Chapter 11. As you can see, they are extremely useful in exposing private `ejbSelect` methods so that they can be invoked by test programs or business logic. All the workbook example programs for Chapter 8 use the custom home methods for this purpose.

Client_81a invokes these queries and displays their output. To run it, invoke the Ant task `run.client_81a`. Remember to set your `JBOSS_HOME` and `PATH` environment variables. The output should look something like this:

```
C:\workbook\ex08_1>ant run.client_81a
Buildfile: build.xml

prepare:

compile:

run.client_81a:
     [java] FIND METHODS
     [java] --------------------------------
     [java] SELECT OBJECT(c) FROM Customer c
     [java] WHERE c.lastName = ?1 AND c.firstName = ?2
     [java] Find Bill Burke using findByName
     [java]    Found Bill Burke
     [java]
     [java] SELECT OBJECT(c) FROM Customer c
     [java] WHERE c.hasGoodCredit = TRUE
     [java] Find all with good credit.  Sacha has bad credit!
     [java]    Bill has good credit.
     [java]    Marc has good credit.
     [java]    Jane has good credit.
     [java]    Nomar has good credit.
     [java]
     [java] SELECT METHODS
     [java] --------------------------------
     [java] SELECT a.zip FROM Address AS a
     [java] WHERE a.state = ?1
     [java] show ejbSelectZipCodes with queryZipCodes
     [java]    01821
     [java]    02115
     [java]    02116
     [java]
```

```
[java] SELECT OBJECT(a) FROM Address AS a
[java] show ejbSelectAll with queryAll
[java]     123 Boston Road
[java]     Billerica, MA 01821
[java]
[java]     Etwa Schweitzer Strasse
[java]     Neuchatel, Switzerland 07711
[java]
[java]     Somewhere Dr.
[java]     Atlanta, GA 06660
[java]
[java]     1 Beacon Street
[java]     Boston, MA 02115
[java]
[java]     1 Yawkey Way
[java]     Boston, MA 02116
[java]
[java]     West Broad Street
[java]     Richmond, VA 23233
[java]
[java]     Somewhere
[java]     Atlanta, GA 06660
[java]
[java]
[java] SELECT OBJECT(C) FROM Customer AS c
[java] WHERE c.homeAddress = ?1
[java] show ejbSelectCustomer using Bill's address.
[java] The customer is:
[java]     Bill Burke
[java]     123 Boston Road
[java]     Billerica, MA 01821
```

Client_81b

The *Client_81b* program gives you a chance to investigate some of the queries illustrated in the EJB book. For an explanation of the details of the tested queries below, please refer to "Simple Queries with Paths" in Chapter 8 of the EJB section of this book. The business logic for this example is implemented in `com.titan.test.Test81Bean`, in the `test81b()` method.

All the EJB QL queries in this example are `ejbSelect` methods. Again, these `ejbSelect` methods are wrapped by custom home methods. This example tests the following Customer EJB QL queries and home methods:

query:	`SELECT c.lastName FROM Customer AS c`
`ejbSelect` **method:**	`ejbSelectLastNames()`
custom home method:	`queryLastNames()`
`ejbHome` **method:**	`ejbHomeQueryLastNames()`
query:	`SELECT c.creditCard FROM Customer c`
`ejbSelect` **method:**	`ejbSelectCreditCards()`
custom home method:	`queryCreditCards()`

ejbHome method: ejbHomeQueryCreditCards()
query: SELECT c.homeAddress.city FROM Customer c
ejbSelect method: ejbSelectCities()
custom home method: queryCities()
ejbHome method: ejbHomeQueryCities()
query: SELECT c.creditCard.creditCompany.address FROM Customer AS c
ejbSelect method: ejbSelectCreditCompanyAddresses()
custom home method: queryCreditCompanyAddresses()
ejbHome method: ejbHomeQueryCreditCompanyAddresses()
query: SELECT c.creditCard.creditCompany.address.city FROM Customer AS c
ejbSelect method: ejbSelectCreditCompanyCities()
custom home method: queryCreditCompanyCities()
ejbHome method: ejbHomeQueryCreditCompanyCities()

Client_81b invokes these queries and displays their output. To run it, invoke the Ant task `run.client_81b`. Remember to set your `JBOSS_HOME` and `PATH` environment variables. The output should look something like this:

```
C:\workbook\ex08_1>ant run.client_81b
Buildfile: build.xml

prepare:

compile:

run.client_81b:
     [java] SIMPLE QUERIES with PATHS
     [java] -------------------------------
     [java] SELECT c.lastName FROM Customer AS c
     [java]    Burke
     [java]    Labourey
     [java]    Fleury
     [java]    Swift
     [java]    Garciaparra
     [java]
     [java] SELECT c.creditCard FROM Customer c
     [java]    5324 9393 1010 2929
     [java]    5311 5000 1011 2333
     [java]    5310 5131 7711 2663
     [java]    5810 5881 7788 2688
     [java]    5450 5441 7448 2644
     [java]
     [java] SELECT c.homeAddress.city FROM Customer c
     [java]    Billerica
     [java]    Neuchatel
     [java]    Atlanta
     [java]    Boston
     [java]    Boston
     [java]
```

```
[java] SELECT c.creditCard.creditCompany.address
[java] FROM Customer AS c
[java]    West Broad Street
[java]    Richmond, VA 23233
[java]
[java]    West Broad Street
[java]    Richmond, VA 23233
[java]
[java]    West Broad Street
[java]    Richmond, VA 23233
[java]
[java]    Somewhere
[java]    Atlanta, GA 06660
[java]
[java]    Somewhere
[java]    Atlanta, GA 06660
[java]
[java]
[java] SELECT c.creditCard.creditCompany.address.city
[java] FROM Customer AS c
[java]    Richmond
[java]    Richmond
[java]    Richmond
[java]    Atlanta
[java]    Atlanta
```

Client_81c

The *Client_81c* program lets you investigate some more queries illustrated in the EJB book. For an explanation of the details of the tested queries below, please refer to "The IN Operator" in Chapter 8 of the EJB section. The business logic for this example is implemented in `com.titan.test.Test81Bean`, in the `test81c()` method.

All the EJB QL queries in this example are `ejbSelect` methods. Again, these `ejbSelect` methods are wrapped by custom home methods. This example tests the following Customer EJB QL queries and home methods:

query:	`SELECT OBJECT( r )` `FROM Customer AS c, IN( c.reservations ) AS r`
`ejbSelect` **method:**	`ejbSelectReservations()`
custom home method:	`queryReservations()`
`ejbHome` **method:**	`ejbHomeQueryReservations()`
query:	`SELECT r.cruise` `FROM Customer AS c, IN( c.reservations ) AS r`
`ejbSelect` **method:**	`ejbSelectCruises()`
custom home method:	`queryCruises()`
`ejbHome` **method:**	`ejbHomeQueryCruises()`

query:	`SELECT cbn.ship`
	`FROM Customer AS c, IN( c.reservations ) AS r,`
	`IN( r.cabins ) AS cbn`

ejbSelect method: ejbSelectShips()
custom home method: queryShips()
ejbHome method: ejbHomeQueryShips()

Client_81c invokes these queries and displays their output. To run it, invoke the Ant task run.client_81c. Remember to set your JBOSS_HOME and PATH environment variables. The output should look something like this:

```
C:\workbook\ex08_1>ant run.client_81c
Buildfile: build.xml

prepare:

compile:

run.client_81c:
     [java] THE IN OPERATOR
     [java] --------------------------------
     [java] SELECT OBJECT( r )
     [java] FROM Customer AS c, IN( c.reservations ) AS r
     [java]    Reservation for Alaskan Cruise
     [java]    Reservation for Alaskan Cruise
     [java]    Reservation for Atlantic Cruise
     [java]    Reservation for Atlantic Cruise
     [java]    Reservation for Alaskan Cruise
     [java]
     [java] SELECT r.cruise
     [java] FROM Customer AS c, IN( c.reservations ) AS r
     [java]    Cruise Alaskan Cruise
     [java]    Cruise Alaskan Cruise
     [java]    Cruise Atlantic Cruise
     [java]    Cruise Atlantic Cruise
     [java]    Cruise Alaskan Cruise
     [java]
     [java] SELECT cbn.ship
     [java] FROM Customer AS c, IN( c.reservations ) AS r,
     [java] IN( r.cabins ) AS cbn
     [java]    Ship Queen Mary
     [java]    Ship Queen Mary
     [java]    Ship Queen Mary
     [java]    Ship Queen Mary
     [java]    Ship Titanic
     [java]    Ship Titanic
     [java]    Ship Titanic
     [java]    Ship Titanic
     [java]    Ship Titanic
     [java]    Ship Titanic
     [java]    Ship Queen Mary
     [java]    Ship Queen Mary
```

Exercise 8.2: Complex EJB QL Statements

The example programs in Exercise 8.2 delve deeper into the complexities of EJB QL. You will learn about arithmetic and logic operators in WHERE clauses as well as other, more complex WHERE-clause constructs. The test programs of this section demonstrate most of the example queries provided in Chapter 8 of the EJB book.

Start Up JBoss

If you already have JBoss running, there is no reason to restart it.

Build and Deploy the Example Programs

Build the examples for this exercise in the *ex08_2* directory, following the same procedure as for earlier exercises.

Examine the JBoss-Specific Files

This exercise introduces no new features in JBoss-specific files. If you think you need to, review Exercise 6.1 of this workbook to understand the JBoss-specific files in this example.

Initialize the Database

The database tables for this exercise will automatically be created in JBoss's default database, HypersonicSQL, when the EJB JAR is deployed, but to initialize all database tables in this example, you must perform the Ant task `run.initialize`:

```
C:\workbook\ex08_2>ant run.initialize
Buildfile: build.xml

prepare:

compile:

run.initialize:
   [java] added Bill Burke
   [java] added Sacha Labourey
   [java] added Marc Fleury
   [java] added Jane Swift
   [java] added Nomar Garciaparra
   [java] added Richard Monson-Haefel
```

As in the preceding exercise, all example business logic is implemented within a stateless session bean—in this case, `com.titan.test.Test82Bean`—and the database initialization code is in that bean's `initialize()` method, which creates all the entity beans for this exercise.

Examine and Run the Client Applications

Each example method of Test82Bean implements the example code fragments shown in the EJB book. Each Test82Bean method is invoked by a small, simple client application.

Client_82a

The *Client_82a* program implements the queries illustrated in the EJB section of this book, in the section of Chapter 8 called "Using DISTINCT." The business logic for this example is implemented in com.titan.test.Test82Bean, in the test82a() method.

The code demonstrates a Customer EJB finder query that returns duplicate responses, then invokes a finder query that uses the DISTINCT keyword to filter out duplicates.

finder method:	findAllCustomersWithReservations()
query:	SELECT OBJECT(cust) FROM Reservation res, IN (res.customers) cust
finder method:	findDistinctCustomersWithReservations()
query:	SELECT DISTINCT OBJECT(cust) FROM Reservation res, IN (res.customers) cust

Client_82a invokes these queries and displays their output. To run it, invoke the Ant task run.client_82a. Remember to set your JBOSS_HOME and PATH environment variables. The output should look something like this:

```
C:\workbook\ex08_2>ant run.client_82a
Buildfile: build.xml

prepare:

compile:

run.client_82a:
     [java] USING DISTINCT
     [java] --------------------------------
     [java] Non-distinct:
     [java] SELECT OBJECT( cust)
     [java] FROM Reservation res, IN (res.customers) cust
     [java]    Bill has a reservation.
     [java]    Sacha has a reservation.
     [java]    Nomar has a reservation.
     [java]    Bill has a reservation.
     [java]    Marc has a reservation.
     [java]    Jane has a reservation.
     [java]
     [java] Distinct:
     [java] SELECT DISTINCT OBJECT( cust)
     [java] FROM Reservation res, IN (res.customers) cust
```

```
     [java]    Bill has a reservation.
     [java]    Sacha has a reservation.
     [java]    Marc has a reservation.
     [java]    Jane has a reservation.
     [java]    Nomar has a reservation.
```

Client_82b

The *Client_82b* program implements the queries illustrated in the EJB book, in the section of Chapter 8 called "The WHERE Clause and Literals." The business logic for this example is implemented in `com.titan.test.Test82Bean`, in the `test82b()` method.

Various Customer and Ship EJB finder queries show how to use string, numeric, and Boolean literals in EJB QL queries.

EJB:	`Customer`
finder method:	`findByAmericanExpress()`
query:	`SELECT OBJECT( c ) FROM Customer AS c` `WHERE c.creditCard.organization = 'American Express'`
EJB:	`Ship`
finder method:	`findByTonnage100000_()`
query:	`SELECT OBJECT( s ) FROM Ship AS s` `WHERE s.tonnage = 100000.0`
EJB:	`Customer`
finder method:	`findByGoodCredit()`
query:	`SELECT OBJECT( c ) FROM Customer AS c` `WHERE c.hasGoodCredit = TRUE`

Client_82b invokes these queries and displays their output. To run it, invoke the Ant task `run.client_82b`. The output should look something like this:

```
C:\workbook\ex08_2>ant run.client_82b
Buildfile: build.xml

prepare:

compile:

run.client_82b:
     [java] THE WHERE CLAUSE AND LITERALS
     [java] --------------------------------
     [java] SELECT OBJECT( c ) FROM Customer AS c
     [java] WHERE c.creditCard.organization = 'American Express'
     [java]    Jane has an American Express card.
     [java]    Nomar has an American Express card.
     [java]
     [java] SELECT OBJECT( s ) FROM Ship AS s
     [java] WHERE s.tonnage = 100000.0
     [java]    Ship Queen Mary as tonnage 100000.0
     [java]
     [java] SELECT OBJECT( c ) FROM Customer AS c
```

```
[java] WHERE c.hasGoodCredit = TRUE
[java]     Bill has good credit.
[java]     Marc has good credit.
[java]     Jane has good credit.
[java]     Nomar has good credit.
[java]     Richard has good credit.
```

Client_82c

The *Client_82c* program implements the queries illustrated in the EJB book, in the section of Chapter 8 called "The WHERE Clause and Input Parameters." The business logic for this example is implemented in `com.titan.test.Test82Bean`, in the `test82c()` method.

The code demonstrates a Customer EJB `ejbSelect` query that uses strings as input parameters to the query and a Cruise EJB finder method that uses a Ship EJB as an input parameter. As in previous sections, the `ejbSelect` query is wrapped in a custom home method.

EJB:	`Customer`
`ejbSelect` method:	`ejbSelectLastNames()`
custom home method:	`queryLastNames()`
`ejbHome` method:	`ejbHomeQueryLastNames()`

query:	`SELECT OBJECT( c ) FROM Customer AS c`
	`WHERE c.homeAddress.state = ?2`
	`AND c.homeAddress.city = ?1`

EJB:	`Cruise`
finder method:	`findByShip()`
query:	`SELECT OBJECT( crs ) FROM Cruise AS crs` `WHERE crs.ship = ?1`

Client_82c invokes these queries and displays their output. To run it, invoke the Ant task `run.client_82c`. Remember to set your `JBOSS_HOME` and `PATH` environment variables. The output should look something like this:

```
C:\workbook\ex08_2>ant run.client_82c
Buildfile: build.xml

prepare:

compile:

run.client_82c:
     [java] THE WHERE CLAUSE AND INPUT PARAMETERS
     [java] --------------------------------
     [java] SELECT OBJECT( c ) FROM Customer AS c
     [java] WHERE c.homeAddress.state = ?2
     [java] AND c.homeAddress.city = ?1
     [java] Get customers from Billerica, MA
     [java]     Bill is from Billerica.
```

```
[java]
[java] SELECT OBJECT( crs ) FROM Cruise AS crs
[java] WHERE crs.ship = ?1
[java] Get cruises on the Titanic
[java]    Atlantic Cruise is a Titanic cruise.
```

Client_82d

The *Client_82d* example program implements the queries illustrated in the EJB book, in the section of Chapter 8 called "The WHERE Clause and CDATA Sections" The business logic for this example is implemented in `com.titan.test.Test82Bean`, in the `test82d()` method. The code demonstrates a Reservation EJB finder method that must be enclosed in an XML CDATA section because it uses the > symbol in the query.

EJB:	`Reservation`
finder method:	`findWithPaymentGreaterThan()`

query:	`<![CDATA[`
	`OBJECT( r ) FROM Rservation r`
	`WHERE r.amountPaid > ?1`
	`]]>`

Client_82d invokes this query and displays its output. To run it, invoke the Ant task `run.client_82d`. The output should look something like this:

```
C:\workbook\ex08_2>ant run.client_82d
Buildfile: build.xml

prepare:

compile:

run.client_82d:
     [java] THE WHERE CLAUSE AND CDATA Sections
     [java] --------------------------------
     [java] ![CDATA[
     [java] SELECT OBJECT( r ) FROM Rservation r
     [java] WHERE r.amountPaid > ?1
     [java] ]]>
     [java]    found reservation with amount paid > 20000.0: 40000.0
```

Client_82e

The *Client_82e* program implements the queries illustrated in the EJB book, in the section of Chapter 8 called "The WHERE Clause and BETWEEN." The business logic for this example is implemented in `com.titan.test.Test82Bean`, in the `test82e()` method. Two Ship EJB finder methods demonstrate how to use the `BETWEEN` keyword in a `WHERE` clause.

EJB:	`Ship`
finder method:	`findByTonnageBetween()`

query: SELECT OBJECT(s) FROM Ship s
WHERE s.tonnage BETWEEN 80000.00 and 130000.00

EJB: Ship

finder method: findByTonnageNotBetween()

query: SELECT OBJECT(s) FROM Ship s
WHERE s.tonnage NOT BETWEEN 80000.00 and 130000.00

Client_82e invokes these queries and displays their output. To run it, invoke the Ant task `run.client_82e`. The output should look something like this:

```
C:\workbook\ex08_2>ant run.client_82e
Buildfile: build.xml

prepare:

compile:

run.client_82e:
     [java] THE WHERE CLAUSE AND BETWEEN
     [java] -------------------------------
     [java] SELECT OBJECT( s ) FROM Ship s
     [java] WHERE s.tonnage BETWEEN 80000.00 and 130000.00
     [java]    Queen Mary has tonnage 100000.0
     [java]
     [java] SELECT OBJECT( s ) FROM Ship s
     [java] WHERE s.tonnage NOT BETWEEN 80000.00 and 130000.00
     [java]    Titanic has tonnage 200000.0
```

Client_82f

The *Client_82f* program implements the queries illustrated in the EJB book, in the section of Chapter 8 called "The WHERE Clause and IN." The business logic for this example is implemented in `com.titan.test.Test82Bean`, in the `test82f()` method.

The code uses two Customer EJB finder methods. One queries for all customers living in Georgia or Massachusetts. The other queries for all customers that do not live in these two states.

EJB: Customer

finder method: findInStates()

query: SELECT OBJECT(c) FROM Customer c
WHERE c.homeAddress.state IN ('GA', 'MA')

EJB: Customer

finder method: findNotInStates()

query: SELECT OBJECT(c) FROM Customer c
WHERE c.homeAddress.state NOT IN ('GA', 'MA')

Client_82f invokes these queries and displays their output. To run it, invoke the Ant task `run.client_82f`. The output should look something like this:

```
C:\workbook\ex08_2>ant run.client_82f
Buildfile: build.xml

prepare:

compile:

run.client_82f:
     [java] THE WHERE CLAUSE AND IN
     [java] --------------------------------
     [java] SELECT OBJECT( c ) FROM Customer c
     [java] WHERE c.homeAddress.state IN ('GA', 'MA')
     [java]    Bill
     [java]    Marc
     [java]    Jane
     [java]    Nomar
     [java]
     [java] SELECT OBJECT( c ) FROM Customer c
     [java] WHERE c.homeAddress.state NOT IN ('GA', 'MA')
     [java]    Sacha
```

Client_82g

The *Client_82g* program implements the queries illustrated in the EJB book, in the section of Chapter 8 called "The WHERE Clause and IS NULL." The business logic for this example is implemented in com.titan.test.Test82Bean, in the test82g() method.

There are two Customer EJB finder methods. One selects all customers that have a null home address. The other selects all customers that do not have a null address.

EJB:	Customer
finder method:	findHomeAddressIsNull()
query:	SELECT OBJECT(c) FROM Customer c WHERE c.homeAddress IS NULL
EJB:	Customer
finder method:	findHomeAddressIsNotNull()
query:	SELECT OBJECT(c) FROM Customer c WHERE c.homeAddress IS NOT NULL

Client_82g invokes these queries and displays their output. To run it, invoke the Ant task run.client_82g. The output should look something like this:

```
C:\workbook\ex08_2>ant run.client_82g
Buildfile: build.xml

prepare:

compile:

run.client_82g:
```

```
[java] THE WHERE CLAUSE AND IS NULL
[java] --------------------------------
[java] SELECT OBJECT( c ) FROM Customer c
[java] WHERE c.homeAddress IS NULL
[java]    Richard
[java]
[java] SELECT OBJECT( c ) FROM Customer c
[java] WHERE c.homeAddress IS NOT NULL
[java]    Bill
[java]    Sacha
[java]    Marc
[java]    Jane
[java]    Nomar
```

Client_82h

The *Client_82h* program implements the queries illustrated in the EJB book, in the section of Chapter 8 called "The WHERE Clause and IS EMPTY." The business logic for this example is implemented in `com.titan.test.Test82Bean`, in the `test82h()` method.

The code uses two Cruise EJB finder methods to illustrate the use of `IS EMPTY`. One returns all the Cruises that do not have Reservations. The other method returns all Cruises that have Reservations.

EJB:	`Cruise`
finder method:	`findEmptyReservations()`
query:	`SELECT OBJECT( crs ) FROM Cruise crs` `WHERE crs.reservations IS EMPTY`
EJB:	`Cruise`
finder method:	`findNotEmptyReservations()`
query:	`SELECT OBJECT( crs ) FROM Cruise crs` `WHERE crs.reservations IS NOT EMPTY`

Client_82h invokes these queries and displays their output. To run it, invoke the Ant task `run.client_82h`. The output should look something like this:

```
C:\workbook\ex08_2>ant run.client_82h
Buildfile: build.xml

prepare:

compile:

run.client_82h:
     [java] THE WHERE CLAUSE AND IS EMPTY
     [java] --------------------------------
     [java] SELECT OBJECT( crs ) FROM Cruise crs
     [java] WHERE crs.reservations IS EMPTY
     [java]
     [java] SELECT OBJECT( crs ) FROM Cruise crs
```

```
[java] WHERE crs.reservations IS NOT EMPTY
[java]    Alaskan Cruise is not empty.
[java]    Atlantic Cruise is not empty.
```

Client_82i

The *Client_82i* program implements the queries illustrated in the EJB book, in the section of Chapter 8 called "The WHERE Clause and MEMBER OF." The business logic for this example is implemented in `com.titan.test.Test82Bean`, in the `test82i()` method.

Two Cruise EJB finder methods demonstrate how to use EJB QL to find whether or not an entity is a member of a relationship.

EJB:	`Cruise`
finder method:	`findMemberOf()`

query:	`SELECT OBJECT( crs ) FROM Cruise crs,`
	`IN (crs.reservations) res, Customer cust`
	`WHERE cust = ?1 ANT cust MEMBER OF res.customers`

EJB:	`Cruise`
finder method:	`findNotMemberOf()`

query:	`SELECT OBJECT( crs ) FROM Cruise crs,`
	`IN (crs.reservations) res, Customer cust`
	`WHERE cust = ?1 ANT cust NOT MEMBER OF res.customers`

Client_82i invokes these queries and displays their output. To run it, invoke the Ant task `run.client_82i`. The output should look something like this:

```
C:\workbook\ex08_2>ant run.client_82i
Buildfile: build.xml

prepare:

compile:

run.client_82i:
     [java] THE WHERE CLAUSE AND MEMBER OF
     [java] --------------------------------
     [java] SELECT OBJECT( crs ) FROM Cruise crs,
     [java] IN (crs.reservations) res, Customer cust
     [java] WHERE cust = ?1 ANT cust MEMBER OF res.customers
     [java] Use Bill Burke
     [java]    Bill is member of Alaskan Cruise
     [java]    Bill is member of Atlantic Cruise
     [java]
     [java] SELECT OBJECT( crs ) FROM Cruise crs,
     [java] IN (crs.reservations) res, Customer cust
     [java] WHERE cust = ?1 ANT cust NOT MEMBER OF res.customers
     [java] Use Nomar Garciaparra
     [java]    Nomar is not member of Atlantic Cruise
```

Client_82j

The *Client_82j* program implements the queries illustrated in the EJB book, in the section of Chapter 8 entitled "The WHERE Clause and LIKE." The business logic for this example is implemented in `com.titan.test.Test82Bean`, in the `test82j()` method.

One Customer EJB finder method is used to query all Customers with a hyphenated name.

EJB:	`Customer`
finder method:	`findHyphenatedLastNames()`
query:	`SELECT OBJECT( c ) FROM Customer c` `WHERE c.lastName LIKE '%-%'`

Client_82j invokes this query and displays its output. To run it, invoke the Ant task `run.client_82j`. The output should look something like this:

```
C:\workbook\ex08_2>ant run.client_82j
Buildfile: build.xml

prepare:

compile:

run.client_82j:
     [java] THE WHERE CLAUSE AND LIKE
     [java] -------------------------------
     [java] SELECT OBJECT( c ) FROM Customer c
     [java] WHERE c.lastName LIKE '%-%'
     [java]    Monson-Haefel
```

Client_82k

The *Client_82k* program implements the queries illustrated in the EJB book, in the section of Chapter 8 called "Functional Expressions." The business logic for this example is implemented in `com.titan.test.Test82Bean`, in the `test82k()` method.

One Customer EJB finder method demonstrates the use of a couple of functional expressions.

EJB:	`Customer`
finder method:	`findByLastNameLength()`

query:	`SELECT OBJECT( c ) FROM Customer c`
	`WHERE LENGTH(c.lastName) > 6 AND`
	`LOCATE(c.lastName, 'Monson') > -1`

Client_82k invokes this query and displays its output. To run it, invoke the Ant task `run.client_82k`. The output should look something like this:

```
C:\workbook\ex08_2>ant run.client_82k
Buildfile: build.xml
```

```
prepare:

compile:

run.client_82k:
     [java] THE WHERE CLAUSE AND FUNCTIONAL EXPRESSIONS
     [java] --------------------------------
     [java] SELECT OBJECT( c ) FROM Customer c
     [java] WHERE LENGTH(c.lastName) > 6 AND
     [java] LOCATE(c.lastName, 'Monson') > -1
     [java]    Labourey
     [java]    Garciaparra
     [java]    Monson-Haefel
```

Client_82m

The *Client_82m* program implements the queries illustrated in the EJB book, in the section of Chapter 8 called "EJB 2.1: Aggregate functions in the SELECT clause." The business logic for this example is implemented in `com.titan.test.Test82Bean`, in the `test82m()` method.

The first query finds the count of all customer Zip codes that are in the Boston, MA area. Most Zip codes in the Boston area start with 0211, so a `LIKE` statement is used. A custom home method from the Customer EJB's home interface is used to wrap the private `ejbSelect` queries defined in the same bean.

```
query:               SELECT DISTINCT COUNT(c.homeAddress.zip)
                     FROM Customer AS c
                     WHERE c.homeAddress.zip LIKE '0211%'
ejbSelect method:    ejbSelectCountOfBostonZips()
custom home method:    countOfBostonZips()
ejbHome method:        ejbHomeCountOfBostonZips()
```

The second gets the maximum value of the `amountPaid` field of all Reservation EJBs. A custom home method from Reservation EJB is used to wrap the private `ejbSelect` queries that are declared within the bean class.

```
query:                 SELECT SELECT MAX(r.amountPaid)
                       FROM Reservation As r
ejbSelect method:      ejbSelectMaxAmountPaid()
custom home method:    maxAmountPaid()
ejbHome method:        ejbHomeMaxAmountPaid()
```

The third query gets the sum of all reservations paid based on a cruise passed in as a parameter. A custom home method from Cruise EJB is used to wrap the private `ejbSelect` queries that are declared within the bean class.

```
query:                 SELECT SUM( r.amountPaid)
                       FROM Cruise c, IN( c.reservations) AS r
                       WHERE  c = ?1
ejbSelect method:      ejbSelectSumReservation(CruiseLocal cruise)
custom home method:    sumReservation(CruiseLocal cruise)
ejbHome method:        ejbHomeSumReservation(CruiseLocal cruise)
```

The final query takes the average of all reservations paid based on a cruise passed in as a parameter. A custom home method from Cruise EJB is used to wrap the private ejbSelect queries that are declared within the bean class.

```
query:                  SELECT AVG( r.amountPaid)
                        FROM Cruise c, IN( c.reservations) AS r
                        WHERE  c = ?1
ejbSelect method:       ejbSelectAveragePaidReservation(CruiseLocal cruise)
custom home method:     averagePaidReservation(CruiseLocal cruise)
ejbHome method:         ejbHomeAveragePaidReservation(CruiseLocal cruise)
```

Client_82m invokes these queries and displays their output. To run it, invoke the Ant task `run.client_82m`. The output should look something like this:

```
C:\workbook...x08_2>ant run.client_82m
Buildfile: build.xml

prepare:

compile:

run.client_82m:
     [java] EJB 2.1 Aggregate Functions
     [java] --------------------------------
     [java] SELECT DISTINCT COUNT(c.homeAddress.zip)
     [java] FROM Customer AS c
     [java] WHERE c.homeAddress.zip LIKE '0211%'

     [java] count of Boston zip codes: 2
     [java] --------------------------------
     [java] SELECT MAX(r.amountPaid)
     [java] FROM Reservation As r

     [java] max amount paid for a reservation: $40000.0
     [java] --------------------------------
     [java] SELECT SUM( r.amountPaid)
     [java] FROM Cruise c, IN( c.reservations) AS r
     [java] WHERE  c = ?1

     [java] Sum of Alaskan Cruise reservations: $40000.0
     [java] --------------------------------
     [java] SELECT AVG( r.amountPaid)
     [java] FROM Cruise c, IN( c.reservations) AS r
     [java] WHERE  c = ?1
     [java] Average of Atlantic Cruise reservations: $10000.0
```

Client_82n

The *Client_82n* program implements the queries illustrated in the EJB book, in the section of Chapter 8 entitled "EJB 2.1: The ORDER BY Clause." The business logic for this example is implemented in `com.titan.test.Test82Bean`, in the `test82n()` method.

One Customer EJB finder method demonstrates the use of ORDER BY with the DESC keyword.

```
EJB:                Customer
finder method:      findByOrderedLastName()
query:              SELECT OBJECT( c ) FROM Customer AS c
                    ORDER BY c.lastName DESC
```

Client_82n invokes this query and displays its output. To run it, invoke the Ant task run.client_82n. The output should look something like this:

```
C:\workbook…x08_2>ant run.client_82n
Buildfile: build.xml

prepare:

compile:

run.client_82n:
     [java] EJB 2.1 ORDER BY Clause
     [java] --------------------------------
     [java] SELECT OBJECT( c ) FROM Customer AS c
     [java] ORDER BY c.lastName DESC
     [java]    Swift
     [java]    Monson-Haefel
     [java]    Labourey
     [java]    Garciaparra
     [java]    Fleury
     [java]    Burke
```

JBoss Dynamic QL

One of the features seriously lacking in EJB QL is the ability to do dynamic queries at run time. This example shows how you can do dynamic queries on Customer EJBs with JBoss CMP 2.0.

First, you must declare an ejbSelectGeneric() method that will invoke your dynamic queries and an ejbHome wrapper method so that the test program can invoke it.

```
public abstract class CustomerBean implements javax.ejb.EntityBean
{
   public abstract Set ejbSelectGeneric(String jbossQl, Object[] arguments)
        throws FinderException;

   public Set ejbHomeDynamicQuery(String jbossQL, Object[] arguments)
      throws FinderException
   {
      return ejbSelectGeneric(jbossQL, arguments);
   }
```

Next, declare your ejbHome wrapper method in *CustomerHomeLocal.java*:

```
public interface CustomerHomeLocal extends javax.ejb.EJBLocalHome
{
```

```
    ...
    public Set dynamicQuery(String jbossQl, Object[] arguments)
       throws FinderException;
}
```

The ejbSelectGeneric() method must be defined in the *ejb-jar.xml* deployment descriptor. Notice that the <ejb-ql> value is empty.

```
<ejb-jar>
 <enterprise-beans>
   <entity>
      <ejb-name>CustomerEJB</ejb-name>
      ...
      <query>
        <query-method>
           <method-name>ejbSelectGeneric</method-name>
           <method-params>
              <method-param>java.lang.String</method-param>
              <method-param>java.lang.Object[]</method-param>
           </method-params>
        </query-method>
        <ejb-ql></ejb-ql>
      </query>
```

Finally, in *jbosscmp-jdbc.xml*, tell JBoss that the ejbSelectGeneric() method is dynamic:

```
<jbosscmp-jdbc>
   <enterprise-beans>
      <entity>
         <ejb-name>CustomerEJB</ejb-name>
         <query>
            <query-method>
               <method-name>ejbSelectGeneric</method-name>
               <method-params>
                  <method-param>java.lang.String</method-param>
                  <method-param>java.lang.Object[]</method-param>
               </method-params>
            </query-method>
            <dynamic-ql/>
         </query>
      </entity>
   </enterprise-beans>
</jbosscmp-jdbc>
```

The business logic for this example is implemented in com.titan.test.Test82Bean, in the test82Dynamic() method.

```
public String test82Dynamic() throws RemoteException
{
  ...
  // obtain Home interfaces
  InitialContext jndiContext = getInitialContext();
  Object obj = jndiContext.lookup("CustomerHomeLocal");
```

```
    CustomerHomeLocal customerHome = (CustomerHomeLocal)obj;
    ...
    Object[] params = {};
    Set customers =
     customerHome.dynamicQuery("SELECT OBJECT( c ) FROM Customer c " +
                               "WHERE c.lastName LIKE 'B%'", params);
    ...
  }
```

The test82Dynamic() method generates a dynamic query string and invokes the dynamicQuery() method defined in the CustomerHomeLocal interface.

Client_82Dynamic invokes test82Dynamic() and displays its output. To run it, invoke the Ant task run.client_82dynamic. The output should look something like this:

```
C:\workbook\ex08_2>ant run.client_82dynamic
Buildfile: build.xml

prepare:

compile:

run.client_82dynamic:
     [java] JBoss Dynamic Queries
     [java] --------------------------------
     [java] SELECT OBJECT( c ) FROM Customer c
     [java] WHERE c.lastName LIKE 'B%'
     [java]    Burke
```

Advanced JBoss QL

In the "Problems with EJB QL" section of Chapter 8, Richard Monson-Haefel talks about some of the limitations of EJB QL. In the JBoss CMP 2.0 implementation, EJB QL is just a subset of a larger JBoss query language. JBoss QL does a great job of filling in some of the gaps in the EJB QL spec. Features such as the ability to use parameters within IN and LIKE clauses are just a few of the enhancements JBoss has implemented. Please review the advanced CMP 2.0 documentation available at the JBoss web site, *http://www.jboss.org*, for more information on these features.

WORKBOOK 7

Exercises for Chapter 9

Exercise 9.1: A BMP Entity Bean

In this exercise, you will build and examine a simple EJB that uses *bean-managed persistence* (BMP) to synchronize the state of the bean with a database. You will also build a client application to test this Ship BMP bean.

Start Up JBoss

If JBoss is already running, there is no reason to restart it.

Initialize the Database

As in the CMP examples, the state of the entity beans will be stored in the database that is embedded in JBoss. JBoss was able to create all tables for CMP beans, but it cannot do the same for BMP beans because the deployment descriptors don't contain any persistence information (object-to-relational mapping, for example). The bean is in fact the only one that knows how to load, store, remove, and find data. The persistence mapping is not described in a configuration file, but embedded in the bean code instead.

One consequence is that the database environment for BMP must always be built explicitly. To make this task easier for the BMP Ship example, Ship's home interface defines two helpful *home methods*.

Entity beans can define home methods that perform operations related to the EJB component's semantics but that are not linked to any particular bean instance. As an analogy, consider the static methods of a class: their semantics are generally closely related to the class's semantics, but they're not associated with any particular class instance. Don't worry if this is not totally clear: Chapter 10 of the EJB book, explains all about home methods.

Here's a partial view of the Ship EJB's home interface:

```
public interface ShipHomeRemote extends javax.ejb.EJBHome
{
    ...
    public void makeDbTable () throws RemoteException;
    public void deleteDbTable () throws RemoteException;
}
```

It defines two home methods. The first creates the table needed by the Ship EJB in the JBoss-embedded database and the second drops it.

The implementation of the `makeDbTable()` home method is essentially a `CREATE TABLE` SQL statement:

```
public void ejbHomeMakeDbTable () throws SQLException
{
   PreparedStatement ps = null;
   Connection con = null;
   try
   {
      con = this.getConnection ();

      System.out.println("Creating table SHIP...");
      ps = con.prepareStatement ("CREATE TABLE SHIP ( " +
                                 "ID INT PRIMARY KEY, " +
                                 "NAME CHAR (30), " +
                                 "TONNAGE DECIMAL (8,2), " +
                                 "CAPACITY INT" +
                                 ")" );
      ps.execute ();
      System.out.println("...done!");
   }
   finally
   {
      try { if (ps != null) ps.close (); } catch (Exception e) {}
      try { if (con != null) con.close (); } catch (Exception e) {}
   }
}
```

The `deleteDbTable()` home method differs only by the SQL statement it executes:

```
...
System.out.println("Dropping table SHIP...");
ps = con.prepareStatement ("DROP TABLE SHIP");
ps.execute ();
System.out.println("...done!");
...
```

We explain how to call these methods in a subsequent section.

Examine the EJB Standard Files

The Ship EJB source code requires no modification to run in JBoss, so the standard EJB deployment descriptor is very simple.

ejb-jar.xml (part I)

```
...
<enterprise-beans>
  <entity>
     <description>
           This bean represents a cruise ship.
     </description>
     <ejb-name>ShipEJB</ejb-name>
     <home>com.titan.ship.ShipHomeRemote</home>
     <remote>com.titan.ship.ShipRemote</remote>
     <ejb-class>com.titan.ship.ShipBean</ejb-class>
     <persistence-type>Bean</persistence-type>
     <prim-key-class>java.lang.Integer</prim-key-class>
     <reentrant>False</reentrant>
     <security-identity><use-caller-identity/></security-identity>
     <resource-ref>
          <description>DataSource for the Titan DB</description>
          <res-ref-name>jdbc/titanDB</res-ref-name>
          <res-type>javax.sql.DataSource</res-type>
          <res-auth>Container</res-auth>
     </resource-ref>
 </entity>
</enterprise-beans>
...
```

This first part of the deployment descriptor essentially tells the container that the Ship bean:

- Is named `ShipEJB`.
- Has a persistence type set to `Bean` because it's a BMP bean.
- Declares a reference to a data source named `jdbc/titanDB`.

Because the bean directly manages the persistence logic, the deployment descriptor does not contain any persistence information. In contrast, this information would have been mandatory for a CMP EJB.

The second part of the deployment descriptor declares the transactional and security attributes of the Ship bean.

ejb-jar.xml (part II)

```
...
<assembly-descriptor>

   <security-role>
      <description>
```

```
            This role represents everyone who is allowed full
            access to the Ship EJB.
         </description>
        <role-name>everyone</role-name>
      </security-role>

      <method-permission>
        <role-name>everyone</role-name>
        <method>
            <ejb-name>ShipEJB</ejb-name>
            <method-name>*</method-name>
        </method>
      </method-permission>

      <container-transaction>
        <method>
           <ejb-name>ShipEJB</ejb-name>
           <method-name>*</method-name>
        </method>
        <trans-attribute>Required</trans-attribute>
      </container-transaction>

    </assembly-descriptor>

   </ejb-jar>
```

All methods of the Ship bean require a transaction. If no transaction is active when a method invocation enters the container, a new one will be started.

In entity beans, transactions are always managed by the container, never directly by the bean. Thus, all work done on transactional resources, such as databases, will implicitly be part of the transactional context of the container.

Examine the JBoss-Specific Files

If you don't include a *jboss.xml*-specific deployment descriptor with your bean, JBoss will take the following actions at deployment time. It will:

- Bind the Ship bean in the public JNDI tree under `/ShipEJB` (which is the name given to the bean in its associated *ejb-jar.xml* deployment descriptor).
- Link the `jdbc/titanDB` data source expected by the bean to `java:/DefaultDS`, which is a default data source that represents the embedded database.

Unless you require different settings, you don't need to provide a *jboss.xml* file. While this shortcut is generally useful for quick prototyping, it will not satisfy more complex deployment situations. Furthermore, using a JBoss-specific deployment descriptor enables you to fine-tune a container for a particular situation.

If you take a look at the *$JBOSS_HOME/server/default/conf/standardjboss.xml* file, you will find all the default container settings that are predefined in JBoss (standard BMP, standard CMP, clustered BMP, and so on). In JBoss, there's a one-to-one mapping between a bean and a container, and each container can be configured independently.

This mapping was a design decision made by the JBoss container developers and has not been dictated by the EJB specification: other application servers may use another mapping.

When you write a JBoss-specific deployment descriptor, you have three options:

- Don't specify any container configuration. JBoss will use the default configuration found in *standardjboss.xml*.
- Create a brand new container configuration. The default settings are not used at all. JBoss will configure the container only as you specify in *jboss.xml*.
- Modify an existing configuration. JBoss loads the default settings from the existing configuration found in *standardjboss.xml* and overrides them with the settings you specify in the *jboss.xml* deployment descriptor. This solution allows you to make minor modifications to the default container with minimal writing in your deployment descriptor.

The Ship bean uses the last option in order to test its behavior with different commit options. As outlined below, this new configuration defines only a single setting (`<commit-option>`). All others are inherited from the `Standard BMP EntityBean` configuration declared in the *standardjboss.xml* file. We'll discuss commit options in a dedicated section at the end of this chapter.

jboss.xml

```
<?xml version="1.0"?>

<!DOCTYPE jboss PUBLIC
      "-//JBoss//DTD JBOSS 4.0//EN"
      "http://www.jboss.org/j2ee/dtd/jboss_4_0.dtd">

<jboss>
...
<container-configurations>
   <container-configuration>
      <container-name>Standard BMP EntityBean</container-name>
      <commit-option>A</commit-option>
   </container-configuration>
</container-configurations>
...
```

Because a single deployment descriptor may define multiple EJBs, the role of the `<ejb-name>` tag is to link the definitions from the *ejb-jar.xml* and *jboss.xml* files. You can consider this tag to be the bean's *identifier*. The `<jndi-name>` tag determines the name under which the client applications will be able to look up the EJB's home interface, in this case `ShipHomeRemote`.

You can also see how the bean refers to a specific configuration, thanks to the <configuration-name> tag.

```
...
   <enterprise-beans>
      <entity>
      <ejb-name>ShipEJB</ejb-name>
      <jndi-name>ShipHomeRemote</jndi-name>
      <configuration-name>Standard BMP EntityBean
      </configuration-name>
      <resource-ref>
         <res-ref-name>jdbc/titanDB</res-ref-name>
         <jndi-name>java:/DefaultDS</jndi-name>
      </resource-ref>
      </entity>
   </enterprise-beans>
</jboss>
```

The Ship bean BMP implementation needs to establish a database connection explicitly. It's the getConnection() method that manages the acquisition of this resource.

ShipBean.java

```
private Connection getConnection () throws SQLException
{
   try
   {
      Context jndiCntx = new InitialContext ();
      DataSource ds =
      (DataSource)jndiCntx.lookup ("java:comp/env/jdbc/titanDB");
      return ds.getConnection ();
      ...
```

The bean expects to find a data source bound to the java:comp/env/jdbc/titanDB JNDI name. That's why the *ejb-jar.xml* file contains the following declaration.

ejb-jar.xml

```
...
<resource-ref>
     <description>DataSource for the Titan DB</description>
     <res-ref-name>jdbc/titanDB</res-ref-name>
     <res-type>javax.sql.DataSource</res-type>
     <res-auth>Container</res-auth>
</resource-ref>
...
```

Then *jboss.xml* maps the jdbc/titanDB data source name to the actual name defined in JBoss.

jboss.xml

```
...
<resource-ref>
  <res-ref-name>jdbc/titanDB</res-ref-name>
```

```
  <jndi-name>java:/DefaultDS</jndi-name>
</resource-ref>
...
```

In any default JBoss installation, `java:/DefaultDS` represents the embedded database.

Build and Deploy the Example Programs

Perform the following steps:

1. Open a command prompt or shell terminal and change to the *ex9_1* directory created by the extraction process
2. Set the `JAVA_HOME` and `JBOSS_HOME` environment variables to point to where your JDK and JBoss 4.0 are installed. Examples:

   Windows:

   ```
   C:\workbook\ex9_1> set JAVA_HOME=C:\jdk1.4.2
   C:\workbook\ex9_1> set JBOSS_HOME=C:\jboss-4.0
   ```

   Unix:

   ```
   $ export JAVA_HOME=/usr/local/jdk1.4.2
   $ export JBOSS_HOME=/usr/local/jboss-4.0
   ```

3. Add `ant` to your execution path.

   Windows:

   ```
   C:\workbook\ex9_1> set PATH=..\ant\bin;%PATH%
   ```

   Unix:

   ```
   $ export PATH=../ant/bin:$PATH
   ```

4. Perform the build by typing `ant`.

As in the last exercise, you will see *titan.jar* rebuilt, copied to the JBoss *deploy* directory, and redeployed by the application server.

Examine the Client Application

In the "Initialize the Database" section earlier in this chapter, you saw how the bean implements the home methods that create and drop the table in the database. Now you'll see how the client application calls these home methods.

Client_91.java

```
public class Client_91
{
   public static void main (String [] args)
   {
      try
      {
         Context jndiContext = getInitialContext ();

         Object ref = jndiContext.lookup ("ShipHomeRemote");
         ShipHomeRemote home = (ShipHomeRemote)
         PortableRemoteObject.narrow (ref,ShipHomeRemote.class);
```

```
// We check if we have to build the database schema...
//
if ( (args.length > 0) &&
     args[0].equalsIgnoreCase ("CreateDB") )
{
   System.out.println ("Creating database table...");
   home.makeDbTable ();
}
// ... or if we have to drop it...
//
else if ( (args.length > 0) &&
          args[0].equalsIgnoreCase ("DropDB") )
{
   System.out.println ("Dropping database table...");
   home.deleteDbTable ();
}
else
...
```

Depending on the first argument found on the command line (CreateDB or DropDB), the client application calls the corresponding home method.

If nothing is specified on the command line, the client will test our BMP bean:

```
...
else
{
   // ... standard behavior
   //
   System.out.println ("Creating Ship 101..");
   ShipRemote ship1 = home.create (new Integer
                      (101),"Edmund Fitzgerald");

   ship1.setTonnage (50000.0);
   ship1.setCapacity (300);

   Integer pk = new Integer (101);

   System.out.println ("Finding Ship 101 again..");
   ShipRemote ship2 = home.findByPrimaryKey (pk);

   System.out.println (ship2.getName ());
   System.out.println (ship2.getTonnage ());
   System.out.println (ship2.getCapacity ());

   System.out.println ("ship1.equals (ship2) == " +
   ship1.equals (ship2));

   System.out.println ("Removing Ship 101..");
   ship2.remove ();
}
...
```

The client application first creates a new Ship and calls some of its remote methods to set its tonnage and capacity. Then it finds the bean again by calling `findByPrimaryKey()` and compares the bean references for equality. Because they represent the same bean instance, they must be equal. We've omitted the exception handling because it deserves no specific comments.

Run the Client Application

Testing the BMP bean is a three-step process that involves:

1. Creating the database table
2. Testing the bean (possibly many times)
3. Dropping the database table

For each of these steps, a different Ant target is available.

Creating the database table

To create the table, use the `createdb_91` Ant target:

```
C:\workbook\ex9_1>ant createdb_91
Buildfile: build.xml

prepare:

compile:

createdb_91:
     [java] Creating database table...
```

On the JBoss side, the BMP bean displays the following lines:

```
...
12:31:42,584 INFO  [STDOUT] Creating table SHIP...
12:31:42,584 INFO  [STDOUT] ...done!
...
```

Once this step has been performed, the actual testing of the BMP bean can take place.

If you're having trouble creating the database, shut down JBoss, then run the Ant build target `clean.db`. This removes all database files and allows you to start fresh.

Testing the BMP bean

To test the BMP bean, use the `run.client_91` Ant target:

```
C:\workbook\ex9_1>ant run.client_91
Buildfile: build.xml
```

```
prepare:

compile:

run.client_101:
     [java] Creating Ship 101..
     [java] Finding Ship 101 again..
     [java] Edmund Fitzgerald
     [java] 50000.0
     [java] 300
     [java] ship1.equals (ship2) == true
     [java] Removing Ship 101..
```

Analyzing the effects of transactions and commit options

Even though it's not particularly related to BMP beans, let's focus on an interesting problem that arises when the client first creates and initializes the bean:

```
ShipRemote ship1 = home.create (new Integer
                   (101),"Edmund Fitzgerald");

ship1.setTonnage (50000.0);
ship1.setCapacity (300);
```

This piece of code generates three different transactions on the server side. The client does not implicitly start any transaction in its code. The transaction starts only when the invocation enters the bean container and commits when the invocation leaves the container. Thus, when the client performs three calls, each one is executed in its own transactional context.

Look at the implications for the BMP bean:

```
14:36:31,730 INFO  [STDOUT] ejbCreate() pk=101 name=Edmund Fitzgerald
14:36:31,780 INFO  [STDOUT] ejbStore() pk=101
14:36:31,840 INFO  [STDOUT] setTonnage()
14:36:31,840 INFO  [STDOUT] ejbStore() pk=101
14:36:31,860 INFO  [STDOUT] setCapacity()
14:36:31,860 INFO  [STDOUT] ejbStore() pk=101
```

As you can see, `ejbStore()` is called at the end of each transaction! Consequently, these three lines of code cause the bean to be stored three times. Worst of all, after any method invocation, the container has no way of knowing whether the state of the bean has been modified, and thus, to be on the safe side, it triggers storage of the bean. Given that there is no read-only method concept in EJBs, calls to get methods also trigger calls to `ejbStore()`:

```
15:03:19,301 INFO  [STDOUT] getName()
15:03:19,311 INFO  [STDOUT] ejbStore() pk=101
15:03:19,331 INFO  [STDOUT] getTonnage()
15:03:19,331 INFO  [STDOUT] ejbStore() pk=101
15:03:19,371 INFO  [STDOUT] getCapacity()
15:03:19,371 INFO  [STDOUT] ejbStore() pk=101
```

In the execution of the test program, `ejbStore()` is called seven times.

You can see that transaction boundaries (i.e., where transactions are started and stopped) directly influence the number of callbacks from the container to the Ship bean, and consequently have a direct effect on performance. We'll now focus on another setting that also affects the set of callback methods the container will invoke on the bean: the *commit option*. The commit option determines how an entity bean container can make use of its cache. Remember from the container configuration section that the bean is currently using commit option A. Let's examine all the options and their effects.

If you select commit option A, the entity bean container is allowed to cache any bean that it has loaded. Next time an invocation targets a bean that is already in the application server cache,* the container will not have to make a costly database access call to load it again.

If you select commit option B or C, the entity bean container is allowed to cache a bean only if it loads that bean during the lifetime of the currently running transaction. Once the transaction commits or rolls back, the container must remove the bean from the cache. The next time an invocation targets the bean, the container will have to reload it from the database.

That extra reloading is costly—but you must use B or C† whenever the data represented by the container can also be modified by other means. Direct database access calls through a console, for example, will cause the container cache to become unsynchronized with the database, leading to incorrect computations and other dire results. A container must not use commit option A unless it "owns" the database (or, more accurately, the specific tables it accesses).

Most of the time, this "black or white" approach isn't satisfactory: in real-world applications, commit option A can be used only very rarely, and commit options B and C will preclude useful cache optimizations. To circumvent these limitations, JBoss provides some proprietary optimizations: an additional commit option, distributed cache invalidations, and even a distributed transactional cache with various locking policies (JBossCache). See the JBoss web site for more information.

The JBoss-proprietary commit option D is a compromise between options A and C: The bean instance can be cached across transactions, but a configurable timeout value indicates when this cached data is stale and must be reloaded from the data-

* We are speaking about the application server cache, not the database cache. While database caches are critical to performance, application server caches can improve it even further.

† The difference between commit option B and C is very small: when a transaction commits, a container using commit option C must effectively throw away the bean instance while a container using commit option B may keep it and reuse it later. This distinction allows commit option B to be used for very specific container optimizations (such as checking whether the data has really been modified in the database and reusing the instance if no modification has occurred, instead of reloading the whole state).

base. This option is very useful when you want some of the efficiency of commit option A, but want cached entities to be updated periodically to reflect modifications by an external system.

Remember that each EJB deployed in JBoss has its own container. Consequently, for each EJB, you can define the commit option that best fits its specific environment. For example, a Zip code entity bean (with data that will most probably never change) could use commit option A, whereas the Order EJB would use commit option C.

After this introduction to commit options, it becomes possible to guess that the container is currently using commit option A without looking at its configuration. Two pieces of evidence lead us to this conclusion:

- The `findByPrimaryKey()` call isn't displayed in the log. The container first checks whether the cache already contains an instance for the given primary key. Because it does, there is no need to invoke the bean implementation's `ejbFindByPrimaryKey()` method.
- `ejbLoad()` isn't called for the bean. At the start of each new transaction, it's already in cache and there is no need to reload it from the database.

Note that only direct access to a given bean (using its remote reference) or `findByPrimaryKey()` calls can be resolved in cache. All other queries (`findAll()`, `findByCapacity()`, and so on) must be resolved by the database directly (there is no way to perform queries in the container cache directly).

To see how different commit options lead to different behavior, change the commit option in *jboss.xml* from A to C:

jboss.xml

```
...
<container-configurations>
   <container-configuration>
      <container-name>Standard BMP EntityBean</container-name>
      <commit-option>C</commit-option>
   </container-configuration>
</container-configurations>
...
```

Run the tests again. You'll see:

```
14:41:29,798 INFO  [STDOUT] ejbCreate() pk=101 name=Edmund Fitzgerald
14:41:30,449 INFO  [STDOUT] ejbStore() pk=101
14:41:30,539 INFO  [STDOUT] ejbLoad() pk=101
14:41:30,599 INFO  [STDOUT] setTonnage()
14:41:30,609 INFO  [STDOUT] ejbStore() pk=101
```

```
14:41:30,659 INFO  [STDOUT] ejbLoad() pk=101
14:41:30,669 INFO  [STDOUT] setCapacity()
14:41:30,679 INFO  [STDOUT] ejbStore() pk=101
14:41:30,709 INFO  [STDOUT] ejbFindByPrimaryKey() primaryKey=101
14:41:30,729 INFO  [STDOUT] ejbLoad() pk=101
14:41:30,750 INFO  [STDOUT] getName()
14:41:30,750 INFO  [STDOUT] ejbStore() pk=101
14:41:30,780 INFO  [STDOUT] ejbLoad() pk=101
14:41:30,790 INFO  [STDOUT] getTonnage()
14:41:30,800 INFO  [STDOUT] ejbStore() pk=101
14:41:30,840 INFO  [STDOUT] ejbLoad() pk=101
14:41:30,850 INFO  [STDOUT] getCapacity()
14:41:30,860 INFO  [STDOUT] ejbStore() pk=101
14:41:30,880 INFO  [STDOUT] ejbLoad() pk=101
14:41:30,900 INFO  [STDOUT] ejbStore() pk=101
14:41:30,910 INFO  [STDOUT] ejbRemove() pk=101
```

Now, in addition to the `ejbStore()` calls you've already seen, you see calls to `ejbLoad()` at the start of each new transaction, and the call to `ejbFindByPrimaryKey()` as well, which reaches the bean implementation because it cannot be resolved within the cache.

Possible optimizations

As you have seen during the execution of the client application, the Ship bean performs many `ejbLoad()` and `ejbStore()` operations. There are two reasons behind this behavior:

- Many transactions are started.
- The Ship bean BMP code is not optimized.

You can reduce the number of transactions in several ways:

- Define less fine-grained methods that return all attributes of the bean in a single data object.
- Add a new create method with many parameters, so a single call can create and initialize the bean.
- Use the Façade pattern: create a stateless session bean that starts a single transaction, then performs all the steps in that one transaction.
- Start a transaction in the client application, using a `UserTransaction` object.

BMP code optimization is a wide topic. Here are some tricks that are frequently used:

- Use an `isModified` flag in your bean. Set it to `true` each time the state of the bean changes (in set methods, for example). In the implementation of `ejbStore()`, perform the actual database call only if `isModified` is `true`. Think about the impact on the test application. All the `ejbStore()` calls resulting from invocations to get methods will detect that no data has been modified and will not try to synchronize with the database.

- Detect which fields are actually modified during a transaction and update only those particular fields in the database. This tactic is especially useful for beans with lots of fields or with fields that contain large amounts of data. Contrast with the Ship BMP bean as it's currently written, where each setXXX() call updates all fields of the database even though only one actually changes.

Note that any decent CMP engine performs many of these optimizations by default.

Dropping the database table

Once you've run all the tests, clean the database environment associated with the BMP bean by removing the unused table. Use the dropdb_91 target:

```
C:\workbook\ex9_1>ant dropdb_91
Buildfile: build.xml

prepare:

compile:

dropdb_101:
     [java] Dropping database table...
```

On the JBoss side, the BMP bean logs the following lines:

```
...
14:40:34,339 INFO  [STDOUT] Dropping table SHIP...
14:40:34,349 INFO  [STDOUT] ...done!
...
```

WORKBOOK 8
Exercises for Chapter 11

Exercise 11.1: A Stateless Session Bean

In this exercise, you will build and examine a stateless session bean, `ProcessPaymentEJB`, which writes payment information to the database. You will also build a client application to test this ProcessPayment bean.

The bean inserts the payment information data directly into the database, without using an intermediary entity bean.

Examine the EJB

This example is based on the Customer and Address EJBs and their related data objects that you used in Exercise 6.3. The present exercise leaves these EJBs unchanged, and focuses on the ProcessPayment stateless session bean.

The ProcessPayment bean has a very simple remote interface. It offers options to process a payment by check, cash, or credit card. Each possibility is handled by a different method.

ProcessPaymentRemote.java

```
public interface ProcessPaymentRemote extends javax.ejb.EJBObject
{
   public boolean byCheck (CustomerRemote customer,
                           CheckDO        check,
                           double         amount)
   throws RemoteException, PaymentException;

   public boolean byCash (CustomerRemote customer,
                          double         amount)
   throws RemoteException, PaymentException;

   public boolean byCredit (CustomerRemote customer,
                            CreditCardDO  card,
                            double        amount)
```

```
        throws RemoteException, PaymentException;
        ...
}
```

Each method's third parameter is a simple transaction amount. The other two are more interesting.

The first is a CustomerRemote interface, which enables the ProcessPayment EJB to get any information it needs about the customer.

It's possible to use EJB remote interfaces as parameters of other EJB methods because they extend EJBObject, which in turn extends java.rmi.Remote. Objects implementing either Remote or Serializable are perfectly valid RMI types. This choice of parameter type makes no difference at all to the EJB container.

The second parameter conveys the details of the transaction in a data object with a type that reflects the form of payment. A data object is a Serializable object that a client and a remote server can pass by value back and forth. Most of the time it is a simple data container, with minimal behavior. For example, the CheckDO class contains the check's number and bar code.

CheckDO.java

```
public class CheckDO implements java.io.Serializable
{
   public String checkBarCode;
   public int checkNumber;

   public CheckDO (String barCode, int number)
   {
      this.checkBarCode = barCode;
      this.checkNumber = number;
   }
```

Focus on the ProcessPayment EJB implementation for a little while. Each remote method first performs validity tests appropriate to the type of payment. Eventually all of them call the same private method: process(), which inserts the payment information into the database. For example, byCredit() implements this logic as shown.

ProcessPaymentBean.java

```
public boolean byCredit (CustomerRemote customer,
                         CreditCardDO   card,
                         double         amount)
throws PaymentException
{
   if (card.expiration.before (new java.util.Date ()))
   {
      throw new PaymentException ("Expiration date has passed");
   }
```

```
    else
    {
       return
          process (getCustomerID (customer),
                   amount,
                   CREDIT,
                   null,
                   -1,
                   card.number,
                   new java.sql.Date (card.expiration.getTime ()));
    }
}
```

If the credit card has expired, the method throws an *application exception*. If not, it simply delegates the chore of inserting the payment information into the database to process(). Note that some parameters passed to process() are meaningless. For example, the fourth parameter represents the check bar code, which means nothing in a credit card payment, so byCredit() passes a dummy value.

The process() method is very similar to the ejbCreate() method of the BMP example in Chapter 10. It simply gets a data-source connection, creates a PreparedStatement, and inserts the payment information into the PAYMENT table:

```
...
con = getConnection ();

ps = con.prepareStatement
   ("INSERT INTO payment (customer_id, amount, " +
    "type, check_bar_code, " +
    "check_number, credit_number, " +
    "credit_exp_date) "+
    "VALUES (?,?,?,?,?,?,?)");
ps.setInt (1,customerID.intValue ());
ps.setDouble (2,amount);
ps.setString (3,type);
ps.setString (4,checkBarCode);
ps.setInt (5,checkNumber);
ps.setString (6,creditNumber);
ps.setDate (7,creditExpDate);

int retVal = ps.executeUpdate ();
if (retVal!=1)
{
   throw new EJBException ("Payment insert failed");
}

return true;
...
```

Note that the returned value is not significant. The method either returns true or throws an application exception, so its return type could as easily be void.

Examine the EJB Standard Deployment Descriptor

The ProcessPayment standard deployment descriptor is very similar to one you've already seen.

ejb-jar.xml

```
...
<session>
  <description>
    A service that handles monetary payments
  </description>
  <ejb-name>ProcessPaymentEJB</ejb-name>
  <home>com.titan.processpayment.ProcessPaymentHomeRemote</home>
  <remote>com.titan.processpayment.ProcessPaymentRemote</remote>
  <ejb-class>com.titan.processpayment.ProcessPaymentBean</ejb-class>
  <session-type>Stateless</session-type>
  <transaction-type>Container</transaction-type>
  <env-entry>
    <env-entry-name>minCheckNumber</env-entry-name>
    <env-entry-type>java.lang.Integer</env-entry-type>
    <env-entry-value>2000</env-entry-value>
  </env-entry>
  <resource-ref>
    <description>DataSource for the Titan database</description>
    <res-ref-name>jdbc/titanDB</res-ref-name>
    <res-type>javax.sql.DataSource</res-type>
    <res-auth>Container</res-auth>
  </resource-ref>
</session>
...
```

Note that the ProcessPaymentEJB's <session-type> tag is set to Stateless and its <transaction-type> tag is set to Container. These settings ensure that the container will automatically manage the transactions and enlist any transactional resources the bean uses. Chapter 16 of the EJB section of this book explains how these tasks can be handled by the EJB itself (if it's a session bean or a message-driven bean).

The descriptor contains a reference to a data source it will use to store the payments. You use this data source the same way you did in the BMP example in Chapter 10.

ProcessPaymentBean.java

```
private Connection getConnection () throws SQLException
{
   try
   {
      InitialContext jndiCntx = new InitialContext ();

      DataSource ds = (DataSource)
      jndiCntx.lookup ("java:comp/env/jdbc/titanDB");
```

```
            return ds.getConnection ();
        }
        catch(NamingException ne)
        {
            throw new EJBException (ne);
        }
    }
```

The *ejb-jar.xml* file also specifies an *environment property*, `minCheckNumber`. Environment properties provide a very flexible way to parameterize a bean's behavior at deployment time. The `<env-entry>` tag for `minCheckNumber` specifies the property's type (`java.lang.Integer`) and a default value (2000). The ProcessPayment EJB accesses the value of this property through its JNDI ENC.

ProcessPaymentBean.java

```
...
InitialContext jndiCntx = new InitialContext ();

Integer value - (Integer) jndiCntx.lookup
                        ("java:comp/env/minCheckNumber");
...
```

One very interesting point to note is that although the ProcessPayment bean works with Customer beans (recall that each remote method's first parameter is a Customer interface), the deployment descriptor doesn't declare any reference to the Customer EJB. No `<ejb-ref>` or `<ejb-local-ref>` tag is needed because the ProcessPayment bean won't find or create Customer beans through the `CustomerRemoteHome` interface, but instead receives Customer beans directly from the client application. Thus, from the ProcessPayment EJB's point of view, the Customer is a standard remote Java object.

Examine the JBoss Deployment Descriptors

The JBoss-specific deployment descriptor for the ProcessPayment bean is very simple. It only maps the data source to the embedded database in Jboss.

jboss.xml

```
<session>
   <ejb-name>ProcessPaymentEJB</ejb-name>
   <jndi-name>ProcessPaymentHomeRemote</jndi-name>
   <resource-ref>
      <res-ref-name>jdbc/titanDB</res-ref-name>
      <jndi-name>java:/DefaultDS</jndi-name>
   </resource-ref>
</session>
```

The `<res-ref-name>` in *jboss.xml* maps to the same `<res-ref-name>` in *ejb-jar.xml*.

Start Up JBoss

If JBoss is already running, there is no reason to restart it.

Build and Deploy the Example Programs

Perform the following steps:

1. Open a command prompt or shell terminal and change to the *ex11_1* directory created by the extraction process.
2. Set the `JAVA_HOME` and `JBOSS_HOME` environment variables to point to where your JDK and JBoss 4.0 are installed. Examples:

   Windows:
   ```
   C:\workbook\ex11_1> set JAVA_HOME=C:\jdk1.4.2
   C:\workbook\ex11_1> set JBOSS_HOME=C:\jboss-4.0
   ```
   Unix:
   ```
   $ export JAVA_HOME=/usr/local/jdk1.4.2
   $ export JBOSS_HOME=/usr/local/jboss-4.0
   ```
3. Add `ant` to your execution path.

   Windows:
   ```
   C:\workbook\ex11_1> set PATH=..\ant\bin;%PATH%
   ```
   Unix:
   ```
   $ export PATH=../ant/bin:$PATH
   ```
4. Perform the build by typing `ant`.

As in the last exercise, you will see *titan.jar* rebuilt, copied to the JBoss *deploy* directory, and redeployed by the application server.

Initialize the Database

As in previous examples, you'll use the relational database that's embedded in JBoss to store payment information. Because the deployment descriptor of a stateless session bean does not contain any information about the database schema that the bean needs, JBoss can't automatically create the database table, as it does for CMP beans. Instead, you will have to create the database schema for the `PAYMENT` table manually through JDBC. Use the `createdb` Ant target:

```
C:\workbook\ex11_1>ant createdb
Buildfile: build.xml

prepare:

compile:

ejbjar:
```

```
createdb:
     [java] Looking up home interfaces...
     [java] Creating database table...
```

On the JBoss console, you'll see:

```
INFO  [STDOUT] Creating table PAYMENT...
INFO  [STDOUT] ...done!
```

If you're having trouble creating the database, shut down JBoss. Then run the Ant build target `clean.db`. This removes all database files and allow you to start fresh.

A `dropdb` Ant target has been added as well, if you want to destroy the `PAYMENT` table:

```
C:\workbook\ex11_1>ant dropdb
Buildfile: build.xml

prepare:

compile:

dropdb:
     [java] Looking up home interfaces..
     [java] Dropping database table...

BUILD SUCCESSFUL
```

To implement the `createdb` and `dropdb` Ant targets, the JBoss version of the ProcessPayment bean introduced in the EJB book defines two new methods: `makeDbTable()` and `dropDbTable()`.

Here's a partial view of the ProcessPayment EJB's remote interface:

```
public interface ProcessPaymentRemote extends javax.ejb.EJBObject
{

    public void makeDbTable () throws RemoteException;
    public void deleteDbTable () throws RemoteException;
}
```

It defines two home methods: the first creates the table needed by the ProcessPayment EJB in the JBoss embedded database, and the second drops it.

The implementation of `makeDbTable()` is essentially a `CREATE TABLE` SQL statement:

```
public void makeDbTable ()
{
   PreparedStatement ps = null;
   Connection con = null;

   try
   {
      con = this.getConnection ();
      System.out.println("Creating table PAYMENT...");
      ps = con.prepareStatement
```

```
            ("CREATE TABLE PAYMENT ( " + "CUSTOMER_ID INT, " +
             "AMOUNT DECIMAL (8,2), " + "TYPE CHAR (10), " +
             "CHECK_BAR_CODE CHAR (50), " + "CHECK_NUMBER INTEGER, " +
             "CREDIT_NUMBER CHAR (20), " + "CREDIT_EXP_DATE DATE" +
             ")" );
         ps.execute ();
         System.out.println("...done!");
      }
      catch (SQLException sql)
      {
         throw new EJBException (sql);
      }
      finally
      {
         try { ps.close (); } catch (Exception e) {}
         try { con.close (); } catch (Exception e) {}
      }
   }
```

The deleteDbTable() home method differs only in the SQL statement it executes:

```
public void dropDbTable ()
{
      ...
      System.out.println("Dropping table PAYMENT...");
      ps = con.prepareStatement ("DROP TABLE PAYMENT");
      ps.execute ();
      System.out.println("...done!");
      ...
}
```

Examine the Client Applications

This exercise includes two example clients. The first simply prepares and creates a single Customer bean, which the second uses to insert data into the PAYMENT table.

Client_111a

Run the first application by invoking the run.client_111a Ant target:

```
C:\workbook\ex11_1>ant run.client_111a
Buildfile: build.xml

prepare:

compile:

ejbjar:

run.client_111a:
     [java] Creating Customer 1..
     [java] Creating AddressDO data object..
     [java] Setting Address in Customer 1...
```

```
[java] Acquiring Address data object from Customer 1...
[java] Customer 1 Address data:
[java] 1010 Colorado
[java] Austin,TX 78701
```

Client_111b

The code of the client application that actually tests the PaymentProcess EJB is much more interesting. First, it acquires a reference to the remote home of the ProcessPayment EJB from a newly created JNDI context:

```
Context jndiContext = getInitialContext ();

System.out.println ("Looking up home interfaces..");
Object ref = jndiContext.lookup ("ProcessPaymentHomeRemote");

ProcessPaymentHomeRemote procpayhome = (ProcessPaymentHomeRemote)
PortableRemoteObject.narrow (ref,ProcessPaymentHomeRemote.class);
```

This home makes it possible to create a remote reference to the stateless session bean:

```
ProcessPaymentRemote procpay = procpayhome.create ();
```

Then the client acquires a remote home reference for the Customer EJB and uses it to find the Customer bean created in the preceding example:

```
ref = jndiContext.lookup ("CustomerHomeRemote");
CustomerHomeRemote custhome = (CustomerHomeRemote)
PortableRemoteObject.narrow (ref,CustomerHomeRemote.class);

CustomerRemote cust = custhome.findByPrimaryKey (new Integer (1));
```

The ProcessPayment EJB can now be tested by executing payments of all three kinds: cash, check, and credit card.

```
System.out.println ("Making a payment using byCash()..");
procpay.byCash (cust,1000.0);

System.out.println ("Making a payment using byCheck()..");
CheckDO check = new CheckDO ("010010101101010100011", 3001);
procpay.byCheck (cust,check,2000.0);

System.out.println ("Making a payment using byCredit()..");
Calendar expdate = Calendar.getInstance ();
expdate.set (2005,1,28); // month=1 is February
CreditCardDO credit = new CreditCardDO ("370000000000002",
                                         expdate.getTime (),
                                         "AMERICAN_EXPRESS");

procpay.byCredit (cust,credit,3000.0);
```

Finally, to check the validation logic, the client tries to execute a payment with a check whose number is too low. The ProcessPayment EJB should refuse the payment and raise an application exception.

```
System.out.println ("Making a payment using byCheck() with a low
                     check number..");
CheckDO check2 = new CheckDO ("111000100111010110101", 1001);
try
{
   procpay.byCheck (cust,check2,9000.0);
   System.out.println("Problem! The PaymentException has
                       not been raised!"); }
catch (PaymentException pe)
{
   System.out.println ("Caught PaymentException: "+
                       pe.getMessage ());
}

procpay.remove ();
```

You can launch this test by invoking the `run.client_111b` Ant target:

```
C:\workbook\ex11_1>ant run.client_111b
Buildfile: build.xml

prepare:

compile:

ejbjar:

run.client_111b:
     [java] Looking up home interfaces..
     [java] Making a payment using byCash()..
     [java] Making a payment using byCheck()..
     [java] Making a payment using byCredit()..
     [java] Making a payment using byCheck() with a low check number..
     [java] Caught PaymentException: Check number is too low. Must be at least 2000
```

At the same time, the JBoss console will display:

```
INFO  [STDOUT] process() with customerID=1 amount=1000.0
INFO  [STDOUT] process() with customerID=1 amount=2000.0
INFO  [STDOUT] process() with customerID=1 amount=3000.0
```

Once you've performed the tests, you can drop the table by invoking the `dropdb` Ant target:

```
C:\workbook\ex11_1>ant dropdb
Buildfile: build.xml

prepare:

compile:

ejbjar:

dropdb:
     [java] Looking up home interfaces..
     [java] Dropping database table...
```

The JBoss console displays:

```
INFO  [STDOUT] Dropping table PAYMENT...
INFO  [STDOUT] ...done!
```

Exercise 11.2: A Stateful Session Bean

In this exercise, you will build and examine a stateful session bean, TravelAgent, which coordinates the work of booking a trip on a ship. You will also build a client application to test this EJB.

Our version of this exercise does not follow the one in the EJB section strictly. Instead of simplifying the beans and their relationships as the EJB section does, we use the beans implemented in Chapters 6 and 7 and thus take advantage of the CMP 2.0 features of JBoss.

Examine the EJB

This exercise is based on the EJBs from Exercise 7.3 and doesn't contain much material that previous sections haven't covered. Nevertheless, a few modifications have been made:

- The Customer EJB again has a remote home and bean interfaces (as in Chapter 6) and exposes its relationship with the Address EJB in the remote interface through a new data object, `AddressDO`.
- The Cabin EJB has a new create method that takes several parameters.
- The Reservation EJB has a new create method that takes several parameters, and has a local reference to the Customer EJB.

The TravelAgent bean's role is to perform all activities needed to book a successful trip. Thus, as in the preceding example, this session bean acts as a coordinator between different EJBs and groups several actions on different beans in the same transaction. Here, though, the bean maintains a conversational state with the client; i.e., each client has a dedicated bean on the server.

In the previous example featuring stateless session beans, the home create method was not allowed to have parameters: providing initialization parameters would be useless, as the bean wouldn't be able to remember them for forthcoming invocations. A stateful session bean, by contrast, maintains a conversational state, so its create methods can have parameters to initialize the bean state. Indeed, the home interface can have several create methods. In this example, however, the TravelAgent home interface declares only one:

```
public interface TravelAgentHomeRemote extends javax.ejb.EJBHome
{
   public TravelAgentRemote create (CustomerRemote cust)
      throws RemoteException, CreateException;
}
```

Furthermore, if you take a look at the remote interface, you can see that methods are correlated around an identical state:

```
public interface TravelAgentRemote extends javax.ejb.EJBObject
{
   public void setCruiseID (Integer cruise)
      throws RemoteException, FinderException;

   public void setCabinID (Integer cabin)
      throws RemoteException, FinderException;

   public TicketDO bookPassage (CreditCardDO card, double price)
      throws RemoteException, IncompleteConversationalState;

   public String [] listAvailableCabins (int bedCount)
      throws RemoteException, IncompleteConversationalState;
}
```

If no conversational state between the client and the server existed, calling `setCruiseId()` would make no sense. The role of this method is simply to populate this conversational state so that future calls can use this data in their processing.

Because this exercise is based on the beans implemented in Chapters 6 and 7, it needs a database schema that includes all the relationships among them, and thus differs from the one in the EJB book. Because the `listAvailableCabins()` method performs direct SQL calls, it must be rewritten to take this new database schema into account:

```
...
Integer cruiseID = (Integer)cruise.getPrimaryKey ();
Integer shipID = (Integer)cruise.getShip ().getPrimaryKey ();
con = getConnection ();

ps = con.prepareStatement (
        "select ID, NAME, DECK_LEVEL from CABIN "+
        "where SHIP_ID = ? and BED_COUNT = ? and ID NOT IN "+
        "(SELECT RCL.CABIN_ID FROM RESERVATION_CABIN_LINK AS RCL,"+
        "RESERVATION AS R "+
        "WHERE RCL.RESERVATION_ID = R.ID " +
        "AND R.CRUISE_ID = ?)");

ps.setInt (1,shipID.intValue ());
ps.setInt (2,bedCount);
ps.setInt (3,cruiseID.intValue ());

result = ps.executeQuery ();
...
```

You may remember that in previous examples we added a method (either home or remote) to the EJB to be able to initialize the test environment. As you can guess, this example uses the same trick. The TravelAgent EJB remote interface has been extended with one method:

```
public interface TravelAgentRemote extends javax.ejb.EJBObject
{
```

```
    ...
    // Mechanism for building local beans for example programs.
    //
    public void buildSampleData () throws RemoteException;
}
```

This method removes any Customer, Cabin, Ship, Cruise, and Reservation EJBs from the database and recreates a basic environment. You can follow this initialization step by step. First, the method acquires references to the remote home of the Customer EJB, and to the local homes of the Cabin, Ship, Cruise, and Reservation EJBs:

```
public Collection buildSampleData ()
{
    Collection results = new ArrayList ();

    try
    {
        System.out.println ("TravelAgentBean::buildSampleData()");

        Object obj = jndiContext.lookup
                   ("java:comp/env/ejb/CustomerHomeRemote");
        CustomerHomeRemote custhome = (CustomerHomeRemote)
        javax.rmi.PortableRemoteObject.narrow (obj,
                                     CustomerHomeRemote.class);

        CabinHomeLocal cabinhome =
        (CabinHomeLocal)jndiContext.lookup
                       ("java:comp/env/ejb/CabinHomeLocal");
        ShipHomeLocal shiphome =
        (ShipHomeLocal)jndiContext.lookup
                      ("java:comp/env/ejb/ShipHomeLocal");
        CruiseHomeLocal cruisehome =
        (CruiseHomeLocal)jndiContext.lookup
                        ("java:comp/env/ejb/CruiseHomeLocal");
        ReservationHomeLocal reshome =
        (ReservationHomeLocal)jndiContext.lookup
                        ("java:comp/env/ejb/ReservationHomeLocal");
```

Then any existing bean is deleted from the database:

```
// we first clean the db by removing any customer, cabin,
// ship, cruise and reservation beans.
//
removeBeansInCollection (custhome.findAll());
results.add ("All customers have been removed");
removeBeansInCollection (cabinhome.findAll());
results.add ("All cabins have been removed");
removeBeansInCollection (shiphome.findAll());
results.add ("All ships have been removed");
removeBeansInCollection (cruisehome.findAll());
results.add ("All cruises have been removed");
removeBeansInCollection (reshome.findAll());
results.add ("All reservations have been removed");
```

The removeBeansInCollection() method is a simple one. It iterates through the specified collection and removes each EJBObject or EJBLocalObject.

Two customers and two ships are created:

```
// We now set our new basic environment
//
System.out.println ("Creating Customers 1 and 2...");
CustomerRemote customer1 = custhome.create (new Integer (1));
customer1.setName ( new Name ("Burke","Bill") );
results.add ("Customer with ID 1 created (Burke Bill)");

CustomerRemote customer2 = custhome.create (new Integer (2));
customer2.setName ( new Name ("Labourey","Sacha") );
results.add("Customer with ID 2 created (Labourey Sacha)");

System.out.println ("Creating Ships A and B...");
ShipLocal shipA = shiphome.create (new Integer (101),
                  "Nordic Prince", 50000.0);
results.add("Created ship with ID 101...");
ShipLocal shipB = shiphome.create (new Integer (102),
                  "Bohemian Rhapsody", 70000.0);
results.add("Created ship with ID 102...");
```

The buildSampleData() method adds a message to the results collection after each significant step, and ultimately returns results so the caller knows what's happened on the server. It then creates 10 cabins on each ship:

```
System.out.println ("Creating Cabins on the Ships...");
ArrayList cabinsA = new ArrayList ();
ArrayList cabinsB = new ArrayList ();
for (int jj=0; jj<10; jj++)
{
   CabinLocal cabinA = cabinhome.create (new Integer
                            (100+jj),shipA,"Suite 10"+jj,1,1);
   cabinsA.add(cabinA);
   CabinLocal cabinB = cabinhome.create (new Integer
                            (200+jj),shipB,"Suite 20"+jj,2,1);
   cabinsB.add(cabinB);
}
results.add("Created cabins on Ship A with IDs 100-109");
results.add("Created cabins on Ship B with IDs 200-209");
```

The method quickly organizes some cruises for each ship:

```
CruiseLocal cruiseA1 = cruisehome.create ("Alaska Cruise", shipA);
CruiseLocal cruiseA2 = cruisehome.create ("Norwegian Fjords",
                                          shipA);
CruiseLocal cruiseA3 = cruisehome.create ("Bermuda or Bust", shipA);
results.add("Created cruises on ShipA with IDs
            "+cruiseA1.getId()+", "+cruiseA2.getId()+",
            "+cruiseA3.getId());

CruiseLocal cruiseB1 = cruisehome.create ("Indian Sea
                                          Cruise", shipB);
```

```
CruiseLocal cruiseB2 = cruisehome.create ("Australian Highlights",
                                           shipB);
CruiseLocal cruiseB3 = cruisehome.create ("Three-Hour Cruise",
                                           shipB);
results.add ("Created cruises on ShipB with IDs "+
             cruiseB1.getId ()+", "+cruiseB2.getId ()+",
            "+cruiseB3.getId ());
```

Finally, some reservations are made for these cruises:

```
        ReservationLocal res =
        reshome.create (customer1, cruiseA1,
                        (CabinLocal)(cabinsA.get (3)),
                        1000.0, new Date ());
        res = reshome.create (customer1, cruiseB3,
                        (CabinLocal)(cabinsB.get (8)),
                        2000.0, new Date ());
        res = reshome.create (customer2, cruiseA2,
                        (CabinLocal)(cabinsA.get (5)),
                        2000.0, new Date ());
        res = reshome.create (customer2, cruiseB3,
                         (CabinLocal)(cabinsB.get (2)),
                        2000.0, new Date ());

        results.add ("Made reservation for Customer 1 on Cruise "+
                     cruiseA1.getId ()+" for Cabin 103");
        results.add ("Made reservation for Customer 1 on Cruise "+
                     cruiseB3.getId ()+" for Cabin 208");
        results.add ("Made reservation for Customer 2 on Cruise "+
                     cruiseA2.getId ()+" for Cabin 105");
        results.add ("Made reservation for Customer 2 on Cruise "+
                     cruiseB3.getId ()+" for Cabin 202");
    }
    ...
    return results;
}
```

Later, you'll see how to call this method to set up the environment.

Examine the EJB Standard Deployment Descriptor

Most of the *ejb-jar.xml* file comprises definitions you've seen in previous examples (entity beans, relationships, the ProcessPayment stateless session bean, etc.). Only two things have been added.

ejb-jar.xml

First, the Customer EJB now has both local and remote interfaces:

```
<entity>
  <ejb-name>CustomerEJB</ejb-name>
  <home>com.titan.customer.CustomerHomeRemote</home>
  <remote>com.titan.customer.CustomerRemote</remote>
```

```
    <local-home>com.titan.customer.CustomerHomeLocal</local-home>
    <local>com.titan.customer.CustomerLocal</local>
    <ejb-class>com.titan.customer.CustomerBean</ejb-class>
    <persistence-type>Container</persistence-type>
    <prim-key-class>java.lang.Integer</prim-key-class>
    <reentrant>False</reentrant>
    <cmp-version>2.x</cmp-version>
    <abstract-schema-name>Customer</abstract-schema-name>
    <cmp-field><field-name>id</field-name></cmp-field>
    <cmp-field><field-name>lastName</field-name></cmp-field>
    <cmp-field><field-name>firstName</field-name></cmp-field>
    <cmp-field><field-name>hasGoodCredit</field-name></cmp-field>
    <primkey-field>id</primkey-field>
    <security-identity><use-caller-identity/></security-identity>
  </entity>
```

Providing the second interface enables the Customer EJB to serve local clients as well as remote ones. Note that the remote and local interfaces do not declare the same methods. For example, it's illegal for a remote interface to expose entity relationships, so they're accessible only via the local interface.

The second addition is the new TravelAgent stateful session bean that is the heart of this exercise:

```
  <session>
    <ejb-name>TravelAgentEJB</ejb-name>
    <home>com.titan.travelagent.TravelAgentHomeRemote</home>
    <remote>com.titan.travelagent.TravelAgentRemote</remote>
    <ejb-class>com.titan.travelagent.TravelAgentBean</ejb-class>
    <session-type>Stateful</session-type>
    <transaction-type>Container</transaction-type>
    ...
```

As you can see, only the value of the <session-type> tag distinguishes the declaration of a stateful session bean from that of a stateless bean.

The deployment descriptor then declares all the beans referenced by the TravelAgent EJB:

```
    ...
    <ejb-ref>
      <ejb-ref-name>ejb/ProcessPaymentHomeRemote</ejb-ref-name>
      <ejb-ref-type>Session</ejb-ref-type>
      <home>
        com.titan.processpayment.ProcessPaymentHomeRemote
      </home>
      <remote>
        com.titan.processpayment.ProcessPaymentRemote
      </remote>
      <ejb-link>ProcessPaymentEJB</ejb-link>
    </ejb-ref>
    <ejb-ref>
      <ejb-ref-name>ejb/CustomerHomeRemote</ejb-ref-name>
```

```
        <ejb-ref-type>Entity</ejb-ref-type>
        <home>
            com.titan.customer.CustomerHomeRemote
        </home>
        <remote>com.titan.customer.CustomerRemote</remote>
        <ejb-link>CustomerEJB</ejb-link>
    </ejb-ref>
    <ejb-local-ref>
        <ejb-ref-name>ejb/CabinHomeLocal</ejb-ref-name>
        <ejb-ref-type>Entity</ejb-ref-type>
        <local-home>
            com.titan.cabin.CabinHomeLocal
        </local-home>
        <local>com.titan.cabin.CabinLocal</local>
        <ejb-link>CabinEJB</ejb-link>
    </ejb-local-ref>
    <ejb-local-ref>
        <ejb-ref-name>ejb/ShipHomeLocal</ejb-ref-name>
        <ejb-ref-type>Entity</ejb-ref-type>
        <local-home>
            com.titan.cabin.ShipHomeLocal
        </local-home>
        <local>com.titan.cabin.ShipLocal</local>
        <ejb-link>ShipEJB</ejb-link>
    </ejb-local-ref>
    <ejb-local-ref>
        <ejb-ref-name>ejb/CruiseHomeLocal</ejb-ref-name>
        <ejb-ref-type>Entity</ejb-ref-type>
        <local-home>
            com.titan.cruise.CruiseHomeLocal
        </local-home>
        <local>com.titan.cruise.CruiseLocal</local>
        <ejb-link>CruiseEJB</ejb-link>
    </ejb-local-ref>
    <ejb-local-ref>
        <ejb-ref-name>ejb/ReservationHomeLocal</ejb-ref-name>
        <ejb-ref-type>Entity</ejb-ref-type>
        <local-home>
            com.titan.reservation.ReservationHomeLocal
        </local-home>
        <local>com.titan.reservation.ReservationLocal</local>
        <ejb-link>ReservationEJB</ejb-link>
    </ejb-local-ref>
    <resource-ref>
        <res-ref-name>jdbc/titanDB</res-ref-name>
        <res-type>javax.sql.DataSource</res-type>
        <res-auth>Container</res-auth>
    </resource-ref>
</session>
```

Examine the JBoss Deployment Descriptor

The *jboss.xml* deployment descriptor contains the JNDI name mapping found in the previous examples. The only new entry is the TravelAgent EJB definition.

jboss.xml

```
<session>
   <ejb-name>TravelAgentEJB</ejb-name>
   <jndi-name>TravelAgentHomeRemote</jndi-name>
   <resource-ref>
      <res-ref-name>jdbc/titanDB</res-ref-name>
      <jndi-name>java:/DefaultDS</jndi-name>
   </resource-ref>
</session>
```

This file defines the JNDI name for the TravelAgent, then maps the data source's JNDI ENC name to the embedded database.

The `listAvailableCabins()` method uses this mapping to execute SQL statements directly against the database, so it must know precisely the names of the tables and fields to use in each query. While *jbosscmp-jdbc.xml* already defines the field-to-column mapping of all CMP beans, it doesn't define the fields and tables used by relationships between these beans. If it doesn't have those definitions, JBoss will use arbitrary names for these tables—not good in this case. To avoid this problem, extend *jbosscmp-jdbc.xml*, adding definitions that map the relationships into the desired tables and columns exactly. For this exercise, we mapped only the relationships used in the SQL query: Cabin-Ship, Cabin-Reservation, and Cruise-Reservation.

jbosscmp-jdbc.xml

Cabin-Reservation is a many-to-many relationship:

```
<ejb-relation>
   <ejb-relation-name>Cabin-Reservation</ejb-relation-name>
   <relation-table-mapping>
      <table-name>RESERVATION_CABIN_LINK</table-name>
      <create-table>true</create-table>
      <remove-table>true</remove-table>
   </relation-table-mapping>
   <ejb-relationship-role>
      <ejb-relationship-role-name
       >Cabin-has-many-Reservations<
      /ejb-relationship-role-name>
      <key-fields>
         <key-field>
            <field-name>id</field-name>
            <column-name>CABIN_ID</column-name>
         </key-field>
      </key-fields>
   </ejb-relationship-role>
```

```
    <ejb-relationship-role>
        <ejb-relationship-role-name
         >Reservation-has-many-Cabins<
         /ejb-relationship-role-name>
        <key-fields>
            <key-field>
                <field-name>id</field-name>
                <column-name>RESERVATION_ID</column-name>
            </key-field>
        </key-fields>
    </ejb-relationship-role>
</ejb-relation>
...
```

Many-to-many relationships always need an intermediate table. The name of this table is defined in the `<table-name>` tag. Then, for each role of the relationship, the `<field-name>` and `<column-name>` tags do the mapping between the CMR field of the bean and the column in the table.

The last two mappings needed are for one-to-many relationships, Cabin-Ship and Cruise-Reservation:

```
...
<ejb-relation>
    <ejb-relation-name>Cabin-Ship</ejb-relation-name>
    <foreign-key-mapping/>
    <ejb-relationship-role>
        <ejb-relationship-role-name
         >Ship-has-many-Cabins<
        /ejb-relationship-role-name>
        <key-fields>
            <key-field>
                <field-name>id</field-name>
                <column-name>SHIP_ID</column-name>
            </key-field>
        </key-fields>
    </ejb-relationship-role>
    <ejb-relationship-role>
        <ejb-relationship-role-name
         >Cabin-has-a-Ship<
        /ejb-relationship-role-name>
        <key-fields/>
    </ejb-relationship-role>
</ejb-relation>

<ejb-relation>
    <ejb-relation-name>Cruise-Reservation</ejb-relation-name>
    <foreign-key-mapping/>
    <ejb-relationship-role>
        <ejb-relationship-role-name
         >Cruise-has-many-Reservations<
        /ejb-relationship-role-name>
        <key-fields>
```

```
            <key-field>
               <field-name>id</field-name>
               <column-name>CRUISE_ID</column-name>
            </key-field>
         </key-fields>
      </ejb-relationship-role>
      <ejb-relationship-role>
         <ejb-relationship-role-name
          >Reservation-has-a-Cruise<
         /ejb-relationship-role-name>
         <key-fields/>
      </ejb-relationship-role>
   </ejb-relation>
```

For each relationship identified by an `<ejb-relation-name>` tag (the name must be the same as the one declared in *ejb-jar.xml*), the mapping of the CMR field to a table column is defined by the `<field-name>` and `<column-name>` tags.

Start Up JBoss

If JBoss is already running, there is no reason to restart it.

Build and Deploy the Example Programs

Perform the following steps:

1. Open a command prompt or shell terminal and change to the *ex11_2* directory created by the extraction process.
2. Set the `JAVA_HOME` and `JBOSS_HOME` environment variables to point to where your JDK and JBoss 4.0 are installed. Examples:

   Windows:
   ```
   C:\workbook\ex11_2> set JAVA_HOME=C:\jdk1.4.2
   C:\workbook\ex11_2> set JBOSS_HOME=C:\jboss-4.0
   ```
   Unix:
   ```
   $ export JAVA_HOME=/usr/local/jdk1.4.2
   $ export JBOSS_HOME=/usr/local/jboss-4.0
   ```
3. Add ant to your execution path.

   Windows:
   ```
   C:\workbook\ex11_2> set PATH=..\ant\bin;%PATH%
   ```
   Unix:
   ```
   $ export PATH=../ant/bin:$PATH
   ```
4. Perform the build by typing `ant`.

As in the last exercise, you will see *titan.jar* rebuilt, copied to the JBoss *deploy* directory, and redeployed by the application server.

Initialize the Database

Because the exercise uses the ProcessPayment EJB from the previous example, the database must contain the PAYMENT table. The createdb and dropdb Ant targets, Java code, and clients here have been borrowed from Exercise 11.1.

If you have dropped the PAYMENT table after running the examples in Exercise 11.1, re-create it now by running the createdb *Ant* target.

```
C:\workbook\ex11_2>ant createdb
Buildfile: build.xml

prepare:

compile:

ejbjar:

createdb:
     [java] Looking up home interfaces..
     [java] Creating database table...
```

On the JBoss console, you'll see:

```
INFO  [STDOUT] Creating table PAYMENT...
INFO  [STDOUT] ...done!
```

If you're having trouble creating the database, shut down JBoss. Then run the Ant build target clean.db. This removes all database files and allows you to start fresh.

The container manages the persistence of all other entity beans used in this exercise, so it will create the needed tables for them automatically.

Examine the Client Applications

This exercise includes three example client applications.

Client_112a

The first client simply calls the TravelAgent bean's buildSampleData() method. To run this application, invoke the Ant target run.client_112a:

```
C:\workbook\ex11_2>ant run.client_112a
Buildfile: build.xml

prepare:

compile:

ejbjar:
```

```
run.client_112a:
  [java] Calling TravelAgentBean to create sample data..
  [java] All customers have been removed
  [java] All cabins have been removed
  [java] All ships have been removed
  [java] All cruises have been removed
  [java] All reservations have been removed
  [java] Customer with ID 1 created (Burke Bill)
  [java] Customer with ID 2 created (Labourey Sacha)
  [java] Created ship with ID 101...
  [java] Created ship with ID 102...
  [java] Created cabins on Ship A with IDs 100-109
  [java] Created cabins on Ship B with IDs 200-209
  [java] Created Alaska Cruise with ID 0 on ShipA
  [java] Created Norwegian Fjords Cruise with ID 1 on ShipA
  [java] Created Bermuda or Bust Cruise with ID 2 on ShipA
  [java] Created Indian Sea Cruise with ID 3 on ShipB
  [java] Created Australian Highlights Cruise with ID 4 on ShipB
  [java] Created Three-Hour Cruise with ID 5 on ShipB
  [java] Made reservation for Customer 1 on Cruise 0 for Cabin 103
  [java] Made reservation for Customer 1 on Cruise 5 for Cabin 208
  [java] Made reservation for Customer 2 on Cruise 1 for Cabin 105
  [java] Made reservation for Customer 2 on Cruise 5 for Cabin 202
```

Now that you've prepared the environment, you can use the other two client applications. *Client_112b* allows you to book a passage, while *Client_112c* gives you a list of the Cabins for a specific Cruise that have a specified number of beds.

Client_112b

The second client starts by getting remote home interfaces to the TravelAgent and Customer EJBs:

```
public static void main(String [] args) throws Exception
{

   if (args.length != 4)
   {
      System.out.println
         ("Usage: java " +
          "com.titan.clients.Client_122b" +
          "<customerID> <cruiseID> <cabinID> <price>");
      System.exit(-1);
   }

   Integer customerID = new Integer(args[0]);
   Integer cruiseID = new Integer(args[1]);
   Integer cabinID = new Integer(args[2]);
   double price = new Double(args[3]).doubleValue();

   Context jndiContext = getInitialContext();
   Object obj = jndiContext.lookup("TravelAgentHomeRemote");
   TravelAgentHomeRemote tahome = (TravelAgentHomeRemote)
```

```
   javax.rmi.PortableRemoteObject.narrow(obj,
             TravelAgentHomeRemote.class);

obj = jndiContext.lookup("CustomerHomeRemote");
CustomerHomeRemote custhome = (CustomerHomeRemote)
   javax.rmi.PortableRemoteObject.narrow(obj,
             CustomerHomeRemote.class);
```

With the home references in hand, it can now get a reference to the customer whose ID was given on the command line. If no customer with this ID exists, an exception is thrown.

```
// Find a reference to the Customer for which to book a cruise
System.out.println("Finding reference to Customer "+customerID);
CustomerRemote cust = custhome.findByPrimaryKey(customerID);
```

The application then creates a TravelAgent stateful session bean and gives it, as part of the transactional state, the reference to the customer, the cruise ID, and the Cabin ID.

```
// Start the Stateful session bean
System.out.println("Starting TravelAgent Session...");
TravelAgentRemote tagent = tahome.create(cust);

// Set the other bean parameters in agent bean
System.out.println("Setting Cruise and Cabin information in TravelAgent..");
tagent.setCruiseID(cruiseID);
tagent.setCabinID(cabinID);
```

It can then book the passage, thanks to a dummy credit card:

```
// Create a dummy CreditCard for this
//
Calendar expdate = Calendar.getInstance();
expdate.set(2005,1,5);
CreditCardDO card = new CreditCardDO("370000000000002",
                                     expdate.getTime(),
                                     "AMERICAN EXPRESS");

// Book the passage
//
System.out.println("Booking the passage on the Cruise!");
TicketDO ticket = tagent.bookPassage(card,price);

System.out.println("Ending TravelAgent Session...");
tagent.remove();

System.out.println("Result of bookPassage:");
System.out.println(ticket.description);

}
```

Test this client application by booking Suite 201 for Mr. Bill Burke on the Three-Hour Cruise aboard the "Bohemian Rhapsody."

Ant doesn't make it particularly easy to pass command-line parameters through to the client. To make this task easier, use one of the scripts that accept command-line parameters in a more customary fashion, available in the *ex11_2* directory.

To book a passage, use the BookPassage.bat (Windows) or the BookPassage script (Unix):

```
BookPassage.bat <customerID> <cruiseID> <cabinID> <price>
Or
./BookPassage <customerID> <cruiseID> <cabinID> <price>

C:\workbook\ex11_2>BookPassage 1 5 201 2000.0
Buildfile: build.xml

prepare:

compile:

ejbjar:

run.client_112b:
     [java] Finding reference to Customer 1
     [java] Starting TravelAgent Session...
     [java] Setting Cruise and Cabin information in TravelAgent..
     [java] Booking the passage on the Cruise!
     [java] Ending TravelAgent Session...
     [java] Result of bookPassage:
     [java] Bill Burke has been booked for the Three-Hour Cruise cruise on ship
Bohemian Rhapsody.
     [java]  Your accommodations include Suite 201 a 2 bed cabin on deck level 1.
     [java]  Total charge = 2000.0

BUILD SUCCESSFUL
```

Client_112c

The last application gives you a list of available cabins for a specific cruise that have a desired number of beds. First, the application verifies that it's been given the correct number of command-line arguments and gets a remote home reference to the Travel-Agent EJB:

```
public static void main(String [] args) throws Exception
{
   if (args.length != 2)
   {
      System.out.println("Usage: java " +
                         "com.titan.clients.Client_122c" +
                         " <cruiseID> <bedCount>");
      System.exit(-1);
   }

   Integer cruiseID = new Integer(args[0]);
   int bedCount = new Integer(args[1]).intValue();
```

```
Context jndiContext = getInitialContext();
Object obj = jndiContext.lookup("TravelAgentHomeRemote");
TravelAgentHomeRemote tahome = (TravelAgentHomeRemote)
   javax.rmi.PortableRemoteObject.narrow(obj,
             TravelAgentHomeRemote.class);
```

Because the session bean is not really dedicated to a specific instance of Customer, but is instead making an SQL query in the database, the client creates a TravelAgent bean with a dummy Customer reference, which will never be used. Then it supplies the Cruise ID:

```
// Start the Stateful session bean
System.out.println("Starting TravelAgent Session...");
TravelAgentRemote tagent = tahome.create(null);

// Set the other bean parameters in agent bean
System.out.println
   ("Setting Cruise information in TravelAgent..");
tagent.setCruiseID(cruiseID);
```

Finally, the application asks for a list of all available cabins with a desired number of beds on a particular cruise and displays the result, if any:

```
String[] results = tagent.listAvailableCabins(bedCount);

System.out.println("Ending TravelAgent Session...");
tagent.remove();

System.out.println("Result of listAvailableCabins:");
for (int kk=0; kk<results.length; kk++)
{
   System.out.println(results[kk]);
}

}
```

To launch this application, you can use the ListCabins.bat (Windows) or ListCabins (Unix) script:

```
ListCabins.bat <cruiseID> <bedCount>
Or
./ListCabins <cruiseID> <bedCount>
```

Ask the system for a list of the two-bed cabins that are available on the Three-Hour Cruise, the one Mr. Bill Burke chose:

```
C:\workbook\ex11_2>ListCabins 5 2
Buildfile: build.xml

prepare:

compile:

ejbjar:
```

```
run.client_112c:
     [java] Starting TravelAgent Session...
     [java] Setting Cruise information in TravelAgent..
     [java] Ending TravelAgent Session...
     [java] Result of listAvailableCabins:
     [java] 200,Suite 200,1
     [java] 203,Suite 203,1
     [java] 204,Suite 204,1
     [java] 205,Suite 205,1
     [java] 206,Suite 206,1
     [java] 207,Suite 207,1
     [java] 209,Suite 209,1

BUILD SUCCESSFUL
```

Suite 201 has two beds but is not shown as available. This omission is correct, because Mr. Bill Burke has booked that suite.

Exercises for Chapter 12

Exercise 12.1: JMS as a Resource

This exercise is entirely based on the beans implemented in Exercise 11.2. You'll modify the TravelAgent EJB so it publishes a text message to a JMS topic when it completes a reservation.

You'll learn how to create a new JMS topic in JBoss, and configure your bean to use JMS as a resource. You'll also build a client application that will subscribe to this topic and display any published message. To complete new reservations, you'll use one of the client applications created for the preceding example.

Start Up JBoss

If JBoss is already running there is no reason to restart it.

Initialize the Database

Because the exercise uses the ProcessPayment EJB used in recent exercises, the database must contain the `PAYMENT` table. The `createdb` and `dropdb` Ant targets, Java code, and clients here have been borrowed from Exercise 11.1.

If you haven't already dropped the `PAYMENT` table after running the examples in Exercise 11.2, do so now by running the `dropdb` Ant target.

```
C:\workbook\ex12_1>ant dropdb
Buildfile: build.xml

prepare:

compile:

dropdb:
     [java] Looking up home interfaces..
     [java] Dropping database table...

BUILD SUCCESSFUL
```

Then re-create the PAYMENT database table by running the createdb *Ant* target

```
C:\workbook\ex12_1>ant createdb
Buildfile: build.xml

prepare:

compile:

ejbjar:

createdb:
     [java] Looking up home interfaces..
     [java] Creating database table...
```

On the JBoss console, the following lines are displayed:

```
INFO  [STDOUT] Creating table PAYMENT...
INFO  [STDOUT] ...done!
```

If you're having trouble creating the database, shut down JBoss. Then run the Ant build target clean.db. This will remove all database files and allow you to start fresh.

The persistence of all other entity beans used in this exercise is managed by the container (CMP), so JBoss will create the needed tables for them automatically.

Create a New JMS Topic

Because the TravelAgent EJB will publish messages in a JMS topic, you'll have to create this new topic in JBoss. This exercise walks you through two different ways to create a new JMS topic: through an XML configuration file and through the JBoss JMX HTTP connector.

Adding a JMS Topic through a configuration file

The most common way to set up a JMS topic is to use an XML configuration file. As you learned in the installation chapter, every component in JBoss is a JMX MBean that can be hot-deployed. This part of the exercise shows you how to write a JMX MBean definition for a new JMS topic.

You can find the JMX configuration file in the *ex12_1/src/resources/services* directory.

jbossmq-titantopic-service.xml

```
<server>
  <mbean code="org.jboss.mq.server.jmx.Topic"
        name="jboss.mq.destination:service=Topic,
              name=titan-TicketTopic">
    <depends optional-attribute-name="DestinationManager"
      >jboss.mq:service=DestinationManager</depends>
```

```
    </mbean>
</server>
```

Each set of MBeans in a JMX configuration file must be defined within a `<server>` tag. An MBean itself is declared in an `<mbean>` tag. The only MBean declaration in this file defines the actual JMS topic you'll use for the example code in this chapter. Each MBean is uniquely identified by its name, called an *ObjectName*. JMX ObjectNames can include any number of key-value parameters to describe the MBean further. In our case, the MBean class representing the JMS topic is declared first (`org.jboss.mq.server.jmx.Topic`), along with its JMX ObjectName (`jboss.mq.destination:service=Topic, name=titan-TicketTopic`). For JMS topic MBeans, a single parameter is useful: `name`. This is where the name of the JMS topic is defined (`titan-TicketTopic`).

One thing to note is that the application server must deploy the `DestinationManager` MBean before any queue or topic is deployed. This dependency is declared in *jbossmq-titantopic-service.xml*'s `depends` tag. JBoss will take care of satisfying this dependency and make sure the `titan-TicketTopic` isn't started until the `DestinationManager` MBean has finished initializing and is ready to provide services to new queues and topics. Copying this file into the JBoss deploy directory will hot-deploy the JMS topic and make it ready for use.

We've defined a `make-topic` Ant target for deploying the topic bean. Run this target to copy *jbossmq-titantopic-service.xml* into JBoss's deploy directory:

```
C:\workbook\ex12_1>ant make-topic
Buildfile: build.xml

make-topic:
     [copy] Copying 1 file to C:\jboss-4.0\server\default\deploy
```

On the server side, the following line is displayed:

```
[titan-TicketTopic] Bound to JNDI name: topic/titan-TicketTopic
```

Adding a JMS Topic through the JMX HTTP connector

An XML configuration file is the preferred means to deploy a JMS topic permanently, but for quick tests and such an alternative approach that uses JBoss's JMX HTTP connector and the `DestinationManager` is sometimes better, because the topic lives in JBoss only until the application server is shut down. First open your browser and go to *http://localhost:8080/jmx-console/*, where you can browse through all deployed JBoss JMX MBeans. Scroll down to the `jboss.mq` section and find in it the MBean service `DestinationManager` (Figure W-8).

Click on the `service=DestinationManager` link and you get a list of the MBean's attributes and operations. One of the operations, `createTopic()`, allows you to create a new JMS topic (Figure W-9).

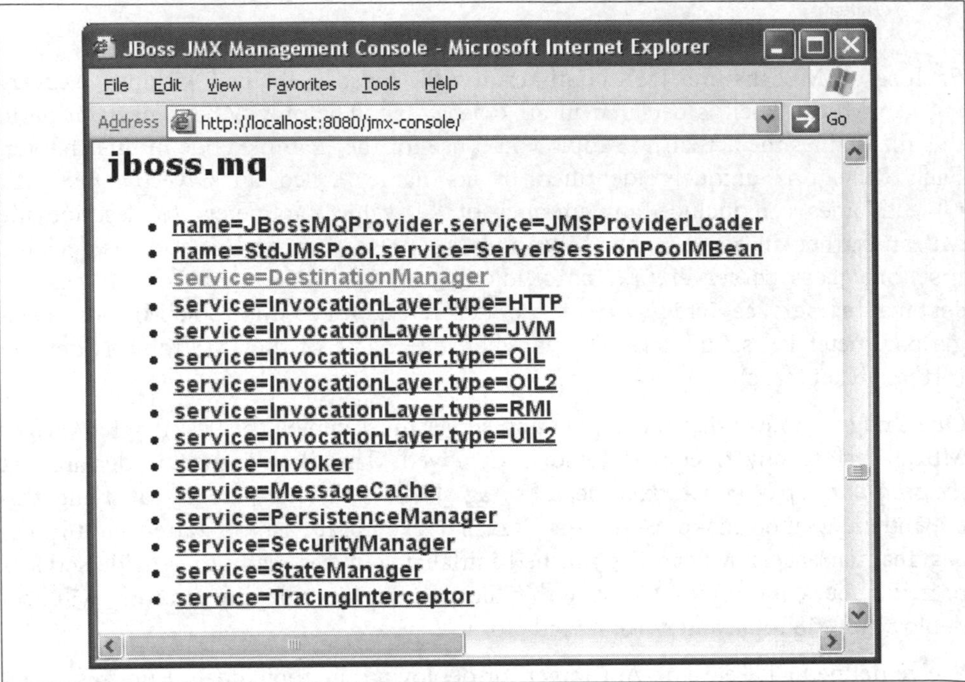

Figure W-8. Finding the `DestinationManager`

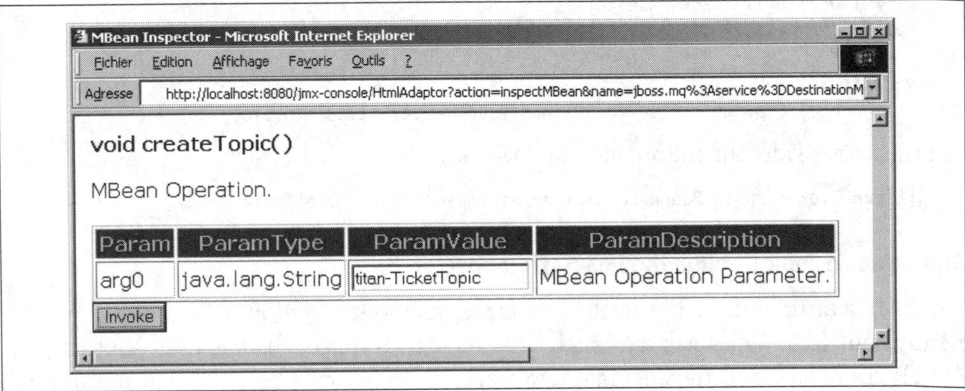

Figure W-9. Naming a new JMS topic

Type the name of the new JMS topic in the text area, and click on the Invoke button associated with the `createTopic()` operation. The Destination Manager will create the JMS topic and display a status message (Figure W-10).

To see your new JMS topic MBean, go back to the home page of the JMX HTTP connector and search for the `jboss.mq.destination` domain. You should be able to see your new topic MBean (Figure W-11).

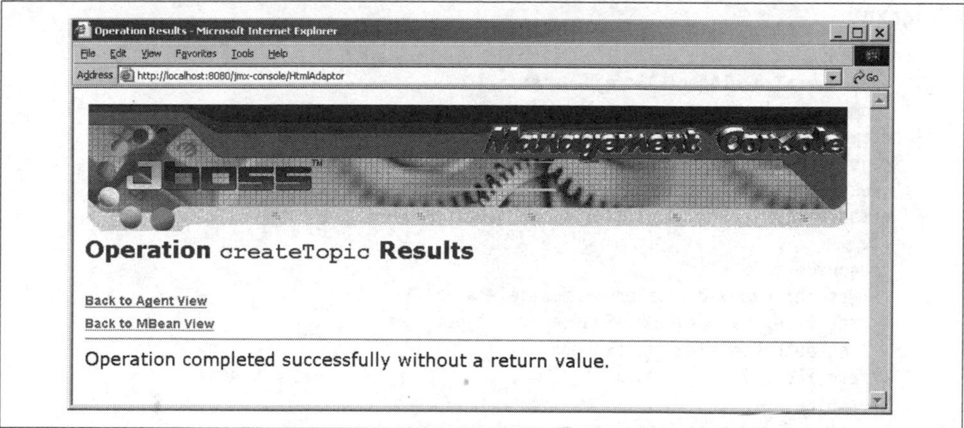

Figure W-10. Confirming topic creation

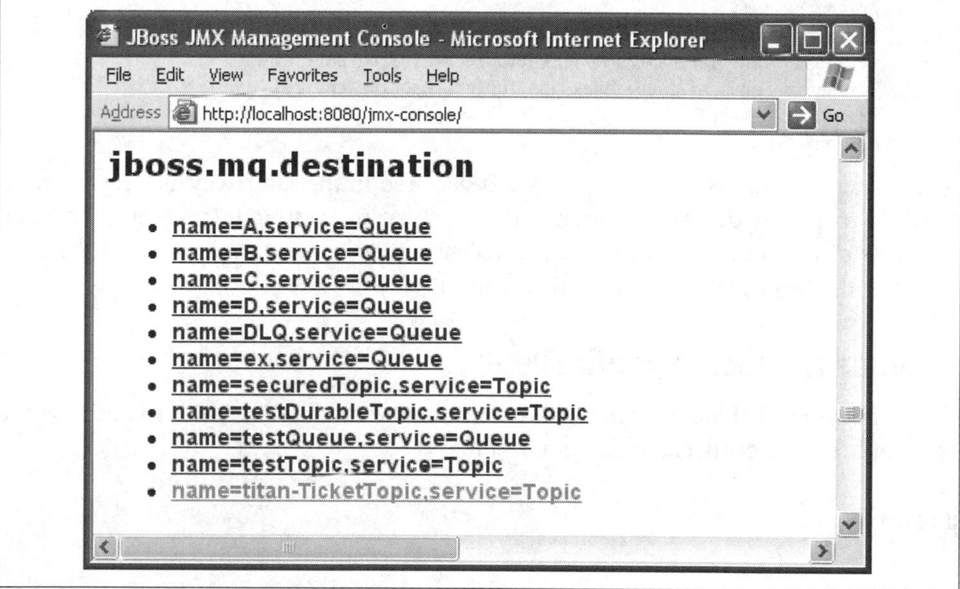

Figure W-11. Finding the new topic

Note that you can use the JMX HTTP connector to see the status of your topics and queues even if you create then in an XML configuration file.

Examine the EJB Standard Files

The *ejb-jar.xml* deployment descriptor is equivalent to the one for Exercise 11.2 except for the TravelAgent EJB. The definition for this bean has been extended to reference the JMS topics you just created.

ejb-jar.xml

```
<session>
  <ejb-name>TravelAgentEJB</ejb-name>
  <home>com.titan.travelagent.TravelAgentHomeRemote</home>
  <remote>com.titan.travelagent.TravelAgentRemote</remote>
  <ejb-class>com.titan.travelagent.TravelAgentBean</ejb-class>
  <session-type>Stateful</session-type>
  <transaction-type>Container</transaction-type>
  ...
  <resource-ref>
    <res-ref-name>jdbc/titanDB</res-ref-name>
    <res-type>javax.sql.DataSource</res-type>
    <res-auth>Container</res-auth>
  </resource-ref>
  <resource-ref>
    <res-ref-name>jms/TopicFactory</res-ref-name>
    <res-type>javax.jms.TopicConnectionFactory</res-type>
    <res-auth>Container</res-auth>
  </resource-ref>
  <resource-env-ref>
    <resource-env-ref-name>jms/TicketTopic</resource-env-ref-name>
    <resource-env-ref-type>javax.jms.Topic</resource-env-ref-type>
  </resource-env-ref>
</session>
```

A reference to a TopicConnectionFactory is declared in the same way as a reference to a DataSource. The definition contains the name of the resource (jms/TopicFactory), the class of the resource (javax.jms.TopicConnectionFactory), and whether the container or the bean performs the authentication.

Examine the JBoss-Specific Files

The TravelAgentEJB definition in *jboss.xml* must be modified as well, to describe the JMS topic references declared in *ejb-jar.xml*.

jboss.xml

```
...
<session>
  <ejb-name>TravelAgentEJB</ejb-name>
  <jndi-name>TravelAgentHomeRemote</jndi-name>
  <resource-ref>
    <res-ref-name>jdbc/titanDB</res-ref-name>
    <jndi-name>java:/DefaultDS</jndi-name>
  </resource-ref>
  <resource-ref>
    <res-ref-name>jms/TopicFactory</res-ref-name>
    <jndi-name>java:/JmsXA</jndi-name>
  </resource-ref>
  <resource-env-ref>
    <resource-env-ref-name>jms/TicketTopic</resource-env-ref-name>
```

```
      <jndi-name>topic/titan-TicketTopic</jndi-name>
    </resource-env-ref>
  </session>
  ...
```

The <resource-ref> entry from *ejb-jar.xml* is mapped in the *jboss.xml* file to the JNDI name java:/JmsXA. If you take a look at the JBossMQ default configuration file in *$JBOSS_HOME/server/default/deploy/jms/jms-ds.xml*, you'll see that the XA connection manager is bound to this name by default.

The last part of the TravelAgent EJB descriptor in *jboss.xml* maps the jms/TicketTopic name from the JNDI ENC of the bean to the topic/titan-TicketTopic JNDI name. This name corresponds to the JMS topic you just created.

Build and Deploy the Example Programs

Perform the following steps:

1. Open a command prompt or shell terminal and change to the *ex12_1* directory created by the extraction process
2. Set the JAVA_HOME and JBOSS_HOME environment variables to point to where your JDK and JBoss 4.0 are installed. Examples:

   Windows:

   ```
   C:\workbook\ex12_1> set JAVA_HOME=C:\jdk1.4.2
   C:\workbook\ex12_1> set JBOSS_HOME=C:\jboss-4.0
   ```

   Unix:

   ```
   $ export JAVA_HOME=/usr/local/jdk1.4.2
   $ export JBOSS_HOME=/usr/local/jboss-4.0
   ```

3. Add ant to your execution path.

   Windows:

   ```
   C:\workbook\ex12_1> set PATH=..\ant\bin;%PATH%
   ```

   Unix:

   ```
   $ export PATH=../ant/bin:$PATH
   ```

4. Perform the build by typing ant.

You will see *titan.jar* rebuilt, copied to the JBoss *deploy* directory, and redeployed by the application server.

Examine the Client Applications

This exercise includes two client applications. You can find the code for them in the *ex12_1/src/main/com/titan/clients* directory.

The first application is the one used in Exercise 11.2 to make a reservation. The Ant target run.client_112b hasn't changed, and needs no review.

The second application is new. *JmsClient_1* subscribes to the titan-TicketTopic JMS topic and displays all messages published on it.

The application first gets an InitialContext, and looks up its TopicConnectionFactory and Topic.

JmsClient_1.java

```
...
Context jndiContext = getInitialContext();

TopicConnectionFactory factory = (TopicConnectionFactory)
   jndiContext.lookup("ConnectionFactory");

Topic topic = (Topic)
   jndiContext.lookup("topic/titan-TicketTopic");
```

The name of the JMS topic is the same as the one you created in Exercise 11.1, but the name of the TopicConnectionFactory is *not* the same as the one used by the TravelAgent EJB.

Remember that the java:/JmsXA connection factory used by the EJB was in the *private* JNDI space of the JBoss JVM (indicated by the java: prefix). Thus, the client application cannot look up this name from its JVM. For external applications, JBoss binds a set of connection factories within the public JNDI tree, each dedicated to a particular message transport protocol.

JBossMQ supports several different kinds of message invocation layers. Each layer has its own ConnectionFactory that is bound in JNDI, as shown in Table W-3.

Table W-3. JBossMQ message invocation layers

Invocation Layer	JNDI name
JVM	java:/ConnectionFactory and
Hyperefficient invocation layer using standard Java method invocation, used for in-JVM JMS clients; external clients cannot use this invocation layer	java:/XAConnectionFactory (with XA support)
RMI	RMIConnectionFactory and
RMI-based invocation layer	RMIXAConnectionFactory (with XA support)
OIL (Optimized Invocation Layer)	ConnectionFactory and
Uses custom TCP/IP sockets to obtain good network performance with a small memory footprint	XAConnectionFactory (with XA support)
UIL2	UIL2ConnectionFactory and
Used by client applications that cannot accept network connections originating from the server	UIL2XAConnectionFactory (with XA support)

We strongly suggest to use the UIL2 invocation layer; it is the most robust and efficient layer currently available.

```
TopicConnection connect = factory.createTopicConnection();

TopicSession session =
   connect.createTopicSession(false, Session.AUTO_ACKNOWLEDGE);
```

```
TopicSubscriber subscriber = session.createSubscriber(topic);

subscriber.setMessageListener(this);

System.out.println
   ("Listening for messages on topic/titan-TicketTopic...");
connect.start();
```

The end of the client application code is the same as in the EJB book.

Run the Client Applications

When you redeployed *titan.jar*, JBoss dropped and recreated the database tables, destroying any existing content. For this reason, you must have Ant execute the `run.client_112a` target to repopulate the database.

The `run.client_112a` target originated in Exercise 11.2, but we've duplicated it in the *ex12_1* directory to facilitate your work.

Here's the output:

```
C:\workbook\ex12_1>ant run.client_112a
Buildfile: build.xml

prepare:

compile:

ejbjar:

run.client_112a:
  [java] Calling TravelAgentBean to create sample data..
  [java] All customers have been removed
  [java] All cabins have been removed
  [java] All ships have been removed
  [java] All cruises have been removed
  [java] All reservations have been removed
  [java] Customer with ID 1 created (Burke Bill)
  [java] Customer with ID 2 created (Labourey Sacha)
  [java] Created ship with ID 101...
  [java] Created ship with ID 102...
  [java] Created cabins on Ship A with IDs 100-109
  [java] Created cabins on Ship B with IDs 200-209
  [java] Created Alaska Cruise with ID 0 on ShipA
  [java] Created Norwegian Fjords Cruise with ID 1 on ShipA
  [java] Created Bermuda or Bust Cruise with ID 2 on ShipA
  [java] Created Indian Sea Cruise with ID 3 on ShipB
  [java] Created Australian Highlights Cruise with ID 4 on ShipB
  [java] Created Three-Hour Cruise with ID 5 on ShipB
  [java] Made reservation for Customer 1 on Cruise 0 for Cabin 103
  [java] Made reservation for Customer 1 on Cruise 5 for Cabin 208
```

```
     [java] Made reservation for Customer 2 on Cruise 1 for Cabin 105
     [java] Made reservation for Customer 2 on Cruise 5 for Cabin 202

BUILD SUCCESSFUL
```

For your new application to receive the message published on the JMS topic, you have to start it first:

```
C:\workbook\ex12_1>ant run.client_121
Buildfile: build.xml

prepare:

compile:

ejbjar:

client_121:
     [java] Listening for messages on topic/titan-TicketTopic...
```

The last line of the output confirms that the client application has successfully subscribed to the topic and is waiting for messages.

Now you need to make some reservations exactly as you did in Exercise 11.2. Open a new shell and use the *BookPassage* script to make a reservation for Bill Burke on the Three-Hour Cruise for cabin 101 at $3,000.00:

```
C:\workbook\ex12_1>BookPassage 1 5 101 3000.0
Buildfile: build.xml

prepare:

compile:

ejbjar:

run.client_112b:
     [java] Finding reference to Customer 1
     [java] Starting TravelAgent Session...
     [java] Setting Cruise and Cabin information in TravelAgent..
     [java] Booking the passage on the Cruise!
     [java] Ending TravelAgent Session...
     [java] Result of bookPassage:
     [java] Bill Burke has been booked for the Three-Hour Cruise cruise on ship
Bohemian Rhapsody.
     [java]  Your accommodations include Suite 101 a 1 bed cabin on deck level 1.
     [java]  Total charge = 3000.0
```

In the JMS subscriber window you started, the following lines should appear:

```
[java] Listening for messages on topic/titan-TicketTopic...
[java]
[java]  RESERVATION RECEIVED:
[java] Bill Burke has been booked for the Three-Hour Cruise cruise on ship Bohemian
Rhapsody.
```

```
[java]  Your accommodations include Suite 101 a 1 bed cabin on deck level 1.
[java]  Total charge = 3000.0
```

Remember from the EJB section of this book that our client application uses a non-durable subscription to the topic. Consequently, all the messages sent while the subscriber client application is not running are lost. That would not be the case if we had used a durable subscription to the topic.

To see the "many-to-many" nature of JMS topics, launch several JMS listener applications at the same time. They will all receive the messages sent to the topic.

Exercise 12.2: The Message-Driven Bean

This exercise is an extension of the preceding one. You'll add a message-driven bean (MDB), `ReservationProcessor`, which plays the same role as the TravelAgent EJB but receives its booking orders through a JMS queue instead of synchronous RMI invocations.

To test the MDB, you'll build a new client application that makes multiple reservations in batch, using a JMS queue that's bound to the MDB. You'll also build a second client application that listens on another queue to receive booking confirmations.

Along the way, you'll learn how to create a new JMS queue in JBoss and configure a message-driven bean (MDB).

Start Up JBoss

If JBoss is already running, there is no reason to restart it.

Initialize the Database

Because the exercise uses the ProcessPayment EJB used in recent exercises, the database must contain the `PAYMENT` table. The `createdb` and `dropdb` Ant targets, Java code, and clients here have been borrowed from exercise 12_1.

If you haven't already dropped the `PAYMENT` table after running the examples in Exercise 12.1, do so now by running the `dropdb` Ant target.

```
C:\workbook\ex12_2>ant dropdb
Buildfile: build.xml

prepare:

compile:

dropdb:
     [java] Looking up home interfaces..
     [java] Dropping database table...

BUILD SUCCESSFUL
```

Then re-create the PAYMENT database table by running the createdb Ant target:

```
C:\workbook\ex12_2>ant createdb
Buildfile: build.xml

prepare:

compile:

ejbjar:

createdb:
     [java] Looking up home interfaces..
     [java] Creating database table...
```

On the JBoss console, the following lines are displayed:

```
INFO  [STDOUT] Creating table PAYMENT...
INFO  [STDOUT] ...done!
```

If you're having trouble creating the database, shut down JBoss. Then run the Ant build target clean.db. This will remove all database files and allow you to start fresh.

The persistence of all other entity beans used in this exercise is managed by the container, so it will create the needed tables for them automatically.

Create a New JMS Queue

This exercise requires two different JMS queues, one for the ReservationProcessor MDB and one to receive booking confirmations.

Adding new JMS queues to JBoss is much like adding new JMS topics. As in the preceding exercise, you have two options, one involving a configuration file, the other the JMX HTTP connector.

Adding a JMS queue through a configuration file

The most common way to set up a JMS queue is to use an XML configuration file. This part of the exercise shows you how to write a JMX MBean definition for a new JMS queue. You can find the JMX configuration file in *ex12_2/src/resources/services*.

jbossmq-titanqueues-service.xml

```
<server>
  <mbean code="org.jboss.mq.server.jmx.Queue"
         name="jboss.mq.destination:service=Queue,
                name=titan-ReservationQueue">
    <depends optional-attribute-name="DestinationManager"
     >jboss.mq:service=DestinationManager</depends>
  </mbean>
```

```
  <mbean code="org.jboss.mq.server.jmx.Queue"
         name="jboss.mq.destination:service=Queue,
               name=titan-TicketQueue">
    <depends optional-attribute-name="DestinationManager"
     >jboss.mq:service=DestinationManager</depends>
  </mbean>
</server>
```

Recall that each set of MBeans must be defined within a `<server>` tag and each MBean declared in an `<mbean>` tag. Because this exercise requires two different queues, we've defined two MBeans. The MBean class that represents a JMS queue is `org.jboss.mq.server.jmx.Queue`. Its `name` property specifies the name of the JMS queue to be created, such as `titan-ReservationQueue` and `titan-TicketQueue`.

Remember also that the application server must deploy the `DestinationManager` MBean before any queue or topic is deployed. This dependency is declared within the `<depends>` tag in *jbossmq-titanqueues-service.xml*. JBoss will take care of satisfying this dependency and make sure the `titan-ReservationQueue` and `titan-TicketQueue` will not be started until the `DestinationManager` MBean has finished initializing and is ready to provide services to new queues and topics. Copying this file into the JBoss deploy directory will hot-deploy these JMS queues and make them ready for use.

To deploy *jbossmq-titanqueues-service.xml*, run the `make-queues` Ant target:

```
C:\workbook\ex12_2>ant make-queues
Buildfile: build.xml

make-queues:
     [copy] Copying 1 file to C:\jboss-4.0\server\default\deploy
```

On the server side, the following lines are displayed:

```
[titan-ReservationQueue] Bound to JNDI name: queue/titan-ReservationQueue
[titan-TicketQueue] Bound to JNDI name: queue/titan-TicketQueue
```

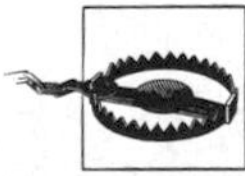

You must deploy the XML file containing the queues *before* you deploy the JAR containing your beans (see below). If you deploy your EJB JAR first, JBoss detects that the MDB's expected queue does not exist and creates it dynamically. Then, when you try to deploy the XML file that contains the queues, an exception arises, and you'll be told you're trying to create a queue that already exists.

Adding a JMS queue through the JMX HTTP connector

Add each of the new JMS queues through the JMX HTTP connector the same way you added the JMS topic in the preceding exercise, with one obvious difference: instead of using the `createTopic()` operation of the JBossMQ server, use the `createQueue()` operation.

Remember that queues and topics created in the JMX HTTP Connector live only until the application server is shut down.

Examine the EJB Standard Files

The *ejb-jar.xml* file for this exercise is based on the one for Exercise 12.1. The only notable difference is the addition of the new ReservationProcessor MDB.

ejb-jar.xml

```
<message-driven>
  <ejb-name>ReservationProcessorEJB</ejb-name>
  <ejb-class
   >com.titan.reservationprocessor.ReservationProcessorBean<
  /ejb-class>
  <transaction-type>Container</transaction-type>
  <message-selector>MessageFormat = 'Version 3.4'</message-selector>
  <acknowledge-mode>auto-acknowledge</acknowledge-mode>
  <message-driven-destination>
    <destination-type>javax.jms.Queue</destination-type>
  </message-driven-destination>
```

The MDB descriptor specifies container-managed transactions and automatic acknowledgement of messages, and that messages will be received from a queue rather than a topic. The descriptor also contains a `<message-selector>` tag that allows the MDB to receive only those messages that conform to a specified format. Then a set of `<ejb-ref>` entries identifies all the beans that ReservationProcessor beans will use during their execution:

```
<ejb-ref>
  <ejb-ref-name>ejb/ProcessPaymentHomeRemote</ejb-ref-name>
  <ejb-ref-type>Session</ejb-ref-type>
  <home>
    com.titan.processpayment.ProcessPaymentHomeRemote
  </home>
  <remote>
    com.titan.processpayment.ProcessPaymentRemote
  </remote>
  <ejb-link>ProcessPaymentEJB</ejb-link>
</ejb-ref>
<ejb-ref>
  <ejb-ref-name>ejb/CustomerHomeRemote</ejb-ref-name>
  <ejb-ref-type>Entity</ejb-ref-type>
  <home>
      com.titan.customer.CustomerHomeRemote
  </home>
  <remote>com.titan.customer.CustomerRemote</remote>
  <ejb-link>CustomerEJB</ejb-link>
</ejb-ref>
<ejb-local-ref>
  <ejb-ref-name>ejb/CruiseHomeLocal</ejb-ref-name>
  <ejb-ref-type>Entity</ejb-ref-type>
```

```
    <local-home>
        com.titan.cruise.CruiseHomeLocal
    </local-home>
    <local>com.titan.cruise.CruiseLocal</local>
    <ejb-link>CruiseEJB</ejb-link>
  </ejb-local-ref>
  <ejb-local-ref>
    <ejb-ref-name>ejb/CabinHomeLocal</ejb-ref-name>
    <ejb-ref-type>Entity</ejb-ref-type>
    <local-home>
        com.titan.cabin.CabinHomeLocal
    </local-home>
    <local>com.titan.cabin.CabinLocal</local>
    <ejb-link>CabinEJB</ejb-link>
  </ejb-local-ref>
  <ejb-local-ref>
    <ejb-ref-name>ejb/ReservationHomeLocal</ejb-ref-name>
    <ejb-ref-type>Entity</ejb-ref-type>
    <local-home>
        com.titan.reservation.ReservationHomeLocal
    </local-home>
    <local>com.titan.reservation.ReservationLocal</local>
    <ejb-link>ReservationEJB</ejb-link>
  </ejb-local-ref>
  <security-identity>
    <run-as><role-name>everyone</role-name></run-as>
  </security-identity>
```

Because the MDB will send a confirmation message to a queue once the booking has been successful, it needs a reference to a `javax.jms.QueueConnectionFactory`, specified in the `<resource-ref>` at the end of the MDB descriptor:

```
  <resource-ref>
    <res-ref-name>jms/QueueFactory</res-ref-name>
    <res-type>javax.jms.QueueConnectionFactory</res-type>
    <res-auth>Container</res-auth>
  </resource-ref>
</message-driven>
```

Note this difference from the preceding exercise: while this bean does send messages to a queue, its descriptor does not contain a `<resource-env-ref>` entry that refers to the destination queue. Why not? In Exercise 12.1, the destination was fixed at deployment time, but in this exercise the destination is not fixed and not even known by the MDB. It is the client application that knows the destination, and transmits it to the MDB by serializing the JMS queue object as part of the JMS message.

Examine the JBoss-Specific Files

No modifications have been made to the CMP entity beans, so the *jbosscmp-jdbc.xml* file is unchanged.

The *jboss.xml* file does need modification to take the new ReservationProcessor EJB into account.

jboss.xml

```
<message-driven>
  <ejb-name>ReservationProcessorEJB</ejb-name>
  <destination-jndi-name
    >queue/titan-ReservationQueue<
    /destination-jndi-name>
  <resource-ref>
    <res-ref-name>jms/QueueFactory</res-ref-name>
    <jndi-name>java:/JmsXA</jndi-name>
  </resource-ref>
</message-driven>
```

The `<destination-jndi-name>` tag maps the MDB to an existing JMS destination in the deployment environment. You should recognize the name of one of the two JMS queues you just created: `titan-ReservationQueue`.

By default, each MDB EJB deployed in JBoss can serve up to 15 concurrent messages.

The `<resource-ref>` tag maps the ConnectionFactory name used by the Reservation-Processor EJB to an actual factory in the deployment environment. This mapping is identical to the one in the exercise for the TravelAgent EJB.

Build and Deploy the Example Programs

Perform the following steps:

1. Open a command prompt or shell terminal and change to the *ex12_2* directory created by the extraction process
2. Set the `JAVA_HOME` and `JBOSS_HOME` environment variables to point to where your JDK and JBoss 4.0 are installed. Examples:

   Windows:

   ```
   C:\workbook\ex12_2> set JAVA_HOME=C:\jdk1.4.2
   C:\workbook\ex12_2> set JBOSS_HOME=C:\jboss-4.0
   ```

   Unix:

   ```
   $ export JAVA_HOME=/usr/local/jdk1.4.2
   $ export JBOSS_HOME=/usr/local/jboss-4.0
   ```

3. Add `ant` to your execution path.

   Windows:

   ```
   C:\workbook\ex12_2> set PATH=..\ant\bin;%PATH%
   ```

   Unix:

   ```
   $ export PATH=../ant/bin:$PATH
   ```

4. Perform the build by typing `ant`.

As in the last exercise, you will see *titan.jar* rebuilt, copied to the JBoss *deploy* directory, and redeployed by the application server.

Examine the Client Applications

In this exercise, you'll use two client applications at the same time. The producer generates large numbers of JMS messages reporting passage bookings, destined for the ReservationProcessor MDB EJB. The consumer listens to a JMS queue for messages confirming the bookings, and displays them as they come in.

The producer first gets the cruise ID and the number of bookings from the command line.

JmsClient_ReservationProducer.java

```
public static void main (String [] args) throws Exception
{
   if (args.length != 2)
      throw new Exception
   ("Usage: java JmsClient_ReservationProducer <CruiseID> <count>");

   Integer cruiseID = new Integer (args[0]);
   int count = new Integer (args[1]).intValue ();
```

The producer then looks up a `QueueConnectionFactory` and two JMS queues from the JBoss naming service. The first queue is the one bound to the ReservationProcessor MDB, to which passage booking messages will be sent. The second is not used directly, as you'll see later.

```
QueueConnectionFactory factory = (QueueConnectionFactory)
  jndiContext.lookup ("ConnectionFactory");
Queue reservationQueue = (Queue)
  jndiContext.lookup ("queue/titan-ReservationQueue");
Queue ticketQueue = (Queue)
  jndiContext.lookup ("queue/titan-TicketQueue");
QueueConnection connect = factory.createQueueConnection ();
QueueSession session = connect.createQueueSession
  (false,Session.AUTO_ACKNOWLEDGE);
QueueSender sender = session.createSender (reservationQueue);
```

The client application is now ready to send `count` booking messages in batch. Among other chores, it has looked up the ticket queue, the JMS queue that the Reservation-Processor MDB will use to send confirmation messages.

For each booking, it then creates a JMS `MapMessage`, assigns the ticket queue into the message's `JMSReplyTo` property, and sets the booking data: Cruise ID, Customer ID, Cabin ID, price, credit card number, and expiration date, and so on. Note that only basic data types such as `String` and `int` can be stored in a `MapMessage`:

```
for (int i = 0; i < count; i++)
{
   MapMessage message = session.createMapMessage ();
```

```
            // Used in ReservationProcessor to send Tickets back out
            message.setJMSReplyTo (ticketQueue);

            message.setStringProperty ("MessageFormat", "Version 3.4");

            message.setInt ("CruiseID", cruiseID.intValue ());
            // either Customer 1 or 2, all we've got in database
            message.setInt ("CustomerID", i%2 + 1);
            // cabins 100-109 only
            message.setInt ("CabinID", i%10 + 100);
            message.setDouble ("Price", (double)1000 + i);

            // the card expires in about 30 days
            Date expDate = new Date (System.currentTimeMillis () +
                                     30*24*60*60*1000L);

            message.setString ("CreditCardNum", "5549861006051975");
            message.setLong ("CreditCardExpDate", expDate.getTime ());
            message.setString ("CreditCardType",
                               CreditCardDO.MASTER_CARD);

            System.out.println ("Sending reservation message #" + i);
            sender.send (message);
         }

         connect.close ();
      }
```

One interesting property that's set in the JMS message header is `MessageFormat`. Recall that the `<message-selector>` tag in the MDB deployment descriptor used this property to specify a constraint on the messages the MDB is to receive.

Once all messages are sent, the application closes the connection and terminates. Because messages are sent asynchronously, the application may terminate before the ReservationProcessor EJB has processed all of the messages in the batch.

The consumer application is very similar to the client application in Exercise 12.1. This time, though, it will subscribe not to a topic but to a queue.

JmsClient_TicketConsumer.java

To receive JMS messages, the client application class implements the `javax.jms.MessageListener` interface, which defines the `onMessage()` method. The main method simply creates an instance of the class and uses a trick to make the main thread wait indefinitely:

```
   public class JmsClient_TicketConsumer
      implements javax.jms.MessageListener
   {

      public static void main (String [] args) throws Exception
      {
```

```
        new JmsClient_TicketConsumer ();

        while(true) { Thread.sleep (10000); }
    }
```

The constructor is very simple JMS code that subscribes the client application to the JMS queue and waits for incoming messages:

```
public JmsClient_TicketConsumer () throws Exception
{
   Context jndiContext = getInitialContext ();

   QueueConnectionFactory factory = (QueueConnectionFactory)
      jndiContext.lookup ("ConnectionFactory");
   Queue ticketQueue = (Queue)
      jndiContext.lookup ("queue/titan-TicketQueue");
   QueueConnection connect = factory.createQueueConnection ();
   QueueSession session =
     connect.createQueueSession (false,Session.AUTO_ACKNOWLEDGE);
   QueueReceiver receiver = session.createReceiver (ticketQueue);
   receiver.setMessageListener (this);

   System.out.println ("Listening for messages on titan-
                        TicketQueue...");
   connect.start ();
 }
```

When a message arrives in the queue, the consumer's onMessage() method is called. The method simply displays the content of the ticket:

```
public void onMessage (Message message)
{
   try
   {
      ObjectMessage objMsg = (ObjectMessage)message;
      TicketDO ticket = (TicketDO)objMsg.getObject ();
      System.out.println ("********************************");
      System.out.println (ticket);
      System.out.println ("********************************");

   }
   catch (JMSException displayed)
   {
      displayed.printStackTrace ();
   }
}
```

Run the Client Applications

When you redeployed *titan.jar*, JBoss dropped and recreated the database tables, destroying any existing content, so you must repopulate the database. Have Ant execute the run.client_112a target.

The run.client_112a target originated in Exercise 11.2, but we've duplicated it in the *ex12_2* directory for your convenience.

```
C:\workbook\ex12_2>ant run.client_112a
Buildfile: build.xml

prepare:

compile:

ejbjar:

run.client_112a:
  [java] Calling TravelAgentBean to create sample data..
  [java] All customers have been removed
  [java] All cabins have been removed
  [java] All ships have been removed
  [java] All cruises have been removed
  [java] All reservations have been removed
  [java] Customer with ID 1 created (Burke Bill)
  [java] Customer with ID 2 created (Labourey Sacha)
  [java] Created ship with ID 101...
  [java] Created ship with ID 102...
  [java] Created cabins on Ship A with IDs 100-109
  [java] Created cabins on Ship B with IDs 200-209
  [java] Created Alaska Cruise with ID 0 on ShipA
  [java] Created Norwegian Fjords Cruise with ID 1 on ShipA
  [java] Created Bermuda or Bust Cruise with ID 2 on ShipA
  [java] Created Indian Sea Cruise with ID 3 on ShipB
  [java] Created Australian Highlights Cruise with ID 4 on ShipB
  [java] Created Three-Hour Cruise with ID 5 on ShipB
  [java] Made reservation for Customer 1 on Cruise 0 for Cabin 103
  [java] Made reservation for Customer 1 on Cruise 5 for Cabin 208
  [java] Made reservation for Customer 2 on Cruise 1 for Cabin 105
  [java] Made reservation for Customer 2 on Cruise 5 for Cabin 202

BUILD SUCCESSFUL
```

At this point, you're going to launch both the client that sends booking messages and the client that receives the tickets as passage confirmations. Launch the consumer *first* by invoking the Ant target run.client_122:

```
C:\workbook\ex12_2>ant run.client_122
Buildfile: build.xml

prepare:

compile:

ejbjar:

run.client_122:
     [java] Listening for messages on titan-TicketQueue...
```

Now start the producer, adhering to the following usage:

```
BookInBatch <cruiseID> <count>
```

where cruiseID is the ID of a Cruise in the database (created when you invoked the run.client_112a Ant target) and count is the number of passages to book.

Book 100 passages on the Alaskan Cruise:

```
C:\workbook\ex12_2>BookInBatch  0 100
Buildfile: build.xml

prepare:

compile:

ejbjar:

run.bookinbatch:
     [java] Sending reservation message #0
     [java] Sending reservation message #1
     [java] Sending reservation message #2
     [java] Sending reservation message #3
     ...
     [java] Sending reservation message #98
     [java] Sending reservation message #99
```

Shortly after the producer starts, the consumer, which has been patiently listening to its JMS queue for booking confirmations, will display:

```
run.client_122:
     [java] Listening for messages on titan-TicketQueue...
     [java] ********************************
     [java] Bob Smith has been booked for the Alaska Cruise cruise
            on ship Nordic Prince.
     [java]  Your accommodations include Suite 100 a 1 bed cabin on
             deck level 1.
     [java]  Total charge = 1000.0
     [java] ********************************
     [java] ********************************
     [java] Joseph Stalin has been booked for the Alaska Cruise
            cruise on ship Nordic Prince.
     [java]  Your accommodations include Suite 101 a 1 bed cabin on
             deck level 1.
     [java]  Total charge = 1001.0
     [java] ********************************
     [java] ********************************
     [java] Bob Smith has been booked for the Alaska Cruise cruise
            on ship Nordic Prince.
     [java]  Your accommodations include Suite 102 a 1 bed cabin on
             deck level 1.
     [java]  Total charge = 1002.0
     [java] ********************************
     ...
     [java] ********************************
```

```
[java] Joseph Stalin has been booked for the Alaska Cruise
       cruise on ship Nordic Prince.
[java]  Your accommodations include Suite 109 a 1 bed cabin on
        deck level 1.
[java]  Total charge = 1099.0
[java] ********************************
```

Note that because the booking confirmation messages are queued, you could start the consumer much later than the producer, rather than before. The confirmation messages sent by the ReservationProcessor MDB would then be stored on the server until the client application starts and begins to listen to the queue.

WORKBOOK 10

Exercises for Chapter 13

Exercise 13.1: EJB Timer Service

In this exercise, you will learn how to use work with the EJB Timer Service. The examples in this chapter match the modifications made to the Ship EJB to enable Timers. This exercise builds off the code within Exercise 12.1, so initialization and deployment should be around the same.

Clean the Database

You need to clean and refresh the database. To do this, shutdown JBoss if you have it running and run `ant clean.db`. Then restart JBoss.

Build and Deploy Example Programs

Perform the following steps:

1. Open a command prompt or shell terminal and change to the *ex13_1* directory created by the extraction process.
2. Set the `JAVA_HOME` and `JBOSS_HOME` environment variables to point to where your JDK and JBoss 4.0 are installed. Examples:

   Windows:
   ```
   C:\workbook\ex13_1> set JAVA_HOME=C:\jdk1.4.2
   C:\workbook\ex13_1> set JBOSS_HOME=C:\jboss-4.0
   ```
   Unix:
   ```
   $ export JAVA_HOME=/usr/local/jdk1.4.2
   $ export JBOSS_HOME=/usr/local/jboss-4.0
   ```
3. Add ant to your execution path. Ant is the build utility.

   Windows:
   ```
   C:\workbook\ex13_1> set PATH=..\ant\bin;%PATH%
   ```
   Unix:
   ```
   $ export PATH=../ant/bin:$PATH
   ```
4. The exercise uses a JMS Topic. Deploy the topic using the following Ant target.
   ```
   $ ant make-topic
   ```

5. Build the EJBs used in this example.

```
$ ant
```

You will see *titan.jar* copied to the JBoss *deploy* directory and redeployed by the application server.

6. Initialize the database.You will see a bunch of entity beans being created.

```
$ ant createdb
```

Examine the Service Code

The scheduleMaintenance, clearSchedule, and ejbTimeout methods from the EJB book have been added to Ship EJB to show the EJB Timer Service in action.

ShipBean.java

```
public void scheduleMaintenance(String descr, Date dateOf) {
   TimerService timerService = ejbContext.getTimerService();
   timerService.createTimer(dateOf, description);
}

public void clearSchedule() {
   TimerService timerService = ejbContext.getTimerService();
   java.util.Iterator timers = timerService.getTimers().iterator();
   while (timers.hasNext()) {
      System.out.println("Cancelling maintenance on ship: " + getName());
      javax.ejb.Timer timer = (javax.ejb.Timer) timers.next();
      timer.cancel();
   }
}

public void ejbTimeout(javax.ejb.Timer timer)   {
   String description = (String) timer.getInfo();

   try {
      InitialContext jndiContext = new InitialContext();
      TopicConnectionFactory factory =(TopicConnectionFactory)
              jndiContext.lookup("java:comp/env/jms/TopicFactory");

      Topic topic = (Topic)
         jndiContext.lookup("java:comp/env/jms/MaintenanceTopic");

      TopicConnection connect = factory.createTopicConnection();
      TopicSession session = connect.createTopicSession(true, 0);
      TopicPublisher publisher = session.createPublisher(topic);

      TextMessage textMsg = session.createTextMessage();
      textMsg.setText(getName() + " " + description);
      publisher.publish(textMsg);
      session.close();
      connect.close();
   } catch (Exception e){
      throw new EJBException(e);
   }
}
```

A stateless session bean has been added to the ship package so that the Ship EJB methods can be called remotely. The scheduleMaintenance and clearSchedule methods look up a Ship EJB and call those methods on that particular entity bean.

ShipMaintenanceBean.java

```
public void scheduleMaintenance(int shipId, int secs, String desc) {
   try {
      ShipHomeLocal shiphome =(ShipHomeLocal)
          jndiContext.lookup("java:comp/env/ejb/ShipHomeLocal");

      ShipLocal ship =
         shiphome.findByPrimaryKey(new Integer(shipId));
      Date dateOfTest = new Date(System.currentTimeMillis()
                               + (secondsToSchedule * 1000));
      ship.scheduleMaintenance(description, dateOfTest);
   } catch (NamingException e){
      throw new EJBException(e);
   } catch (javax.ejb.FinderException e){
      throw new EJBException(e);
   }
}

public void clearSchedule(int shipId) {
   try {
      ShipHomeLocal shiphome =(ShipHomeLocal)
          jndiContext.lookup("java:comp/env/ejb/ShipHomeLocal");

      ShipLocal ship =
         shiphome.findByPrimaryKey(new Integer(shipId));
      Date dateOfTest = new Date(System.currentTimeMillis()
                               + (secondsToSchedule * 1000));
      ship.clearSchedule();
   } catch (NamingException e){
      throw new EJBException(e);
   } catch (javax.ejb.FinderException e){
      throw new EJBException(e);
   }
}
```

Examine the Client Code

There are four client programs used to run the examples. The programs are in the `com.titan.clients` package. *InitDB.java* calls code in TravelAgentEJB to create all the entity beans needed for this example. *JmsClient_1.java* listens on the MaintenanceTopic for published messages from the ejbTimeout method in ShipEJB. *MaintenanceScheduler.java* initiates a call to the ShipMaintenance EJB to schedule maintenance. *CancelMaintenance.java* initiates a call to the ShipMaintenance EJB to clear the maintenance schedule. We don't walk through the code for these programs because they are a quite straightforward example of invoking on a stateless session bean.

Run the Example

The first thing you must do to run the example is start up the JMS client that listens for maintenance messages. Launch another console window and initialize its environment as described above. Start the JMS client by executing the following Ant target:

```
C:\workbook\ex13_1>ant run.watcher
```

You should see the following displayed on the console:

```
C:\workbook\ex13_1>ant run.watcher
Buildfile: build.xml

prepare:

compile:

ejbjar:

run.watcher:
     [java] Listening for messages on topic/titan-MaintenanceTopic...
```

Next, you can schedule maintenance to a ship by running the `ScheduleMaintenance` script. There is one provided for both Windows and Unix. To run this script, you need to provide a ship ID (101 or 102), the time in seconds for when you want the maintenance scheduled, and finally a description of the maintenance that will be scheduled:

```
C:\workbook\ex13_1>ScheduleMaintenance 101 5 propellar
```

After five seconds, you should see the JMS client console window show up with the scheduled maintenance:

```
C:\jboss\workbook\ex13_1>ant run.watcher
Buildfile: build.xml

prepare:

compile:

ejbjar:

run.watcher:
     [java] Listening for messages on topic/titan-MaintenanceTopic...

     [java]  MAINTENANCE SCHEDULED:
     [java] Nordic Prince propeller
```

You can cancel any maintenance by running the `CancelMaintenance` script before the `ejbTimeout` executes. There is one provided for both Windows and Unix. To run this script, you need to provide a ship ID (101 or 102):

```
C:\workbook\ex13_1>CancelMaintenance 101
```

WORKBOOK 11

Exercises for Chapter 15

Exercise 15.1: Web Services and EJB 2.1

In this exercise, you will learn how to use JAX-RPC's client and server-side programming model with EJB 2.1. You will expose a stateless session bean as a web service. You will also investigate how to connect to and invoke on an existing web service from within EJB code. The stateless session bean that is exposed models the TravelAgentEndpoint in Chapter 15 of the EJB book. The supporting code for the rest of this exercise is borrowed from the exercises for Chapter 11 (Workbook 8). This exercise also introduces another stateless session bean that acts as a JAX-RPC client to the TravelAgentEndpoint EJB.

Initialize Your Environment

Perform the following steps:

1. Open a command prompt or shell terminal and change to the *ex15_1* directory created by the extraction process.
2. Set the `JAVA_HOME` and `JBOSS_HOME` environment variables to point to where your JDK and JBoss 4.0 are installed. Examples:

   Windows:
   ```
   C:\workbook\ex15_1> set JAVA_HOME=C:\jdk1.4.2
   C:\workbook\ex15_1> set JBOSS_HOME=C:\jboss-4.0
   ```
   Unix:
   ```
   $ export JAVA_HOME=/usr/local/jdk1.4.2
   $ export JBOSS_HOME=/usr/local/jboss-4.0
   ```
3. Add ant to your execution path. Ant is the build utility.

   Windows:
   ```
   C:\workbook\ex15_1> set PATH=..\ant\bin;%PATH%
   ```
   Unix:
   ```
   $ export PATH=../ant/bin:$PATH
   ```

Clean the Database

You need to clean and refresh the database. To do this, first shutdown JBoss if you have it running and then run the `ant clean.db`.

Build and Deploy Example Programs

JBoss implements web services integration using the Apache Axis project *http://ws.apache.org/axis/*. One of the more annoying things about web services and EJB is creating a WSDL document based on a Service Endpoint interface. To alleviate this work, Axis has a nice tool called Java2WSDL that allows you to automatically generate a WSDL document based on a plain Java interface. If you examine the *build.xml* file, you can see an ant target devoted to invoking this utility.

build.xml

```
<target name="wsdl" depends="compile">
  <java classname="org.apache.axis.wsdl.Java2WSDL" fork="yes" dir=".">
    <classpath refid="classpath"/>
    <arg value="-lhttp://localhost:8080/ws4ee/services/TravelAgentService"/>
     <arg value="-uLITERAL"/>
     <arg value="-sTravelAgentEndpoint"/>
    <arg value="-o${src.resources}/META-INF/travelagent.wsdl"/>
    <arg value="com.titan.webservice.TravelAgentEndpoint"/>
  </java>
  <copy file="${src.resources}/META-INF/travelagent.wsdl" todir="${src.resources}/
client/META-INF/" />
</target>
```

The `-l` switch tells Java2WSDL the default service location URL that will be used by a client connection. The `-uLITERAL` switch tells Axis to generate WSDL with RPC/Literal messaging. No one takes the default RPC/Encoded messaging seriously anymore as it doesn't interoperate very well. The `-o` switch just specifies where the WSDL file should be generated. The class name of the Service Endpoint Interface (it can be any Java interface) must be specified as an argument and must also be within the classpath.

In this exercise there are two EJB *jar* files. One is *titan.jar*, which contains TravelAgentEndpoint and other supporting EJBs; the other is *titan-client.jar*, which contains the EJB that will be connecting to TravelAgentEndpoint as a JAX-RPC client. Both of these *jar*s require the *travelagent.wsdl* file to do their things.

To do the build, perform the following steps:

1. Generate the `WSDL` documents:

   ```
   $ ant wsdl
   ```

2. Compile and deploy the *ejb jar*s:

   ```
   $ ant ejbjar
   ```

You will see *titan.jar* and *titan-client.jar* built, copied to the JBoss *deploy* directory, and redeployed by the application server.

So where's the JAX-RPC stub generation? The spirit of JBoss has always been to avoid any precompilation step. If you have run any of the other examples in this book, you will have seen that there is not any stub generation for EJBs either. At deployment time, JBoss automatically generates dynamic proxies to handle all web service communication both with clients and services.

Examine the Server Model

To illustrate how to expose a stateless session bean, the TravelAgentEJB from Exercise 4.2 has been extended. This first thing to be done was to define a Service Endpoint interface the web service will implement. This interface is defined in *src/main/com/titan/travelagent.*

TravelAgentEndpoint.java

```
package com.titan.webservice;

public interface TravelAgentEndpoint extends java.rmi.Remote {
   String makeReservation(int cruiseId, int cabinId,
                          int customerId, double price)
          throws java.rmi.RemoteException;
}
```

This interface is taken directly from Chapter 15 of the EJB book. Next, you have to define all the deployment descriptors. These files reside in src*/resources/META-INF.*

ejb-jar.xml

```
<session>
  <description>
     A Web Service reservation service
  </description>
  <ejb-name>TravelAgentEjbEndpoint</ejb-name>
  <service-endpoint>
     com.titan.webservice.TravelAgentEndpoint
  </service-endpoint>
  <ejb-class>
     com.titan.webservice.TravelAgentBean
  </ejb-class>
  <session-type>Stateless</session-type>
  <transaction-type>Container</transaction-type>
  <ejb-ref>
...
```

This XML is taken directly from Chapter 15 of the EJB book and added to the definition of the other supporting EJBs.

travelagent_mapping.xml

```
<java-wsdl-mapping
  xmlns="http://java.sun.com/xml/ns/j2ee"
  xmlns:xsi="http://www.w3.org/2001/XMLSchema-instance"
  xsi:schemaLocation="http://java.sun.com/xml/ns/j2ee
              http://www.ibm.com/webservices/xsd/j2ee_jaxrpc_mapping_1_1.xsd"
  version="1.1">
  <package-mapping>
    <package-type>com.titan.webservice</package-type>
    <namespaceURI>
        http://webservice.titan.com/TravelAgentEndpoint
    </namespaceURI>
  </package-mapping>
</java-wsdl-mapping>
```

The endpoint we are exposing follows the guidelines for a simple mapping file. The `namespaceURI` element is a little different from Chapter 15 of the EJB book because it should match the generated WSDL document.

webservices.xml

```
<webservices
   xmlns="http://java.sun.com/xml/ns/j2ee"
   xmlns:xsi="http://www.w3.org/2001/XMLSchema-instance"
   xmlns:titan="http://www.titan.com/TravelAgent"
   xsi:schemaLocation="http://java.sun.com/xml/ns/j2ee
                http://www.ibm.com/webservices/xsd/j2ee_web_services_1_1.xsd"
                    version="1.1">

<webservice-description>
   <webservice-description-name>
      TravelAgentService
   </webservice-description-name>
   <wsdl-file>META-INF/travelagent.wsdl</wsdl-file>
   <jaxrpc-mapping-file>
      META-INF/travelagent_mapping.xml
   </jaxrpc-mapping-file>
   <port-component>
      <port-component-name>TravelAgentEndpoint</port-component-name>
      <wsdl-port>titan:TravelAgentEndpoint</wsdl-port>
      <service-endpoint-interface>
          com.titan.webservice.TravelAgentEndpoint
      </service-endpoint-interface>
      <service-impl-bean>
          <ejb-link>TravelAgentEjbEndpoint</ejb-link>
      </service-impl-bean>
   </port-component>
 </webservice-description>
</webservices>
```

This is a standard *webservices.xml* descriptor. It links the WSDL file, mapping file, Service Endpoint interface, and TravelAgentEndpoint EJB all together. The important part of this file as it pertains to Jboss is the `<webservice-description-name>`. JBoss binds all deployed web services under the */ws4ee/services/<webservice-description-name>* URL. For this example, it would be under */ws4ee/services/TravelAgentEndpoint*. You can also view all endpoints by going to the base URL */ws4ee/services* (Figure W-12).

Figure W-12. Listing the deployed services

Examine the Client Model

TravelAgentClientEJB is a stateless session bean that illustrates how to invoke a web service from within EJB code. It simply exposes the same interface as TravelAgent-Endpoint EJB and implements it by delegating to the TravelAgentEndpoint interface, invoking over the wire via a SOAP invocation.

TravelAgentClientBean.java

```
public String makeReservation(int cruiseId, int cabinId,
                              int customerId, double price)
        throws java.rmi.RemoteException {
   try {
      javax.naming.Context jndiContext = new InitialContext();
      Object obj =
          jndiContext.lookup("java:comp/env/service/TravelAgent");
```

```
        javax.xml.rpc.Service svc = (javax.xml.rpc.Service) obj;
        TravelAgentEndpoint endpoint = (TravelAgentEndpoint)
                                svc.getPort(TravelAgentEndpoint.class);

        return endpoint.makeReservation(cruiseId, cabinId,
                                        customerId, price);

     } catch (Exception e) {
        e.printStackTrace();
        throw new EJBException("failed");
     }
  }
```

Since the spirit of JBoss is to avoid stub generation, the preferred method for clients is the Dynamic Proxy API as JBoss will automatically set up all proxies at deploy time. `TravelAgentClientBean.makeReservation` is an example of this. A generic proxy is registered for the service reference and you can get a proxy to any endpoint interface you want by passing in a Java Class parameter to the `getPort` method.

ejb-jar.xml

```
<session>
  <ejb-name>TravelAgentClientEJB</ejb-name>
...
     <service-ref>
          <service-ref-name>service/TravelAgent</service-ref-name>
          <service-interface>
             javax.xml.rpc.Service
          </service-interface>
          <wsdl-file>META-INF/travelagent.wsdl</wsdl-file>
          <jaxrpc-mapping-file>
             META-INF/travelagent_mapping.xml
          </jaxrpc-mapping-file>
     </service-ref>
  </session>
```

The `<service-ref>` element is standard. One thing to note is that the `<service-qname>` element can be left out if the WSDL file contains only one service definition. The other deployment descriptors are the same descriptors as in the server model.

travelagent.wsdl

```
<wsdl:service name="TravelAgentEndpointService">
   <wsdl:port name="TravelAgentEndpoint"
       binding="impl: TravelAgentEndpointSoapBinding">

      <wsdlsoap:address location="http://localhost:8080/ws4ee/services/
         TravelAgentService"/>

   </wsdl:port>
</wsdl:service>
```

The address location in the *TravelAgentEJB.wsdl* file is the URL used by the Dynamic Proxy created in the listCabins method.

Run the Client Application

The client application is made up of two clients. The first client initializes the entity beans and database tables that are needed for this exercise.

```
C:\workbook\ex15_1>ant createdb
Buildfile: build.xml

prepare:

compile:

createdb:
  [java] Calling TravelAgentBean to create sample data..
  [java] All customers have been removed
  [java] All cabins have been removed
  [java] All ships have been removed
  [java] All cruises have been removed
  [java] All reservations have been removed
  [java] Customer with ID 1 created (Burke Bill)
  [java] added credit card: 4300000000000000 for Bill
  [java] Customer with ID 2 created (Labourey Sacha)
  [java] Created ship with ID 101...
  [java] Created ship with ID 102...
  [java] Created cabins on Ship A with IDs 100-109
  [java] Created cabins on Ship B with IDs 200-209
  [java] Created Alaska Cruise with ID 0 on ShipA
  [java] Created Norwegian Fjords Cruise with ID 1 on ShipA
  [java] Created Bermuda or Bust Cruise with ID 2 on ShipA
  [java] Created Indian Sea Cruise with ID 3 on ShipB
  [java] Created Australian Highlights Cruise with ID 4 on ShipB
  [java] Created Three-Hour Cruise with ID 5 on ShipB
  [java] Made reservation for Customer 1 on Cruise 0 for Cabin 103
  [java] Made reservation for Customer 1 on Cruise 5 for Cabin 208
  [java] Made reservation for Customer 2 on Cruise 1 for Cabin 105
  [java] Made reservation for Customer 2 on Cruise 5 for Cabin 202
  [java] Creating database table...
```

The second client is a MakeReservation script that can be run from the command line. There is a script provided for both Unix and Windows. The arguments for the script are a cruise ID, cabin ID, a customer ID, and finally a price for the reservation. You can pull three of the arguments from the output of `run.createdb`:

```
C:\workbook\ex15_1>MakeReservation 1 106 1 5000.00
Buildfile: build.xml

prepare:

compile:
```

```
ejbjar:

run.client:
     [java] reservation 5 completed.
```

Here we are, back at the dock, our "EJB on JBoss" cruise complete! We really hope you've enjoyed the voyage and that we'll soon meet you on JBoss's forums for some more exciting adventures.

APPENDIX

Database Configuration

This appendix describes how to set up database pools for data sources other than the default database embedded in JBoss, Hypersonic SQL. It also shows you how to set up your EJBs to use these database pools. For illustration purposes, we've modified Exercise 6.1 to configure and use an Oracle connection pool with JBoss.

Set Up the Database

To deploy a database connection pool, JBoss requires a datapool configuration file. The configuration file is very simple, yet can be used for almost all standard datapool setups.

Basic Setup

The first step is to download the JDBC driver classes for your database. Copy your database's JDBC JAR file to *$JBOSS_HOME/server/default/lib*. For example, the Oracle JDBC class files are contained in *classes12.zip*.

The JBoss distribution includes example database connection-pool files, in the directory *$JBOSS_HOME/docs/examples/jca*. The name of each file ends in *-ds.xml*. For this exercise, we've copied the *oracle-ds.xml* configuration file to *exAppendixA/titandb-ds.xml* and modified it accordingly.

To deploy this connection pool, you must copy *titandb-ds.xml* to the *$JBOSS_HOME/service/default/deploy* directory. Note that the name of this config file must end with *-ds.xml*, or JBoss will not deploy it.

Database connection pools are among the many things that can be hot-deployed in JBoss, simply by plopping the pool's XML configuration file into the *deploy* directory.

Examine some of the configuration parameters this file defines.

titandb-ds.xml

```
<datasources>
  <local-tx-datasource>
    <jndi-name>OracleDS</jndi-name>
```

The <jndi-name> tag identifies the connection pool within JNDI. You can look up this pool in JNDI with the java:/OracleDS string. The class of this bound object is javax.sql.DataSource.

```
    <connection-url
     >jdbc:oracle:thin:@localhost:1521:JBOSSDB</connection-url>
```

The <connection-url> tag tells the Oracle JDBC driver how to connect to the database. The URL varies depending on the database you use, so consult your database JDBC manuals to find out how to obtain the appropriate address.

```
    <driver-class>oracle.jdbc.driver.OracleDriver</driver-class>
```

The <driver-class> tag tells JBoss and the base JDBC classes the name of Oracle's JDBC driver class they need to instantiate and use.

```
    <user-name>scott</user-name>
    <password>tiger</password>
  </local-tx-datasource>
</datasources>
```

Finally, the <user-name> and <password> tags are used when connecting to the Oracle database.

Examine the JBoss-Specific Files

The example code for this appendix has been borrowed from Exercise 6.1 of this workbook. It is fairly easy to configure the EJBs from this exercise to use the Oracle connection pool you created above. Simply point the data source to java:/OracleDS and use the Oracle8 database mapping.

jbosscmp-jdbc.xml

```
<jbosscmp-jdbc>

  <defaults>
    <datasource>java:/OracleDS</datasource>
    <datasource-mapping>Oracle8</datasource-mapping>
    <create-table>true</create-table>
    <remove-table>true</remove-table>
  </defaults>

  <enterprise-beans>
    <entity>
      <ejb-name>CustomerEJB</ejb-name>
      <table-name>Customer</table-name>
```

```
      <cmp-field>
        <field-name>id</field-name>
        <column-name>ID</column-name>
      </cmp-field>
      <cmp-field>
        <field-name>lastName</field-name>
        <column-name>LAST_NAME</column-name>
      </cmp-field>
      <cmp-field>
        <field-name>firstName</field-name>
        <column-name>FIRST_NAME</column-name>
      </cmp-field>
      <cmp-field>
        <field-name>hasGoodCredit</field-name>
        <column-name>HAS_GOOD_CREDIT</column-name>
      </cmp-field>
    </entity>
  </enterprise-beans>

</jbosscmp-jdbc>
```

Start Up JBoss

In this variation of Exercise 6.1, you must restart JBoss,so recognizes the JDBC JAR file you copied into the *lib* directory. Review the *JBoss Installation and Configuration* chapter at the beginning of this workbook if you don't remember how to start JBoss.

Build and Deploy the Example Programs

To build and deploy the example for this chapter, you must configure the file described above, *titandb-ds.xml*, to conform to the database you're using.

Perform the following steps:

1. Open a command prompt or shell terminal and change to the *exAppendixA* directory created by the extraction process.
2. Set the `JAVA_HOME` and `JBOSS_HOME` environment variables to point to where your JDK and JBoss 4.0 are installed.Examples:

   Windows:
   ```
   C:\workbook\exAppendixA> set JAVA_HOME=C:\jdk1.4.2
   C:\workbook\exAppendixA> set JBOSS_HOME=C:\jboss-4.0
   ```
   Unix:
   ```
   $ export JAVA_HOME=/usr/local/jdk1.4.2
   $ export JBOSS_HOME=/usr/local/jboss-4.0
   ```
3. Add `ant` to your execution path.

   Windows:
   ```
   C:\workbook\exAppendixA> set PATH=..\ant\bin;%PATH%
   ```
   Unix:
   ```
   $ export PATH=../ant/bin:$PATH
   ```
4. Perform the build by typing `ant`.

You will see *titan.jar* rebuilt, copied to the JBoss *deploy* directory, and redeployed by the application server. The build script copies *titandb-ds.xml* to the *deploy* directory as well, which triggers deployment of the customer database pool.

Examine and Run the Client Applications

There is only one client application for this exercise, *Client_61*. It's modeled after the example in Chapter 6 of the EJB book. It will use information you supply in the command-line parameters to create Customer EJBs in the database.

To run the client, first set your `JBOSS_HOME` and `PATH` environment variables appropriately. Then invoke the provided wrapper script. You must supply data on the command line, specifiying a primary key, first name, and last name for each Customer. For example:

```
Client_61 777 Bill Burke 888 Sacha Labourey
```

For the sample command, the output should be:

```
777 = Bill Burke
888 = Sacha Labourey
```

The example program removes the created beans at the conclusion of operation, so there will be no data left in the database.

Index

Symbols

Numbers

A

We'd like to hear your suggestions for improving our indexes. Send email to *index@oreilly.com*.

B

C

D

E

F

G

H

I

J

L

M

N

O

P

Q

R

S

T

About the Authors

Richard Monson-Haefel is a Senior Analyst for The Burton Group and is one of the world's leading experts in Enterprise JavaBeans. He helped develop the specifications for EJB 2.1, EJB 3.0, and J2EE 1.4, and served on the JCP Executive Committee, which oversees all JSRs (specifications) developed for the J2SE and J2EE platforms.

Richard is a founder of the Apache Geronimo Project (an open source J2EE Application Server) as well as the OpenEJB project (an open source EJB container). He is the award-winning author of three best-selling editions of *Enterprise JavaBeans* (O'Reilly), *J2EE Web Services* (Addison-Wesley), and the coauthor of *Java Message Service* (O'Reilly). You can learn more about Richard at his web site, *http://www.monson-haefel.com*.

Bill Burke is the Chief Architect of JBossGroup, LLC. Bill has more than 10 years experience implementing and using middleware in the industry. He was one of the primary developers of Iona Technology's Orbix 2000 CORBA product and has also designed and implemented J2EE applications at a few Internet startups. Besides hanging with his wonderful wife, Bill can often be found cheering for the New England Patriots at Gillette Stadium with his dad.

Sacha Labourey is General Manager of JBoss (Europe) and one of the core developers of JBoss Clustering. He holds a master's degree in computer science from the Swiss Federal Institute of Technology and was the founder of Cogito Informatique, a Swiss company specializing in the fields of application servers and middleware. To prove to himself he is not a computer addict, he regularly goes on trips to the Alps to extend his Rumantsch vocabulary.

Colophon

Our look is the result of reader comments, our own experimentation, and feedback from distribution channels. Distinctive covers complement our distinctive approach to technical topics, breathing personality and life into potentially dry subjects.

The animals on the cover of *Enterprise JavaBeans*, Fourth Edition, are a wallaby and her joey. Wallabies are middle-sized marsupials belonging to the kangaroo family (*Macropodidae*, the second-largest marsupial family). They are grazers and browsers, native to Australia and found in a variety of habitats on that continent. Female wallabies have a well-developed anterior pouch in which they hold their young. When they are born, the tiny, still-blind joeys instinctively crawl up into their mothers' pouches and begin to nurse. They stay in the pouch until they are fairly well-grown. A female wallaby can support joeys from up to three litters at once: one in her uterus, one in her pouch, and one that has graduated from the pouch but still returns to nurse.

Like all *Macropodidae*, wallabies have long, narrow hind feet and powerful hind limbs. Their long, heavy tails are used primarily for balance and stability and are not prehensile. Wallabies resemble kangaroos, but are smaller: they can measure anywhere from less than two feet to over five feet long, with the tail accounting for nearly half of their total length. Oddly enough, although they can hop along quite quickly (reaching speeds of up to 50 km/h), it is physically impossible for wallabies to walk backward!

The three main types of wallaby are brush, rock, and nail-tailed. There are 11 species of brush wallaby (genus *Macropus*), including the red-necked and pretty-faced wallabies, and 6 named species of rock wallaby (*Petrogale*). Brush wallabies usually live in brushland or open woods. Rock wallabies, which are notable for their extreme agility, are usually found among rocks and near water. There are only three species of nail-tailed wallaby (*Onychogalea*), which are so named because of the horny growth that appears on the tip of their tails. Two of these species are endangered—although they were once the most numerous type of wallaby, their numbers have been seriously depleted by foxes and feral cats. Aside from hunting and habitat destruction, predation and competition by introduced species such as these are what threaten wallabies today.

Colleen Gorman was the production editor and copyeditor for *Enterprise JavaBeans*, Fourth Edition. Leanne Soylemez was the proofreader. Reg Aubry and Mary Anne Weeks Mayo provided quality control. Julie Hawks wrote the index.

Hanna Dyer designed the cover of this book, based on a series design by Edie Freedman. The cover image is an original engraving from *The Illustrated Natural History: Mammalia*, by J.G. Wood, published in 1865. Emma Colby produced the cover layout with QuarkXPress 4.1 using Adobe's ITC Garamond font.

David Futato designed the interior layout. This book was converted by Julie Hawks to FrameMaker 5.5.6 with a format conversion tool created by Erik Ray, Jason McIntosh, Neil Walls, and Mike Sierra that uses Perl and XML technologies. The text font is Linotype Birka; the heading font is Adobe Myriad Condensed; and the code font is LucasFont's TheSans Mono Condensed. The illustrations that appear in the book were produced by Robert Romano and Jessamyn Read using Macromedia FreeHand 9 and Adobe Photoshop 6. The tip and warning icons were drawn by Christopher Bing. This colophon was written by Rachel Wheeler.

Whenever possible, our books use a durable and flexible lay-flat binding. If the pagecount exceeds this binding's limit Perfect Binding is used.

Related Titles Available from O'Reilly

Java

Ant: The Definitive Guide
Eclipse: A Java Developer's Guide
Hardcore Java
Head First Java
Head First Servlets & JSP
Head First EJB
J2EE Design Patterns
Java and SOAP
Java & XML Data Binding
Java & XML
Java Cookbook
Java Data Objects
Java Database Best Practices
Java Enterprise Best Practices
Java Enterprise in a Nutshell, *2nd Edition*
Java Examples in a Nutshell, *3rd Edition*
Java Extreme Programming Cookbook
Java in a Nutshell, *4th Edition*
Java Management Extensions
Java Message Service
Java Network Programming, *2nd Edition*
Java NIO
Java Performance Tuning, *2nd Edition*
Java RMI
Java Security, *2nd Edition*
Java ServerPages, *2nd Edition*
Java Serlet & JSP Cookbook
Java Servlet Programming, *2nd Edition*
Java Swing, *2nd Edition*
Java Web Services in a Nutshell
Learning Java, *2nd Edition*
Mac OS X for Java Geeks
NetBeans: The Definitive Guide
Programming Jakarta Struts
Tomcat: The Definitive Guide
WebLogic: The Definitive Guide

Keep in touch with O'Reilly

1. Download examples from our books

To find example files for a book, go to:

www.oreilly.com/catalog

select the book, and follow the "Examples" link.

2. Register your O'Reilly books

Register your book at *register.oreilly.com*

Why register your books?
Once you've registered your O'Reilly books you can:

- Win O'Reilly books, T-shirts or discount coupons in our monthly drawing.
- Get special offers available only to registered O'Reilly customers.
- Get catalogs announcing new books (US and UK only).
- Get email notification of new editions of the O'Reilly books you own.

3. Join our email lists

Sign up to get topic-specific email announcements of new books and conferences, special offers, and O'Reilly Network technology newsletters at:

elists.oreilly.com

It's easy to customize your free elists subscription so you'll get exactly the O'Reilly news you want.

4. Get the latest news, tips, and tools

www.oreilly.com

- "Top 100 Sites on the Web"—PC Magazine
- CIO Magazine's Web Business 50 Awards

Our web site contains a library of comprehensive product information (including book excerpts and tables of contents), downloadable software, background articles, interviews with technology leaders, links to relevant sites, book cover art, and more.

5. Work for O'Reilly

Check out our web site for current employment opportunities:

jobs.oreilly.com

6. Contact us

O'Reilly & Associates
1005 Gravenstein Hwy North
Sebastopol, CA 95472 USA

TEL: 707-827-7000 or 800-998-9938
(6am to 5pm PST)

FAX: 707-829-0104

order@oreilly.com
For answers to problems regarding your order or our products. To place a book order online, visit:

www.oreilly.com/order_new

catalog@oreilly.com
To request a copy of our latest catalog.

booktech@oreilly.com
For book content technical questions or corrections.

corporate@oreilly.com
For educational, library, government, and corporate sales.

proposals@oreilly.com
To submit new book proposals to our editors and product managers.

international@oreilly.com
For information about our international distributors or translation queries. For a list of our distributors outside of North America check out:

international.oreilly.com/distributors.html

adoption@oreilly.com
For information about academic use of O'Reilly books, visit:

academic.oreilly.com